SLAVERY AND SOCIAL DEATH

SLAVERY AND SOCIAL DEATH

A Comparative Study

Orlando Patterson

Harvard University Press
*Cambridge, Massachusetts, and
London, England*

Library of Congress Cataloging in Publication Data

Patterson, Orlando, 1940–
Slavery and social death.

Includes bibliographical references and index.
1. Slavery. 2. Slaves—Psychology. 3. Slaveholders—
Psychology. I. Title.
HT871.P37   306′.362   82-1072
ISBN 0-674-81082-1 (cloth)   AACR2
ISBN 0-674-81083-X (paper)

For Nerys

... dissymlaf gwreic a bonedigeidaf i hannwyt a'y hymdidan oed.

The Mabinogi

Preface

THERE IS NOTHING notably peculiar about the institution of slavery. It has existed from before the dawn of human history right down to the twentieth century, in the most primitive of human societies and in the most civilized. There is no region on earth that has not at some time harbored the institution. Probably there is no group of people whose ancestors were not at one time slaves or slaveholders.

Why then the commonplace that slavery is "the peculiar institution"? It is hard to say, but perhaps the reason lies in the tendency to eschew what seems too paradoxical. Slavery was not only ubiquitous but turns out to have thrived most in precisely those areas and periods of the world where our conventional wisdom would lead us to expect it least. It was firmly established in all the great early centers of human civilization and, far from declining, actually increased in significance with the growth of all the epochs and cultures that modern Western peoples consider watersheds in their historical development. Ancient Greece and Rome were not simply slaveholding societies; they were what Sir Moses Finley calls "genuine" slave societies, in that slavery was very solidly the base of their socioeconomic structures. Many European societies too were genuine slave societies during their critical periods. In Visigothic Spain, late Old English society, Merovingian France, and Viking Europe, slavery—if not always dominant—was never less than critical. The institution rose again to major significance in late medieval Spain, and in Russia from the sixteenth century to the end of the eighteenth. Slaves constituted such a large proportion of the Florentine population during the fourteenth and fifteenth centuries that they significantly transformed the appearance of the indigenous Tuscan population. Late medieval and early Renaissance Venice and Genoa were extremely dependent on slave labor, and the Italian colonies of the Mediterranean during the late Middle Ages not only were large-scale plantation slave systems but, as Charles Verlinden has shown, were the models upon which the advanced plantation systems of the Iberian Atlantic colonies were based. These, in turn, were the testing grounds for the capitalistic slave systems of the modern Americas.

The late Eric Williams may have gone too far in his celebrated argument that the rise of capitalism itself could be largely accounted for by the enormous profits generated by the slave systems of the Americas. But no one now doubts that New World slavery was a key factor in the rise of the West European economies.

Europe, however, was hardly unique in this association of civilization and slavery. The rise of Islam was made possible by slavery, for without it the early Arab elites simply would not have been able to exploit the skilled and unskilled manpower that was essential for their survival and expansion. Even more than the Western states, the Islamic world depended on slaves for the performance of critical administrative, military, and cultural roles.

The same holds true for Africa and certain areas of the Orient. In both the pagan and Islamic regions of precolonial Africa advanced political and cultural developments were usually, though not always, associated with high levels of dependence on slavery. Medieval Ghana, Songhay, and Mali all relied heavily on slave labor. So did the city-states of the Hausas, Yorubas, and Ibibios, the kingdoms of Dahomey and Ashanti at their peak, the caliphate of Sokoto, and the sultanate of Zanzibar.

Oriental societies are unusual in world historical terms for the relatively low level of association between periods of high civilization and the growth of slavery. Even so, it is easy to underestimate the role of slavery in this part of the world. The institution existed in all oriental systems, and slaves played significant roles in the palatine service and administration. In fact, it is in the oriental state of Korea that we find one of the most extraordinary cases of economic dependence on slaves among all peoples and all periods. Large-scale slavery flourished there for over a thousand years up to the nineteenth century. For several centuries the servile population was proportionately higher than the one in the U.S. South at its peak of dependence on slavery in the nineteenth century.

In the Western world the paradox is compounded by another historical enigma. Slavery is associated not only with the development of advanced economies, but also with the emergence of several of the most profoundly cherished ideals and beliefs in the Western tradition. The idea of freedom and the concept of property were both intimately bound up with the rise of slavery, their very antithesis. The great innovators not only took slavery for granted, they insisted on its necessity to their way of life. In doing so, they were guilty not of some unfathomable lapse of logic, but rather of admirable candor. For Plato and Aristotle and the great Roman jurists were not wrong in recognizing the necessary correlation between their love of their own freedom and its denial to others. The joint rise of slavery and cultivation of freedom was no accident. It was, as we shall see, a sociohistorical necessity.

Modern Western thinkers, especially since the Enlightenment, have found such views wrong, disturbing, and deeply embarrassing. The embarrassment was not confined to those who puzzled over the ancient world: it was to reach its zenith in the most democratic political constitution and social system ever achieved by a Western people—the experiment called the United States. Americans have never been able to explain how it came to pass that the most articulate defender of their freedoms, Thomas Jefferson, and the greatest hero of their revolution and history, George Washington, both were large-scale, largely unrepentant slaveholders. Slavery, for all who look to Enlightenment Europe and revolutionary America as the source of their most cherished political values, is not the peculiar institution but the embarrassing institution.

Our distress, however, stems from a false premise. We assume that slavery should have nothing to do with freedom; that a man who holds freedom dearly should not hold slaves without discomfort; that a culture which invented democracy or produced a Jefferson should not be based on slavery. But such an assumption is unfounded. We make it only because we reify ideas, because we fail to see the logic of contradiction, and because in our anachronistic arrogance we tend to read the history of ideas backward.

I show in this book that slavery and freedom are intimately connected, that contrary to our atomistic prejudices it is indeed reasonable that those who most denied freedom, as well as those to whom it was most denied, were the very persons most alive to it. Once we understand the essence and the dynamics of slavery, we immediately realize why there is nothing in the least anomalous about the fact that an Aristotle or a Jefferson owned slaves. Our embarrassment springs from our ignorance of the true nature of slavery and of freedom.

Exposing and removing our misconceptions about a subject is a necessary part of any attempt to comprehend it. This book, however, is not a study in the history of ideas; it seeks an understanding of a social fact. It will attempt to define and explore empirically, in all its aspects, the nature and inner dynamics of slavery and the institutional patterns that supported it.

Two sets of societies provided the data for this work. The first, and far the more important, comprises all those societies in which slavery attained marked structural significance, ranging from those in which it was important for cultural, economic, or political reasons, or a combination of all three, through those in which it was critical though not definitive, to those in which it was the determinative institution. It is these societies on which we have the richest data both quantitatively and qualitatively, and they are the basis of most of the textual discussion in this book. There is as yet no consensus among students of slavery on a terminology. I have followed others in using the phrase "large-scale slave societies" to describe the groups I have considered; I have also sometimes used Finley's term "genuine slave societies."

One of the mistakes frequently made in comparative research is the exclusion of all societies in which the object of one's inquiry, even though it may occur, does not attain marked systemic importance. I have tried to avoid this as an unwarranted delimitation of the data base. If one's concern is with the internal structure of a given process, if as in this work one is attempting to describe and analyze exhaustively its nature and inner dynamics, then to restrict oneself to those cases in which the process in question attained structural significance is to build a wholly inadmissible bias into one's account of the process.

For it is often the case that the most systemically or externally significant manifestations of the process are not the most typical. There are some kinds of events which, when they happen, are always structurally important: from the social universe, one may cite revolutions; from the biological universe, cancer. But this is certainly not the case with very many processes. To take another analogy from biology, the typical viral infection is often a structurally minor event. A biologist attempting to analyze the nature of viruses who restricts himself to cases of chronic viral pneumonia will end up with a highly distorted account. Slavery is a case in point from the social universe. Its typical occurrence is in contexts where it does not have much structural importance. If I am to understand the universal features of the internal structure of slavery, I am obliged to give due weight to a consideration of it under those conditions where it is of minor significance.

Another reason for considering the structurally subordinate cases is of less concern in this work, but should nonetheless be noted. If one confines oneself to major cases only, to the structurally important cases, one remains unable to answer what is perhaps the most serious structural problem, namely, how and under what conditions the process in question ceases being unimportant and becomes important. It is a mistake to think that one can answer the question from a set of major cases. One can only explain how the process becomes structurally *more* important, not how it became important in the first place. It is often assumed, as a response to this problem, that the factors explaining the movement from structural importance to even greater structural importance are identical with those explaining its movement from unimportance to importance, or worse, from nonexistence to minor or significant existence. This may be true of some processes (although I cannot think of any offhand), but it is not true of *most* processes, and it is certainly not true of slavery. The movement from nonbeing to being, and structurally, from nonsignificance to significance, frequently involves different sets of explanatory conditions, but they usually share the quality that mathematicians and some physicists call a "catastrophe." An exploration of the nature and causes of catastrophic changes in the external systemic relations of slavery is not one of the objectives of this work. However, sound comparative analysis requires attention not only to the minor, typical, and advanced cases but to the circumstances that account for changes in the structural significance of the process.

In order to be able to make statements about the entire range of slave-holding societies, I have employed George P. Murdock's sample of world societies. If Murdock's list of 186 societies is a valid approximation of the full range of human cultures, then drawing on the slaveholding societies in this sample should provide a reasonable basis for formulating general statements.

There has been an enormous growth in slavery studies in recent years. Indeed, the most important developments in quantitative historical methods have been disproportionately concentrated in this area. Almost all have centered on the Atlantic slave trade and the slave systems of the modern Americas, although there are indications that the focus is beginning to shift to other areas, especially Africa. Traditional historians, particularly in Europe, have analyzed the institution of slavery in the ancient and medieval world for over a hundred fifty years, and such studies continue today at almost as rapid a pace as studies of modern slavery.

It is clearly impossible to read every scholarly work produced on every slaveholding society. I do not pretend to have done so, nor can I claim to have acquired a full understanding of the wider social contexts of the large-scale slave societies discussed in this book. After twelve years of concentrated comparative study (mainly of secondary materials), preceded by six years of intensive archival work on what was once my special area of interest—the British Caribbean slave societies, especially Jamaica—I remain painfully aware of the gaps in my knowledge of this global institution.

In spite of the narrow concerns of the vast majority of slave studies, important theoretical contributions have been made. My debt to those who have paved the theoretical way and have provided models of comparative analysis is amply demonstrated in my notes. The fact remains, however, that no global analysis of the institution of slavery has been attempted since H. J. Nieboer published his classic study over three-quarters of a century ago. Furthermore, Nieboer's work was largely confined to the study of preliterate societies and his focus, unlike mine, was on the conditions under which slavery existed—its external relations, so to speak. Nieboer was fully aware of his neglect of the internal issues and in his concluding chapter specified what he called the "outlines of a further investigation of the early history of slavery," which could almost pass for a table of contents of my own work. This book, in short, is a response to a scholarly challenge laid down eighty years ago. It is my hope that I have done some small justice to so worthy a challenger.

* * *

I HAVE INCURRED many intellectual debts in the production of this work. One of the greatest is to Stanley Engerman, whose help and advice have been quite extraordinary. Not only did he offer detailed textual criticism at various stages, but he gave enormously helpful general criticism of both a theoretical and a practical nature, to say nothing of amiable encouragement. It has been my unusual good fortune to have so generous a friend and colleague, and I am extremely grateful.

All who engage in comparative studies live in apprehension of the specialist, and no group of specialists is more to be feared than the students of ancient Greece and Rome—not because they are more hostile to generalists than other specialists, but because their subject has more traps and pitfalls for the unwary comparativist than any other. I have been extremely fortunate in the assistance I have received from several scholars in this area. I want to single out Peter Garnsey of Jesus College, Cambridge, who read and commented on the manuscript and during my year at Cambridge University, when most of the first draft was written, was a constant source of friendly support.

All of us who work on the comparative study of slavery are in intellectual debt to Sir Moses Finley. My study of classical slavery began with his works; so did my fascination with the wider historical sociology of the ancient world. Above all, his theoretical writings constituted the intellectual springboard for my own reflections on the nature of slavery and slave societies. His personal encouragement of my work persuaded me that a nonspecialist could with benefit immerse himself in the vast secondary and translated primary sources on the classical world; at the same time, his sharp and incisive criticisms of my manuscript and exposure of my blunders kept me fully aware of the scholarly minefield through which I picked my way.

Another classicist, Dr. Valerie Warrior, read my work with the greatest care and offered judicious revisions and technical assistance in the translation and interpretation of critical passages from the classical texts. My colleague John Padgett offered useful criticisms of the theoretical aspects of the work. I am grateful also to another colleague, Gosta Esping Anderson, for his kindness in translating an important Swedish text.

I took most of the advice I received, though not all. Any factual errors or lapses of logic in this work are entirely my own.

Financial support was provided by a grant from the National Endowment for the Humanities, a fellowship from the Center for Advanced Study at Princeton, and a grant from the Guggenheim Foundation. A visiting fellowship to Wolfson College, Cambridge University, enabled me to use the facilities of that institution during my sabbatical year there.

Many research assistants have aided me over the years, and I am deeply indebted to them. Paul Chen, at the time a graduate student at Harvard, translated literally hundreds of pages of important texts for me. His fluency in Chinese and Japanese (as well as in English), and the meticulous care with which he translated and interpreted the texts, effectively compensated for my inability to read these languages. Russell A. Berman was extremely helpful in my study of the secondary sources on slavery in the ancient Near East and classical world. Maurie Warren labored with me for months on the anthropological data on slavery in the preliterate world and was invaluable as a first coder of these materials. Tong Soo Chung, a former student, interpreted important Korean texts and provided a useful coding of the Korean materials. Murray Dalziel, Hiroshi Ishida, and Don Katcher were reliable and skillful programmers. Karen Lee typed repeated drafts with a speed and accuracy excelled only by her patience.

I have used many libraries in the preparation of this work and am grateful to their staffs, especially those at Harvard, Princeton, Cambridge University, and the University of the West Indies. I should like to single out for special praise the Tozzer Library at Harvard University's Peabody Museum of Archaeology and Ethnology; my work has been immeasurably aided by the extraordinary facilities there. Nancy J. Schmidt and her superbly competent and gracious staff have given invaluable assistance over the years.

Last and most significant is the debt I owe Nerys Wyn Patterson. As a student of medieval Celtic societies, she not only provided me with innumerable references to valuable sources on Celtic slavery, but translated and interpreted important Welsh and old Irish texts. As a historical anthropologist, she has been an invaluable colleague willing to listen to my latest interpretations and theories and to offer sober criticisms and illuminating insights. As my wife, she has refused to bear with traditional wifely fortitude the frustration of living with a spouse obsessively engaged in a twelve-year project. Her impatience has been my salvation: it has been good to be reminded every so often that there really are other important things in the world besides understanding the nature of slavery.

Contents

Introduction:
The Constituent Elements of Slavery   *1*

I The Internal Relations of Slavery

1 The Idiom of Power   *17*
2 Authority, Alienation, and Social Death   *35*
3 Honor and Degradation   *77*

II Slavery as an Institutional Process

4 Enslavement of "Free" Persons   *105*
5 Enslavement by Birth   *132*
6 The Acquisition of Slaves   *148*
7 The Condition of Slavery   *172*
8 Manumission: Its Meaning and Modes   *209*
9 The Status of Freed Persons   *240*
10 Patterns of Manumission   *262*

III The Dialectics of Slavery

11 The Ultimate Slave   *299*
12 Slavery as Human Parasitism   *334*

Appendix A:
Note on Statistical Methods   *345*
Appendix B:
Slaveholding Societies in the Murdock World Sample   *350*
Appendix C:
The Large-Scale Slave Systems   *353*
Notes   365
Index   484

Introduction

The Constituent Elements of Slavery

ALL HUMAN RELATIONSHIPS are structured and defined by the relative power of the interacting persons. Power, in Max Weber's terms, is "that opportunity existing within a social relationship which permits one to carry out one's will even against resistance and regardless of the basis on which this opportunity rests."[1] Relations of inequality or domination, which exist whenever one person has more power than another, range on a continuum from those of marginal asymmetry to those in which one person is capable of exercising, with impunity, total power over another. Power relationships differ from one another not only in degree, but in kind. Qualitative differences result from the fact that power is a complex human faculty, although perhaps not as "sociologically amorphous" as Weber thought.

Slavery is one of the most extreme forms of the relation of domination, approaching the limits of total power from the viewpoint of the master, and of total powerlessness from the viewpoint of the slave. Yet it differs from other forms of extreme domination in very special ways. If we are to understand how slavery is distinctive, we must first clarify the concept of power.

The power relation has three facets.[2] The first is social and involves the use or threat of violence in the control of one person by another. The second is the psychological facet of influence, the capacity to persuade another person to change the way he perceives his interests and his circumstances. And third is the cultural facet of authority, "the means of transforming force into right, and obedience into duty" which, according to Jean Jacques Rousseau, the powerful find necessary "to ensure them continual mastership." Rousseau felt that the source of "legitimate powers" lay in those "conventions" which today we would call culture.[3] But he did not specify the area of this vast human domain in which the source of authority was to be found. Nor, for that matter, did Weber, the leading modern student of the subject.[4] In Chapter 2 I show that authority rests on the control of those private and public symbols and ritual processes that induce (and seduce) people to obey because they feel satisfied and dutiful when they do so.

With this brief anatomy of power in mind we may now ask how slavery is distinctive as a relation of domination. The relation has three sets of constituent features corresponding to the three facets of power. It is unusual, first, both in the extremity of power involved, and all that immediately implies, and in the qualities of coercion that brought the relation into being and sustained it. As Georg Hegel realized, total personal power taken to its extreme contradicts itself by its very existence, for total domination can become a form of extreme dependence on the object of one's power, and total powerlessness can become the secret path to control of the subject that attempts to exercise such power.[5] Even though such a sublation is usually only a potential, the possibility of its realization influences the normal course of the relation in profound ways. An empirical exploration of this unique dimension of the dialectic of power in the master-slave relationship will be one of the major tasks of this work.

The coercion underlying the relation of slavery is also distinctive in its etiology and its composition. In one of the liveliest passages of the *Grundrisse,* Karl Marx, while discussing the attitudes of former masters and slaves in postemancipation Jamaica, not only shows clearly that he understood slavery to be first and foremost "a relation of domination" (his term and a point worth emphasizing in view of what has been written by some recent "Marxists" on the subject) but identifies the peculiar role of violence in creating and maintaining that domination. Commenting on the fact that the Jamaican ex-slaves refused to work beyond what was necessary for their own subsistence, he notes: "They have ceased to be slaves, . . . not in order to become wage labourers, but, instead, self-sustaining peasants working for their own consumption. As far as they are concerned, capital does not exist as capital, because autonomous wealth as such can exist only either on the basis of *direct* forced labour, slavery, or *indirect* forced labour, *wage labour.* Wealth confronts direct forced labour not as capital, but rather as *relation of domination*" (emphasis in original).[6] It is important to stress that Marx was not saying that the master interprets the relationship this way, that the master is in any way necessarily precapitalist. Indeed, the comment was provoked by a November 1857 letter to the *Times* of London from a West Indian planter who, in what Marx calls "an utterly delightful cry of outrage," was advocating the reimposition of slavery in Jamaica as the only means of getting the Jamaicans to generate surplus in a capitalistic manner once again.[7]

Elisabeth Welskopf, the late East German scholar who was one of the leading Marxist students of slavery, discussed at great length the critical role of direct violence in creating and maintaining slavery.[8] Force, she argued, is essential for all class societies. Naked might—violence, in Georges Sorel's terminology[9]—is essential for the creation of all such systems. However, organized force and authority—what Welskopf calls "spiritual force"—usually obviated the need to use violence in most developed class societies where nonslaves made up the dominated class. The problem in a slaveholding society, however, was that it was usually necessary to introduce new persons to the status of slaves because the former slaves either died out or were manumitted. The worker who is fired remains a worker, to be hired elsewhere. The slave who was freed was no longer a slave. Thus it was necessary continually to repeat the original, violent act of transforming free man into slave. This act of violence constitutes the prehistory of all stratified societies, Welskopf argued, but it determines both "the prehistory and (concurrent) history of slavery." To be sure, there is the exceptional case of the Old South in the United States, where the low incidence of manumission and the high rate of reproduction obviated the need continually to repeat the violent "original accumulation" of slaves. While Welskopf does not consider this case (her concern is primarily with the ancient world), her analysis is nonetheless relevant, for she goes on to note that the continuous use of violence in the slave order was also made necessary by the low motivation of the slave to work—by the need to reinforce reward with the threat and actuality of punishment. Thus George P. Rawick has written of the antebellum South: "Whipping was not only a method of punishment. It was a conscious device to impress upon the slaves that they were slaves; it was a crucial form of social control particularly if we remember that it was very difficult for slaves to run away successfully."[10]

But Marx and the Marxists were not the first to recognize fully the necessity or the threat of naked force as the basis of the master-slave relationship. It was a North Carolina judge, Thomas Ruffin, who in his 1829 decision that the intentional wounding of a hired slave by his hirer did not constitute a crime, articulated better than any other commentator before or after, the view that the master-slave relationship originated in and was maintained by brute force. He wrote:

> With slavery . . . the end is the profit of the master, his security and the public safety; the subject, one doomed in his own person, and his posterity, to

live without knowledge, and without the capacity to make anything his own, and to toil that another may reap his fruits. What moral considerations such as a father might give to a son shall be addressed to such a being, to convince him what it is impossible but that the most stupid must feel and know can never be true—that he is thus to labour upon a principle of natural duty, or for the sake of his own personal happiness. Such services can only be expected from one who has no will of his own; who surrenders his will in implicit obedience in the consequence only of uncontrolled authority over the body. There is nothing else which can operate to produce the effect. The power of the master must be absolute, to render the submission of the slave perfect.[11]

Justice Ruffin may have gone a little too far in what Robert M. Cover describes as "his eagerness to confront the reality of the unpleasant iron fist beneath the law's polite, neutral language."[12] He certainly underestimated the role of "moral considerations," to use his term, in the relationship. But his opinion did penetrate to the heart of what was most fundamental in the relation of slavery. As we shall see when we come to the comparative data in Chapter 7, there is no known slaveholding society where the whip was not considered an indispensable instrument.

Another feature of the coercive aspect of slavery is its individualized condition: the slave was usually powerless in relation to another individual. We may conveniently neglect those cases where the slave formally belonged to a corporation such as a temple, since there was always an agent in the form of a specific individual who effectively exercised the power of a master.[13] In his powerlessness the slave became an extension of his master's power. He was a human surrogate, recreated by his master with god-like power in his behalf. Nothing in Hegel or Friedrich Nietzsche more frighteningly captures the audacity of power and ego expansion than the view of the Ahaggar Tuaregs of the Sahara that "without the master the slave does not exist, and he is socializable only through his master."[14] And they came as close to blasphemy as their Islamic creed allowed in the popular saying of the Kel Gress group: "All persons are created by God, the slave is created by the Tuareg."[15]

These Tuareg sayings are not only extraordinarily reminiscent of Ruffin's opinion but of what Henri Wallon, in his classic study, wrote of the meaning of slavery in ancient Greece:

The slave was a dominated thing, an animated instrument, a body with natural movements, but without its own reason, an existence entirely absorbed in another. The proprietor of this thing, the mover of this instrument, the soul and the reason of this body, the source of this life, was the master. The master was everything for him: his father and his god, which is to say, his authority and his duty ... Thus, god, fatherland, family, existence, are all, for the slave, identified with the same being; there was nothing which made for the social person, nothing which made for the moral person, that was not the same as his personality and his individuality.[16]

Perhaps the most distinctive attribute of the slave's powerlessness was that it always originated (or was conceived of as having originated) as a substitute for death, usually violent death. Ali Abd Elwahed, in an unjustly neglected comparative work, found that "all the situations which created slavery were those which commonly would have resulted, either from natural or social laws, in the death of the individual."[17] Archetypically, slavery was a substitute for death in war. But almost as frequently, the death commuted was punishment for some capital offense, or death from exposure or starvation.

The condition of slavery did not absolve or erase the prospect of death. Slavery was not a pardon; it was, peculiarly, a conditional commutation. The execution was suspended only as long as the slave acquiesced in his powerlessness. The master was essentially a ransomer. What he bought or acquired was the slave's life, and restraints on the master's capacity wantonly to destroy his slave did not undermine his claim on that life. Because the slave had no socially recognized existence outside of his master, he became a social nonperson.

This brings us to the second constituent element of the slave relation: the slave's natal alienation. Here we move to the cultural aspect of the relation, to that aspect of it which rests on authority, on the control of symbolic instruments. This is achieved in a unique way in the relation of slavery: the definition of the slave, however recruited, as a socially dead person. Alienated from all "rights" or claims of birth, he ceased to belong in his own right to any legitimate social order. All slaves experienced, at the very least, a secular excommunication.

Not only was the slave denied all claims on, and obligations to, his parents and living blood relations but, by extension, all such claims and obligations on his more remote ancestors and on his descendants. He was truly a genealogical isolate. Formally isolated in his social relations with those who lived, he also was culturally isolated from the social heritage of his ancestors. He had a past, to be sure. But a past is not a heritage. Everything has a history, including sticks and stones. Slaves differed from other human beings in that they were not allowed freely to integrate the experience of their ancestors into their lives, to inform their understanding of social reality with the inherited meanings of their natural forebears, or to anchor the living present in any conscious community of memory. That they reached back for the past, as they reached out for the related living, there can be no doubt. Unlike other persons, doing so meant struggling with and penetrating the iron curtain of the master, his community, his laws, his policemen or patrollers, and his heritage.

In the struggle to reclaim the past the odds were stacked even more heavily in favor of the master than in the attempt to maintain links with living relatives. One of the most significant findings of Michael Craton's study of the oral history of the descendants of the Worthy Park plantation slaves of Jamaica was the extraordinary shallowness of their genealogical and historical memory.[18] The same is attested by the recorded interviews with American ex-slaves.

When we say that the slave was natally alienated and ceased to belong independently to any formally recognized community, this does not mean that he or she did not experience or share informal social relations. A large number of works have demonstrated that slaves in both ancient and modern times had strong social ties among themselves. The important point, however, is that these relationships were never recognized as legitimate or binding. Thus American slaves, like their ancient Greco-Roman counterparts, had regular sexual unions, but such unions were never recognized as marriages; both groups were attached to their local communities, but such attachments had no binding force; both sets of parents were deeply attached to their children, but the parental bond had no social support.

The refusal formally to recognize the social relations of the slave had profound emotional and social implications. In all slaveholding societies slave couples could be and were forcibly separated and the consensual "wives" of slaves were obliged to submit sexually to their masters; slaves had no custodial claims or powers over their children, and children inherited no claims or obligations to their parents. And the master had the power to remove a slave from the local community in which he or she was brought up.

Even if such forcible separations occurred only infrequently, the fact that they were possible and that from time to time they did take place was enough to strike terror in the hearts of all slaves and to transform significantly the way they behaved and conceived of themselves. Nothing comes across more dramatically from the hundreds of interviews with American ex-slaves than the fear of separation. Peter Clifton, an eighty-nine-year-old ex-slave from South Carolina, was typical when he said: "Master Biggers believe in whippin' and workin' his slaves long and hard; then a man was scared all de time of being sold away from his wife and chillun. His bark was worse than his bite tho', for I never knowed him to do a wicked thing lak dat."[19]

Isaiah Butler, another South Carolina ex-slave, observed: "Dey didn't have a jail in dem times. Dey'd whip em, and dey'd sell 'em. Every slave know what 'I'll put you in my pocket, Sir' mean."[20]

The independent constituent role of natal alienation in the emergence of slavery is vividly illustrated by the early history of slavery in America. Winthrop D. Jordan has shown that in the early decades of the seventeenth century there were few marked differences in the conception of black and white servitude, the terms "slave" and "servant" being used synonymously. The power of the master over both black and white servants was near total: both could be whipped and sold.[21]

Gradually there emerged, however, something new in the conception of the black servant: the view that he did not belong to the same community of Christian, civilized Europeans. The focus of this "we-they" distinction was at first religious, later racial. "Enslavement was captivity, the loser's lot in a contest of power. Slaves were infidels or heathens."[22] But as Jordan argues, although the focus may have changed, there was really a fusion of race, religion, and nationality in a generalized conception of "us"—white, English, free—and "them"—black, heathen, slave. "From the first, then, vis-à-vis the Negro the concept embedded in the term Christian seems to have conveyed much of the idea and feeling of *we* as against *they*: to be Christian was to be civilized rather than barbarous, English rather than African, white rather than black."[23] The strangeness and seeming savagery of the Africans, reinforced by traditional attitudes and the context of early contact, "were major components in that sense of *difference* which provided the mental margin absolutely requisite for placing the European on the deck of the slave ship and the Negro in the hold."[24]

Although using different symbolic tools, much the same sense of apartness, of not belonging, emerged in other cultures to differentiate the genuine slave from other forms of involuntary servants over whom almost total power was exercised. Yet the natal alienation of the slave was not necessarily expressed in religious, racial, or even ethnic terms. Among primitives, as we shall see, alienation from one's natal ties was all that was necessary. Sometimes law alone, superimposed on the slave's sense of not belonging, was sufficient. Indeed, it was Moses Finley, drawing on the Greco-Roman experience, who was among the first to emphasize what he called the "outsider" status of the slave as a critical attribute of his condition.[25] He did not make the mistake that Henri Lévi-Bruhl had earlier made, of generalizing from the Roman experience to the conclusion that the social alienation of the slave was necessarily an ethnic one.[26] Insofar as Roman slaves were foreigners, Finley argued, they were outsiders twice over, clearly allowing for the reduction of locally recruited slaves to the status of outsiders.

I prefer the term "natal alienation," because it goes directly to the heart of what is critical in the slave's forced alienation, the loss of ties of birth in both ascending and descending generations. It also has the important nuance of a loss of native status, of deracination. It was this alienation of the slave from all formal, legally enforceable ties of "blood," and from any attachment to groups or localities other than those chosen for him by the master, that gave the relation of slavery its peculiar value to the master. The slave was the ultimate human tool, as imprintable and as disposable as the master wished. And this is true, at least in theory, of all slaves, no matter how elevated. Paul Rycaut's classic description of the Janissaries as men whom their master, the sultan, "can raise without Envy and destroy without Danger"[27] holds true for all slaves in all times.

The incapacity to make any claims of birth or to pass on such claims is considered a natural injustice among all peoples, so that those who were obliged to suffer it had to be regarded as somehow socially dead. Callicles in Plato's *Gorgias* goes to the heart of the matter when he says:

> By the rule of nature, to suffer injustice is the greater disgrace because the greater evil; but conventionally to do evil is the more disgraceful. For the suffering of injustice is not the part of a man, but of a slave, who indeed had better die than live; since when he is wronged and trampled upon, he is unable to help himself, or any other about whom he cares.[28]

All slaves of all times and places were forced to suffer the natural injustice of which Callicles spoke. But nowhere in the annals of slavery has their condition been more poignantly expressed than by an American ex-slave, a Mr. Reed, who was interviewed by Ophelia Settle Egypt of Fisk University in about 1930.

> The most barbarous thing I saw with these eyes—I lay on my bed and study about it now—I had a sister, my older sister, she was fooling with the clock and broke it, and my old master taken her and tied a rope around her neck—just enough to keep it from choking her—and tied her up in the back yard and whipped her I don't know how long. There stood mother, there stood father, and there stood all the children and none could come to her rescue.[29]

How, we may ask, could persons be made to accept such natural injustice? The question applies not only to the victims but to those third parties not directly involved in the slave relation who stood by and accepted it. Denying the slave's humanity, his independent social existence, begins to explain this acceptance. Yet it is only a beginning, for it immediately poses the further question: how was the slave's social death, the outward conception of his natal alienation, articulated and reinforced?

Chapter 2 will attempt to answer this question by means of comparative data. There it will be shown that the master's authority was derived from his control over symbolic instruments, which effectively persuaded both slave and others that the master was the only mediator between the living community to which he belonged and the living death that his slave experienced.

The symbolic instruments may be seen as the cultural counterpart to the physical instruments used to control the slave's body. In much the same way that the literal whips were fashioned from different materials, the symbolic whips of slavery were woven from many areas of culture. Masters all over the world used special rituals of enslavement upon first acquiring slaves: the symbolism of naming, of clothing, of hairstyle, of language, and of body marks. And they used, especially in the more advanced slave systems, the sacred symbols of religion.

Natal alienation has one critical corollary that is an important feature of slavery, so important indeed that many scholars have seen it as the distinguishing element of the relation. This is the fact that the relation was perpetual and inheritable. James Curtis Ballagh's assessment sums this up for many scholars: "The distinguishing mark of the state of slavery is not the loss of liberty, political or civil, but the perpetuity and almost absolute character of that loss, whether voluntary or involuntary."[30] He then showed, from the case of Virginia, how in legal terms the crucial emerging difference between indentured servants and slaves during the seventeenth century was the consolidation of the view that "all negroes and other slaves shall serve *durante vita,*" beginning with the passage of the 1661 act of the Assembly, which stated that blacks, unlike white indentured servants, "are incapable of making satisfaction [for the time lost in running away] by addition of time."[31]

Ballagh was wrong, however, in his assumption that the inheritability of slavery was the "natural consequence" of the life bondage of the slave, although in fairness we should point out that he was shrewd enough not to commit the easy error of deriving inheritability from the totality of the master's power. It is easy to show in purely empirical terms that neither absolute power nor lifetime subjection to such power necessarily imply the inheritability of such status. The most obvious case is that of prisoners serving life sentences. Some oriental societies, especially China, did reduce the children of such convicts to slavery, but they were the exceptions.[32] More telling perhaps is the case of debt-bondage. In many societies the masters of debt-servants had as complete control over them as they did over slaves, including the right to sell them. The distinction, often made, between selling their labor as opposed to selling their persons makes no sense whatever in real human terms. Debt-servitude was, for all practical purposes, usually lifelong in societies where it was found, since the debtor's labor only repaid the interest. Still, despite the totality of the master's power and the expected lifelong servitude of the debtor, his status was almost never inherited by the debtor's children, even those born after servitude began.[33] Clearly then, there was no "natural" development from total power and lifelong subjection to hereditary servitude.

The hereditary factor only entered in when the servant lost his natal claims to his own parents and community. Having no natal claims and powers of his own, he had none to pass on to his children. And because no one else had any claim or interest in such children, the master could claim them as his own essentially on the grounds that whatever the parents of such children expended in their upbringing incurred a debt to him. Not by virtue, then, of his lifetime power over the slave did the master claim the latter's issue, but by virtue of the absence of any third party's interest in the child, the absence of the child's capacity to assert a claim on any such third parties, and the claim that necessarily accrued to the master with the parent's expenditures for childrearing.

The peculiar character of violence and the natal alienation of the slave generates the third constituent element of slavery: the fact that slaves were always persons who had been dishonored in a generalized way. Here we move to the sociopsychological aspect of this unusual power relationship. The slave could have no honor because of the origin of his status, the indignity and all-pervasiveness of his indebtedness, his absence of any independent social existence, but most of all because he was without power except through another.

Honor and power are intimately linked. No one understood this more than Thomas Hobbes. In the chapter of *Leviathan* in which he sets out to define his central concept—power—and related conditions, Hobbes devotes more than two-thirds of his effort to a detailed disquisition on the nature of honor. Fully recognizing that honor is a social-psychological issue, Hobbes wrote: "The manifestation of the Value we set on one another, is that which is commonly called *Honouring,* and *Dishonouring.* To Value a man at a high rate, is to *Honour* him; at a low rate, is to *Dishonour* him. But high, and low, in this case, is to be understood by comparison to the rate that each man setteth on himself."[34] The link between honor and power is direct: "To obey, is to Honour; because no man obeys them, whom they think have no power to help, or hurt them. And consequently to disobey, is to Dishonour." Somewhat cynically, Hobbes observes that it really does not matter "whether an action . . . be just or unjust: for Honour consisteth onely in the opinion of Power."[35]

As usual, Hobbes overstates his case; and his materialism prevents him from recognizing important dimensions of honor which, if anything, might have strengthened his argument. In Chapter 3 I shall explore the concept of honor in depth, and in the light of modern studies. Hobbes, however, gives us a useful starting point, for he was basically right in recognizing the significance of honor as a critical aspect of the psychology of power. Furthermore, his emphasis on the concept as a social-psychological process, as distinct from a purely psychological one, is still far in advance of, say, the reductionist utilitarianism of John Stuart Mill, who speaks of "the sense of honour" as "that feeling of personal exaltation and degradation which acts independently of other people's opinion, or even in defiance of it."[36] Nor does Mill ever make the critical connection between honor and power that came so easily to the more incisive mind of Hobbes.

The slave, as we have already indicated, could have no honor because he had no power and no independent social existence, hence no public worth. He had no name of his own to defend. He could only defend his master's worth and his master's name. That the dishonor was a generalized condition must be emphasized, since the free and honorable person, ever alive to slights and insults, occasionally experiences specific acts of dishonor to which, of course, he or she responds by taking appropriate action. The slave, as we shall see, usually stood outside the game of honor.

The honoring of the master and the dishonoring of the slave were the outward product of their interaction. We can say little or nothing about the private lives of the members of either group. Certainly we know next to nothing about the individual personalities of slaves, or of the way they felt about one another. The data are just not there, and it is the height of arrogance, not to mention intellectual irresponsibility, to generalize about the inner psychology of any group, be they medieval Jewish merchants, New England Puritan farmers, or Scythian slave policemen in Athens.

What we do know a great deal about, however, is the political psychology of the everyday life of masters and slaves in their relationships with one another. The interaction was complex and fascinating, fraught with conflict and perversity. It was Hegel who first explored in depth the dialectics of this political psychology.[37] Eugene Genovese, paraphrasing Hegel, has argued that "the slaveholder, as distinct from the farmer, had a private source of character making and mythmaking—his slave. Most obviously, he had the habit of command, but there was more than despotic authority in this master-slave relationship."[38] I disagree with Genovese on what is critical in the interaction, just as I do with Hegel on his stance that the slave stood interposed between his master and the object his master desired (that which was produced).[39] This may have been partly true of the capitalistic antebellum U.S. South, but as the comparative data will show, in a great many slaveholding societies masters were not interested in what their slaves produced. Indeed, in many of the most important slaveholding societies, especially those of the Islamic world, slaves produced nothing and were economically dependent on their masters or their master's nonslave dependents.

What was universal in the master-slave relationship was the strong sense of honor the experience of mastership generated, and conversely, the dishonoring of the slave condition. Many masters, especially among primitives, acquired slaves solely for this purpose. But even if the motivation was chiefly materialistic, the sense of honor was still enhanced. The traits Genovese attributed to the southern slaveholder—"his strength, graciousness, and gentility; his impulsiveness, violence, and unsteadiness[,t]he sense of independence and the habit of command [which] developed his poise, grace and dignity"[40]—hold for the way in which all slavemasters conceived of themselves, whether they were Toradja tribesmen in the central Celebes, ancient Greek intellectuals, or Islamic sultans. What they actually were is a matter on which I do not feel qualified to comment.

The counterpart of the master's sense of honor is the slave's experience of its loss. The so-called servile personality is merely the outward expression of this loss of honor.[41] And it is truly remarkable how consistent are the attributes of the expression of generalized dishonor not only among all slaves but among all oppressed peoples. There is, for example, the crushing and pervasive sense of knowing that one is considered a person without honor and that there simply is nothing that can be done about it. As Sosia observes in Plautus' *Amphitryo,* "It's not just the work, but knowing you're a slave, and nothing can alter it."[42] There is, too, the outward expression of self-blame. "You know," observes Phaniscus in Plautus' *The Ghost,* "slaves get the masters they deserve."[43] One finds this view repeated constantly by American ex-slaves in their interviews. "De Massa and Missus was good to me but sometime I was so bad they had to whip me," said Victoria Adams.[44] "It was always for something, sir. I needed de whippin'," recalled Millie Barber.[45]

More tragic than the victim's outward acceptance of blame as part of the dynamics of interaction with the master was his tendency to express psychological violence against himself: the outward show of self-hatred in the presence of the master, which was prompted by the pervasive indignity and underlying physical violence of the relationship. In Plautus' most mature play, *The Rope,* Palaestra, a slave anticipating escape from her condition, begins to cry, exclaiming "Oh life and hope." She is roguishly comforted by Trachalio, who tells her, "Just leave it all to me." To this Palaestra retorts, "I could if I had no force to fear, force which forces me to do violence to myself."[46] It does not matter whether these were Plautus' words or the words of the Greek playwright he was adapting. Whoever wrote them knew, in a profound way, what slavery really meant: the direct and insidious violence, the namelessness and invisibility, the endless personal violation, and the chronic inalienable dishonor.

It was in the interaction between master and slave that such feelings were expressed and played out. Clearly, no authentic human relationship was possible where violence was the ultimate sanction. There could have been no trust, no genuine sympathy; and while a kind of love may sometimes have triumphed over this most perverse form of interaction, intimacy was usually calculating and sadomasochistic.

Occasionally we get a glimpse of the relationship in action from incidents recalled by American ex-slaves. This is how Grace Gibson from South Carolina described the moment when she was given as a present to her young mistress:

> I was called up on one of her [Miss Ada's] birthdays, and Marster Bob sorta looked out of de corner of his eyes, first at me and then at Miss Ada, and then he make a little speech. He took my hand, put it in Miss Ada's hand, and say: "Dis your birthday present, darlin'." I make a curtsy and Miss Ada's eyes twinkle like a star and she take me in her room and took on powerful over me.[47]

Frederick Douglass, undoubtedly the most articulate former slave who ever lived, repeatedly emphasized as the central feature of slavery the loss of honor and its relation to the loss of power. After physically resisting a brutal white who had been hired by his exasperated master to break him, Douglass, whose spirit had nearly broken and who had run the risk of being executed for his resistance, recalls that he felt "a sense of my own manhood . . . I was nothing before, I was a man now."[48] And he adds in a passage for which this chapter may be read as an extended exegesis: "A man without force is without the essential dignity of humanity. Human nature is so constituted that it cannot honor a helpless man, although it can pity him; and even that it cannot do long, if the signs of power do not arise."[49]

At this point we may offer a preliminary definition of slavery on the level of personal relations: *slavery is the permanent, violent domination of natally alienated and generally dishonored persons.* The chapters of Part I are devoted to an elaboration of this statement.

Even at this most elementary level of personal relations it should be clear that we are dealing not with a static entity but with a complex interactional process, one laden with tension and contradiction in the dynamics of each of its constituent elements. The power of the master, in its very extremity, tended to become sublative; the slave's natural love for and attachment to kinsmen worked against the master's attempt to deny him all formal claims of natality; and the master's need for honor and recognition was both enhanced and undermined by the dishonoring of the slave and the latter's own effort to eke out some measure of pride and dignity in the face of the master.

However, it is not solely on the level of personal relations that we should examine slavery. Like all enduring social processes, the relation became institutionalized. Patterned modes of resolving the inherent contradictions of the relation were developed. Such modes were no less dynamic in their operation than were the constituent elements. On the institutional level the modes of recruitment, enslavement, and manumission were all intimately interrelated. The desocialized new slave somehow had to be incorporated; but the process of incorporation created new contradictions, which usually made necessary the process of manumission. One of the major tasks of this work will be to disclose the dynamics of this institutional process.

Parts I and II, therefore, explore cross-sectionally the peculiar features of slavery as a personal relation and as an institutional process. A significant problem with all attempts at discovering inductively the invariant dynamics of any given process is the inclination to neglect what may be called the limiting cases. By these I refer not to the extreme cases, which are fully accounted for in our samples, but to those apparently borderline cases that challenge the conceptual stability of the processes one has identified. It is always tempting to cut corners and simply exclude any limiting cases. Analysis of such cases, however, is essential to any comparative study, for both substantive and methodological reasons. In Part III of this book I examine the extraordinary phenomenon of palatine slavery. By showing how and why these elites were indeed genuine slaves, I shall not only have secured and more boldly defined the boundaries of my analysis, so to speak, but in the process raised issues that illuminate the interior analytic landscape I have previously explored.

These issues lead to my concluding analysis. Here I do not merely summarize my major findings; I integrate them into a final rendering of slavery as a special form of human parasitism. In so doing I bring into focus, and I hope illuminate, the domain of freedom, which inevitably shadows any attempt to understand the structure and meaning of slavery.

I

THE
INTERNAL
RELATIONS
OF SLAVERY

1

The Idiom of Power

"MAN'S REFLECTION on the forms of social life," wrote Marx, "and consequently, also, his scientific analysis of these forms, takes a course directly opposite to that of their actual historical development. He begins, *post festum,* with the results of the process of development ready to hand before him." The result is that the objects of social inquiry "have already acquired the stability of natural self-understood forms of social life, before man seeks to decipher, not their historical character, for in his eyes they are immutable, but their meaning—the categories of bourgeois economy consist of such like forms."[1]

In the course of my preliminary discussion of the constituent elements of slavery it must have appeared extraordinary that I made no reference to the notion of property—extraordinary because almost all early and modern definitions of slavery employ the term. The omission, however, was quite deliberate. The notion of property certainly has an important place in any discussion of slavery, as I hope to make clear shortly—but it is in no way one of the constitutive elements. The fact that the property concept has almost universally been considered constitutive is a classic instance of the *"post festum"* problem identified by Marx, which plagues so much of modern social analysis.

How then does the notion of property relate to the problem of slavery? An answer to this question takes us immediately back to the problem of power, more properly to the first of its three aspects—the forms and trans-formations of coercive action.

The Idiom of Power and the Concept of Property

Human beings have always found naked force or coercion a rather messy, if not downright ugly, business, however necessary. As Niccolò Machiavelli observed, it is the "beastly" part of power.[2] The problem has always been to find some way to clothe its beastliness, some idiom through which it can be made immediately palatable to those who exercise it. By the idiom of power I mean the principal way in which power is immediately interpreted in socially and cognitively acceptable terms. It is the way in which power is most meaningfully presented to, and understood by, those who wield it and by the members of their community. It is not necessarily a form of mystification, although one form of it certainly is. In most preindustrial societies individuals are usually fully aware of what it stands for. Nor is the idiom a form of legitimation, although it paves the way for it.

The idiom of power has two aspects—one purely social, the other conceptual. To begin with the social aspect, in the course of human history there have been two polar extremes in the idiomatic handling of the coercive aspect of power. One has been the tendency to acknowledge human force openly, then to humanize it by the use of various social strategies such as fictive kinship, clientship, and asymmetric gift exchanges. The other extreme has been the method of concealment, in which coercion is almost completely hidden or thoroughly denied. Indeed, it is even presented as the direct opposite of what it is, being interpreted as a kind of freedom.

Marx has given us our basic insight into the two extremes by contrasting the direct personal dependence of feudal societies with the "fantastic form" of concealment of real power in capitalism brought about by the mediation of property and the "fetishism of commodities."[3] I shall call the two polar types the personalistic and the materialistic idioms. In the personalistic idiom, power is direct—or nearly so—and is frequently transparent. Individuals are directly dependent on others and usually have others dependent on them. Among the most primitive societies such as hunter-gathering bands and acephalous village communities there is hardly even the need for an idiom, since power (insofar as it exists) is greatly diffused and relatively evenly distributed. In most hunter-gathering bands leadership is usually "titular," to use Robert Lowie's phrase. It almost never rests on the control of coercive force, but on its opposite—namely, the capacity for peacemaking and oratory.[4] "Personal prestige and the ability to inspire confidence," writes Claude Lévi-Strauss, "are the foundation of leadership."[5]

Direct relations of subjection in the personalistic idiom emerge on a structurally significant scale among more advanced premodern systems, where what Marshall Sahlins calls "chiefly power" finds its place. Even where the personalistic idiom translates a highly unequal distribution of power, it remains "simple and transparent." There is translation, but little concealment. Although power relations are not mystified, they are humanized; and here the principle of kinship plays a crucial role. Even in very advanced premodern societies we find a tendency to assimilate the direct domination of one person by another to at least a fictive kin relation. But kinship, whether real or fictive, is at most a veil, never a cloak. No dependent in such societies ever loses sight of the stark and obvious fact that he or she is directly dependent on a more powerful party—nor do the fictive patron and his real blood relations.[6]

Quite the opposite is true of the materialistic idiom. Here, as in the most extreme case of modern capitalism, relations of dependence are "disguised under the shape of social relations between the products of labor." Commodities are seen as autonomous entities, divorced entirely from labor and the unequal relations of laborer and capitalist who produced them. The power relationship is no longer viewed as power over persons but as power over commodities.[7]

Between these two extremes there is a continuum, which Marx clearly recognized, for he notes that in the early stages of simple commodity production the fetishism of commodities exists, although it is easy to see through; as the production process becomes more complex, power over individuals is increasingly mediated through power over goods until the point is reached where the basic power relationship is largely, though never completely, obscured.

It is possible to find traces of the fetishism of commodities even in simple societies where the personalistic idiom is dominant, as well as marked traces of direct, personalistic power where the materialistic idiom prevails. Thus, the late Czech sociologist Franz Steiner has shown how goods of practical, utilitarian value are "translated" into items of ritual and ceremonial value when used as the basis of power in several preliterate societies.[8] On the other hand, cases of transparent personalistic power are not hard to find in advanced capitalist societies—relations between blacks and whites (as well as between sharecropping whites and their landowners) in the U.S. South, not to mention those between many husbands and wives all over the industrial world, are cases in point.

In all societies, of course, there is a distinction between what is actually going on and the mental structures that attempt to define and explain the reality. I do not mean normative patterns, for these are merely prescriptive. I refer, rather, to what Lévi-Strauss has termed "a culture's homemade models," developed to *explain* the actual social processes.[9] At their most sophisticated, such native models may take into account the variance between practice and norm and also provide "explanations" for such variance. It is the difference, for example, between the legal codes and the jurisprudence of a culture, and their application to actual legal practice and procedure. The mental structures have some basis in reality, although their explanatory power varies considerably from one culture to another. More important, they not only reflect with varying degrees of accuracy the reality that informs them, but in turn feed back on and shape the ordering of that reality.

The conceptual aspect of the idiom of power, the category of thought that constitutes what Marx would call its "self-understood form," is the notion of property. What is property? The conventional definition is that it is anything owned by a person or corporation. But this begs the question. What is ownership? Immediately we open a pandora's box filled with at least two thousand years of jurisprudential clutter. The prevailing view of ownership, which persists as a fundamental legal concept in continental civil law and is now universally employed as a *social* concept even in countries such as Britain and America in spite of its irrelevance to common law, is the Roman view that it is a set of absolute rights in rem—things, usually tangibles, sometimes also intangibles. The whole weight of Anglo-American jurisprudence, as well as the sociology and economics of property, comes down heavily against the validity of such a concept. Why is this? Because, first, in sociological and economic terms (as in the view of common law) there can be no relation between a person and a thing. Relations only exist between persons. Second, relations between persons with respect to some object are always relative, never absolute.

Property in modern socioeconomic terms is, as W. B. Friedmann indicates, "a bundle of powers"; it refers to "the degree of control that a physical or corporate person exercises over an aggregate of tangible things, be they land, shares, claims, or powers of disposal."[10] The anthropologist E. Adamson Hoebel, drawing on the legal philosophy of W. N. Hohfeld and a wealth of anthropological data, arrives at much the same conclusion. Hoebel notes that there are two essential aspects of property, "(1) the object, (2) the web of social relations, which establishes a limiting and defined relationship between persons" with respect to the object.[11] He follows Hohfeld in seeing the object as being of far less significance in the definition of property than the relation.[12] The object, further, may be anything, *including other human beings.* Finally, almost all social scientists who have addressed the subject directly, as well as many jurists, have concluded that the notion of rights and duties has no place whatever in the conception of property. They add nothing to the more appropriate concepts of claims and powers. The most devastating criticisms have come from Scandinavian jurists such as Anders V. Lundstedt, Karl Olivecrona, and Alf Ross.[13] "Rights" and "duties," they have shown, are essentially fictitious. There is nothing in the social reality of property as we have defined it above that in any way requires the concept of either a right or a duty. The terms are, of course, "ideologically loaded," as

Ross has argued, and for this reason remain useful in the rhetoric of both the courtroom and the marketplace, but they are both redundant and mystical.[14]

There is no direct relationship, I must add, between the growing complexity of the notion of property and the growing complexity of socioeconomic systems. The complex, absolute (and essentially fictive) conception of property developed by the Romans and perpetuated in the legal-economic categories of modern civil law are in no way required by modern capitalism, as the case of Anglo-American common law with its simpler, more "primitive" relativist conception of property indicates. Indeed, this is one of those ironical cases where the more primitive (or earlier) conception has proved more appropriate to modern economic conditions than later, more complex developments.[15]

Property and Slavery

We must now focus all of this discussion on the problem of slavery. The first danger to which our analysis alerts us is the error of all attempts to define slavery in modern legalistic terms. Yet the vast majority of works employ just such an approach. It would be tedious to give a long list of such definitions;[16] we note only a few of the better known. For J. K. Ingram "the essential character of slavery may be regarded as lying in the fact that the master was owner of the person of the slave."[17] H. J. Nieboer, perhaps the most prominent author on the subject, also emphasizes property.[18] Perhaps the most frequently cited definition is that given by the League of Nations committee on slavery: "the status or condition of a person over whom any or all the powers attaching to the right of ownership are exercised."[19] More recently, James L. Watson has deliberately rejected anthropological advances in the definition of the subject by harking back to Nieboer, claiming "that the property aspect of slavery must be accepted as primary—this is what distinguishes slavery from all other forms of dependency and involuntary labour."[20]

My objection to these definitions is not that I do not consider slaves to be property objects. The problem, rather, is that to define slavery *only* as the treatment of human beings as property fails as a definition, since it does not really specify any distinct category of persons. Proprietary claims and powers are made with respect to many persons who are clearly not slaves. Indeed any person, beggar or king, can be the object of a property relation. Slaves are no different in this respect.

If we must use the property concept (an approach I prefer to avoid because of the inevitable confusions), we need to be more specific. We must show not simply that slaves are a category of persons treated as property objects, but as Moses Finley cogently demonstrates, that they are a *subcategory* of human proprietary objects.[21] The fact that we tend not to regard "free" human beings as objects of property—legal things—is merely a social convention. To take the most obvious example, an American husband is part of the property of his wife. We never express it this way, of course, for it sounds quite ghastly. Nevertheless, in actual and sociological terms a wife has all sorts of claims, privileges, and powers in the person, labor power, and earnings of her husband—as every third husband in America has painfully discovered in the divorce courts.[22] We need hardly add that husbands also have proprietary claims and powers in their wives, powers that they all too frequently exercise with naked violence.

These examples also reveal the speciousness of the ownership concept in definitions of slavery. It is often contended that a person does not own his or her spouse, whereas a master does own his slave. This distinction, however, is an exercise in semantics. If we do not accept the Roman and civil law conception of absolute ownership, then ownership, stripped of its social and emotional rhetoric, is simply another name for property; it can only mean claims and powers vis-à-vis other persons with respect to a given thing, person, or action. This is what a master possesses with respect to his slave; it is also exactly what a person possesses with respect to his or her spouse, child, employee, or land. The fact that a man does not say he "owns" his wife, or that she is part of his property, is purely conventional, as it is conventional for a master to say that he "owns" his slave, or that the slave is part of his property. To be sure, this convention is subjectively meaningful though objectively spurious. But the subjective meaning of the convention is an aspect of the slave's lack of honor. It is *impolite* to say of one's spouse or one's debtor that they are part of one's property. With slaves politeness is unnecessary.

Another fallacy that we can quickly dispose of is the common definition of a slave as someone without a legal personality. "The conventional legal explanation of personality," writes G. B. J. Hughes, "is that a person in law is an entity which may be the bearer of rights and duties."[23] Even if we rephrase the words "rights" and "duties" in realist terms—the *stricto sensu,* for example, of the technical terminology of Hohfeld—we find that the idea of the slave as someone without a legal personality has no basis in legal practice. It is a fiction found only in western societies, and even there it has been taken seriously more by legal philosophers than by practicing lawyers. As a legal fact, there has never existed a slaveholding society, ancient or modern, that did not recognize the slave as a person in law. All we need do to demonstrate this is to examine the legal response in slaveholding societies to the delicts of slaves: in all cases the slave is held legally and morally responsible, as we shall demonstrate in Chapter 7.

Many modern students of slavery, in failing to see that the definition of the slave as a person without a legal personality is a fiction, have found irresistible a popular form of argument that amounts to a red herring. The argument has a standard formula. The scholar, usually not very well informed about comparative legal practice, declares as a legal fact that the slave is defined and treated by the slaveholding class as a person without legal or moral personality. He then digs into his data and comes up with "proof" that the slave is indeed treated as a person in law—for is he not punished for his crimes? and are there not laws restricting the powers of the master? Thus there is, we are told, a fundamental problem posed by slavery, the so-called conflict between the treatment of the slave as a thing and as a human being. The formula ends with some ringing piece of liberal rhetoric to the effect that human dignity is irrepressible: "You may define a person as a thing," goes the flourish, "but you cannot treat him as one" (or some such pious statement). The whole formula is, of course, a piece of irrelevance. No legal code I know has ever attempted to treat slaves as anything other than persons in law. The irrelevance, I might add, springs from the confusion of jurisprudence with law. It is unfortunate that most students of slavery tend to be as knowledgeable about jurisprudence as they are ignorant of law.

Closely related to the definition of slavery as property rights in man is the view, held by some Marxists, that slavery is distinctive in that slaves are the only group of persons who constitute disposable capital—the only group of persons in whom capital is invested and who can be bought and sold on the market.[24] The first part of this claim can be quickly discarded. One need only cite that whole branch of modern economics known as the study of human capital to indicate its speciousness. When any firm, ancient or modern, invests funds in the training of persons whose skilled labor it later hopes to exploit for profit, it is doing nothing other than investing capital in persons.

More deserving of attention is the claim that only slaves are capable of being bought and sold. This claim, however, is also incorrect on purely empirical grounds. On the one hand, in the vast majority of premodern slaveholding societies there was usually a prohibition on the sale of all slaves beyond the second generation. The houseborn slave was considered so intimate and close a member of the household, or when not in the household so special a dependent, that masters would rather go into debt or pawn one of their free dependents than sell that slave. Indeed, such an act was usually considered so dishonorable that it resulted in a severe loss of face and prestige by the master. Nor was this always left to the sanction of public opinion. In many highly developed slave systems it was forbidden by law to sell a slave of the third or later generation.

On the other hand—and perhaps more tellingly—there were many societies in which "free" (or at any rate definitely nonslave) persons were capable of being sold. In imperial and modern China up to the early part of the present century, for example, it was common practice to sell certain categories of nonslave persons such as concubines and children—especially girls. In imperial China a distinction was always drawn between the continued "honorable" status of these individuals and the dishonored slaves, and it was a serious offense to sell such a person without making her status known to the purchaser.[25] The sale of concubines, and even daughters, continued into the 1940s.[26] (It is probable too that in early Rome children were sold into nonslave statuses.[27])

More important is the practice of bride sale all over traditional Africa and other parts of the world, where bride-price is an essential part of all marital transactions. Western anthropologists, compensating for earlier racist interpretations, have bent so far backward in denying the commercial aspect of these transactions that they have positively distorted the truth. But as anthropologist Robert F. Gray has demonstrated,[28] this overcompensation by liberal anthropologists, however laudable, completely misses the point. Both African men and women regard the exchange of brides as a sale—in addition, of course, to recognizing its other, equally important social and emotional functions. The women, in particular, make it clear that they take pride in the amount of goods or money paid for them and in no way feel that they have been demeaned by the fact that they were sold. The only source of humiliation would be the eventuality that a very low bride-price had been paid for them. These women would be universally horrified to learn that their sale in any way implied that they were slaves.

It is tempting to interpret the strong distaste for the sale of free persons as a peculiarly Western concern, but even this would be wrong. For it is a fact that in what is reputedly one of the world's most advanced societies—the contemporary United States—certain categories of persons annually are put up for auction and sold to the highest bidder. I refer to professional athletes, especially football stars. While the terms of the transaction differ, there is no substantive difference in the sale of a football idol such as Joe Namath by his proprietors, the New York Jets, to the Los Angeles Rams, and the sale of a slave by one proprietor to another. Namath would no doubt be as amazed and distressed as the betrothed bride of Africa to learn that his sale implied anything slavelike about him. (So, no doubt, would be the millions of Americans who count themselves among his fans.)

What do professional American athletes and the brides of tribal Africa have in common that makes it absurd for us to call them slaves in spite of the fact that they are bought and sold? Before answering this question, let me dispose of two popular though erroneous explanations. It is commonly thought that what is purchased in the case of a slave transaction is the "raw body" of the slave, whereas in the case of athletes, employees, and tribal wives not their bodies but their services are purchased or hired. This distinction has subjective meaning, but it makes no sense in physical or economic terms. When one buys or hires a person's labor, by implication one purchases the person's body for the negotiated period. There is no such thing as a disembodied service, only the discreet willingness to suspend all disbelief in such disembodiment. Present-day employers, it is true, do not demand of potential employees that they stand naked on an auction block being prodded and inspected by the employers and their physicians. But when an employer requires a medical certificate from a worker or professional athlete before hiring him, he is not only soliciting the same kind of information as a slavemaster inspecting his latest cargo of bodies, he is betraying the inherent absurdity of the distinction between "raw bodies" and the services produced by such bodies. There is certainly an important difference in the way the information is gathered, but the difference has to do with respect for the employee, recognition of his dignity and honor; it is in no way a confirmation of the fiction that there is a real difference between hiring a person's body and hiring his services.[29] Sidney W. Mintz argues that Marx was bothered by this problem, hence his tendency to waver between a recognition of wage labor as distinctive in that the worker sells his disembodied labor as a commodity, and a rejection of this view in favor of the worker as a wage slave.[30]

A second common error is the assumption that all nonslave persons have a choice in the sale and withdrawal of their services, whereas slaves do not. This might usefully distinguish slaves from most wage earners, but not from other forms of bonded laborers. Serfs, indentured servants, peons, and debt-bondsmen had no say in the purchase and sale of their labor. Nor for that matter did contracted professional athletes in the United States up until 1975 (not if they wanted to remain professional athletes). As late as 1970 the Supreme Court of the United States upheld, in the Curt Flood case, the notorious reserve clause that enabled proprietors to sell and buy athletes against their will. In addition to his antitrust claim, Flood made three other arguments in support of his case, one of them being that "the reserve system is a form of peonage and involuntary servitude in violation of the antipeonage statutes and the Thirteenth Amendment."[31] Many sportswriters directly compare the reserve clause to slavery, Alex Ben Block's comment on the issue being typical: "After the Civil War settled the slavery issue, owning a ball club was the closest one could come to owning a plantation."[32] The reserve clause has been defined as "a rule (or agreement between all clubs) that the baseball services of each player are in effect the permanent property, unless assigned, of the team holding the player's contract."[33]

Although the sale of a player is often euphemistically referred to as the sale of his "contract," the expressed views of players, proprietors, and sportswriters alike leave us in no doubt that it is the player's body and services that are sold. Typical of the proprietors' attitude is that of Philip K. Wrigley, chewing gum magnate and owner of the Chicago Cubs. In 1938 Wrigley hired a researcher to investigate the reflexes of his players, and he later commented on the experiment as follows: "We figured if we could measure the physical characteristics and reflexes of an established player, we could test prospects and know what to look for. If you want to make the best knives in the world you buy the finest steel. You can go out and spend $250,000 for a ballplayer and he may not be able to cut butter."[34] Just as significant is the fact that the Internal Revenue Service accepts as legitimate accounting practice the depreciation of players "over their estimated useful life in computing taxable income."[35]

American professional athletes, then, are depreciating proprietary assets in whom capital is heavily invested, who may be bought and sold like any other object of property. They now have a say in their sale and purchase, but until December 1975 their bodies when used to secure a livelihood in their chosen occupation (for many, the only occupation they knew) were part of the permanent assets of their proprietors. As professional athletes they had no voice whatever in their sale and purchase, nor in the price paid for them.

And yet these professional athletes are not slaves, and were not even during the era of the reserve clause. Why is this? What, in other words, are the real differences between slaves and nonslaves who are nonetheless salable even against their will? The first difference is the relative power of the parties concerned and the origins of their relationship. The proprietor's power is limited by the fact that nonslaves always possess some claims and powers themselves vis-à-vis their proprietor. This power has its source not only in central authorities (where they exist) but in a person's claims on other individuals. Even in early Rome where the pater familias had enormous power over his wife and children, the father could not kill the children without justification and "a wife in manu remained very much under the jurisdiction of her blood-relatives."[36] The slavemaster's power over his slave was total. Furthermore with nonslaves, the proprietor's powers, however great, were usually confined to a specific range of activities; with slaves, the master had power over all aspects of his slave's life.

The power relationship also differs in its origins. The crucial difference here, however, lies not in the fact that nonslaves always had some choice in initiating the relationship but, as we saw in the Introduction, in the fact that only slaves entered the relationship as a substitute for death. Serfs and peons, for example, were obliged to enter and remain in the relationship with their lords as a result of the latter's monopoly of the means of production.

Slaves also differ from contracted athletes and bond servants in their alienation from all ties of natality and in their lack of honor and publicly recognized repute. As indicated earlier, it is the latter that partially dictates the necessity for the fiction of disembodied labor.

While the constituent elements of slavery are the same for all kinds of social orders, the fact remains that this specific configuration of elements will be understood differently in different socioeconomic systems. Any attempt to understand comparatively the nature of slavery, or any other social process, if it fails to take account of such contextual variations, must remain of limited value.

This is where our discussion of the idiom of power becomes critical. The remainder of this chapter analyzes the nature of slavery in the context of the continuum between the two polar extremes of the idiom of power. I also explore how and why the conception of slavery in one idiomatic context has come to dominate and confound our comparative understanding of its basic nature.

The Idioms of Power and Slavery

Let us begin with the nature of slavery and of slave status in societies where the personalistic idiom is dominant. Most important is the fact that the conception of the slave as a person without power, natality, and honor does not create in the personalistic idiom the antithetical status that Westerners call "freedom." In almost all non-Western slaveholding societies there was no such status in law as a "free" person. Indeed, there was no word for freedom in most non-Western languages before contact with Western peoples. Instead of defining slaves and nonslaves in polarized terms, people in societies where the personalistic idiom was dominant perceived the status of persons along a single dimension of power: that of claims and powers in other persons. All persons were seen as the objects of property. Individuals differed in the degree of power, claims, and privileges others had in them and in the counterbalancing set of claims, powers, and privileges they had in others.

In human terms this was seen as the amount of protection a person had and the number of his protectors. The Ashanti of West Africa neatly illustrate the point. "If you have not a master," goes a popular proverb, "a beast will catch you." And according to another: "When a chicken separates itself from the nest, the hawk will get it." Robert S. Rattray, in his classic ethnography of the Ashanti, elaborates as follows:

> It will have been observed already that a condition of voluntary servitude was, in a very literal sense, the heritage of every Ashanti; it formed indeed the essential basis of his social system. In West Africa it was the masterless man and woman who ran the imminent danger of having what we should term "their freedom" turned into involuntary bondage of a more drastic nature.[37]

Voluntary servitude, however, was not slavery. Rattray takes pains to point out that if we are to understand the institution of slavery in a society such as the colonial Ashanti where the personalistic idiom was dominant, it is essential that we "banish from our thoughts the familiar pictures conjured up in our minds by the popular conception of slavery as it existed in Europe and America prior to its abolition," and he adds:

> In that country [Ashanti] there existed no person or no thing without a master or owner. There is a well known proverb which runs: ... If there be a debt in the village that owns no master (i.e. for which no one can be found responsible), it is a debt of the head of the village; if there be a thing in a village without an owner, it belongs to the head of the village.[38]

Clearly, it was not enough to have a great deal of protection, for that the slave of a powerful master had. A slave was powerless in relation to another precisely because he had to depend *exclusively* on a single person for protection. A person departed from the condition of slavery to the degree that he was able to spread the source of his protection as wide as possible—without, at the same time, making it too diffuse. Thus the real antithesis to slavery in societies where the personalistic idiom of power was dominant was what may be called countervailing power. People did not seek to be "free" (in the modern Western "bourgeois" sense of isolation from the influence of others) in such systems because, ironically, this was the surest path to slavery. Rather they sought to become embedded in a network of protective power.

In societies, then, where the personalistic idiom of power prevailed, the most unslavelike person was the one in whom a small number of claims, powers, and privileges were spread over a large number of persons; the slave, on the other hand, was someone in whom a large number of claims, privileges, and powers were concentrated in a single person. This implied an important proprietary status as far as the slave was concerned. The slave could not claim or exercise direct powers of property; all such claims had to be made through the master. Thus we are led back to the conclusion that property is indeed an important (though secondary) factor in defining both the legal and the socioeconomic status of the slave, with this critical difference: the slave was a slave not because he was the *object* of property, but because he could not be the *subject* of property.[39]

We must now turn our attention to the other end of the continuum of the idiom of power and consider that point on the continuum where the shift begins in critical fashion away from the personalistic toward the materialistic. To quote Marshall Sahlins, it is the transition from a system of property in which "a right to things [is] realized through a hold on persons" to one in which "a hold on persons [is] realized through a right to things."[40]

This transition finds its earliest complete expression in the Roman socioeconomic order, with, of course, important precursors. The Roman economy was, by modern standards, a simple one, although more advanced than any other in the premodern world. Naked power remained important, but incorporated extremely complex development toward a materialist idiom of power. In socioeconomic terms, power was mediated through wealth, especially land and slaves.[41] On the cognitive level, we find the emergence of a startlingly new legal concept: the idea of absolute ownership of things. The

Greek laws of property were, according to Douglas M. MacDowell, "simple and primitive by comparison with the elaborate property laws of Roman and later systems."[42] There was no linguistic distinction between ownership and possession among the Greeks although, in practice, they might have been aware of it. It is perhaps misleading to speak of the Greek property system as being more primitive since, ironically, from the viewpoint of modern Anglo-American common law, the less elaborated and more relativistic Greek system was actually closer to modern practice than was the Roman.[43] The significant point about the Roman law of property, with its emphasis on absolute dominion in tangible things, was the fact that it fitted nicely with the realities of an economy of simple commodity production. As Otto Kahn-Freund observed in his introduction to Karl Renner's work:

> The Roman dominium, the legal norm safeguarding to the individual the absolute unfettered control over a tangible thing, tallied precisely with the economic and social function of property ... The conception of ownership was the mirror of a society in which wealth mainly consisted of tangible things, things which formed a functional unit ... Legal and economic property coincided: The notion of ownership applied to, and was the corollary of, a functional microcosm, an *universitas rerum*.[44]

The notion of absolute property became pivotal in private law. It conceptualized, reflected, and supported both production and power without the need for support from other areas of culture. Another quotation from Kahn-Freund expresses this well: "Property, then, the central institution of private law, fulfilled in the system of simple commodity production the functions of providing an order of goods, and, in part, an order of power. It did so without any essential aid from other institutions."[45]

It seems not unreasonable to argue that slavery played a critical role in this development—that the Romans were led to elaborate (that is to say, make fictive) the laws of property to the degree that they did chiefly because of the problems posed by large-scale slavery in their midst. The laws of slavery, W. W. Buckland tells us, are "the most characteristic part of the most characteristic intellectual product of Rome." Furthermore, "there is scarcely a problem which can present itself, in any branch of law, the solution of which may not be affected by the fact that one of the parties to the transaction is a slave, and outside the region of procedure, there are few branches of the law in which the slave does not prominently appear."[46] The critical role of slavery in the development of Roman law is perfectly understandable in light of the major role of slaves in the economy.[47] Slaves along with land were the major sources of wealth. Of the two, land was without doubt the more important; but slaves were the more flexible and problematic.

The development of the Roman doctrine of absolute ownership presents us with a fascinating paradox. The Romans, whom we celebrate for their legalistic innovations, in elaborating the doctrine of dominium or absolute ownership, were actually creating a legal fiction and thereby distorting the concept of property when viewed from the perspective of comparative law. Modern civil law continues to confound and be confounded by this ingenious fiction. English common law, on the other hand, largely escaped the Roman fiction, precisely because its law of property grew directly out of its primitive Anglo-Saxon and feudal notions of property.[48]

Our analysis now prompts us to ask two important questions: Did the Romans know that they were creating a fiction in developing the doctrine of dominium? If so, why did they do it? I am inclined to think that the Romans knew exactly what they were doing when they developed the doctrine of dominium; they were too legally clever not to have been aware of it. Why then did they do it? The answer, as I have already suggested, is found in a single word: slavery. While it is true that Greek civilization was based on slavery, the degree of socioeconomic dependence on the institution was apparently far greater in late republican and imperial Rome than at any period of Greek history. Greek slavery was overwhelmingly urban and industrial; Roman slavery had a major impact on both its urban and rural economic sectors.[49] This unprecedented state of affairs created all sorts of social problems, as can be easily imagined. First, given the number of slaves in the Roman midst, it was vitally important that the issue of their status be settled.[50] An unambiguous way had to be found for differentiating human beings classified as chattel from human beings classified as nonchattel. It should be all too obvious that any confusion on the matter would have been socially disastrous. It may be wondered why was it that the Greeks, who had a highly developed system of slavery in their critical urban sectors, did not find it necessary to resolve the problem in the same way. My feeling is that the Greeks did not find the problem as socially urgent as the Romans, because of the highly particularistic nature of the Greek civilization. Two more crucial social divisions obviated the need for legal precision: the distinction between citizen and noncitizen, reinforced by the distinction between Greek and non-Greek. It is true that Greeks occasionally enslaved fellow Greeks, but normally there was considerable reluctance to do so. More important, each Greek state jealously guarded the privilege of citizenship. What these two critical social divisions meant was that in spite of the large number of slaves, there was never any problem of confusing slaves with persons who really mattered—not nonslaves who were not citizens (metics), but freeborn, ethnically superior Greek citizens.[51]

In Rome the situation was quite different. From relatively early times, Rome was a highly inclusive society. The long-standing practice of granting citizenship to manumitted slaves was quite extraordinary. Clearly there were no preexisting social divisions to insulate the freeborn population, as was the case in Greece. The Romans had no choice but to turn to law for social clarification. However, when the Romans of the expanding slave economy of the late republic turned to the ancient proprietary action (the *legis actio sacramento in rem*), they saw all too clearly that this essentially relativistic principle of property would not do as a means of distinguishing slaves from other persons. In other words, they saw clearly what any modern Anglo-American lawyer or Ashanti elder would have seen, that all human beings can be the object of property and that, strictly speaking, property refers to a set of relationships between persons.[52]

In searching for a solution to this problem, the Romans invented the legal fiction of dominium or absolute ownership, a fiction that highlights their practical genius. It is not as jurists that we should applaud the Romans, but as applied sociologists. Let us see how dominium worked. First, by emphasizing the categories of persona (owner) and res (thing) and by rigidly distinguishing between corporeal and incorporeal things, the Romans created a new legal paradigm in which there could be no room for ambiguity in deciding what was and what was not the object of property. An object could only be a tangible thing. More important, the fiction now emerged that was to haunt continental Western law for the next two thousand years: property was no longer a relation between persons but a relation between persons and things. And this fiction fitted perfectly its purpose, to define one of the most rapidly expanding sources of wealth, namely slaves. The three constituent elements of the new legal paradigm—*persona, res,* and *dominium*—modeled directly the three constituent elements of the master-slave relationship—master, slave, and enslavement. There is yet another aspect of the notion of dominium that points clearly to the role of slavery in its development. More than just a relation between a person and a thing, dominium was absolute power. And this absolute power involved not simply the capacity to derive the full economic value of a thing, to use (*usus*) and enjoy its fruits (*fructus*), as well as "to use it up" (*ab-usus*), to alienate it, but perhaps most significantly, as the Danish legal historian C. W. Westrup notes, it has the psychological meaning "*of inner power over a thing* beyond mere control."[53] If it is difficult to explain why the Romans would want to invent the idea of a relation between a person and a thing (an almost metaphysical notion, quite at variance with the Roman way of thinking in other areas), it becomes impossible to comprehend why they should want inner psychic power over it unless we understand that, for most purposes, the "thing" on their minds was a slave.

Although there is controversy over the nature of the primitive Roman law of property, the consensus is that, whatever may have preceded it, the concept of dominium was not fully developed before the end of the republican era. The use of the term "dominium" in its classic sense emerged only in the first century B.C., and the other term for absolute property—"proprietas"—came even later.[54]

The etymology of the word "dominium" further supports our hypothesis. When the word "dominus" first appeared in the third century B.C., it did not mean owner but, significantly, slavemaster.[55] It was between this period and the end of the first century B.C. that the Roman slave order rapidly developed and reached its highest point of socioeconomic permeation. It can be no accident that the shift in the meaning of "dominium" from slaveholding to the holding of all objects of property in an absolute sense perfectly correlates with the changeover of the Roman economy from one in which slaves were simply one of many objects of property to a society in which slaves became one of the two most important sources of wealth and objects of property. I am not saying that the emergence of large-scale slavery was the only factor explaining the development of the absolute conception of ownership, but we can reasonably guess that it was the decisive one.

By means of the doctrine of dominium, then, the condition of slavery was transformed into a condition of powers in rem. Hence the most common conception of the slave among the Romans became, by the end of the republic, that of a thing—the idea of "thingness" in law being emphasized as never before, specifically for this purpose. The slave was above all a res, *the only human res.*[56] The cardinal attribute of the condition of slavery was that the slave was a person subject to dominium.

If my interpretation of the development of the Roman doctrine of absolute property is correct, it is seen at once how misguided are modern attempts, drawing mainly on this tradition, to define slavery in terms of the civil law concept of ownership or absolute property. Such definitions not only confuse legal fiction with legal and sociological realism; worse, they read the history of human thought backward. It is not the condition of slavery that must be defined in terms of absolute notions of property, as is so often attempted; rather it is the notion of absolute property that must be explained in terms of ancient Roman slavery.

The Contradictions of Slavery

The coercive problem of slavery occasioning the Roman fictive legal "solution" that was to influence all subsequent Western conceptions of slavery and the continental law of property was part of a wider, more fundamental set of problems posed by this relation in all kinds of social orders, and to these I now return.

Earlier, I observed that in its coercive aspect slavery was less problematic in societies where the personalistic idiom was dominant. It would be a mistake, however, to claim that slavery was never problematic in such societies. The main advantage of having slaves in these, as in all other kinds of societies, was their inherent flexibility. Because slaves were natally alienated, they could be used in ways not possible with even the most dominated of nonslave subordinates with natal claims.

Whatever the prevailing idiom, slaves could always be used either as direct objects of domination or as an indirect means of dominating others. In many primitive societies where there was little differentiation in the possession of wealth, slaves were usually the major (sometimes the only) form of wealth that made such differentiation possible. Claude Meillassoux and others have shown how in many parts of pre-European West Africa masters used slaves not only as direct objects of domination, but as a primary means of reproducing and accumulating wealth both in persons (more slaves) and in goods. This was done by exploiting the female slaves' reproductive and farming capacity, and the farming and military capacity of the male slaves. In many of these societies the primary objective was not to increase the consumption of goods but to convert wealth into power over nonslaves.[57] As Igor Kopytoff and Suzanne Miers neatly expressed it with respect to the less centralized parts of Africa, there was not a mass consumption society with ever-increasing demand for commodities, but a society with a mass demand for persons as retainers in the escalating demand for power.[58] Power over slaves, then, was both the direct exercise and enjoyment of power and an investment in the means of reproducing and accumulating power over others. In being so used, slavery was clearly problematic for the prevailing personalistic idiom with its humanized fictive kinship expression. Since the slave obviously did not belong, to define him as a junior fictive kinsman undermined the authenticity of fictive kin assimilation with respect to nonslave retainers. The relation gave the master an advantage in the competition for status and power, but it was an advantage that broke the rules of the game and threatened to undermine the ideological expression of the prevailing idiom.

When we move to the other extreme of this idiom of power, we find that slavery was equally problematic—but for the very opposite reason. In the modern capitalistic slave systems of the Americas, especially that of the U.S. South, the slave relation stands out as a direct, personal mode of domination in the midst of the prevailing indirect idiom. It is this, we suspect, which led Eugene Genovese to claim that the South was precapitalistic.[59] It has now been persuasively demonstrated, however, that this society was thoroughly capitalistic.[60] Slaves, because of their total flexibility, could be used as the perfect capitalistic work force as easily as they could be (and were) used as the perfect noncapitalistic retainer, concubine, or soldier.

The problem that slavery created for the U.S. South and other capitalistic slave systems, therefore, was not economic but, as in primitive societies, ideological. The relation, even while promoting capitalism, undermined its major ideological rationalization: the indirect idiomatic mode expressed in the notion of a free wage labor force. The use of personally dominated individuals for the production and reproduction of wealth exposed the reality behind the so-called free labor. The laborer came to see his work for others for what it really was—alienation from the means of production and exploitation by the employer. Faced with the stark reality of personal power exercised over slaves, the worker could easily see that his much-vaunted freedom to change employers was simply a meaningless freedom to change masters.

In this way the free laborer became dangerously radicalized by the presence of slavery. Nonslave workers universally tended to despise work for others in all societies where a critical mass of slaves was used.[61]

It would be a mistake to say that slavery demeaned labor per se. What Moses Finley showed for ancient Greece held equally for the modern Americas: it was labor for others that was shunned, not labor in itself.[62] Furthermore, it is not strictly correct to argue that slavery *caused* the contempt for labor; rather it *exposed* the demeaning nature of such labor. From a Marxian perspective, all labor for others who appropriate the means of production involves alienation and exploitation. It is, by its very nature, demeaning. When the ideological camouflage is stripped from slavery, a crisis is created for the capitalist class. We can see this in the mass migration of free white labor from the Caribbean at the end of the seventeenth century as slave labor expanded rapidly,[63] and it is evident in the mass migration of free farmers from the latifundia areas of Italy during the period of the late republic.[64]

The master class, to be sure, has various ways of responding to such a crisis. It may simply allow the exodus of free workers to run its course, resulting in a total slave order in which almost all workers are slaves and all nonlaborers masters or their agents, as happened in the Caribbean. Or the master class may contain the expansion of the slave sector, allowing room for free persons to work on their own and exploiting them in other, more indirect ways. This happened in Roman Italy and in the U.S. South. In addition, the slave relationship provides its own partial resolution. The definition of the slave as an outsider, as the enemy within who is socially dead, allows for solidarity between master and nonslave as honorable members of their community vis-à-vis the dishonored slave. Such resolutions, however, are rarely complete. Often they create further problems and thereby establish a new cycle of crisis and response. But these are issues to be explored at greater length elsewhere.

2

Authority,
Alienation,
and
Social Death

ALL POWER STRIVES for authority. A. Geoffrey Wood-
head, in his study of Thucydides and the nature of power, observes that
"there remains a need for spiritual and moral support, a need to say that an
action is 'right' . . . whatever the realpolitik behind the action."[1] In our examination of the property concept in the last chapter we saw that the master-slave relationship cannot be divorced from the distribution of power
throughout the wider society in which both master and slave find themselves. Total power or property in the slave means exclusion of the claims
and powers of others in him.

If the master sought to exclude as far as possible all other claims and
powers in his slave, it nevertheless remains true that he needed both the recognition and the support of the nonslave members of his community for his
assumption of sovereign power over another person. An isolated master
faced grave risks. Plato, who knew what he was talking about on this issue,
shrewdly pointed out that a slave owner within his community had nothing
to fear from his slaves because the entire state was ready to defend each individual citizen. But if he and his immediate family with more than fifty
slaves were transported to the middle of a desert where no freeman could
come to his defense, that citizen would be in great fear for his own life and
that of members of his family, and he would try to ingratiate himself with
the slaves by making promises and offers of freedom.[2]

Actually, the situation was more complex than this, for the danger the master faced was not merely physical. In all slaveholding societies the slave posed grave moral and spiritual dangers. Most slave populations have been so small that they were rarely considered a serious political menace; their danger lay in their capacity to offend supernaturally. The master's task, then, had both a negative and a positive aspect. On the negative side, he had to defuse the potential physical and spiritual threat posed by his slave's presence. And on the positive side, he had to secure extracoercive support for his power. Both were achieved by acquiring the thing we call authority.

Authority as Symbolic Control

What was involved in the acquisition of authority? From the community at large, authority came with the institutionalization of the slave relationship. It was achieved by incorporating it into the normative order. As Siegfried Lauffer puts it, the power relationship (*Gewaltverhältnis*) that formed the basis of the slave relationship had to become a rights relationship (*Rechtsverhältnis*).[3] Those who were not directly involved with the relationship—though indirectly influenced by it—had to come to accept it not just grudgingly, but as the normal order of things (as did the nonslaveholding Greek, Roman, Hausa, or antebellum southern farmer). Nor was it only the nonslaveholding "freeman" whom the master wished to acknowledge his authority. The arrogance of power knows no bounds, for the master desired too that the slave recognize his authority, as well as his right to dominate him. To the extent that he did, to that degree was he able to walk fearlessly into the desert with his slave. And the truth is that many masters succeeded. As the history of the slaveholding peoples of the Sahara shows, many a master accompanied by his slave knew, for long periods of their lives, only each other and the desert.

Understanding how this happens is no easy matter. Most social scientists faced with the problem of authority are content to cite a few well-known passages from Weber—the acknowledged authority on the subject—then continue blithely with their analysis. There is too much that is unsatisfactory in Weber's analysis for us to take this course. He tells us that authority has three sources: law, charisma, and tradition.[4] Law, however, cannot be a source of authority, for it is merely that complex of rules which has the coercive power of the state behind it. As the Scandinavian and other modern jurists have pointed out, to define law as normative rules is to evade the crucial issue.[5] Law itself begs for the thing we call authority; and as every student of jurisprudence knows, one of the major sources of law, and of law's authority, is tradition. Nor does Weber's notion of charisma get us very far. By its very nature, this is an exceptional phenomenon. No doubt there was the occasional master who was genuinely charismatic, but in general masters were no more endowed with unusual personal qualities than other persons, including their slaves.

We are left only with tradition. Weber was on the right track here, but unfortunately was too vague. What does tradition mean? And why should the traditional automatically convey authority? By tradition Weber was obviously referring to the total complex of norms, values, ideas, and patterned behavior we call culture. I agree that somewhere in this vast universe of received human experience is to be found the source of authority; but where?

The answer, I think, has been provided by students of symbolic anthropology, beginning with Meyer Fortes' critique of Weber.[6] Fortes and other British anthropologists, especially Raymond Firth, have argued that symbols, both private and public, constitute a major instrument of power when used directly or indirectly. Herein lies the source of authority. Those who exercise power, if they are able to transform it into a "right," a norm, a usual part of the order of things, must first control (or at least be in a position to manipulate) appropriate symbolic instruments. They may do so by exploiting already existing symbols, or they may create new ones relevant to their needs.

The full mechanics of this process of symbol appropriation is beyond the scope of the present work; what I shall do is examine the nature of symbolic control in the case of the master-slave relationship. Symbolic processes, like so many other areas of human experience, have both an intellectual and a social aspect. On the intellectual level symbolic thought attempts to explain, in the language of symbols, a given area of actual experience. It is essentially mythic, similar in intellectual form to the validating concepts and beliefs of religion. The social aspect of symbolic behavior refers to the ritual processes by means of which symbolic ideas are acted out in terms of real human interactions. Such actions invariably are highly formalized and ceremonial. Where the experience being symbolized extends over a long period of time, there is a tendency for a clearly defined symbolic pattern to develop: critical stages in the developmental process, and especially the transition from one stage to the next, are given special ritual expression. The celebrated work of Arnold Van Gennep examined, for example, the various ritual expressions of the human life cycle among a variety of peoples.[7] Similar rites of passage may be found in lasting relationships—and slavery, as we shall see, is one such case.

A final theoretical point to note is the contribution of Victor Turner who, in his masterful treatise on the Ndembu and in later theoretical writings, developed the concept of the dominant symbol.[8] Mythic and ritual processes by nature are multivocal, ambiguous, diffuse, and sometimes downright incomprehensible. Within a given cultural domain, however, a dominant symbol—a major mythic theme, a key ritual act—stands out as pivotal. By its emergence it makes possible an internal interpretation of the symbolic process on both the intellectual and the social level.

Slavery, I intend to show in this chapter, is a highly symbolized domain of human experience. While all aspects of the relationship are symbolized, there is overwhelming concentration on the profound natal alienation of the slave. The reason for this is not hard to discern: it was the slave's isolation, his strangeness, that made him most valuable to the master; but it was this very strangeness that most threatened the community and that most exercised that "primacy of feeling and willing over thinking" which is at the core of the symbolic mind. On the cognitive or mythic level, one dominant theme emerges, which lends an unusually loaded meaning to the act of natal alienation: this is the social death of the slave. On the ritual level, the enslavement process is expressed in terms of well-defined rites of passage.

The Two Conceptions of Social Death

If the slave no longer belonged to a community, if he had no social existence outside of his master, then what was he? The initial response in almost all slaveholding societies was to define the slave as a socially dead person. Claude Meillassoux and his associates have most thoroughly explored this aspect of slavery. They reject the simplistic materialist view, which fails to take account of this problem—which indeed does not even recognize the existence of the problem.[9] From the structural viewpoint, Meillassoux argues, slavery must be seen as a process involving several transitional phases. The slave is violently uprooted from his milieu. He is desocialized and depersonalized. This process of social negation constitutes the first, essentially external, phase of enslavement. The next phase involves the introduction of the slave into the community of his master, but it involves the paradox of introducing him as a nonbeing. This explains the importance of law, custom, and ideology in the representation of the slave relation. Summarizing his own views and those of his associate Michel Izard, Meillassoux writes: "The captive always appears therefore as marked by an original, indelible defect which weighs endlessly upon his destiny. This is, in Izard's words, a kind of 'social death.' He can never be brought to life again as such since, in spite of some specious examples (themselves most instructive) of fictive rebirth, the slave will remain forever an unborn being (non-né)."[10]

There is much of value in this analysis, although it exaggerates to make the point. It goes astray, or at any rate is likely to mislead, mainly in its overemphasis of external sources and conquest as the initiating act of enslavement. It is simply not the case that "the condition of slavery never results from an internal process of social differentiation." Meillassoux is here drawing too narrowly on his field experience in West Africa, in much the same way that an earlier French theorist, Henri Lévy-Bruhl, was led to the same conclusion by generalizing from the single experience of Roman slavery.[11] Slavery among the primitive Goajiros of Venezuela, the large-scale slavery in Korea from the Koryŏ period to nearly the end of the Yi dynasty, and Russian slavery during the seventeenth and eighteenth centuries are three cases of slavery operating in different contexts and on very different scales as the result of a process of internal differentiation.

In almost all premodern slaveholding societies, at least some slaves were locally recruited. The problems these slaves posed were no different from those presented by the more dramatically disrupted captives. What was different, however, was the manner of their social death. I suggest that there were two ways in which social death was represented and culturally "explained," depending on the dominant early mode of recruiting slaves. Where the earliest and most dominant mode of recruitment was external, the cultural mode of representing social death was what I shall call *intrusive* and this was likely to continue even where, later, most slaves were internally recruited. The second way in which social death was represented may be called *extrusive*, and this too was determined by the earliest dominant means of recruiting slaves. It persisted even if, later, there was a shift to external sources.

In the intrusive mode of representing social death the slave was ritually incorporated as the permanent enemy on the inside—the "domestic enemy," as he was known in medieval Tuscany.[12] He did not and could not belong because he was the product of a hostile, alien culture. He stood, on the one hand, as a living affront to the local gods, an intruder in the sacred space (the cosmicized circle, as Mircea Eliade would say, that defined the community).[13] The views of the Bella Coola Indians of British Columbia and of the Nias of Indonesia are not only nearly identical, but typical of all peoples. The Bella Coola were fond of saying that "no slaves came to earth with the first people," and Thomas F. McIlwraith comments: "To the Bella Coola, who still consider a man's power in the land as dependent to a considerable extent on his ancestral myth, a slave's greatest misfortune lay in the fact that he had no ancestral home, and hence no rights . . . A slave was a stranger in a strange land, unsupported by a chain of ancestors reaching back to the beginning of time."[14] Similarly Peter Suzuki reports that among the Nias "the slaves are not mentioned in any ancestral myth, have no place in the world-tree, thus lack religion and consequently, a place in the cosmos. They have no past nor future, living as they do, on the whims and mercy of their masters. They live on the fringes of the cosmos and are viewed as being almost on a par with animals."[15]

On the other hand, the slave was symbolic of the defeated enemy, the power of the local gods, and the superior honor of the community. Because of the association of the slave with the enemy in this mode of representing social death, we are not surprised to find that slavery was associated with the military, and that the terminology of slavery took on a military flavor in many such societies. Among the Kwakiutl Indians of the northwest coast of

America, "a slave is designated by the expression 'q!aku q!ak'o,' " the basis of which is the root "q!ak," meaning "to cut off the head." U. P. Averkieva observes:

> The custom of cutting off the heads of slain enemies and carrying them away as a sort of trophy, which existed side by side with [the practice] of enslavement, bears witness to the fact that, whereas in the distant past an enemy [taken prisoner] had his head cut off, because, as yet, there was no place in society for a slave, he later began to be inducted into slavery.[16]

The Ashanti of West Africa, like the peoples of early Mesopotamia, referred to slaves as people of a foreign country. Indeed, *adonke,* the general term for slave in Ashanti, was the same term for all foreign northerners; and in the Third Dynasty of Ur the word for slave literally meant man or woman of the mountain, the area from which the earliest slaves came.[17]

The Greek word for slavery, *doulos,* is still an etymological mystery, but it is significant that in spite of the highly commercial nature of Greek slavery in classical times and the fact that from the sixth century B.C. on the vast majority of slaves were bought at slave markets rather than captured, the agent of the state responsible for the public regulation of slaves was the war archon.[18] The Roman experience was even more revealing. P. R. C. Weaver, in his discussion of the *servus vicarius,* tells us that the term "is derived, *as is much of the domestic terminology of Roman slavery,* from military usage and organization" (emphasis added). A common term for slave was "captivus."[19] Roman law fully represented the intrusive conception of the slave. The Roman captured by the enemy lost all claims as a Roman citizen, but if he escaped and found his way back home, the principle of *postliminium* applied: he was fully restored to his original status, subject to a few restrictions and occasionally to a redeemer's lien.[20] The idea of social death was also given direct legal expression in Roman law. The slave was *pro nullo.* We learn, too, from the comedies of Plautus and Terence that the slave was one who recognized no father and no fatherland.[21]

Hebrew slavery in law and practice, in both ancient and medieval times, was highly intrusive. Fellow Jews could be and were enslaved in biblical times, but the slave was conceived of as the quintessential enemy within. In Leviticus we read:

> And as for thy bondsmen, and thy bondsmaids, which thou shalt have of the nations that are round about you, of them all shall ye buy bondsmen and bondsmaids. Moreover of the children of the strangers that do sojourn among you, of them shall ye buy, and of their families that are with you, which they have begotten in your land; and they shall be your possession. And ye shall make them an inheritance for your children after you, to hold for a possession; of them shall ye take your bondsmen forever.[22]

The foreign slave according to Maimonides "is like land in regard to the acquisition of title," and one who was a minor "is like cattle, and one may acquire title to him by the modes whereby title to cattle . . . is acquired."[23]

Medieval Christendom from its very early days defined all pagans and infidels who resisted conversion as enemies who could justly be enslaved if taken in war. Like the Hebrews, the medieval Christian nations permitted the enslavement of fellow Christians and denied that the conversion of slaves obliged masters to manumit them.[24]

It is in Islamic religious and social thought that we find the purest expression of the intrusive conception of social death. The outsider was foreigner, enemy, and infidel, fit only for enslavement after the jihad, to be incorporated as the enemy within. Legally the Muslim is not permitted to enslave coreligionists, although, as we shall see, many ways were found to get around this injunction. As a cultural mode of representation, however, the image of the slave as the captured enemy and internalized outsider in a state of social death was firmly fixed in Islamic thought. The most frequent expression for female slaves in the Qoran is "that which your right hand possesses." The slave is primarily "a person taken captive in war, or carried off by force from a foreign hostile country, and being at the time of capture an unbeliever."[25] Ali Abd Elwahed argued forcefully that in contrast to the basically ethnic conception of the slave's distinctiveness found in western slave societies, both ancient and modern, the Islamic world's conception was based on religious differences. He admitted that there were strong traces of racism in both the political and legal thought of the Arabs, but insisted that in their "collective representations" slavery was the result of captivity occasioned by just wars against the infidel.[26] Similarly, M. G. Smith has emphasized this difference in the representation of slavery among Islamic and West Indian slavemasters.[27] More recently, Paul Lovejoy has called attention to the need to distinguish between ideology and practice in the interpretation of slavery among Islamic peoples.[28] Quite apart from the problem of confusing ideology with reality, an overemphasis on the religious content of the Islamic mode of representing the social death of the slave has tended to obscure the more important common element in the Western and Islamic representations: the fact that they are both intrusive.

In sharp contrast with the intrusive conception of death was the extrusive representation. Here the dominant image of the slave was that of an insider who had fallen, one who ceased to belong and had been expelled from normal participation in the community because of a failure to meet certain minimal legal or socioeconomic norms of behavior. The destitute were included in this group, for while they perhaps had committed no overt crime their failure to survive on their own was taken as a sign of innate incompetence and of divine disfavor. Typical of the extrusive representation of social death among primitives were the Goajiro of Venezuela, among whom slavery was essentially "a consequence of the violation of the code of social order."[29] Among advanced archaic civilizations the Aztecs, Egyptians, and Chinese were typical. The Aztecs, while they took many prisoners of war, used them mainly in their religious ceremonies or else resettled them. Slavery was viewed as being of internal origin, and the slave was someone who had fallen as a result of destitution or criminality.[30] In pharaonic Egypt the terminology of slavery contrasted strikingly with that of early Mesopotamia in that it did not refer to the slave as a foreigner. Egyptian terminology accurately reflected the internal source of slavery and the fact that it arose primarily from destitution. To the Egyptians this status amounted to social and legal death, as 'Abd al-Muhsin Bakīr clearly shows.[31] And it was into this status that captives who were enslaved were assimilated. Significantly, the Egyptian word for captive, literally translated, meant "living dead."[32] China throughout its long recorded history held firmly to an extrusive conception of slavery. The slave was conceived of as a criminal, and the prisoner of war, if enslaved, was legally and ideologically assimilated to the status of the internal criminal.[33]

In none of the above-mentioned societies do we find really large-scale slavery, so it may be wondered whether the extrusive mode of representing slavery applies only to social systems in which the institution did not attain marked structural significance. This, however, is not the case. There are two quite dramatic cases of advanced societies highly dependent on slavery in which the institution was intrusively represented: these are Korea during the Koryŏ and Yi dynasties, and Russia from the late seventeenth century to near the end of the eighteenth century.

Although it is not generally known even among scholars specializing in the study of slavery, both Korea and Russia relied heavily on slaves not only in their economic sectors but for the performance of administrative roles, and Korea at varying periods had slave populations that constituted more than 30 percent of its total population.[34]

In Korea during the Koryŏ period slavery had a "moral . . . connotation"; slaves were persons from whom heaven had withdrawn its favor. In 1300 King Chungnyŏl of Korea responded in alarm to a draft of a plan by a Chinese, Kno-li Chi-su, to reform the system of slavery. The king explained thus: "Our ancestors have instructed us that these servile elements are of a different race and therefore it is not possible for them to become common people—to oppose the instructions of our ancestors is to endanger our social order."[35] Five hundred years later the conception of the slave was much the same. Both Susan Shin and Edward W. Wagner, from their studies of the census data of the late seventeenth century, found that social mobility was "overwhelmingly downward" and that the slave who stood at the bottom of the hierarchy was essentially someone who had fallen there.[36]

In Russia we find another important slaveholding society with an extrusive conception of slavery. One of the earliest sets of laws dealing with slavery in Russia dates back to the second half of the twelfth century.[37] The law listed three ways in which persons became slaves and it is significant that they excluded capture at war. This exclusion has puzzled Russian historians, and all sorts of theories have been advanced to explain the presumed omission, the most widely accepted being that the clauses in question dealt only with cases where a person becomes a slave by his own action. This may be the correct explanation, but equally plausible is another: in the same way that the enslaved prisoner of war in imperial China was assimilated to the status of a person who had become a slave as the result of conviction for a capital offense, so in Kievan Russia the captive may well have been assimilated to the dominant extrusive conception of the slave as an internally fallen person.

Even more revealing is the controversy surrounding the connotation of the term "izgoi." The term referred to aliens and freedmen but, significantly, its primary meaning was "a man who has lost his former status and is in need of special protection." In this regard it applied as much to orphaned princes and bankrupt merchants as to destitute ex-slaves and aliens.[38] Thus we find the alien being assimilated to the status of the fallen insider rather than the other way around.

After its virtual disappearance during the early seventeenth century slavery began to expand again during the era of Peter the Great and continued doing so until Russia became one of the most important of the European slaveholding states, including those of the New World. It remained unique among the European slave systems, however, in maintaining a highly extrusive conception of slavery. As in imperial China, slavery was very closely tied to the penal system and the slave was conceived of as someone who had committed a capital offense. Not all criminals became slaves, but the *kátorshniki* and *poseléntsi* who were sentenced to a lifetime of hard labor and forced colonization were public slaves in every sense of the term. "Both were by their sentences deprived of all civil rights. In the eyes of the law they were nonpersons; their property was distributed to their heirs; their wives could remarry since all family relations had been annulled by the sentences."[39]

The extrusive conception of slavery applied equally to private slaves who served their masters in urban areas. Earlier we saw how the three monotheistic religions reinforced an intrusive conception of slavery. It is therefore highly significant that Russia was the only Christian state whose church did not help to define the slave as a converted infidel. The Orthodox church, according to Richard Hellie, "condoned, and in fact, encouraged, the enslavement of Orthodox by Orthodox," and it did not object to the enslavement of Orthodox Christians by members of other faiths.[40] This becomes all the more extraordinary when we realize that in Muscovy national consciousness was expressed mainly in religious terms: "the Orthodox Church played a central role in the rise and consolidation of the Muscovite state."[41]

With slavery retaining its highly extrusive character in Russia, the slave was never the enemy within but the internally fallen. Ideological elaboration of the difference between slave and free did not seek the aid of religion but defined the gulf in terms of what Hellie calls "simulated barriers." One of these barriers is most revealing. Slave owners invented genealogical "claims of foreign origin for their clan." They claimed to be foreigners of noble dynastic origins "reigning over another people."[42] Almost all of these claims were false, but it is remarkable that the Russian slaveholder, instead of defining his slave as the captured foreigner within his land, chose exactly the opposite course in defining himself as the foreigner of noble ancestry. This of course is consistent with an extrusive conception of slavery, where the slave is the insider who has fallen.

We may summarize the two modes of representing the social death that was slavery by saying that in the intrusive mode the slave was conceived of as someone who did not belong because he was an outsider, while in the extrusive mode the slave became an outsider because he did not (or no longer) belonged. In the former the slave was an external exile, an intruder; in the latter he was an internal exile, one who had been deprived of all claims of community. The one fell because he was the enemy, the other became the enemy because he had fallen. At one extreme, even when prisoners of war became the major source of slaves in China during the period of the Northern dynasties, the representation of the slave as the internally fallen, the criminal, persisted; at the other extreme, in dynastic Mesopotamia as late as the Third Dynasty of Ur, when the vast majority of slaves were internally recruited, the intrusive representation of the slave as the defeated enemy, the people "from the mountain," endured.

It is precisely this persistence of one conception of slavery during periods when we might normally expect the other which explains many otherwise puzzling aspects of the study and treatment of the subject of slavery. Let me illustrate with one important example. It is almost universally believed by European and American writers and readers of history that slavery was abolished in the northern part of Western Europe by the late Middle Ages. Yet in France, Spain, England, and the Netherlands a severe form of enslavement of Europeans by Europeans was to develop and flourish from the middle of the fifteenth century to well into the nineteenth. This was penal slavery, beginning with galley slavery and continuing with its replacement by the Bagnes, or penal slavery in public works. Both were slavery in every sense of the term. They developed as substitutes for the death penalty at a time when there was not a prison system in Europe to accommodate the huge number of persons found guilty of capital offenses. To be sure, the growing incidence of such offenses was largely a reflection of the increase in the number of acts legally so defined. Indeed, there is growing evidence that the legal redefinition of crime and the resulting increase in penal and public slavery was largely determined by the need to regulate labor.[43]

It is truly extraordinary that European scholars have either neglected this whole aspect of the subject or defined it as something other than slavery when they have recognized it. When we look for reasons, it is too easy to claim that there has been a conspiracy of silence, or worse, a deliberate attempt to distort the historical facts. My own feeling is that there has been a genuine failure to recognize the institution for what it was owing to the pervasiveness of the intrusive conception of slavery in the Western intellectual consciousness. The same framework may explain the neglect of modern Russian slavery by West European scholars. Galley slavery and slavery in the Bagnes are immediately recognizable to anyone who understands the institutions in extrusive terms. When the King of France issued a royal letter to his judicial authorities requesting them to provide for the galleys "all malefactors . . . who have merited the death penalty or corporeal punishment, and also those whom they could conscientiously declare to be incorrigible and of evil life and conduct,"[44] he was issuing a call for more public slaves in much the same way that an oriental or Russian monarch would have done. The only difference was that the oriental or Russian ruler would have known that he was requesting more slaves and felt no qualms about it, whereas the French king, with his intrusive view of slavery, either believed he was requesting some other category of labor or conveniently persuaded himself that he was.[45]

Liminal Incorporation

Although the slave might be socially dead, he remained nonetheless an element of society. So the problem arose: how was he to be incorporated? Religion explains how it is possible to relate to the dead who still live. It says little about how ordinary people should relate to the living who are dead. This is the final cultural dilemma posed by the problem of slavery. James H. Vaughan, in his analysis of slavery (*mafakur*) among the Margi of Nigeria, has addressed this problem with considerable insight.[46] He tells us that traditional Margi society was "in theory, a closed system, recognizing birth as the only method of recruitment." Any outsider was an intruder into this social space and must remain an alien; but, equally, the insider who committed some capital crime offended the gods and his ancestors and in so doing broke society's invisible boundaries and made himself an alien.

The population of slaves among the Margi comprised both types of aliens, although the dominant representation of their social death was intrusive. The rich diversity of groups surrounding the Margi make them particularly aware of their social space. As Vaughan observes: "They are sensitive to a unifying 'Marginess'—largely consensual—that distinguishes them from the numerous other societies around them," and slaves are those who have breached "the boundaries of this closed system." The institution of slavery "bestows a rational—even utilitarian—place upon the anomaly of the permanent resident alien, by giving him an institutional marginality." Furthermore:

> The outstanding general characteristic of *mafakur* is that all *mafa*, without regard to political position, private influence, or wealth, hold in common a status that in structural terms is fundamentally and irrevocably intermediate with regard to membership in Margi society. But it is equally apparent that, despite their marginal status, their roles are fully integrated into society.[47]

Thus slavery involved two contradictory principles, marginality and integration, and Margi society reconciled this contradiction by "formalizing the marginality." Hence Vaughan calls the institution "limbic" (I prefer the more common anthropological term "liminal") "for its members exist in the hem of society, in a limbo, neither enfranchised Margi nor true aliens." But the Margi also enslaved local offenders, and these too were assimilated to the same limbic or liminal status of the institutionalized outsider. The criminal "remained in the society: a part of it, yet apart from it. He was not [physically] expelled, for that would be less humiliating . . . Rather, it was the loss of identity and normality that was so objectionable to the proud Margi."

Institutionalized marginality, the liminal state of social death, was the ultimate cultural outcome of the loss of natality as well as honor and power. It was in this too that the master's authority rested. For it was he who in a godlike manner mediated between the socially dead and the socially alive. Without the master, as the Tuareg insist, the slave does not exist. The slave came to obey him not only out of fear, but out of the basic need to exist as a quasi-person, however marginal and vicarious that existence might be.

There were other gains to the master, as well as to the other members of the community, in the slave's liminality. The marginal person, while a threat to the moral and social order, was often also essential for its survival. In cultural terms the very anomaly of the slave emphasized what was most important and stable, what was least anomalous in the local culture of the non-slave population. This was particularly true of small-scale, highly integrated societies with little class division among the nonslave population.

Theda Perdue makes this point in her discussion of the precontact phase of Cherokee slavery. Before they adopted the institution of plantation slavery from the whites, the Cherokees kept slaves; but they contributed nothing to the economic, political, or social life of their warfare-oriented communities. Why then were slaves kept? Perdue's explanation is that the tradi-

tional belief system of the Cherokees rigidly categorized the social and physical universe. As with all systems of categorization, however, there were
many anomalies that simply did not fit. The Cherokee way of handling such
exceptions was to emphasize them, on the principle that it was precisely
what stood at the margins that emphasized the boundaries. The slave acquired the same cultural significance among them as the bear—a four-
footed animal, which nonetheless had the human habit of standing on its
hind legs and grasping with its two front paws—or the *Uktena,* the mythical
beast, "which had the body of a snake, the antlers of a deer and the wings of
a bird." Similarly the *atsi nahsa'i,* or slaves, were utterly anomalous; they
had the shape of human beings but had no human essence whatever, since
humanness was defined in terms of belonging to a clan. The slave, in not
belonging, emphasized the significance of belonging; in being clanless, emphasized the clan as the only basis of belonging; in being deviant, "helped
establish and strengthen group identity among the Cherokees."[48]

We get a fascinating glimpse of the symbolic significance of the liminal
slave in a more complex social system fraught with conflict in the Anglo-
Saxon epic, *Beowulf.*[49] Beowulf's world was one riddled with internal feud-
ing and external warfare. It was also a social order with a highly developed
class system, in which an aristocratic warrior class lived off the surplus generated by its servants. Slavery and the slave trade were an integral part of
this world. Indeed, literally the first event we come across in the prologue is
a reference to the Danish hero Shild, who "made slaves of soldiers from
every land, crowds of captives he'd beaten into terror."

In addition to social division there was a fundamental cleavage in the
moral order of the world of Beowulf, between the old paganism and the
newly acquired and not yet fully integrated Christianity. In the poem this is
expressed in terms of the conflict between the forces of good and those of
evil. This is not a tidy organic world; evil and conflict are ever present and
recognized as such:

> The world,
> And its long days full of labor, brings good
> And evil; all who remain here meet both.[50]

The role of the slave in Beowulf's last and greatest battle is replete with
symbolic meaning. First, it is significant that it was a runaway slave, beaten
by his master, who in searching for a place to hide found "the hidden path"
to the sleeping dragon, "awoke him from his darkness and dreams and
brought terror to his [Beowulf's] people."[51] There is thus a forceful juxtapo-
sition of the most pronounced social conflict (that between master and brutalized slave), with the most deep-seated moral conflict (that between Christianity and the lurking forces of evil and paganism, symbolized by the
hidden "heathen treasure" and the dragon that protects it).

> So mankind's enemy, the mighty beast
> Slept in those stone walls for hundreds
>   of years; a runaway slave roused it,
> Stole a jeweled cup and bought
> His master's forgiveness, begged for mercy
> And was pardoned when his delighted lord took
>   the present
> He bore, turned it in his hands and stared
> At the ancient carvings. The cup brought peace
> To a slave, pleased his master, but stirred
> A dragon's anger.[52]

Not only is there a symbolic association of social and moral conflict, but in the role of the slave as guide to the dragon's evil world we find one of the most remarkable statements of the slave's liminal status. It is significant that the slave was not counted among the twelve men who went to the dragon's den. And there might be some hint of his anomalous nature in the fact that he was the *thirteenth* person. It was precisely because he was marginal, neither human nor inhuman, neither man nor beast, neither dead nor alive, the enemy within who was neither member nor true alien, that the slave could lead Beowulf and his men across the deadly margin that separated the social order above from the terror and chaos of the underground, between good and evil, between the sacred world of the Christian and the profane world of the pagan.

A consideration of the important role of the slave's liminality brings us to an important feature of slavery that is often misunderstood. Although the slave is socially a nonperson and exists in a marginal state of social death, he is not an outcaste. The point must be emphasized in view of the easy use often made of the caste concept in interpreting American slavery and its postemancipation consequences.[53]

With the noteworthy exception of temple slaves, enslaved persons are never relegated to the status of an outcaste group, nor are they ever stratified as one of several castes in any of the societies that have a complex hierarchy of castes. Before explaining why, let us look at the nature of the relationship between caste and slavery.

The *Ethnographic Atlas* (see Appendix B) classifies the 186 societies of the Murdock World Sample with respect to "caste stratification." The four groupings are societies where:

(1) Caste distinctions of any kind are absent or insignificant.
(2) There are one or more despised occupational groupings (whether smiths or leather workers or whatever else), distinguished from the general population, regarded as outcastes, and characterized by strict endogamy.
(3) There is ethnic stratification in which a superordinate caste withholds privileges from and refuses to intermarry with a subordinate

caste (or castes), which it stigmatizes as ethnically alien (for example, as descended from a conquered and culturally inferior indigenous population, from former slaves, or from foreign immigrants of different race and/or culture).

(4) Complex caste stratification exists, in which occupational differentiation emphasizes hereditary ascription and endogamy to the near exclusion of achievable class status.

The main advantage of this classification is that it takes account of both the narrow and the wide definitions of caste. Many scholars would hold that the term "caste" strictly applies only to societies in category (4), confined mainly to India and the related societies of Southeast Asia.[54] Others, who hold to the more general interpretation of the caste concept, would include societies in category (2) along with (4) as legitimate cases.[55] My own position is closer to the second, with the important qualification that for me caste additionally connotes some notion of ritual purity and pollution as a means of maintaining social distance. The existence of "hereditary endogamous groups" that are "socially differentiated by prescribed behavior" is a necessary but not sufficient criterion for defining castes, for this description is true of almost all class systems. In the light of this definition it is clear that I do not accept category (3) of the *Ethnographic Atlas* grouping as containing genuine caste systems, since ethnic differentiation need not be reinforced by notions of ritual purity and pollution.

With these observations in mind we can now examine the relationship between the presence or absence of slavery and types of caste stratification. This is reported in Table 2.1. The table is highly significant ($p = 0.002$), although there is no strong overall relationship. Most slaveholding societies, we see, do not have castes of any kind. Yet slavery is not incompatible with the existence of castes. There is a weak overall relationship with slavery as the dependent variable: the moderately strong association with occu-

Table 2.1   The relation of slavery to caste stratification, as delineated by the Murdock *Ethnographic Atlas*.

Presence or absence of slavery	Type of society			
	Caste absent	Occupational groupings	Ethnic stratification	Complex caste differentiation
Slavery absent:				
Number	114	6	1	4
Percent	66.3	3.5	0.6	2.3
Slavery present:				
Number	33	10	2	2
Percent	19.2	5.8	1.2	1.2

NOTE: Chi square = 14.17, with three degrees of freedom. Significance = 0.0027.

pational castes is balanced by a rather weak relation with complex caste systems.

More important is what is revealed by the ethnographic data on those societies which have both slavery and caste. In none of them (the rare cases of temple slavery excepted) were slaves either outcastes or segregated as distinct castes. Typical of slaveholding societies with occupational castes were the Margi, the Somali, and the Koreans. The rich historical and anthropological data on these societies indicate that slaves were held to be distinct from the caste groups in question.[56] There was never any marriage, or even illicit sexual relations, between the outcaste group and ordinary persons, whereas such relations were common between "free" males and slave women. It is typical of the boundary-crossing capacity of slaves that among the Somali they were the only persons who could have sexual relations and marry with both ordinary "free" Somalis and the outcaste Sab group. Furthermore, the outcaste groups could never lose their caste status, nor did they want to, while in all these societies slaves could be manumitted and become "free" persons. Third, the outcaste groups were usually segregated. The Korean paekchŏng, for example, had a high degree of internal autonomy, living in their own communities as an organized outcaste group. Slaves were never segregated simply because they were slaves. Fourth, the outcaste groups all had a monopoly of certain occupations in which they specialized; slaves were never confined to particular jobs. In all premodern societies they performed virtually the entire range of occupations, and even in modern capitalistic slave systems recent studies have indicated that the range of their occupations was much wider than previously thought.[57] Perhaps the most important difference is that while slaves may have been held in contempt, they were never avoided or feared because it was felt that they were polluting. The Sab of Somalia and the paekchŏng of Korea, however, were avoided for this reason.[58]

It is not difficult to understand why slaves were never assimilated to the status of outcastes. Slavery, we have seen, was primarily a relation of personal domination. There was an almost perverse intimacy in the bond resulting from the power the master claimed over his slave. The slave's only life was through and for his master. Clearly, any notion of ritual avoidance and spatial segregation would entail a lessening of this bond. Second, the assimilation of the slave to the status of an occupationally specialized caste would undermine one of his major advantages—the fact that he was a natally alienated person who could be employed in any capacity precisely because he had no claims of birth. Slaves universally were not only sexually exploited in their role as concubines, but also in their role as mother-surrogates and nursemaids. However great the human capacity for contradiction, it has never been possible for any group of masters to suckle at their slave's breast as infants, sow their wild oats with her as adolescents, then turn around as adults and claim that she was polluted.

Indeed, the comparative data indicate that in societies with highly developed notions of ritual pollution one of the main reasons for keeping slaves was that they were nonpolluting and thus a major means of circumventing pollution norms. Among the Maori, for instance, every free person had *tapu*, a complex set of prohibitions that were the laws of the gods. Breaking these severely endangered the individual, since he lost his *mana* (power) and became vulnerable to supernatural forces. According to Elsdon Best:

> The shadow of *tapu* lay over the Maori from birth until death, his very bones and their resting place remained *tapu* for all time. The higher the rank of a person the more *tapu* was he. It is interesting to note that slaves were held to be free from *tapu* and yet no explanation is given as to their condition of welfare and their survival, why they did not perish in such a defenceless condition.[59]

They did not perish, we now know, because as natally alienated persons they were socially dead. "Even though he [the slave] had once been a chief in another tribe," Raymond Firth tells us, "his capture removed him from the *mana* of the gods and in things spiritual he ceased to count." In this liminal state he could cross boundaries prohibited to other persons and could perform the vital task of preparing the master's food, which if done by a mortal would result in certain spiritual and possible physical death.[60]

For much the same reasons we find in Nepal that slaves, while "politically the most debased section of Nepalese society," were nonetheless sometimes selected from the higher castes. "Indeed, in order to perform the various duties imposed on domestic servants, to be permitted to cross the threshold of an owner's dwelling, it was imperative for the slave to enjoy a degree of ritual purity conferred only by membership in certain castes." Paradoxically, even Brahmins were enslaved without losing caste.[61]

A consideration of the relation of slavery to caste leads us back to where we began: the liminality of the slave is not just a powerful agent of authority for the master, but an important route to the usefulness of the slave for both his master and the community at large. The essence of caste relations and notions of ritual pollution is that they demarcate impassable boundaries. The essence of slavery is that the slave, in his social death, lives on the margin between community and chaos, life and death, the sacred and the secular. Already dead, he lives outside the mana of the gods and can cross the boundaries with social and supernatural impunity.

The Rituals and Marks of Enslavement

Symbolic ideas are usually given social expression in ritualized patterns. Let us look now at the ritual aspects of the natal alienation of the slave. For all but the most advanced slave systems the acquisition of a slave is a very special event in the master's household. Even where slaves number as much as a quarter of the total household, their acquisition may be a once-in-a-life-time event for the members, especially if the pattern of slaveholding is highly skewed. It was common for people in the premodern world to give ritual expression to special events and when one of those events involved the incorporation of a person defined as socially dead, it is easy to recognize that the event should not proceed without ceremony. The ritual of enslavement incorporated one or more of four basic features: first, the symbolic rejection by the slave of his past and his former kinsmen; second, a change of name; third, the imposition of some visible mark of servitude; and last, the assumption of a new status in the household or economic organization of the master.

Many cultures obliged the new slave to make a symbolic gesture of rejecting his natal community, kinsmen, ancestral spirits, and gods—or, where the slave was of local origin, of rejecting his own kin group and ancestral spirits in favor of those of his master. The ceremony was often simple and brief, but it was always deeply humiliating, sometimes even traumatic, for the slave.

Among the cannibalistic Tupinamba of South America we find slavery in its most primitive form. Most captives were eventually eaten, but in the many years between capture and execution the captives lived as the slaves of their captor and were usually well treated. Before they entered their captor's village the captives were stripped, dressed as Tupinamba, and decorated with feather ornaments. They were led to the graves of persons who had recently died and forced to "renew" or cleanse the bodies. The captives then performed a vital ritual function. They were given the weapons and other belongings of the deceased to be used for a time, after which they were handed over to the rightful heirs. "The reason for this," according to Alfred Métraux, "was that touching the belongings of a dead relative was fraught with dangers, unless they were first defiled by a captive."[62] Being socially dead, the captives were able to move between the living and the dead without suffering the supernatural harm inevitably experienced by the socially alive in such boundary crossing. After this ritual the prisoners were taken to the village, where their captivity was celebrated in song and dance, the captives themselves being forced to participate and "to dance in front of the hut where the sacred rattles were kept."[63]

Among the more complex Germanic peoples of early medieval Europe, the new slave of local origin placed his head under his master's arm and a collar or strap was placed around his neck.[64] We find a variant of this in late Anglo-Saxon England, where a man who through poverty was forced to sell himself into slavery had to place his head between his new master's hands; a billhook or an oxgoad was then given him to symbolize his new condition. This led to a special way of referring to enslavement, as when a Northumbrian mistress spoke of "all those people whose heads she took in return for their food in the evil days."[65] The expression gives a clue to the meaning of the ceremony; a man's head is associated with his mind and will and it is these, in addition to his labor, that the master takes.

If we look instead at traditional Africa, we find some interesting parallels and differences. The objective of the rituals was the same: to give symbolic expression to the slave's social death and new status. But the emphasis was less on personal and spiritual labor and more on the social use of the slave incorporated as a permanent marginal into a network of affiliation after a ritual break with his old kin ties and ancestral protectors. The Imbangala of northwestern Angola are typical.[66] All slaves, whether acquired from outside of Kasenje or within its boundaries, were considered alien to local lineages. In a special rite of passage the slave was first "cleansed" of his natal ties, by means of a medicine that denuded him of ancestral protection. Significantly, however, the medicine also eliminated any memory among the master's lineage of the slave's ancestry, so the very act of separation paved the way for the possible assimilation of the slave's descendants. This was followed by a dangerous purgatorical period in which the new slave was spiritually exposed, lacking the protection of both former and prospective ancestral spirits. Finally, the slave was incorporated (though not adopted) into the master's lineage via a naming ceremony in which he became an "alien dependent," protected once again, but without the full complement of names that was the birthright of every true member of the lineage.

The initiating ritual varied regionally, although its symbolic and practical objectives remained the same. Among the Kwanyama of southwestern Angola the rite was called *elyakeko,* which literally meant "to tread upon something." The captive was taken by the parents of the warrior to the whetstone kept in all Kwanyama houses:

> The father takes the stone and holds it in his hand, while his wife pours water over the whetstone, water which the father forces the prisoner to drink. After this has been done, the prisoner's master takes the stone and beats the victim on the top of the cranium with it, "to prevent him from having thoughts of escape." As the stone is motionless by nature, the Kwanyama believe the person so treated comes to possess the same quality.[67]

Similarly, among the Tiv of central Nigeria, "the purchaser and the man's agnates split a chicken which was held to sever the slave from his kin, thus making it impossible for him to run away, 'for he would have no place to go.' "[68] Some African groups like the Aboh offered sacrifice to special shrines, and feasted;[69] others, such as the Ila, assigned the new slave "a spirit associated with a deceased member of the patrilineal group" and in a communal ritual the ancestors were informed of the newly affiliated slave and their protection was sought.[70] The length of time for full adjustment to their new status varied with the kind of slave: it was usually easier for women, but occasionally the path was smoother for men (as among the Ila). Whatever the variations, in all African traditional societies the newcomer, unless he was a "trade slave" destined for resale, was forced to deny his natal kin ties and acquire certain fictive kin bonds to the master and his family. The exact meaning of his new ties will be examined later.

The initiating ceremony served much the same purpose among kin-based societies in other parts of the world. Among the Kachin of highland Burma, for example, the shaved head of the new slave was rubbed with ashes from the master's hearth prior to his incorporation into the master's clan.[71] Shorn of the memory of his past, the slave received the ashes of his master's ancestral spirits. As a final example, we may take the Toradja of the central Celebes.[72] As soon as he was brought into his master's house, the slave was given a meal made of the same kind of food his master normally ate, "so that his life spirit will be tranquil." The meal was usually served on the cover of a pot that was meant to help the slave forget his former attachments. Next, a little basket of rice, eggs, ubi, and coconut was prepared and was turned above the head of the slave seven times to the left and seven times to the right. The basket was then placed on the slave's head and the master invoked as follows: "You, so-and-so, wherever your life spirit may have gone, to your relatives left behind, here is rice which I give to you; eat it so that he may settle down on you and you may have a long life." The slave ate the contents, after which a priestess usually came and invoked long life for the new slave. The symbolism here is self-evident and needs no commentary. Once again it involved the loss of independent social existence—of the slave's "life spirit"—the placating of the lost spirits and protection against them, and the incorporation of the slave into the marginal existence of the permanent alien.

In large-scale slave systems where the slave became a unit of production outside the household economy we do not, of course, find such elaborate initiating rituals of enslavement. The newcomer was usually handed over to a trusted older slave to be taught the necessary skills to survive in his new environment. This is not to say, however, that ritual did not play a part even here. For we know that even in the brutal capitalistic slave plantations of the modern Caribbean, slaves had a rich ritual life and found their own ways of incorporating the new recruit.[73] The same was very possibly true of slaves on the latifundia of ancient Rome, given the rich and intense religious life of the slave population. But if the slave was not incorporated privately by his master, there was still the need to incorporate him publicly, to give ritual expression to his presence as a large and significant, and potentially dangerous, element in the body politic. We shall see later that in such large-scale systems this task was performed by the state religion.

The second major feature of the ritual of enslavement involved the changing of the slave's name. A man's name is, of course, more than simply a way of calling him. It is the verbal signal of his whole identity, his being-in-the-world as a distinct person. It also establishes and advertises his relation with kinsmen. In a great many societies a person's name has magical qualities; new names are often received upon initiation into adulthood and into cults and secret societies, and the victim's name looms large in witchcraft and sorcery practiced against him. As Ernst Cassirer observed: "The notion that name and essence bear a necessary and internal relation to each other, that the name does not merely denote but actually *is* the essence of its object, that the potency of the real thing is contained in the name—that is one of the fundamental assumptions of the mythmaking consciousness itself."[74] Thus it is understandable that in every slave society one of the first acts of the master has been to change the name of his new slave. One must reject any simplistic explanation that this was simply a result of the master's need to find a name that was more familiar, for we find the same tendency to change names when slaves come from the identical society or language group as their masters.

There are several reasons for the change of name. The changing of a name is almost universally a symbolic act of stripping a person of his former identity (note for example the tendency among modern peoples to assign a new formal identification, usually a number, to both prisoners of war and domestic convicts). The slave's former name died with his former self. The significance of the new name, however, varied from one kind of slave culture to another. Among most kin-based societies the slave took the clan name of his new master. This was the first act in the creation of fictive kin ties. The situation was different, however, among that small group of kin-based societies where the slave was not incorporated into the household economy but was exploited separately, in a protocapitalist sector, and in most of the advanced premodern slave systems. Here the new name was often a badge of inferiority and contempt. Sometimes the names were either peculiarly or characteristically servile. A Greek name in republican Rome, for example, often indicated slave status or ancestry, and many traditionally Roman names eventually became favorite slave names, cognomens such as Faustus, Felix, Fortunatus, and Primus.[75] In Russia masters and slaves used the same names to a greater degree, which is understandable in the light of the local origins of most slaves: nonetheless, certain names such as Kondratii and Matrona became typical slave names.[76] In other societies such as China, those of the ancient Near East and pharaonic Egypt, the absence of family names was the surest mark of slavery.[77] Much more humiliating, however, were those cases in which insult was added to injury by giving the slave a name that was ridiculous or even obscene. Among the Duala of the Cameroon, slaves were given such names as "Irritation"; and among the Aboh of Nigeria, there were names like "Bluebeard" and "Downcast."[78] The Nootka of the northwest coast of America, the Icelanders, and the Kachin of highland Burma are all typical of peoples who took special delight in giving to female slaves names that demeaned both their status and their sex.[79]

Much the same pattern existed in the Americas, where the assignation and use of names was an important focus of conflict between masters and slaves. In the U.S. South slaves were sometimes whipped for using the forenames of important whites. The pompous classical names preferred by many planters were resented by most slaves, except when they were reminiscent of African names. Slaves usually changed their surnames after manumission, although sometimes, for purposes of protection, they kept the names of their ex-masters if they were important persons. Apparently many slaves selected their own surnames, which they used among themselves.[80] In doing so they often took the names (or "entitles" as they called them) of distant ancestors or former masters, in a direct symbolic rejection of their present master. Herbert G. Gutman insists that most slaves had surnames, and that the choice of a different name involved, on the one hand, a rejection of the "intimacy" of the ties of paternalism claimed by the master and, on the other hand, "served to shape a social identity independent of slave ownership."[81] This has become a highly contentious subject, one that has generated more heat than the points at issue merit. My own reading of the literature, including slave narratives and interviews, suggests that while there were many variations both within and between regions, most slave surnames in the United States were those of the owners and changed with a change of owner. Nor can the fact that slaves had no legal claim to surnames be dismissed as irrelevant "legalism" any more than can the fact that they had no legal claim to their own persons or labor.

The situation in Latin America was similiar to that uncovered in South Carolina by Peter Wood: the masters chose the names, but during the colonial period often selected African names; later the African names were replaced by Spanish ones. Thus in Colombia:

> The Spanish usually retained the *bozales'* African tribal names, or their place of origin in Africa, as the blacks' surnames. Second-generation slaves might retain this African surname but usually either had no surnames, took the surnames of their masters, or were designated *criollos* (born in America).[82]

A census taken in Colombia in 1759 showed that almost 40 percent of the slaves had only one name; 30 percent had the surname Criollo, and the remainder had African tribal or regional surnames such as Mina, Congo, Mandingo, and Caraba. Blacks "were more likely to assume their owners' surnames following manumission than while they remained in captivity."[83]

Much the same pattern existed in other parts of Latin America. In Mexico, for example:

> All African slaves ... were given a first name and were identified by that name. The names most commonly used included Juan, Antón, Francisco, Diego, Sebastian, and Hernando for males, and María, Isabel, Magdalena, Ana, and Catalina for females. Some slaves had a last name as well (usually that of the master)—slaves who were given only a first name were often identified by the addition of their tribal or their national origin ... Other

slaves, such as Juan Viejo (old man) and Juan Tuerto (one-eyed), had a nickname appended to the first name.[84]

The pattern of naming in the Caribbean also was very similar to that of Spanish America and colonial South Carolina. In Jamaica, African day-names and tribal names were either selected in their pure form or adapted as English names. During the nineteenth century these African names acquired pejorative meanings: Quashee, a day-name that originally meant "Sunday" in Akan, came to signify a stupid, lazy slave; and Cudjo, which was the Akan day name for "Monday," came to mean a drunkard.[85] Even a change to purely English or Creole names did not involve any lessening of degradation: slaves were given either classical names such as Phoebe and Cyrus, or insulting nicknames. On Worthy Park estate, for example, they had such names as Beauty, Carefree, Monkey, Villain, and Strumpet. These names were certainly imposed on the slaves by their masters or overseers, for as Craton notes: "To a significant degree, all these single slave names were distressingly similar to those of the estate's cattle, so that it is almost possible to confuse one list with another in the Worthy Park ledgers."[86] Toward the end of the eighteenth century an increasing number of slaves acquired a surname and usually at the same time changed their forename. This was permitted after baptism and may well have been one of the major incentives for Christianization in Jamaica. Whatever the reason, by the time of abolition most slaves had two names, usually English, with the surname being that of respected whites on the plantation or in the area.[87] Where children acquired surnames, these were rarely given before their tenth year "and very often these names reflect those of the whites on the estates (even when they were not the fathers)."[88]

Finally there were the French Antilles. While naming practices there were similar in broad outline to those in the British Caribbean, there were a few noteworthy variations.[89] Slaves were given a new name on the slave ships during the passage from Africa, yet among themselves they used their African names. A few days after arriving on the plantation each slave was given a nickname, which became his official name and was the one used by the planters. Apparently slaves continued among themselves to use other names as their Christian names, with the planters' names becoming their surnames. This tendency was much greater among males than females, the women for the most part using the single name given by their masters.

The slaves had a third name, acquired after baptism—usually that of a saint. This name was rarely used by the slaves themselves and almost never by the masters. Its main role was to indicate baptismal status.

As for the names themselves, French masters too used names of classical figures and names from literature. The blacks themselves apparently preferred names from the military lexicon such as Alerte, Jolicoeur, Sans-souci, and Fanfaron. The nicknames or second names given by the masters referred either to some physical characteristic of the slave (Longs-Bras, Con-querico, Torticolis, Hautes-Fesses) or to their area of origin (Fantu, Mina, Senegal). In some instances the African day-name was used, as in the British Caribbean and colonial South Carolina, but the masters, being French, insisted on a translation, so that the slaves were called Mercredi, Vendredi, and so on.

There was the same tendency in the French Antilles for African first names to be replaced by Creole names with the passing of the eighteenth century. The slaves late in that century had more opportunities to choose their names because of the much higher proportion of absentee owners and the rapid turnover of overseers. When they had a choice, they almost never selected the names of their owners: instead they used the names of ancestors who had belonged to another master, or an area of Africa, or colonial heroes and theatrical and literary figures known to be abolitionists, or—most commonly—of saints.

The slave's name was only one of the badges of slavery. In every slave-holding society we find visible marks of servitude, some pointed, some more subtle. Where the slave was of a different race or color, this fact tended to become associated with slave status—and not only in the Americas. A black skin in almost all the Islamic societies, including parts of the Sudan, was and still is associated with slavery. True, there were white slaves; true, it was possible to be black and free, even of high status—but this did not mean that blackness was not associated with slavery.[90] Perceived racial differences between masters and slaves could be found in a significant number of other societies ranging from the Ethiopians, the Bemba, and even the Lozis of Africa, to the Gilyaks and Lolos of eastern Asia.

Another way slaves were identified was by the ornaments they were either obliged or forbidden to wear. Usually a special kind of clothing was specified among peoples like the Ashanti and Chinese, and among peoples such as the Ibos as well, certain forms of jewelry were forbidden. Tlingit slave women could not wear the lip plug favored by free women. Obvious racial distinctions made it unnecessary to enforce clothing prohibitions on the slaves of the Americas and other areas of the modern world, although there were such rules in some areas.[91] The Greeks did not require their slaves to wear special clothes, but apparently (as in America) the slaves' style of dress immediately revealed their status.[92] Rome is fascinating in this regard. The slave population blended easily into the larger proletariat, and the high rate of manumission meant that ethnicity was useless as a means of identifying slaves. A ready means of identification seemed desirable, however, and a special form of dress for slaves was contemplated. When someone pointed out that the proposal, if carried out, would lead slaves immediately to recognize their numerical strength, the idea was abandoned.[93]

The presence of tattoos also identified slaves. They were universal in the ancient Near East, although apparently removable.[94] Surprisingly few societies in the premodern world branded slaves and when they did, as in China, Hellenistic Egypt (where it was eventually forbidden by law), and Rome, only incorrigible runaways were marked. In late medieval and early modern Europe, however, branding of galley and other public slaves was the norm. In France, from the middle of the sixteenth century, persons condemned to galley slavery were first publicly whipped and then the letters GAL were burned into their shoulders. Between 1810 and 1832, when branding was abolished, all public slaves (especially those sent to the Bagnes) were branded with the letters TP (Travaux perpétuels).[95] The branding of public slaves was not abolished in Russia until 1863. The *kátorshniki* were branded in a particularly grisly manner: the letters KAT were punctured on their cheeks and forehead, and gunpowder was rubbed into the wounds.[96]

Throughout the Americas slaves were routinely branded as a form of identification right up to the second half of the eighteenth century. Thereafter, although branding became mainly a form of punishment used on runaways and insubordinate slaves, it did not disappear as a means of identification, even in the United States. As late as 1848 a Kentuckian master identified a runaway female slave by announcing that she was branded "on the breast something like L blotched."[97] And South Carolina not only allowed branding until 1833, but mutilated slave felons by cropping their ears.[98] Branding as a customary form of identification only began to decline in the Caribbean during the last decades of the eighteenth century under abolitionist and missionary pressure. The LP mark with which slaves were branded on their shoulders in Worthy Park during the eighteenth century is still used today as a means of identifying the estate's cattle.[99]

Latin America showed much the same pattern, except that branding of runaways as a form of identification continued until well into the nineteenth century and may even have increased in Cuba during the expansive years at the middle of the century. Occasionally the branding of slaves backfired. In the Minas Gerais area of Brazil, runaway slaves who formed *quilombos,* or Maroon communities, were branded F on their shoulders if and when recaptured. Among the slaves themselves, however, the F brand became "a badge of honor rather than of infamy," and recaptured slaves proudly displayed it to their more cautious but admiring fellow sufferers. When the masters learned of this they replaced branding with a more gruesome form of punishment: the Achilles tendon on one foot was severed.[100]

Sometimes it was the absence of marks that identified slaves, as among the Yorubas who forbade slaves to scar themselves with Yoruba tribal marks; at other times it was the presence of such tribal marks that immediately betrayed the slaves, as among the Ashanti, who did not tattoo themselves like the many neighboring peoples they captured and enslaved. And one could always tell a Mende slave woman by the fact that her hands were not black with dye, since only nonslave women had the leisure and prerogative to dye cloth.[101]

There is one form of identification that deserves special attention, since it is found in the great majority of slaveholding societies: this is the shorn or partly shorn head. In Africa we find the shorn head associated with slaves among peoples as varied as the Ila and the Somali. In China, in highland Burma, among the primitive Germanic peoples, the nineteenth-century Russians, the Indians of the northwest coast, and several of the South American and Caribbean tribes, the heads of slaves were shorn (in the ancient Near East so was the pubic hair of female slaves). In India and pharaonic Egypt slaves wore their hair shorn except for a pigtail dangling from the crown. The Mossi of West Africa were unusual in that the head of the slave was periodically shaved by the master considering selling him, and the practice strongly influenced his final decision on the matter. According to A. A. Dim Delobsom: "Depending on where the hair starts to grow, whether well back on the head, at the forehead, or near the ears, the interpretation varies as to how the slave is to be regarded: as a dangerous being; as a lucky or unlucky influence on the family owning him."[102] Numerous other examples could be cited. The shaving of the slave's head was clearly a highly significant symbolic act. Of all the parts of the body, hair has the most mystical associations.[103] On the private or individual level, there is hardly a culture in which hair is not, for males, a symbol of power, manliness, freedom, and even rebellion; and for women, the crowning expression of feminine beauty. The shorn head is, conversely, symbolic of castration— loss of manliness, power, and "freedom." Even in modern societies we tend to shave the head of prisoners, although the deep symbolic meaning is usually camouflaged with overt hygienic explanations.

On the public or social level, the shorn head in premodern societies usually signified something more: it was a common symbol of transition, especially in the case of mourning the dead. The association between death, slavery, and the shorn head was made explicit for us by the Callinago Caribs of the Lesser Antilles, many of whom were wiped out by the Spaniards soon after their conquest of the islands. Raymond Breton, who visited them in the middle of the seventeenth century, wrote as follows:

> The women cut their hair upon the death of their husbands, and husbands cut their hair upon the death of their wives. The children cut their hair upon the death of their father or mother. The hair is cut for the period of a year. *The slaves have their hair cut all the time and are never allowed to let it grow. They have their hair cut to the neck which means that they are in mourning* (emphasis added).[104]

It is not unreasonable to conclude that the shorn head of the slave was one aspect of a stark symbolic statement: the man who was enslaved was in a permanent condition of liminality and must forever mourn his own social death.

How then do we explain the absence of the shorn head in the large-scale slave systems of the Americas? The answer, I feel, is highly revealing of the symbolic role of hair not only in slave relations but in race relations as well. First, there is the obvious fact that the masters were white and the slaves black—a somatic difference that obviated the need for the more common badges of slavery. Contrary to the common view, it was not so much color differences as differences in hair type that become critical as a mark of servility in the Americas.

Color, despite its initially dramatic impact, is in fact a rather weak basis of ranked differences in interracial societies.[105] There are several reasons. For one thing, the range of color differences among whites and among blacks is greater than is normally thought. Dark Europeans, especially Latins, are not far removed from many Africans who come from areas other than the classic West African "jet-black" zone. The differences diminish even more when we take into account the permanent suntan acquired by most whites working in the tropics. Furthermore, the color differences are quickly blurred by miscegenation, which diminishes the significance of color much faster than is usually imagined. Very soon, therefore, in all slave societies of the Americas, there were numbers of slaves who were in fact lighter than many European masters: the probability that the mulatto slave offspring of an African mother and a very blond Cornish or Irish father was lighter than the average dark Welsh overseer was significantly above zero. Within a couple of generations the symbolic role of color as a distinctive badge of slavery had been greatly muted—though, of course, not eliminated.

Variations in hair were another matter. Differences between whites and blacks were sharper in this quality than in color and persisted for much longer with miscegenation. Hair type rapidly became the real symbolic badge of slavery, although like many powerful symbols it was disguised, in this case by the linguistic device of using the term "black," which nominally threw the emphasis to color. No one who has grown up in a multiracial society, however, is unaware of the fact that hair difference is what carries the real symbolic potency.[106] In the Americas, then, blacks' hair was not shorn because, very much like the Ashanti situation where the slaves came with a readymade badge (their tribal taboos), leaving the hair as it was served as a powerful badge of status. Shaving it would have muted the distinction.

Significantly, in those mixed-blood slaves where the hair type was European, we find a reversion to the premodern tendency of resentment of the slave's long hair on the part of the masters, not to mention excessive pride on the part of the slave. A telling instance of this comes from nineteenth-century Barbados. In 1835 the governor issued an order to the effect that all slaves convicted of crimes "shall have their hair cut off, and their heads washed, for the better promotion of cleanliness." This was a new practice, coming less than four years before the complete abolition of slavery. The governor, following European practice, no doubt introduced the order for genuinely hygienic purposes. However, it provided masters and, more frequently, mistresses with a golden opportunity to put "uppity" mixed female slaves in their place—as we learn from a September 1836 entry in the journal of John Colthurst, special magistrate of Barbados:

> Speaking of the practice of shaving the heads of apprentices, a young quadroon woman who had conducted herself very improperly to her mistress, was brought up about a fortnight before my arrival in the island, and convicted by my predecessor of insubordination, and sentenced to labour on the tread mill for fourteen days, and her head (as a matter of course) to be shaved. This was accordingly done, and on the expiration of her punishment, she was sent home to her mistress, in all respects tamed and amenable, until she found she was laughed at by her fellow servants for the loss of her hair which, like all others of her particular complexion, is usually extremely beautiful, and of wavy and glossy black, and in the utmost profusion and great length. To replace her hair, she purchased false curls, and exhibited a beautiful front. Ere long, however, the circumstance of the original shaving of her head, and which she of course laid all to her mistress' account, created another quarrel, for which she was again brought up before me, in full curl. The charge was proven and another punishment was the consequence—solitary confinement for six days. If this woman's head had not been shaved in the first instance, it is clear there would not have been any necessity of a second application to the Special Magistrate. Therefore my objection to punishments of degrading nature, for it appeared in evidence upon this trial that whenever she put her hand to her head, after her return home from her first punishment, and found it bald, she flew into a rage, and swore she would be revenged.[107]

No doubt the female slaves of ancient Mesopotamia must have flown into similar though silent and repressed rages when they felt their shorn pubic hair, as did the male slaves of all the premodern slaveholding systems when they felt their bald or half-shorn heads. In the Americas the master class thought it achieved the same objective by making African hair the badge of servility. With mixed-race mulatto slaves they may well have succeeded; but with those who retained their African features the degree of symbolic success was questionable. As the shrewd magistrate Colthurst commented: "The negro laments over the loss of his lamb's wool much more than any fashionable young man in England would, having lost the most exquisite crop of hair in the world."[108] Unfortunately it was the mulattoes who were to define the symbolic meaning of hair in postemancipation and modern Caribbean societies. But that is another story.[109]

Fictive Kinship

I have several times referred to the practice of incorporating the slave as a fictive kinsman of his master in kin-based societies, and even in many of the more complex premodern systems. It is time to clarify exactly what this means. On the surface the relationship appears to be a straightforward adoption. All over the world we find the master being addressed as "father" and the slave as "son" or "daughter," and in matrilineal societies we find the term for the social father being used (that is, the term for "mother's brother," while slaves are referred to by the master as "sister's son"). This fictive kin relation extends also to other members of the master's family.

It would be a great mistake, however, to confuse these fictive kin ties with the claims and obligations of real kinship or with those involving genuine adoption. Some anthropologists are rather careless about making this distinction.[110] Relations, we are told, are always warm and intimate; it is difficult to detect any difference between the "adopted" slave and other young members of the family. No wonder some interpreters have concluded that slavery does not exist in these traditional societies, or that the traditional patterns of servitude are best called something else.

In order to avoid confusion it is best that we distinguish between two kinds of fictive kinship, what I shall call adoptive and, following Meyer Fortes, "quasi-filial."[111] Fictive kin ties that are adoptive involve genuine assimilation by the adopted person of all the claims, privileges, powers, and obligations of the status he or she has been ascribed. Fictive kin ties that are quasi-filial are essentially expressive: they use the language of kinship as a means of expressing an authority relation between master and slave, and a state of loyalty to the kinsmen of the master. In no slaveholding society, not even the most primitive, is there not a careful distinction drawn between the genuinely adopted outsider (who by virtue of this act immediately ceases to be an outsider) and the quasi-filial slave (who is nonetheless encouraged to use fictive kin expressions in addressing the master and other members of his family).

Thus among the pre-European Cherokees, for instance, a captive who was not tortured and put to death was either adopted or enslaved and there was no confusion on the matter. Persons adopted were "accorded the same privileges . . . as . . . those whose membership derived from birth."[112] Of the Tallensi slaves of West Africa, Fortes wrote: "Homeless and kinless, they must be endowed with a new social personality and given a definite place in the community. But the bond of actual paternity cannot be fabricated; the fiction is a makeshift and always remains so."[113]

At best, the slave was either viewed as an illegitimate quasi-kinsman or as a permanent minor who never grew up. He might be "of the lineage," but as the Imbangala of Angola illustrate, he was never *in* it.[114] Among the Ashanti, children of slaves remained slaves "forever" in spite of the adoption of the master's clan name, and while such children were preferred for political purposes (and well treated), their slave origins were never forgotten. They were laughed at in private, and people referred to them as having a "left-handed" clan affiliation. Old family slaves who became too familiar were put in their place, as several Ashanti proverbs indicate. For example: "If you play with your dog, you must expect it to lick your mouth."[115]

The Imuhag group of Tuaregs is instructive in this respect. We find here the standard pattern of fictive kin assimilation and the slave's adoption of the master's clan name. However, a slave's status as a fictive daughter did not get in the way of the master's taking her as his concubine or even his wife. Furthermore, the social distance between free and slave was great, in spite of the fictive kin bond. Masters in general distrusted their slaves, both male and female.[116] Female slaves were frequently accused of witchcraft, and we know from the anthropological psychology of witchcraft that such accusations invariably reflect an underlying fear and distrust of the accused.[117]

Even where there was considerable intermarriage between slave and free, in this way replacing fictive kinship with real, the assimilation of the slave was still not assured. As Polly Hill points out, the assimilation of *gandu* slaves (those on special slave farms) into the Nigerian Hausa society "was probably quite limited owing to the breakup of most *gandu* estates by the time the grandsons had reached marriageable age, if not before."[118]

One of the problems with many anthropological accounts of slavery in kin-based societies is that the emphasis on the structural aspects of social life often leads to a neglect of the purely human dimension. This is a serious drawback when it comes to understanding the real meaning of slavery, especially for slaves. Precisely because economic and class differences between masters and slaves were often not marked, the interpersonal and psychological dimensions of powerlessness became all the more important. It was deeply humiliating to be a slave in a kin-based society, and the indignity was no less because unaccompanied by class differentiation. Indeed, it may have hurt a good deal more. The latifundia slave could at least explain his degradation in terms of the economic parasitism and exploitation of his master. The slave in the kin-based society had no such external explanations. His degradation sprang from something presumably innate to his very being. And the degradation heaped upon him came in little ways, sometimes minor, sometimes cutting, but with the cumulative effect of a piranha assault.

Occasionally an anthropologist gives us a rare glimpse of this aspect of exploitation in a kin-based society. In his fine study of the Cubeo Indians of the northwestern Amazon, Irving Goldman records the following incident in the life of a servant girl who had been "adopted":

> The little girl, about nine, was addressed as "daughter" but held the status in the household of a servant. She took on the heaviest chores and was almost never free to play. Her lowly status was truly stigmatized by her lack of possessions. She was the only child among the Cubeo whom I have ever seen

unadorned . . . The children in the household enjoyed beating her as a way of teasing her, rather than wickedly. She took their pinchings and cuffings good-naturedly, on the whole, and had learned to pretend not to notice. Once, in the presence of the headman, her "father," the children were overdoing their teasing. She looked imploringly at the headman. Finally, she caught his eye and he said to her, "It is all right for you to run away." He saw no need to reprimand his own children.[119]

The distinction between adoptive and quasi-filial kinship helps us to understand why it is that even in the highly capitalistic slave systems of the Americas it was still possible to find the master-slave relationship expressed in "kinship" terms. Indeed, quasi-filial kinship became embroiled in the ongoing covert struggle for authority and dignity between masters and slaves, and it was often difficult to distinguish between genuine expression of affection, sheer duplicity, and psychological manipulation.

Two examples will illustrate. In the U.S. South the masters encouraged children to see them as the "Big Pappy," always benevolent, kind, and indulgent. Strict discipline was left to, and expected from, the slave child's parents. The slave children grew up making unfavorable comparisons between real parental authority and the quasi-filial paternalism of the master. The resulting erosion of the paternal bond was, of course, reinforced by the mortifying subjection of the slave parents to punishment before their children. As Genovese concludes: "If the tendency to worship the master and scorn the parents did not take a greater toll than it apparently did, the credit belongs to the slave parents, whose love for their children went a long way toward offsetting the ravages inherent in this scenario."[120]

We find quite a different scenario in Jamaica. In the absence of a cohesive master-class culture, relations between masters and slaves either lacked authority or were on the verge of losing it. Slaves, even here, employed quasi-filial kin terms, but often in sardonic ways, with their aggressive intent only lightly veiled. When the popular gothic novelist Monk Lewis, an absentee slave owner from England, toured his plantations in the early nineteenth century, he was overwhelmed by the reception from the slaves:

In particular, the women called me by every name they could think of. "My son! my love! my husband! my father! You no me massa, you my tat" [father], said one old woman.[121]

Lewis might have been temporarily overwhelmed, but he was hardly deceived, as he later noted. Nor were any but the most naive of the masters who were so addressed. The use of quasi-filial kin terms not as an expression of loyalty or of subordination, but as a thinly disguised form of sarcasm signaled the failure of authority in this most brutal of slave systems.

Religion and Symbolism

The social death of the slave and his peculiar mode of reincarnation on the margin of his master's society was reinforced by the religious institutions of kin-based societies. As we have seen, the slave was usually forced to reject his own gods and ancestral spirits and to worship those of his master. Even so, he was frequently excluded from community-wide ritual practices: while it was all right for him to worship his master's ancestral spirits, he was not allowed to participate in cults that were associated with political power and office.

Among more advanced slaveholding systems religion played an even greater role in the ritual process of incorporating the slave to his marginal status. Most ritual activities became the specialized preserve of religious institutions. And in both its structural and ritual aspects religion reflected the more centralized nature of political power.[122] In the same way that the state had to develop a specialized set of laws to deal with the secular problems of the slave, so the state cult needed to develop a more specialized set of rules and beliefs to represent the condition of slavery.

Religion never played the important role in the development of Greek slavery that it did among the Roman, Islamic, or many Christian peoples. The practice of having the slave worship at the Greek family hearth continued well into the classical period. This hardly met the religious needs of the slaves any more than it would have sufficed for their masters. But slaves again were largely excluded from the extrahousehold religious cults of their masters. What is more, restraints were placed on their attempts to develop their own cults. The religious isolation and confinement of their slaves hardly bothered the Greek masters, for they did not care for any form of incorporation of slaves into the Greek community. Franz Bömer, one of the leading authorities on the religious lives of slaves in antiquity, tells us:

> The fact is that Greek slaves, and not only those from Delphi but from everywhere ... wander like creatures who are dumb, like human bodies without face or profile, without individuality or self-consciousness, and most important, without a noticeable expression of any religious life, be it collective or personal ... The slaves of the Greeks are diametrically opposed to the religious wealth and vivaciousness of the slaves in Rome, who, in fact, could even convince foreign slaves to forget the gods of their native lands and accept Roman ways. Roman religion was stronger in the world of the little man.[123]

The contrast may be a little overdrawn, but the basic point is certainly correct. Roman slaves had more freedom in every part of their lives than Greek slaves. The Greek *polis* was an ethnically exclusive unit, whereas Rome was, from relatively early on, an ethnically and politically open system. It was not just slaves who were excluded from the Greek community, but all foreigners.

There were three respects, however, in which Greek religion aided in the adjustment of the slave to his social death. Along with women, slaves were allowed to participate in the state cult of Eleusis. The second important representation of slavery in Greek religion was the saturnalia-type festivals associated with a variety of cults. During these festivities (the oldest being the Cronia ritual) there was a reversal of roles in which slaves ate, drank, and played with their masters.[124] The late British anthropologist Max Gluckman has suggested that such rites of reversal both vented feelings of tension in conflict-ridden relationships and reaffirmed the rightness of the established order: "The acceptance of the established order as right and good, and even sacred, seems to allow unbridled license, even rituals of rebellion, for the order itself keeps this rebellion within bounds. Hence to act the conflicts, whether directly or by inversion or in other symbolical forms, emphasizes the social cohesion within which the conflicts exist."[125] It may be speculated that these rituals of reversal involved not just a means of releasing the tension inherent in the master-slave relationship, and thereby maintaining order, but emphasized the social death of the slave and his total alienation from Greek life. By playing the master, the slave came to realize, however fleetingly, what it was really like to be not just a free man, but more, a truly free man—that is to say, a Greek. When the playing was over and the roles were reversed to normal, the slave would know then with the sinking feeling of the morning after that socially and politically he was dead. The master, in his turn, learned from the role reversal not compassion for his slave, but the bliss it was to be free and Greek. The Cronia, then, was really a death and resurrection ritual: for the master, it was an affirmation of the life principle and freedom; for the slave, it was a confirmation of his living death, powerlessness, and degradation.

The third, perhaps most important, way in which Greek religion related to the condition of slavery was by sacred manumission. The problem of manumission will be discussed at length in a later chapter; I am concerned here only with the role of religion in its legitimization. Sacred manumission was the technique of selling the slave to a god who, by not exercising his proprietary powers, allowed the slave to behave like a free man. The interesting thing about this practice is how secular it actually was. Religion was brought in as a means of legitimizing the manumission transaction only where formal legal mechanisms were absent. Where (as in Athens) legal mechanisms existed, we find no trace of sacred manumission. Bömer demolishes the traditional view that Apollo was a defender of slaves and the great symbol of Greek humanity. The idea of finding freedom in servitude to a god remained alien to Greek thought. The slave who was sold to Apollo was not given his freedom by the god; he merely acquired a de facto freedom by virtue of the fact that the god did not exercise his proprietary powers. This was a neat way of solving the problem created by the naturalistic theory of slavery. If the slave was by nature fit for nothing else, how could he become free? If he was socially dead, how could he be made socially alive? It was not possible. Thus selling the slave to a god salvaged the idea of his slaveness and the permanence of his servile status. Apollo was no defender of slaves, no oasis of universal humanity in the desert of Greek chauvinistic tyranny; on the contrary, he was the ideological salvation of the most inhuman product of the Greek mind—the Aristotelian notion of innate slavishness. Bömer's brilliant exposure of this false pretender to the sacred throne of humanism deserves to be quoted at length:

> The light that surrounded Apollo was cold and hard, and this coldness and hardness characterized his essence. He was no "divine friend of man" who could console the unlucky, the wounded and the homeless. These people found help later from Asclepius and Sarapis, and often consciously turned away from Apollo. This ruthless aspect, not the humane one, of the Delphic god revealed itself simultaneously in the enslavement of small groups . . . and in the Delphic form of sacral manumission.[126]

A fascinating aspect of Apollo is the fact that this god, who became the very embodiment of the "Hellenic Spirit," was of non-Greek origin. This has intrigued and puzzled students of Greek religion, especially the fact that the god was in all likelihood of barbaric, Asiatic origins. The main support for the Asiatic origin of Apollo, W. K. C. Guthrie tells us, is "the fact that at most of his great cult-centers in the mainland of Greece he appears as an intruder."[127] That the most Greek of Greek gods should be of barbaric origin offers ample room for speculation; equally tantalizing is the thought that there may be some connection between the intruder status of this god in the realm of the supernatural and the significance of his social role in the life of the vast number of intrusive slaves who were so essential to the socioeconomic fabric of Greek civilization.

Rome was different, and the slaves' religious life a great deal better. Not that Roman masters were any less cruel; they may have been even more brutal. Rather, Rome had a culture that was far more inclusive, with institutions that were incomparably more flexible, and in no area more so than religion. In primitive Rome and even as late as midrepublic times, slaves participated in the religion of the household, especially in the Lares cult. Originally the head of the cult was the paterfamilias. But as the latifundia replaced the household farm, the master withdrew from this role. By Cato's day the slave villicus or overseer directed the cult. With urbanization and the further growth of the latifundia, toward the end of the republic the Lares cult became increasingly attractive to slaves and freedmen.[128] The saturnalia and matronalia (festivals in honor of Mars and Hera originally celebrated by married women) were also important ritual supports for the slaveholding system from early times, the former quite possibly influenced by Greek traditions.[129]

As the gesellschaft principle of social organization replaced the gemeinschaft principle in Roman life, ritual specialization increased further. The slave-oriented cults, however, could only initiate the new slaves into the slave sector. There remained the urgent need to incorporate the slave and still more, his descendants, into the wider community. Several kinds of religious organizations were adapted to meet both the specific ritual needs of the slaves and the wider superstructural problem of somehow representing the slave system in supernatural terms.

There were, first, the interclass cults. In Jupiter, Juno, and especially Silvanus, we find originally Roman deities who were associated by the slaves with eastern counterparts with which they were more familiar. Many of the cults were of foreign origin—a good number of them brought to Rome by the slaves themselves. Most notable was Mithras, famous for the rapidity with which it attained popularity and the equality of master and slave in the performance of ritual practices.[130]

In the institution of the collegia, which constituted the organizational aspect of worship, the slave found not only a church but "a social club, a craft guild, and a funeral society";[131] and in holding one of the many offices, he or she experienced some vicarious sense of importance. The names of some of these colleges are very revealing. In the light of what we have said about slavery as a state of social death, it is not unreasonable to suppose that when the members of one college called themselves "comrades in death," they were referring not solely to their coming physical death.[132]

Finally, there was the role religion played in relating the slave and slavery to the wider sociopolitical order. Here it was the state cults that were critical. According to Bömer, during the republican era Jupiter Libertas had a special appeal to slaves because of the association of the god with freedom, but the evidence is slender and controversial.[133] Of much greater interest was the phenomenon of emperor worship and the extraordinary role of the slaves and ex-slaves in the imperial cults. The earliest of these, the Augustan Lares, was in fact a revival of the dying Lares cult to which the emperor added his own imprint. Keith Hopkins argues that this cult had been started by ex-slaves, Augustus simply institutionalizing the informal local celebrations into a state cult devoted partly to his worship. "The cult provided rich ex-slaves, as organizers of the cult, with a prestigious and public outlet for social display. And it allowed emperor worship to flourish at street level."[134] It was not long, however, before emperor worship was accepted at all levels of society. It was a major legitimizing force among slaves for the simple reason that the emperor's cult introduced into Roman law the alien principle of asylum for slaves. The granting of the right of appeal to Caesar's statue was one of the few ways in which the state intervened between master and slave. The state was, of course, sensitive to this intrusion on the authority of the master, and in practice very few slaves attempted such an appeal. But in enhancing the authority of the emperor in the eyes of all, including even the meanest of slaves, the legitimacy of the system as a whole was reinforced. What the master lost in individual authority, the slave system as a whole gained, embodied as it was in the divine protective power of the deified emperor.[135] Still, as Moses Finley has pointed out: "In so one-sided a relationship, in a world in which there was little hope of material success for the majority of the free population (let alone the slaves), and in which the earthly power was now pretty close to despotism, fear rather than love was often the dominating emotion behind worship, at best fear and love together. Religion became increasingly centered on salvation in the next world, whereas it had once been chiefly concerned with life in this one."[136]

Among the religions of salvation, Christianity was to emerge slowly, then dramatically, over the next three hundred years as the religion par excellence, one that could forge a moral order which appealed to and united emperor and subject, master and slave.[137] A discussion of the means by which it achieved this is beyond the scope of the present work. It is generally accepted that Christianity found many of its earliest converts among the slave populations of the Roman Empire, although the fact is surprisingly difficult to authenticate.[138] What is certain, however, is that the slave experience was a major source of the metaphors that informed the symbolic structure of Christianity.[139]

The most cursory examination of "the three terms which are the keywords" of the Apostle Paul's theology (according to J. G. Davies) immediately reveals the extraordinary role of the slave experience as a metaphoric source. These key words are redemption, justification, and reconciliation.[140] Redemption quite literally means release from enslavement. Through Christ the believer is emancipated from sin. Justification means that the believer has been judged and found not guilty, in much the same manner as the slave who has received the most perfect of manumissions, the restoration of his natality with the legal fiction that he had been wrongfully enslaved. "Reconciliation or Atonement means the bringing together of those who have been separated," in much the same way that the manumitted slave is reborn as a member of a community. Paul in fact went so far as to use the idea of adoption to describe the relationship between redeemed man and God. "Redeemed, justified, reconciled, man is elevated from the status of slave to that of son, and becomes 'an heir through God' of the promised salvation."[141]

What Ambrosio Donini calls "the myth of salvation" became the unifying master concept of organized Christianity, and it is most powerfully evoked in the dominant symbol of the religion, that of the death and resurrection of Christ.[142] Man fell into spiritual slavery because of his original sin.

Slavery, which on the level of secular symbolism was social death, became on the level of sacred symbolism spiritual death. When, however, we question what Christ's crucifixion meant, we find two fundamentally different symbolic interpretations. One explanation, which has profoundly conservative spiritual and social implications, held that Christ saved his followers by paying with his own life for the sin that led to their spiritual enslavement. The sinner, strictly speaking, was not emancipated, but died anew in Christ, who became his new master. Spiritual freedom was divine enslavement. Here was a confluence of two old ideas: the Near Eastern and Delphic notion of freedom through sale to a god, and the Judaic idea of the suffering servant and sacrificial lamb. It was not a very tidy symbolic statement, and it accounts in part for the occasional impenetrability of Paul's theology. He had this interpretation in mind, for example, when he made remarks such as the following: "The death that he died, he died unto sin once: but the life that he liveth, he liveth unto God."[143]

There was a far more satisfactory and at the same time more liberating symbolic interpretation of the crucifixion. The slave, it will be recalled, was someone who by choosing physical life had given up his freedom. Although he could, of course, have kept his freedom and died, man lacked the courage to make such a choice. Jesus, "his savior," by his death made this choice for him. It is this feature that was completely new in the religious behavior and death of Jesus. What it meant in symbolic terms was that Jesus did not redeem mankind by making mankind his slave in the manner of the old pagan religions. Rather, he annulled the condition of slavery in which man existed by returning to the original point of enslavement and, on behalf of the sinner about to fall, gave his own life so that the sinner might live and be free.

It is remarkable that Paul held also to this radically different interpretation of the crucifixion. The contradiction was directly paralleled by the well-known ethical contradiction of his theology. As Maurice Goguel has pointed out, Paul had two irreconcilable religious ethics.[144] One was the pre-Christian and essentially Judaic ethic of law and judgment, in which obedience to divine law, and judgment according to one's social and religious actions, were of the essence. The other was the ethic of the justified man. In this ethic Christ's death redeemed mankind of the burden of sin; the believer, through faith, was immediately emancipated. The first ethic corresponded to the conservative use of the slave metaphor; the second to the more liberal conception of slavery and emancipation. Paul tried to hold both these positions at the same time and thereby placed the believer, as Goguel points out, in the impossible position of one "who must struggle to realize in fact what he is in principle."[145] And he asks: "How can we now speak of a judgment for those who are in Christ, and therefore cannot be subject to condemnation?"[146]

The answer was to abandon the liberal view of emancipation and to canonize the essentially pre-Christian interpretation of salvation as reenslavement to a god, in the triumph of the conception of the believer as the slave of God and of Christianity as a theological transmutation of the order of slavery. Whatever other factors explain Christianity's conquest of the Roman world, there seems little doubt that the extraordinary way in which its dominant symbolic statements and meanings are informed by the experience of slavery was a major contributing factor. For the same reason too, Christianity was to provide institutional support and religious authority for the advanced slave systems of medieval Europe and of the modern Americas.

Christianity was not alone among the major world religions in legitimizing slavery. Earlier we noted the contradiction in Islam between the rationalization of slavery as a means of converting the unbeliever and the continuing enslavement of the converted. We find the same contradiction in Judaism and Christianity. The slave, in the city of the Christian God, was declared an insider, an integral part of the brotherhood of man in the service of God; but the slave, in the city of man, remained the archetypical outsider, the eternal enemy within, in a formalized state of marginality.

At first sight the contradiction is not obvious. Indeed, the opposite seems to be the case: the exclusion of the slave on the secular level was symbolically compensated for by his inclusion in the sacred community. The contradiction between marginality and integration, which slavery created, was apparently resolved by relegating each to a separate domain of cultural existence. But this theological solution on the part of a monotheistic slaveholder class works only where there is hegemonic imposition of a rigid dualism in the socioreligious ideology. This was exactly what happened in medieval Christendom under the conservative spell of Saint Augustine.[147] But Judaism and Islam were too this-worldly and too strongly monistic for such an interpretation to be taken seriously.[148] And the rise of Protestantism dealt a death blow to the neat symbolic compromise of the Middle Ages. Augustinian dualism lingered in the symbolic representation of Latin American slavery: hence the apparent anomaly that has baffled so many Anglo-American historians, that of a Catholic church stoutly declaring slavery a sin, yet condoning the institution to the point where it was itself among the largest of slaveholders.[149]

The Anglican masters of the Caribbean avoided the problem altogether by abandoning religion or making a mockery of it, both for themselves and for their slaves—clergymen in nineteenth-century Jamaica being "the most finished debauchers in the land."[150] As Richard S. Dunn has pointed out, the refusal of the English planters in the West Indies to convert their slaves to Christianity, in contrast with contemporary Latin masters, "can largely be explained by Protestant versus Catholic conversion techniques."[151] Protestantism by its very nature demanded the liberating conception of the crucifixion, with its emphasis on personal choice and freedom. Realizing this, the West Indian masters did everything possible to keep their slaves in ignorance of their creed—giving in only when, a few decades prior to abolition, they found their policy to be too easy a target in the propaganda war of the abolitionists.

How then do we account for the Protestant slave South where, during the late eighteenth and the nineteenth centuries, both masters and slaves were highly religious? It is clear that the special version of Protestantism that triumphed in the South and the peculiar socioeconomic features of the system together explain its unusual course of development.

Until nearly the end of the eighteenth century the U.S. South did not differ markedly from other Protestant slave systems. Masters were generally hostile to the conversion of their slaves, fearing—like their Caribbean counterparts—that the nature of their creed with its emphasis on instruction in the gospels, personal choice, and spiritual liberation would, if adopted by their slaves, undermine the masters' authority. As late as 1782 slaves in Georgia were still being whipped savagely for preaching,[152] and while Albert Raboteau may have overstated the case in claiming that "the majority of slaves . . . remained only minimally touched by Christianity by the second decade of the nineteenth century," he was not far wrong.[153]

Two major developments explain the remarkable change that took place during the nineteenth century. One was the great religious awakening that culminated in the religious conversion of the South from classical Protestantism to revivalist fundamentalism.[154] The second was the emergence in the South between 1790 and 1830 of a full-fledged slave system, a total commitment to the institution as an essential feature of the region's socioeconomic order, and the realization that if slavery was to function effectively the system had to be reformed. In Genovese's words, "whereas previously many slaveholders had feared slaves with religion, now they feared slaves without religion even more. They came to see Christianity primarily as a means of social control . . . The religious history of the period formed part of the great thrust to reform slavery as a way of life and to make it bearable for slaves."[155]

Fundamentalist Protestantism was peculiarly suited to such a reform. Its emphasis on conversion as a sudden spiritual transformation rather than the result of reflection and instruction; its oral rather than literary missionary techniques; its other-worldliness, especially its insistence on salvation as a purely spiritual change, the rewards of which are to be achieved in the hereafter; its emphasis on piety and obedience, and on the sinfulness of the world and the flesh; made it a creed that the masters could confidently regard as a support for, rather than a subversion of, their authority.[156]

Nevertheless, it would be simplistic to interpret the role of religion in the slave South solely in terms of an opiate for the masses, a device used by the master class as an agent of social control. In the final analysis it was indeed just that, and there is abundant evidence that the master class cynically devised a "theology of slavery" in a crude attempt to rationalize the system. But as recent studies have shown, slaves quickly recognized the crude ideological strategy of their masters. Olli Alho's detailed analyses of the slave narratives "indicate that the carefully constructed theology of slavery built up by the whites became in many plantations nothing more than a joke" among the slaves.[157]

The slaves found in fundamentalist Christianity paths to the satisfaction of their own needs, creating the strong commitment to Christianity that has persisted to this day. In so doing they created an institutional base that provided release and relief from the agonies of thralldom, and even offered some room for a sense of dignity before God and before each other. Having said all this, I must emphasize that the religion they experienced was the same as that of their masters in all its essential doctrinal and cultic aspects; that while the spirituals they sang may have had a double meaning with secular implications, it is grossly distorting of the historical facts to claim that they were covertly revolutionary in their intent; and, most important of all, it is irresponsible to deny that however well religion may have served the slaves, in the final analysis it did entail a form of accommodation to the system.

In all of this I am in complete agreement with Genovese's penetrating interpretation of the role of religion in the slave South.[158] Where I differ from him, and from others such as Lawrence W. Levine[159] and Albert J. Raboteau who with equal skill and persuasion have emphasized the creative and positive side of religion for the slave, is in my interpretation of the specific means by which fundamentalist Christianity became at one and the same time a spiritual and social salvation for the slaves and an institutional support for the order of slavery.

To appreciate where we differ it is necessary to return to the nature of Christianity and to specify the peculiar doctrinal features of fundamentalism. Pauline Christianity, as we saw, was theologically dualistic, containing an ethic of judgment and an ethic of the justified person that were in constant tension with each other. These two ethics in turn were symbolically expressed in two contrasting interpretations of Jesus' crucifixion. Roman Catholicism resolved the tension by eliminating what I call the liberating pole of Pauline dualism, emphasizing the ethic of judgment and obedience; classic Protestantism resolved it by eliminating the conservative pole and by strongly reviving the ethic of the justified person.

What then is distinctive in fundamentalism? My answer is that it restored *both* poles and returned fully to Pauline dualism with all its contained tension and its contextual shifting from one ethical and symbolic pole to the other. If we do not understand this distinctive doctrinal feature of fundamentalism, we cannot fully appreciate how the religion could have spiritually sustained both slaves and masters as well as the system as a whole. We will also fail to comprehend the symbolic life of the slaves themselves.

If we next seek the major doctrinal and symbolic components of slave religion, we find that the fundamentalism of the slaves was, like that of all southerners, essentially Pauline in its overwhelming preoccupation with Christ and the crucifixion and in its ethical and symbolic dualism, its paradoxical tension between the ethic of judgment and the ethic of the redeemed sinner. Further, it is precisely this dualism that explains the apparent paradox that the religion of the slaves, doctrinally one with that of their masters, nonetheless allowed for the spiritual support of both groups and of the system as a whole.

Jesus and his crucifixion dominate the theology of the slaves and not, as recent scholars have claimed, the Israelites and Exodus story.[160] Not only is the theme of the crucified Christ explicitly central and dominant, but even when figures from the Old Testament are referred to (including Moses), closer examination reveals that the allusion is really to Jesus. Although Alho does not make the connection to Pauline theology, it is striking that his most important finding concerns the dualistic conception of Jesus in the religion of the slaves—that of Jesus as Messiah King and Jesus as comforting savior. He concludes his interpretation with a reference to an insightful contemporary observer: "The difference between the two main identities of Jesus reminds one of what T. W. Higginson wrote in his camp diary about the religious behavior of his black soldiers; softness, patience, and meekness on the one hand, hardness, energy, and daring on the other, seems to be reflected in the dualistic way in which the spirituals picture the figure and roles of Jesus."[161]

We can now explain how fundamentalism, a single religion, performed the contradictory roles it did in the slave South. Both masters and slaves adhered to Pauline ethical dualism, with its sustained "eschatological dissonance."[162] And in exactly the same way that Paul and the early Christians shifted from one pole of their doctrinal dualism to another as occasion and context demanded, so did the masters and their slaves. Thus the masters, among themselves, could find both spiritual and personal dignity and salvation in the ethic of the justified and redeemed sinner. The crucified Jesus as redeemer and liberator from enslavement to sin supported a proud, free group of people with a highly developed sense of their own dignity and worth. Similarly, the slaves in the silence of their souls and among themselves *with their own preachers,* could find salvation and dignity in this same interpretation of the crucified Lord. When the theologian Olin P. Moyd insists that "redemption is the root and core motif of black theology" and that it means essentially liberation from sin and confederation within the fellowship of black worshippers, it is, I suspect, to this end of the Pauline dualism that he is referring.[163]

As with the masters, the slave dualism had another pole. This is the ethic of law, judgment, and obedience, the ethic that found symbolic expression in the other Jesus, the more Judaic Messiah King who judges, who demands obedience, and who punishes the wicked and rewards the righteous. This is the Jesus who saves not by annulling slavery but by divine enslavement. To live with this Jesus demands, as Goguel tells us, watchfulness, obedience, and stoic acceptance.

Both masters and slaves held also to this conception of Jesus and, like Paul and the early Christians, shifted to this symbolic code in dealing with, and coming to terms with, all authority relations—not only the one between master and slave but, among the masters between male and female, upper class and working class, parent and child, and among the slaves between parent and child. In this way fundamentalism, by reverting to Pauline dualism, provided the slave South with the perfect creed, one much more subtle in its support for the system than most of the masters thought. The crude theology of slavery that the masters tried unsuccessfully to preach in the plantation mission was really quite unnecessary. Nor was it necessary for master and slave to have two separate religions. Christianity, after Paul, had already constructed an extraordinarily shrewd creed with a built-in flexibility that made it possible for emperor and slave to worship the same god without threatening the system, but also without denying all dignity to the oppressed.

In the U.S. South there developed the last and most perfectly articulated slave culture since the fall of the Roman Empire. The religion that had begun in and was fashioned by the Roman slave order was to play the identical role eighteen hundred years later in the slave system that was to be Rome's closest cultural counterpart in the modern world. History did not repeat itself; it merely lingered.

3

Honor
and
Degradation

NEAR THE MIDDLE of the first century B.C., the mime-writer and epigrammatist Publilius Syrus triumphed over his rival Laberius in a dramatic contest of verbal skill ordered by Caesar. A major factor contributing to his success must certainly have been what J. Wight Duff and Arnold M. Duff described as his "gift of understanding Roman psychology."[1] Publilius' comprehension of the Roman mind came from a very special perspective, that of the underdog—that sharp, incisive insight and sardonic wit honed on bitter experience which gives the most trusted and intelligent members of an oppressed class a distinctive access to the mind of their oppressors. For Publilius had been a slave of Syrian origin, brought possibly from Antioch as a youth, who by sheer force of intellect and verbal skill in the language of his master won both his freedom and the adoration of the populace. As we examine the remnants of the maxims extracted from his mimes, it comes as no surprise that a disproportionate number of them are concerned with the nature of honor and the indignities of submission. When he wrote that "the height of misery is to live at another's will," the words came from deep in the suffering of his own earlier life.[2]

Publilius knew how to play on the deepest weaknesses, anxieties, and conceits of the various categories of persons in his audience. He no doubt had the slaveholders in mind when he inserted in one of his mimes, "Honor

scarce ever revisits the mind it has quitted";[3] and it was to placate the freedmen that he threw in, "None ever loses honor save him who has it not."[4] But
I strongly suspect that it was for the slaves who looked on from the fringes
that he coined his finest maxim: "What is left when honor is lost?"[5] There
was no need to elaborate, for everyone—master, freedman, and most of all
slave—at once knew the answer.

And so would the members of all other societies in all other times. The
idea that a person's honor is more valuable than his life, and that to prefer
life to honor betrays a degraded mind, comes close to being a genuinely universal belief. It is a theme that haunts Western literature. Pascal need not
have been influenced by Publilius when over fifteen hundred years later he
expressed the view that "he would be infamous who would not die to preserve his honor." The most cursory search will quickly turn up numerous
similar passages, from Shakespeare's Richard the Second proclaiming,
"Take honor from me and my life is done," to Nietzsche's superman declaring, "One should die proudly when it is no longer possible to live proudly."
And even where writing is not to be found, the proverbs and oral traditions
of all preliterate peoples, including every headhunting and cannibal tribe I
know, would reveal an almost identical belief: that to choose life over honor
is infamy. As Marcel Mauss has observed: "Even in really primitive societies
like the Australian the 'point of honour' is as ticklish as it is in ours . . . Men
could pledge their honour long before they could sign their names."[6]

Yet it was the choice of life over honor that the slave or his ancestor
made, or had made for him. The dishonor of slavery, I have already argued,
was not a specific but a generalized condition. It came in the primal act of
submission. It was the most immediate human expression of the inability to
defend oneself or to secure one's livelihood. It was not part of the institutionalization of slavery, for its source was not culture. The dishonor the
slave was compelled to experience sprang instead from that raw, human
sense of debasement inherent in having no being except as an expression of
another's being.

What the captive or condemned person lost was the master's gain. The
real sweetness of mastery for the slaveholder lay not immediately in profit,
but in the lightening of the soul that comes with the realization that at one's
feet is another human creature who lives and breathes only for one's self, as
a surrogate for one's power, as a living embodiment of one's manhood and
honor. Every slavemaster must, in his heart of hearts, have agreed with
Nietzsche's celebrated declaration: "What is good? Everything that
heightens the feeling of power in man, the will to power, power itself. What
is bad? Everything that is born of weakness. What is happiness? The feeling
that power is *growing*, that resistance is overcome."[7]

We are far removed from the ostentatious ironies of Nietzsche when we
turn to the essays of Francis Bacon; but in his own quiet, almost serenely

self-assured way, for his own time, Bacon made the same point when he wrote, "Discreet followers and servants help much to reputation. *Omnis fama a domesticiis exeant* [All reputation proceeds from servants]."[8] A story from the Icelandic sagas provides another illustration. It concerns the behavior of the crafty slave overseer Atli, who without permission lavishly entertained the shipwrecked Vebjorn and his men throughout the winter at his master's expense. When the master, Geirmund, finally learned of his slave's extravagance, he was understandably outraged and demanded an explanation. The cunning Atli responded that "he wanted to show how great-minded and generous his master must be, and how great an estate he must have, when one of his thralls dared to do such a thing without his permission. Geirmund was so pleased with the answer that he gave the thrall his freedom and also the farm he had managed."[9]

The Nature of Honor

In this chapter I propose to show that, first, in all slave societies the slave was considered a degraded person; second, the honor of the master was enhanced by the subjection of his slave; and third, wherever slavery became structurally very important, the whole tone of the slaveholders' culture tended to be highly honorific. (In many societies the sole reason for keeping slaves was in fact their honorific value.)

Before considering the comparative data, we need to clarify the concept of honor by drawing on the rich anthropological literature on the subject. Happily, a *communis opinio* has emerged and is well expressed in the work of Julian Pitt-Rivers.[10] He argues that honor is a complex notion having several facets: "It is a sentiment, a manifestation of this sentiment in conduct, and the evaluation of this conduct by others, that is to say, reputation. It is both internal to the individual and external to him—a matter of his feelings, his behavior, and the respect he receives." The way in which these facets of behavior are related is cogently put: "Honor felt becomes honor claimed, and honor claimed becomes honor paid." Only those who aspire to honor can be dishonored: "Those who aspire to no honor cannot be humiliated."

What this immediately implies is that those who do not compete for honor, or are not expected to do so, are in a real sense outside the social order. To belong to a community is to have a sense of one's position among one's fellow members, to feel the need to assert and defend that position, and to feel a sense of satisfaction if that claimed position is accepted by others and a sense of shame if it is rejected. It is also to feel that one has a right to take pride in past and current successes of the group, and to feel shame and dishonor in its past and present failures.

Modern anthropologists have confirmed Thomas Hobbes' insight that the sense of honor is intimately related to power, for in competing for precedence one needs power to defend one's honor. Still, it is one's sense of honor that often drives one to acquire the instruments of power in the first place. It is foolish to insist too strongly on a single causal direction, and even worse to adopt a vulgar materialistic interpretation of the relationship. It is true, as John Davis observes, that honor "describes the distribution of wealth in a social idiom, and prescribes appropriate behaviour for people at various points in the hierarchy"; in this sense "it entails acceptance of superordination and subordination." But, he goes on to note, honor "is closely associated with integrity: the whole man is contemplated."[11] Pitt-Rivers finds that "the claim to honor depends always in the last resort, upon the ability of the claimant to impose himself. Might is the basis of right to precedence, which goes to the man who is bold enough to enforce his claim, regardless of what may be thought of his merits." It is for this reason that "courage is the sine qua non of honor, and cowardice its converse."[12]

Because honor envelops "the whole man," it is seen as an intimate personal quality relating to both his physical and characterologic attributes. A person's will and intentions are the two vital ingredients in any assessment of his honor by others. Is he a man of his word? Is his oath inviolable? Can he assert his will as a man of honor? "The essence of honor is personal autonomy," and to be in another's command, Pitt-Rivers adds, "restricts it." Furthermore, a freely established relation of dependence with a more powerful patron can be the basis for expanding one's honorific claims vis-à-vis one's equals. The client's attachment also firmly establishes him in a place within the hierarchy of honorable statuses. He belongs and is one with his patron as a member of *their* society. The patron needs him as much as he needs the patron, and this is fully understood by both parties.

The idea that honor is personal autonomy takes us to the philosophical core of this most elusive of social concepts. For the real mystery of honor lies in the fact that although its existence is revealed, and its claims proven in acts of honor, such acts are always considered epiphenomenal. This should be evident from the common observation that two persons may perform the same act, yet the behavior of one is considered honorable while that of the other is not. Acting honorably is not the same thing as *being* honorable; it is not enough to abide by a code of honor. Honor is never evaluated in teleological terms. Like Immanuel Kant's "good" which is nothing if not a "good will,"[13] honor is nothing except the honorable will. Nor does the fact that one is honored make one honorable. One need not even be a human being to be honored; in India millions of persons daily honor the cow. Understanding this aspect of honor is critical, if what I have to say later is not to be misunderstood. There have been slaves who have been honored or whose acts have been considered honorable, yet who have remained despised as persons without honor.

Finally, we must take account of the important role of honor as a distinctive feature of certain cultures. The sense of honor is present in all human societies—in some to the point where it becomes a dominant value. Following Plato, we may call the culture of such societies, and the character syndrome in which honor and pride are excessively developed, timocratic.[14]

Honor and Slavery among Tribal Peoples

Let us begin with the Tupinamba of South America, a primitive, warlike group among whom slavery existed in its most elementary form. Economic motives were wholly absent in the enslavement of captives. Slaves were kept for two purposes only: as a living exhibition of the master's honor and valor in war, and ultimately as meat for the cannibalistic orgy that might take place as long as fifteen years after capture. Between being taken prisoner and being eaten, the captive "recognize[d] himself as a slave and a defeated man, he follow[ed] the victorious man, serve[d] him faithfully without having to be watched."[15]

The slave among the Tupinamba was constantly aware of the fact that he was a doomed person. Even if he escaped, his own tribe would not take him back. His sense of degradation was as intense as his master's sense of glory. A Tupinamban slave told Father Evreux that what really bothered him was not the prospect of being eaten,

> but not to be able to take revenge before dying on those who are to eat me. I remember that I am the son of an important man in my country . . . Now I see myself as a slave without being painted and no feathers attached to my head, my arms, around my waist, as the important people of my country are decorated, then I want to be dead.[16]

While slaves among the primitive Germanic peoples may not have been physically consumed, it is no exaggeration to say that they were socially consumed (as they were to be in all other slaveholding societies). Carl O. Williams' observation on slavery in ancient Iceland is pertinent:

> The class of the lowly is the source from which the master class draws its livelihood and leisure. Thraldom is a degree of cannibalism. It is a system of man feeding upon man. The master is a human parasite, who, by the right of might, has secured his fellow-men in the bonds of thraldom in order to feed upon them and to use them for the satisfaction of his appetites.[17]

What the slave mainly fed was the master's sense of honor and his sexual appetite, for the economic role of the slave was quite marginal among most of the continental Germanic tribes.[18] Among these peoples, however, the sense of honor was highly developed, each nonslave member of the community having a specific honor price determined by his position in the kin group and the group's position in the wider community. Slaves were regarded, above all, as people without honor. This could take rather amusing turns. For instance, if a member of the community verbally abused another he could expect savage retaliation, sometimes resulting in death; slaves, however, could verbally abuse anyone if they were so inclined, because "the abusive language of a slave cannot injure anybody's honor. If his abuses become offensive, the slave must be looked on only as the mouthpiece of the lord."[19] Of course, if the slave made a nuisance of himself he could be killed on the spot, but the matter of honor was irrelevant. If the freeman chose to laugh the matter off as the simple rantings of a crazy brute, there was no loss of honor.

This was true of all the Germanic tribes, with minor variations. Much the same situation prevailed among the Norwegians and their Icelandic offshoot. "No one," declared the Icelander Hóvamól, "should put faith in a sick calf or in a self-willed thrall."[20] It was a mortal insult among the Icelanders to call someone a thrall, for it amounted to saying that they were without honor. To do so was a *fullrettisord* (a gross verbal insult requiring atonement) and invariably resulted in bloodshed.[21] As among other Germanic peoples, the injury or murder of a thrall required compensation to the master, but the compensation was in no way viewed as part of an honor price payment. The master might, if so inclined, view the injury as an offense to his own honor, but even then "the offense was of no grave consequence—only a matter of a boot of twelve aurar [the value of twelve cows] for each thrall."[22]

The same situation existed among the Welsh and Anglo-Saxons. To be sure, the Welsh laws required a *sarhed,* or honor payment, for injuries to slaves; but a closer examination of the laws reveals that the payment was to be made in kind not to the slave but to his master, and the goods specified all related to materials for the improvement of the slave's working capacity. Even where a slave woman was sexually abused, the sarhed was to be paid not to her or her common-law slave spouse, but to the master.[23] A similar situation existed among the Anglo-Saxons during the seventh century. The honor price for raping a "birele" or household slave, H. R. P. Finberg tells us, was "appointed in proportion *not to her feelings* but to her master's rank: 12 shillings or 240p for a nobleman's, 6 shillings or 120p for a commoner's" (emphasis added) and so on down to the "twenty-five shillings women" or "grinding slave." The money apparently went to the master.[24]

If we move now to the impressive body of data on domestic slavery in sub-Saharan Africa,[25] there is unambiguous support for our argument. All traditional African societies were extremely alive to the role of honor in people's lives. Where large-scale slave systems existed, honor became a dominant value. The classic examples were the Nigerian pre-European states such as Bornu and Hausaland, the Amhara of Ethiopia, and the nineteenth-century Ashanti.[26] In the great majority of traditional African societies, however, stratificatory systems were not highly developed and classes were either absent or not "well defined."[27] However, precisely because such classes and status groups were not well developed, individual competition for honor and prestige was rampant—as is well known to students of preindustrial societies.[28] The less centralized were such societies, the greater their emphasis on prestige ranking of individuals. (The extreme was the highly formalized recognition of honor found among the largely acephalous Ibos.[29])

In the struggle for prestige, what was critical in *all* African societies was the number of dependents an ambitious man could acquire. Kinship and affinal alliances were the two major techniques for accumulating dependents, but a third important means was the institution of slavery. Among many African tribes this was often the sole reason for the acquisition of slaves, there being little or no economic difference between the condition of slaves and their masters and no such thing as a slave class.[30]

Typical of the African situation were the Mende, who kept considerable numbers of slaves for both social and economic reasons and on the whole treated them well, so well indeed that it was difficult for an outsider to distinguish between free and slave. The primary social difference between the two groups was the honorlessness of the slaves, a condition that the free man was reluctant to point out in the presence of strangers, knowing how crushing it would be to the slave. Thus J. J. Grace tells us that the *nduwanga* or slave group was subjected to "a prescribed code of conduct which made their inferior status clear." He cites T. S. Alldridge, a former trader and official in Mende country, who wrote: "Slaves merely cringe up and place their hands one on each side of their master's hand, and draw them back slowly without the fillip while the head is bowed."[31] The loss of honor was most evident among aged slaves. In no other part of the world was age more respected and honored than in traditional African societies. But old Mende slaves never received this respect: "They were minors who would never receive the respect due to a mature adult."[32]

Nowhere in Africa was the association between slavery, the timocratic character, and the conception of the slave as a degraded person more pronounced than in the large-scale slave societies of the Fulani. In his brilliant study of Fulani society in Jelgobi (on the Upper Volta), Paul Riesman shows how the strong image the Fulani have of themselves is negatively defined largely in relation to their stereotype of the despised *maccube* (slaves) and ex-slaves.

> In Fulani eyes, it is among "captives" or ex-slaves that one finds most clearly expressed everything that is the opposite of Fulani. According to this stereotype, "captives" are black, fat, coarse, naive, irresponsible, uncultivated, shameless, dominated by their needs and emotions. These qualities are innate and manifest the servile condition, for the Fulani cannot imagine that a descendant of slaves could have better qualities than his ancestors.[33]

The term *pulaaku* means everything that is ideally Fulani, and Riesman found that the best way to define it was simply to "make a list of antonyms of the terms which define the stereotype of the *maccudo*. It follows that the Fulani should be: light-skinned, slender, refined, subtle, responsible, cultivated, endowed with a sense of shame, and master of his needs and of his emotions." The Fulani ideal is strongly expressed in Fulani epic poetry, in which the "very word *pulaaku* has a meaning which obliges us to put the accent on the social: *pulaaku* means not only 'the qualities appropriate to a Fulani' but also at the same time the group of Fulani men possessing these qualities." In other words, there is not only a timocratic character, but a timocratic group and culture. Significantly, Riesman finds that the Somali bard's use of the term *pulaaku* "is an exact structural equivalent of the English word 'chivalry' and, like it, designates at once certain moral qualities and a group of men possessing these qualities."[34]

Among the Indians of North America hereditary slavery of any significance existed, with only a few exceptions, mainly on the northwest coast. There the condition of the slave was unenviable—but rarely for economic reasons, since the considerable surplus generated from rich fishing beds meant that the consumption patterns of masters and slaves were much the same. Slaves, however, were utterly without power or honor. What Robert E. Stearns wrote of the Kassi tribe in the late nineteenth century was true of the entire northwest coast during this period, that "they treat their slaves as if they were dogs; they look on them as a possession outside the human category. For a master to kill a dozen slaves is nothing; it merely demonstrates his wealth and his power."[35]

In the potlatch ceremony, for which these peoples are best known, the killing of slaves often reached frightful proportions, especially among the Tlingit.[36] There is no reason for us to become entangled here in the vexatious problem of the potlatch, a subject on which American anthropologists have been waging intellectual war since the turn of the century.[37] Incontestably though, the ceremony was closely tied to the Indians' excessively developed sense of prestige and honor (whatever other functions it may have served), and the slaughter, freeing, or donation of slaves was its high point. Although slaves served some economic functions, as in Africa and South America, their primary function was to support the honor and power of their masters.

Perhaps the most remarkable instance of the association between slavery and both honor and degradation among preliterate tribal peoples is the Toradja tribes of the central Celebes. This group of tribes is instructive for two reasons: first, some had a highly developed system of slavery with a large slave class, while others did not, hence valuable comparisons can be made; and, second, the relationship between slavery and culture was direct.

The first lesson we draw is that among the tribes with a slave standing work had become dishonorable.[38] Second, while decisions were made in a democratic consensual manner among the tribes that kept no slaves, decision making among the slaveholding tribes was highly autocratic: "The manner in which a Lage chief handles matters testifies to a feeling of power that has developed through mastery over his slaves, but from which the free in the society also feel the influence." Third, childrearing patterns were strongly influenced by the large number of slaves: children in the slaveholding groups were far more obedient and grew up to be far more authoritarian than did those of the nonslaveholding tribes. Fourth, the sexual exploitation of slave women and the resulting "licentiousness of many female slaves made the free women more prudish."[39]

What resulted from all this was an almost perfect example of the timocratic character among the slaveholders, in sharp contrast to the highly sensitive, give-and-take attitude of members of nonslaveholding tribes. According to N. Adriani and Albert C. Kruyt:

> Slavery has put its stamp on the character of the various Toradja tribes. The To Lage and the To Anda'e, who always had to be mindful of keeping their prestige high with regard to their slaves, had in this way achieved a great deal of self-control, through which they made a more civilized impression on the foreigner than did the To Pebato who, not knowing this pressure, behaved more as they are, let themselves go more . . . The feeling of responsibility that is characteristic of the To Lage must also be a consequence of keeping slaves, since the lord answered for his slaves and was responsible for their deeds.[40]

At the same time, the personality of the slave was considered to be totally opposite from that of the master, and the slave's behavior tended to conform to the master's view of him. How he actually felt, of course, the ethnographers do not tell us, but their description of his social character is typical of the political psychology of slavery in all times and all places:

> There was indeed a great difference in character and disposition between the free and the slaves. The slave is so accustomed to not being allowed to have any free will that he has a great deal of passiveness and indifference. One therefore cannot depend on him. The slave has little feeling of responsibility for his deeds; if he has done something wrong, his master is there to pay the fine for him. In the rice field or at the salt-making place, he is equally indolent everywhere, because he knows that he does not work for himself, and only the presence of his master will move him to moderate effort. Because he is not heard at deliberations over political or social matters, he is dull and indifferent about everything that happens in the village and tribe. Because of all this slaves are often rude, and *aba mbatoea,* "slave manners," is tantamount to improper behavior.[41]

Honor and Slavery among Advanced Premodern Peoples

The situation was much the same among the slaveholding peoples of the advanced civilizations, although there was not always the same direct causal link between slavery and the development of timocratic character and culture.

Throughout all the advanced oriental societies the sense of honor was heavily stressed.[42] It was ideologically elaborated among the Chinese and the many peoples they influenced in the distinction between base and ignoble or dishonorable persons. All imprisoned criminals lost honorable status and were "base," and E. G. Pulleyblank propounds the generally accepted view that "it was at least partly a result of the penal origin of slavery that slaves were termed *chien* ('base,' 'ignoble') as opposed to the normal population who were called *liang,* 'good.' "[43] Criminals, while assimilated to the status of slaves, were not all slaves; for the condition of some of them was only temporary. Furthermore, it was always illegal in China to reduce a "good" or "honorable" person to slavery, although this dictate did create some rather tricky legal problems. The same was true of Korea, where "the good people consisted of Yangban [aristocrats] and commoners," while the "base" consisted "primarily of slaves" (although certain polluting caste members were also base).[44] The Gia-Long code of the ancient Vietnamese spelled out this distinction in fine detail as it applied to persons in genuine slavery as opposed to those in debt-servitude. Hired or pledged persons, the law stated, "are on the same footing as persons of honorable status and are considered as 'any persons whomsoever'; one may not consider them equivalent to those who are slaves in perpetuity."[45] In relation to their owners and the families of their owners, pledged persons and others in debt-bondage had little power and were totally dependent economically. In that respect their condition resembled slavery, but it would be a great mistake to confuse them with slaves, for they were not without honor. Dang Trinh Ky comments, "In social life, in relations with strangers, they are always considered as 'any persons whomsoever' and 'honorable.' They have never lost their dignity or liberty."[46]

In ancient India we find the same conception of the slave as a "base" person, which is not surprising in view of the Buddhist influence on this mode of conceptualizing the absence of honor.[47] While not conceptualized in the same way, the base condition of the slave was even more pronounced in the pre-Buddhist era. In the Rigveda the slave is not even considered a human being.[48] During all the periods of ancient India the term "dasa," meaning slave, was always a term of abuse, and according to Katualya it was a crime to call someone "dasa" or "dasi."[49]

In considering the ancient Greeks, we encounter not only one of the two most advanced slave systems of antiquity but, not accidentally, a society in which, on the one hand, the degraded condition of the slave was consciously articulated and, on the other hand, the culture was highly timocratic. I am certainly not suggesting that large-scale slavery was the cause of the honorific nature of classical Greek culture. The world of Odysseus, as Finley has shown, had an extremely honorific culture with slavery being of only marginal significance.[50] What I do maintain is that in classical Greece, slavery and the timocratic character were mutually reinforcive. The preexisting timocratic value system, along with new economic forces, encouraged the development of large-scale slavery. At the same time, the enormous growth of slavery not only reinforced the timocratic character of the ruling class but stimulated its diffusion among all classes, for by the classical period these were societies in which even the destitute felt deprived if they could not afford a slave.[51]

Few would disagree with Alvin Gouldner when he says that "a central, culturally approved value of Greek life, embedded in and influencing its systems of stratification is an emphasis on individual fame and honor," and that the contest for power and honor in ancient Greece, as in most honorific cultures, was largely a zero-sum game, "in that someone can win only if someone else loses."[52]

It is not difficult to imagine the extraeconomic role of slaves in such a society. After reviewing the intellectual evidence, Robert Schlaifer sums up the popular conception of the slave as one who was "completely without honor, shame or any sound element at all."[53] The slave was a stock character in Greek comedy and even Joseph Vogt, after reviewing the literary evidence, was obliged to conclude that "slaves were irrevocably degraded in the eyes of the public."[54] Where the slave was not cast in his usual role as a lazy, cowardly buffoon, it is significant that he was merely an onlooker to tragedy. He himself never experienced tragedy, and was never "allowed to participate in anything even remotely connected with suffering or responsibility."[55] While it is true that the law of hubris held it an offense to outrageously insult a slave, G. R. Morrow goes too far in claiming that it implied either respect or unusual protection for the slave.[56] As he himself observes, fourth-century orators found it anomalous that this law should apply to slaves, "for what honor has a slave to lose?"[57] The law during the classical period must certainly have been a dead letter, since the court was made up of the citizen body and its verdicts strongly reflected public opinion. What is more, the slave had no legal standing and could not bring charges in this court. It is difficult to conceive of a situation in which a third party would bring charges on a slave's behalf against a free person, in view of the fact that the accuser faced a stiff penalty if less than a fifth of the court supported the charge.[58]

There was little humanity in the conception of the slave in classical Greece, and Finley has effectively demolished attempts by some classicists to suggest that the slave was treated as something more than an utterly degraded figure.[59] "Both male and female slave were an 'unfree body,' *andra-poda*, 'human-footed stock,' "[60] and like their Mende counterparts, old slaves could anticipate no respect: "One of the favorite etymological jokes was to derive the word for 'boy' and 'slave' from the word for 'to strike'; thus even an old slave could be addressed as 'boy' because he was beaten so often."[61]

While it is easy to show the existence side by side of a highly timocratic elite culture and a degraded slave condition, it is quite another matter to demonstrate how the two related to each other. Indeed, all we can do is speculate on the nature of the relationship. The best guess is that the large-scale slavery and the timocratic culture of classical Greece had independent historical sources before they came to reinforce each other. The contempt for working for others—and among the ruling class, working at all—must certainly have encouraged the growth of slavery. Further, it is not unreasonable to speculate that slaves did more than help in meeting material needs, they also satisfied a psychological need to dominate. As Victor Ehrenberg observes: "Free men and women frequently indulged their pride towards slaves without restraint. The master was always the absolute lord and owner, the *despotes.*"[62]

Slaves, moreover, may well have had a direct effect on the character formation of the Greek middle and upper classes, in view of their important role in bringing up the children of their masters. But Finley has, quite reasonably, expressed reservations about drawing conclusions from this function about the attitudes of masters and slaves toward each other.[63] I fully agree that the use of male and female governesses and nursemaids in no way encourages "humanity" on the part of a master class toward the class of people who rear them; the experience of black southerners in the United States should have made that clear to even the most anticomparativist of classicists. At the same time the southern experience suggests that a dependence on slaves for childrearing does have some effect on the character formation of the children involved; that, in short, it reinforces arrogance and authoritarianism and supports the timocratic syndrome.[64] When, further, one takes account of the peculiar status of women in classical Greek culture, the ready availability of female slaves as sex objects, and the apparent tendency of the father to absent himself as much as possible from the home,[65] it appears that among upper-class Greeks of this era the role of household slaves in the formation of the timocratic character was not unimportant.

We now move to a consideration of the ancient Roman experience, which for four reasons is critical to my argument. First, Rome evolved the most complex slave system of all the peoples of the premodern world. Second, the Romans, like the Greeks, had a remarkably developed sense of honor. Third, Rome presents the unusual, though by no means unique, case in which significant segments of the slave population—the Greeks and other hellenized slaves—were acknowledged by their masters as culturally superior. Finally, in Rome a group of slaves and freedmen exercised extraordinary power in both the executive and administrative branches of the imperial government. This last feature of Roman society is so critical a test of my hypothesis that I shall consider it separately in a later chapter.

How did the Roman conception of slavery respond to this environment? Did the acknowledged superiority of Greek culture create an exception to the rule I am here maintaining, that slaves are always regarded as persons without honor? To answer these questions, the legal system is as good a place to begin as any; for it is here that we find the traditional notions of *dignitas* or *honor* not only persisting, but acquiring new significance by the period of the late republic, as Peter Garnsey demonstrates in his excellent study of social status and legal privilege in ancient Rome.[66]

The entire legal system, Garnsey shows, was based on the principle of privilege. There was a dual legal structure, one for those who had privilege and another for those who did not. The privileged were tried in a different court, and the penalties they received differed from those meted out to the nonprivileged who had committed the same offense. There were several channels of privilege; these included birth, Roman citizenship, wealth, and proximity to power. However, the main channel of legal privilege was "the possession of *honor* or *dignitas,* which derived from character, birth, office, and wealth."[67] Dignitas, according to Cicero, is "honorable prestige. It merits respect, honor and reverence."[68] And, Garnsey elaborates, "emphasis is placed on moral qualities, manner of life and the esteem which they evoke—or rather command."[69]

The Greeks, we have seen, had their own highly developed sense of honor and we know that the Romans greatly respected their civilization. In Horace's famous phrase, "Captive Greece held her captor captive."[70] Modern historians attest to the accuracy of this aphorism. Chester G. Starr, to cite a typical view, marvels that "the degree to which the conqueror bent culturally before the conquered and humbly admitted his own inferiority in thought and tongue was extraordinary."[71] Did the Roman master, then, accept the Greek slave's highly developed conception of his own honor?

He did not. However much the Roman master admired his Greek slave, the one thing he always denied him was a confirmation of his sense of honor. Indeed, he went further: he denied the very existence of honor in Greek culture, seeing this as one of its major failings. The opening passage of Garnsey's work states that the Romans viewed punishment not only as a deterrent and correction, but as something aimed at "the preservation of honor, when the dignity and prestige of the injured party must be protected, lest, if the offense is allowed to go without punishment, he be brought into contempt and his honor be impaired."[72] Of special interest in this statement is the fact that the Romans made a point of contrasting their own view of punishment with that of the Greeks. Plato's theory, they argued, however admirable in other respects, was flawed by its failure to recognize the principle of honor as the crucial element in the infliction of punishment.

It is one thing, however, to comment from afar on the intellectual products of another people and quite another to hold a similar view about them face-to-face. Just what was the attitude of the Romans toward their Greek slaves? The closer the relationship, it seems, the greater was the tendency to deny the quality of honor to the vanquished Greeks. Contact between Romans and Greeks went back to Etruscan times; still, the available data, which are quite limited, suggest that until the end of the fourth century the prevailing feeling was one of mutual indifference.[73] As late as 200 B.C. the Roman state had no eastern policy to speak of. Understandably, Greek attitudes began to change first. By 268 B.C. the reputation of the Romans as a people of good faith and integrity was well advanced among the Greeks.[74] Increasingly, Rome came to be regarded with awe and admiration. Perhaps the best expression of this sentiment was Melinno's "Hymn to Rome," written in the early part of the second century B.C.[75]

The Roman attitude toward the Greeks changed in just the opposite direction. By the start of the second century B.C. "no Greek could help being distressed by the almost universal contempt shown, at least in public utterances, toward his nation."[76] In stark contrast to the identification of the Roman name with good faith among the Greeks, the term *Graeca fides* among the Romans came to mean uncreditworthiness.[77] The Greek classicist Nicholas Petrochitos has made a special study of Roman attitudes toward the Greeks, and his findings fully support my argument.[78] The Romans, he shows, soon developed a set of stereotypes about the Greeks, which centered on what they considered to be the six main failings of the Greek character: (1) *volubitas,* a tendency to prefer formal facility in speech to substance; (2) *ineptia,* a proclivity for inappropriate or excessive behavior, a readiness to elaborate on subjects of which they knew nothing; (3) *arrogantia* and *impudentia,* related according to Cicero to "irresponsibility, deceitfulness and an aptitude for flattery"; (4) deceitfulness, singled out as a particularly unpleasant trait; (5) a weakness for excessive luxury and ostentation. But it was the sixth quality that the Romans most despised: *levitas.* Embracing "aspects of instability, rashness and irresponsibility," it connoted "absence of good faith, honor and trustworthiness" and was "a prominent element in the popular conception of Greek character."[79] Cicero, in a celebrated case, tried to win support for his plea by impugning the credibility of the Greek witnesses on this basis, and Petrochitos comments that *"levitas* here is that lack of credibility which is the consequence of subordinating standards of honor and duty to personal and unworthy motives, and it is attributed by Cicero to the Greeks as a people."[80] The Romans made a point of contrasting the traditional Roman qualities of *gravitas* and *dignitas* with the Greek *levitas.*

Finally, it was from the relationship between Roman master and Greek slave that the diminutive *graeculus* came, especially from the household context in which the Greek slave performed the role of tutor. The tutor may have been admired for his intellectual excellence, but the affection was always tinged with contempt. The term *graeculus* seems to have suggested "Greek unmanliness" and also "general worthlessness." Petrochitos concludes: *"Graeculus* is thus a word of unique type, a diminutive formed from an ethnic name; it reflects the special quality of the relationship of Roman and Greek; by nature of being a diminutive it can express a variety of attributes from the mildly patronizing to the openly contemptuous."[81] Like the American term "sambo" and the Jamaican "quashee," graeculus could sometimes be a term of endearment without losing its undertone of contempt. Significantly, this insulting term first appeared in Cicero's time, when the system of slavery was at or near its peak in the Roman socioeconomic order. The Romans, we know, were not a particularly chauvinistic people. In fact, with the possible exception of the ancient Persians, they were among the least chauvinistic peoples of all time.[82] A good deal of the carping at the Greek way of life sprang from Roman defensiveness about their own culture, which in many areas had benefited from Greek influence; thus the lack of honor attributed to the Greeks in their midst must have come from the master-slave relationship and the tendency to view all eastern slaves (many of whom ended up in the household) as Greeks. In other words, the causal chain did not run from a stereotype about the Greeks as a people without honor to a stereotype of the eastern slave as a person without honor but rather in the opposite direction: Greeks as a group came to be regarded as persons without honor because the great majority of slaves in face-to-face contact with Roman masters were either ethnic Greeks or hellenized peoples.

That the Romans were fully aware of the distinction between free Greeks and slave Greeks is made clear in their efforts to find proper tutors for their children. Most Romans found it cheap and convenient to hire or buy a slave tutor. As in Greece, though, there was always concern about the effects of this means of education on the character of the Roman child. The problem was a favorite theme of Roman moralists, especially Juvenal. And, of course, it was the stuff of Roman comedy; the relationship between the *adolescens* and the *servus callidus,* the intriguing slave, was always the funniest part of these plays.[83] The point is well illustrated by a humorous exchange between a free Greek teacher and a Roman father who was evidently caught in the dilemma of choosing between the quality of his son's education and its inordinate expense, a dilemma that two thousand years of educational reform has yet to resolve:

"How much will you charge to teach my son?" the father asked Aristippus.

"A thousand drachmae," replied Aristippus, who obviously had a high opinion of his worth.

"But I can buy a slave for that," returned the father, to which the sharp-witted Aristippus rejoined: "Then you will have two slaves—your son and the one you buy."[84]

What held for the civilized and culturally admired Greek slaves held even more for other slaves. The typical slave in the Roman view was a "vocal instrument," a nonperson to be used sexually, disciplined with the whip, and questioned in court only under torture since his word was utterly without honor. At the same time the Roman master, even more than his Greek counterpart, took special delight in possessing a large retinue of slaves. Nothing more enhanced his sense of honor and his reputation in the eyes of his peers. And, as in all slave societies, even the poor who may have owned no slaves felt a sense of honor in the presence of slaves. In this sense the system was self-regulating; it "fed on itself," as Keith Hopkins indicates: "The presence of substantial numbers of slaves in Roman society defined free citizens, even if they were poor, as superior. At the same time, free citizens' sense of superiority probably limited their willingness to compete with slaves, to work full time as the overt dependents of other citizens. Yet rich men, by definition, needed dependents. Slavery permitted the ostentatious display of wealth in the palaces of the rich without involving the degradation of the free poor."[85]

The Roman master, it should be emphasized, demanded more than mere obedience from his slave. Seneca no doubt spoke for his class when he drew the distinction between *ministerium,* which is the performance by the slave of what he is obliged to do, and *beneficium,* which is what was performed "not by command but voluntarily."[86]

What was true of ancient Rome held equally for the slaveholding societies of the Islamic world, especially those of the Arabs, all of whom had highly timocratic cultures.[87] Perhaps more than in any other part of the premodern world, slavery there was not only a state of dishonor, but one in which a major function of the institution was to support the dignitas of the master. The modern ethnography on the Arabs and other Middle Eastern peoples presents innumerable instances of this. A few examples will suffice.

Harry St. John Briger Philby, who traveled in Saudi Arabia during the 1930s, recalled how a slave, Shabban, was sent by his master with a present of two sheep for Philby's dinner. "I naturally proffered the usual money gift," he wrote, "and was somewhat taken aback at his absolute refusal to accept it. That was certainly unusual though very credible. He visited me several times during the afternoon, and proved to be a person who combined strength of character with a manner of great charm. And though only a slave and practically a full-blooded Negro, he *seemed to exercise the authority of his master by proxy, as to the manner born"* (emphasis added).[88]

All masters, especially Arabs, desired slaves such as Shabban. When they did find one, they were prepared to protect him more carefully than their own son—for their honor was thoroughly invested in this human possession. Harold H. P. Dickson, who visited Kuwait during the early part of this century, observed: "They [the slaves] know that their lord will avenge himself on any stranger who harms his slave, more than if he were his own son. This is literally true, for to kill or kidnap a man's slave affects his honor, not so the slaying of his son."[89] And as Sylvia Bailes, who cites this passage, adds: "It should be noted, of course, that the Kuwait master is not actually concerned about his slave, but rather about his honor."[90]

Even where the Arabs developed large-scale plantation slavery, as they did in Zanzibar, the psychosocial significance of slaveholding remained at least as great as its economic value. As Frederick Cooper points out, this so puzzled European observers that they branded the Arab planters as indolent and unambitious.[91] Economic success, however, was only one element of the highly timocratic slave-based culture of the Arab elite. The term that was central to the Zanzibari elite's definition of its identity was *heshima,* which meant "respect." In more concrete terms heshima meant, in addition to being prosperous, having a large retinue of slaves, a good family background, and an aristocratic demeanor. "Having dependent followers had long been an important component of power and prestige. The increasing economic importance of slaves was added to their social value—whether the clove industry prospered or stagnated, the slaves' labor helped provide subsistence while their presence conveyed prestige."[92]

Cooper, in emphasizing the paternalistic ethos in Zanzibar, the integrative tendencies of the society, and the manifest ideology of Islam (which defined the slave as socially inferior but equal in the sight of God), comes uneasily close to neglecting the inherent degradation of slave status.[93] Slavery was more than simply "subordination"; it was considered a degraded condition, reinforced by racist attitudes among the Arab slave owners.[94] In Zanzibar, as in all other Arab states, it therefore was forbidden to enslave fellow Arabs.

Roger F. Morton, in his study of Arab slavery on the Kenya coast, emphasized the role of racism in the master's view of slaves, and there is no reason to believe that the Arabs of Zanzibar were any different: "Rendered inferior by birth, occupation, and color, slaves became natural objects of abuse for the Muslim free-born."[95] Furthermore, what Finley says of ancient Greece and Rome holds equally for Zanzibar and the Kenya coast during the nineteenth century: whatever the relationship between masters and slaves, the fact that slaves could be and were subject to corporal punishment was an implicit statement of their degradation. In Muslim East

Africa, as in the ancient world, slaves were (with very few exceptions) the only category of persons subject to whipping by private persons. In East Africa, as in the U.S. South, their degradation meant that all free persons regarded them as fit subjects for abuse. It was not just in Georgia that slaves, once outside the protective power of their masters, found themselves victims of mob violence; it happened also in Malindi and Mombasa.[96]

There can be no doubt that the slaves themselves regarded their condition as a degraded one. While they have left little verbal account of their feelings, their actions speak directly to the point. In spite of the paternalism of the Zanzibari and coastal Kenyan slave orders, slaves ran away in droves, risking severe exploitation by the strange peoples of the interior and even more murderous retaliation by their masters if and when they were recaptured.[97]

Honor and Slavery in the U.S. South

What is true of premodern slavery holds equally for the slave regimes of the Americas. E. D. Genovese's claim that "the old South came closest of all New World slaveholding regimes to producing a genuine slave society" might be open to challenge, but he certainly is correct in arguing that the master class of the Old South developed to its highest degree a slaveholder's ideology.[98]

By no accident did this ideology expand into the most elaborate and deliberately articulated timocracy of modern times. One part of the ideology referred to the master's own conception of himself, and it is generally agreed that its pivotal value is the notion of honor, with the attendant virtues of manliness and chivalry. The historian Clement Eaton, himself a southerner, writes of the southern slave plantocracy that "despite their faults the Southern aristocracy had resplendent virtues that seem archaic in our industrial society today—their code of personal and regional honor, their devotion to a cause and their appreciation of chivalric conduct."[99] It was not in spite of, but because of their faults, especially their slavedriving, that they possessed these "resplendent virtues."

The same held for their love of freedom. When Samuel Johnson asked, "How is it that we hear the loudest yelps for liberty among the drivers of negroes?"[100] he betrayed a rare failure of irony, not to mention a superficial grasp of the history of the idea of liberty. There was nothing at all hypocritical or anomalous about the southerner's highly developed sense of honor and freedom. Those who most dishonor and constrain others are in the best position to appreciate what joy it is to possess what they deny. It is important to emphasize the connection between slavery and timocracy in the Old South, for the link is sometimes denied by historians. Rollin G. Osterweis argues correctly that "the civilization of the Old South rested on a tripod—

cotton and the plantation system forming one leg, Negro slavery a second," and what he calls "the chivalric cult" constituting the third.[101] He correctly identifies its essential features: an excessively developed sense of honor and pride, militarism, the idealization and seclusion of women, and regional nationalism. While he recognized the role of slavery in the development of this cult, he claimed that its significance lay mainly in providing the planter class with enough leisure to be receptive to romantic ideas from Europe. Thus he interprets the chivalric cult as "a manifestation of the romantic movement." European ideas no doubt contributed to the southern intellectual expression of its timocratic culture, but it is to reify ideas excessively to claim that southern timocracy was a manifestation of European romanticism.

Even though it is not possible to authenticate any direct causal relationship between slavery and timocracy in the slave systems of Greco-Roman antiquity, there can be no doubt about the direct link between the two in the culture of the slave South. One of the most definitive statements of the relationship is provided by John Hope Franklin. First, he correctly emphasizes the notion of honor—not romanticism—as the central, articulating principle of southern life and culture.

> It was something inviolable and precious to the ego, to be protected at every cost. It promoted extravagance, because of the imputation of poverty which might follow retrenchment. It sanctioned prompt demand for the redress of grievance, because of the imputation of guilt that might follow a less precipitate policy. It countenanced great recklessness of life, because of the imputation of cowardice that might follow forgiveness of injuries. The honor of the Southerner caused him to defend with his life the slightest suggestion of irregularity in his honesty or integrity; and he was fiercely sensitive to any imputation that might cast a shadow on the character of the women in his family. To him nothing was more important than honor. Indeed, he placed it above wealth, art, learning, and the other "delicacies" of an urban civilization and regarded its protection as a continuing preoccupation.[102]

Second, Franklin shows how the notion of honor diffused down to all free members of the society from its ruling-class origins.[103] Third, and most important, he demonstrates the direct causal link between the southern ruling class's excessively developed sense of honor and the institution of slavery.[104] More specifically, he shows how the master's sense of honor was derived directly from the degradation of his slave, beginning in childhood and continuing through life in his despotic exercise of power. Franklin leaves no doubt concerning the veracity of Thomas Jefferson's observation that the relationship between his fellow slave owners and their slaves was "a perpetual exercise of the most boisterous passions, the most unremitting despotism on the one part; and degrading submission on the other."[105]

Nor was the connection lost on other, less celebrated southerners. The Alabama lawyer Daniel R. Hundley, for example, wrote in 1860 that "the natural dignity of manner peculiar to the Southern Gentleman, is doubtless owing to his habitual use of authority from his earliest years," and he goes on to give the classic rationalization for this means of achieving "dignity" when he adds, "for while coarser natures are ever rendered more savage and brutal by being allowed the control of others, refined natures on the contrary are invariably perfected by the same means, their sense of the responsibility and its incident obligations teaching them first to control themselves before attempting to exact obedience from the inferior natures placed under their charge."[106] Perhaps the most brutally cogent statement of the inexorable link between southern slavery and timocracy was given by the Confederate soldier who described his flag as the symbol of "an adored trinity—cotton, niggers and chivalry."[107]

The other side of southern timocracy was the ideology of "Sambo," the degraded man-child that, to the southerner, constituted the image of the slave. Stanley Elkins summarizes this stereotype as follows: "Sambo, the typical plantation slave, was docile but irresponsible, loyal but lazy, humble but chronically given to lying and stealing; his behavior was full of infantile silliness and his talk inflated with childish exaggeration. His relationship with his master was one of utter dependence and childlike attachment: it was indeed this childlike quality that was the very key to his being. Although the merest hint of Sambo's 'manhood' might fill the Southern breast with scorn, the child, 'in his place', could be both exasperating and lovable."[108] As a description of how the typical southern master felt about his slave, this is quite accurate. An almost identical stereotype of the slave existed in the Caribbean.[109] And how reminiscent it is of the ancient slaveholder's Graeculus conception of his slave. The stereotype is, in fact, an ideological imperative of all systems of slavery, from the most primitive to the most advanced. It is simply an elaboration of the notion that the slave is quintessentially a person without honor. The key to Sambo, Elkins rightly notes, is the total absence of any hint of "manhood," which in turn is a perfect description of the dishonored condition.

The existence of the Sambo ideology in the South, as in all other slave systems, is further proof of my claim that slaves are universally treated as dishonored persons. The Sambo ideology, however, is no more realistic a description of how slaves actually thought and behaved than was the inflated conception of honor and sense of freedom an accurate description of their masters. What was real was the *sense* of honor held by the master, its denial to the slave, its enhancement through the degradation of the slave, and possibly the slave's own feeling of being dishonored and degraded.

Beyond this it is difficult to generalize, for the degree to which a master class is prepared to defend its honor against rebelling slaves or invading outsiders, and the degree to which a slave population will accommodate to or reject its dishonored condition, are functions of the peculiar structure, internal strength, and external constraints of the slave system in which they find themselves. In some cases, as among the slaveholders of the emirates of northern Nigeria during the nineteenth century, the sense of honor and its peculiarly Islamic elaboration proved to be highly functional in perpetuating the system.[110] In other instances, such as the antebellum South, the exaggerated sense of honor and quixotic chivalry of the ruling class proved to be the major cause of its undoing. Among some slave populations the condition of dishonor as well as the sense of being so dishonored might, given the right revolutionary opening, prove to be an important asset in the struggle for emancipation, as it was in parts of the Greco-Roman world during the second and first centuries B.C.,[111] in the dead lands of lower Mesopotamia during the late ninth century,[112] and in many areas of the Caribbean and Latin America between the seventeenth and nineteenth centuries. In countless other situations the viability of the slave system, the solidarity of the ruling class, and the absence of revolutionary openings dictate that the slave population nurse its sense of dishonor, accept its dishonored condition, or find alternative means of expressing or sublimating its grievances.[113]

There is absolutely no evidence from the long and dismal annals of slavery to suggest that any group of slaves ever internalized the conception of degradation held by their masters. To be dishonored—and to sense, however acutely, such dishonor—is not to lose the quintessential human urge to participate and to want a place.[114] Indeed, it is precisely this irrepressible yearning for dignity and recognition that is hardest to understand about the condition of slavery. The fundamental problem posed by slavery may be simply stated as one of incentive and mutual recognition. The master not only forces the slave to serve him with the threat and the actuality of physical violence, he heaps insult upon injury by continually degrading him. Why does the slave obey? Why does the master so wantonly appear to undermine his own best interest by degrading his slave? What really is going on?

Hegel and the Dialectics of Slavery

It is this fundamental dilemma that so intrigued Hegel.[115] An examination of his analysis is instructive not only for the profound insights it offers, but for what we can learn from a critique of its limitations.

The master's domination of the slave is seen by Hegel as a paradigm of inequality: "The one is independent whose essential nature is to be for itself, the other is dependent whose essence is life or existence for another. The former is Master, or Lord, the latter is Bondsman."[116] The master's existence is enhanced by the slave's, for in addition to existing on his own account his consciousness is mediated through another consciousness, that of the slave. In other words, another person lives through and by him—becomes his surrogate—and the master's power and honor is thereby enhanced. The master's independence becomes the real—the only—basis of the slave's thralldom. By negating the slave's existence, the master seems to solve one of the most pressing problems of a free and equal relationship: the frustration that the other, if he is free, is also strongly desirous of winning confirmation of his identity from ego. Both are struggling to gain the other's confirmation of their superior identity. All free relationships amount to a "life-and-death struggle."

Slavery appears to solve this dilemma. The slave cannot negate the master, for whatever he does is done on behalf of his master. The slave dies, it is true, but he dies in the master; so the master becomes autoconfirming, so to speak. But this one-sided and unequal form of recognition soon reveals its limitations. At precisely the point where the master achieves lordship, he finds that he has become dependent on his slave. He cannot be sure even of his own existence, since the reality of his domination rests on the unreality of that which he masters: the slave, whom he has socially killed and rendered non-essential by making him merely an extension of himself. Further, the slave cannot confirm his honor, cannot offer recognition, because he is not worthy. This is what Alexandre Kojève, in his celebrated commentary, calls the master's "existential impasse."[117]

The opposite, Hegel thought, was true of the slave: "Just as lordship showed its essential nature to be the reverse of what it wants to be, so too, bondage will, when complete, pass in the opposite of what it immediately is."[118] The slave, by his social death, and by living "in mortal terror of his sovereign master" becomes acutely conscious of both life and freedom. The idea of freedom is born, not in the consciousness of the master, but in the reality of the slave's condition. Freedom can mean nothing positive to the master; only control is meaningful. For the slave, freedom begins with the consciousness that real life comes with the negation of his social death. (What I am here calling the negation of social death is what Hegel, with his usual verbal extravagance, calls "extraneous alien negation.") Freedom—life—is a double negation; for his condition is already a negation of life, and the reclamation of that life must therefore be the negation of this negation.

Nevertheless, freedom is more than just a double negation. It is continuously active and creative. The slave, in his social death, is already once transformed. The life he strives to regain cannot be the life he lost. In his enslavement the slave has become a new man for his master; in his struggle for freedom and in his ultimate disenslavement the slave, Hegel believes, becomes a new man for himself. And here is the most surprisingly radical insight in all of Hegel's work, the insight that was to have so profound an effect on Marx and on generations of subsequent radical thinkers.[119] How does the slave become positively free? How does he make a new man of himself? "Through work and labour," answers Hegel, "this consciousness of the bondsman comes to itself"; for labor "is desire restrained and checked, evanescence delayed and postponed; in other words labour shapes and fashions the thing." Consciousness, through work, creates object, becomes externalized, and passes "into something that is permanent and remains. The consciousness that toils and serves accordingly comes by this means to view that independent being as its self." He adds, by way of conclusion, "Thus precisely in labour where there seemed to be merely some outsider's mind and ideas involved, the bondsman becomes aware, through this rediscovery of himself by himself, of having a being and a mind of his own."[120]

Hegel is partly right and partly wrong in arriving at this conclusion. Ironically, he is wrong precisely where most commentators, including Marx and Kojève, have considered him most insightful. There is nothing in the nature of slavery which requires that the slave be a worker. Worker qua worker has no intrinsic relation to slave qua slave. This does not mean that the slave cannot be *used* as a worker. Indeed, his slaveness, especially his natal alienation, made possible his effective exploitation as laborer in conditions where no other kind of laborer would do. But this does not in any way mean that slave necessarily implies worker. I have repeatedly stressed that most slaves in most precapitalist societies were not enslaved in order to be made over into workers; they may even have been economic burdens on their masters.

Further, I disagree totally with the view that slavery created an existential impasse for the master. In the first place, the master could and usually did achieve the recognition he needed from other free persons, including other masters. In almost all large-scale slaveholding societies, not to mention those in which slavery was not structurally important, there was a sizable class of free nonslaveholding persons; indeed they usually constituted the majority of all persons in such societies. As we have seen, the nonslaveholding free group invariably came to adopt elements of the timocratic character of the master class. The poorest free person took pride in the fact that he was not a slave. By sharing in the collective honor of the master class, all free persons legitimized the principle of honor and thereby recognized the members of the master class as those most adorned with honor and glory.

Beyond this, the degradation of the slave nurtured the master's sense of honor, both in his childhood training by slave nannies and, throughout his life, as a ready object for the exercise of his sense of power.[121]

In a small but important minority of large-scale slave societies, however, almost all free persons were masters. This was true of the total slave systems of the Caribbean and the equally brutal though isolated instance of Dutch East Indian slavery in the Banda group of the Spice Islands to the south of Ceram.[122] In these societies we do find something approaching Hegel's crisis of honor and recognition among the master class. Other than themselves, there was only the brutally used and utterly despised class of slaves to recognize the prestige of the masters. Faced with this dilemma, the master class did two things. In the slave society where they procured their wealth, they abandoned all claims to honor and any attempt to develop a timocratic culture. Slavery, they recognized, degraded both master and slave. Hence they dropped all pretensions to culture and civilization and simply indulged their appetites. The slave women whom they whipped in the fields during the day became their bedmates during the night. There were no attempts to build great manors decorated with idolized wives. More often than not, the mistress of the large stone hovel that passed for a great house in the Caribbean was herself a slave. Since there was no one to confirm honor, it was simply thrown to the winds.

But there was another solution. The successful master, as soon as he made his fortune, would pack up and flee the degraded source of his wealth. He would return to Europe, where he could ostentatiously display his wealth, proclaim his honor, and have it confirmed by the free population of the metropolis. It is this which largely explains the high rate of absenteeism among successful members of the planter class in the Caribbean.[123]

Thus in criticizing Hegel's failure to take account of the free nonslaveholding members of the master's society, we arrive at an extremely important, if paradoxical, conclusion about the nature of slave-based timocratic cultures: namely, that they are possible only where slavery does not totally dominate the society. A truly vibrant slave culture, if it is to avoid the crisis of honor and recognition, must have a substantial free population. Conversely, a society with only masters and slaves cannot sustain a slave culture.

Leaving aside such extreme cases as the British Caribbean slave societies and those of the Banda Islands, we must still answer the very basic questions set forth earlier about the reasons for the slave's degradation and the benefits to the master. I have said that Hegel was partially right in the answer he gave; specifically, in that he pointed to one solution to the dilemma. Confronted with the master's outrageous effort to deny him all dignity, the slave even more than the master came to know and to desire passionately this very attribute. For dignity, like love, is one of those human qualities that are most intensely felt and understood when they are absent—or unrequited.

Slavery, for the slave, was truly a "trial by death," as Hegel called it. Out of this trial the slave emerged, if he survived at all, as a person afire with the knowledge of and the need for dignity and honor. We now understand how very superficial are assertions that the slave internalized the degraded conception of him held by the master; or that his person was necessarily degraded by his degraded condition. Quite the opposite was the case, Hegel speculated, and what evidence there is fully supports him.

Thus whenever we hear the voice of the slave himself, or whenever we hear from chroniclers and analysts who attempt to probe behind planter-class ideology into the actual feelings of the slave, what invariably surfaces is the incredible dignity of the slave.[124]

This leads us to one of the most remarkable features of slavery. What does the master make of the slave's yearning for dignity, itself part of his wider yearning for disalienation and relief from the master's all-embracing power? In all but a handful of slaveholding societies the master exploits this very yearning for his own benefit. How?

He does so by manipulating it as the principal means of motivating the slave, who desires nothing more passionately than dignity, belonging, and release. By holding out the promise of redemption, the master provides himself with a motivating force more powerful than any whip. Slavery in this way was a self-correcting institution: what it denied the slave it utilized as the major means of motivating him.

The slave constantly struggled with his master for recognition, for survival. Somewhat like Saint Augustine, who found in the very depth of grief over his friend's death that he was "at once utterly weary of life and in great fear of death"[125] and in this way came to love life even more, so did the slave in the weariness of his degradation and social death come to a passionate zeal for dignity and freedom.

The dialectic does not end here. The slave's struggle made it necessary that the master, in order to make slavery workable, provide an opportunity for the negation of slavery. The conflict between master and slave became transformed from a personal into an institutional dialectic, in which slavery, as an enduring social process, stood opposite to and required manumission as an essential precondition.

How did this come about? What were the institutional mechanisms that brought slavery into being and, in order to sustain it, generated further mechanisms for its negation? And what of that handful of societies that resisted this institutional dialectic and denied manumission? Why did they reject this resolution? How was the dignity of the slave, which sprang from his degradation, expressed and contained in such systems? To an exploration of these and related problems we now turn our attention.

II

SLAVERY
AS AN
INSTITUTIONAL
PROCESS

4

Enslavement
of "Free"
Persons

IN THE STUDY of the sources of slaves two closely related but separate issues are invariably confused: the problem of how persons became slaves, and the problem of how slaveholders acquired slaves. The means by which persons were enslaved are legion and include many that were peculiar to certain societies. The overwhelming majority, however, may be grouped under eight heads:

(1) Capture in warfare
(2) Kidnapping
(3) Tribute and tax payment
(4) Debt
(5) Punishment for crimes
(6) Abandonment and sale of children
(7) Self-enslavement
(8) Birth.

The first seven means, involving persons who were born free and subsequently were reduced to slavery, will be considered in this chapter. Birth, the most important method of enslavement, will be discussed separately in Chapter 5. Then, in Chapter 6, we shall look at the various means of acquisition.

Capture in Warfare

Throughout history, captivity in warfare has been one of the major means by which persons have been reduced to slavery. It is easy, however, to exaggerate the role of warfare as a source of slaves. If we are to place captivity in warfare in proper perspective, we need to clarify certain important and neglected issues. The first is the distinction between captivity in warfare as a *current* means of enslavement and as an *original* means of enslavement. By current means of enslavement, I mean its relative significance for a slave population at a given moment in time. By original means of enslavement, I refer to its role in the enslavement of the ancestors of a slave population observed at any given moment. The complicating factor is enslavement by birth. Captivity in warfare, even when a major factor in the enslavement of the ancestors of all persons born as slaves, usually declined in relative significance as the proportion of the slave population enslaved through birth increased.

A second important point is that captivity in warfare should not be confused with enslavement by means of such captivity. This is a major problem in the literature on slavery, largely because of the frequent and wholly erroneous assumption that the fate of most prisoners of war was enslavement. It is simply not true that the majority of persons captured in warfare have been enslaved, even if only premodern societies are considered. What is more, it is incorrect to assume that even if a society keeps slaves in great numbers it will enslave all or most of its captives. There are several reasons for this. One is the logistics of warfare. Having a large number of prisoners is an encumbrance for an army in the field. Even if it was decided to profit from the enslavement of prisoners, it could still be a formidable problem for soldiers to return home with a batch of chained slaves. The best course of action was to sell the prisoners to traders as soon as possible, even when there was a strong demand for slaves in the home society of the victors. Accounts of ancient warfare and slavery sometimes foster the misleading impression of Roman, Carthaginian, and Grecian officers marching home accompanied by thousands of slaves, with eager expectations of employing them on their latifundia or home farms. This must rarely have happened, even where the officers owned slaves.

Before assessing the role of warfare as a means of enslavement, let us consider the more common experiences of captives. The alternatives were immediate massacre; torture and sacrifice, sometimes culminating in cannibalism; ransom; prisoner exchange; temporary imprisonment; serfdom; impressment in the victor's army; colonization; and simple release.

There is no relation between the level of development of a victorious group and its treatment of prisoners. The Tupinamba and the Aztecs, for instance, differed vastly in sociopolitical complexity but treated their prisoners in much the same way, both engaging in highly ritualized, sadistic slaughter and cannibalism.[1] Torture, massacre, ransom, and all the rest might be employed along with enslavement. This was true not only of primitive tribes such as the precontact Cherokees and other Indians of southeastern North America, as well as those of the northwestern coast,[2] but of highly advanced peoples. The Carthaginians ritually sacrificed thousands of prisoners.[3] The ancient Greeks and Romans throughout their history massacred not only soldiers in the field but defenseless inhabitants of captured cities. Human sacrifice of prisoners was practiced occasionally by the Romans from 225 B.C. until its abolition by the Senate in 97 B.C., and even was recognized as a form of ritual sacrifice.[4]

Ransom, however, was the more common fate of prisoners of war. Among the Nkundu and the Luvale of central Africa, the person who was primarily responsible for starting a war had to find the means of ransoming anyone taken during hostilities, otherwise he himself ended up as the slave of the aggrieved kinsmen, a salutary check on adventurous spirits.[5] Among all the advanced states of Africa, Asia, and Europe upper-class captives were usually ransomed. As one would expect, the higher the rank of the captive, the greater was his ransom. Sometimes this could be quite excessive: during the Third Dynasty of Ur vast and ruinous sums were asked for upper-class officers.[6] Among many peoples prisoners were taken mainly with the intent of exchanging them for their own members taken in previous battles, or for purely commercial purposes: Icelandic warriors made a tidy sum by this means,[7] and the Kerebe of Tanzania took slaves mainly to exchange them for cattle, which interested them far more than the "two-footed stock" preferred by the Greeks.[8] Warfare for the Margi of northern Nigeria "served largely as a wife-recruiting and ransom collecting institution."[9] Among Islamic peoples captured coreligionists were, by law, offered for ransom and not enslaved, but this regulation was not always observed and even if it were, negotiations sometimes went on interminably.[10] Between Christians and Muslims, of course, religious scruples worked against the captive.[11] From medieval through early modern times the North African Muslim states relied on captives as an important source of both income and slaves. In early modern Algiers, according to Ellen Friedman, "the labor services of captives as well as ransoms paid for them were critical to the Algerian economy."[12]

In many advanced premodern societies prisoners of war were incorporated into the victors' societies in a dependent status other than slavery. This tendency was most marked in the ancient Near East and Orient. The practice existed side by side with the institution of slavery. Indeed, for this very reason it was long assumed that in ancient Mesopotamia and China both, all prisoners of war were automatically enslaved. Many authorities still make this assumption,[13] but it has been strongly challenged by recent scholarship. Because China and Mesopotamia are the two best-known and most controversial cases, it is worth examining them at some length.

Chinese scholars are divided on the destiny and role of the vast numbers of prisoners taken in the many wars of the ancient Chinese. What may be called the "hard-line" periodization view, best represented by the works of Chou ku-Cheng,[14] holds that large-scale slavery existed in ancient China and that the vast majority of slaves originated as prisoners taken from defeated clans. On the whole, however, even those Marxist scholars who insist on a period of large-scale slavery tend to argue against the view that prisoners of war were the major source of slaves. Kuo Mo-jo, the most eminent of the Marxists, is rather vague on this issue in his frequently cited discussion of the role of sacrifice.[15] Less equivocal is Tung Shu-yeh who, while claiming that slaves at one period constituted as high as 25 percent of the total population, nonetheless asserts that very few were recruited from among the prisoners of war—crime and debt being the main sources.[16] Finally, among Communist scholars, there is the lengthy discussion by Chien Po-tsan who, against his colleagues, promulgates the view that there could not have been large-scale slavery during the eastern and western Han dynasties because prisoners of war were not available in quantity. Wars with the barbarians, he argues, were fought to establish commercial routes through central Asia, to expand the empire, and to force the conquered to pay tribute. The taking of prisoners of war was incidental, engaged in principally as a form of intimidation and revenge. It was highly exceptional for prisoners to be given to officers as a form of payment or encouragement.[17]

Western scholars tend to disagree with almost all these interpretations. The standard position is that of C. M. Wilbur.[18] He observes that while in the former Han dynasty "thousands of the enemy were captured . . . it cannot be lightly assumed that these prisoners were enslaved."[19] He concludes:

> What became of the thousands and probably hundreds of thousands of prisoners of war is a historical enigma. Some were enslaved but there is no evidence of this on a large scale. Han histories simply neglect to tell what happened to the prisoners taken in wars against the Hsuiung-nu, against the oasis states of the northwest, the Koreans, and the kingdoms of south China. It is not even possible in most instances to distinguish numerically or proportionately between enemy slain and captured. This seems significant: it was apparently a matter of indifference to the state whether enemy soldiers were captured or killed. This would hardly have been the case if prisoners of war had been economically important as a source of slaves.[20]

E. G. Pulleyblank throws some light on the enigma by emphasizing the fact that "no sharp distinction" was made between prisoners of war and ordinary convicts, especially during the Han and earlier periods. He notes, further, that prisoners of war were not sold by the state but were given away to officials.[21] He is less inclined than Wilbur to think that they were not enslaved in substantial numbers.

The most likely conclusion is that the Chinese treated prisoners of war differently during different periods of their vast history. Up to the end of the

Han dynasty the most likely practice was to enslave only a minority and to use the rest as colonists or for other purposes. After this, there was an increasing tendency to enslave the great majority of prisoners of war. By the period of the Northern dynasties (A.D. 386–618) "significant evidence is available to leave little doubt that . . . enslavement of captured or surrendered enemies, on combat duties or otherwise, was common practice."[22] Prisoners of war were still used for other purposes: they were "placed in bonds, regrouped and then impressed into the victorious army, [and] settled in the victor's sparsely populated areas," but the evidence is clear that "conquered civilians were reduced to slavery en masse."[23]

An almost identical problem is faced by students of early Mesopotamia. Isaac Mendelsohn argues the traditional view that the vast majority of prisoners of war were enslaved, although he notes also that there were alternate uses.[24] Until a decade or so ago Russian students of Mesopotamia, under the dominant influence of academician V. V. Struve, dogmatically assumed that all prisoners of war were enslaved and that this was the primary source of slaves in the presumed large-scale slave systems of the area.[25] In recent years, however, most Russian scholars have done a complete about-face on the issue. I. M. Diakonoff holds that most male prisoners of war in early Sumer times were killed and that they were never employed as slaves in significant numbers during later periods.[26] I. I. Semenov is typical of the most extreme reaction against Struve and the Stalinist school. "What happened to them?" he asks of the prisoners of war in ancient Mesopotamia, then answers:

> In our view, a direct, unconditional identification of prisoners of war with slaves is erroneous. Prisoners of war, in and of themselves, are not yet slaves: they are still only people torn out of the system of relationships existing in the society to which they belonged, and thus separated from the means of production . . . In the ancient Eastern societies, prisoners of war, when there were more of them than could be used in domestic and auxiliary work, were usually settled on the land.[27]

Most Western scholars adopt much the same position. I. J. Gelb argues forcefully that it was simply not practical to enslave prisoners of war in ancient Mesopotamia. Instead, after being branded and kept for a short period as prisoners, "they were generally freed and resettled or utilized for specialized purposes of the crown, such as the personal guard of the king, mercenaries, and a movable force."[28] Gelb, however, may have gone too far in the opposite direction in denying altogether the use of prisoners of war as slaves on a significant scale.[29]

The true situation would seem to be more like that which existed over time in China. At all times some prisoners of war were used as slaves, but from the earliest period on which we have records up to the end of the Baby-

Ionian dynasties only a small proportion were reduced to slavery. However, as in China, an increasing number were enslaved with the passing centuries, and by the neo-Babylonian period there is reason to believe that the majority were being enslaved. The Soviet scholar Dandamayev may have overstated his case somewhat in claiming that large-scale slavery existed in the Achaemenid empire during the sixth century B.C., although the evidence he presents strongly suggests that at that time slave labor was heavily used on the domains of the Persian upper class throughout the empire.[30]

Neither China nor the ancient Near Eastern states ever developed large-scale slave systems, so an appropriate question is whether the fate of prisoners of war was substantially different where the combatants came from societies that relied heavily on slavery. Pierre Ducrey's study of the treatment of prisoners of war among the ancient Greeks is instructive in this regard.[31] Ducrey examined 120 cases of warfare involving Greeks from earliest times to the Roman conquest. He found 24 cases of massacre, 28 cases of general enslavement, and 68 cases in which prisoners seem to have suffered nothing more severe than simple detention followed by release.[32]

One must be careful in generalizing from these figures; they tell us nothing about the number of persons involved in each engagement, and the limitations of the data and the sample are obvious. Even so, it is surprising that in less than a quarter of the cases mentioned in the sources are captured soldiers sold into slavery. In spite of the tremendous demand for slaves in the ancient Greek world, the pattern of treatment of prisoners seems not to have departed significantly from what prevailed in imperial China and the ancient Near East.

Ducrey draws attention to an important distinction in the discussion of prisoners of war: between soldiers captured in open engagement, and the defenders and citizens of a captured city.[33] The ancient sources, if not read carefully, give the impression that the inhabitants of conquered cities were routinely reduced to slavery or carried off en masse to slave markets. Ducrey found, however, that many of these claims were either improbable or too vague for us to be sure just what happened to the inhabitants of the captured cities. Where the sources are clear, the general conclusion to be drawn is that when a Greek city was besieged, its survival as a political entity was at stake rather than the survival or liberty of its citizens. In most cases the attackers and the besieged arrived at an accord that did not involve enslavement.

The Greek experience points to an important general tendency in the history of enslavement: there is a strong tendency on the part of a conquering group not to enslave a conquered population en masse and in situ. This, however, is no more than a strong tendency, to which there have been many exceptions. The exceptions bring us to a second generalization, which can be stated in much stronger terms: attempts by a conquering group to enslave a conquered population en masse and in situ were almost always disastrous failures.

When a people was conquered, it was by definition the conquerors who were the outsiders to the local community and the conquered who were the natives. In this situation one of the fundamental elements of slavery—natal alienation—was almost impossible to achieve either intrusively or extrusively. By the nature of the case, the conquered native population could not be natally alienated in intrusive terms, for it was the master class who would be the intruders. It was equally difficult to natally alienate a native population extrusively, since in this case the moral community (insofar as it existed) was defined by the conquered. A community could hardly be expected to accept the idea of itself as having fallen. Nor was the strategy of divide and partially enslave likely to work, because such an act was likely only to make heroes of those selected for enslavement.

There were other, purely practical reasons why the attempt to enslave a native population was likely to fail. First, there was the solidarity of the bulk of the population with the enslaved. Second, the enslaved were on their own social and physical ground and could easily survive by running away. Furthermore, they were more likely to find refuge in this situation than in the more usual cases where they were genuine outsiders or defined as morally fallen.

Most conquering groups were sufficiently aware of these problems not to attempt to enslave a conquered group in situ. If a conquering elite wished to maintain (or introduce) on a large scale the institution of slavery, there was a variety of options. One was to take over the slave population of the conquered group, if such a slave group already existed. A second option was to bring in slaves from the outside and deliberately refrain from locally enslaving the conquered population. The most dramatic instance of this was perhaps the Dutch policy toward the conquered Khoikhoi of South Africa during the period of large-scale slavery from the late seventeenth century to the early nineteenth.[34]

The Greeks employed all these measures and more. Perhaps the most typical strategy was the behavior of the Spartan Kallikratidas after he had captured the Athenian garrison at Methymna on Lesbos. He sold all the captured soldiers as well as the captive slaves into slavery, but freed the citizens.[35] In more extreme cases the entire population would be either deported or sold away into slavery, and new colonists brought in with their own slaves. This, for example, was the fate of the Poteidaians after they surrendered to the Athenians in 430 B.C. There were many cases of large-scale transportation of conquered populations in Sicily, as in 483 B.C. when Gelon, the tyrant of Syracuse, after destroying Megara sold the common folk into slavery but declared members of the upper class citizens of Syracuse.[36]

A similar range of strategies was employed by the Romans. The fate of the population of a conquered city depended on whether or not the city had been in revolt and on whether it was taken by storm, had surrendered before being stormed, or had surrendered after the battering rams had touched its walls.[37]

For our purposes the most important conclusion to be drawn from the numerous references to the conquest of cities and other types of states in Greco-Roman antiquity is a negative one. Although there are frequent references to enslavement, there is not a single unambiguous case of the mass of the free members of a conquered people being successfully enslaved in situ. The closest the ancient world came to such a situation was Spartan helotry. This is a controversial subject, and at least one reputable historian of ancient Greece has declared categorically in a widely used text that "they [the helots] were very thoroughly slaves, and are often called by the standard Greek word *douloi*." Unfortunately, Antony Andrews, who made this assertion, did not tell us what he meant by the term "slaves."[38] From our definition of slavery, however, it is clear that the helots were not slaves—whatever the merits of Critias' remark, cited as supporting evidence by Andrews, "that in Sparta the free were more free and the slaves more fully slaves than elsewhere."[39] The distinctive feature of slavery is not the degree of oppression involved; were this the case, the British proletariat at the middle of the nineteenth century would have been as much slaves as the blacks of the U.S. South, not to mention the countless millions of the Asian rural poor. But as Finley has pointed out, the helots remained nonslaves in the collective nature of their bondage and in the fact that they were a "subject *community*" (emphasis added),[40] which in essence means that they belonged, and had rights of birth, however attenuated, including custodial claims in their parents and children. Their status as Greeks was never lost; it was only politically suspended. Nothing better attests to their nonslave status than a comparison of their fate after emancipation in 371 B.C. with that of black Americans after emancipation in 1865. "The Messenians," Finley tells us, "were at once accepted by the Greeks generally as a proper Greek community";[41] almost a century and a half after legal emancipation, black Americans are still struggling for acceptance in the community of which they are, as a group, among the oldest members.

The reluctance to try to enslave a conquered native population, I have said, is only a tendency. There have been several noteworthy attempts at mass enslavement in the annals of slavery, all ending in failure. The most sustained and, not surprisingly, the most frightening, was the European attempt to enslave the Indian populations of the Americas.

In both North and South America all such attempts ended unsuccessfully, although they lasted much longer than is generally acknowledged. The decimation of the Indian populations throughout the Americas following attempts to enslave them or force them into encomienda relations and reservations is well known; it is the extent of the genocide that has been fully appreciated only in recent years.[42]

Nowhere were the attempts more extreme and the consequences more disastrous than in that familiar theater of European imperial horrors, the Caribbean. Hispaniola was Spain's first colony, with a large Indian population of over a million souls when it was discovered by Columbus. In sixteen years it was reduced to about fifty thousand, by 1520 there were hardly ten thousand persons, and by 1550 under two hundred fifty.[43] Jamaica was even less fortunate. Its Arawak population was wiped out within a decade. The story was much the same in the other islands. Slavery, of course, was not the only cause of this destruction; disease and famine were the prime factors. Yet it is important not to underestimate the role of slavery both directly and indirectly in the demoralization and social destruction of the native population. As Kenneth R. Andrews observes: "Altogether these disruptive aspects of the conquest and exploitation of the Indians must be considered not merely as subordinate allies of the microbes but as major forces in the work of destruction."[44] This was most evident in the Central American region of the Caribbean. In Panama the notorious portage of the isthmus called the *trajin* resulted in untold suffering and death for the Indian slaves who carried silver and other goods for their masters.[45]

In what kinds of slaveholding societies, then, did prisoners of war constitute the major means of enslavement? First, we find that captivity in warfare was always the most important means of enslavement among kin-based or tribal societies. This held true whether or not such societies themselves engaged in warfare, since external trading of slaves constituted one of the earliest forms of trade. Captivity in warfare remained important even where slavery became structurally very important in such societies, because descendants of slaves tended to be assimilated to nonslave status. To be sure, there were a few cases of kin-based societies with highly developed slave systems that did not rely heavily on war captives for their slaves (for example, the Toradja of the central Celebes[46]), but these were highly exceptional cases. More typical were the Maoris of New Zealand,[47] nearly all the pre-European African societies with advanced slave sectors,[48] and the slaveholding Indians of the American northwest coast.[49]

A second group in which captivity in warfare was the dominant means of enslavement comprises a subset of advanced societies with large-scale slavery during only the formative period of their developing slave sectors. There are two unambiguous cases in the premodern world: the ancient Greek slave systems, especially Athens, between the sixth and the end of the fifth century B.C.,[50] and Rome during the third and second centuries B.C.[51]

The pattern of change in both civilizations was complex. In Rome during the first two centuries of the empire a small though still significant proportion of the slave population would have been reduced to their condition as a result of captivity in warfare, but this proportion may well have increased periodically from the end of the second century of our era.[52] In ancient Greece, too, the secular downward trend in the proportion of the slave population reduced to their status through warfare would have been disturbed periodically during unusually unstable military situations: for example, during the Peloponnesian wars (431–404 B.C.), the unsettled period during and after the Social War in the middle decades of the fourth century B.C., and during the early decades as well as the last half-century or so of the Hellenistic period.[53]

All the slave societies of the Americas, and possibly those of the capitalistic slave systems of Mauritius and the other Mascarene Islands, fall into this group.[54] They vary, of course, in the length of time during which prisoners of war dominated the slave populations. Assuming that most externally acquired slaves in the Americas before the end of the seventeenth century were captives of warfare, whether waged deliberately for slaves or not, we find that the Spanish colonies were the first to witness significant reductions in the proportion of their populations enslaved by this means, although the change to birth as the major means of enslavement was to take over two centuries.[55] The colonies of North America surpassed all others in the rapidity with which enslavement by birth overtook captivity in warfare.[56] Colonies of the non-Latin Caribbean showed the slowest rate of change, a factor that was to have disastrous consequences for the slaveholder class.[57]

It cannot, of course, be assumed that even during this early period all (or even most) African slaves in the New World were taken as prisoners of war. Some undoubtedly were enslaved as a punishment for crimes, but these must have constituted a tiny proportion of exported slaves.[58]

It has also been claimed that the majority of persons sold to the European slavers on the West African coast were already slaves when captured.[59] This argument is morally specious and in all probability factually inaccurate. Even if it were true, it merely takes the problem of the original means of enslavement one step backward, for we are still entitled to ask how these slaves were originally enslaved. It is highly likely that prior to the start of the eighteenth century the answer was captivity in warfare.[60]

The third group of societies are those advanced systems with significant levels of slavery in which captivity was the dominant original means of enslavement and remained the dominant current means throughout the period of slavery. This was true of the Iberian Peninsula right down to the ending of slavery in early modern times.[61] Included in this group are France during Merovingian and Carolingian times,[62] as well as the large-scale slave systems of the Italian colonies of the Mediterranean during the late Middle Ages and early modern times (especially Cyprus, Crete, and Sicily).[63] The bulk of the societies falling into this category are the Islamic slave systems, especially those of Saharan and sub-Saharan Africa, of North Africa and Muslim Spain.[64] The strong reliance on prisoners of war as a means of enslavement in these societies is explained by a combination of factors: the Is-

lamic emphasis on the jihad and enslavement as a means of recruiting manpower, and the high rate of manumission requiring a constant inflow of outsiders to replace and to increase the slave populations.[65]

Kidnapping

Among premodern peoples it is frequently difficult to distinguish so-called
warfare from kidnapping raids by small "war parties" on neighboring
groups. We have separated kidnapping from warfare on the grounds that it
was not usually a communal affair and might be directed either at a neigh-
borhood group with whom there was no overt state of warfare or at members of the kidnappers' own group. Kidnapping was also conducted with the
sole aim of acquiring captives, whereas this was often only a by-product of
warfare. The distinction, however, cannot be too rigidly held. What Henry
Ormerod observes of the ancient world held equally for most premodern
societies: "It is . . . difficult to apply the modern conception of the 'politically
organized society' to early conditions of ancient life. It was only as a result of
a long process of development that the ancient world came to distinguish
between foreigner and enemy, piracy and privateering, lawful trade and
kidnapping."[66]

In kin-based, small-scale societies kidnapping ranked a close second to
captivity in warfare as a major means of enslavement, both original and
current. According to I. J. Gelb, piracy and abduction (what he calls piracy
slavery) represented "the main source of servile labor of ancient Mesopotamia and the Ancient Near East in general."[67] This may be too sweeping a
generalization. Gelb does not take sufficient account of persons enslaved by
birth. It is best to qualify the statement by saying that kidnapping was the
most important original means of enslavement, and continued as one of the
major current means, during all periods of Mesopotamian antiquity.

Kidnapping, especially piracy, also ranked close to captivity in warfare
as an original and current means of enslavement among all the ancient and
medieval slaveholding societies of the Mediterranean. The area was ideally
suited to this form of enslavement, as Ormerod and others have shown.[68]
Indeed, before modern times the area was plagued by piracy in all but one
period of history, the first two centuries A.D. Individuals at sea and inhabitants of coastal towns were ceaselessly ravaged by pirates, Caesar being perhaps the most celebrated victim. The Greeks were both captors and captives
in this nefarious traffic; for they captured fellow Greeks as well as barbarians. Kidnapping at sea and on land was rampant during the Persian wars.
The practice subsided with the naval supremacy of Athens, which effectively policed the eastern Mediterranean during the middle decades of the
fifth century B.C. With the outbreak of the Peloponnesian wars, however,
kidnapping soared to new heights of atrocity. Not only were the citizens of

all the belligerent states at risk, but the rights of neutrals were notoriously neglected. The heavy reliance on mercenaries simply worsened the situation, for these soldiers saw warfare, kidnapping, and privateering as equally attractive forms of employment. The situation was so bad that even Athenian generals engaged in an early form of the protection racket, guaranteeing the safety of coastal cities against kidnapping for a heavy price.

Although Alexander attempted to clear the sea of pirates after 331 B.C., he was only partially successful and the effort collapsed after his death. During the last decades of the fourth century and throughout the next two centuries kidnapping became chronic, with certain peoples such as the Cretans and the Illyrians surpassing even their own notorious reputations as pirates and robbers.

After the Punic wars Rome assumed the role of policeman of the Mediterranean, but until the start of the Christian era her record was marred by inconsistencies and duplicity. Indeed, perhaps the worst period in the annals of piracy and land-based kidnappings occurred during the second half of the second century B.C. and the last hundred years of the republic. Ormerod suggests that Rome's negligence in controlling the pirates, especially those of Cilicia, was deliberate, motivated by the growing demand for slaves in the still expanding latifundia.[69] Only when trade came almost to a standstill did Rome act. The result was that the Mediterranean was secure from pirates and other kidnappers during the first two centuries A.D. Not so the outer seas. Arab pirates were rampant in the Red Sea throughout antiquity and medieval times, and the Black Sea coast remained infested. Even during these first two centuries, then, a substantial proportion of newly arrived slaves in Rome and other Mediterranean slaveholding societies were the victims of kidnappers.[70]

Throughout medieval Europe kidnapping remained a major source of slaves, sometimes rivalling warfare in importance. The Vikings plagued the coastal cities of the North Sea, capturing people from one area and selling them to another, with the Irish, Welsh, and northeast Britons and Slavs being particularly subject to their raids. The massive rise in the slave population of Christian Spain during the late thirteenth, fourteenth, and early fifteenth centuries was largely made possible by piracy and privateering, which became the most important original and current source of slaves during this period.[71]

Many of the slaves recruited to work on the large-scale sugar plantations of the Mediterranean islands from the thirteenth century must have been kidnapped, although it is difficult to distinguish them from genuine prisoners of war. They came from Greece, Bulgaria, Turkey, and the Black Sea region as well as from Africa.[72]

In order to develop irrigation works, and later to settle the Madeiran Islands during the early fifteenth century, large numbers of slaves were kidnapped from the Canary Islands by the Portuguese. More were kidnapped to work the sugar plantations of the Azores and Cape Verde Islands, so that by the end of the fifteenth century the Canary Islands, estimated to have had a population of about one hundred thousand when first discovered in the fourteenth century, had been nearly decimated.[73]

Piracy flared up again in the western Mediterranean with the expansion of the Ottoman Empire during the late sixteenth century, and for the next two hundred years Christians and Muslims captured one another, enslaving many of their captives. The North African states, especially Algiers and Morocco, came to depend heavily for manpower and external revenues on the "little war" of piracy conducted by the so-called Barbary pirates, especially during the eighteenth century.[74]

But it was not only in Europe and the other slaveholding states of the Mediterranean that kidnapping was important. It was the major original and current means of enslavement in Southeast Asia, where its maritime version, piracy, was highly developed. Kidnapping (including piracy) was the second most important source of slaves in Burma and Thailand.[75] A substantial number of slaves in China, right up to modern times, were originally taken by pirates, especially on the Korean coast.[76] And in Japan piracy was rampant and a primary source of slaves up to the Moramachi period.[77]

In Africa the advanced slave systems established by the Arabs on the east coast, especially in Zanzibar and Kenya, relied entirely on organized kidnapping as the original means of enslavement and as the most important current means of enslavement during most of the nineteenth century.[78] The same was true of the slave regimes established by the Portuguese and the Dutch in southern Africa.[79]

All societies strongly forbade internal kidnapping and sale of free persons. In ancient and medieval Europe it was usually a capital offense; but the continuous enactment of laws against the practice indicates that it was never completely eliminated.[80] In China, while it was also always a capital offense, the laws seem to have been far less effective than in Europe. This was particularly so in the period of the Northern dynasties (A.D. 386–618), when thousands of local citizens were reduced to slavery by semiautonomous war lords.[81] Even more ruthlessly kidnapped were the aborigines of the borderlands "who had never been considered equals of the Chinese and would be arbitrarily enslaved."[82]

It is this same feeling of ethnic distinctiveness that explains two other important instances where internal kidnapping constituted a major means of enslavement: the emirates of the Sudan and the indigenous semi-Islamized states of pre-European Malaysia. The Islamic emirs, sultans, and noble families who ruled the many petty states of northern Nigeria and other areas of the Sudan not only raided the African pagans on their borders but frequently turned on the subjected tribes within their own state boundaries, even when they were known to be converted Muslims. Raiding was so much a part of life for them and so essential to their wealth that they strongly resisted early British attempts to stamp out the practice. As one emir proudly put it: "Can you stop a cat from mousing?"[83] It is, of course, forbidden by Islamic law to enslave fellow Muslims, and technically it was also illegal to enslave members of the raiders' own state, especially when such raiders were sworn to protect the subjected tribes. However, the viciously predatory rulers of these unfortunate Africans easily got around both prohibitions. They either simply ignored them or justified the raids on the grounds that the captured groups were really pagans. And they circumvented the problem of raiding their own subjects by tacitly agreeing to raid across one another's boundaries with the understanding that there would be no retaliation as long as the captives were Negroes.[84]

The situation was even more blatant among several of the pre-European states of Malaysia, where there was not even an attempt to find excuses. In Perak, for example, the raja made annual raids on his own villages and seized every nubile girl who took his fancy. Less organized raids involving both males and females were also common. Again, this outrageous disregard for their own subjects was due to racial, ethnic, and (in the case of the pagan tribes) religious differences between rulers and ruled.[85]

We come, finally, to the colonial slave regimes of the modern Europeans. In the case of the large-scale slave system of the Banda Islands established by the Dutch and the Perkenier-family descendants during the seventeenth and eighteenth centuries, there is no doubt whatever that kidnapping constituted the sole original and most important current means of enslavement. Even before the arrival of the Dutch, piratical kidnappings and enslavement of peoples were common in this part of the world. When the native population died out, the inhabitants of the neighboring chains of islands, especially Sangir, were raided for slaves; as the demand grew, people were kidnapped from as far away as Arakan on the west coast of Burma.[86]

The situation is more complex with respect to the more than 11.5 million Africans transported to the slave regimes of the Americas. Were they primarily prisoners of war or victims of kidnapping raids? Earlier I suggested that during the establishment of these slave systems most of the externally recruited slaves were prisoners of war. While the proportion of externally recruited slaves declined over the course of the late seventeenth and eighteenth centuries, the fact remains that when the total number of Africans transported is considered in absolute terms, the vast majority came during the eighteenth and nineteenth centuries.[87] So we still need to ask whether they were mainly prisoners of war or kidnapped.

To attempt an answer to this question we must take account of several factors: the various time periods over which the slave trade lasted; the areas of Africa from which the slaves came; and whether the so-called wars on the coast were fought essentially to acquire slaves or for other purposes.

To begin with the third factor, Philip Curtin has proposed that for the west coast of Africa during the eighteenth century most wars were waged deliberately in order to acquire slaves. The Senegambia region departed from the norm, in that purely political factors motivated warfare somewhat more frequently than economic ones.[88]

Henry Gemery and Jan Hogendorn take much the same position, arguing that the large-scale use of African slaves in the Americas was at least partly promoted by a highly elastic supply of slaves on the west African coast. They argue, further, that the low market price for slaves before the coming of the Europeans suggests that the taking of slaves at that time was incidental to warfare. As the demand increased during the eighteenth century, more and more wars were waged for the primary purpose of taking slaves.[89]

We may now ask a crucial question: should we dignify the aggressive assaults and raids on neighboring peoples, waged exclusively for the purpose of acquiring slaves, with the term "warfare"? My answer is an unequivocal no. The more closely we examine these so-called wars, the more we come to realize that they were nothing more than sordid kidnapping expeditions incited by no other motive than the desire for the goods and money being offered by European traders and their agents.[90] True, there were important political consequences of many of these raids, especially in the Guinea coastal area, but these were strictly by-products of the organized kidnappings. In southwest Africa there were no such complications. For virtually the entire period of Portuguese devastation of this vast area, almost all Africans taken were captured in raids—most as in the rest of Africa conducted by African middlemen, but many by the Portuguese themselves.[91]

J. D. Fage has estimated that less than a third of all Africans taken over the entire course of the trade were kidnapped, while a little more than half were genuine prisoners of war.[92] I suggest instead the following conclusion, based on more recent scholarship.[93] Of the 1.6 million Africans brought to the New World before the end of the seventeenth century, as many as 60 percent may have been the captives of genuine warfare, while slightly less than a third were kidnapped. Of the estimated 7.4 million transported between 1701 and 1810, the proportions were reversed—that is, over 70 percent were kidnapped and under 20 percent were the victims of genuine wars. Many of those kidnapped were taken in raids organized by the rulers of centralized polities such as Dahomey and Ashanti, which had advanced politically primarily as a result of the economic stimulus of slave raiding and trading.[94] However, it seems highly probable that the majority were kidnapped in smaller, individually organized raids such as those described by the Efik trading chief, Antera Duke, in the region that is now the Calabar province of Nigeria.[95]

The nineteenth-century picture is more complicated. Between 1811 and 1870 about 2.4 million slaves were brought to the New World, the vast majority going to Brazil and the Spanish Caribbean, especially Cuba. The early decades of the century were times of political turmoil in Guinea, so it can definitely be said that the majority of captives coming from this region were genuine prisoners of war.[96] This was true, for example, of the large number of Yorubas who ended up on the expanding slave plantations of Cuba.[97] Most of the slaves who left Africa in the nineteenth century, however, wound up in Brazil (over 1.2 million of the total of about 2.4 million); we know the majority of these came from southern Africa and that almost all of them were kidnapped.[98] We may conclude that for the nineteenth century a little over 60 percent of the slaves brought to the New World were kidnapped, while a little under 30 percent were genuine prisoners of war.

In all, then, the overwhelming majority of slaves brought to *all* regions of the New World were kidnapped persons, with no more than 30 percent being genuine prisoners of war. After 1700, prisoners of war outnumbered kidnapped persons in only a few regions during certain brief periods (Jamaica during the first quarter of the eighteenth century, Brazil during the first two decades of the nineteenth century, and Cuba during the first half of the nineteenth century).

One final issue must be addressed in connection with enslavement by captivity in warfare and by kidnapping: it concerns sexual bias. A common view is that among more primitive peoples where slavery was not very important, there was a strong preference for women, but that with more advanced social systems and slave formations, the bias shifted toward the taking of male captives. The comparative data suggest otherwise. It is true that women were taken more frequently than men among small-scale, kin-based peoples—although there are many exceptions. For example, among the Kerebe of Africa "male captives were as welcome as females,"[99] and the Ibos apparently took men and women in equal numbers.[100] Nonetheless, what Finley says of Homeric Greece holds true for most small-scale societies: "There was little ground, economic or moral, for sparing the lives of the defeated men. The heroes as a rule killed the males and carried off the females, regardless of rank."[101]

It turns out, however, that this sexual bias in favor of women holds true for the great majority of peoples. There was certainly a decline in the tendency among more advanced peoples to kill off their male captives, especially when there was an economic need for slaves; but before the Atlantic slave trade we rarely find more males being captured than females, and the practice of massacring male captives remained prevalent even where they were also enslaved.

What determined sexual bias in the taking of captives was not the level of development of the society or the degree of structural dependence on slavery, but the use to which slaves were to be put (especially in the dominant mode of production), purely military considerations, and the problem of security in the captor's society. It is obvious that women and children were easier to take than men; they were also easier to keep and to absorb in the community. In addition, in most premodern societies women were highly productive laborers and, especially in Africa, they were frequently the main producers.[102] Even where men had traditionally monopolized the productive sector, slave women were absorbed as workers.

After examining a hundred cases of the aftereffects of conquest in ancient Greece between the sixth and the second century B.C., Pierre Ducrey found that the practice of enslaving the women and children and killing the men was no longer "normal" but was still quite common.[103] The situation was not much different among the Romans. Indeed, some authorities suggest that their practices seem to have been closer to what we find among primitives. Mars M. Westington concluded his study of atrocities in Roman warfare by observing that "the slaughter of adult males and the enslavement of women and children is tersely mentioned with the regularity of a fugal theme."[104] This is clearly an exaggeration, contradicted by some of Westington's own evidence and later research; the male slaves on the latifundia had to come from somewhere. Nonetheless, the primitive practice of massacring the men and enslaving only the women and children was clearly attested in numerous instances.[105]

With the rise of the Islamic states we find a systematic effort to capture as many men as women in order to supplement the conquering armies of Islam and reinforce their manpower.[106] Once these states were established, the age-old practice of favoring female over male captives returned. Among the great majority of Islamic peoples after the ninth century, female captives and kidnapped persons fetched a higher price than males, even where slavery was economically important.[107]

Often radical shifts in sexual preference took place over time in certain societies, depending on changes in the demand for and uses of slaves. During the earliest periods of Mesopotamian and Egyptian history there was a decided preference for female prisoners, males being killed on the spot; later the bias moved in favor of males.[108] According to the Soviet classicist J. A. Lencman, there was an important shift away from the tendency to take mainly female slaves between the world depicted in the *Iliad* and that depicted in the *Odyssey*. After noting that female captives were mentioned 11 times as against male captives once in the *Iliad,* in contrast with 46 references to female slaves and 34 references to males in the *Odyssey,* Lencman speculates that there was a higher incidence of kidnapping in the world of Odysseus (pillage being conducted mainly to capture slaves and other booty), while the taking of slaves was largely a by-product of genuine warfare in the *Iliad.*[109] I need hardly belabor the dangers of such evidence, if evidence it is. Lencman, however, makes a very good point in the course of this otherwise questionable speculation: a deliberate shift in favor of male slaves strongly suggests that kidnapping is the major means of enslavement. With this in mind, let us look at one area where there was a marked tendency toward such shifts in sexual bias in the selection of slaves, namely, the slaveholding and trading peoples of West Africa.

Such shifts are found there only after the contact with Europeans. The Aboh, who traditionally had taken women and children, with the coming of the Europeans took both sexes, keeping the women and children for themselves and selling the males to the Europeans.[110] The Vai, before 1826, took only women and children. Between 1826 and 1850 they took mainly men, to meet the demand on the coast. When the Atlantic trade dried up in about 1850, they returned to the practice of killing male captives and taking only women and children.[111] This changing sexual bias was even more pronounced among the Duala of West Africa, who until 1700 took mainly women and children, to meet their own traditional domestic needs; then between 1700 and 1807 shifted to an emphasis on males, to meet the needs of the European traders; after 1807 returned to an emphasis on women and children when the export trade declined; then, with a shift in their own mode of production at the turn of the century, changed once again to the acquisition of mainly male captives, a pattern that continued until 1920, when slavery was finally abolished.[112]

What all this demonstrates beyond any reasonable doubt is that the supply of slaves was highly elastic on the west coast of Africa, even to the point of being sex specific. The vast majority of Africans brought to the New World were not prisoners taken in wars either of their own making or of anyone else's. As Equiano and other African ex-slaves who wrote their autobiographies so often insisted, the slaves were stolen from their homes by European-supported thieves.[113]

Tribute and Tax Payment

Enslavement as a result of being part of tributary or tax payments is obviously related to warfare but should not be confused with either captivity or kidnapping. The vassal state may never have engaged in warfare with the state to which it paid tribute; it may have voluntarily offered tribute as a means of preventing attacks or simply as a goodwill gesture to the more powerful state.

Most of the advanced premodern peoples who kept slaves on a large scale obtained some of them at some time by this means. It was unusual, however, for significant proportions of a slave population to be obtained as tribute, especially where slavery was of marked structural importance. Rome is a good case in point. The Roman economy by the period of the early empire was "basically a money economy," as Richard Duncan-Jones points out, and tribute payments in cash were preferred (although payments in corn were common).[114] Tribute payment in slaves was important during only one period, the late second and first centuries B.C., when Roman tax farmers plundered the eastern provinces and took persons as slaves in such vast numbers "that when Nicomedes of Bithynia was asked for a contingent at the time of the Cimbrian wars he replied that the majority of his subjects had been carried off by the tax farmers and were now in slavery."[115]

The Islamic states and several of the advanced pagan states of Africa stand out as the slaveholding peoples who relied most heavily on tribute to establish and augment their slave populations. Although most of the slaves in the early Abbasid slave armies were bought, considerable numbers were obtained as tribute.[116] According to Ibn Xurdâdhbih, between the years A.D. 826 and 828 two thousand captives of the Turkish tribe Guzz were sent from the province of Xurâsân as part of their tax payment.[117] A considerable number of the elite slave corps found throughout the Islamic world came as tribute, the most celebrated being the Ottoman janissaries, who were recruited by means of the *devshirme* (tribute of children from the Christian subjects of the empire).[118] A large number of the public and private slaves of Muslim Africa were similarly obtained.[119] Among pagan states with advanced slave sectors Ashanti and Oyo were the two that relied most heavily on tribute.[120]

Where did the tributory slaves come from? Often they were persons who were already slaves in the tribute-paying state. Sometimes, however, the unfortunate slave was already part of a tribute paid by another vassal state in an international pecking order. Thus in the mid-nineteenth century the emir of Adamawa (the primary slave center of the Fulani) was paid approximately five thousand slaves by his vassal states, of which he sent two thousand to the sultan of Sokoto.[121] Similarly Bornu, itself a tribute-paying state, received tribute in slaves from the Kwararafa kingdom, which in turn received slaves from its own vassal states.[122] Equally elaborate was the tribute system extending from the Guinea coastal state of Popo to the Ardra, who in turn paid to the Oyo, who were sometimes in vassalage to yet more powerful states.[123]

Many vassal states, too weak to impose tribute on others, did not have enough slaves to meet their quota so were obliged to send their own "free" people as part of the tribute. Thus when Korea became a client state of the Mongols in the thirteenth century, most of the slaves sent as tribute were free persons.[124] The same was true of many of the subjected peoples who paid tribute to the Aztecs.[125] But few societies have had a longer or more unhappy history as tribute payers than the Nubians. They provided slaves both from among themselves and from their southern neighbors as tribute to the viceroy of Egypt from the Nineteenth to the Twentieth dynasties, especially during the viceroyalty of Kush. Over two thousand years later the Nubians were still paying tribute in slaves to foreign conquerors. After the negotiated truce with the Arabs in A.D. 651–652 (called the *Baqt* by Arab historians) a tribute in slaves was demanded by the Arabs. The terms are instructive. According to the Arab geographer Magrizi, it required that "each year you are to deliver 360 slaves which you will pay to the Iman of the Moslems from the finest slaves of your country, in whom there is no defect. [There are to be] both male and female. Among them [is to be] no decrepit old man or woman or any child who has not reached puberty. You are to deliver them to the Wali of Aswan."[126] The insistence on slaves without defects touches on a problem that must have plagued all such payments. Indeed, wars were sometimes fought over the quality of the slaves sent as tribute. In the nineteenth century "the custom of the king of Bagirmi of sending his oldest, ugliest and most useless slaves to Wadai was one of the provocations which moved the king of Wadai to attack him in 1870."[127]

Debt

Debt as a source of slaves must be examined with the greatest caution for, on the one hand, debt is usually a reflection of other causes such as poverty and, on the other hand, so-called debt-slavery has to be carefully distinguished from true slavery. Even so, it very often happens that persons get into debt not from poverty, but as a result of risks that were in no way pressing. While the distinction between slavery and debt-servitude is important, the fact remains that in all societies where debt-slavery existed, the possibility of the debt-slave falling into permanent slavery was always present. Debt, in short, may have been a direct or an indirect cause of slavery.

Among the less commercially developed peoples, debt tended to create slaves by indirect means. Throughout traditional Africa, for example, the practice of pawning was widespread. Usually it was not the debtor, but a member of his family, who was pawned or pledged as security for a loan. The Ashanti were typical. The pawn was usually a woman, often the niece of the debtor—his jural daughter in this matrilineal society. Most such pawns were restored to freedom, since most debts were repaid. Still, it occasionally happened that the debtor was unable to repay his loan on time and, given the high interest rate (50 percent a month according to one source!) got deeper and deeper into debt to the point where he simply could not repay the debt. When this happened, the pawn became a genuine slave.[128]

Much the same situation prevailed among the tribal peoples and petty states of pre-European Malaysia, where debt may well have been the major source of slavery. The interest rate among the more primitive Bataks was a whopping 100 percent—"folding the debt" is the vivid local expression. Persons also fell into debt-servitude and later slavery, as a result of high bride-price and passion for gambling.[129] The situation was not much better among the more centralized Islamic states. One notorious practice among the Arab rulers of these states, especially in Perak, was the imposition of spurious and heavy fines on the native population which the fined person had no means of paying. He would then go into debt-servitude to the raja and eventually, with the accumulation of heavy interest, fall into permanent slavery.[130]

Debt as a direct cause of slavery was more common among the commercially more advanced peoples. It was one of the most important sources of slavery in ancient Mesopotamia,[131] and the second most important among the ancient Hebrews,[132] the premodern Koreans,[133] and the premodern Thai.[134]

The enslavement of persons for debt, or the sale of oneself or one's relatives to repay a debt, was specifically forbidden among a wide range of peoples. Sometimes only the practice of "reducing" the pawn or debt-servant was forbidden. Among the nineteenth-century Damagaram of Zinder, Nigeria, "no individual could reduce another to slavery because of debt."[135] Islamic law forbade enslavement for debt although, as we have seen, the prohibition was frequently circumvented. Debt-servitude was rampant in Hesiodic Greece and was the source of much unrest. In Athens one of Solon's major reforms was to abolish the practice and, in so doing, reduce the possibility of citizens falling into genuine slavery as a result of destitution.[136] Many other Greek states followed Athens' lead, but there were exceptions such as Gortyna in Crete. Further, in most Greek states a prisoner of war ransomed by a fellow citizen remained a slave to his ransomer until he repaid the debt. Citizens who did not pay their taxes could also be made public slaves. And in most Greek states metics, especially freedmen, could be reduced to slavery for debt. In the oriental regions of Hellenistic Greece the pre-Greek tradition of enslavement for debt continued after the Greek conquest.[137] Roman law too was very harsh on debtors. In early Rome judgment-debtors might eventually fall into slavery, but as W. W. Buckland points out, "the position of *iudicatus* in early law is in some points obscure . . . and the system was very early obsolete."[138] At all times, defaulting debtors were subject to compulsory labor.[139]

In several societies the prohibition of enslavement as a result of debt was part of a wider prohibition on the enslavement of free natives except for capital offenses. In both China and Vietnam the sale of one's self or one's wife or relatives into permanent servitude was forbidden.[140] However, the pawning and pledging of persons was permitted, and this provided an escape route that was frequently exploited. The sale of persons, as such, was not illegal: what was illegal was the failure to ensure that a sold person did not fall into perpetual servitude by making it clear to the purchaser that the person being sold was "good" and not "base." It is easy to see how such a law would frequently be broken. Court cases on the matter ended up in long arguments, which sought to establish whether the purchaser bought the "good" person honestly thinking he or she was "base" or whether the seller had taken sufficient care to make the status of the sold person known.[141]

Punishment for Crimes

The enslavement of criminals who had committed capital offenses and other serious crimes was practiced in the great majority of premodern slave systems and in several European states down to the nineteenth century. Among a number of primitive peoples it ranked as the primary source of slaves— usually only where slavery existed on a small scale. It was an important source, for example, among the Ibos of West Africa and the Goajiros of northern South America. Among more advanced premodern societies crime tended to be of less significance as a source of slaves. It was minor in the ancient Near East. In ancient Greece penal enslavement existed but was largely confined to metics, foreigners, and freedmen in central Greece; it was never a significant source of slaves. In Hellenistic Egypt it was of more economic importance; but since the main crime for which persons were penally enslaved was insolvency to the state, the difference between this source of slaves and enslavement for debt was slight.[142]

In Rome penal slavery was a far more established institution: "a person convicted of crime and sentenced in one of certain ways suffered *capitis deminutio maxima,* and became a slave. It was essentially capital punishment, and the *capitis deminutio* had all its ordinary results."[143] Not all forms of capital punishment involved the reduction to penal slavery, and only some categories of persons were affected (usually lower-class freemen). Only when the sentence was lifelong was it slavery, and a distinction was drawn between temporary penal servitude in the mines and permanent slavery.

One variant in Rome harks back to the most primitive roots of slavery: persons who were condemned to die became penal slaves during the interval between their sentence and their execution. This was particularly true of persons condemned to die *ad gladium* and *ad bestias.* Goods belonging to the *servus poenae* (penal slaves) technically had no owner, and only the emperor could manumit him or her. Such pardons, the so-called *indulgentia generalis,* were not uncommon, and although the pardoned person was restored to the status of freeman he had certain liabilities. It must be emphasized that in Rome the enslavement of criminals was essentially a penal matter: as a source of slaves it was insignificant. Penal slaves did perform economic roles—mainly in the mines—but their contribution to the Roman economy was slight.[144]

In several oriental societies penal slavery was a significant source of both public and private slaves. It provided the bulk of slaves among the ancient Vietnamese, for instance, although slavery was never of any real importance there.[145] In Korea, which had the most advanced slave system in the Orient—and one of the most developed anywhere in the premodern world—penal slavery was never a major source of slaves.[146] It was of greater significance in Japan. Here, prior to the sixth century A.D., the two primary sources were prisoners of war and the kinsmen of criminals (as well as the criminals themselves). However, as slavery gained in economic significance during the sixth and seventh centuries, these were replaced by poverty and destitution as the principal sources.[147]

In China penal enslavement was the foremost source of slaves. Strictly speaking, the enslavement of the families of condemned persons was the only recognized source of slaves in Chinese law. As we have seen, there were many other sources; but these were usually either illegal or extralegal. Significantly, those prisoners of war who were enslaved were first assimilated to the status of convicts. Unlike Rome, the strong emphasis on familial responsibility in China meant that a person's wife and kinsmen were fully liable for his criminal actions. The number of such kinsmen varied but at times the law became draconian, involving the entire clan of a convicted person. Before the Han period the convicted person was always executed and his family enslaved. After this there was a growing tendency to enslave both the offender (in the case of the lesser capital offenses) and his family. Pulleyblank argues persuasively that penal slavery, being the origin of both public and private slavery in China, gave the institution its name, and influenced "Chinese conceptions of the nature of slavery and ... the legal position of slaves."[148] The slave was always viewed as a criminal and, as such, base (*chien*) and subject to physical mutilation. This is why the sale of "good" persons into slavery was so abhorred in Chinese law. It also explains why kidnappers of free persons immediately branded them. This was the surest sign of their criminal origins and made them much easier to sell. C. M. Wilbur argues that a distinction was always made in Chinese law between convicts and slaves; Pulleyblank, while agreeing that the distinction existed in law, argues that in practice it did not. China is unusual too in that penal slaves often ended up in the hands of private owners. Usually presented as gifts, they were sometimes simply seized by unscrupulous officials and officers. As in Rome, only the emperor could manumit penal slaves; but the issue was complicated because so many were in private hands. Apparently the manumission of penal slaves by private owners was condoned though never recognized in law.[149]

J. Thorsten Sellin, drawing on previous works, shows that there was a threefold relationship between slavery and the penal system in the history of Europe.[150] First, slavery remained a form of punishment throughout the Middle Ages, though penal slaves did not serve as an important source of slaves even where the institution remained important. Second, over the medieval centuries the nature of punishment of free persons was strongly influenced by the kind of punishment originally inflicted only on slaves. Slavery, in other words, had an increasingly retrogressive effect on the treatment of convicted persons. In the words of Gustav Radbruch: "To this day, the criminal law bears the traits of its origin in slave punishments . . . to be punished means to be treated like a slave. That was symbolically underscored in olden times when to flogging was joined the shaving of the head, because the shorn head was the mark of the slave . . . Slavish treatment meant . . . not just a social but a moral degradation. 'Baseness' is thus simultaneously and inseparably a social, moral, and even aesthetic value judgment . . . the diminution of honor, which ineradicably inheres in punishment to this day, derives from slave punishments."[151]

There was also a third relationship. Penal slavery became from the late Middle Ages down to the nineteenth century a means of recruiting labor for the mines, the galleys, and other public works, especially in Spain, France, Italy, and Russia. In quantitative terms, the number of such slaves was never great among the Western Europeans;[152] in Russia, however, from the late seventeenth century on, it was one of the major sources of slaves in what was a very large-scale slave system (even if one excludes the so-called serfs, most of whom were genuine slaves). Punishment for crimes was the source of nearly all the vast number of public slaves who worked in the mines and developed the Siberian hinterland.[153]

Penal slavery was prohibited in Islamic law. Indeed, the introduction of Islam to a country usually terminated this means of enslavement.

Slavery was often a punishment for capital offenses, whatever these might be. Typical of the list of persons considered criminal, and hence enslaved, in a primitive society is that of the Ibos. The roster included adulterers, those who sold or rented communal property, "quarrelsome person[s] whose headstrong activities might lead to war," very disobedient children, thieves, sorcerers, those accused of witchcraft, and any seizable members of a divorced woman's family where her bride-price had not been returned.[154] The list is usually much shorter among more advanced peoples: those who committed treason and particularly horrible crimes such as patricide (in the case of Rome), and (in Greece) persistently promiscuous daughters, metics who enrolled as citizens or refused to pay the metic tax, freedmen who failed to live up to their obligations to their patrons, and foreigners who married Athenian women.[155] In some societies unscrupulous rulers were occasionally tempted to increase the number of crimes for which persons might be executed or enslaved. In West Africa the list grew with the expansion of the Atlantic slave trade. A number of Africans who ended up on the shores of the Americas were tricked into slavery. A common practice was for several of the many wives of an unscrupulous chief to seduce unwary young men, then accuse them of committing the capital offense of adultery with the wife of the chief. The practice became known among the Sherbro as "woman damage."[156] Rarely was it more than a minor source of slaves.[157] In early modern

Europe we find a similar increase in the number of crimes punishable by enslavement in the galleys.[158]

Abandonment and Sale of Children

This was a widespread source of slaves but apart from the ancient Mediterranean it was rarely a major one. Among kin-based preliterate peoples it was often due to poverty; just as frequently it resulted from some attribute of the child, such as birth defects to which taboos were attached. Twins, slightly deformed children, those born with peculiar birthmarks, breech babies, and the like might be either killed or exposed. The only unambiguous case I know in which exposure of infants became the major source of slaves was among the Fulani of Borgou in northern Benin, Nigeria, during the nineteenth century. The Batomba of Borgou, who did not practice slavery to any significant degree, had the custom of killing any child whose first tooth appeared in the upper jaw because such a child was felt to bring "disaster, illness, and death to his family." Occasionally a child was spared if a certain tribal official, the *gossiko,* was available and willing to raise it, but the vast majority were left to die from exposure. When the immigrant Fulani arrived, they eagerly picked up these children and reared them as slaves. In time the Batomba hosts would simply hand the children over to their Fulani guests, who used them not only as shepherds and domestics but to perform the agricultural duties they themselves despised.[159]

While never a major source, the exposure and sale of infants was not unimportant in the ancient Near East and the Orient. In China the vast majority of such infants were girls, reflecting not only the strong cultural preference for boys (in this respect the practice is closely associated with female infanticide), but also the greater demand for female slaves mainly for domestic and sexual purposes. Most of these girls eventually ended up as concubines or prostitutes. This form of slavery continued in China right down to the twentieth century, where it was disguised as a form of adoption—the so-called Mui-tsai institution.[160]

Poverty was the main reason for sale and exposure in the ancient Near East, and during periods of hardship it became a not unimportant source of slaves. The practice was referred to as being "placed in a pit" or "thrown to the mouth of a dog," terms that grimly indicate the outcome if the child was not fortunate enough to have been enslaved.[161]

It is in the ancient Mediterranean and adjacent lands that child exposure became a significant source of slaves. Although forbidden in one or two of the Greek city-states (Thebes, for example), it was permitted in most and was a common though never major source during classical times. It was of more significance in the Hellenistic world and in Asia Minor, and was to increase in significance during the period of Roman rule. In Rome itself the practice was negligible during republican times but became a primary source of slaves from the period of early empire on. William V. Harris claims that "no other source within the empire can have made a major contribution to filling the gap left by slave-born slaves."[162] Poverty was not the only reason for exposure. In Rome, as in other parts of the world, persons from all classes exposed unwanted children, again with girls being exposed at a disproportionately higher rate.[163]

Both Babylonian and Roman law remained ambiguous on the issue of exposed children, especially concerning the restoration of their status as free persons. The only section of the Babylonian code that applied to child exposure, despite its frequency, was the edicts on adoption. From these it has been inferred that the child could be taken back by its parents at any time before it became an adult, but not thereafter.[164] Roman law, in keeping with its basic rule that free persons could not be reduced to slavery except for capital offenses, maintained that the foundling who was saved and brought up as a slave could reclaim her or his freedom if free birth could be proven. The burden of proof, however, was on the slave, and since it was virtually impossible to secure such proof the law really amounted to very little. What is more, in the Greek-speaking part of the Roman empire it was required that a ransom be paid for the cost of upbringing, should such a person be lucky enough to prove his free birth. (I should add that the Roman emperors consistently refused to recognize the legality of this rule.)[165]

Self-Enslavement

Poverty was, of course, one of the main reasons for self-sale, and we have already noted that in several advanced societies such as China and Japan it was at times a major source of slaves. In Russia between the seventeenth and nineteenth centuries self-sale as a result of poverty was the most important reason for enslavement among the mass of domestic slaves. Richard Hellie goes so far as to call Russian (private) slavery a welfare system.[166]

Yet there were reasons other than poverty why persons sold themselves. Sometimes it was because of political rather than economic insecurity. Strangers who found themselves cut off from their kinsmen in tribal societies often sought self-sale into slavery as the only path to survival. This was quite common, for example, in the Kongo during the unsettled years of the nineteenth century.[167] In primitive Germany it was often the only means whereby isolated persons could procure land and protection.[168] Another cause of self-enslavement was the sale of self and relatives in order to escape either military services or prohibitive taxes—whether in cash, kind, or corvée labor. This was not infrequent in China, especially during oppressive regimes but it was the most marked in Korea. Indeed, during the Yi dynasty (A.D. 1392–1910) self-enslavement was the single most important source of slaves.[169]

There were a few peoples among whom individuals might sell their relatives, wards, and unwanted wives and children not out of economic necessity but for pure economic gain. The Ainu, for example, were notorious among the neighboring Siberian tribes for this practice.[170] We must, however, view such claims with great caution, for they often turn out to be self-serving propaganda among the slave-purchasing and slave-trading groups. Greco-Roman talk had it that the peoples of Asia Minor eagerly sold their wives and relatives into slavery out of sheer greed, but there is no proof of this.[171] The Slavs suffered the same stereotype during medieval times.[172] And one must treat with equal caution the claim of Islamic traders that the nomadic peoples of Asia, especially the Turks, avidly sought out the traders in order to sell their relatives and fellow tribesmen.[173]

Finally, enslavement resulting from marriage to a slave must be viewed as a form of self-enslavement. In many primitive societies, as well as in most of the oriental and European slaveholding societies from ancient to modern times, we find this as a minor form of enslavement.[174] In most cases it was free women marrying slaves, who paid the penalty of their freedom. Even where the laws prohibited it, men usually found ways of marrying slave women with impunity.

5

Enslavement
by
Birth

ENSLAVEMENT BY BIRTH was, naturally, the consequence of earlier forms of enslavement, but in all societies where the institution acquired more than marginal significance and persisted for more than a couple of generations, birth became the single most important source of slaves. Of the great majority of slaveholding societies the stronger claim may be made that birth during *most* periods was the source of *most* slaves.

The discussion of other means of enslavement has implied estimates of the relative significance of birth, which will not be repeated. However, in view of certain common misconceptions concerning the capacity of slaves to reproduce themselves, a few crucial remarks may clear up some popular confusions. First, it is essential to distinguish between the biological and the social reproduction of a slave population. By "biological" I refer to the capacity of a slave population to produce a number of persons equal to or greater than itself, whatever the status of the succeeding generation. The only issue is whether the total number of deaths is balanced or exceeded by the total number of births. By "social" reproduction of a slave population I refer to the degree to which it is able to reproduce itself when, in addition to birth and death, nonnatural factors are taken into account, the most important being manumission and the immigration/emigration rates.

As we shall see in Chapter 10, most slave populations had high manumission rates. One major consequence was that many slave populations that were biologically self-reproductive were nonetheless socially *non*reproductive, because of the social leakage of persons from slave to "free" status. This was the case with many (perhaps most) Islamic slave societies and with most of the Spanish-American slave societies during the eighteenth century. The Mexican and Peruvian populations, for example, virtually disappeared by the end of the eighteenth century not because they were not biologically reproductive, but because of the social loss due to manumission.[1]

A second important point is that where there is a large influx of externally acquired slaves, the claim that a slave population is nonreproductive may well be based on a demographic illusion. In such situations the excess of deaths over births may be entirely a function of the abnormal age structure of the population brought about by the large number of adults—especially adult males—in the population. It is not incorrect, but it is certainly misleading, to say that such populations fail to reproduce themselves naturally. Age-specific mortality and fertility rates may be quite normal. This was true, for instance, of the Cuban and English-speaking slave populations during the nineteenth century.[2] The failure to distinguish between age-specific and general rates of birth and death has led to unwarranted generalizations about slave populations' failing to reproduce out of despair with their lot. True, there have been a few such cases but they are rare in the annals of human slavery. The instinct to reproduce usually triumphs over despair, so that the exceptional cases become all the more poignant. Which were these exceptional cases? The one unambiguous instance is Jamaica during the second half of the eighteenth century. Here all the available data suggest that not only was the mortality rate abnormally high but, more extraordinarily, slave women absolutely refused to reproduce—partly out of despair and outrage, as a form of gynecological revolt against the system, and to a lesser extent because of peculiar lactation practices.[3] The other exceptional cases we can only guess at, given the poor quality of the available evidence. From the ancient world the slave population of rural Rome during the last two centuries of the republic seems likely,[4] as from the modern world does the slave population of the coffee region of Brazil during the nineteenth century.[5]

A third point to be stressed is that even if a slave population is biologically nonreproductive, birth may still remain the single most important source of slaves. There is a tendency among historians to leap from the (correct) observation that birth failed to meet the total demand for slaves to the (often incorrect) assertion that other factors were more important. The simple mathematics of reproduction contradict this thesis. The traditional view of historians of ancient Rome that "most of the need for slaves" was met by birth after the completion of the aggressive wars in the early empire has recently been sharply disputed.[6] I do not have enough information on ancient

Rome to argue the issue in meaningful statistical terms, but the experience of Jamaica during the eighteenth century may be instructive. We have already observed that the Jamaican slave population during most of the eighteenth century was unusual for its biological and social nonreproductivity. Between the end of the seventeenth century and the middle of the eighteenth, the enormous growth of the slave population was due to the massive importation of slaves from Africa. Males outnumbered females to a degree greater than any estimate ever suggested for the slave population of imperial Rome. And yet by the end of the 1760s Creole slaves outnumbered Africans. In other words, in spite of a demographic environment significantly worse than that of Rome during the period of the early empire, birth remained the most important source of slaves.[7] Thus the comparative data strongly support the traditional view expressed by historians such as W. W. Buckland and R. H. Barrow that birth was "in historic times, by far the most important of the causes of slavery."[8]

Let us turn now to the more important factors that influence the social reproduction of slave populations, specifically the social and legal patterns affecting the inheritance of slave status. The manner in which birth determined status was exceedingly complex, varying across cultures as well as within the same society over time. What complicates the issue is the fact that in all slave societies in which the number of slaves was of any significance, free persons interbred with slaves, thus making it difficult to determine the status of the offspring of mixed parentage. Sometimes these were free, sometimes slave; sometimes they occupied an intermediate status, depending on the sex, status, and power of the free parent as well as the relationship between father and mother. A consideration of the factors determining slave status at birth cannot be divorced from those determining free status, since once slavery was established not all persons born free were necessarily the children of parents both of whom were free.

There were five ways in which slave status was determined by birth: (1) by the mother only, regardless of the father's status; (2) by the father only, regardless of the mother's status; (3) by the mother *or* the father, whoever had the higher status; (4) by the mother or the father, whoever had the lower status; and (5) by neither, the child always being free regardless of the status of either or both parents. The last case, of course, refers to incipient (nonhereditary) slavery and is not, strictly speaking, genuine slavery as we understand and use the term. Such cases are, however, important in any attempt to comprehend the origins of slavery. Next we observe that where both parents were free, there were several possibilities for determining the status of the child, for a *category* of free persons may be determined by birth through, or inherited from, the mother only (matrilineal societies); the father only (patrilineal societies); both parents (double unilineal and bilateral); or optionally from either parent, that of the one with the more favorable status being stressed.

When we consider these two sets of rules of inheritance of status—one determining slave/free status and one determining categories of free status—a useful distinction emerges among slaveholding societies: there was one group, the majority, in which the rules determining the inheritance of status for the children of parents both of whom were free differed from those determining the inheritance of slave/free status, while in the second group the rules of status determination were the same whether slave/free status or category of free status was being determined. In other words, there were some slaveholding societies in which, say, father's status determined category of free status but slave/free status was determined by mother's status, while in others the fact that father's status determined category of free status among the children of free parents also meant that father's status determined child's status even if the mother was a slave. A moment's reflection will indicate that where there was a high incidence of mixed unions (which was true of the vast majority of slaveholding peoples), it made a huge difference to the progeny of such unions and to the number of slaves recruited by birth whether the rules of determination were similar or different.

A careful examination of the comparative data reveals that all known slaveholding societies fall, *empirically,* into seven main groups when classified in terms of the joint operation of the rules determining categories of free status for the children of free parents and categories for the children of parents one or both of whom were slaves. I have followed the convention of kinship studies in designating each such class by the name of the society that was most typical of it: *Ashanti, Somali, Tuareg, Roman, Chinese, Near Eastern,* and *Sherbro.* In the discussion that follows I concentrate on the "ideal type," so to speak, and conclude with examples that conform to that type. *The fact that societies belong to the same type in no way implies any historical link between them.*

The Ashanti Pattern

The rule of status inheritance for children of nonslave parents in this group was unilineal, uterine (basically matrilineal), and the same for the children of parents who were either mixed (one slave, one free) or were both slave. The Ashanti provide the classic case. The children of the union of two slaves belonging to the same master remained slaves of the parents' master. The children of the union of two slaves of different masters also remained slaves, but belonged to the master of the mother. Among the Ashanti there was a special name for the children of two slaves, *nnonkofo mienu mma* or sometimes *afono mma.* The children of the union of a male slave and a free woman were always free and were in no way under the potestas of their slave father or his master. The children of the union of a free man and a female slave were always slaves and were known as *Kanifa,* or half-Akan. Although they grew up to consider themselves Ashanti, they were still slaves unless they were formally adopted. The child whose father was the master of his mother was of special importance to the matrilineal Ashanti, for only over such children did the biological father have complete authority (the potestas of the natural children of a man by his nonslave wife were held by his wife's brother). According to R. S. Rattray, "the children of these children in the female line were considered slaves forever."[9] The need for such children was an important reason for slavery in many matrilineal societies.

The Ashanti pattern was the direct consequence of structural principles typical of matrilineal societies. Hence it was found not only among all other Akan-speaking groups but, with the notable exceptions of the Tuareg of the Sahara and the Merina of Madagascar, in all matrilineal slaveholding societies. To cite some of the more important cases, the pattern was found among the Mende, who claimed the children of their female slaves on the proverbially expressed grounds that "mine is the calf that is born of my cow." Although far more ruthless than the Ashanti in claiming the children of their female slaves, sometimes to the point of disrupting their marital unions, Mende masters tended to manumit their slave concubines, and as such, their children by them, to a greater degree.[10] We find the same pattern among the Imbangala of Angola, of whom J. C. Miller writes: "Because one's primary social standing derived from the mother under Imbangala rules of matrilineal descent, the child of mubika [slave] mother (whatever the status of the father) assumed the mubika status."[11] It is the same with the important slaveholding nineteenth-century Kongo group, the Mbanza Manteke, among whom permanent slave lineages were produced from the progeny of female slaves.[12]

The slaveholding Indian tribes of the northwest coast of America are of special interest because, while sharing strikingly similar cultural patterns, they differed in terms of the rule of status inheritance among nonslaves. The more northern tribes—the Tlingit, Haida, and Tsimshian—inherited status matrilineally, and here we find the Ashanti pattern with respect to the children of slaves and of mixed parentage. Rank distinctions were even more marked in these societies than among the Akan, so that even the children of a chief and a female slave could not expect ever to be manumitted. Indeed, a highly ranked person who married a lowly ranked "free" person ran the risk of being killed.[13] Under these circumstances it was extremely rare for a free woman to bear children for a slave. Both woman and child were disgraced in the unlikely event that this happened.[14] Among the Bella Coola Indians mixed unions in which the mother was the nonslave were less uncommon. In such cases the kinsmen of the woman always bought and freed the slave father of her child and both during pregnancy and after there were elaborate purification ceremonies and gift giving undertaken to wash away the "stain" of slavery from the child. Significantly, if the father was the nonslave and wealthy, similar ceremonies might be performed should he wish to elevate the status of his child, but the status of such children was always precarious no matter how powerful and wealthy their fathers.[15]

Among the Goajiro of South America the pattern was strikingly Ashanti, although it had elaborations of its own. Nonslave women always produced nonslave children, regardless of the status of the father. Sometimes, however, the master might pay the bride-price for a free woman to marry one of his slaves. Even when this was done the children still belonged to the mother and her kin group. The master of the slave husband was compensated for his bride-price payment by being given the bride-price of the first daughter of the union.[16]

The Somali Pattern

In this group status was determined by the father (whatever the status of the mother), and when both parents were slaves, the ownership of the child still was determined by the slave father. The Migiurtini Somali are the prototype of this relatively unusual pattern. Among them the child of the union of two slaves remained a slave but, unlike the Ashanti, the child always belonged to the master of the father. The master of the slave husband paid a nuptial gift to the master of the slave bride, and this legally compensated for the ownership of the children of the slave woman.[17] The children of the union of a slave woman and a free man were free if the father acknowledged paternity.[18] Unions between slave males and "free" women were so strongly prohibited that they were nearly unthinkable. However, there was a low-caste, nonslave group among the Somali, the *Sab,* with whom male slaves were allowed to intermarry, and here the same rules applied: the children of a female Sab and a male slave were slaves, while those of a male Sab and a female slave became Sab.[19]

The rigidly patrilineal principle of the Migiurtini Somali was rather unusual among slaveholding groups. The Margi of northern Nigeria, who today live in the states of Gondola and Bornu, were another case in point. James H. Vaughan tells us that in this patrilineal society "the status of the mafa [slave] is hereditary in the male line."[20] Most slaves were women. There was, however, an important office filled by a person known as the *birma,* a kind of acolyte to the king, which was always held by male slaves. Birmas were permitted to marry free women and, strictly speaking, their children were slaves of the king. However, in the case studies detailed by Vaughan it turns out that both the king and one of his sons who married daughters of their birma paid the latter bridewealth. Vaughan could get no satisfactory answer from his informants to this "seeming anomaly."[21]

Some Ibo groups among whom slavery was a well-established institution came close to the Somali pattern. Among most tribes marriage between slave and free of whatever sex was strictly forbidden. However, in the Okigwi area of Ndizogu it was possible for slave men to marry free women as long as the latter were from some remote village. The parents of the bride were compensated for the loss of status by the much higher bride-price they received for their daughter in such marriages. The children of such unions became slaves of the father's master. Among other Ibo groups if a married woman had a child by a slave lover, the child inherited the status of his legal father—the woman's free husband—and was therefore free.[22]

During certain periods and certain areas of the ancient and modern world there were cases that may be classed as Somali. In Homeric Greece "it was the father's status that was determinative" for both free and slave.[23] In certain of the Greek states this pattern held throughout the ages of antiquity. Indeed, status inheritance seems to have become increasingly Somali in ancient Crete. According to J. Walter Jones:[24]

> The children are free or slaves according as to the spouse, whose home it is, is free or slave, so that if a free man goes to live with a slave wife the children are slaves of the master in whose household the mother lives. Later, however, children of a free man by a slave wife were always free in Crete whether he went to live with her or not.

In the modern Americas we find a Somali pattern in Maryland between 1664 and 1681, where the father determined the status of the child for both free persons and slaves. Although the Roman rule was adopted in 1681, the courts of Maryland were inclined to ignore it in the unusual cases where the rule worked on behalf of the slaves.[25] Although it is nowhere explicitly stated, the same situation may have prevailed in early Virginia. It was not until 1662 that an act was passed that defined the status of the child according to that of the mother. According to A. Leon Higginbotham: "Prior to passage of this statute it had been an open question as to whether the normal doctrine of English law would be applicable—that the status of a child would be dependent on the status of the child's father," and since a similar act was not passed in New York until 1706 it may be assumed that at least in some cases the Somali rule applied.[26] During the seventeenth century the Somali rule held in the French Antilles up to 1681, and in South Africa for a few years after that.[27]

The Tuareg Pattern

The Tuareg of the Sahara stood, literally, in a class by themselves. They were doubly idiosyncratic in that, first, they were the only Islamic people with a matrilineal pattern of status inheritance for the children of "free" parents, and second, they were the only matrilineal people among whom the status of the children of mixed parents was patrilineally determined. Both peculiarities are directly attributable to the major role of slavery in the socioeconomic life of this group.

Following Islamic practice, the children of a master and his slave concubine were "free," and if a Tuareg noble married the slave of another man "he could claim nobility for the children by paying a high bridewealth to the original owner."[28] Pierre Bonte, who worked among the Kel Gress group, tells us that this frequently happened, "the children generally having the status and rights of the father."[29] The assumption of full hereditary rights on the part of the children of slave wives, however, was peculiar to the Kel Gress and did not hold for the Kel Ahaggar group. It should be noted that this kind of status inheritance would have been quite impossible among the Ashanti or any other matrilineal slaveholding group. More in keeping with the matrilineal principle is the fact that the children of two slaves belonged to the master of the female slave, although the master of the male slave paid a bride-price to the master of the female and became her fictive father-in-law.[30]

In summary, the pattern is one in which status was inherited matrilineally by the progeny of intracaste unions but was inherited patrilineally among those of intercaste unions. Murdock is certainly correct in his hypothesis that this peculiar arrangement was developed to preserve the purity of race and to prevent the transmission of proprietary powers to the substantial number of persons of mixed blood, and hence of slave/free ancestry.[31]

The Roman Pattern

This was the classic pattern found in many highly developed slaveholding systems and in most of the Western slave societies. The rule of status inheritance differed for the children of free and of mixed parentage, and custodial powers differed with respect to the children of parents who were both free and those whose parents were both slaves. W. W. Buckland describes the Roman case with his customary clarity: "The general principle is simple. The child born of female slave is a slave, whatever be the *status* of the father; if the mother is free the child is free, whatever the *status* of the father."[32] The law further states that "the slave issue belongs to the owners of the mother at the time of the birth, not at the time of conception." Roman law provided a rationale for this rule. According to Gaius, it was the rule of the *ius gentium:* where there was no connubium, the child took the status of the mother.[33]

The Roman pattern should not be confused with the Ashanti, in spite of some superficial resemblance. The Ashanti pattern had a single principle of status inheritance for the children of both free and mixed parents, whereas the Roman pattern used different principles: patrilineal for the free, matrilineal for the slave. Emanating from this was another crucial difference: free women among the Ashanti did not lose rank or the right to determine the status of their children if they produced children by slaves.

As with all the patterns, exceptional situations did develop. There were a few cases where free women could give birth to slaves: (1) the child of a free woman who cohabited with a slave in agreement with the latter's owner that any issue would be the slave of the owner, and (2) the child of a free woman who cohabited with a slave knowing him to be one. Hadrian abolished the first rule but, oddly, not the second. The apparent anomaly is explained by the fact that the second law was more concerned with the proscription of unions between free women and slaves. Cohabiting free women became slaves, and the law grew progressively harsher on the issue. Their children became slaves according to the general rule.[34] There were also cases where the child of an *ancilla* (female slave) was free. Among other exceptional cases, if the mother was free anytime between conception and birth, and was legally married, the child was free; but if the pregnancy was *volgo conceptio,* the child became a slave.[35] The general rule was that the law operated in the interest of the unborn child. Thus if the mother was a slave at the time of birth but was already entitled to manumission, with the delay in her emancipation resulting from administrative factors, the child would be free.

The Roman pattern of status inheritance was widespread in both the Western world and parts of the oriental world. Most Western societies, whether influenced by Roman law or not, had this pattern, and it was characteristic of many Indo-European slaveholding peoples. In ancient India up to the period of the Buddha, the Roman rule prevailed and was so strongly maintained that even the son of a king by a slave concubine could have been reduced to slavery. The rule, however, changed drastically in Mauryan times.[36]

The Athenian experience conformed in general to the Roman pattern but, as Glenn R. Morrow observes, it is a "little more difficult to determine and seems to have varied in different periods."[37] The rule was apparently Roman during the fifth and fourth and later centuries B.C., although there is reason to believe that in certain special cases children of slave mothers and free fathers were freed. Significantly, Plato took a harsher stand on this issue and would have had the children of mixed parentage inherit the status of the slave parent.[38]

The Roman pattern held among many central and northern Germanic peoples, who applied it with extreme rigidity. Early Norse law punished cohabitation with a slave by a free person of either sex with enslavement to the master of the slave.[39] During later periods, the laws were relaxed and a free woman who bore a child for a slave could pass on her free status to the child, whereas a free man, even a master of the mother, could not do so except under unusual circumstances.[40] The pattern changed again in Sweden at the end of the twelfth century, as we shall see. "Thrall born of thrall was thrall" went the Icelandic saying.[41] In Icelandic law the child of a free woman and a thrall was free but could not inherit. A man had to emancipate his thrall concubine if their child was to be free. Should the child be conceived before the mother was manumitted, the child was free but declared a bastard and could not inherit.[42]

Much the same pattern seems to have existed among the Celts, although the legal texts provide little information on the subject. From the law covering the relation between free Welsh and servile foreigners we deduce that the situation was of the Roman type. We know from the *Book of Iorwerth* that children of free Welsh women and servile foreigners could be given the free status of the mother if the mother so chose. Ironically, it appears that this status was only given the child when the servile foreign father rejected his paternity. Servile foreigners were sometimes quite prosperous, which explains both the pregnancy and the woman's frequent preference for penurial status for her child.[43] The child of a servile foreign woman and a free Welsh father, according to the same laws, took the status of the mother.[44]

Not all the Germanic and Celtic peoples followed the Roman rule. We have little information on the tribal Irish, but the ancestral myth of the most famous of the Irish royal families—Uí Neill—may have some significance. The reputed ancestor of the family, Niall Noígiallach (Niall of the nine hostages)—who, legend has it, lived in the early fifth century—was the son of Eochu Mugmedon ("lord of slaves") and a British slave girl. This definitely suggests a non-Roman, possibly a Somali, pattern of status inheritance, at least among the royal families.[45]

Several Germanic groups that rose to power in the wake of the Roman empire also had non-Roman patterns, especially the Lombards and Visigoths. So did Christian Spain from the thirteenth century on.

At the same time, the Roman pattern was by no means peculiar to the Indo-European peoples. During the height of Japanese slavery we find not only the general rule that the children of a slave woman were slaves belonging to her master regardless of the status of the father, but, strikingly, a regular exception to the rule which held that the children of a free woman who cohabited with a slave were the slaves of the master of the father.[46]

The Chinese Pattern

The Chinese pattern contrasts in many striking ways with the Roman. As in the Roman model, the rule differed for the children of free parents and those of mixed parents, but in almost every other respect the models were unlike. Niida Noburu has discussed the issue at length, deliberately highlighting the contrasts with the Roman pattern.[47] From the period of the Han dynasties on, the basic Chinese rule was that in cases where the parents were of different statuses, the offspring of the union became a slave. In other words, the principle of *deterior condicio* operated: the child always took the status of the parent with the lower status. Between the eighth and twelfth centuries A.D. if a freewoman had a child by a slave, the child became a state slave and the woman was severely punished. However, in the event that a commoner girl had married a slave in the genuinely mistaken belief that he was "good" (that is, not a slave), the child remained free. During the Yuan period (roughly the thirteenth to fourteenth centuries A.D.) slaves and "good" persons were allowed to intermarry, but the wife always assumed the status of the husband—that is, slave women married to "free" men became free, while "free" women married to slaves became slaves. What this amounted to was an exception to the basic rule, in that the issue of such marriages followed the status of the father. There was, however, a regular exception to this exception. If a slave was married to a freeman and had an illegitimate child, the child followed the status of the mother, whereas if the mother was the free partner and had an illegitimate child, the child remained free.

It is interesting to note that the legal logic behind both the exception and the exception to the exception in Chinese law was identical to the logic of the general Roman rule of the *ius gentium,* which stated that where there was connubium the child took the status of the father and where there was none it took that of the mother. Because the Chinese of this period allowed intermarriage, the rule had markedly different social consequences. Though late in the development of slavery, the laws of Yuan can be interpreted as an extension and humanization of earlier Chinese practice. Prior to the thirteenth century A.D., women were always strongly prohibited from having relations with slaves and, as we have seen, the children of such illegal unions became slaves. The practice, however, did take place and the reforms of the thirteenth century simply gave it legal sanction. The woman and her child still paid a penalty in that both continued to be reduced to slavery. The major differences were the privatization of the penalty (the child now became the slave of the father's master) and the humanization of the sanction: instead of punishing the slave and banishing the woman, the lovers and their child were allowed to form a recognized union (though one that would produce permanently "base" or slave issue). The new regulations of Yuan were also an extension and humanization of the far more frequent unions in the opposite direction: those where "free" males entered into concubinage with slave women. Concubinage was long recognized in the law, and frequently the children of such unions were emancipated.[48] The new rules simply elevated such unions to the status of full marriages, the children of which became fully legitimate heirs.

The Chinese case nicely illustrates why it is that we should not rely exclusively on law in interpreting the practices of a people. The basic rule of *deterior condicio*—that the child always takes the status of the lower parent—strikes one as harsh, and if practice had conformed strictly to law there would have been very few freed slaves in Chinese history. Practice, however, never did conform exactly to the dictates of law; in the end, it was law that during the thirteenth and fourteenth centuries finally gave way to practice by legitimizing both exception and exception to the exception.

In practical terms Wang Yi-T'ung seems correct in arguing that over the full course of Chinese history, "the status of slave progeny is rather ill-defined and consequently permits a high degree of fluidity in Chinese slave institutions."[49] In fact, it was this unusual fluidity that partially accounts for the persistently small proportion of slaves in China in spite of the vast numbers of persons enslaved: "This lack of genealogical force sharply distinguishes Chinese slavery from the conventional consummate pattern [and] ... was one of the chief factors which prevented China from becoming static, and it may have given comfort and hope to those who aspired to freedom and higher social activity."[50] This statement, true of China, could apply equally to any number of slaveholding societies such as Rome and almost all of the Islamic world.

What happened where there were no humanizing exceptions to the basic Chinese rule either in law or practice? The cases in point are most instructive. We expect that if such a severe restriction of the major means of manumission prevails, the slave population will accumulate to a considerable degree, and this is exactly what we find. In Korea where the rule applied prior to the Yi dynasty (though only partially during the Koryŏ period), we find the most advanced slave system in the Orient and one of the most developed anywhere in the premodern world. Let us examine it more closely.[51]

From very early, birth became the major source of slaves in the Koryŏ period. Considerable attention was therefore paid to slave/free unions with a view to restricting any generational "leakage" from the slave population. The rule of status inheritance was frequently debated and repeatedly changed, rarely in favor of the slave. The Chinese rule of *deterior condicio* was rigidly applied throughout most of the Koryŏ period and began to change only with the Mongol invasions of the thirteenth century. Amelioration reached its height during the reign of Kongmin Wang (1352–1374), and in the very last year of the Koryŏ period the Roman pattern was made law. The year was hardly out when the new Yi dynasty reverted to the Chinese pattern. This continued until 1669, when once again there was a change from Chinese to Roman type; but there was considerable unhappiness with the switch, and five years later the rule was changed back to the Chinese type. Between 1674 and 1731 the rule of status inheritance kept alternating between Chinese and Roman until the Roman pattern was finally enacted in 1731. By this time, of course, the landowning class had shifted from slavery to other more profitable forms of dependent labor. Exceptions were always made for the children of high officials and their favored slave concubines, many of whom were freed along with their children.

It is significant that in the two instances where the Chinese pattern was found among a primitive people—the To Lage and To'Onda'e tribes of the Toradja group of the Celebes, and the Merina of Madagascar—there was also the highest proportion of slaves, the servile group rising to over 50 percent of the population in some Toradja tribes.[52]

The basic Chinese pattern was followed by several of the barbarian groups that inherited the Roman Empire. In Visigothic Spain the principle of deterior condicio was rigidly applied.[53] The same was true of Lombardic law right up to the end of slavery in the early modern period. In medieval Tuscany the legal situation was a strange mixture of Roman and Lombard law as well as local custom. The dominant pattern, however, was Lombardic, and the rule was that "children born of parents of unequal status took that of the parent of inferior rank: the child was considered a slave if either of his parents was unfree."[54]

Finally, there was the American case of South Carolina, where a statute of 1717 "for the Better Governing and Regulating of White Servants" contained certain clauses that made the state's pattern Chinese rather than Roman, as elsewhere in North America. All children of female slaves were to be slaves. If a free woman, white or otherwise, had a child by a slave, the child "was condemned to servitude for the 'indiscretions' of his parents."[55]

The Near Eastern Pattern

The earliest recorded pattern of status inheritance, this was the dominant form among all the slaveholding societies of the ancient Near East. It was also the most liberal. The rule may be simply stated. When the parents were both free, the child inherited the father's status. Where one of the parents was free and the other a slave, the child inherited the status of the free parent whatever the sex, as long as the father acknowledged paternity. In sharp contrast with the *deterior condicio* principle of the Chinese, the principle of *melior condicio* was operative here. As far as the marital status of the parents was concerned, this pattern required of free men and women only the power to acknowledge and pass their status on to their children. How they actually did so might vary: in the ancient Near Eastern prototype it was done either by marriage to the slave partner by the free person of either sex without any penalty being suffered by the free partner or by freeing the concubine mother of the child, or by simple adoption of the child.[56] Free women did not lose their freedom, nor were they punished for simply bearing children for slaves, although of course the practice was viewed with some disfavor and illegitimacy was strongly prohibited. A free woman could marry certain privileged categories of slaves and although, in view of her husband's status, she could not become a *mater familias,* her children could not be claimed as slaves by her husband's master.

The major exception to this generally liberal pattern of status inheritance was the Sirqu, the temple slaves of ancient Babylonia. This was a hereditary caste and could not be manumitted. In stark contrast to secular slaves, the basic Chinese pattern of inheritance applied rigidly.[57]

The Near Eastern pattern is not only the earliest, but possibly the most widely distributed, pattern of status inheritance among the advanced premodern slaveholding societies. One of the main reasons is that the pattern was incorporated, in its essentials, into Islamic law and in this way was diffused throughout the world with the spread of Islam. The Tuareg, as we have already seen, was one of the few Islamic slaveholding groups that did not conform to this rule. The key factor in the operation of this pattern among Muslims is the Islamic law of concubinage, which holds that a slave woman becomes free along with her children as soon as she bears a son for her master. Islamic law and practice were, of course, far less liberal when it came to the union of free women and slaves. Even so, it is noteworthy that the direct counterpart to the king's slaves of ancient Babylonia, the Islamic Mamluks, could also marry free women; with respect to the ordinary slave population, the prohibition in practice did not severely distort the pattern inasmuch as most slaves in most Islamic lands were females. (The exceptional Tuareg remain peculiar even in this respect, since among certain groups of them, where female status was high, free women could marry slaves if they chose.[58])

There were only two important European instances of the Near Eastern pattern, both of which emerged independently during the thirteenth century. In Sweden, when the laws of Ostergotland and Svealand were codified, it was stated that "the child follows the better half"; as Joan Dyste Lind comments, "regardless of which parent was the free person, the child would be free."[59] It is still not clear whether this rule had always prevailed in these parts of Sweden or whether it was simply a part of the general amelioration of slavery that was taking place. In Spain at about the same time, the harsh Visigothic law (which, as we have already indicated, was of the Chinese type) was changed to approach a pattern that was almost Near Eastern. The new rule was that the child of a Christian and of his Saracen slave or the slave of another master should be baptized, and if the Christian were the master of the slave the child also would be freed. Additionally, the child of a Jewish-owned slave and a Christian would be baptized and immediately freed without any indemnity to the master.[60] Religion obviously had a role in this development, and not often from the best of motives. At the same time, we cannot rule out a possible Moorish influence. If religion was the sole factor operating, its purpose would have been achieved simply by insisting on baptism of the child of mixed parentage. The automatic manumission of the child of a slave concubine is so distinctly Islamic, and more generally Near Eastern, and so alien to the traditional pattern of Visigothic and early Christian Spanish law, that one is not rash in assuming some influence.

In legal theory the majority of the slaveholding systems of modern Spanish America conformed to the Roman pattern of status inheritance, but in practice the rule was much closer to the Near Eastern pattern, with the important exceptions of nineteenth-century Cuba and sixteenth-century Mexico and parts of Brazil. The children of virtually all mixed unions inherited the status of the free parent (invariably the father). Where free women (usually freed women and Indians, but occasionally lower-class whites) cohabited with slaves, the women and their children remained free.[61] This may have been a continuation of the Near Eastern pattern found beginning in thirteenth-century Spain, but there need have been no historical continuity. A high incidence of miscegenation between masters and slaves, in combination with a less proletarian and more household use of slaves, will tend to generate a Near Eastern pattern.

Even where slaves were used in a highly capitalistic manner and the legal norm was rigidly Roman, a Near Eastern pattern occasionally applied to the children of certain categories of slaves. This was the case, for example, in the British slave colonies of the Caribbean during the late eighteenth and early nineteenth centuries. Partly because of the shortage of white women in the islands, it was normal for white overseers and even some managers of the absentee-owned plantations to take black and mulatto concubines. There was no legal requirement that these women and their children be freed and many, perhaps the majority, of them remained slaves. However, where ties of sentiment developed between the master and his concubine, the woman and their children were manumitted and even inherited from the father, so much so that frequent laws were passed in late eighteenth-century Jamaica limiting the amount of money that could be inherited by such children. While the group of so-called free coloreds that resulted from these unions was to constitute an important social class in the late slave and post-emancipation periods, for the vast majority of slaves, including those who had temporary liaisons with whites and the resulting children, the Roman pattern prevailed. At no time was there any attempt to change this strongly sanctioned rule.[62]

The Sherbro Pattern

Not many societies conformed to this type of status inheritance, where there was no fixed rule of status inheritance among the children of nonslave or "free" parents. Children chose the status of the parent whose line carried the greater status, although they tended to favor the father's side. The same flexibility applied to slaves, except that it was the master of the slave's parent who took advantage of the flexibility rather than the offspring. Among the

Sherbro of Sierra Leone "an individual's claim to be a member may be made through either a male or a female link, although there is a patrilineal preference. The matrilateral connection is usually stressed when the mother's or father's mother's group is of high status."[63]

The inheritance of slave status here is ambiguous. In keeping with the dominant stress among the nonslave population, the child's status was usually determined by the father. Women of *ram* (free) status who married slaves produced slave children, hence unions of this kind were unusual. Even though slaves were generally described as "those whom we would not marry," a benevolent master wishing to reward a loyal and useful male slave would take advantage of the flexibility of the inheritance rules by providing him with a wife from his (the master's) own ram. The children of such unions could not inherit status patrilineally like most other slaves, but were considered "*ram de,* freeborn through their mother."[64]

Although he is not explicit on the matter, we may deduce from Arthur Tuden's discussion of slavery among the Ila that the Sherbro pattern held.[65] It seems likely too that a Sherbro-type flexibility with similar patrilineal stress held for the *tyeddo,* or slaves of the Wolof of Senegambia.[66]

Early Bermuda evinced an illiberal version of the Sherbro pattern that applied only in cases where a child was born of slaves belonging to different masters. The first such child went to the master of the mother, the second to the master of the father, and so on. Only quasi-Sherbro, this example conforms to the pattern in its flexibility but differs in that the parent's gender determined only the master of the child, not his or her slave/free status.[67] The practice was highly reminiscent of the distribution of children of serfs belonging to different masters in medieval France.[68] One other variant of the Sherbro pattern did influence the status of the child, and it was the practice that prevailed among the Iban tribe of Borneo. From Brooke Low's classic account of the group during the nineteenth century we learn that "where the parent is free on one side, and the other parent either an *in* or *out*door slave, the first child follows the fortunes of the father, the second that of the mother, and so on in succession, and this rule is unalterable."[69]

6

The Acquisition of Slaves

SLAVEHOLDERS ACQUIRED SLAVES either directly, using any of the means enumerated in Chapters 4 and 5, or indirectly—that is, from third parties via trade, gifts, or closely related payments in kind, or when the slaves were used as money. The most important of the indirect means of acquisition are considered in this chapter.

External Trade

External trade always played a major role in the indirect acquisition of slaves. Few would challenge this statement in the case of the advanced premodern and modern slave systems. What may seem surprising, however, is that it holds too for the most primitive of the societies where slavery was important.

Slaves often constituted the earliest article of trade, especially of external and long-distance trade, among primitive peoples. The only commodity simple peoples could usually offer to more advanced peoples for the luxury goods they desired was fellow human beings. This becomes evident in studies of the indigenous West African markets and trade. Summarizing the findings of his own work and that of his colleagues, Claude Meillassoux concludes that the slave was both a commodity and a producer in West

Africa. Sometimes the slave was involved with trade purely as a commodity, especially in the destructive trade with the Europeans. In intra-African trade, the slave figured both as commodity and as producer. Slaves were also vital in long-distance overland commerce as porters and in the capture of more slaves.[1] This, however, was true mainly of the more advanced societies. In the simpler lineage-based communities "goods circulate through a network of kinship, affinity, and clientage, through prestation, redistribution, or gift exchange. Wealth as an instrument of social control is a privilege of rank or of birth."[2] In such small-scale communities trade was sometimes a threat to the established order and was therefore circumscribed. Hence imported goods "acquire a social and political content which makes it difficult to transform them into trade commodities." Slaves were prestige goods and at best a "means of social reproduction," rarely a means of production. In the Sudan the use of slaves as producers for external trade was always accompanied by the rise of both a warrior and a merchant class.[3]

The archeological data on neolithic Europe strongly suggest that slaves were among the earliest articles of trade.[4] One of the most striking articles recovered from the Llyn Cerrig Bach find in Anglesey was a slave-gang chain, leaving no doubt that slave trading was a well-established practice in the La Tene culture of the Celts during the first century of our era.[5] This trading continued down to the Viking period, as we shall see.

Among the Indians of the northwest coast of America there was a well-developed pattern of long-distance trade in which slaves were the principal items of commerce. One reason was the propensity of slaves from neighboring or even moderately distant tribes to run away and rejoin their own groups. Thus the price of a slave was largely determined by the distance of his point of origin from the final buyer's home. Large-scale slave marts dotted the coastline. The Dalles, a slave mart, became the Delos of aboriginal North America. Trade moved in two directions: from the south up to the Dalles came slaves who were exchanged for other goods that came from the north; the slaves were then traded farther north.[6]

It should by now be clear that slavery was intricately tied up with the origins of trade itself, especially long-distance trade, the bartering of slaves for prestige goods often being the sole form of commercial activity. As the demand for slaves grew, slave-trading systems expanded in both organizational complexity and distance between areas of recruitment and areas of use.

Throughout recorded history, even to the first half of this century, slave-trading systems have always existed to meet the widespread demand for slaves. Five systems stand out in terms of the volume of trade and the distances involved: the Indian Ocean; the Black Sea and Mediterranean; the medieval European; the trans-Saharan; and the transatlantic. A few general remarks on these trading systems are warranted.

THE INDIAN OCEAN TRADE

Perhaps the oldest slave trade of all, the commerce in the Indian Ocean had both an east-west and a north-south axis (see Map 1).[7] As early as the Eighteenth Dynasty (1580 B.C.) ships were sailing from Egypt to northern Somaliland (the land of Punt) with the specific aim of obtaining slaves.[8] There is reference to trade in slaves from East Africa to Alexandria in the early second century A.D.[9] The large number of black slaves in the Persian Gulf area attests to a slave trade preceding the rise of Islam. This trade was intensified as Islam grew, and Arab traders for slaves in increased numbers began establishing posts on the East African coast as far south as Zanzibar, probably as early as the ninth century.

The volume of trade, especially during the nineteenth century, was much larger than is normally believed. Indeed, the East African trade during the nineteenth century was significantly larger than the Atlantic slave trade during the nineteenth (or seventeenth) century. R. W. Beachey estimates a total volume of 2.1 million slaves exported at that time, not counting the "fringe numbers."[10] Between 1800 and the mid-1820s approximately five thousand slaves per annum were exported, and about the same number held during the last quarter of the century. During the middle half of the century, when the trade was at its peak, some twenty thousand slaves each year were exported south of the Horn; and between the mid-fifties and the end of the seventies more than thirty-five thousand were exported annually from the northern half of East Africa. The vast majority went to the slaveholding societies of the Middle and Near East. For example, for most of the nineteenth century between fifteen and twenty thousand slaves were exported annually into Mecca and Medina from the African part of the Red Sea. The Portuguese may have taken as many as two hundred thousand slaves from the region during the last decades of the eighteenth century, and approximately the same numbers were absorbed by the advanced plantation systems of the Arabs on the East Coast itself. Other authorities estimate the total volume of the trade between the years 800 and 1800 at three million. Thus during its entire history the trade involved the acquisition and sale of approximately five million persons.

THE BLACK SEA AND MEDITERRANEAN TRADE

The Black Sea and Mediterranean slave trade was another of the oldest and most important in the history of slave acquisition (see Map 2). Despite its importance for the ancient economies, we know very little about it other than that it rose to prominence toward the end of the seventh century B.C. Before our era the southern regions of the Black Sea and Asia constituted the single most important source of slaves, although significant numbers also

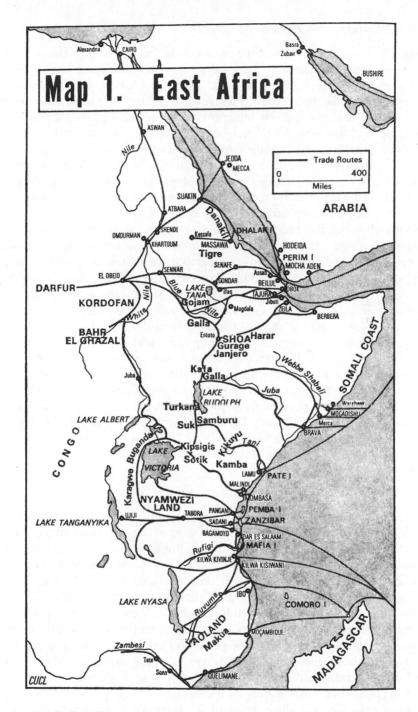

Map 1 The Indian Ocean slave trade. From Joseph E. Harris, *The African Presence in Asia* (Evanston, Illinois: Northwestern University Press, 1971), p. 4.

came from the north.[11] From the period of the Pax Romana to the end of the ancient world, the northern and northwestern areas became more important. One recent estimate places the total number of slaves legally traded annually during the period of the Principate at 250,000. We have no idea what proportion of this trade was intraprovincial and what proportion interprovincial, but it is a reasonable guess that the vast majority of the slaves traded in Rome and other parts of the empire came from within the empire itself.[12]

This trading system did not end with the fall of the western Roman Empire, but supplied the highly developed slave system of Visigothic Spain as well as early medieval France.[13] With the Muslim conquest, the demand for slaves through this system abated somewhat in what was left of Christian Spain, although the Moors continued to rely on it for their labor supply. From the thirteenth to the late fifteenth century, however, Christian Spain once again relied on this trading system to increase its slave population. The typical slave in Spain prior to the thirteenth century was Saracen, but from then on slaves came from Greece, Sardinia, Russia, the Crimea, and especially from among the Turks, Armenians, and Balkan peoples. There were also slaves from Africa and the Canary Islands.[14]

The traffic also supplied slaves from these same regions to Mediterranean France between the thirteenth and fifteenth centuries. But the revival of demand was most pronounced in the Italian city-states and in their slave colonies in the Mediterranean islands of Cyprus, Crete, Rhodes, and Sicily. Tartars and other peoples from the shores of the Black Sea as well as Greeks, Bulgarians, Russians, Turks, and Africans were supplied to the Italian plantation owners in vast numbers. Italian and Jewish traders dominated this trade, although Frenchmen played a role also.[15]

THE MEDIEVAL EUROPEAN TRADE

The European slave trade that flourished from the early ninth century to the middle of the twelfth was small in scale compared to the other major trading systems.[16] The trade routes ran in all directions, but there were two principal routes—one western, in the North Sea and across the English Channel; the other eastern, involving sea, river, and overland transport (Map 3). Although the Vikings dominated all of these routes, other peoples were also involved, especially after the tenth century. In Western Europe before that time Anglo-Saxons and Vikings were raiding and trading peoples from all over Western Europe. The Celtic peoples of the British Isles and the Scandinavians themselves were the main victims. Large numbers of Welsh and Irish were raided and sold to Iceland in order to augment the labor force during the period of settlement; at the same time they, along with Scandinavian slaves, were bought in quantity by Norwegian masters to restore the losses in manpower created by the emigration to Iceland. The Welsh, like

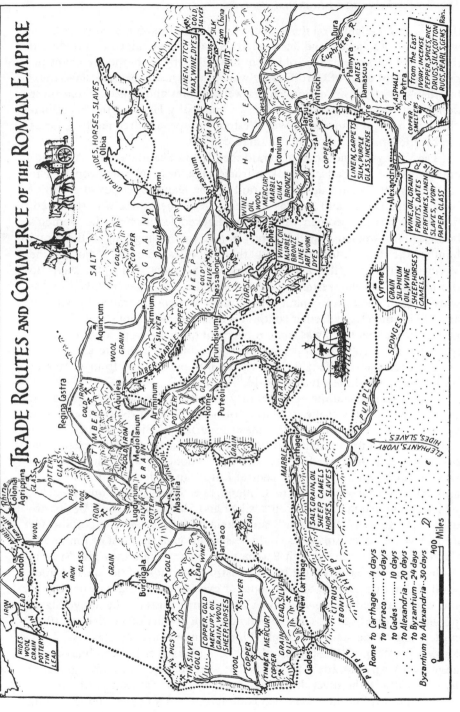

Map 2 The Black Sea and Mediterranean slave trade. From Charles Alexander Robinson, Jr., *Ancient History: From Prehistoric Times to the Death of Justinian* (New York: Macmillan Co. 1951), p. 565. Copyright © 1951 by the Macmillan Co.

the African middlemen on the west coast of Africa eight hundred years later, were to be both victims and dealers in this trade. They raided and traded in the interior for slaves, then sold them to the Viking seaborne merchant pirates. The port cities of Cardiff and Swansea may have begun as slave-trading marts. But the two major centers were Dublin and Bristol. From these depots and from their own home bases, especially Hedeby, the Scandinavian merchants spread out all over Western Europe, and frequently as far as the Mediterranean, selling their human cargoes.

The Vikings did not scruple to raid their fellow Scandinavians. A considerable number of thralls were taken from neighboring Nordic peoples. The Icelandic poet Valgard describes a raid on the Danes by a mixed group of Norwegians, Danes, and Swedes wherein "the Danes, those who still lived, fled away, but fair women were taken. Locked fetters held the women's bodies. Many women passed before you [the conquering king of the pirate band] to the ships, fetters bit greedily the bright-fleshed ones."[17] Nor did the Vikings hesitate to sell Scandinavian as well as Slavic and Celtic slaves to the Muslims. On the western route some of these slaves were taken southward to Lyons and on to Spain, where many were again traded by Muslim and Jewish merchants farther south and east to the Muslim states. There is also evidence that there was some movement of slaves from south to north, for the "blue men" who appeared in Ireland in A.D. 859 were almost certainly African slaves brought there by the intrepid Vikings from Arabia or some other part of the Muslim world.[18]

After the middle of the ninth century the heaviest traffic in slaves was on the eastern route. It was then that the Volga and Dnieper rivers were opened up mainly "as slave routes to the eastern market."[19] Birka, situated on the northwest part of the island of Bjorkö in Lake Mälar, not only became the pivotal point in this trade but until it was abandoned in about the year 1000 was crucial for all northern and central European trade.[20] From here slaves and fur could be sent south to Gotland, the South Baltic, and Hedeby, which dominated the western route; silver and Slavic slaves could be distributed north and west for use in Scandinavia itself; and, most important, fur and a few Scandinavian slaves could be sent through the Gulf of Finland to the Volga, then south through Russia to Bulghar, where they met Muslim traders from the east. It must be emphasized that most of the slaves traded south did not come from Scandinavia, or even from the Slavs of the Baltic, but were gathered on the way down in terrifying raids on the native Slavic populations that lived closer to the market. The distinction between warfare, piracy, and trade was completely blurred among the Vikings. As P. H. Sawyer points out: "Most if not all of the Kuffic silver in Scandinavia was acquired by way of trade. The goods that were sold were probably gathered by violence, and the silver that reached the Baltic was at least partly distributed by piracy, but there was also commerce."[21] It was the Viking raiding

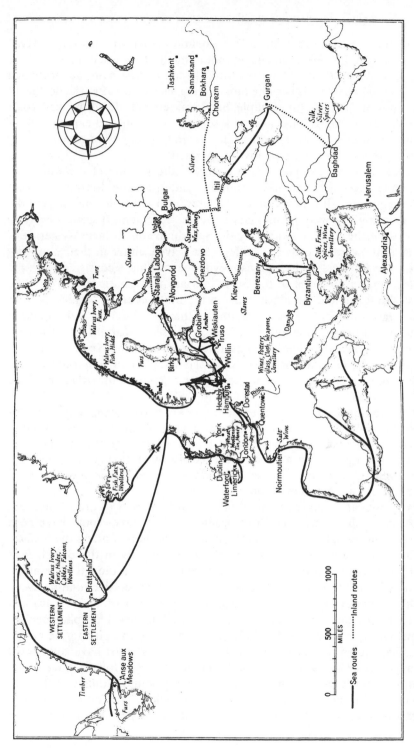

Map 3 The European slave trade. From Gwyn Jones, *A History of the Vikings* (London: Oxford University Press, 1968), pp. 160–161.

and trading of Slavs that led to the common root for the term "slave" throughout the European languages, not to mention its use as one word for slave in Arabic. Still, the Slavs like the Celts to the west paid the Norsemen back in kind. Their raids became more daring, especially after the decline of Viking power. In 1135, for example, Slavic raiders plundered the west-coast Swedish city of Kungahälla and took some seven thousand captives, all of whom were sold into slavery (although, as with so many other contemporary figures, this number seems greatly exaggerated).[22]

It is impossible to make any estimate of the volume of the European slave trade. Recent studies have tended to underplay the destructiveness of the Viking raids.[23] It is now commonly agreed, for example, that most of the raids into England were preliminary stages of settlement. It seems likely too that most of the slaves captured by the Scandinavians in their Western European raids were used by the raiders themselves, either in their home societies or as laborers in the regions they settled.[24] This is consistent with the best explanation for one of the Scandinavian numismatic mysteries, "the rarity of English and Frankish coins in the ninth century," which Sawyer finds "extraordinary."[25] His reasoning is that the English and Frankian coins gathered in plunder and as tribute were used as capital for settlement in these same areas, so that the coins never reached Scandinavia. In keeping with the Viking pattern of mixed raiding, slaving, plunder, and trade, a great many of these coins were also used to buy slaves to assist in settlement of the plundered areas.

This is reinforced by recent evidence on the carrying capacity of ninth- and tenth-century Viking ships.[26] The extravagant estimates of earlier scholars have been considerably scaled down: for long raiding voyages the average ship during the ninth century carried no more than thirty-two men. Ships in Scandinavian and other Western European home waters carried more, but not a great many more.

What we can conclude from all this is that in Western Europe the heaviest traffic in slaves involved short distances. Most slaves could have been captured and bought for the Scandinavian home market along the Scandinavian shores. Similarly, the slaves of the settlements in the British Isles could have come mainly from other parts of this area, although there might also have been a shunting system, essential to avoid excessive running away, similar to that of the indigenous slave-trading systems of West Africa and among the Indians of the northwestern coast of America. The "blue men" of Ireland and the "bright-fleshed," flaxen-haired boys and girls in the homosexual and heterosexual harems of the Muslim East must have constituted an insignificant fraction of the total volume of the European slave trade.

It is, as noted earlier, impossible to offer any sound estimate of the volume of the European slave trade during this period. The following guesses are at least suggestive. J. C. Russell has estimated the population of Western

Europe around 950 at 22.6 million.[27] My own estimate is that the lower limit of the slave population of Western Europe at this time was 15 percent of the total. This is highly conservative; in England a little over a century and a quarter later, when slavery was on the decline, the slave population averaged almost 10 percent of the total and in the western regions over 20 percent.[28] The slave population in parts of Scandinavia was likely to have been at its highest point during this period. The Icelandic settlement had reached its climax by about 930, creating a critical labor problem in both Iceland and Norway. In other parts of Western Europe the population decline during the first half of the tenth century would have intensified the demand for slaves.[29] Thus we can estimate the total slave population of Western Europe at this time at approximately 3.39 million. From what we know of slavery in the kind of societies that existed then in Western Europe, we can confidently assume that the slave population was both socially and biologically reproductive. The annual demand for slaves, in that case, would have existed only to meet the needs of new settlements and to compensate for social "leakage" due to manumission. This could not have exceeded 1 percent of the total slave population in any given year.[30] Hence the annual volume of the Western European trade could not have been greater than a total of 33,900 slaves at the middle of the tenth century. It is difficult to even guess at the volume of trade on the eastern routes, although it certainly must have been much greater. At the very least, then, the total volume of the trade at its height must have been between 67 and 68 thousand slaves annually.

THE TRANS-SAHARAN TRADE

The trans-Saharan slave trade lasted for almost thirteen centuries. As Philip D. Curtin has pointed out: "Islam and commerce was first associated in West Africa because Islam came across the Sahara carried by merchants, and contacts on the Sahel were between merchants."[31] From as early as the ninth century, highly profitable trade diasporas were established to take advantage of the demand in the North African and Mediterranean states for African slave laborers and African goods.

The four main routes to the Mediterranean coast (see Map 4) were from "Timbuktu to Morocco, Kano to Air and Ghadames, Bornu to Fezzan, and Wadai to Benghazi."[32] The slaves carried in this trade eventually found themselves in almost all the Islamic slaveholding societies of North Africa and the Middle and Near East, with the main areas of ultimate purchase being Egypt, Morocco, Libya, Tunisia, and Algeria, in that order. Estimates of the volume of the trade vary considerably. Curtin claims that it was particularly large during the last quarter of the seventeenth and first half of the eighteenth centuries,[33] while most others view the nineteenth century as the period of greatest traffic. The most systematic evaluation of the direct and

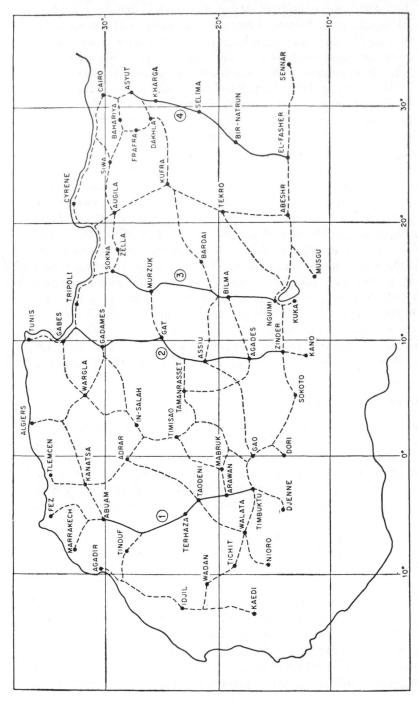

Map 4 The trans-Saharan slave trade. From George Peter Murdock, *Africa: Its People and Their Culture History* (New York: McGraw-Hill Co., 1959), p. 128. Copyright © 1959 by McGraw-Hill Book Company, Inc. Used with the permission of McGraw-Hill.

indirect statistical data is that of Ralph A. Austen, who estimates that between A.D. 650 and 900 some 450,000 persons were transported in this trade; between 900 and 1400 approximately 2.8 million persons; another 2.4 million were carried away between 1400 and 1800; and during the nineteenth century about 1.2 million.[34] It is striking that the total number of persons acquired in this trade is well over half those taken to the Americas in the Atlantic slave trade, and that when the East African total of five million persons is added, the total volume of African slaves acquired by Muslim masters is greater than the total acquired by Europeans in the Americas (even after making allowances for upward revision of Curtin's estimate of the transatlantic trade).

There were, however, important differences. The rate of acquisition was much slower in the trans-Saharan and East African trading systems; and the overall mortality rate was higher. However, the pattern of mortality also differed. The mortality rate en route in the Saharan trade was between 3 and 7 percentage points greater than that of the Atlantic trade, but the mortality rate before embarkation on the middle (transatlantic) passage was much greater than that involved in the enslavement of persons destined for the trans-Saharan passage. The proportion of men enslaved was also much larger in the Atlantic trade. And, not least of all, the experiences of Africans after reaching their final destinations were radically different in the two systems: in the Americas the slaves were mainly absorbed in capitalistic systems as a rural proletariat; in the Muslim world they were used largely as domestics (although one should be careful not to underestimate the nondomestic and rural uses of slaves in these societies).

The trade declined toward the end of the nineteenth century, under direct pressure on the suppliers by the European colonial powers in Africa and diplomatic pressure on the Muslim states of the Mediterranean and Turkey. However, the slave trade was never completely abolished. A UNESCO report on Mauritania in 1960 claimed that a quarter of one of the largest tribes of the country were slaves, many recruited through the trans-Saharan slave trade.[35] A much reduced but significant flow of slaves also found its way across the Sahara to the states of the Arabian peninsula, which continued to hold slaves right up to the 1960s and may, indeed, still have a few. In 1960 the trade to Saudi Arabia ran "from villages in the French Sudan, the High Volta, the Niger Provinces and the region of Timbuktu . . . across Africa to the coast at Port Sudan or Suakin and thence across the Red Sea by dhow to Lith, a port south of Djedda."[36]

THE TRANSATLANTIC TRADE

The last and greatest of all slave trading systems—the Atlantic—began as a diversion from the trans-Saharan and Mediterranean systems. The earliest

groups of Africans to land in the New World came from the Iberian peninsula, to which they had been delivered by the traders of the Mediterranean
system. And the earliest group of Africans coming directly from Africa was
recruited from the Senegambian coast, from traders primarily involved with
the trans-Saharan trade.[37] Very early, however, the demand for slaves in the
New World outgrew the capacity of these two ancient slave-trading systems.

Almost all the Western European peoples were involved at one time or
another with the enormously profitable transatlantic slave trade. The Scandinavian role, though not insignificant, was minor compared with the major
slave-trading states: the Portuguese, Dutch, English, and French.[38] Although Spain was an important consumer of the slaves carried by this traffic, its role in the actual commerce was small. This was not because of humanitarian considerations, but simply because its resources were stretched
too thinly controlling its vast empire in the Americas. The Portuguese were
the first to develop the trade on a significant scale, but by the end of the sixteenth century their monopoly was being seriously challenged, mainly by
the Dutch; by the end of the seventeenth century the English and French too
were heavily involved.

The slaves were recruited almost entirely from the western coast of
Africa, from the Senegambian region down to Angola (see Map 5). Except
during the last decades of the trade in the nineteenth century, the coastal
belt of tribes (extending no farther than two hundred miles inland) was the
principal source. Certain African tribes therefore lost far more people than
others. Up to the end of the eighteenth century most slaves came from the
tribes of the Guinea coast region, an area that, in spite of its large number of
tribes and languages, had marked underlying cultural uniformities. In the
next century most slaves came from southwestern Africa and, to a lesser extent, from Mozambique and central Africa.

A whole new subspecialty of historical studies has developed around the
problems posed by the demography of the slave trade, largely stimulated by
Philip Curtin's census.[39] Curtin's estimate of 9.5 million persons (plus or
minus 20 percent) imported to the New World by this traffic is widely used,
but most recent studies relying on archival data have tended to increase his
figure. It is safer to say that between 11 and 12 million Africans (plus or
minus 20 percent) were imported to the New World.

Figures 6.1 and 6.2 summarize the most striking features of this traffic.
Most slaves came to the New World during the eighteenth century. The
United States, which imported the smallest percentage of Africans, by 1825
had the largest proportion of slaves in the hemisphere. The Caribbean slave
societies, on the other hand, which imported over 40 percent of all Africans
brought to the New World, had less than 20 percent of the slave population
of the hemisphere by 1825. The difference is due to the remarkable rate of
natural increase of the U.S. slave population compared to the equally

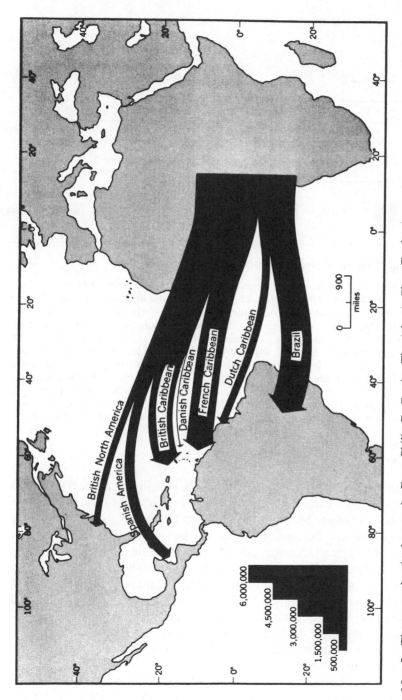

Map 5 The transatlantic slave trade. From Philip D. Curtin, *The Atlantic Slave Trade: A Census* (Madison: University of Wisconsin Press, 1969), p. 125.

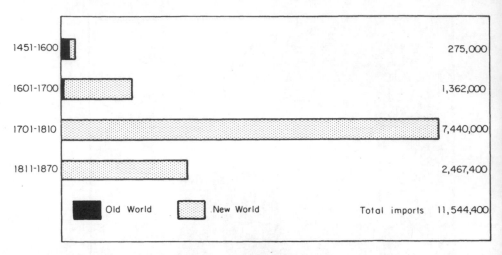

Figure 6.1   Imports of Negro slaves by time and region.

SOURCE: Adapted from Robert W. Fogel and Stanley L. Engerman, *Time on the Cross* (Boston: Little, Brown, 1974), vol. 1, p. 16. Revised estimates are based on Roger Anstey, "The Volume and Profitability of the British Slave Trade, 1761–1807," in Stanley L. Engerman and Eugene D. Genovese, eds., *Race and Slavery in the Western Hemisphere,* (Princeton, N.J.: Princeton University Press, 1974), pp. 3–31; Patrick Manning, "The Slave Trade in the Bight of Benin, 1640–1890," in Henry A. Gemery and Jan S. Hogendorn, eds. *The Uncommon Market: Essays in the Economic History of the Atlantic Slave Trade* (New York: Academic Press, 1979), pp. 107–141; D. Eltis, "The Direction and Fluctuation of the Transatlantic Slave Trade, 1821–1843," in Gemery and Hogendorn, *The Uncommon Market*, pp. 273–298; and Herbert S. Klein, *The Middle Passage: Comparative Studies of the Atlantic Slave Trade* (Princeton, N.J.: Princeton University Press, 1978).

remarkable rate of natural decrease of the Caribbean and other New World slave populations. These shifts in the proportions resulted from both higher death rates and lower birth rates in the Caribbean, although the latter was the more important. Better diet, shelter, and general material conditions account for the higher U.S. birth rate. Continued reliance on the slave trade partially explains the higher death rate in the Caribbean, since the larger proportion of Africans compared to Creoles meant a smaller number of women (less than 40 percent of the Africans brought over were women) and an older population. Differences in lactation practices between the two regions also account for the higher fertility rate of the American slaves; the greater fertility was also in part the result of a lower relative reliance on the slave trade in the United States.[40]

Regarding the organization of the slave trade itself and the experience of slaves on the middle passage, recent works suggest the following. First, there

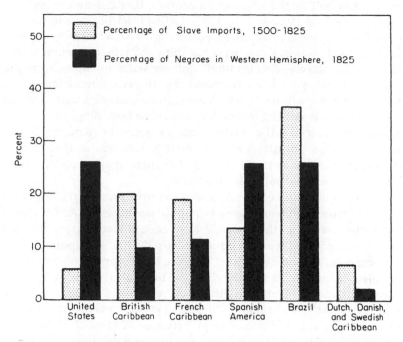

Figure 6.2   A comparison of the distribution of the Negro population (slave and free) in 1825 with the distribution of slave imports, 1500–1825.

SOURCE: Robert W. Fogel and Stanley L. Engerman, *Time on the Cross* (Boston: Little, Brown, 1974), vol. 1, p. 28 (© 1974 by Little, Brown and Co., Inc.). By permission of Little, Brown and Co.

was a remarkable similarity in the organization and functioning of the trade among all the European nations who participated in it. The most individualistic trading nation was Portugal, which relied less on the triangular pattern that linked Europe, Africa, and the New World into a single trading system, and more on a direct two-way traffic between southwestern Africa and Brazil from the second third of the nineteenth century on. Second, mortality rates were equally high among all the trading nations, one estimate of the average annual mortality rate during the eighteenth century being 13 percent. However, there was a general decline of this rate during the eighteenth century. An important recent finding is that "tight packing" of the slaves in the ships was not the major cause of mortality on board, but the length of time at sea, the quality of food and water during the passage, and epidemics and health conditions at the point of embarkation in Africa.[41] (This does not take account of mortality in Africa before embarkation, a point we shall return to later.)

The price of slaves in Africa averaged between 3 and 4 pounds sterling during the last half of the seventeenth century, rose during the eighteenth century to a peak of 18 pounds in 1740, declined sharply during the 1740s, then oscillated upward to about 17 pounds in 1770, when it began to fall again.[42] Richard Nelson Bean, who has done the most thorough work on these prices, has drawn several rather controversial conclusions from them. One is that there was a direct relation between price fluctuations and the varying volume of the trade. Wars, changing transport costs, and other political factors were the shifting forces that influenced both supply and demand for slaves: "In each case the market acted as would be expected from the basic maximization postulates of price theory. This was as true in the response of African slavers to the stimuli of changed market conditions as it was in the reactions of the British planters."[43]

Bean's second major conclusion is derived from the first. He argues that if the slave trade had created greater population losses in Africa than the rate of natural increase, there should have been a much larger rise in the price of slaves coupled with an equally sharp decline in exports. That, he claims, was contradicted by the joint increase in both price and volume. Not everyone would wish to so confidently draw this conclusion from price series data. Even more controversial is Bean's claim that the "European contact, even inclusive of the drain imposed by slave exports, may well have meant that there were more Africans alive in Africa in 1800 or 1850 than would have been the case had all Europeans left Africa strictly alone."[44] Curtin has pointed out that in Africa slaves were sold by their African middlemen captors "for much less than the cost of reproduction," and the appropriate economic model for estimating the effects of the trade is not the "fishery industry" preferred by Bean but "burglary."[45] Other later studies on the vexatious question of the effects of the trade on Africa strongly contradict Bean's extraordinary claim. Henry A. Gemery and Jan S. Hogendorn, in particular, have shown that even with the very best set of assumptions, West Africa suffered not only severe net economic losses but incalculable demographic and social losses. Millions of slaves, for instance, died between being captured and being forced on board the slave ships. In order that the slave masters of the Americas might acquire 11 to 12 million slaves, at least 24 million persons were originally enslaved in Africa.[46]

Internal Trade

Apart from the external slave trade, masters could acquire slaves by means of an internal slave trade. This type of trade, drawing on locally born slaves, was actually quite unusual in the history of slavery. In premodern slave systems, however advanced, there was a universal reluctance to sell locally born slaves. Such a sale was usually a form of punishment in most slaveholding societies, especially in the case of persistent runaways. In imperial

Rome, for example, some slaves were undoubtedly acquired in internal trading but the numbers involved were insignificant.[47]

It is only in the Americas that one finds internal slave trading on a significant scale. The two most notable cases are the United States South and Brazil during the nineteenth century, especially after the conclusion of the Atlantic slave trade. Recent studies indicate, however, that there was a minor internal slave trade in Jamaica after 1807.

With the expansion of cotton production and the corresponding shift of economic focus within the U.S. slave South from the northeastern to the central and southwestern states, an interregional movement of slaves took place. It has been estimated by R. W. Fogel and S. L. Engerman that between 1790 and 1860 some 835,000 slaves moved from the northeastern states of the Old South to the new Deep South. The same authors, somewhat more controversially, estimated that only 16 percent of these slaves were sold from one master to another, the remaining 84 percent actually moving with their masters.[48] The popular view that slaves were specially bred for this trade has been vehemently opposed, although it still has supporters.[49]

From very early on there was an internal slave trade in Brazil. It was of minor significance until 1850, when the abolition of the Atlantic slave trade combined with the rise of the coffee plantation stimulated an internal trade that according to Robert Conrad was "strikingly similar to that which developed in the United States under comparable circumstances."[50] The superficial resemblances were indeed remarkable. In the same way that the rise of cotton created a demand for slaves in the Deep South, so did the rise of coffee create a tremendous demand for slaves in the central and southwestern states of Rio de Janeiro, São Paulo, and Minas Gerais. In like manner slaves were shifted from the older northeastern states to the newly opened ones. Conrad goes so far as to argue that the drainage of slaves from the northeast of Brazil "compelled" farmers of this region "to make an earlier transition to a free-labor system" and encouraged them to challenge the whole system of slavery.[51]

This thesis, however, has been challenged by Herbert S. Klein, who argues that the interprovincial seaborne trade in Brazil transported only five to six thousand slaves annually during the 1850s, 1860s, and early 1870s; that the main function of this trade was to supply a limited number of skilled slaves from the northeast and extreme south to the south central states; and that this trade was simply not of sufficient volume to account for either the decline of slavery in the northeast or its increase in the central states.[52]

It is interesting to note that Klein's revisionist thesis is similar to that of Fogel and Engerman with respect to the American South. The two slave societies are still held by Klein to be similar in the pattern of internal slave trading, but in ways quite different from the traditional positions of Conrad and Frederick Bancroft.[53] The cliometricians have deemphasized the inter-regional movement of slaves; yet it is important to note that they have not proven (or attempted to prove) that there was not an important internal slave trade. Rather, it would seem that the internal slave trade was over-whelmingly intraprovincial or intrastate rather than interprovincial or inter-state. Unfortunately, interest has centered more on the problem of interre-gional movements than on internal slave trade regardless of the kinds of movement involved. Available work on both Brazil and the United States suggests that when intraregional trade is taken into account internal trading was indeed significant.

The scale of the internal slave trade was much smaller in the Caribbean, although the pattern was similar. The end of the British Atlantic slave trade in 1807 was followed by a small, insignificant interisland trade.[54] In the case of Jamaica, the internal trade was not a great deal more significant than the interisland trade. Between 1829 and 1932 only 4,838 slaves moved from one parish to another, amounting to only 1.5 percent of the total slave popula-tion. As in the United States there is no evidence of systematic breeding; most of the movements were to adjoining parishes, and most may not have involved sales. As in Brazil, most of the slaves who were moved interregion-ally were nonpredials, and the trade may have involved mainly a more effi-cient utilization of the skilled and domestic urban slaves.[55]

Bride and Dowry Payments

The other principal indirect means of acquiring slaves was through dowry and bride-payments. Slaves as bride-payments can be quickly dealt with, since this practice was confined to those preliterate tribes which circulated brides among groups against a countercirculating transfer of goods.[56] Where slaves existed they sometimes constituted a part of the bride-payment. What is surprising, however, is that the practice was not as common as one might have suspected among slaveholding peoples with bridewealth marriages. The Dahomeans, for example, had elaborate bride-payments but there is no mention of slaves in the list of goods presented as payment.[57] Livestock tended to occur far more frequently as a standard item throughout Africa. Sometimes the high cost of slaves explained their absence in the bride-pay-ment: among the Ibos the standard price of a female slave was one and a half times the bridewealth of the average maiden.[58] There were cases, how-ever, where the bride-price was considerably higher than the price of the slave, yet slaves were not mentioned as part of the bridewealth (for example, among the Duala of the Cameroons).[59]

For whatever reason, the use of slaves as bride-payments is attested in only a minority of slaveholding societies that had this custom. Among a few peoples it was an essential part of the bride-payment. For example, among the Mende, slaves "formed an invariable and important part of bride-wealth." In view of the fact that the bridewealth was high and slavery very important, a considerable number of slaves must have been acquired in this way.[60] Among the Tuareg, slaves—especially newly acquired ones—were often part of the bridewealth of their masters;[61] and among the predominantly patrilineal Wolof of Senegambia, it is curious that slaves acquired as bridewealth were inherited matrilineally, whereas bought slaves were inherited patrilineally.[62]

Perhaps the most dramatic case of the acquisition of slaves through bridewealth was that of the Nkundu of the Kongo, a primitive tribe among whom slavery was traditionally indispensable, not for economic reasons but because no marriage was truly legitimate until the bride-price was completed by the payment of the *bosongo* (which comprised, on average, two slave women, but in some cases as many as five to ten slaves).[63] "The strength of the marriage," goes a traditional Nkundu saying, "is to be found in the slave." It is also said that "by means of the *bosongo* the woman completely becomes the wife." The bosongo of the Nkundu is one of the most curious reasons in the history of the institution for the emergence of slavery on a significant scale.

Far more widespread was the practice of including slaves in the bridal dowry. The dowry, because it is found mainly among advanced peoples, figures as a mode of acquisition among all civilized slaveholding societies. In the ancient Near Eastern societies it must have been a significant means of acquiring slaves; it was the custom of the wealthy, especially in Babylon, to include several slaves in the dowry of their daughters. Slaves were included in the dowry in pharaonic Egypt; in India from ancient to modern times; among all the slaveholding peoples of ancient, medieval, and early modern Europe; and among all the slaveholding societies of the Americas.[64]

As with bride-payments, some very odd customs occasionally surround the use of slaves as dowry. In ancient Rome, being given as a dowry or pledge automatically made a man a slave.[65] Among the early Icelanders we find this curious law:

> A free woman engaged to be married was considered free from physical and other defects if she would bring a price not lower than that of a female thrall. But if it was found that she had such defects as would lower the price were she a female thrall, the punishment for the one who, with "knowledge of her defects, betrothed her to a man," was outlawry in the first degree.[66]

Slaves as Money

The acquisition of slaves as bride-payment or dowry is closely related to the use of slaves as money, and this constitutes yet another way in which slaves were acquired. Money, as is well known, has several functions: it is a unit of accounting or a standard of value, a method of payment, a medium of exchange, and a means of storing wealth. In primitive and archaic economies, as Karl Polanyi and his students have emphasized, "the various functions of money are institutionalized separately"—that is, one kind of object could be used as a unit of value, another for making payments, and so on. Multifunctional money is a very modern phenomenon.[67]

The interesting thing about slaves is that in many primitive and archaic societies they constituted the closest approximation to modern multifunctional money. In the ancient Near East, slaves were sometimes used instead of metal as a standard of value and a medium of payment for (among other things) brides, houses, and fines.[68] In Burmese society until a century ago, slaves "were the currency in which a husband was compensated for the violation of his wife—two slaves for a poor but free woman, four for the wife of a merchant, eight for that of a rich man, fifteen for that of a lesser mandarin, and so forth."[69]

In both pagan and Muslim Africa, slaves were often used as money. Among the Mende of West Africa, slaves were exchanged for bags of salt and cattle: "A single slave was worth from three to six cows and a man, woman or child, were all considered as one 'head' of money. This was equivalent, later in the century, in 1890, to 3 pounds sterling."[70] Slaves were similarly used in Yorubaland and parts of Central Africa.[71] Among Muslim traders slaves were commonly "a store of value, albeit one which medical hazards made extremely risky," as well as units of value and a common form of payment, especially of debts and fines.[72]

It was in early medieval Ireland and Iceland, however, that we find the most complex employment of slaves as money. In Ireland the *cumal*, or female slave, was the highest unit of value.[73] A cumal was equivalent to 6 to 8 *seoit*, and a *set* was worth between 3 and 8 cows. A cumal was also equivalent to 3 ounces of silver. It was the standard unit of value for fines. Thus in homicide cases the value of the life of a free man (the *eric* fine) was reckoned at 7 cumala. It perhaps is significant, however, that the honor price was reckoned and paid in other forms of money. The cumal, in addition, was used as a measure of the value of land. There has been some uncertainty in the past concerning whether the cumal was used as a method of payment, but Marilyn Gerriets has definitively established that the cumal did also serve this function of money.[74] Interestingly, the *mug*, or male slave, was never used as a unit of value, but was sometimes utilized as a form of payment. The use of the female slave as a form of money during medieval times strongly suggests that she played an important economic role in early pre-Christian Ireland, but declined in economic significance by the pre-Norman period, her role as money being a vestige of her former economic value.

With values of half a cumal frequently attested in the texts, it may be wondered just how half a human being was possible. There was no problem, of course, where the cumal was being used only as a unit of value: half a cumal would simply be interpreted in terms of, say, 1½ ounces of silver, or between a cow and a calf and 4 cows. But how was the problem handled if the cumal was also serving as a form of payment? A simple and elegant explanation has been offered.[75] In keeping with the pattern found in other tribal systems where slavery existed, the enslavement of women was rarely lifelong. The Irish therefore also reckoned the value of a cumal, in substantive terms, at 7 years labor by an able-bodied woman. Hence half a cumal would mean the payment of 3½ years labor by an able-bodied woman.

We have less information on early Iceland, but it is well established that female slaves were used as both units of value and forms of payment, and that, as in Ireland, silver and cows were also used as units of value. The equivalences were very precisely worked out by the Icelanders and did not differ significantly from those of the Irish. Thus: "1 very strong and big male thrall = 24 aurar = 24 cows; 1 average male thrall = 12 aurar = 12 cows; 1 female thrall (for concubine) = 12 aurar = 12 cows; 1 female thrall = 8 aurar = 8 cows."[76]

It may seem extraordinary that a human being should be used as money, and inhuman that the value she defined was only 8 cows. But in the comparative annals of slavery the Irish and the Icelanders placed a very high value indeed on their female slaves—as did the Danes, among whom an enslaved nun during the ninth century was valued at a horse with its gear, "not cheap," as Eric Oxenstierna correctly comments.[77] In sixteenth-century Burma, 40 Indian slaves was the going price for a horse.[78] In 1870, a normal year at the Kuka market on Lake Chad, a young adult man was worth the same as a good riding horse, although a young girl was worth a little more and a eunuch twice as much. However, in the glutted Bagirmi market of the Sudan two years later, women were being sold for 5 dollars; not long after, a cow was valued at 10 slaves, a young male slave at 6 chickens.[79] And as late as the third decade of the present century in the unadministered parts of northern Burma, especially in the triangular region, "slaves were so plentiful as to be worth no more than a few pigs."[80]

IN THE LAST three chapters I have employed several analytic categories and reported a number of new findings. The most fundamental distinction is between the means of enslavement and the means of acquisition. Past failures either to recognize or to consistently apply this distinction have led to considerable confusion regarding the sources and distribution of slaves. Many eminent and otherwise very cautious scholars, for example, have discussed the subject under categories such as "warfare," "trade," "kidnapping," "birth," and the like, without any apparent awareness of the nonexclusiveness of these categories. Invariably, discussions either imply (erroneously) that persons enslaved by means of warfare were directly acquired by the slaveholders of the victorious society, or, more frequently, they ignore the issue of the disposal of enslaved captives as noncontroversial.

With the aid of another distinction, between original and current means of enslavement, I have explored the relative contribution of prisoners of war and found that while enslavement by this means was generally important as an original means, it was unusual for it to rank as the most important current means of enslavement. For all but a small subset of significant slaveholding societies, birth was by far the major current means of enslavement. In this regard, the distinction between the social and biological reproductivity of a slave population has proved to be a useful analytic aid.

The most important substantive contribution of these three chapters has been the identification and illustration of the seven major rules of inheritance of slave status. No doubt future research will refine and add to these rules. Since no one previously has attempted to identify and systematically discuss them, it would be surprising if, in this first effort, all the important types have been exhausted and all the relevant issues explored.

In analyzing the means of acquisition, I have distinguished between direct and indirect means. Examination of the direct means has involved a reanalysis of the data on warfare and captivity. Contrary to conventional scholarly and popular opinion, my finding is that enslavement was not the normal fate of the vast majority of captives, even when captured or conquered by armies from societies with highly developed slave systems and a persistent demand for slaves. Slaughter, ransom, temporary imprisonment, colonization, impressment, and simple release were all at various times, separately or together, the more common fate of captives. Even during those special periods of history where most slaves in a growing large-scale slave society were enslaved as a result of captivity, most captives still did not suffer this fate. The vast majority of persons conquered or captured in battle by Greek armies during the classical period, or by Roman armies during the militaristic triumphs of the last three centuries before Christ, did not suffer enslavement. And the same was true of those who fell before the conquering armies of Islam.

Of special importance is my finding that it was unusual for a conquering group to attempt to enslave on a mass scale, on their home territory, the free members of a conquered population. Where such attempts were made, the long-term consequences were always disastrous.

Trade, we have shown, was next to birth the most important means of acquiring slaves. The other indirect means (bride and dowry payments and the use of slaves as money), though widespread, were minor compared with trading. A review of the five major slave-trading systems in human history disclosed many surprising parallels and historical continuities. What stands out most strikingly was the extraordinary centrality of the Mediterranean. This sea, with the nations that surround it, has consistently played a critical role in slave-trading systems, sometimes throughout their entire course.[81] The Mediterranean, central to the development of human civilization and lovingly celebrated in Euro-American historiography,[82] from the viewpoint of human oppression has been a veritable vortex of horror for all mankind, especially for the Slavic and African peoples. The relationship was in no way accidental.

7

The
Condition
of Slavery

HAVING EXAMINED how human beings were enslaved and acquired, we need now to analyze their fate. We want to know how slaves adjusted to their masters and to their new condition, and how masters used their power in the relationship with their slaves. We must inquire too into the way this relationship was accepted by the society at large. In short, we need to look at what factors determined the adjustment, treatment, and institutionalization of slaves.

The adjustment of the slave to his condition involved two basic kinds of relationships: that between master and slave and that between slave and community. Mediating these two relationships was a third, that between master and community. How the master treated the slave and how the slave responded depended, first, on factors intrinsic to the master-slave relationship. We may see these as the *private determinants* of the relationship. But the master, however independent he may have wished to be in his relations with his slave, needed his community to both confirm and support his power. The community, through its agents, wanted this support reciprocated, if only to safeguard the interests of its members. These constituted the *public determinants* of the master-slave relationship. Some sprang wholly from the nature of the community, independent of the master's position. Yet the relationship between the master and his community was never a static one. The master wanted to influence public attitudes and deflect attempts to interfere with his proprietary claims on his slaves. His ability to do so depended upon his power and influence; this itself was partly determined by the newfound importance he derived from possessing slaves.

Nor was the slave a wholly passive entity. He might, in relative terms, be powerless; but he always had *some* choice. He might react psychologically, play the slave, act dumb, exasperate. He might lie or steal. He might run away. He might injure or kill others, including his own master. Or he might engage in armed revolt. Barring all these, he might destroy his master's property by destroying himself. To be sure, only a small minority of slaves ever made such drastic choices. Most chose simply to behave with self-respect and do the best they could under the circumstances. Nevertheless, I know of no slaveholding societies in which some slaves at some times did not rebel in some manner. Even where the slave remained completely docile, the very totality of his master's power over him made his master dependent on him. While he might not have been a person of value, he was a thing of value—perhaps the only thing over which the master had true power. The master's whole manhood might have been invested in him. Parasitic domination was a real possibility wherever slavery existed, as we shall see in a later chapter.

LET US CONSIDER FIRST the factors that were intrinsic to the master-slave relationship. The most important of these was the use to which the slave was put. Slaves, of course, have performed every known task. However, there was usually a primary use for which they were acquired, and the condition of the slave was to a large extent determined by this purpose: they might have been acquired for prestige, political, administrative, ritual, sexual, marital, or economic reasons. It should be obvious that if slaves were acquired as secondary wives, concubines, or homosexual lovers, their material comfort (if not their peace of mind) generally would have been better than those acquired to perform agricultural or mining jobs. The primary use of the slave also determined whether he or she would be permitted to marry and rear a family. Whereas the denial of custodial power was an invariant attribute of the slave condition, in practical terms there was considerable leeway in the degree to which slave families were allowed to remain stable. There was little variation among slaveholding societies with respect to the sexual claims and powers of masters over female slaves: I know of no slaveholding society in which a master, when so inclined, could not exact sexual services from his female slaves. What did vary considerably was the protection of slave women, and of slave unions, from interference by third parties.

Where used as workers, the way in which slaves were integrated into the work force was another critical factor in determining their treatment. The fate of slaves on highly regulated latifundia or plantation-type farms differed radically from the lot of those incorporated as tenant farmers, and both differed from the kind of treatment experienced by household slaves or slaves of small family farmers.

Another important determinant was the mode of acquisition. In almost all slaveholding societies a distinction was made between the slave bought as an adult and the slave born in the household (or acquired as a child and brought up in the master's household). Ties of sentiment usually developed between the master (and his family) and the housebred slave. The uses to which slaves were put interacted in important ways with their mode of acquisition in determining their condition. This was particularly the case in advanced precapitalist slave systems. Thus in ninth-century Iraq there were many slaves by birth who served as menials in the households of their lords and were treated with indifference, while the slaves acquired as adolescents or even as young adults and trained as soldiers became the trusted aides and confidants of their masters. This was true of all the Islamic slaveholding societies, as we have already seen, but it was equally true of other areas. The king's slaves in Thailand; the eunuchs and other officials of many Roman, Byzantine, Chinese, and African courts; and the Greek tutors and clerks of Roman households are only a few examples of slaves acquired as adults who were much better treated and more highly regarded than slaves born in the household.

To take a celebrated example from the private life of Cicero, we learn from Susan Treggiari that slaves or freedmen such as his secretary Spintharus, his accountant Hilarus, and his letter carriers Aegypta and Phaetho were all warmly regarded by their master and, later, patron; while he demanded "loyalty, affection, and not uncommonly self-sacrifice" from them, he in turn "treated his *liberti boni* with some consideration for their own claims, with gratitude for their hard work and devotion, and with genuine affection."[1] Educated slaves who were useful to Cicero were all manumitted. At the same time Treggiari shows that "Cicero and other authorities rarely name the humbler slaves" and may not even have known their names, although several of them were born in his household. The litter bearers who remained loyal up to the moment of Cicero's assassination, the groom, cook, and maid of all work remain anonymous, and the only case of a laborer who was emancipated "is contemptuously dismissed as *'operarius homo'* after he played truant from his work, and is not named."[2]

Closely related to these two variables is a third: the residence of the slave. It cannot be assumed that all slaves by birth were based in the master's household, any more than it can be assumed that all bought slaves were lodged outside the household. Both assumptions tend to be true of small, kin-based societies, but even among tribal pastoralists and many chiefdoms, and certainly in more advanced societies, many slaves acquired at birth grew up in separate quarters. In pastoral societies slaves were often segregated in slave villages where they specialized in agriculture, while other slaves, many of them bought as adults, were kept as retainers in the household. This pattern held among all the early states of the Sudan, as well as the emirates of northern Nigeria, right up to the end of the nineteenth century.[3]

While it is certainly true that slaves of the household, whether born in the household or not, tended to assimilate their master's culture at a faster rate than those quartered elsewhere, it must not be assumed that the household slave was necessarily better treated than the tenant or field slave. Nonetheless, being in the household had the advantage of proximity to the comforts of the master, and the slave who won the master's favor was indeed privileged. In favor of the house-born slave too was the fact that in most precapitalist slave societies masters were reluctant to sell such slaves, hence they were spared one of the major risks of slavery, that of sudden and arbitrary disruption in their lives. Among the Mende, for example, it was considered shameful to sell a house slave.[4] Sanctions against such sales were not formalized among the more commercially advanced peoples. However, while an unscrupulous or financially embarrassed master could sell house-born slaves within his society, among a number of such advanced precapitalist cultures there were legal prohibitions on the sale of slaves abroad, especially house-born slaves. In both ancient Mesopotamia and Palestine slaves could not be sold to foreigners or gentiles. And in Egypt during Roman times, where we find considerable data on the *oikogeneis,* or house-born slave, the sale for export of house-born children of slaves incurred severe legal penalties.[5]

Proximity to the master also carried enormous risks and disadvantages. The slave was under the constant supervision of the master and therefore subjected to greater and more capricious punishment and humiliation than those housed elsewhere. This was particularly true of the female slave, who in every slaveholding society, from the most primitive to the most advanced, ran the additional risk of the jealousy and vengeance of the "free" women of the household, especially the master's senior wife. The famous adage should have run: hell has no fury like a free wife scorned in favor of a slave.

In contrast, the slave who lived apart, while materially more insecure and more exposed to the vindictiveness of free third parties, had a much greater measure of independence. Most slaves in most societies valued this partial "freedom" far more than the dubious material delights of the great house. There is abundant evidence from ancient Greece, Rome, and elsewhere that the condition most coveted by the slave was to be able to live on his own and hire himself out or otherwise provide for himself.

A fourth factor bearing on the condition of the slave was his original means of enslavement. Its direct influence, however, was weak. It was of far greater importance in its impact on the public determinants of the slave's condition, that is, in its effect on how the society at large responded to the slave and permitted his adjustment to public life and communal activities. A captive from a traditional enemy would clearly have more problems with the community at large than, say, a local person who fell into slavery as a result of destitution. Still, this cut both ways. In several societies, for example medieval Wales and the Toradjas of the central Celebes, the captive was regarded with less disrespect than the local person who had fallen into slavery, because the former was less responsible for his condition.

Another cluster of variables influencing the condition of the slave relates to his personal characteristics. To begin with race, we note that there were fifty-five societies in the world sample on which adequate data were available. Of these 75 percent had populations in which both slaves and masters were of the same mutually perceived racial group, 21 percent had populations in which masters and slaves were of different racial groups, and 4 percent had populations in which some slaves were of the same racial group as their masters while others were not. It has often been remarked that slavery in the Americas is unique in the primary role of race as a factor in determining the condition and treatment of slaves. This statement betrays an appalling ignorance of the comparative data on slave societies. A great deal, of course, depends on what one means by race. I take the racial factor to mean the assumption of innate differences based on real or imagined physical or other characteristics. In these terms, there have been numerous slaveholding societies where race was socially important; it is not at all obvious, though, how race influenced the condition of slaves.

Throughout the Islamic world, for instance, race was a vital issue. The light-skinned Tuareg and related groups had decidedly racist attitudes toward the Negroes they conquered.[6] Throughout the Islamic empires, European and Turkish slaves were treated quite differently from slaves south of the Sahara Desert.[7] In pre-European Malaysia, the Arab rulers viewed the conquered native population with utter contempt.[8] In Han and later China, the darker and physically distinct border peoples were considered racially inferior to the heartland Chinese; not only were they considered natural slaves, but their harsh treatment was tolerated whereas such treatment of a truly Chinese slave would be punishable by law.[9] The border peoples, however, responded in kind. As late as the early twentieth century the Lolos of Taliang Shan kidnapped and enslaved Han Chinese even though they were under the sovereignty of China. In a remarkable inversion of racial stereotype the Lolos called their upper-class members "black Lolos" and the subject population "white Lolos." White skin, so highly prized among the Han Chinese, was despised by the swarthy black Lolos and became a mark of servility and a way of identifying the Han slaves.[10]

Among the medieval Scandinavians, where blond hair, white skin, and blue eyes were the somatic ideal, the stereotype of the thrall was so consistently different that one is tempted to think that most of their slaves came from the darker European or even Asian peoples (although we know that this was not the case): "The thralls were said to be ugly. The thrall mentioned in the *Rígspula* had swarthy skin, a hideous countenance, and a flat nose."[11] Foreign slaves who conformed to the Icelandic racial ideal were more favorably regarded. This, for example, was true of Freystein, a thrall belonging to Thorkel Gaetisson: "He was neither ugly nor hard to manage like other thralls, but, rather, gentle and of good manners and more handsome than almost anyone else, wherefore he was called Freystein the Fair." More important than the color of their skin, however, was the belief that thralls as a group were innately inferior in mental qualities and other personal attributes. This is well illustrated by the story of Hjor, the Norwegian king, and his wife Ljufvina, a Russian princess whom he had captured. Ljufvina gave birth to twins but did not like them because they were swarthy. She therefore exchanged them for Lief, a lighter-skinned child of her bondswoman by a thrall. The king, however, disliked Lief, finding him lacking in manliness. One day the queen asked a poet to evaluate the three children as they played together. He immediately recognized the nobility of the twins and the slave origins of Lief, whereupon the queen took back her twins.[12]

It is not true either, as is so often claimed, that race was not an issue in the classical world. Although it was certainly of less importance than in the modern Americas or parts of the Islamic world, it did operate in a fairly significant way. We have already observed that in Greece and Rome slaves came from almost every racial group; and "Ethiopians," as most Africans were called, were very much present. Nor should one underestimate the somatic differences between the lighter, blue-eyed, northern slaves and their darker, curly-haired, brown-eyed, Roman masters. The important question, of course, is not the mere presence of physical differences but their sociological significance for Greeks and Romans. Certainly, when one considers the striking emphasis the Greeks placed on physical beauty in both sexes, especially males, it would be sociologically unlikely that somatic factors did not figure in their treatment of slaves. A beautiful young boy slave who came close to the Greek physical ideal would almost certainly end up as the homosexual lover of his master. Physically attractive women and less "virginal" but still pretty boys ran a far greater risk than their less handsome counterparts of being forced into the lucrative prostitution trade in which many Greek and Roman masters engaged.[13]

Those who, to Greco-Roman eyes, were less physically attractive races, were spared such fates; but aversion to them may well have been expressed in other ways. Frank M. Snowden, Jr., is right in claiming that the racial factor weighed less heavily for blacks in antiquity than it did for those in the Americas, but he exaggerates when he suggests that there was little racial prejudice.[14] There is not much literary evidence to go on, but if the occasional asides of the satirist Juvenal are reliable, strong racial antipathy was not uncommon in Rome.[15] From the portrayals of blacks in sculpture and painting with their features persistently caricatured as bestial and grotesque, it seems safe to conclude that Negro features were not an asset in the slave-holding societies of the Greco-Roman world.[16]

Racial difference from the master did not, of itself, always work against the slave. Among the Arabs and Ottoman Turks white slaves were specially prized.[17] Men as well as women of different races were recruited for sexual purposes.[18] In nineteenth-century Egypt, Caucasian slave women were the most prized members of the harems of the upper classes.[19] Nor was a black skin always a disadvantage. In imperial China and Islamic India, black slaves were valued for their exotic appearance and fetched the highest prices.[20] And young black pageboys were the rage in the boudoirs of eighteenth-century England and France, although what they did with their leisured mistresses as they grew older is best left to the imagination.[21]

More important than race, and more widespread in its repercussions, was the ethnic difference between master and slave. Through its interaction with this variable the means-of-enslavement factor could be most effective: prisoners of war were more apt to be of a different ethnic and religious group than slaves originally obtained by other means. But this was only a tendency: wars were often fought between peoples who are ethnically close.

This raises the interesting question of the reluctance of peoples to enslave those with whom they shared a common culture and felt a sense of ethnic identity. From the comparative data on this problem we may draw two conclusions. First, it was simply not the case that slavery within the ethnic group never existed—that, as Henri Lévi-Bruhl claimed, endoservitude was an impossibility.[22] Slaves were recruited from within the community in a significant number of slaveholding societies. There was, nonetheless, a universal reluctance to enslave members of one's own community, hence the need to redefine them as outsiders. Yet the ethnic group is often wider than the community or the state, and where such cross-societal ethnicity existed it is useful to inquire whether there was a reluctance to enslave fellow ethnics. The data suggest that while there was indeed such a reluctance, different groups responded to the dilemma in different ways. The most common response was either to kill or to ransom or sell elsewhere-enslaved fellow ethnics, but not to enslave them. Upper-class black Lolos were always killed when captured by fellow Lolos in their intraethnic skirmishes.[23] The agricultural Vai of West Africa were constantly at war with one another. Before the European demand for slaves on the coast, Vai captives were always either killed or ransomed, and only the defeated group's slaves or non-Vai subjects were taken into slavery. With the European demand for slaves on the coast, Vai captives routinely were sold there.[24] Among the Tuareg there was a carefully observed agreement that fellow Tuaregs when captured would either be released or ransomed and only Negro captives would be enslaved.[25] The ancient Greeks clearly agonized over the issue and were generally loath to enslave fellow Greeks from other states, but where Greeks from hostile states were taken in war and were not ransomed, they were enslaved.

What all these choices amounted to was a distinct class bias in the enslavement of fellow ethnics. Upper-class and wealthy persons from hostile states, tribes, or clans were usually ransomed or killed. The fate of lower-class or less prosperous persons was more varied: where an external market existed, they were sold away from the region; otherwise they were either killed (especially among less advanced peoples) or were reluctantly enslaved. Among classless, acephalous, slaveholding peoples intraethnic slavery was rarely prohibited.[26]

While the ethnic factor was important in determining who became enslaved, it had surprisingly little influence on the treatment of slaves. Data were obtained on fifty-seven of the slaveholding societies in the sample of world cultures. In 75.4 percent slaves and masters were of different ethnic or tribal groups; in 15.8 percent the two were of the same ethnic group; and in 8.8 percent some slaves were from the same group as their masters, while others were from other ethnic groups. Ethnicity did not significantly correlate with any of the variables that attempt to measure the treatment and condition of slaves.

Another attribute of slaves that influenced their condition was gender. It should not be assumed that female slaves were always acquired primarily for sexual purposes. Among most of the more developed slaveholding societies of Africa, women—both free and slave—played a major role in food production. Even where the traditional female role was minor, slave women were utilized as farmers. For this reason sex was not as critical a factor as might be imagined, and the sex ratio of the slave population related to the overall treatment of slaves in a wholly unexpected way, as we shall see. Regardless of treatment, women were more easily assimilated into the community than men, for reasons examined earlier.

Skill also played a part in determining the condition of the slave. The captive who possessed skills that were in short supply in his master's community, or the slave of the house who was trained into such skills, was obviously more valued by his master and was likely to have been much better treated. In many slaveholding societies slaves were acquired with the specific purpose of introducing skills to the slaveholding group. Slaves who knew how to carve totem poles, for example, were greatly prized among the Tlingit and were often hired out to individuals who were indifferent carvers.[27] Greek society came to rely heavily on skilled craftsmen for its urban industries, and this fact, more than any other, determined the character of Greek slavery (not to mention its overall economy).[28] The same was even more true of Rome, where skilled and literate slaves came to dominate not only urban industries, but education, the arts, theater, and literature.[29]

And perhaps to an even greater degree the same held for the Islamic empires, especially in their early periods. According to Samuel S. Haas, slaves were "the leading elements" in the cultural transformation of the Islamic peoples between the period of Muhammad and the fourteenth century. Apart from their role in politics and warfare, slaves "exerted strong influence in the realms of public administration, religion, arts and crafts, music, poetry, grammar and learning in general."[30]

Many of the striking similarities between Greco-Roman and Islamic slavery derive from the reliance on skilled slaves—features such as the high incidence of manumission, the urban character of the institution, and the absence of any strong tendency to impose caste attributes on the slave or freedman populations.

Even where slaves were not a dominant part of the economy, the skills they introduced could have major implications for the particular culture. Toward the end of the fifteenth century, as an example, many new technologies were introduced to Europe via Italy by Asian slaves, including the vertical-axle windmill, the hot-air turbine, and a new type of governor.[31]

While the possession of a skill in great demand usually worked to the benefit of the slave, this was not always the case. Specialists of various sorts in Africa and other parts of the precapitalist world were often despised and feared and constituted an outcaste group. Slaves with such skills, while valued economically, would naturally suffer the special contempt shared by all those who practiced their craft.[32]

Another important variable determining the treatment of slaves was the relative size of the slave population. The relationship is both interesting and complex and will be discussed at some length shortly.

Two other independent variables are worth mentioning, to conclude this portion of the discussion. One is the level of absenteeism among slave owners. My earlier study of slavery in Jamaica showed that one of the major factors determining the condition of the slaves in this large-scale system was the high level of absenteeism among masters with large holdings.[33] In exploring whether the same held for precapitalist slave systems, I found, first, that genuine absenteeism existed in only a small proportion of all slave societies: 6 percent of those in the Murdock sample of world cultures, and no more than 10 percent of all societies with significant levels of slavery. Among the economically less advanced peoples, genuine absenteeism existed mainly among pastoralists such as the Somali, certain Arab tribes, and the Manchu.[34]

It is important to distinguish between absenteeism proper and the simple living apart of the master class, which we find in those situations where slaves were employed as tenant farmers. A considerable number of small-scale precapitalist societies utilized slaves in such tenant settlements: most of the Germanic tribes who kept slaves,[35] and many African groups such as the Tuareg,[36] the Ashanti,[37] the Sherbro,[38] and the Mende. What Kenneth Little says of these satellite slave villages among the Mende holds for all the others, that "legally speaking the slaves could be described as tenant settlers."[39] The Hausa were a borderline case, with their vast slave villages some three thousand strong. Most of these comprised enslaved tenant farmers, but several were organized along more formal lines, with direct supervision that brought them closer to the latifundic pattern.[40] I. M. Diakanoff's term, "pseudo-latifundic," used to describe some kinds of large farms manned by enslaved tenant farmers in the ancient Near East, is highly suggestive though problematic.[41]

Whether the owner was a genuine absentee or not, the tenant-farming arrangement usually worked to the benefit of the slaves; they controlled the means of production, usually organized their own schedule of work, and had a fair degree of autonomy in conducting their personal lives. The impact of absenteeism only became significant when it occurred in combination with a latifundic or plantation type of socioeconomic organization, or with large-scale mining. Although the combination was infrequent, when it arose, the consequences were invariably disastrous for the lives of the slaves. The most notable cases in the precapitalist world were the Laurium mines of Athens during the fifth century B.C.; southern Italy and Sicily during the period of the late republic and early empire; the slave system of the dead lands of lower Iraq during the Abbasid caliphate, especially during the late eighth and early ninth century A.D.; many of the slave estates of Visigothic and Muslim Spain; the Italian slave plantations on the Mediterranean islands during the late medieval and early modern periods; the royal slave plantations of nineteenth-century Dahomey, West Africa; the Arab-owned absentee slave farms of nineteenth-century coastal East Africa; and in the Orient the large slave estates of the city-based slave owners of Korea during the Koryŏ and, to a lesser extent, the early Yi periods. It is in these and the slave plantations of the Indian Ocean colonies, the Banda Islands of Indonesia, the Mascarene Islands of the Indian Ocean, eighteenth-century South Africa, and the modern Americas that the spiritual, social, and material condition of the slaves reached its lowest level.

Finally, a negative finding is worthy of note, if only because it was given such prominence in the work of the early comparative students of slavery, especially H. J. Nieboer. From the emphasis placed on the classification of societies according to their dominant mode of subsistence (hunter-gatherers, fishers, pastoralists, agriculturalists) one would believe this variable to be important in accounting for variations in the treatment of slaves. My own analysis suggests that mode of subsistence had no effect whatever on the way in which slaves were treated.

LET US NOW EXAMINE more precisely the influence of these independent variables on a select number of factors that reflect the treatment of slaves by their masters and other nonslave persons.

The Peculium

In all slaveholding societies the master had nearly exclusive proprietary claims and powers over the person, labor, possessions, and progeny of his slaves. The fundamental feature of slavery, in law, was the fact that the slave could not be a proprietor: he or she was, quintessentially, a property-less person. From this fundamental disability flowed, both in legal and in socioeconomic terms, all the other manifold disabilities of the slave.

However, it is also true that in all slaveholding societies the slave was allowed a *peculium*. The peculium may be defined as the investment by the master of a partial, and temporary, capacity in his slave to possess and enjoy a given range of goods. The peculium differed from genuine property in that, first, it never included *all* the proprietary capacities. The master always reserved a claim on the possessions of the slave. The slave, however, was allowed the usufruct of the possessions in question and could exercise certain powers and privileges over them in his relation to all third parties. In rare cases such powers and privileges may even have extended to the master, although never to the point of denying the master's ultimate claim on the possessions. The fact that the master reserved this ultimate claim meant, in theory, that the slave was not permitted to dispose of the peculium. Practice invariably followed legal precept here. Yet masters often gave their slaves permission to dispose of the less important movables in the peculium, as well as some of the income generated from any capital assets. Slaves were also frequently allowed to trade and engage in business, using their peculium if the objective was to enlarge it.

The peculium was always a temporary possession. This too was implied in the claim on the property reserved by masters in all slaveholding societies. The usufruct could be withdrawn at any time, but the nearly universal tendency was for the slave to enjoy it for the course of his lifetime. On his death the possessions reverted to the master, who reassigned the peculium to whichever slave he wished. Usually it was in his best interest to reassign it to a descendant or kinsman of the slave, but I know of no slave society in which slaves had a recognized power or privilege to endow legacies or to inherit them.

There was considerable variation among slaveholding societies in the objects over which possession might be given a lifetime usufruct. Where slaves worked the land in allotted parcels, it was understood that this was only for their keep and for the benefit of their masters. They were usually allowed to include in the peculium what remained from the produce of the land after they had provided for themselves and their masters, but the land itself was almost never considered theirs. Of course, in most lineage-based societies land itself was not part of the exclusive property of a single individual: even nonslave persons had only a usufructory claim on it. The difference between the slave and the nonslave was that the nonslave was usually entitled by birth to such a usufruct, whereas the slave used it only at the pleasure of, and in the interest of, his master.[42]

Occasionally one finds what appear to be exceptions to the general prohibition of the inclusion of land in the peculium. The two most striking cases are Korea during the Koryŏ period and Russia during the sixteenth and early seventeenth centuries. Closer inspections of these two cases, however, raise questions about whether they were indeed exceptions. Ellen Unruh, who discusses the Korean case,[43] tells us that "by mid-Koryo, slaves appear to have been permitted to own and dispose of property, i.e. land," and she rightly finds the practice "unusual." She argues that to assume that the ownership of land "negates the slaveness of the Korean slave" is to adopt an ethnocentrically Western view of both slavery and liberty. "Has materialism so warped our thinking," she asks, "that liberty is interpreted as the liberty to make money and own property?" The important point, she observes, is that "slaveness has a moral, not a material, connotation." What was objected to in Korean law and practice was not the simple ownership of land but the ends to which the slave directed such ownership. If he used his possession to acquire the trappings of an honorable person and to deny his inherent baseness, then the law came down on him with all its force.[44]

Our suspicions are reinforced when we examine the second supposed exception. Richard Hellie observes that some slaves in Muscovy "were allowed to own other slaves, landed estates and urban property."[45] However, only a small minority of slaves—what he calls "elite slaves"—were so privileged (2.4 percent). These slaves constituted a managerial class for the landowning elite, and their existence was the direct result of the law code of 1550 that stewards had to be slaves. Hellie speculates that "they provided second-level managerial and other highly skilled talent in a society in which people of high status were unwilling to subordinate themselves to anyone else." It is questionable whether these persons were, strictly speaking, slaves. Most of them were so-called registered slaves (*dokladnoe*). Hellie lists seven categories of slaves, only the first two of which were "hereditary" and "full" slaves. By implication the registered slaves were neither, which automatically excludes them from the group of persons who are the object of this study. Most so-called slaves in Muscovy were "limited-service contract slaves" or indentured servants. Here is another transitional situation, in which the demands for a more flexible labor force at both the managerial and working-class levels were met by an adaptation of traditional patterns of bonded labor. The registered slaves of Muscovy were really bonded retainers, a temporarily nonfree but strictly nonslave group substituting for the free managerial class which Russia, in its slow and painful transition to capitalism, was reluctant to encourage. Significantly, there is no mention of "full" or hereditary slaves owning land. We must conclude that, like Korea, a case has still to be made that this was an exception to the general tendency of slaveholding groups to deny slaves possessions in land as part of their peculium.

The restriction on land was less of a problem for slaves in the urban sectors of the commercially more advanced slaveholding societies. Slaves in the ancient Near East, in the Greco-Roman economies, all over the Islamic world, and in medieval Europe performed every kind of economic activity that free men engaged in—and often did much better financially than the latter. Gifted slaves sometimes earned vast sums as bankers and agents of their masters in all these societies, and in many of the city-states of nineteenth-century West Africa. In sixteenth-century Seville skilled blacks engaged in all the artisan crafts, and their competition was deeply feared by the city's guilds.[46]

While land was generally excluded from the peculium, slaves were almost always included. The *servus vicarius* (slave of a slave) was a universal occurrence. I know of no slave society in which slaves who could afford them were denied the purchase of other slaves. The fact may seem surprising at first, but on further reflection it ceases to be so. If slaves were the extension of a man's person and honor, so were his slaves' slaves. There could be few greater testimonies to a man's power than the fact that even his slaves possessed slaves. At the same time, nothing more confirmed the loyal slaves' acceptance of the condition of slavery and their own enslavement to the master than their willingness to own slaves themselves. The servus vicarius was the best way of making it clear to all that slavery was part of the natural order of things. Undoubtedly, too, the servus vicarius fulfilled for the slave a function more akin to the modern psychological usage of the term "vicarious": the wealthy slave vicariously experienced the status of his master in his relationship with the slave. While this undoubtedly was good for the psychological relationship between the owner of the vicarius and his own master, it was not so good for the vicarius who, often as not, was very much the scapegoat. If we set aside such unusual cases as the vicarii of the imperial slaves of Rome and the Arab caliphates (to be considered in Chapter 11), no condition on earth was less enviable than that of the servus vicarius.

In theory, it would seem that slaves should not be able to redeem themselves with earnings from their peculium: the master, after all, was being paid for one part of his property (his slave) with another (his slave's peculium). In practice, most slaveholding societies found ways of getting around this nice legal problem.[47]

Societies varied in their rules pertaining to the disposal of the peculium when the slave was sold or when he bought himself, although there was not much of a problem in practice. In many premodern societies the slave who accumulated a peculium worthy of the master's notice was not likely to be a slave the master would want to sell. The surest sign anywhere of a "good and loyal slave" was a slave with a large peculium. And where the slave bought his own freedom, it usually cost him his entire peculium. If a slave had saved for years to purchase his freedom, it would hardly have been in his interest to save beyond the sum and time when he could redeem himself. In Rome, where unusual cases were most likely to occur, the slave's peculium usually went with him when he was sold, "and so it would on manumission *inter vivos* unless expressly withheld."[48]

Recognition of the slave's peculium was very nearly universal. Societies varied only in the degree to which the peculium was legally or socially sanctioned. In the ancient world the Cretan state of Gortyna is held by some to be unusual in legally sanctioning the peculium (although the interpretation of Gortyn laws and the extent to which they were actually applied is highly problematic).[49] Less ambiguous was the West African case of Ashanti during the period reconstructed by Rattray (the late nineteenth and early twentieth centuries). He tells us:

> Slaves could and often did amass considerable wealth and attain to considerable power. A master encouraged his slave and helped him in every way to do so, because ultimately everything the slave possessed went to the master. A master could not deprive his slave of his self-acquired property. An Ashanti proverb sums up the situation tersely, thus ... A slave may eat to repletion while his master remains hungry, but what the slave has, is, after all, only wind in his stomach.[50]

In an earlier work Rattray observes: "Lands were also granted to a favorite household slave for life with reversion to the donor, but the slave's children, as long as they served the household, were often in practice allowed to continue to occupy and use the land after the death of the original grantee."[51] The Ashanti master in exceptional cases also allowed a slave child to inherit.[52]

The practice is easily explained in the case of the Ashanti. The society was matrilineal, but patrilineal blood ties (the *ntoro* principle) remained strong. A slave child by a slave woman had no formal matrilineal connections. Every "free" Ashanti dreaded the prospect of extinction of his line and his household. If the master had no matrilineal heirs except a slave child, he preferred to allow the slave to inherit over patrilineal blood relations; the slave, "having no *abusa*, or in other words no other home, when he came into an inheritance carried on the old master's home at the same spot and the rites of honor of the departed spirit."[53]

The universality of the peculium is not difficult to explain. It solved the most important problem of slave labor: the fact that it was given involuntarily. It was the best means of motivating the slave to perform efficiently on his master's behalf. It not only allowed the slave the vicarious enjoyment of the capacity he most lacked—that of owning property—but also held out the long-term hope of self-redemption for the most diligent slaves. The master lost nothing, since he maintained an ultimate claim on the peculium, and he had everything to gain. The ancients recognized this as much as the masters of all other large-scale slave systems. Varro, writing in the first century B.C. in his treatise on agriculture, advised that "the [slave] foremen are to be made more zealous by rewards, and care must be taken that they have a bit of property [peculium] of their own, and mates from among their fellow-slaves to bear them children; for by this means they are made more steady and more attached to the place. Thus, it is on account of such relationships that slave families of Epirus have the best reputation and bring the highest price."[54]

Manipulable statistical data on the peculium were obtained by separating the societies in the sample of world cultures into two groups: those in which the peculium was recognized, strongly sanctioned, and encouraged, and those where it was weakly sanctioned, had no status in law, and was not especially encouraged. Of the forty-four societies on which there were adequate data, 70.5 percent fell into the first group and 29.5 percent into the second. Cross-tabulation of this variable with others showed that the minority of societies that did not sanction or encourage the peculium were the most brutal in the overall treatment of slaves. Masters could kill slaves with impunity to a greater degree, and they were more inclined to provide for the slave rather than to allow the latter to provide for himself. Crimes against slaves either went unpunished or were punished to a far lesser degree than crimes against nonslaves.

Neither race, ethnicity, nor size of the servile population relate in any significant way to attitude toward the peculium. There is, however, some association with the prevailing mode of subsistence. Fishing communities were most inclined to curtail the peculium, while pastoralists were most likely to recognize and encourage it. In fishing communities slaves customarily were used to perform menial tasks under the direct supervision of their masters. The basic resource, fish, was acquired without a great deal of effort or complex planning and execution. There was therefore little need to motivate the slave. In pastoral societies, on the other hand, slaves were usually kept as agricultural specialists and often left for long periods on their own. There was an urgent need to motivate them to work on their own, and the peculium with its prospect of eventual self-redemption was always the best way of doing so.

Marriage and Other Unions

It has been claimed by an eminent student of comparative slavery that marriage is incompatible with chattel slavery.[55] I cannot fully agree with this view. The compatibility of marriage and slavery depended on the nature and sociological significance of wedlock in a given society as well as the number of marital arrangements permitted. If a society had only one kind of marriage, and the institution was defined in such a way that it automatically implied the legitimacy of progeny and the custodial powers of parents, then by definition marriage would be incompatible with slavery. Many societies in both the premodern and modern world, however, recognize a range of permissible unions between adults. Some of these may be quite consistent with slavery; others may not be. It is best to remember that, sociologically, marriage and the family are closely related but different institutions; the former regulates the sexual unions of adults, the latter provides the framework within which children are born and reared. Usually marriage legitimizes not just the cohabitation of the parents but the status of their children. Still, there are many notable exceptions among so-called free populations. In Islamic societies the children of concubines are "legal" children even though the parents remain unmarried, and the same is true in many other societies. In Jamaican and Puerto Rican law all children are legal even though most unions are illegal. Hence primary familial bonds may be initiated and are legal where there is no marriage among parents. And, conversely, it is possible for legally married parents to produce children who are not legally their own: this is exactly what happens in a matrilineal society where a person is the legal child of his mother's brother and not of his biological father, in spite of the fact that the latter is legally married to his mother.[56]

The range of options open to both masters and slaves was wide, and no simple assertion concerning the incompatibility of slavery and marriage is tenable. In 97 percent of the societies falling in the sample of world cultures, masters recognized the unions of slaves. In not a single case, however, did such recognition imply custodial powers over children. The Mende is one of the few lineage-based societies in which masters were found to discourage unions. According to John J. Grace: "Some owners were so afraid of the growth of family feeling among their *nduwonga* that they forbade a slave woman to have successive children by the same man."[57] Even where marriages among slaves were not recognized, it was unusual to find such deliberate discouragement of regular unions in the precapitalist world. The Laurium mines of Attica during the fifth century B.C., the slave latifundia of late republican Rome (although, as we learn from Varro, foremen were allowed to have common-law wives), and the dead lands of lower Mesopotamia in late ninth-century Iraq were notable—and exceptional—instances of this attitude among the more advanced of the precapitalist slave systems.

In most lineage-based societies the slave either paid no bride-price, or the bride-price (usually well below that of a free woman) was paid by his master. Invariably the slave had to seek the permission of his master before taking a wife, especially when she belonged to another master. This was so even among the Ashanti, where slave marriage was strongly sanctioned.

The Islamic legal traditions are among the most liberal in the precapitalist world. Most authorities deny that an adult male slave could contract a marriage of his own volition, but if a slave was a Muslim he was considered legally competent to marry after receiving his master's permission. The master reserved the power to compulsorily marry off his male or female slaves in all Islamic traditions except that of the Mālikis. In this tradition adult male slaves could marry of their own accord; however, the master reserved the power to ratify such unions and to terminate them by repudiation. Male slaves were allowed two wives in most traditions and were permitted to divorce them.[58] Because slaves could not acquire the legal status of spouses, they could not in the full sense commit adultery or fornication. For this reason they were spared the death penalty in such offenses. At the same time, fornication could not be committed against them. Spouses did not have custody over their children.[59]

One should be careful not to idealize the Islamic situation. Even though it was better than most arrangements for slaves, it still left a great deal to be desired. In all Islamic societies the slave woman was at the sexual mercy of her master, in both law and practice. The law forbade masters to break up families, but where economic factors required it, masters found all sorts of ways of getting around such religious prohibitions. A few Islamic states even discarded the religious precepts altogether. The Somali master reserved and frequently exercised his power to sell the mother separately from her children, and of course "the morality of the slave women was not safeguarded by any law."[60]

Let us consider some typical cases from the non-Islamic world, moving as usual from less to more advanced societies. Among the Ashanti a male slave was allowed to pay the *asida,* or bride-price, and when he did so he could claim damages for adultery against anyone. What is more, if the master was the culprit, he paid twice the usual amount and was publicly humiliated for so debasing himself.[61] Even so, the children of slaves belonged to the master unless the mother was a free woman.[62] The laws of Hammurabi say a good deal about slaves, but almost nothing about the marriages of slaves to each other. The laws only touch the subject briefly in reference to the marriage of certain classes of official slaves to free women.[63] Other evidence strongly suggests that family ties were not always respected and that although the sale of families as a unit was "not uncommon" there was nothing to prevent ruthless masters from selling spouses separately.[64] The documents on the Third Dynasty of Ur, as analyzed by Bernard J. Siegel, imply that while marriages between slaves were "commonplace," the slave did not have the right to protest the sale of his or her child by the owner, "in other words [that] he did not have the *potestas* over his own children."[65]

In imperial China the slave family, in particular the slave wife, was protected against third parties but not against the economic or sexual demands of the unscrupulous master. Slaves were considered bound to each other by the laws of filial piety, and masters were encouraged not to separate them. It is revealing, however, that the slave family was typically much smaller than the average nonslave family and that slaves had no surnames.[66]

William Westermann asserts that slaves in Athens who lived apart could marry and found their own households, but this is sheer speculation;[67] moreover, such slaves constituted only a minority of all slaves. Roman legal theory, which probably did not depart much from practice, certainly influenced most subsequent slaveholding societies in the Western world. Slave marriages were not recognized in law; slaves could not establish *connubium,* only *contubernium,* and the master had the power to interfere as he saw fit. In Cato's day there seems to have been relatively little respect for the contubernium, but by Varro's day and thereafter it was more like a common-law marriage. As R. H. Barrow observes, by the early empire the *"ius gentium* [was] triumphing over the *ius civile"* and jurists were "as ready as the slaves themselves to speak of *maritus, uxor, filius, pater* within the boundaries of slavery."[68] The slave, however, never became a paterfamilias and could never exercise potestas.

The triumph of Christianity did lead to a significant improvement in the marital and familial condition of slaves in the late empire and during the Middle Ages. A law of Constantine passed in A.D. 334 forbade the separation of slave families. Slave marriages were given religious sanction although not legal confirmation. In seventh-century English society if one of a slave couple gained his or her freedom, the free party was allowed to buy the freedom of the one still enslaved or else marry a new partner.[69] According to Marc Bloch, religious validation of slave marriages was one of the important religious actions which "gave its aid to the general movement that transformed slavery."[70] One must be careful not to exaggerate, just the same. The church throughout the Middle Ages justified slavery as part of the law of man and the consequence of sin. While it required the baptism of slaves, it sanctioned the sale of Christians (except to Jews and Muslims). It encouraged masters to respect the integrity of slave marriages and families, and one finds an occasional law that reinforced such entreaties. On the whole, though, the master remained supreme in his power over the marital and familial lives of his slaves. Throughout Europe an unscrupulous master could always sexually abuse his female slave, married or not; and at no time did the slave father have custody over his child.[71]

Throughout the modern Americas the unions of slaves and the integrity of their households rarely received legal sanction. Nor was the church any more effective in this regard than it was during the late ancient and middle ages. (There were exceptional cases, such as portions of nineteenth-century Brazil.) The actual stability of unions and households varied with the kind of slave economy, with the demand and supply of slaves, and with the sex ratios of both the slave and free populations, issues we have already discussed. Where the plantation economy was dominant, demand for slaves high, external supplies available, and males in the majority among both masters and slaves, slave unions and households tended to be highly unstable (the U.S. South before 1808 being an important exception). This was true of the French and British Caribbean and many sections of Brazil up to the last quarter of the eighteenth century.

In cases where the plantation system was dominant and the demand for slaves high, but external supplies were either curtailed or cut off, the resulting high cost of slaves made their natural reproduction both profitable and necessary. For these reasons stable unions and households were encouraged, sometimes even required, by the master class. The U.S. South during the nineteenth century is the best-known case. However, the same situation occurred in the British and French Caribbean during the last decades of the eighteenth century and in the early nineteenth century[72]

Finally, where the plantation system was not dominant and external supplies were available and kept up with demand, the unions and households of slaves tended to be more stable, and the risk of arbitrary dissolution was small though never totally absent. This was true of most of Latin America after the eighteenth century, the main exceptions being the mining areas and those regions in which the plantation system became dominant.[73]

The Murder of Slaves

Because slavery is always a relationship that rests ultimately on force, it is hardly surprising that in every slave society the master has the power to inflict corporal punishment. As a matter of fact, throughout the precapitalist world and in a good many modern societies the paterfamilias has the power to physically castigate his wife, children, and servants. Recently an English court ruled that a man has the right to punish his wife by slapping her on the behind. The problem, then, is how far a master was entitled to go in his disciplinary actions. Two questions must be differentiated: the master's right of life and death over his slaves (the *jus vitae necisque*) and his overall treatment of his slaves. The two often vary together; that is, where masters could kill their slaves with impunity, they tended to treat them harshly. But this is only a probability: there were many instances where masters could kill their slaves under special circumstances, or even whenever they pleased, yet in general treated their slaves relatively well. This was the case, for example, among the marsh Arabs of southern Iraq where a master was permitted to kill his female slave at will because he owned her "in blood and bone." This power, however, was rarely exercised. On the contrary, the female slave was well treated, since more often than not she was her master's concubine.[74]

Societies varied considerably in the degree to which their legal codes or customs permitted the murder of slaves by their masters. At one extreme were societies in which not only did the laws recognize such a power, but the masters frequently exercised it. Among the Goajiros of South America, for example, masters could "at any time . . . kill any of their slaves, man or woman."[75] Nothing in the annals of slavery, however, can match the Indians of the U.S. northwest coast for the number of excuses a master had for killing his slaves and the sheer sadism with which he destroyed them. Among the Aleut slaves were killed simply to placate the grief of their masters when a son or nephew had died accidentally. At such times "they drowned them in water, threw them off a cliff in the sight of their parents, in whose despair and bereavement they hoped to find their consolation."[76] Alternatively, slaves were killed to celebrate some special event such as a son's becoming a shaman.[77] In almost all these tribes slaves were killed upon the death of their owners, especially when the latter were important persons: among the Tlingit, the selected slaves were bound hand and foot and thrown alive on the funeral pyre.[78] When a new house was to be built, they were killed and buried beneath the posts;[79] at ceremonies of initiation, especially into the cannibal society of the Kwakiutl (according to Franz Boas), the body was torn into little pieces and eaten by the initiates.[80] But it was during the potlatch ceremony culminating in the ritualized exchange and destruction of property that the murder of slaves became a veritable carnage, in which "rival leaders attempted to surpass one another in the number of slaves killed."[81]

The murder of slaves for ritual purposes was, of course, widespread. It existed, at some time, on every continent and in the early periods of every major civilization. Vast numbers of slaves were buried, often alive, with the earliest Chinese emperors.[82] In Japan, between the second and third centuries B.C., as many as a hundred slaves were buried with an empress.[83] The practice was widespread in the ancient Near East,[84] and among most early European and Asian peoples.[85] We have a vivid account of one such gruesome ceremony of the Vikings from an Arab ambassador who lived among them in the early tenth century.[86] The Aztec slaughter of thousands of prisoners of war and slaves bought for the purpose is well known,[87] as is the similar ritual slaughter by the Dahomeans[88]—although in both cases allowance must be made for exaggeration and propagandistic bias in the original sources. The ritual murder of slaves, it should be noted, does not necessarily imply that masters had the capacity to kill slaves in other contexts. Among the Margi of Nigeria[89] and the Ashanti of Ghana,[90] who practiced human sacrifice, a master who indiscriminately put his slave to death could suffer the death penalty himself.

At the other extreme were slaveholding societies in which the murder of slaves was punished in the same way as the murder of free persons. In some of the Southeast Asian states such as ancient Vietnam and Thailand, masters

who killed their slaves could be punished "according to law."[91] Ancient Hebrew law was far superior to the other codes of the ancient Near East in this
regard: "if the slave died on the same day that he was beaten by his master,
the death was treated as murder."[92] In medieval Europe the influence of the
church led to the enactment of penalties for the murder of slaves by their
masters. Excommunication for two years was the penalty laid down by the
Council of Epaone in 517, and Theodore, archbishop of Canterbury, prescribed a penance of seven years for a mistress who killed her slave in anger.
It was rare, however, for masters to suffer the same penalty for killing one of
their slaves as for killing a free person. Although the master's right of life
and death was limited in thirteenth-century Spain, the penalty was still
light.[93] And whatever the formal position taken in religious or civil law, it
was extremely unusual to find a master in practice suffering the death penalty for the murder of his slave. Here and there we come across the exceptional case. In Siena one Giovanni de Sutri, a man-at-arms, was in 1436
"sentenced by the Podesta to have his head cut off, for having killed his own
slave with a knife, 'contra forman juris et statutorum Senensis.' " More typical was the case of Bartolomeo de Prata, who two years later was sentenced
to pay a moderate fine for the same offense.[94]

Most slaveholding societies fall between these two extremes. Ancient
Athens is typical. From the seventh century on, the murder of slaves was a
legal offense, although the penalty was much less severe than for the murder
of a free person. The law, however, was meaningless because the murdered
slave's kinsmen, invariably also slaves, had no way of bringing a case
against the master. Glenn Morrow, who tried his best to interpret the data in
a favorable light, was forced to conclude that "the murder of a slave could
often escape without punishment."[95] In Rome it was not until the first century A.D. that some restraint was placed on the power of the master to kill his
slave, and this was only with regard to the practice of sending one's slaves to
fight with wild beasts. More meaningful curbs came with Antoninus in the
middle of the second century.[96]

The Greek and Roman experiences point to the major problem of the
slave in the vast majority of slaveholding societies, from the most primitive
to the most advanced: slaves were not allowed to be witnesses or to swear
oaths, except under very special circumstances such as the trial of their master for treason. Even in these exceptional cases the slave's evidence was
usually taken under torture. In oriental and Western law slaves were allowed to take their masters to court only on matters relating to their own
emancipation. A few post-Roman law codes added the capacity to go to
court over disputes relating to the peculium, but actual cases were rare indeed. So too were cases involving contracts between masters and their
slaves: one such case, described by Charles Verlinden as a "very curious"
one in the history of the peculium, took place in Spain in 1284.[97] The truth is

that in almost all slaveholding societies the master—in practice, if not in legal theory—had unlimited power, including that of life and death, over his slave. The Roman jurist Gaius was right in declaring that the *jus vitae necisque* (right of life and death) belonged to the *jus gentium*.[98]

To examine the legal capacity of masters to kill their slaves, I assembled data on forty-five of the societies in the sample of world cultures and coded them by whether the penalty for killing a slave was (1) the same as that for the murder of a free person; (2) not the same, but very severe; (3) mild, amounting to no more than a small fine; or (4) negligible—the master was able to kill his slave with impunity. I found that nine societies (20 percent) fell into the first group; two (4.4 percent) into the second; six (13.3 percent) into the third; and twenty-eight (62.2 percent) into the fourth group.

There are some interesting correlates to this variable. Where masters are allowed to kill their slaves with impunity, there is a greater tendency not to sanction the peculium; crimes against slaves are punished less severely than crimes against nonslaves; masters rely more heavily on captivity and kidnapping as the means of enslavement; and there is less tendency to rely on birth and punishment for crimes as sources. Race, ethnicity, and dominant subsistence patterns were found to have no influence on the legal capacity of the master to kill his slave.

One rather odd relationship stands out. The legal capacity to kill one's slave is closely associated with a low proportion of males in the servile population. Since there is an equally surprising relationship between this variable and others measuring the treatment of slaves, it is best to look at all the relevant factors before attempting to explain it.

Crimes against Slaves by Third Parties

So far we have considered only the treatment of the slave by his master. What about the delicts of third parties against slaves? Here laws were likely to be more important in influencing practice, for the master had a vested interest in the protection of his slave property. Proprietary self-interest, however, benefited the slave in very limited ways. There were many crimes against the person of the slave for which the master did not consider it worth his while to seek redress, for example, the rape of a female slave which resulted in no damage to her working capacity, or the mortifying verbal abuse or slap in the face of a male slave. In no slaveholding society was the honor or dignity of the slave taken into account in law or practice. The comparative data show, further, that in most slaveholding societies delicts against slaves were penalized not in the interest of the slave but in order to protect the master's property. Murder was the one major exception, for most societies considered the killing of a slave by a third party not only an assault on another man's property but sinful. Even with murder, it was usually the case that punishment beyond the payment of damages was rarely very severe. Sometimes the emphasis on compensation to the master for the injury of the slave by a third party had bizarre and tragic consequences for the slave. Among the Bedouins of the Sinai, damage to a slave short of murder was compensated in the same way as damage to a woman, and this could be very expensive. For the murder of a slave, however, there was a fixed payment: two camels. Hence it was common to hear members of the Towara tribe saying that if you injured a slave "it was cheaper to kill him outright."[99]

Rarely did the slave receive any compensation for his injuries; when he did it was a mere pittance, almost an insult. In Iceland, for example, as among all the Germanic peoples, no wergild was paid to the kinsmen of the thrall when he was murdered, only to the master; and if the thrall received a heavy blow from someone other than his master, he was given a compensation of three aurar, equivalent to three cows (an average male slave was worth twelve aurar).[100]

The Greek view of the matter was typical of many precapitalist (especially tribal) peoples. The murder of a slave was considered a form of ritual pollution requiring religious purification for the good of the community rather than for any consideration of the injustice done the slave,[101] a view found in several tribal slaveholding groups.[102] On Greece, Glenn Morrow writes: "That it was something more than a punitive fine, something less than death—this is about all we can infer as to the penalty for murdering a slave."[103]

A slave could no more give evidence against a free third party than he could against his master.[104] Only the master could take legal action against the third party for injuring or murdering his slave, and in actuality it was rare for him to do so. Slaves could lodge information with a magistrate on which prosecution against a free person, his master or anyone else, could be based, but it is not clear how much good this did the slaves.[105] The information would be useless unless a free person was prepared to stand witness on behalf of the injured slave. It is improbable that any Athenian would testify against another free citizen; in the unlikely event that such a person existed, it would obviate the need for the slave to lodge the information in the first place. Clearly the provision was meant for slaves to act as spies against their masters and other free persons who had committed serious crimes against the state. It was not, and could not have been meant, for the benefit of the slaves as Morrow implies.

The Russian classicist E. Grace has shown that Athenian homicide laws respecting slavery emerged slowly as part of the development of laws discriminating between citizens and noncitizens. She speculates that the legal autonomy of the master grew with the emergence of large-scale slavery.[106] She also argues that slaves were not treated as a homogeneous group. "How he would be dealt with as a killer, the extent and type of intervention by public authority in prosecuting his punishment, might well depend upon whose slave he was, a citizen's, a metic's or an altogether foreigner's."[107] His treatment as a criminal would also depend on the status of his victim, "in particular whether or not he was a citizen. The shedding of a citizen's blood, even perhaps the blood of a citizen's slaves, could have different legal consequences from those obtaining when the victim too was an outsider."[108] We know almost nothing about the nature or relative degree of punishment meted out to slaves, as opposed to nonslaves. It does appear that slaves were subject to torture more often than other groups, and such torture was as much a form of punishment as it was a means of gaining information.[109]

The principle of privilege was an entrenched feature of Roman law (as we have already seen). Until the early empire, the victimized slave could seek redress only through his master. The rule that a slave could not give evidence against a free person except for special cases in the public interest (and then, under torture) was progressively modified under the empire. The murder of slaves by freemen without cause was punished first by banishment and later by execution.[110] For lesser injuries against the slave, compensation had to be made to the owner, and from very early we find operating in Roman law the near universal principle that crimes against slaves were punished less severely than comparable crimes against freemen. The Laws of the Twelve Tables, for instance, laid down that the punishment for breaking a slave's bones was half the fine due when the victim was a freeman.[111] Criminal slaves were either handed over to their victims or punished by their masters, but a senatorial decree of A.D. 20 put a stop to this: slaves from then on were tried in the same manner as the lowest-ranked free persons.[112] As in Greece, distinctions were made among slaves and their victims in the treatment of both the crimes and the injuries of slaves. The slaves of powerful patricians were clearly out of bounds for proletarian bullies. We shall see in Chapter 11 that the *familia Caesaris,* itself a heterogeneous group, had privileges other slaves did not.

This sort of status distinction in the treatment of slaves is found in nearly all premodern and modern slave societies. Among lineage-based societies, for example, the royal slaves of the Igala kingdom of West Africa, especially the *amonoji* (palace eunuchs who protected the person and ritual space surrounding the king), held a privileged status vis-à-vis other slaves.[113] And among the Somali, nothing short of blood payment was demanded if the killer of a man's slave was a member of the outcaste Sab, whereas only money compensation was demanded if the killer or injurer was a fellow Somali freeman.[114] In the pre-European Islamic states of Malaysia the murder of an ordinary slave by a freeman usually went unpunished except for payment of the slave's market price, whereas the murder (or even the injury) of one of the raja's slaves was punishable by death.

Ethnic factors also played a part. Members of the Arab ruling class were never punished for the murder or injury of a slave, whatever the latter's status, only members of the indigenous Malay community.[115] More privileged too were the government and church-owned slaves of Visigothic Spain. Skilled household slaves there, the *idonei,* could expect better treatment from free third parties than the *rustici,* or rural slaves.[116] And in thirteenth-century Spain, with its bewildering variety of races, ethnic groups, and creeds, the condition and treatment of slaves both as victims and as criminals varied widely. Orthodox Greek slaves, for example, had a special status in law compared with other slaves, and Jewish and Muslim masters had greatly delimited powers over their slaves compared to their Christian counterparts.[117]

The Delicts of Slaves

No slave society took the position that the slave, being a thing, could not be held responsible for his actions. On the contrary, the slave usually paid more heavily for his crimes when the victim was a freeman. It was different, however, when slaves committed crimes against one another. The penalties then were usually much lower than those for crimes among freemen or involving freemen and slaves. Islamic law was typical in holding that the *talio* (an eye for an eye) did not apply to slaves. The reason had little to do with any concept of reduced responsibility; rather, it was out of consideration for the owner's interests. If a master had already lost one of his slaves at the hands of another, he was hardly inclined in the name of some abstract sense of justice to deprive himself of the services and value of the offender. A beating was about as much punishment as he was prepared to inflict if the determination was left to him (as it usually was, with respect to crimes committed among slaves of the same master).[118] Where the offense involved slaves belonging to different masters, the tendency almost always was for the masters to settle the matter between themselves, unless there were additional grievances. Roman imperial law was unusual in having the courts take over the punishment of slaves for serious crimes against other slaves, and it was noteworthy that this development came relatively late.

Although in theory the slave had no will beyond that of his master, in no slave society was the master held responsible for criminal actions, especially murder, committed by his slaves against free third parties—unless, of course, he ordered the crimes. The criminal slave was usually handed over to the relevant state authorities, or, where there were no formal legal organizations, he was delivered to the victim's kinsmen. Treatment in Iceland was typical: "The thrall was held responsible by the law for the deeds of violence he was accused of having committed. The placing of this responsibility on him is the best evidence that he was considered to be a human being *relative to his crime* . . . It was not due to any benevolence on the part of the masters toward the thrall that he was considered to be a human being when he was in the toils of the law. This law is a punitive measure, promulgated for the purpose of safeguarding the rule of the master class," and only in exceptional cases was he given an opportunity to prove his innocence.[119] The position of alienation of responsibility adopted in Visigothic Spain, derived from Roman and Germanic laws, is true of all slave societies in their response to the master's responsibility for crimes committed by his slaves against free third parties.[120] Even among the Ashanti, with their extreme form of the principle that the head of the household is totally responsible for the actions of its members, an exception was made for the murder of third parties by slaves. "A master is not killed for the murder of his slaves," goes the validating legal proverb.[121] The Fanti, another Akan group, echo the same principle in their maxim, "A slave does not commit murder for the master."[122]

The issue becomes somewhat more complex with respect to the torts of slaves involving third parties, or lesser crimes punishable by fines. The slave was expected to pay the fine or compensation from his peculium, but if the peculium could not cover it, the master often had to pay, then confiscate the slave's peculium and make up the balance in other, no doubt punitive, ways. Far more complex were cases involving commercial transactions between slaves and free persons. If it was clearly understood that the slave was acting with his master's permission, but on his own behalf, then only his peculium was liable for forfeiture. The law courts of all commercially advanced slave holding societies permitted slaves to engage in such transactions, Rome being the classic case.[123] The master, of course, was the person sued, since the slave was not allowed to engage in contracts, to be sued or to sue, but apart from unusual cases the master could only be sued *"dumtaxat e peculio,* up to but not in excess of the value of the slave's *peculium."*[124] However, in slaveholding societies that had any measure of commercial activity, trusted and skilled slaves acted as agents on their master's behalf. Where the matter was clear-cut and the slave understood to be an agent, there were few problems: the master was obviously liable and the slave's peculium did not enter the picture. But the issue was often anything but clear-cut. The peculium of the slave might have been consolidated with other areas of the master's property and thorny legal problems created if and when liability had to be assessed. A vast section of Roman commercial law was devoted to this problem. The general rules that evolved were, first, that the slave, being a person without authority and powerless, "could not transfer *dominium*. If he sold and delivered possession passed but no more." Second, "a slave [had] no authority to make his master's position worse."[125] It is easy to see the kind of opportunities these rules offered to unscrupulous owners.

The Overall Treatment of Slaves

In view of the many factors that influenced slavery in any given society, some means of assessing the overall treatment of slaves was highly desirable. I therefore developed a four-point scale to code those societies in the world sample on which reliable data were available. Fifty-eight societies were coded on the following points: (1) whether there were some legal restraints on masters and third parties in their relations with slaves, and in practice slaves were treated well; (2) whether there were no formal restraints, but in practice slaves were treated well; (3) whether there were some formal restraints, but in practice slaves were treated badly; and (4) whether there were no formal restraints, and in practice slaves were treated badly or brutally. The following frequency distribution emerged:

Societies	Legal restraints; treatment mild	No legal restraints; treatment mild	Legal restraints; treatment harsh	No legal restraints; treatment harsh
Number	29	17	3	9
Percent of total	50	29	5.5	15.5

We see that the treatment of slaves was judged mild in nearly 80 percent of the societies.

The relative size of the slave population does not in itself significantly influence the treatment of slaves. Where there are few slaves, there is a greater tendency for them to be integrated into the households of their masters and into the traditional work patterns alongside nonslave persons. Where the number of slaves grows larger, the rest of the population is obliged to take a more formal interest in them—if not for the slave's well-being, at least to prevent the expression of antisocial and wantonly cruel behavior, which may spill over into the relations between free persons and offend communal norms. As the slave population grows, however, there is an increasing tendency to segregate it, usually in specialized productive activities. This development cuts both ways as far as treatment of the slaves is concerned. Where mining, latifundia, or plantation-type farming systems prevail, the slave tends to become merely a unit of production. The typical slave is in a large holding and has little personal contact with his master. Overseers, themselves frequently slaves, control him. The whip becomes the major impetus to work, and brutality increases. The classic cases here are the non-Latin Caribbean slave societies, nineteenth-century Cuba, and the plantation belt in Brazil; and with respect to mining, the Laurium mines of ancient Athens and many though not all those of the Americas. In many societies with large slave populations the slaves are used as tenant farmers. While there are often "supervisors," their role and functions tend to be different from those of the slave overseers of the Americas. Slaves have a high level of social and economic independence in such systems. The best examples are the slave systems of the Sokoto caliphate during the nineteenth century. Ethnicity was found to bear no relation whatever to the treatment of slaves, and the fact that slaves were of a different race from their masters did not significantly influence their treatment, even where masters had strongly racist views.

As we indicated earlier, it was surprising to find that societies in which female slaves outnumbered males were those in which masters were most likely to be able to kill their slaves with impunity. It was found too that crimes against slaves were less punished in societies where female slaves outnumbered males. At the same time it was found that the sex ratio of the slave population was not significantly related to the overall treatment of slaves. How do we explain these relationships?

It is important to note, first, that female slaves outnumber males in 54 percent of all the slaveholding societies in the Murdock sample; they are equal in number to men in 17 percent; and number less than males in only 29 percent of the sampled societies. Yet the sex ratio of the slave population bears no relation whatever to the proportion of the population enslaved, nor to racial and ethnic differences, nor to the mode of organization of the slave population. These negative findings are consistent with the absence of any significant relationship between the sex ratio of the slave population and the overall treatment of slaves.

The clue to the peculiar set of relationships between the sex ratio and the more specific variables is the fact that societies with more female slaves tended, to a greater degree than those with more males, to be ones in which household production prevailed. In such societies the master, as *patria potestas,* usually had the power to discipline to the point of death all members of the household, not only slaves but wives, children, junior kinsmen, and retainers. We are dealing here with typical kin-based slaveholding societies such as those described in Homer, primitive and early republican Rome, many traditional African societies, and many of the less advanced Islamic and oriental societies. At the same time it is in precisely these societies that the female slave was very rapidly assimilated to the status of junior wife or fictive kinsman. She may have been killed with impunity, for she belonged in "blood and bone," but under the master's potestas this happened no more frequently than it did to "free" persons.

The Slave as an Active Agent

So far the slave has figured in our discussion as a passive creature largely at the mercy of forces beyond his control. Within the law of all slaveholding societies, this was pretty much how he was conceived. The slave, of course, could always act outside the framework in which he was legally or even socially defined. In taking account of him as a criminal, I have already indicated that in no slave society did the slave accept his lot or his legal definition. In another work I have considered the slave as rebel.[126] It is significant that the slave as an active agent was recognized only when he behaved in a criminal manner. Are there any exceptions to this general rule? Was the slave's capacity to act on his own behalf ever recognized in law, apart from the very special cases discussed earlier? The answer is yes.

There were three actions of a positive, willful nature that many slaveholding societies recognized. These were the capacities of the slave to defend himself from the murderous assaults of free third parties; to seek sanctuary; and, in extreme cases, to change masters.

SELF-DEFENSE

While the slave was rarely allowed to seek redress in court for injuries done him by third parties, a significant minority of slave societies allowed him to defend himself from unprovoked attack and even, in some cases, to defend his woman. Quite apart from any appeal to simple justice, such defenses were legally implied in the universal existence of laws that forbade others to damage a free man's property: in defending himself, the slave was defending his master's interests. In medieval Iceland a thrall was permitted to kill a freeman who attempted to violate his "bedfellow" or to harm his own person. However, the thrall stood a very slim chance of ever committing such an act of defense; every free Icelander went about armed to the teeth, whereas thralls were rarely allowed to carry arms of any sort. In Norway this "right" was somewhat backhandedly given: the thrall was permitted to throw a bucket of water over the couple who had offended him. As Peter Foote and David M. Wilson comment, "The contempt for the seducer here only matches the contempt for the thrall."[127] Slaves were allowed to defend themselves and their women in traditional Malay law, especially in Jahore, "for it is written that no married woman shall be made light of; this is the law of custom, but by the law of God whoever kills shall himself be killed."[128] The female slave could also be protected from sexual abuse by her spouse in China, Korea, Vietnam, and among the Ashanti, but in all these cases the slave faced the same problem as his Icelandic counterpart: he was usually unarmed, and he had no way of defending himself in court against a later charge of injury by the freeman in the event that the latter had not been killed. Where it existed, this was a privilege which none but the most daring slave would choose to exercise. In any event it was a privilege found in only a minority of slaveholding societies. Most forbade the slave to defend himself by force except at the order of his own master.

SANCTUARY

The capacities to seek sanctuary and to change masters were closely related, in that the granting of sanctuary was sometimes followed by a change of master and, alternatively, the slave's plea to another master to buy him often amounted to a plea for sanctuary. For purposes of clarity, however, the two will be considered separately here.

Sanctuary was most frequently granted by religious organizations. The Ashanti and the Nyinba, a Tibetan-speaking Nepalese group, were typical. Among the Ashanti "a slave could run away and seek sanctuary by throwing himself on the mercy of a god (e.g., Dente) or the *'samonfo'* (ancestral spirit) at some Barim (mausoleum)"; and among the Nyinba a harrassed slave sought sanctuary in the temple of the local deity of a neighboring village.[129] The practice was widespread in ancient Greece: in Gortyna, it seems the slave in sanctuary could be protected even against the force of law; in Athens, it was the only procedure a slave could invoke on his behalf. The custom was so entrenched in Hellenistic Greece that it continued unabated during Roman times, much to the annoyance of Roman administrators. A Roman praetor once was forcibly prevented from removing a slave from the shrine of Diana at Ephesus and Tacitus complained of the abuse of sanctuary in Asia.[130] But the Romans themselves, by the time of Tiberius and possibly earlier, came to allow the slave to seek sanctuary not only in the old religious manner, but at statues of the emperor as well.

While the Christian church took over the pagan custom of offering sanctuary to slaves, it never had the same power or desire to protect the slave in sanctuary.[131] An incident recorded by Gregory of Tours reveals the ineffective high-mindedness that characterized the church, not only during the late empire but throughout the Middle Ages. Two slaves who had been forbidden to wed fled to the church in order to get married and to seek sanctuary. The master demanded them back, indicating that he intended to punish them. "You cannot receive them back," said the priest, "unless you pledge that their union shall be permanent, and that they remain free from all corporal punishment." The master promised, the slaves were released, and as soon as they were back in their master's clutches they were severely punished.[132] The only time the church really went out of its way to help the slave was when the latter had absconded from a Jewish master. And, as Iris Origo observes, this was wholly because of religious bigotry, for slaves were on the whole better treated by Jewish masters.[133]

In some societies lay officials and even ordinary freemen could offer sanctuary. The statue of the emperor was in fact a secular form of sanctuary, although it had overtones of emperor worship. In the pre-European Malay states a slave in trouble could become a hostage of the raja, a practice the rajas did not discourage, since the slaves thereby became their own.[134]

There were also cases of influential lay individuals offering sanctuary.

Among the Sherbro of Sierra Leone, a slave could seek the intervention of an influential third party who would "sit near" him as his protector. To regain his slave, the master had to get a group of officials to "beg" the slave to return. The officials would then accompany the slave to his master, but would only turn him over after the master had publicly spoken well of the slave and indicated his sincerity by offering small gifts to the officials. A fascinating aspect of this practice is that it was the same procedure used to regain a disgruntled wife who had fled to the sanctuary of her own family.[135]

According to Lombard law, any free man could offer sanctuary to a slave.[136] This may have worked in tribal times, but from the severe penalties inflicted on free persons harboring runaways in Tuscany during the fourteenth and fifteenth centuries, it is clear that only the most foolhardy or powerful Lombard lord would perform such a function.[137]

CHANGE OF MASTERS

Finally, we come to the privilege of changing masters. The Ashanti sum up the normal attitude of most slaveholding peoples in one of their bluntest proverbs: "A slave does not choose his master." Yet this was not always the case. Even among the Ashanti, a slave who felt extremely badly used could, as a last resort, swear an oath that some other master must buy him.[138] The capacity to change masters was found in several advanced, large-scale slave societies—although the degree to which law was reflected in practice is questionable. By the middle of the second century A.D. cruelly used slaves in Rome could not only seek sanctuary at the statue of the emperor but, in theory, request too that they be sold to another master. Spanish law and its Latin American variant also required that a cruelly treated slave be sold to another master. Still, it was unusual for such action to be taken on the slave's behalf in either Spain or Latin America. The Colombian Chocó during the eighteenth century was one such exception. Even in Colombia the courts took this action only in cases of excessive brutality. Furthermore, the slave had no say in the choice of the master to whom he was sold. The action was more a mild punishment of the master than a "right" of the slave.[139]

The ability to change masters was surprisingly widespread because of a peculiar Islamic custom that permitted it. The custom, sometimes in odd forms, was found all over Muslim Africa, the Middle East, and Islamic Asia. The most common version was for the disgruntled slave to go to the compound of the master he wished to have buy him and cut a piece of flesh from the ear of that master's camel or horse. The owner of the slave was then required to compensate for the damage by handing the slave over to the offended master.[140] A more bizarre variant found among the Wolof and the Sereer involved cutting off either the ear of the intended master's horse or the ear of the intended master himself![141] In parts of Saudi Arabia it was the property of the present, not the intended, master that was mutilated. According to an Arab custom known as *beja,* the owner of a house was responsible for any delict committed in front of it. Disgruntled slaves took advantage of this by bringing the camel of their present master to the door of the intended master's household and slaying it there. "Usually the man in front of whose house the slaying occurs [preferred] to repay one camel and gain a slave, rather than kill the slave and suffer dishonor from a broken custom."[142]

Although this curious practice was widespread throughout the Islamic world, it is extraordinary that its origins are unknown. Koranic law enjoins the master to provide for the welfare of his slave or else sell him to another, but there is nothing in the Koran or early religious traditions that would account for this strange mode of changing the master. The French anthropologist André Bourgeot, who has worked among the Imuhag group of the Tuaregs, offers a symbolic and historical explanation. He argues that the custom is a symbolic reaction against the mutilation of slaves during the pagan days of the Arabs, a practice soon condemned by Islam as the inspiration of the devil. Hence, cutting the ear of the camel symbolizes bad treatment and un-Islamic behavior, by harking back to the pagan practice of slave mutilation. The former master for this reason is not permitted to intervene, and the flight of his slave represents both a social and an economic loss. The act, Bourgeot further claims, is an incipient form of individual rebellion on the part of the slave, though one couched in religious rather than political terms.[143]

This interpretation is attractive and may well hold for the Tuareg and other Islamic peoples. The problem is that several pagan or other non-Islamic peoples have a closely related practice. An almost identical custom is found among the Toradja-speaking pagans of the central Celebes. N. Adriani and A. C. Kruyt, who lived among these peoples at the turn of the century, found that a slave who was wronged and wanted to change his master went to the residence of another lord and either broke up some of his furniture or burned pieces of his clothing. The practice was called *mepone,* which literally means to climb up to another's house. When the master came for his slave he had to pay a buffalo for him, and this was meant to teach the master a lesson. But if the slave really wanted to have his master changed, he would destroy so much of the intended master's property that the present master had no choice but to turn him over to the offended master as compensation. Another method involved cutting a lock of hair from a member of the intended master's household and then burning it.[144] Although some groups of the Toradja were subject to Islamic influence, the pagan tribes studied by these authors were not; so we may rule out any diffusionary explanation. Furthermore, we find a basically similar practice halfway around the world from the Toradja. Among the pagan Ila of Central Africa, a dissatisfied slave who could not find another master to buy him would go to a neighboring village and insult the head of the kin group by throwing ashes on him. The fine for this outrage was two beasts, but the slave was usually accepted as a compensation if that was his intention.[145] The comparative data, then, offer no support for Bougeot's symbolist explanation.

The practice, I would argue, is better explained in terms of the general condition of slavery itself. The slave everywhere was held as an extension of his master, a vocal instrument without will except where this worked against the slave. By performing this act of mutilation, the slave achieved three objectives in one fell swoop. First, he succeeded in changing his master. Second, he gained revenge against the master, in that the latter always came out a net loser. (It is significant that when the damage was to the intended master's property, it was only superficial; but when, as in Saudi Arabia, the damage was done to property belonging to the present master, it was real and substantial—a camel was slain, no doubt the master's favorite.) Third, the slave, if only temporarily, asserted his will. This was indeed an act of individual rebellion—not political, to be sure, but not religious either. Rather, it belonged to the category that Albert Camus calls existential. It is not by accident that Camus opens his great work, *The Rebel,* by citing the slave rebel as the archetypal existential rebel. By saying no, the slave set limits beyond which he could not and would not be demeaned. He demanded a recognition of his humanity *not only in a manner that worked against him*—for every slave came to realize existentially what Camus arrived at intellectually: that it is not possible to deny another person his humanity, the worst the oppressor can do is recognize it negatively and exploitatively—but in a manner that worked for him, in his own interest. This was the true interpretation of the practice. Seen in this light, it is not a peculiar custom of Islamic culture but an imperative of the slave condition.

The fact cannot be gainsaid, however, that exchange of masters was found overwhelmingly in Islamic lands. Why is this? The answer is that Islamic law enjoins the master to change his slave if the latter is excessively unhappy with his treatment. The normal method of changing masters was simply for the slave to demand such a change, which the master was duty bound to honor. The custom of abusing the proposed master's property was used only when the master refused to obey the dictates of his religion. Thus, far from being a symbolic harking back to pagan times, the custom was an affirmation of Islamic religious law. This law, however, only made possible the expression of the practice; indeed, the custom was obviated if the law was followed. Islamic law does not explain the custom as such; it only explains the *frequency of its occurrence* in Islamic societies. The practice itself is explained by factors inherent in the condition of slavery.

At the same time, the absence of any requirement in the other major religions to sell an unhappy slave explains the infrequency of the practice elsewhere. This does not mean that the imperatives of slavery were not present in such societies, or that the slave's yearning for vengeance and the positive affirmation of his will were not as pressing. It is, rather, that they had to be expressed in other ways. The ground rules laid down by the master class determined how the slave reacted, how he manipulated or, when necessary, broke the rules. The fact that an extremely unhappy slave could have his master changed was an important safety valve. Other slaveholding peoples have had other safety valves—liberal laws on the peculium, a high rate of manumission, a sufficient incidence of slaves allowed to hire themselves out and live apart from their masters, effective forms of sanctuary, fictive kinship assimilation, adequate physical treatment, to list some of the more familiar. And still other slaveholding societies had no safety valves at all, relying mainly on brute force.

Conclusions

The limited nature of the data on most premodern slaveholding societies obliges us to rely not only on gross indexes of the condition of slavery but also (perhaps too heavily) on legal norms. For most slaveholding societies we simply do not know how often slaves were beaten and for what reasons, much less the internal factors that determined the frequency of the use of violence. Nor can we compare treatment in terms of such "welfare" variables as diet, clothing, housing, and health. And of course we know almost nothing directly about the way slaves felt about their condition in the great majority of such societies.

With all their limitations, however, the data nonetheless allow us to infer certain general statements about the condition of slavery. The most important conclusion is that the master-slave relationship was not a static one in which an active master constantly got his way against a wholly passive slave. In spite of the extreme power of the master, certain constraints were inherent in the very nature of this relationship. One was the self-interest of the master himself. The whole point of keeping slaves was to get them to serve him, in whatever capacity he chose, to the best of their ability. To achieve this objective the master could use various combinations of punishments and rewards. Slavery was unusual in the extraordinary extent to which the slave could be punished for not serving—even to the extreme of murder. But a dead slave, or one incapacitated by brutalization, was a useless slave. This stark fact, plus the recognition that incentives usually work more effectively than punishment in inducing service, was enough to encourage most masters in all slaveholding societies to search for the best balance between reward and punishment.

The second category of constraints was the slaves themselves. Powerless, isolated, and degraded in the eyes of nonslaves they may have been, but they struggled constantly to set limits beyond which they would not be expected to go. In so doing, they could regularize their relationships with the persons who parasitized them and carve out some measure of predictability, if never legitimacy, in their social behavior.

Both masters and slaves, then, had to adjust to one another. Just how much the master would concede in order to gain, and just how much of the master's parasitism the slave would take before declaring a limit, varied considerably both within slaveholding societies and between them. It is trite—and untrue—to say that the relationship that emerged varied with the character of the master. For even on an individual level the condition of the slave varied with the character of the slave also, as well as with the social and economic circumstances that impinged on the dynamics of the interaction between slaveholder and slave.

The experience of the U.S. South, which presents us with a richer body of data than any other slaveholding society (including the testimony of hundreds of ex-slaves), fully supports this general conclusion. From his study of the W.P.A. and Fisk University slave narrative collections, Stephen C. Crawford found that in spite of the total legal power of the masters, self-interest and the determination of the slave to survive as best he or she could created an environment in which slaves could even "significantly control their personal probability of punishment."[146] Self-interest dictated that punishment was not used mainly as a labor promoter but as a form of social control. Slaves also had some option in the kind of household structures they established, and appropriate choice of such structures could reduce the risk of punishment of children and sale away from family and friends.[147]

None of this, of course, implies that the system was not oppressively weighted against the slave. Beyond the character of the master, there were other key features in the environment that the slaves could do nothing about. One was the size of the farm unit on which they lived, another was its location. Both were crucial in determining the condition of slaves in the United States,[148] as they were in all other advanced slave systems. Large farms meant a higher level of whippings, less contact with owners, fewer chances therefore to manipulate the political psychology of the relation, and more work. But even if the slave had some choice in the size and location of the farm on which he lived, he would still be faced with a no-win situation. Small farms, while physically less demanding, offering more opportunities to acquire skills, and allowing far more contact with (and manipulation of) the owner, had their own special horrors. More personal contact meant greater exposure to sexual exploitation for slave women, including the not infrequent experience of gang rape by adolescent kinsmen of the owner. The probabilities of family breakup as the result of such sexual exploitation, and of being sold away, were also greater on such farms.[149]

These examples give some idea of the complexities of both the relationship itself and the conditions that influenced it. In macrosociological terms the U.S. South, as I have repeatedly emphasized (and will have reason to do again), was rather unusual. But it shared with all slaveholding societies certain imperatives of the interaction between slaveholder and slave. Among these was the fact that in southern slavery, as in all other slaveries, there was a constant struggle between master and slave in the effort of the former to gain as much as possible for himself with the least possible loss, including the self-defeating loss of his slave, and the effort of the latter to minimize the burden of his exploitation and enhance the regularity and predictability of his existence. It is a mistake to characterize such a highly asymmetric interaction as one of "give-and-take," as Crawford does in his otherwise impressive study.[150] Husbands and wives give and take, sometimes; employers and wage earners, maybe; masters and slaves, never. What masters and slaves do is struggle: sometimes noisily, more often quietly; sometimes violently, more often surreptitiously; infrequently with arms, always with the weapons of the mind and soul.

In this conflict, as we have seen in Chapter 3, there was resentment on both sides—expressed in ideological stereotypes by both sides. But from time to time masters who wrote about slaves and their condition broke through the barriers of their own prejudices and saw the relationship as it was, not only for themselves but for their slaves. Even in ancient India, where the ideological mystification of exploitation was taken to greater lengths than in almost any other society, masters nonetheless realized that slaves worked under duress and that behind all the rhetoric and religious reinforcement, naked force was the ultimate and essential sanction. During the Buddhist period masters realized that slaves worked resentfully even in the performance of religious work, despite the fact that all such work was considered meritorious when done by anyone, slave or free. In a celebrated passage from Majjhima Nikaya the slaves who were ordered to deputize for their masters in a very sacred ritual were seen as resenting the compulsion and "with tears in their faces, weeping, they [went] about their jobs."[151] Nor were the masters of the Buddhist period always deceived by either their own version of the "Sambo" ideology or by the aggressive duplicity of their slaves, for as another master observed: "O Bhante, our slaves . . . do another thing with their bodies, say another with their speech and have a third in their mind."[152] The master then went on to explain what he meant by this, and in doing so went straight to the heart of the social and psychological struggle inherent in the relationship:

> On seeing the master, they rise up, take things from his hands, discarding this and taking that; others show a seat, fan him with a hand fan, wash his feet, thus doing all that needs be done. But in his absence, they do not even look if oil is being spilled, they do not turn to look even if there were a loss of

hundreds or thousands to the master. (This is how they behave differently with the body.) . . . Those who in the master's presence praise him by saying, "Our master, our lord," say all that is unutterable, all that they feel like saying once he is away. (This is how they behave differently in speech.)[153]

Masters and mistresses who saw beyond their ideological camouflage came to the same conclusion everywhere. The women of the master class usually saw what was going on better than their menfolk, because they had more time and leisure to reflect on the slave relation; but perhaps also because when they did reflect, their own condition as women in a timocratic culture gave them a better understanding of the struggle that underlay the apparent give-and-take of surface realities. It is no wonder that some of the best accounts of the interpersonal aspects of slavery in the antebellum South come from the diaries of women. Mary Boykin Chesnut, writing in the midst of the Civil War, tells of her first recognition of the reality beneath the surface: "They go about in their black masks, not a ripple of an emotion showing; and yet on all other subjects except the War they are the most excitable of all races. Now Dick might be a very respectable Egyptian Sphynx, so inscrutably silent is he. He did begin to inquire about General Richard Anderson. 'He was my young Master once. I always will like him better than anybody else.' "[154]

Deep down, Chesnut undoubtedly knew what lay behind the mask, but it was too much for her to spell out, even in her diary. It is to the poet son of two runaway slaves, Paul Lawrence Dunbar, that we must turn for the answer:

> We wear the mask that grins and lies,
> It hides our cheeks and shades our eyes,
> This debt we pay to human guile;
> With torn and bleeding hearts we smile.[155]

8

Manumission:
Its Meanings
and Modes

WE TURN NOW to the circumstances of release from the
condition of slavery. The transition from slave to freed status posed many
critical problems for a slaveholding society. What did manumission mean?[1]
By what means did the transformation take place? How was the freedman
incorporated into the society? In addition to these more cultural problems,
social and statistical issues are involved. What were the conditions favoring
manumission both within and between societies? Why were some slaves
manumitted while others in a given society were not? And why did some
slaveholding societies show a much higher rate of manumission than others?
These questions will be explored in the next several chapters.

The Meaning of Manumission

What was manumission, and how was it to be achieved? Unsuspected problems of extraordinary complexity arise when one tries to answer these apparently simple questions. Given the way in which slaves were legally and
socioeconomically defined, there was no obvious way in which they could
have been released from their condition. I call this the inalienability problem, and it is in examining the various ways in which the same or different
peoples came to terms with it that we arrive at an understanding of the true

nature of manumission.

The problem may, for purposes of analysis, be divided into three parts: there is a conceptual issue; there is a cultural problem, which encompasses symbolic factors as well as legal or customary modes; and there is a social problem, which focuses on the status of freedmen.

The first two issues will be considered in this chapter and the problem of status in the next.

THE CONCEPTUAL PROBLEM

Common sense has it that the slave or someone else simply buys his freedom from the master. Such a view, itself narrow and problematic, is true only of the advanced capitalistic slave systems of the modern world. Almost no pre-capitalist slave system—including imperial Rome—considered the matter as simple as this. Precisely because Rome had an advanced legal system but was also precapitalist, it highlights the problem in many striking ways. It was not altogether clear to Roman jurists that the sale of freedom was possible. Two reasons can be found for this view, and they apply as much to other precapitalist cultures as to ancient Rome.

First, if everything the slave is and enjoys belongs to the master, then by definition it is never possible for the slave to buy back his freedom from his own resources. The peculium, it may be recalled, always belongs ultimately to the master, who allows his slave to enjoy its usufruct as long as he remains a slave. It is not possible for a third party, either, to buy back the slave's freedom, for that third party must either pay for the slave with money passed to him by the slave, in which case the master is cheated, or else pay for the slave with his own funds, in which case the problem of alienating slave from master is not solved but simply passed along to the third party, who now owns the slave.

There is a second and more profound problem, namely, that it is impossible to express the idea of manumission in terms of any appropriate legal-economic category. The most obvious legal institution is conveyance, but as W. W. Buckland and others have shown, the manumission transaction is only analogous to conveyance, it is not identical to it.[2] In conveyance there is a seller with something to sell and a buyer who wants that particular thing. The buyer exchanges something else, say money, for the thing desired. The seller, on acquiring the money, transmits the thing to the buyer. What the seller hands over and what the buyer receives are one and the same thing. Clearly, this is not what happens in a manumission transaction, even where the slave or someone else pays dearly for the slave's release. For the master does not convey dominium or power to the slave; he merely releases him from his dominium. As Buckland puts it, "What passes to the man is not what belonged to the master, his liberty and *civitas* are not subtractions from those of the *dominus,"* hence "what is released is something other than what is acquired."[3] There surely has been a transaction, but whatever it is, it most certainly is not a sale as understood in Roman and all other legal codes.

What is it then? Buckland proposes that the real meaning of manumission is that "it is not a transfer of dominium; it is a creation of a civis."[4] Buckland is on the right track but leaves many questions unresolved. He is partly right in seeing manumission as a creation—but only partly so, for it is much more than that. Furthermore, while the thing created might have been a *civis* in the special case of Rome, this was not the case in most slaveholding societies, so the second half of his solution is of little value to someone concerned with slavery in comparative terms. The matter of *what* has been created remains unresolved.

THE CULTURAL PROBLEM

In order to come to terms with these issues we must turn to the cultural problems posed by the release from slavery. It is by cultural and symbolic means that the question, What has been created? is answered and at the same time the nature of the transaction is resolved. Since the slave is natally alienated and culturally dead, the release from slavery has certain implications in terms of symbolic logic. As enslavement is life-taking, it follows logically and symbolically that the release from slavery is life-giving and life-creating. The master gives, and in giving he creates. It must always be the case that the master gives up something, so that the slave may gain something else. The master would seem to gain nothing. Hence he incurs a loss. What results from this deliberate loss is a double negation: the negation of the negation of social life, resulting in a new creation—the new man, the freed man. Manumission, then, is not simply an act of creation: it is, rather, an act of creation brought about by an act of double negation initiated by the freely given decision on the part of the master to part with something—his power—for nothing. To be sure, the slave often gives something too: his redemption fee. But not only does this not pay for what the master loses—his power—it is not even possible for it to pay for anything, for whatever the slave gives already belongs to the master. Hence, even when the slave pays, he is really not paying for his freedom. It is usually conceived of as making a gift offering in gratitude for the master's *freely given decision* to release him from slavery, however that release is arranged.

THE THEORY OF GIFT EXCHANGE

The whole complex of ideas and interactions involved in the release from slavery amounts to a classic instance of the anthropology of gift exchange. A distinguished line of anthropologists from Marcel Mauss and Bronislaw

Malinowski through Raymond Firth and Marshall Sahlins has demonstrated the enormous significance of gift exchange not only as a utilitarian premarket means of exchanging and redistributing goods, services, and other resources, but as a means of striking new social compacts and reconfirming old ones.[5] Gift exchanges range in complexity from simple diadic relationships to intricate systems of interaction involving many persons over long periods. Mauss uses the term "prestation" to define such systems, and the most elaborate ones, having implications for the entire social order, he calls systems of "total prestation."[6]

Mauss's arguments may be formalized as follows. There is a utilitarian component, which refers to the material exchange of goods and other resources resulting in a net balance or imbalance as the case may be. And there is an ideological component, which is the conscious rationalization and moral expression of what is actually going on. The ideology of the prestation departs in varying degrees from its reality. In some cases the variance may be minor and quite transparent. It is often held, for example, that a gift is freely given, without any thought of reciprocation, when in fact everyone knows that all kinds of obligations are established by the act. It may even be held that the value of the gift offered is of no importance whatever, only the spirit in which it is given. In this regard modern societies are considerably more hypocritical and mystifying than primitive ones, since in the latter the exact value of the gift was frequently spelled out in great detail. At the other extreme, the ideology of the prestation may interpret the actual transaction as the very opposite of what is actually happening. The recipient may be looked upon as the person who benefits most, and the giver as the person who has magnanimously given far more than he can ever hope to receive; in reality, the very opposite may be the case.

Manumission, we shall soon see, is one such kind of prestation. The symbolic component establishes the gift exchange as "a social compact." It synthesizes the ideological and the utilitarian components as counterpoised elements in a single ritual process. Ritual not only mediates between the two other components, but further mediates between the specific interaction and the total system of interactions that make up the entire exchange system. In this way each subprocess of prestation is given social and moral significance. Speaking of the category of prestation in which there is what he calls "balanced reciprocity," Sahlins has written that "the striking of equivalence, or at least some approach to balance, is a demonstrable forgoing of self-interest on each side, some renunciation of hostile intent or of indifference in favor of mutuality. Against the preexisting context of separateness, the material balance signifies a new state of affairs . . . Whatever the utilitarian value, and there need be none, there is always a 'moral' purpose."[7]

Mauss's major contribution was his analysis of the dialectic of the ritual process that transmits and generalizes the utilitarian and ideological components of the gift exchange. All prestations, he showed, involve three kinds of obligations: there is an obligation to give presents, which in many precapitalist societies was not only morally motivated but may have been a material necessity. This, however, determines that there is a counteractive obligation to receive, since not to do so might not only be an insult to the giver, but (again more in premarket systems) would be an unpardonable break in the chain of exchanges that establishes a moral order, substitutes for a market, and also ensures redistribution. But to fulfill one's obligation to receive can only be resolved in the synthetic obligation to repay the debts imposed by the receipt of gifts, for "the gift not yet repaid debases the man who accepted it."[8] If the relationship is an ongoing one, it is clear that repayments both complete and initiate a cycle of gift exchanges in a continuous dialectical progression that moves forward lineally for the two persons interacting, but concurrently spreads out laterally to all persons interacting in the total system of prestation—in other words, to the community at large.

Later scholars have considerably refined Mauss's analysis, although in some instances the profundity of Mauss's original insights has been missed, partly because of the highly elliptical style in which he wrote. Firth and Sahlins,[9] in particular, have rid the original analysis of its mystical aspects, though in strikingly different ways. Firth emphasizes that Mauss's analysis is, in its entirety, more applicable to premodern societies than to modern ones; in the latter, notions of political morality, not to mention the operations of the market, either obviate or impose deliberate restraints on the obligations to give, receive, and repay. Firth's distinction between different kinds of gifts is also useful, especially his categories of the *earnest*, a gift that is "an indication of what is further to come, or what may further come if certain conditions are met by the recipient," and the *token*, which may serve symbolically either as "an index of commitment" or as a rejection of any such commitment.[10]

Both Firth and Sahlins emphasize the fact that gift exchanges are frequently asymmetrical. Sahlins' distinction between "balanced" and other kinds of reciprocity may be useful for schematic purposes. It seems to me, however, that Mauss was only too aware of these distinctions.

THUS WHILE IT IS TRUE that on the utilitarian level prestations vary considerably in their degree of symmetry, on the ideological level all exchanges are interpreted as balanced and fair. This is true even in an advanced capitalist society, where the ideology of the free market in labor insists on a "balance" and "fairness"—which in reality is anything but balanced. I have already discussed in an earlier chapter Marx's analysis of the way in which the fetishism of commodities acts as a powerful ideology of equal exchange in the face of the actual inequality of exchange involved. I suggest that Mauss's analysis of gift exchange is the precapitalist counterpart of such an ideology.

Once he established the utilitarian dialectic of giving, receiving, and repaying, Mauss shifted the focus of his analysis to the wider dialectic of generalized exchange in premodern societies.

One aspect of Mauss's analysis that has received more attention from students of comparative religion than from mainstream anthropologists concerns gift exchange between man and god. This takes the form of sacrifice. As Mauss notes: "Sacrificial destruction implies giving something that has to be repaid."[11] Mauss argues that such sacrificial exchanges between man and gods (or spirits of the dead) may have been the very first prestations. The gods and spirits of the dead "in fact are the real owners of the world's wealth. With them it was particularly necessary to exchange and particularly dangerous not to; but, on the other hand, with them exchange was easiest and safest."[12] Sacrifice is not just the earliest but the fullest realization of prestation systems, "for the gods who give and repay are there to *give something great in exchange for something small.*" I have added emphasis to the last passage, for it clearly indicates Mauss's understanding of the asymmetry that underlies the ideological and symbolic symmetry of all gift exchanges. Clearly, men do not outwit the gods in getting something great for something small—they only think they do. In the end, however, everything returns to the gods. The asymmetry works on their behalf. What Mauss is suggesting here—though he is at his most elliptical—is the fascinating fact that both parties may think that they have benefited disproportionately, and indeed may have done so, given their respective points of view. What one gains is wholly relative to one's status, aspirations, and needs. And who is to say that the person who thinks he has gained has *not* in fact gained? It is in this sense that all prestations are reciprocally balanced.

Finally, Mauss makes the important observation that there is often a close relationship between gift exchanges among men, on the one hand, and among men and gods on the other, the two reinforcing each other. He notes of the potlatch of the northwestern American Indians: "It is not simply to show power and wealth and unselfishness that a man puts his slaves to death, burns his precious oil, throws coppers into the sea, and sets his house on fire. In doing this he is also sacrificing to the gods and the spirits who appear incarnate in the men who are at once their name-sakes and ritual allies."[13] Mauss sees the origin of almsgiving in prestation, which serves the double purpose of being an offering to the gods while perpetuating prestation among men. I shall have more to say on this tantalizingly brief "note" of Mauss's shortly, for, as we shall see, the origins of manumission itself can be explained in terms of these double-purpose man-god/man-man prestations.

The Rituals of Redemption

To return now to release from slavery, I want to examine a sample of release ceremonies among a wide range of peoples in order to show how the principle of prestation permeates them all. After this preliminary review, I shall examine the data in a more detailed and systematic way, to isolate the main patterns of release within and between the different slaveholding societies.

The Kongo community of Mbanza Manteke (in Zaire) during the nine-teenth century is a good case with which to begin, for it is typical of the ex-treme category of societies in which the inalienability problem was insol-uble. Once a person became a slave, there was no way ever of releasing him from this condition, even though he might have been released from a partic-ular master or even from his master's community. "A slave is a slave for-ever" was the rule. The release from a particular master and his clan "was always possible providing that the slave's owners and his original clan would cooperate; the standard ritual required that the slave be marked with chalk as a sign of redemption and that a pig called 'the pig of rubbing with chalk' be transferred to the ex-owners. But the 'redeemed' slave was then consid-ered to be the slave of his original clan and could never recover first-class citizenship—that is, access to authority."[14]

The release ceremony was obviously a gift exchange. It is significant, however, that the exchange was not between master and slave but between the master and the slave's former clan members. The transaction involved another transition for the slave—hence the chalk mark, a common symbol of such transitional conditions in Africa. The chalk is also a symbol of death, which the slave continued to experience socially. A significant number of other primitive societies hold the view that social death, like its physical counterpart, is irrevocable, even for the slave returning to his natal clan.[15]

At the other extreme, and typical of all advanced slaveholding groups, is the Roman law of *postliminium*, by which the slave who returned home was fully restored to his old status. Most societies fell within these two extremes in providing some possibility of release from slavery. Typical of kin-based societies were the Kerebe of Tanzania. In addition to the usual compensa-tion (one cow), slaves had to send a gift of a hoe or a goat to the omukama, or chief, and "the person being released from servility was taken to a cross-road where his head was shaven to symbolize the loss of servility."[16] We have already seen that the shaving of the head is a common symbol of tran-sition and death and hence of enslavement. Here the shave again symbolizes transition. It also symbolizes death, only now the double negation implied in the death of the social death of the slave. This is reinforced by the cross-roads, another symbol of transition and a common location for ritual events the world over. Nor should we neglect the more obvious symbolic meaning of the crossroads as a sign of free choice. The Kerebe and the Romans of the principate stand at two extremes of sociocultural complexity in the pre-modern world. Yet it is significant that among the Romans freedmen played a disproportionate role in the Lares cult, which was closely associated with crossroads and intersections. Indeed, when the genius of Augustus became the object of religious honors and the Lares cult adapted for this purpose (becoming the *Lares Augusti*), it was freedmen assisted by slaves who were in charge of the rites. J. H. W. Liebeschuetz' explanation for the prominent role of freedmen in this cult in both its older and its Augustan forms is un-persuasive—that it "was appropriate since freedmen formed a high propor-tion of the population of Rome." Clearly their role must be accounted for in terms of the deep and widespread symbolic association of the emancipated with the cult of the crossroads. And it becomes evident that the shrewd em-peror had adapted this particular cult in order to make a powerful symbolic statement to his people—that loyalty to his person and his genius was iden-tical with freedom.[17]

Inasmuch as the human head looms large in the ritual of enslavement, we are not surprised to find it in prominence in the ritual of redemption. One of the most archaic of the Frostathing laws of Norway mandated that "if a slave takes a tenancy or farms for himself, he must make his freedom feast, each man with ale brewed from three measures, and slaughter a wether—a freeborn man is to cut its head off—and his master is to take his neck-redemption off his neck." Significantly, the Norse word for free, *frials,* is derived from *frihals,* which means "free-neck."[18] In ancient India during the period of the Tipitaka the manumission ritual was simple but potent: "A master desirous of freeing a slave would wash his head and declare him to be a *bhujissa,* a freeman." Sometimes, however, the master simply ordered the slaves to "wash their heads themselves and consider themselves free."

A further development took place in India between the second century B.C. and the fourth century A.D. Slavery had been considerably mitigated, and manumission and its implications were both significant and well-de-fined. The ceremony, accordingly, was more elaborate. "A master desirous of manumitting his slaves will take away a jar full of water from the shoul-der of that slave and will break it. He will then shower some parched grain and flowers on the slave's head and repeat thrice, 'You are no longer a *dasa.'* This act symbolized the cessation of his duty of carrying water. With this cessation all servile duties were discontinued for him."[19]

I suggest that this is only the most manifest layer of meaning in a com-plex, evocative rite. Water is the symbol of purification and of regeneration in India, as in many other cultures. The breaking of a jar of water clearly implies both the destruction and the rebirth inherent in the act of manumis-sion. There is the same binary opposition in the act of showering the slave's head with parched grain and flowers. Rice, of course, is used in rite-of-pas-sage ceremonies all over Asia, especially as a fertility or birth symbol. But note that here the rice is parched, another striking opposition, for parched rice is dead. Thus at one stroke have been expressed both the idea of death and the idea of renewal. The social death of the slave is destroyed as in a broken jar or a handful of parched rice. In both there is the simulation of a sacrificial act: the broken body of the jar, the burned rice. The slave dies as slave. Death is negated and there is the hint of renewal, of new bloom, in the flowers thrown on the slave's head.

It is among the medieval Germanic peoples, especially the Scandinavians, that we find the idea of manumission as gift exchange most richly expressed in symbol and ideology. Agnes Wergeland writes of the German master's view that "freedom was, after all, more in the nature of a gift than a purchase, and was also most of the time called by that name."[20] To be sure, he did receive a payment from the slave, but "to the master, the fee would not compensate for the loss of a permanent laborer, and the slave could thus not be said to have really paid for his freedom."

In modern capitalistic slave systems, even though slaves paid dearly in one way or another for their freedom, that freedom itself was still regarded as a gift from the master or mistress. The *cartas,* or letters of manumission, written by masters during the colonial period of Brazil are very revealing. Stuart B. Schwartz found that "statements within the letters—and the pride with which masters granted manumission even to the old and infirm—indicate that slaveowners saw the act of manumission as a charitable gesture no matter what its conditions or terms."[21] In the U. S. South, where the manumission rate was one of the lowest of all slave systems, those few masters (mainly in the cities and border states) who allowed their slaves to buy their freedom "understood that freedom was the greatest gift they could give their slaves, and they consciously used it as a mechanism of control and a means of encouraging divisions among blacks."[22]

The premodern world exhibits some striking parallels in the rituals of release. The "English mode," for example, consisted in "transferring the slave from the hand of the master to that of another freeman, who manumitted, as a symbol of the separation from the lord. This was always done in the presence of the assembled free. The liberated was then shown the open road and door to signify that nobody could restrain him, and he was given a freeman's sword and spear." More common was the ceremony found among the Langobards: "The slave amid clashing of arms in the assembly [*gairpinx*] was passed from the hand of the lord to other freemen till the fourth was reached. He then declared him free and completed the act by leading him to a crossway, bidding him to be at liberty and to go where he wished. The slave was then given arms and was henceforth a full free Langobard."[23] The Germans, like many tribal peoples, required the presence and confirmation of the entire local community in all acts of partial manumission; where full manumission was involved, the king's presence was required among certain groups. Among the Franks, "the slave was liberated before the assembled freemen by the king [originally the lord] knocking a penny from the slave's hand so that it flew over his head. This was a sign that his services and dues were dispensed with." The Germans distinguished between different degrees and stages of manumission. Perhaps the most characteristically Germanic ritual of redemption was that known as the liberation beer. This came when a partially free slave wished to complete his freedom. Wergeland writes that "this was a festivity prepared by the [manumitted] slave to celebrate and at the same time to make public his release. Here, in the presence of company sufficiently numerous to witness the act, he was to offer the lawfully demanded fee, which in this case must be nominal since it represented only one-fourth of what was looked upon as his suitable market value."[24] Closely related to this rite but more elaborate was the ceremony performed for the child of a master and a slave at the point when he was to become a full and free member of the community. At a social gathering an ox was slaughtered and a large quantity of beer brewed. A shoe was then made from the skin of the right forefoot of the ox, and the formal legitimation of the child began: first the father, then the child to be completely manumitted, then the nearest heir, followed by the rest of the family, all stepped into the shoe, "each pronouncing at the same time the appropriate formula which indicated the particular meaning of the ceremony."[25]

A final example is the manumission ritual of early Babylonia, which involved the cleansing of the forehead of the slave and then turning him or her to face the rising sun. The Ugaritic custom was to pour oil on the slave's head. Manumission was often conducted in the presence of a priest or judge, and the fully manumitted slave was made "like a son of the city." The exact nature and meaning of the ceremony of cleansing the brow is a source of some controversy. G. R. Driver and J. C. Miles claim that the cleansing of the brow (in which a slave-mark was literally removed) and the turning of the slave toward the rising sun were "two parts of a simple religious rite, [which] usually took place in the temple of the sun god Samas." It is generally agreed that the cleansing ceremony involved the use of water and was a form of purification, water being very important in the ritual of Babylonia. However, scholars are not in agreement on whether the ceremony also involved dedication to a god, as in ancient Greece.[26]

All these ceremonies emphasize the same themes—the communal nature of the act of manumission, the fact that the manumitted gains power that he formerly lacked (represented for example in the handing over of weapons), the acquisition of the capacity to compete for honor (represented in the German case in the passing of the individual from one freeman to another or in the ritual of stepping in the same shoe), the attainment of will and autonomy (represented by the crossroad), the negation of social death and transition to a new status, and most important, the concept that the master or his clan makes a gift of freedom and that what the slave pays is merely an offering, a gift exchange. No slave, of course, took all this literally. Still, the ceremony was for all of them deeply meaningful and the idea of giving, receiving, and repaying was gratefully accepted. The ideology of gift exchange and the symbolism of free choice were one set of things; the reality of what the slave actually paid, and was required to continue paying, was quite another. To understand the totality of what transpired in the various rituals of release, we must now examine the data more systematically.

The Modes of Release

There were various modes of release from slavery, and most societies at any given time employed several of them. Manumission was not itself a constant: in a given society what a slave achieved through manumission varied. Some slaves achieved full manumission at once, others attained it over time, still others remained for the rest of their lives in a twilight state of semimanumission. The different modes of release reflected such differences in the kinds of manumission.

The modes of release varied too according to which party initiated the release and according to the factors that motivated both slave and master. In some cases, both wished to remain closely tied to each other; in other cases, the slave wished to be as far removed from the master as possible, to the point of returning home or migrating to another more favorable society; and in others, it was the master who wished the ex-slave to remove himself. Different modes of release might be used depending on the expected outcome.

The final variable was the legal and cultural idiom employed in rationalizing and legitimizing the release. Special problems perhaps existed, which had to be resolved before the master was capable of releasing his or her slave, even if he were willing. For example, minors were not usually permitted to manumit in ancient Rome and the French West Indian colonies during the eighteenth century, and in many societies mistresses were forbidden to manumit their male slaves in order to marry them. Exceptions were usually found in special modes of manumission that circumvented the legal prohibition. Or the mode could simply be a cultural survival, a functionally obsolete method that persisted from a previous period when it was meaningful. This was true of *manumissio censu* (a form of political manumission) during the late republic and the early imperial period of ancient Rome.

With a few isolated and culturally peculiar exceptions, the modes of release throughout the slaveholding world were basically of seven types: (1) postmortem; (2) cohabitation; (3) adoption; (4) political; (5) collusive litigation; (6) sacral; and (7) purely contractual.

POSTMORTEM MANUMISSION

The postmortem mode was one of the most widespread, and most likely was one of the earliest modes. By it I mean the release of the slave at the death of his master, whether by written will, or by verbally expressed desire, or by heirs on behalf of the deceased master. There are many reasons why post-mortem manumission was so common and so early to develop. The master who freed his slave after his death incurred no personal cost to himself. There was, of course, a cost to his heirs, but this was more than compensated for by the second factor accounting for the popularity of this mode: it was one of the most effective means of motivating the slave to accept his role and effectively perform his assigned task, whatever it was. The mere possibility of postmortem manumission motivated all slaves in a large household, even if eventually only one or two were manumitted.[27]

The origins of this mode and the fact that it was one of the earliest forms of manumission among most peoples was closely related to the primitive practice of using slaves as sacrificial victims and as gift exchange among persons. We have seen that slaves were killed for three main reasons: as sacrifice to the gods or ancestral spirits; to accompany the master in the afterlife; and to display the master's prestige, power, and wealth, either during his life or at his death. The three uses are clearly interrelated: the same gift can serve the double purpose of an exchange among men and between men and gods. In the same way that the slaughter of slaves at potlatches was as much for the benefit of impressing men as for a sacrifice to the gods, so the burial of slaves with their masters may have served as much for accompaniment of the master to the world of the dead as it did for a sacrifice to the ancestral spirits and gods whom the master was about to join. Indeed, such mortuary sacrifices may even have served a third function: to impress the living with the honor, prestige, and wealth of the deceased.

Illustrative of such multivocal gift exchanges between men and gods, combined with spiritual accompaniment in the afterlife and a final display of honor and wealth, is the beautiful and brutal story of the Icelandic princess Bryndhild, who did not wish to live after her beloved Sigurd had died. She had her eight male and five female slaves killed, and before committing suicide herself, she ordered: "Bedeck the pyre with shields and hangings, variegated Welsh [foreign] cloth and Welsh corpses. Let the hun [that is, Sigurd] be burned on the side of me; on the other side, my servants with their precious ornaments and two hawks." The Welsh corpses were "to honor the dead." She added: "Then will our procession not appear mean and poor, for it shall be followed by five female thralls and eight male thralls of gentle birth reared by me."[28]

Among a great many peoples who sacrificed slaves coexisted the practice of freeing some slaves on the ceremonial occasions when others were sacrificed. What this immediately suggests is that the killing and the freeing of a slave were symbolically identical acts—an identification that makes a good deal of sense. To own a slave, after all, meant simply that one had exclusive proprietary powers in him; and such powers were equally destroyed whether the slave was killed or given away or freed. The principle of gift exchange was served by all three forms of proprietary destruction: in the first, the killing of the slave, the exchange was with a deity or spirit; in the second it was with the slave himself; in the last it was with a third party. Furthermore, giving the slave to himself sometimes also served the dual exchange function between master and slave and between master and god.

The comparative data allow us to observe this process of substitution during the transition stage when sacrifice and emancipation both were practiced, as well as later, when human sacrifice of the slave had been totally replaced by manumission. Let us examine the process among three widely separated groups: the Garos of India, the Toradjas of the central Celebes, and the Indians of the northwest coast of America.

Several observers have established that human sacrifice of slaves was common "in olden times" among the Garos. When this practice was abolished, it was replaced by the sacrifice of an animal—a bull in some areas, a goat in others—at the cremation of the corpse. However, in direct reference to the earlier practice of sacrificing a slave, "a living slave [was] tied to the leg of the corpse from the day of the decease to the hour of the cremation. He or she was then released from further servitude."[29]

Among the Toradjas the development of manumission from the sacrificial murder of the slave at the death of the owner is readily observed. Of its earliest form we learn that at the death of a prominent person a slave was bought from a neighboring tribe for the sacrifice, or if the tribe of the deceased was at war, a head-hunting expedition would go in search of heads. In a second development that began later but ran *concurrently with the first,* a slave was designated the *tandojai,* the person who took food to the deceased and guarded his body from the werewolf to prevent the latter from eating it. The tandojai would speak to no one during this period, and he was free to take food for the dead master from anyone. It was said that "the *tandojai* lives like a death soul who now has a death soul in service." Sometimes instead of assigning a slave as tandojai, a piece of his ear was removed and the blood running from it was rubbed on the coffin. Where the slave was made a tandojai, however, he was always freed after the funeral services; significantly, he led a solitary life and people feared him. In other areas, especially after the arrival of the Dutch, a later development seems to have been the simple guarding of the grave by a slave who was then freed a hundred days after the funeral. The Toradja case clearly indicates that such substitutions were not due to European influences and prohibitions, since they existed alongside the continuing practice of human sacrifice and before Dutch contact.[30]

We find the same striking evidence of the identification of sacrifice with manumission among many of the American northwest coastal tribes where manumission at ceremonial occasions, especially mortuary ones, was often the only mode of release from slavery. Among the Tlingit, slaves were both sacrificed and freed at potlatches and at feasts for the social reception of children; for example, the slave girl who attended her young mistress during the period of her seclusion before she was brought out into society was freed after the burning of the young mistress' old clothes.[31] A slave who disappeared at the cremation of his master was usually considered free, as was the slave who dressed the master in his funeral robe.[32] Among the Nootka, it was the custom to give away some slaves, in addition to killing some, upon the death of a chief.[33]

It does not seem unreasonable to speculate that in many instances of postmortem manumission the identification of release with the sacrificial murder of slaves has survived. We know, for example, that among the Aztecs postmortem manumission was the most common mode of release, and given the important role of the ritual sacrifice of slaves in this society, it is certainly not unreasonable to assume that postmortem release was a continuation of the earlier practice of identifying the killing and freeing of slaves as parallel symbolic acts. The later Christian practice of testamentary manumission substituted easily for this tradition.[34] In much the same way, the Islamic practices of testamentary manumission seem to have replaced— without an intervening period of pagan postmortem manumission—the earlier Wolof and Sereer practice of human sacrifice at the death of the master, which continued as late as the sixteenth century.[35]

What of the origins of testamentary manumission, the postliterate form of the postmortem mode, in Christianity and Islam? The Western mode of testamentary manumission preceded Christianity by many centuries and was simply adopted and sanctified by the early church. The problem, then, is to explain the origins of the practice in pre-Christian times. Unfortunately, there are few data, so it is impossible to do more than speculate. Postmortem manumission may well have developed as a substitute for human sacrifice, in much the same way that it emerged among many contemporary primitives. We have already seen that the custom of human sacrifice at the death of important persons was practiced among the primitive Europeans, as it was in the ancient Near East, the Orient—and, indeed, all other parts of the world. Primitive Rome was no exception.

The circumstantial evidence is very suggestive. Manumission *in testamento* was one of the earliest modes of manumission in ancient Rome and must have long preceded the Twelve Tables, since the Law of the Twelve Tables, which refers to it, takes the form of a confirmation of existing practice. In early times the will was ratified by the primitive assembly. David Daube notes that "the element of public control would be present." He argues forcefully that manumission "*testamento* and *vindicta* must have preceded *censu.*" The same arguments also point to the historical primacy of manumission testamento over vindicta. As Daube points out, "In the history of law private actions authorized by the community preceded 'community-initiated or state actions.'" Furthermore, "a head of a family, a *pater familias,* was stronger and more independent in the primitive, small, loosely organized society than later in a developed and numerous state."[36] Of all the modes of manumission, testamento was the most private. Partly for this reason it did not require any legal convention, only social confirmation. Thus, the very legal maturity of manumission vindicta—maturity in the sense of employing a rather sophisticated legal fiction, to be discussed below—suggests that it was the less archaic of the two. This was also the basis of Appleton's inference that manumission in testamento was the oldest mode in ancient Rome: an inference that Buckland rejects, claiming that "the contrary conclusion seems more reasonable."[37] Buckland gives no reason for this contention; perhaps he assumed that the existence of a legal fiction is indicative of a more archaic form. If so, he was wrong: fictitious litigation is the surest sign of legal maturity, as anyone acquainted with primitive law will attest.

The comparative, circumstantial, and internal legal evidence all point to the historical primacy of manumission in testamento in primitive Roman law. Whether or not this earliest form of manumission developed, in turn, from an earlier custom of symbolically identifying the sacrifice of slaves with their release must remain a matter for speculation. Consider, however, the evidence we do have. We know that the primitive Romans kept slaves, and that the institution of slavery was of great antiquity. We know that the primitive Europeans performed human sacrifice at the death of slave owners, and we have no reason to believe that the Romans were any different on this score. Indeed, apparently under Gaulish influence, there was a revival of the practice of human sacrifice in 225 B.C. when several captives, including two Gauls, were buried alive. Instances of human sacrifice occurred for the next three hundred years, although outlawed by the Senate in 97 B.C. The primitive practice of substituting an animal for a human being when human sacrifice was no longer allowed is attested in historical times, most notably the offering of a goat as surrogate for a human victim in the cult of Vediovis.[38]

Whatever its origins, testamentary manumission was the most popular mode of release from slavery throughout Roman antiquity. R. H. Barrow summarizes the main reasons as follows: "Manumission by will had advantages: it retained the services of slaves to the very last moment in which their owner could use them; it kept the slaves in a suspense of good conduct to the end. Trimalchio made no secret of the provisions of his will: 'my object in making them known is simply that my household may love me as if I were dead.' The manumitter departed from life in a comfortable glow of self-righteousness, which he may have earned by this one deed. He could rely on the grudging gratitude of those who may have hated him, and could trust that a suitable gathering of mourners would lend more than mere respectability to his funeral."[39]

There was, however, a great deal more involved than Barrow imagined. Such manumissions may have been a vestigial gift exchange with the gods, a last sacrificial repayment before departing this world (though in a highly symbolic way). It is important to emphasize that there was never, either in primitive or classical times, any notion of piety involved; this would have been alien to Roman religious conceptions, as it would have been to all other pagans. Second, such manumissions were forms of gift exchange between the dead man and his successors, for anything that enhanced his prestige must have enhanced the prestige of his successors. Significantly, sacrifice of slaves used to perform very much the same function. T. C. Ryan, in his study of the economics of human sacrifice in Africa, found that the most likely model to explain the incidence of sacrifice was that of gift exchange, even where enhancement of the donor's prestige was also involved. He concludes: "Sacrifices at the funeral obsequies of an important person, while sending his favorite slaves to attend him in the hereafter, also asserted the wealth and power of his successor."[40] Exactly the same could be said for the release of slaves at the death of the master.

There was a third gift exchange involved, again largely on the symbolic level, though powerfully so: that between deceased master and slave. The master's death was the occasion for the release of the slave. It is a short step from this to the position that the master had died so that the slave might be free, that is, might be born again into social life. This placed the ex-slave under the deepest possible obligation to repay the gift of the master by honoring him for the rest of his life, and of course also honoring and serving his successors. The slave's manumission may also have had an even deeper symbolic meaning. The slave was an extension of the master's self, a view given legal expression in many slave codes (one of the most noteworthy being that of early modern Russia).[41] The freeing of the slave at the death of the master may well have had a death-defying and recreative meaning: the master's spirit resurrected in the living person of his favorite surrogate. If this was so, it placed the manumitted slave under an even greater obligation: he had to be not only grateful, but a faithful vehicle of the deceased man's spirit. Whether such symbolic meanings existed among the late republican and early imperial Romans is problematic. The symbolism of Christianity, and its enormous success in the Roman world, strongly suggest that such meanings were present in the later empire. Certainly many primitives held such views: among several tribes, for instance, the slaves freed at the death of the master were greatly feared.

There was one last critical development in the symbolic meaning of postmortem manumission: the radically new conception of the relation between man, god, and the cosmos. Robert N. Bellah and others have shown how the development of the great world religions entailed a collapse of the cosmological monism of both primitive and archaic religions. The world was no longer seen as a single cosmos in which men and gods participated in sacred and profane fields, but rather as two sharply polarized cosmos—one centered on the present world, the other on the life hereafter. The major ethical implications of this cosmological dualism were, on the one hand, rejection of the present world as evil and man as inherently unworthy, and on the other hand, emergence of the idea of salvation as the central religious preoccupation. Ritual and sacrifice remained prominent but, as Bellah tells us, they took on a new significance; they were no longer directed so much at fulfilling obligations to the gods by establishing harmony with the cosmos, but at the primary goal of salvation, that of saving man from his original evil and sinfulness and ensuring a place in heaven rather than hell in the other cosmos, which is entered at death.[42]

How did this development influence the interpretation of manumission? The impact was tremendous, but the various world religions came to a recognition of the relationship in different ways. Releasing one's slave from slavery eventually was seen as a pious act that would be rewarded in heaven: it was almost an ethical imperative in any transcendental ethical creed that emphasized humanism, individualism, and salvation, as did all the major world religions. And indeed, they all came to this view in time.

To begin with Christianity, what is immediately striking is the length of time it took to realize this imperative, and the circumstances under which the realization came about. Until the end of the Roman Empire, Christianity had no influence whatever on the meaning and motivation of this form of manumission. Even after it had become an official creed, Christianity remained indifferent to manumission in general. To be sure, the church, from as early as the third century, encouraged the ransoming of captives, but this was motivated by a horror of Christian souls being enslaved by heathens, not by any aversion to slavery per se. Manumission in the church was encouraged from the fifth century on, but the emphasis was on manumission *inter vivos.* The objective was to invest most manumissions with Christian ceremony. As late as the sixth century the church had yet to develop any notion of the virtuousness of manumission, and there was no conception whatever of the special virtue of testamentary manumission.

It was not until the start of the seventh century that we find the first forcefully articulated theological statement that manumission *in general* was an act of piety; it came from Saint Gregory the Great, who took to their logical conclusion the reservations sounded earlier by Chrysostom and Cyril of Alexandria. Even so, there was no attempt to single out testamentary manumission as the form that was most expressive of piety.[43] All of this changed dramatically during the ninth and tenth centuries. At last manumission was not only encouraged but viewed as good for the soul. Piety and salvation were especially ensured by testamentary manumission. The following formulaic statements attached to testamentary manumission are typical:

"While Almighty God gives us health in this life, we ought frequently to think of the salvation of our souls—and so I, for the good of my soul, and to break off my sins that God may pardon me in future, have released my slave ——— and have given him his peculium." Or the following: "It behooves every man in this life to think of the good of his soul, and so I, in God's name, having regard to God and the redemption of my soul, manumit etc., etc." Or finally: "He who releases the bondservice due to him may hope that he may receive a reward in the future from God, and so for my eternal retribution I manumit, etc. etc."[44]

How do we explain this extraordinary change in the religious perception of manumission? Our concern here is not with the influence of Christianity on the *frequency* of manumission, but on its *rationale* or ideology. Why did Christianity wait seven hundred years before reinterpreting the meaning of manumission, and nearly nine hundred years before encouraging testamentary manumission as a form of piety that was good for the reception of the soul in the afterlife? The answer is simple. Early medieval Christianity was fully involved with the problem of converting the heathen peoples of both central and northern Europe, especially the Germanic tribes. The sacrifice of slaves, as well as their manumission at the death of the master, were well-established pagan practices among these primitive Europeans. And the advocates of the new religion were determined to stamp out all forms of paganism, including the sacrifice of slaves at their master's death. Hence the manumission of slaves at their master's death, which already existed as a sacrifice substitute, was reinforced and encouraged; but where the pagan practice of postmortem manumission was meant to honor the departed in this life or serve as a final offering to the pagan gods, the meaning was changed to securing the salvation of the soul of the departed in the next world. The shift of meaning was easily understandable to the pagans, since it was already partly for this purpose that the slaves were sacrificed. By assimilating the pagan meaning of postmortem sacrifice to the Christian meaning of piety and redemption of soul through the encouragement of testamentary manumission, the church was able to achieve two critical objectives simultaneously: it kept the pagan practice of postmortem manumission, but changed its meaning to the Christian one of salvation of the soul in the afterlife; and it kept a good part of the meaning of the pagan practice of postmortem sacrifice of slaves—assistance of the master in his passage to the hereafter—while abolishing the practice itself. Although this transformation is easily documented from the history of all the central and north European peoples, it is best observed in medieval Sweden where Christianization was "gentle and tentative" and where the abundance of testamentary evidence shows clearly how the church introduced "an important second incentive for emancipation: to free a slave was meritorious in the eyes of God and contributed toward the earning of salvation."[45]

Much the same process occurred in the relation of Christianity to modern pagan peoples. The same reinterpretation, for example, quickly took place among the Aztecs, and also among the tribes whose practices of postmortem manumission and sacrifice have already been discussed. But acculturation is always a two-way process. Christianity may have gained more than it lost in this neat piece of theological reinterpretation; still, it would be wrong to assume that the priests had it all their own way. There was compromise. The primitive mind did bend the faith, if only in a small way, to its own manner of thinking. We may speculate that, to the converted, primitive testamentary manumission became a powerful binary symbol. The socially dead slave was made into a socially alive person. The master's death became the occasion for a life-creating act, which pleased not only the men he left behind but the new god he was to meet. The element of sacrifice to the god persisted, only in its more sophisticated form of sacrifice in property. The element of gift exchange was still present—a life here on earth was exchanged for a life there in heaven. Christianity had already anticipated this interpretation: the Crucifixion was an enormously powerful and multivocal symbol. It may have been altogether too powerful and too primitive for the sophisticated urban world of civilized Rome. Thus Paul, when asked to give his views on manumission, made the following paradoxical reply: "Regarding the matter of which you wrote me, the slave who is called by the Lord is a freedman of the Lord, likewise the free man who is called is a slave of Christ. You have been bought for a price, be not slaves of men. Let each man, brothers, remain beside God in that status in which he was called."[46] This theological obscurantism left the early fathers utterly confused. Paul himself may have been none too clear about what he meant.

Much the same process took place in the spread of Islam and its relations, first to the pagan Arabs and later to the other pagan peoples it converted to its faith. The Arabs of Muhammad's day had, like the Romans of the early empire, already abandoned the human sacrifice of slaves and practiced only postmortem manumission. But like the Romans and Greeks, such manumission was directed mainly at the enhancement of the deceased master's good name and honor. We know that Muhammad and his followers accepted the existence of slavery as part of the social order, but much more quickly than Christianity, Islam sought to humanize the institution. To this end, Muhammad not only encouraged manumission inter vivos, but established as a cardinal principle the idea that manumission, especially the testamentary mode, was a pious act that was good for the master's soul. Indeed, Islam went even further. Not only was the master enjoined to free his slaves in the hope of reward in the afterlife, but his heirs were enjoined to do so, for the "freeing of a slave on behalf of a person who is dead is profitable for the dead."[47] And there is abundant evidence that Islam, like Christianity among the Germanic pagans, reinterpreted the traditional practice of the sacrifice and release of slaves among the pagan peoples of Africa and Asia it proselytized. We have already cited the case of the Wolof of the Gambia, who sacrificed slaves as late as the sixteenth century, then replaced this practice with the Islamic doctrine of manumission as a form of piety and redemption for the maltreatment of slaves.

THE COHABITATIONAL MODE

This mode of manumission, by means of marriage or concubinage, was the most common form among lineage- or kin-based preliterate peoples, and it was also the most common mode in the Islamic world, especially in Africa and the Middle East. The reasons are not hard to find. It was easy for men in most precapitalist societies to identify the status of a female slave with that of free concubine or junior wife. The difference in status usually had no material consequences for the woman, although it did for her children. Manumission of, and cohabitation with, female slaves was not only allowed but actively encouraged in Islam. Slaves and concubines were the only women with whom a Muslim was allowed to have either premarital or extramarital sexual relations. While the number of wives was limited to four, the number of concubines remained limitless. A childless concubine could be sold, but rarely was.[48] Once a concubine gave birth to a child by her master, she became in most Islamic states an *umm walad* and could not be sold. On her master's death, such a woman customarily was freed. All children born of legal concubinage were legitimate and usually inherited equally with children born in wedlock. The master had to acknowledge paternity, although in all legal traditions except the Hanafis, he was obliged to do so if the concubine was already umm walad.[49] Islam also encouraged men who were too poor to acquire free wives to marry converted female slaves instead, although "such unions suffer only half the punishment for adultery reserved for formally free wives."

Practice followed religious precept quite faithfully throughout the Islamic world, although there were occasional exceptions. (In Somalia, for example, the concubine was not usually freed after bearing a son, although she was given an allowance.[50]) The free concubine and her free sons are part and parcel of Islamic history and society. Many Islamic rulers have been the children of slave concubines, and the course of Islamic history has been decisively influenced by this pattern of manumission.[51]

Manumission by means of concubinage and marriage is by no means peculiar to the Islamic world. Typical of the preliterate world are the Sena of Mozambique, among whom "marriage between *akporo* [slaves] and free Sena were a form of institutionalized manumission."[52] Free Sena of both sexes could and did marry slaves. But even among preliterates, only a minority of peoples permitted free women to marry slaves; and among advanced peoples with highly developed slave systems, the practice usually was strongly forbidden. Yet it would be a great mistake to assume that advanced premodern peoples *always* prohibited marriage between free women and slaves. The average male slave everywhere generally was unable to marry a free woman because he could not afford to do so. Even where there was disdain for such marriages, exceptions were often made for prosperous slaves or those of powerful owners. In imperial Rome, where strong sanctions were imposed against free women marrying slaves, exceptions were made for the more powerful slaves of the emperor. The important point, however, is that marriage to a free woman did not necessarily bring with it free status for the male slave as it invariably did in the case of the female slave married to a free man. Women rarely confer status on their husbands, even in matrilineal societies where they determine the status of their children.

To return to the more normal practice of manumission by means of marriage to a free man or concubinage with the master, we find that the practice was widespread throughout the world, in both precapitalist and modern times. China presents an interesting case. Contrary to Islamic practice, free women could also become concubines. What is more, it was possible to sell a free concubine, as long as her honorable or nonslave status was made clear. Hence, it was even easier to identify the status of slave lover with that of free concubine. As in the Islamic world, the children of concubines often attained considerable status in the imperial hierarchy, sometimes becoming emperors themselves, and there are occasional cases of former concubines becoming empresses.

What our analysis of the comparative data suggests is that, first, it is extremely unusual to find a slaveholding society in which freemen, especially masters, were prohibited from—or in practice, refrained from—cohabiting with female slaves with the inevitable result of producing children by these women. Indeed, I know of only one case in the entire annals of slaveholding societies in which female slaves were not sexually exploited and in which masters were strongly and effectively prohibited from cohabiting with their slaves. This is the extremely austere Gilyak of southeastern Siberia. Female slavery was an important part of their domestic economy up to the end of the nineteenth century, and possession of these human chattels was both an index of great wealth and a sign of prestige. The slave women, though economically and socially valuable for their masters, were viewed with disdain as persons, and a master who cohabited with one of them immediately lost status and incited great indignation in his community. This moral prohibition reinforced the domestic exploitation of the female slaves, for as Leopold von Schrenck, who studied the Amur group during the mid-nineteenth century explained, the sexual contempt in which the slave women were held meant that the wives of the master entertained no feelings of jealousy toward them and welcomed them as workhorses within the household while they, the wives, performed the more pleasant handicraft tasks. Without doubt this sexual avoidance of slave women was largely due to racial scorn for the Ainus, from whom most of them were purchased.[53]

Second, the sexual exploitation of slave women by their masters often resulted in ties of affection between them; and obviously, those ties were reinforced when the slave woman bore a child for the master. Many societies in addition to those advocating Islam automatically freed the concubine, especially after she had had a child. About a third of all non-Islamic societies fall into this category. In addition to the Sena, examples are the Nkundo, the Ibos, the ancient Vietnamese, the ancient Mesopotamians, Swedes certainly by the late thirteenth century (and possibly earlier), and the French Antilles up to about the end of the seventeenth century.

Ancient Mesopotamia is of special interest. The Hammurabi code required the manumission of a female slave and her children on the death of the owner. It was customary for a wife who was sterile to give her husband a slave concubine in order to bear him children. Such *assatum* or concubines did not have the special slave tattoo and could not be sold, but their status was ambiguous; they remained the slave of the master's wife while serving as the master's concubine. As one would expect, this was an emotionally charged situation that often led to tensions, especially after the concubine bore a child and became (inevitably) forward in her relations with her mistress. Apparently, prosperous and caring fathers gave such slave-maids at the time of their daughters' marriages to ensure that their daughters were not divorced on the grounds of sterility. The biblical story of Hagar, given to Abraham by his sterile wife, Sarah, ended in jealousy and grief, and this may well have been the fate of many such triangular relationships. The ménage à trois hardly ever works, especially when a slave or servant is involved. C. R. Driver and J. C. Miles suggest that such Hagar-type concubinage occurred in the ancient Near East mainly where the wife was a priestess. Apparently in the late Babylonian period concubines remained slaves and could even be sold.[54]

In the second group of non-Islamic societies there was no legal requirement to free the concubine, but in practice it was usually done. Most non-Islamic societies fall into this group: the Mende, the Aboh, the Karebe of Africa, the peoples of ancient India and pharaonic Egypt, and the slaveholding societies of classical and medieval Europe. We have little evidence about concubinal relationships in classical Greece, although there are clear indications of its existence in the *Iliad* and the *Odyssey*. The record of the Delphic manumissions in the second and first centuries B.C. suggests that freedom through concubinage with a master or other freeman was not uncommon. According to Keith Hopkins, we simply do not know where slave women procured the substantial sums demanded for their release in the Delphic manumissions; concubinage with a third party is a reasonable guess.[55] While we can only speculate on the instances of concubinal manumission in ancient Greece, ancient Athens must have been one of the rare cases where male slaves achieved freedom by this means. It is well established that there was an unusually high incidence of homosexuality among the slaveholding class, and it may have been that a substantial number of slaves bought for exclusively sexual purposes were males. Hence ties of sexual affection resulting in manumission may have applied as much to males as to females. The young boy slaves and youth freed in the will of the Peripatetics perhaps were cases in point. It is hard to see what other purpose they could have served in the philosophers' households and for what other reason they should have been so favored in their masters' wills.[56]

Much less exotic was the Roman experience. Indeed, the traditional practice of manumitting concubines and their children was framed into law by Justinian, who provided that the concubine of a man who died without indicating her status in his will should be freed along with her children.[57]

The practice of manumitting the concubine and her children continued throughout the Middle Ages and was also widely practiced in the slaveholding societies of the Americas, the Mascarene Islands of the Indian Ocean, and the Banda Islands at the southern end of the Moluccas. The view that there was a greater tendency toward concubinage in Latin America as opposed to the northwest European slaveholding societies is a myth, although it is true that manumission rates were higher in most of the Latin American slave societies. Concubinal manumission was not uncommon in the English-speaking and French Caribbean slave societies. Indeed, genuine concubinage amounting to common-law marriage was found as frequently in the British, French, and Dutch Caribbean as in other areas of the Americas, including Spanish America. The Jamaican and French planters were sometimes as eager to manumit and endow their illegitimate offspring and their concubines as any Islamic master. Indeed, so much wealth was being passed on to the freed colored class that legislation had to be passed repeatedly to limit the amount of money that freed colored offspring could inherit. The frequency with which the laws were reenacted attest to their ineffectiveness. It should be emphasized, however, that while a disproportionate number of freed persons were the concubines and children of their former masters, this group of societies differs radically from those of the ancient Near East and the Islamic states in that there was no automatic legal manumission of such persons, and, more important, the vast majority of concubines and slave progeny did not receive their freedom. South Africa and the French Antilles during the second half of the seventeenth century did have laws or official edicts requiring manumission of the progeny of concubines, but recent works have demonstrated that while there were indeed a few such manumissions and even marriages between masters and their concubines, on the whole the laws were largely ineffectual.[58]

There is, finally, a small group of slaveholding societies in which slave women, while sexually exploited, were rarely freed. In the premodern world the overwhelming majority were kin-based matrilineal societies. Slave concubines and wives were highly desired in such societies, as a means of acquiring children over whom the father had complete control. Hence, such concubines and their children tended to remain slaves. The Ashanti and Imbangala in Africa were two noteworthy examples. Other instances will be cited in the next chapter, when we discuss freedman status. In the modern world, South Africa during the eighteenth and early nineteenth centuries and the U.S. South during the eighteenth and nineteenth centuries are the most striking cases.

ADOPTION

From concubinal manumission we move to adoption as a mode of release from slavery. This is also an ancient and widespread mode, though by no means a universal one. In sharp contrast with concubinage, adoption as a means of manumission is conspicuous for its absence in the numerous Islamic slaveholding societies. The main reason, no doubt, is that Muhammad, while he did not abolish adoptions, significantly transformed the traditional custom, one that was basically similar to the fictive kin assimilation found all over the world. Muhammad himself recommended clientage as a more suitable form of bond between nonrelatives: "If ye know not their fathers, let them be as your brethren in religion and your clients."[59] Subsequent Islamic law came to recognize only one form of filiation: what is known as *iqrâr* or "acknowledgment," which, while closely resembling adoption, has certain important differences. For example, a man cannot acknowledge another who is not at least twelve and a half years younger than he is; nor can he acknowledge a person whose parents are known. This automatically excludes the very group of slaves who are most likely to qualify for manumission—the houseborn. Favored slaves purchased from pagan lands, however, were not infrequently acknowledged, especially if the master had no heir.

Outside of Islamic lands, adoption was practiced among the great majority of premodern peoples although it was rarely a very important form of manumission. The mode was very common among preliterate peoples. We have seen earlier that the slave was marginally reintegrated in many such societies as a junior member of the family. Thus, emancipation by adoption was simply an extension of the assimilative process begun during enslavement. There was usually, however, a definite point indicated by a rite of passage in which a slave ceased to be a slave and became a fully adopted member of his master's family. Often the adoptive process took place over several generations, so that a descendant of a slave after a certain generation was automatically considered a full member of the community. Among the

Katchin of highland Burma, for example, the *mayan* or slave had the status of an illegitimate son—between a rich man and a poor son-in-law. Absorption increased by blood the ties that strengthened over the generations, and when the mayan was to be manumitted, he was "ceremonially received into the clan of which he [was] a real blood member."[60]

It is striking that such automatic intergenerational adoption took place even where there was marked hostility toward the adoption of first-generation slaves. The group that best illustrates this pattern is the Gilyaks. We have already seen that first-generation slaves among them were viewed with total contempt. Masters, however, procured spouses for their slaves, and according to Lev Schternberg, the son of two slaves was considered "free to the neck," that is, only his head was free. The grandchildren of slaves were said to be "free to the belt," the great-grandchildren were "free to the feet," and all descendants of slaves of the fourth generation were considered "pure." They became *k: khal,* or kinsmen of their masters, and could sue anyone who called them slaves. "Pure," however, seems to have been a relative term. Such manumitted persons, while pure in law, still were stigmatized and treated condescendingly.[61]

K. Nwachukwu-Ogedengbe, in his study of slavery among the nineteenth-century Aboh, an Igbo-speaking group of the lower Niger, brings out the difference between the initial fictive kin absorption of slaves and marginals and the status of the genuinely adopted freed slaves, and emphasizes the fact that such adoptions were highly unusual. He writes: "Although the slave was absorbed into the kinship system he was not included in the inheritance regulations governing true kinship relations. No property passed to him upon his master's death except at the will of the master's heirs. The only exception was an adopted slave *ukodei* on whose behalf the special ritual of igoya n'obii [to admit into the lineage through ritual sacrifice] had been performed. It must be emphasized that the *ukodei was not a pseudokinsman but a kinsman in the fullest meaning of the term.* The status of *ukodei* was, however, conferred *only in exceptional cases*—for example, in the absence of a natural heir who could sacrifice at the shrine of the deceased master" (emphasis added).[62] Almost exactly the same observation could be made of the medieval Scandinavian communities. The child by a slave woman, if he was to be fully freed rather than having his descendants gradually absorbed intergenerationally, "had to go through a full ceremony of adoption into the family before he had equal rights of inheritance or received and paid a full share in atonement."[63]

Adoption may therefore have come about in two ways, by a gradual intergenerational process taking anywhere from two to five generations, or in a single stroke. The latter was usually attended by more ceremony, and the assimilation of the individual and his descendants was apparently more complete than in the intergenerational case. Even so, in both instances it would seem that the blemish of having a slave ancestor was never completely erased, even though the sanctions against any verbal abuse of the descendants may have been so strong that it was expressed only among intimates. Among a wide range of tribal peoples we find the adoption rite being repeated after long intervals in order to "cleanse" the ex-slave of all status pollution and to reaffirm the community's acceptance of his changed status. Among many primitive Germanic groups the manumission of the slave had to be announced to the assembly of free persons twice in twenty years, after which no one could contest the change of status. And among the northwest coast Indians, when a free woman took the unusual step of marrying a slave (invariably a shotgun marriage), not only was the slave's freedom bought and her husband formally adopted into the woman's kin group, but ritual cleansing ceremonies were conducted for the unborn fetus and were repeated later during various periods of the child's lifetime.

A more direct contractual type of adoption was practiced among most of the literate and politically advanced premodern peoples. Although not mentioned in the Hammurabi code, release by adoption was one of the two most common forms of manumission in ancient Mesopotamia. According to Isaac Mendelsohn, "Release by adoption was fundamentally a business transaction, a quid pro quo proposition. The manumitted slave entered into a sonship [or daughtership] relation with his former master. The relationship terminated with the death of the manumitter." The release by adoption of a female slave was often accompanied by her marriage to a free man, in which case the couple was supposed to support the manumitter until his or her death. Adoption was rarely an act of generosity.[64]

In the Greco-Roman societies, adoption was somewhat unusual. Given the ethnically exclusive nature of Greek society, this is not surprising. The practice existed in early Roman society but was extremely unusual even during the late republican era. By the period of classical law, it had completely died out. Manumission by adoption was equally rare in the romanized areas of medieval Europe, and of course it was virtually nonexistent in the modern Americas.

POLITICAL MANUMISSION

In one sense a form of adoption, political manumission occurs when the state or agent of the community (in the person of the chief, sultan, or ruler) adopts the former slave as a full-fledged member of the community with or without the consent of the owner. There were many reasons why the central authority or ruler of the community may have wished to manumit slaves, the most common being exceptional acts of valor on the part of the slave, usually in warfare. Typical was the old Norse law that "when common danger calls all (free and slave) to arms in the defense of the country the slave who succeeds in slaying an enemy in battle is free."[65] As we shall see in Chapter 10, slaves were often freed by the state in order to make them eligible to become soldiers in societies where as slaves they were strictly forbidden to bear arms. Slaves who revealed treasonable acts on the part of their master or others also were frequently rewarded with their freedom, although this obviously was a dangerous practice if the charge failed to hold up. In ancient Greece the presentation of facts (as distinct from testimony) by slaves on such matters was one of the few occasions on which the slave could participate in the legal process. Where the state owned slaves, it could release them either on an individual basis or by a general pardon.

In Greece, Rome, and in most other premodern societies ownership and release of such slaves presented few special problems. The situation was different in China, and to some extent Korea, where a large proportion of slaves in private hands were actually state owned, with their usufruct granted to favored officials. Whether the private masters of such slaves had the power to manumit them remained an unresolved legal problem in imperial China. More complicated were the periodic large-scale pardons of a substantial number of slaves, both privately and publicly owned, by Chinese emperors in occasional fits of magnanimity. From the continuing presence of slaves (and other evidence) it would seem that both the restrictions on the manumission of state-owned slaves by private masters and the manumission of privately and even publicly owned slaves in response to imperial decrees were frequently neglected.[66] Slaves were sometimes freed by the state when badly mistreated by their masters. This was not uncommon in some Islamic lands, since the Koran requires it, but it was also the case in a number of non-Islamic societies.

Whatever the reason, manumission by the state was often the most complete method—and from the slave's point of view, the one that granted him the fullest integration into the society. Among the Germanic peoples freedman status was often hemmed in by considerable civil disability. A major exception was the slave freed by the king for exceptional merit; he was immediately made a full member of the community and given arms. A similar situation prevailed among the Somalis, where freed persons usually were at a considerable disadvantage. However, where a person was manumitted by a decree of a sultan, he became a full member of the Somali community with none of the usual restrictions on his freedom. His natality was fully restored and he could, for example, marry a freeborn Somali woman.[67] In ancient Rome too, only the emperor could restore natality—that is, exercise the legal fiction that the former slave was born a freeman, whatever may have actually been the case, or that he had never been enslaved.

If we are to accept the complex and subtle arguments of David Daube on the nature of early Roman manumission, *manumissio censu* (in which the slave was freed by being enrolled by the censor) was a distinctive form of political manumission. Unlike other modes where the master released the slave and gave up what belonged to him, here the state selected and incorporated the slave as a citizen. Daube writes: "In *manumissio censu,* enrollment, incorporation by the State, came first, and liberty from the master was in strictness, only a consequence of that act. The master did not give up what had been his: he lost it, as a result of a political act."[68] Usually the master agreed to this act, but the censor had the right to register the slave against his master's will. While manumissio censu developed after other modes of manumission, it may have been the earliest mode of granting the freedman citizenship: the other modes merely granted release from slavery. Only much later did citizenship come automatically with the granting of manumission by Roman masters using all the different modes. When this happened—during the late republic—there was no longer any special need for manumissio censu, and by the period of the empire it had become obsolete. Buckland argues that its successor in the later imperial period was *manumissio in sacrosantis ecclesiis,* in that "it retains a trace of that element of public control which is dying out in the other forms.[69]

COLLUSIVE LITIGATION

The collusive mode of manumission was one of the earliest secular ways of circumventing the inalienability problem of release from slavery. It was a legal fiction, a form of collusive litigation that had much the same concept behind it in both Greece and Rome. In Athens it took the form of a simulated trial in which the slave was tried for abandoning his master, and thereby his status as slave, with a predetermined verdict of acquittal. The acquittal was proof that the person was not a slave. It did not imply, however, that the slave, so freed, was a citizen. He became, instead, a metic.[70] In Rome, where the procedure was known as *manumissio vindicta,* it took the form of an *adsertor libertatis* claiming the slave to be a free man before a magistrate. The master, as in Greece, made no defense, and the slave was declared free. This mode, incidentally, was accompanied in ancient Rome by an unparalleled ritual: the master held the slave by one of his limbs, slapped his cheek, then turned him around.[71] Buckland, like most other commentators, has expressed complete mystification at this extraordinary practice. Actually the practice of striking something or someone being alienated from its possessor, as a symbolic way of severing ties with it, is widespread. Mauss's explanation is that something owned is felt to possess an element of one's self in it and that therefore some symbolic means was necessary to break the bond when it was sold or given away. He found this to be true even of the France of his day, where numerous "customs show how it is necessary to detach the thing sold from the man who sells it, a thing may be slapped, a sheep may be whipped, and so on." For Mauss such rituals were vestiges of the previous practice of the gift exchange, lingering in formal legal exchange. Indeed, what he writes of such vestiges in modern France would hold even more for survivals in ancient law and society, barely removed from the natural economy in which prestations formed the dominant pattern of exchange: "The theme of the gift, of freedom and obligation in the gift, of generosity and self-interest in giving, reappear in our own society like the resurrection of a dominant motif long forgotten."[72]

It is noteworthy that in Greece collusive litigation was the most common mode of manumission except for Delphi. It was, for example, the typical mode in Athens. In Rome it ranked second only to testamentary manumission.[73]

SACRAL MANUMISSION

The origins and development of sacral manumission are not at all clear, although the subject has received considerable scholarly attention. It may have existed in the ancient Near East, although the evidence is inconclusive. It was, however, the most popular form of manumission in Delphi and thus is firmly associated with the Greek world. It is important to emphasize that sacral manumission was not the most popular form of manumission *throughout* Greece. It is merely the one about which we happen to have substantial evidence. It was not, so far as we know, practiced at any of the major Greek cities such as Athens, Corinth, or Thebes, where collusive litigation and testamentary manumission seem to have been the standard modes of release.[74]

According to Bömer, there were two kinds of sacral manumission: fiduciary consecration and fictive sale to a god. In consecration, the older of the two forms, the manumitter initiated the process in the *hope* that the god would free the slave; in fictive sale to the god, the slave initiated the process (practically, though not legally) under the *condition* that the god would free him.[75]

Though not the first to do so, the Delphic priests articulated most clearly what was entailed by manumission in terms of four basic freedoms: "[legal] status, personal inviolability, the right to work as one pleased, and the privilege of going wherever one wished."[76] There is no source in Delphi older than 201 B.C. Bömer rejects F. Sokolowski's thesis that sacral manumission originated in the practice of the slave's seeking asylum in the temple.[77] Another hypothesis is that sacral manumission may have developed from the genuine sale of slaves to the temple—in other words, temple slavery. Bömer expresses some doubt about this view, on the grounds that there were none of the expected transition forms between temple slavery and the fictive process of sacral manumission.[78] To argue from silence is always dangerous, but the comparative data support Bömer's skepticism. It is striking that wherever we find temple slavery, there is always a strong prohibition on the sale of such slaves. This was true, for example, of the temple slaves of ancient Mesopotamia, the *sirqu*, who became a hereditary caste of slaves and who were the only group of slaves barred from manumission.[79] It is significant that the slaves of the early and medieval churches were usually the last to be freed in the transition from slavery to serfdom.[80] In Burma we find that the temple slaves were a despised hereditary caste and could not be manumitted, even by the ruler.[81] And to cite a final case, the Osu, or cult slaves among the Ibos, were the one group who could never be assimilated. Even today descendants of Osu slaves, even upper-class Osus, suffer the stigma of their ancestry—unlike the descendants of other slaves.[82] Clearly there is something extraordinary about the status of the temple slave.[83]

I am therefore fully inclined to accept Bömer's thesis that sacral manumission developed not before, but after secular manumission in Greece, and I certainly agree with his rejection of the neoevolutionary assumption that the secular always follows the sacred form in the development of institutions. Sacral manumission developed as a substitute for adequate legal processes, as a way of giving sanction and ceremony to a purely secular legal act. The "guarantees were stronger when the participants considered the gods involved, while the essence of the operation was legal."[84] The best support for this is the fact that when the authority of the state was strong (as in Athens, Corinth, and Thebes) there was no need for, and no surviving evidence of, sacral manumission. Hence, sacral manumission was essentially a consequence—and a late one—of small communities with poorly developed political and legal traditions, or of the decline of the *polis.*[85]

The Delphic manumissions are extremely revealing about such practices in the ancient world. As Hopkins observed, they constitute the "hardest" set of data we have on almost any subject in antiquity. They reveal not only the "degraded" condition of slaves, but the fact that slaves paid dearly for their freedom.[86] The average price of 400 drachmas at the end of the third century was the equivalent of what it would cost "to feed a poor peasant family for over three years." Freedom usually had to be bought in installments. What slaves got in return was often of dubious material value. The down-payment terms (*paramonē*)—which we shall come to later—made freedom often little more than an "illusion," according to Hopkins. What is more, the prices were constantly rising during the last two centuries before Christ.[87]

THE FORMAL CONTRACTUAL MODE

We come, finally, to purely contractual manumission. Most forms of manumission, of course, had a contractual element. We have seen that Babylonian adoptions were largely business documents. Even so, they were a legal fiction, as was manumissio vindicta in Rome. We are thinking here of what

Weber called legal-rational contracts, those that completely ignore the need to circumvent the conceptual problem posed by manumission. Buckland suggested that Roman manumissio testamento rapidly developed into just such a contract. While it was a highly developed legal contract, it nonetheless retained "nonrational" symbolic elements.

Formal contractual manumission really grew out of various types of informal manumission that made their appearance during republican times. Two such forms were (1) a simple verbal declaration by the master that the slave was free, and (2) the writing of a letter of manumission before witnesses. Neither was valid during the republic.[88] Justinian formalized these methods, giving some of them the same validity as manumission vindicta. Among the most important of the new, formal methods were *per epistolam,* in which a letter of manumission by the master was witnessed by free persons; *inter amicos,* similar to the earlier version except that it was also signed by a magistrate; and simply destroying the slave's papers in the presence of five witnesses.[89] They became more popular and more fully developed during the late ancient world and the Middle Ages, though perhaps were never the most important modes until rather late. In thirteenth-century Spain, for example, manumission by will remained extremely popular;[90] over the years manumission by church authorities gradually became the dominant mode. It is only in the modern world that the legal-rational mode became dominant.

The situation was different in Islamic lands. We have already seen that testamentary and concubinal manumissions were the most common, but from Muhammad's day on, purely contractual manumission was provided for and encouraged. The Islamic practice, called the kitāb in the Koran, resembled the Greek paramonē system: the slave paid for his freedom in equally spaced installments. Most Islamic authorities insisted on the installment mode of payment, only the Hanafis sanctioning a single payment. The master could not sell the slave during the period of his payment. When the *mukataba,* as such a slave was called, completed his payment, he was free, and a rebate was usually given him.[91]

I BEGAN this chapter by observing that the release from slavery posed three kinds of problems: the conceptual issue of how to define the transaction in meaningful terms; the cultural problem of giving symbolic and ritual expression to the transaction as well as customary form; and the more social problem of creating a new status for the freed slave. Having explored the first two of these areas, I turn in the next chapter to the third.

9

The
Status
of Freed
Persons

THE ACT OF MANUMISSION creates not just a new person and a new life, but a new status—into which we must now inquire. The freedman must establish two kinds of relationships: with his former master, and with society at large (more particularly, with free men other than his former master). The two are closely related. Indeed, the single most important factor determining the condition of the freedman in the society at large will be the nature of his relationship with his former master.

The Freedman and the Ex-Master

There is a remarkable uniformity among the slaveholding peoples of the world with regard to this relationship. Almost universally the former master has established a strong patron-client bond with his freedman. In most societies this bond has been sanctioned by law. Actually, the intrasocietal variation in the nature and strength of the patron-client relationship tends to be greater than the intersocietal variation; that is, in any given society the nature of the dependence of the freedman upon his former master was affected by economic matters, such as the price the slave paid for his freedom (in the event a price was paid) and the terms of the payment, as well as the sex of the slave (women usually being more bound than men), his or her occupation, and the nature of the preexisting master-slave relationship.

When we look across societies, the similarities were impressive. Everywhere the freedman was expected to be grateful for the master's generosity in freeing him, however much he may have paid. This followed naturally from the universal conception of manumission as a gift from the master. In Rome a freedman could be charged with the crime of ingratitude and, if guilty, could be reenslaved. Much the same pattern existed throughout medieval Europe. Other societies were less legalistic about the matter but no less demanding. Everywhere in the premodern world the freedman had to honor his former master, and everywhere certain social obligations were expected of him. "Patronage belongs to the emancipator," goes the Islamic saying. Indeed, one must see the relationship between ex-slave and ex-master as something quite distinct from the normal patron-client relationship, entered into freely and voluntarily by nonslave persons. The relationship between ex-slave and ex-master was always stronger and always carried with it a certain involuntary quality that was quite distinctive. It cannot be viewed in isolation from the relationship it replaced. For this reason I propose to use the Arabic term *wala* to distinguish this relationship from clientship among free persons.[1]

In many lineage-based societies the freedman was assimilated, though in an inferior capacity, into his master's lineage or clan or family. Almost invariably in these cases the freedman continued to function within the same economic context as previously. He had little choice. Land was corporately owned, and access to it was determined by kin ties. This financial dependence was not usually a hardship, since enslavement in such societies was not primarily economic in origin. Freedman status with respect to the master tended to have mainly social and psychological implications. The freedman became legally competent, could sue and be sued (usually not his former master). He could now own property and had custodial powers over his or her children. The ex-slave could marry without the ex-master's consent, and the range of potential spouses was wider—though rarely as large as it was to persons who were never enslaved.

In Islamic societies the freedman and his descendants established a hereditary bond of kinship with the former master and his descendants. Both patron and client were referred to as *mawala* in the wala relationship. In China, filial piety and respect were expected from the freedman. In the ancient Near East, the freedman reputedly was not truly free until his master's death, so strong was the bond. In the advanced slave systems of Greece and Rome, ties between patron and client were equally strong, sometimes assimilated to the relationship between parent and child. Many Greek freedmen spent the rest of their lives paying off the remainder of the mortgage for their freedom, the result being that they remained firmly attached to their ex-masters. Freed persons were frequently required to obey and respect their former owners and to serve them for the rest of their lives. Sometimes these obligations were transferred to the ex-master's heirs. In Athens if a patron successfully sued his freedman for disobedience, the latter was returned to slavery; however, if the patron lost, the freedman became absolutely free. Between 340 and 320 B.C. there were approximately fifty such cases each year.[2]

There were marked variations in the kind and strength of the wala relationship. In the relatively complex urban economy of the Greek city-states, opportunities existed for some slaves who so desired to break the bonds completely, either by moving to another part of the country, to another part of the city, or entirely away from the country. The tremendous range of occupations of slaves meant that some slaves were better able to take advantage of their freedom than others. Rural slaves were not only far less likely to be manumitted than urban ones, but in the unlikely event that they were, their dependency ties remained much stronger because they were less capable of surviving on their own.[3]

Before Islam, nowhere was the wala relationship more elaborately prescribed both in law and in practice than in ancient Rome during late republican and imperial times.[4] There were three kinds of claims that the patron could make on his freedman. First, there was the *obsequium*. This basically meant the showing of proper reverence and gratitude to the patron and his kinsmen. It is not clear whether this attitude was legally enforceable during republican times. Susan Treggiari argues that it could have been legally enforced only if it had been stipulated at the time the manumission contract was drawn up. Otherwise the claim had moral sanction only, albeit this was powerful. During imperial times obsequium increasingly became a legally enforceable claim of the patron.

The second and more practically significant claim of the patron was the *operae*. This was the obligation of the freedman to work for the patron, which "sprang, not from the status of *libertus*, but from an oath which the freedman took after manumission."[5] Almost all masters insisted on such an oath. In classical law it was legally enforceable and automatic, but even from republican times it was strongly established "that operae was naturally owed to the patron in gratitude for the supreme gift of freedom." The operae referred to units of days-work, hence it was possible to specify a certain number of operae per year, or even the total number of operae due. The freedman was expected to perform work for which he was qualified, except that he was not required to perform tasks that endangered his life even if, as a slave, he had been trained to do so. Operae claims could be transferred by the patron to another person and were passed on to the patron's heirs.

The third kind of claim the patron had on his freedman was the right to half, and in some cases all, of the freedman's estate on his death. These claims were also inheritable by the patron's heirs.

The patron's claims on his freedwomen—his *libertae*—were even stronger than those on his liberti since, in addition, they were under his *tu-*

tela. What, in practical terms, this meant was that he or his heirs always inherited the entire estate of his libertae.

The wala relationship was supposed to be reciprocal. But since the obligations of the freedperson were conceived as expressions of gratitude for the gift of freedom—however great the material rewards that may have accrued to the ex-master—it is understandable that the patron's obligations were few and vaguely defined: he was to protect and aid his freedpersons as best he could.

In view of the symbolism of gift exchange inherent in the act of manumission, it is not surprising to learn that in spite of its enormous economic significance for both patron and freedman, the Roman wala relationship ultimately rested on moral rather than legal force. Reinforcing the law, at times even functioning without it, was the powerful Roman sentiment of *fides* (trust, faith, honor, loyalty, allegiance). Treggiari concludes her analysis with the observation "that the whole structure of obligations and rights between patron and freedman rested on the moral concept of *fides* and that the law sought to strike a balance between conflicting interests."[6]

As in the Greek city-states there were considerable individual and regional variations in the kinds of balance struck between patrons and freedmen. A few talented and lucky ex-slaves were able to buy themselves completely out of the indignities of spiritual and economic dependence. Others, the great majority, had no choice but to prolong the relationship for the rest of their lives and, what is more, pass it on to their children—gaining, in return, the gift of freedom, a gift that may have been materially meaningless but nonetheless meant moral worth, belonging, and self-respect. Furthermore, in the isolated case of Rome, it also meant, if the master was a Roman citizen, the remarkable gift of citizenship, a privilege that has no parallel in the history of slavery.

Roman law greatly influenced most of the slaveholding systems of medieval continental Europe, so it is no surprise to find a replication of the patterns just described in Visigothic and later in Christian Spain, as well as in France, medieval Italy, and the large-scale slave systems of the Mediterranean islands during late medieval and early modern times.[7] There were, to be sure, variations based on peculiar local customs or pre-Roman law, but the general pattern was to adopt Roman practice and to codify in law what earlier Roman practice had left principally to moral suasion.

The northern Europeans require special comment, in view of the lateness of the Roman legal influence. Here, as elsewhere, the wala relationship was strongly enforced in both traditional law and custom. As Thomas Lindkvist points out in his study of the *landbor* and related classes in the Nordic countries during the early Middle Ages, the freedman remained under a strong bond of personal dependency throughout the Scandinavian lands, and his relation to the ex-master was sharply differentiated from that of other semifree persons to their lords. The relationship was inherited by the heirs of the patron and continued for as much as two generations among the descendants of the freedman. The control of the patron seems to have been even stronger than among the central and southern Europeans: for example, he continued to have a say in the freedman's marriage. As in other parts of the world, there were some variations in the amount of control. Freedmen who could afford and were permitted the ritual liberation beer party were under no more obligation than other full members of the patron's family, which is not to say that a dependency relationship did not persist. However, intrasocietal variations in the degree of dependence were much smaller in these essentially rural Nordic countries; almost all freedmen joined the economic, if not the social, ranks of tenant farmers.[8]

Intersocietal variations in the wala relationship were much greater than intrasocietal. At one extreme, the laws of Jutland and Sjaelland suggest that freedmen were under no further obligation to their former masters, and this is explicitly stated in the Sjaelland laws after 1215. At the other extreme were the Norwegians, among whom the freedman remained under the tight control of his former master:

> A man in this situation had no freedom of movement, he owed his patron certain dues in labor for one year, he had to consult him on any business, including marriage, and he shared any atonement for injury with him. If he conspired against his former master or joined his enemies or took part in a law suit against him or "spoke to him as if on an equal footing," then he forefeited his property and returned to servitude. On the other hand, the patron took responsibility for the freed slave's maintenance and gave him general support.[9]

In certain parts of Norway the wala continued for four generations, only those descendants born of the fifth generation being free of the dependency.

We come finally to the modern world. Here, as everywhere else, ties of economic dependency with the ex-master were the norm. However, there were important differences in the degree to which the wala was institutionalized and legally enforceable. In only a small minority of American societies was there a universal application of a formalized wala: among these were the slave societies of the Dutch Antilles. According to Harry Hoetink, "freed slaves and their offspring were obliged to show all honor, respect, and reverence to their former master, his wife, children and their descendants. Offences against his former master could result in the freedman's reversion to slavery."[10] In the Spanish Americas and colonial Brazil the wala was never legally formalized. However, masters did manumit slaves on condition that the freedmen perform the equivalent of the Roman operae: "Slaves were freed, for example, on condition that they continue to work for their former masters for a certain period of time each day; or a black owned by a partnership might become, say, one-third free upon manumission by one of the partners, in which case he would divide his time between his own occupations and continuing service to the partnership."[11] We also find conditional manumissions that were highly reminiscent of the contractual obligations imposed on freedmen in medieval Scandinavia. "In rural areas, some masters freed large numbers of blacks but made sure that they became tenants. The former were thereby freed of the costs of slavery, assured of a fixed annual rent from the lands involved, and at the same time kept a pool of labor to draw upon at harvest time."[12]

The situation was much the same in colonial Brazil, where slaves were not only frequently manumitted on condition that they perform certain tasks but an individual could be and was reenslaved "as the law decrees for repaying by ingratitude the favor of having been granted his freedom."[13]

Nevertheless, even in Latin America conditional manumission in the strict legal sense of partial freedom until clearly specified conditions were met constituted a minority of all cases (in some areas a substantial minority). In Buenos Aires between 1776 and 1817, such manumissions made up 10.9 percent of all cases; in Bahia between 1813 and 1853 they constituted 22.5 percent; in Paraty, Bahia, between 1789 and 1822 they made up 42.5 percent; in Lima between 1580 and 1650 the figure was 18.4 percent; and in Mexico City between 1580 and 1650 it was 24.3 percent.[14] When one adds to these percentages those of slaves manumitted gratis, the total in all of these societies except Buenos Aires ranges between 52 percent (Lima) and 66 percent (Paraty). And when it is recalled that slaves manumitted gratis were nearly always under powerful moral pressure, not to mention economic and political pressure, to display gratitude and respect to their manumitters, it is seen that the wala existed in practical terms for the majority of freedmen. As for the remainder, what Stuart B. Schwartz observes of all freedmen in colonial Bahia would have held true of freedmen throughout Latin America, that their manumission was "ultimately conditional in that a *liberto* was always subject to reenslavement"; even if such laws were rarely put into practice, "the very threat of enforcement may have been enough to produce the desired result of social control."[15]

The wala relationship was least formalized in the more highly capitalistic slave systems of South Africa, the British Caribbean, and the U.S. South. In South Africa during the less vicious period of the late seventeenth century, "quite a number were freed unconditionally," according to A. J. Böeseken, although many freedmen were subject to specified operae and other conditions, some of them quite extraordinary: one Paul de Kock, for example, was freed on condition that during consecutive periods totaling more than five years he serve two men, both of whom lived in Batavia, several thousand miles away from South Africa.[16]

In the eighteenth century the South African pattern came to resemble its southern U.S. counterpart. There were very few manumissions, but the great majority (84 percent) were wholly unconditional: "freed slaves did not become thinly disguised indentured servants."[17] What is most revealing is the difference in the experience of privately owned slaves and of the semipublicly owned slaves of the Dutch East India Company. The company manumitted its slaves at twelve times the rate of the private owners but "imposed the harshest conditions on its freed slaves."[18] This intrasocietal difference in the experience of slaves in South Africa highlights an important intersocietal pattern about which I shall have more to say in the next chapter, namely, the higher the rate of manumission, the stronger and more formalized the wala, and vice versa.

The fact that the wala was not legally enforceable in most areas of the New World meant that those freedmen who wished to break the ties could do so. A few did, but only a minority; while many more would have liked to, they were hampered by the same set of constraints that applied to their Greco-Roman counterparts: the purchase of their freedom may have left them penniless or indebted; their lack of urban skill may have confined them to rural areas, where their lack of land meant that they could only turn to the ex-master for help; even where they had a skill, they may have been confined by their white competitors to the lowest-paying jobs, so-called "nigger work"; and, perhaps most important of all, affective ties to kinsmen and other loved ones still in slavery often dictated that the most expedient course of action was to maintain ties of dependency with the ex-master. A factor that was of special importance—though not unique—to South Africa and the U.S. South was racist hostility on the part of free whites to the mixed-race or black freedman; the ex-master was often the only source of protection in a society whose laws were not only unsympathetic, but whose minimal protections were not enforced.

Ira Berlin's study demonstrates that while "free Negroes often went out of their way to break the bonds of dependence," very few in fact succeeded in doing so.[19] At the same time it was rare to find legally enforceable wala obligations in the United States or in the non-Dutch Caribbean. In South Carolina during the 1830s freed slaves were required to have legal guardians from the white population; these need not necessarily have been the former master. In any case, the purpose of the law was not to strengthen the personal bond between freedmen and former masters, but to police the former.[20]

In the United States, as in other parts of the New World, manumission was highly selective, favoring those slaves who were most likely to want to maintain the ties of dependence.[21] In the urban areas of the South, especially the older parts of the antebellum South, most of those freed were women with sexual ties to the master; in the rural areas most of those freed were men, but it was precisely in these agricultural areas that freedmen were most at the economic mercy of the ex-master. Berlin chronicles the desperate economic marginality of the male freedmen, most of whom remained in farming, in a "vicious cycle of debt and de facto servitude."[22]

Certain generalizations may be made with regard to the freedman/ex-master relationship as it existed in all societies. Masters rarely lost much in tangible terms—economic or political—by manumission and usually gained a great deal. Invariably the ties of dependency continued, usually fully institutionalized in the wala relationship throughout the premodern world, but in only a minority of cases in modern slave systems. Whatever the primary reasons for original enslavement, these continued to be served after manumission. If the main reason had been economic, economic ties persisted; if the main motive had been political, such ties were reinforced; if the primary motive had originally been sexual, invariably the former master continued to enjoy sexual satisfaction. If, as in most primitive societies, slaves had been mainly prestige goods, the freedmen joined the household of the ex-master and further enhanced his dignity and honor.[23]

The Freedman and the Freeborn

The status of the freedman in the community at large is the second major area to be considered. In a comparison across societies it is useful to distinguish between the political-legal status of the freedman and what may be called his prestige ranking. By the latter is meant the respect with which the freedman was viewed—the degree to which he was accepted as an equal who fully belonged to the community. Full political-legal capacity does not necessarily imply full social acceptance. Alternatively, there are a few cases where the freedman was fully accepted in prestige terms, yet did not achieve full legal and political capacity—this usually occurred where the ex-slave was a native-born person who fell into slavery for political or military reasons. A classic example is the Roman captured by the enemy who, after being ransomed, was freed postliminium but was subject to certain limitations with respect to his ransomer.

Let us begin with the problem of prestige ranking. Nominally granted almost complete equality, politically and legally, with "free" persons, freedmen nonetheless remained stigmatized. Even among people such as the Sena, who went as far as possible in incorporating the manumitted slave, freedmen were still "treated condescendingly by junior kinsmen," were obliged to perform the most unpleasant tasks, and were first to be sold if the family faced starvation in a time of economic crisis.[24] The stigma of former slavery meant that the freedman was rarely perceived as an equal. Only time could blot out the memory of the debased condition he experienced as a slave. Hence, full freedom came only to his descendants. How long this took varied from one society to the next.

In well over 80 percent of all significant slaveholding societies freedmen suffered some civil disability. Honored with the nominal status of citizenship, in practice they remained second-class citizens. In almost all societies ex-slaves were barred from the most important leadership roles in the community. (We exclude here, of course, the special case of palace slaves and freedmen, to be considered in Chapter 11.) Occasionally an ex-slave became a minor chief, as among the Mende, but such cases were always considered exceptional by the people themselves and could sometimes lead to trouble. The Duala of the Cameroon provide an instructive illustration. During the nineteenth century a captive married the daughter of a chief and produced a ruling family of one of the major Duala towns, Deido, but as Ralph A. Austen tells us, "The subsequent history of Deido is marked by particularly severe conflict with other Duala towns, culminating in the unprecedented execution of the chief, Charley Dido."[25]

Even where freedmen were relied on to fill executive and administrative roles, it is important to recognize that the great majority of freedmen were excluded from such positions. Igor Kopytoff and Suzanne Miers make the important point that a range of slave statuses did not necessarily reflect significant mobility. Some slaves may have been acquired specifically for official tasks, others to work as laborers—and the latter may not have had the slightest chance of rising to the ranks of the former. The same holds for freedmen. In imperial Rome it was almost impossible for a freedman of a private master (the vast majority of all freedmen) to rise to the position of an imperial freedman, since these were recruited from within the *ordo* of the *familia Caesaris*. This was even more true in the Islamic caliphate and the Ottoman empire, where slaves were recruited for military and administrative roles from specific areas with very ascriptive criteria on race and ethnicity. A despised African Zandj who against all odds managed to win his freedom in ninth-century Iraq stood no chance of achieving the military or executive rank of the Turkish Mamluk freedman. The janissaries of the Ottoman empire were all white, the children of Christian subjects.

I have repeatedly emphasized that slavery was not a static institution. From the moment the slave entered his status, changes began to take place in his relations with his master and with the rest of the community. Kopytoff and Miers neatly sum up this process by applying the common sociological distinction between intergenerational and intragenerational mobility to three dimensions of the slave's relationship: the slave's legal status, his affective marginality, and his worldly success.[26] They observe that changes along these three dimensions may occur during the lifetime of a single slave, that is, intragenerational or what they call "lifetime mobility," which must be distinguished from "changes that his offspring and descendants will experience, that is, intergenerational mobility." Then they add: "The rather obvious distinction must be kept in mind because such statements as 'the slave becomes integrated into the lineage in several generations' have sometimes been taken as showing the flexible and benign nature of a slave system. It should be remembered that intergenerational flexibility can coexist with rigid statuses into which each generation may be frozen."[27] These points are well taken and are fully supported by the comparative data.

However, we come upon another ambiguity in the anthropological literature on slavery. Emphasis on the fluidity and intergenerational nature of slave status tends to give the impression that the freedman, once manumitted, was fully integrated, and this was far from being the case. In Charles V. Monteil's discussion of slavery among the Bambara,[28] for instance, he tells us that the status of slaves was not fixed, but generally passed through three stages. The children of slaves "born in the house" (*wolo-so-u*) had a privileged position—by which he means privileged vis-à-vis other slaves, although this is only implied. The third generation, he adds, "were ipso facto freed (*dyongoron-u*)," and he adds, "They have played an important role in native society." Maybe so, but were they really equal to freeborn Bambara? Significantly, Monteil slips and refers to this third generation as "another category of slaves." The very fact that the freedman belonged to a specially designated category of persons—*dyongoro*—suggests that he was indeed different, and we can deduce from the marked sensitivity to status among the Bambara (fully documented by Monteil) just how insecure must have been the place of the freedman. What was true of the Bambara was true of virtually all slave-owning societies, and what it amounts to is this: freedman status was not an end to the process of marginalization but merely the end of the beginning—the end of one phase, slavery, which itself had several stages. Freedman status began a new phase: the ex-slave was still a marginal, but the process was now moving toward demarginalization socially, and disalienation in personal terms. The new phase may itself have taken several generations, although as with slavery, for a fortunate few the process may have been short-circuited and the freedman immediately declared free. This was true, for example, of Somali slaves freed by the sultan as a reward for exceptional acts, and true of those Roman slaves who by imperial edict were granted the status of ingenuus (locally born free persons). By their very nature such cases were highly unusual.

As a marginal person the freedman continued to be viewed as something of an anomaly and, like all persons in transitional states, was regarded as potentially dangerous. The community took an active interest in him not only for economic reasons, to ensure that he did not become a public burden, but also for social and symbolic reasons.

We have already seen how in western Norway during the Middle Ages the ties of dependency with the master lasted for four generations. Paralleling this dependency was the contempt in which the freedman and his descendants were held for carrying the lingering stain of slave ancestry. The image of the thrall as nasty, ugly, foul, stupid, cowardly, and inferior had been racist pure and simple; in exactly the same way, the attitude to the freedman was racist until the fifth generation, when at last "the stain" was removed and the descendant became "pure."

The New World slave societies differed from this situation only in degree. In the French slave colony of Saint Domingue during the second half of the eighteenth century, when hostility to the freedmen was especially strong, a book that had the official blessing of the French government declared, "Interest and security demand that we overwhelm the black race with so much disdain that whoever descends from it until the sixth generation shall be covered by an indelible stain."[29] It is very tempting, on the basis of passages such as these, to hasten to the conclusion that New World slavery was unique in the additional burden of racism that slaves and freedmen bore. But this identification of a given group with slavery was as old as slavery itself; freedmen in all parts of the world suffered this perception of them as being stained by both slavery *and* the group with which they were identified. Han freedmen among the Lolos were stained with descent from Chinese blood. Among the Ashanti the freedman who was of foreign ancestry was stained with both his slavery and his northernness. In the medieval Muslim world "Zandj" meant slave as well as black, and both "stained" the freedman and his descendants. Throughout medieval Europe "slave" and "Slav" became so indistinguishable that "Slav" came to mean "slave," a linguistic fate that did not befall the words "Negro" or "black" in any of the European languages (even if there has been a sociological identification of blacks with slave status).

In spite of these worldwide uniformities there have been variations between slave societies in the kind and pace of social reception of the freedman. What has determined such variations? Without doubt one of the most important factors has been the degree of institutionalization of the wala relationship, the extent to which the relationship has been formalized and given legal-cultural sanction. Among the other variables that interact to determine political-legal status and prestige of the freedman the most important are race, the social formation of the community, and the demographic composition of the population—especially the sex ratio of the master class and the proportion of the total population who are slaves. The mode of manumission, itself closely related to these factors, operates independently in determining the freedman's acceptance.

As a result of the joint operation of these variables, I find the slaveholding societies of the world to be grouped into six types.

(1) In the first group of societies, the freedman and his dependents retained close ties of dependency with the former master and his family for generations—indeed, in perpetuity. Over time the ex-slave was physically absorbed into the former master's family. While there were always exceptions, freedmen's descendants usually constituted the "poor relations" of the family. The degree and pace of absorption depended largely on whether the original ex-slave was a native who had fallen into slavery or an ethnic outsider. Race was not a factor, since both groups belonged to the same race. The freedmen and their descendants were legally full-fledged members of the community by virtue of being members of the former master's family.

There was usually little or no economic exploitation of the freedman or his descendants, given the fact that these societies were usually small-scale subsistence systems with little class development. I include here the great majority of lineage-based and other preliterate societies that kept slaves. There is, however, an important subdivision of this group. The freedman and his descendants were more deeply absorbed and the stigma more rapidly erased in patrilineal societies than in matrilineal ones. In matrilineal societies the vast majority of freedmen and their descendants could be easily recognized by virtue of the patrilineal origins of their clan name. If a slave concubine was the ancestral freedperson, her descendants had to trace their ancestry back to her master, who would have been the ancestral male. The major exception was the rare case in which the freedman or woman was originally a native free person who had fallen into slavery and was later restored to freedom, in which case he or she would have simply rejoined the matrilineal group. Among the Yao and Ashanti the stigma of slavery persisted for many generations for this reason. In most kin-based societies, however, the freedman and his descendants were physically absorbed in two or three generations. And in some, such as the Ila, almost all stigma was gone by the second generation.

(2) In a second group of societies, the fate of the freedman is determined mainly by the interaction with the wala relationship of gender and the mode of manumission. The majority of freed persons were women who were absorbed as concubines or wives. Their children were wholly absorbed into the family of the master, and the stigma of slavery disappeared within a generation or two. Male freedmen and their spouses and descendants experienced a separate fate. Ties of dependency, often economic and political, remained strong and perpetual. The freedman and his descendants become a distinct status group intermediate between slaves and free men, sometimes living in separate areas, sometimes maintaining strong economic relations with the former master's family and close physical proximity to them. Although such freedmen may have been formally considered citizens of their society, they continued to suffer the disabilities that all dependent groups experience: they were culturally assimilated but socially excluded.

Race and sex operated jointly to produce two opposing effects. Where, as was usually the case here, the slaves were of a different racial group, female slaves who became concubines were freed along with their children and were fully absorbed by the master class. Concubinage was legal and children of these unions inherited equally with other children. Male freed persons, however, were racially excluded. Barred from marrying women of the ex-master's race, they tended to take their wives from freedwomen of their own race, often buying them out of bondage or being given them for this purpose. The strong wala relationship established bonds of solidarity with the dominant race. There was no sense of solidarity with the slave group. Ironically, there often was strong prohibition against marriage or concubinage between males of the master class and freeborn women who were children of this freedman caste, even though there was a high rate of concubinage and even formal marriage with females of the slave class. The "estate" nature of such freedmen standings was usually reinforced by racial or somatic differences, although the genetic absorption of slave concubines tended toward some degree of somatic convergence. Reflecting this convergence was a marked sensitivity to somatic differences among all groups.

This second group subsumes all the Islamic slaveholding societies (including those of the Sudan and the Sahel) with the exception of the racially homogeneous black African communities who advocate Islam.

(3) In the third group of societies, there was little or no perceived racial difference between masters and slaves, although strong ethnic differences may have existed. The wala relationship was highly formalized in law. The freedman was made a citizen and had full legal capacity with respect to persons other than his ex-master and the latter's family. There was a highly centralized social formation and the freedman was given citizenship, even though he was barred from certain of the highest and most prestigious positions. The freedman experienced some stigma; but this varied with his skill, education, and wealth, and whether he lived in a rural or urban area. The stigma was completely gone after two generations.

Rome was the classic instance of this kind of society. The assimilation of freedmen was particularly impressive in view of the fact that almost all slaves were of foreign ancestry. But we should be careful not to exaggerate. In theory the liberti of a Roman citizen were citizens. But as Treggiari has shown,[30] custom, law, and prejudice together ensured that they were second-class citizens. They could not stand for office in Rome and were usually prevented from holding offices in other Italian towns; they were apparently excluded by custom from magistracies elsewhere. The sons of freedmen suffered few if any of these civil disabilities. They became senators, held magistracies, and were admitted to the ranks of the equestrian offices. Nonetheless, the stigma of slavery still was suffered by the sons of freedmen, as the frequently cited case of the poet Horace attests.[31]

China, Korea, and Vietnam also fell into this group. The freedman was restored to full citizenship within his lifetime, although the stigma took longer to be erased (about three generations). Chinese history is full of successful descendants of slaves who were slandered by their half-relatives. Typical of these was Ts'ui Tao-ku, the son of a former slave during the period of the Northern dynasties (A.D. 386–618), who was so ill used by his half-brothers that his father gave him some money and packed him off to government service in the south. Ts'ui made good, and after a successful career returned home and, in triumph, held a banquet for the local officials. His cruel half-brothers would not be reconciled and insulted him by forcing his mother, now a freedwoman, to serve the dinner at the banquet.[32]

The ancient Near Eastern societies must also be included in this category. In Mesopotamia and in pharaonic Egypt the freedman was made a "son of the city" or a "freedman of the land of Pharaoh," both of which are taken to mean citizenship; this was accompanied by a wala relationship that lasted until the master's death. Jacob Rabinowitz[33] finds the parallels between Rome and the ancient Near East so striking that he claims that Roman manumission laws were influenced by those of Mesopotamia, a view that Ernst Levy rejects as "unwarranted in every respect," adding caustically that "a device which other nations were able to introduce was certainly not beyond the reach of Romans."[34]

Bernard Siegel makes an extreme claim for the Third Dynasty of Ur. "There is," he states, "considerable documentary evidence for manumission and freedom, which when once established, completely freed the slave from the stigma of his former status."[35] If this is indeed the case, then the Third Dynasty of Ur ranks as an unparalleled instance of tolerance toward the exslave.

We should also include in this third group the freedmen of India during the Buddhist period. Dev Raj Chanana favorably contrasts their fate with that of freedmen in Greece and Rome. He errs in lumping Greece and Rome together and paints an exaggeratedly bleak picture of the Roman freedman; and the evidence he cites for the extremely favorable status of the Indian freedman is none too persuasive. He concludes by telling us that the social integration of the Indian freedman "once he had been manumitted was immediate and complete."[36] I take this with the same skepticism as I do Siegel's assessment of freedmen in the Third Dynasty of Ur.

All these societies, then—Rome, ancient China, India during the period of Buddha, ancient Egypt, ancient Mesopotamia, and medieval Korea— constitute a special group in which the political and social status of the freedman was relatively most favorable: wala relations were formalized and strong, but not excessively demanding. Citizenship, though perhaps second-class, was achieved by the freedman, and the stigma of slavery disappeared within two or three generations.

(4) In the fourth group of societies, we find that although economic ties of dependence, as always, continued to be strong, there was no institutionalization of the relationship between ex-master and ex-slave. The freedman was, at least in theory, free to go where he pleased. Although agriculture continued to be the economic base, these societies had a strong urban and mercantile character. A considerable proportion of slaves, in some cases the majority, were located in the urban or industrial sectors and performed the full range of occupations. The economic condition of the freedman was determined by the kind of relationship he or she worked out with the former master and by his sectoral location: that is, whether rural, small farming, latifundia or plantation, mining, or urban commercial. There was, however,

an interesting and distinctive relationship between the political-legal and prestige status of the freedman on the one hand, and the rate of manumission and condition of slaves on the other hand. The overall rate of manumission tended to be high in this group of societies (freedmen and their descendants made up between 25 and 50 percent of the total population), but the freedman was rigidly excluded from full or even partial citizenship even though he participated fully in the economic life of the community. There was a strong and persisting stigma attached to freedman status, and this continued for generations. Indeed, the freedman group came to form a separate caste. Many were descendants of members of the master class and cherished their ethnic, racial, or class ties, using them as a means of separating themselves from the slave group. Unlike the Islamic group, there was no physical absorption of the children of concubines and no formal recognition of the concubinal relationship.

I include in this group the slave societies of ancient Greece, especially Athens and Delphi; all the slave societies of Latin America except Cuba during the nineteenth century; the Dutch commercial colony of Curaçao; and South Africa during the eighteenth century. Although it may seem extraordinary to include Greece here, this is only because of the conventional view (which I have already criticized) that racial differences between masters and slaves in Latin America differentiate these societies sharply from those of the Greco-Roman world.

A significant common feature of this category of slave societies is that despite the large freedman population in the urban areas, there was relatively little economic conflict between freedmen and the free artisan group. This, as we shall see, contrasts strikingly with some of the other groups of societies. There are several reasons for this relative absence of economic hostility. One is the fact that all these societies had continuously expanding urban economies. The demand for skilled and semiskilled labor always outpaced the available supply, so that slave labor did not unduly depress the wages of the free. Second, most of the urban slaves were in fact owned in relatively small holdings by people who were barely coping, or by the free artisans themselves who either employed them in their own workshops or allowed them to hire themselves out. The artisan class, then, did not see the slave population as competitors, but in many cases as a vital part of its labor force. At the same time, in order to motivate its slave working force, it resorted to the technique of manumission with, of course, strong economic ties of dependency. The kind of work the slaves performed also allowed them to acquire a peculium large enough to buy their freedom. Since the artisan class, then, partially created the freedman class to serve its own interests, it was hardly in a position to resent it. Third, and perhaps most important, was the attitude toward labor. In ancient Greece, as in preabolition Latin America and eighteenth-century South Africa, all forms of labor were viewed with some contempt: they were banausic. What the free Greek artisan, like his Latin American counterpart, desired more than anything else was to accumulate enough wealth so that he could retire early from the despised artisan crafts. Unlike regions such as the United States South, there was no categorization of some crafts as worthy to be reserved for freemen and others as unworthy and fit only for slaves. In Greece all skilled work, including even architecture, was viewed with contempt.[37] The distaste for labor, including the "banausic" skills, may have been less extreme in Latin America and South Africa, but it was nonetheless present.[38] It is no accident that the best pieces of eighteenth-century South African architecture that have survived are all the work of freedmen or slaves—or that in both Lima and Buenos Aires freedmen were able to become masters of craft guilds.[39]

The inclusion of eighteenth-century South Africa in this group of societies may seem surprising. Although the fact is not well known, eighteenth-century South Africa was a large-scale slave system, "a complete microcosm of that of the Americas," as Lewis J. Greenstein has observed.[40] South African slave society did not closely approximate any single New World slave society. Economically, it resembled seventeenth-century Peru and Mexico in its combination of large hacienda-type farms where most of the slaves worked and in having an extremely important urban center, Cape Town, the seat of the highly autocratic Dutch East India Company.[41] Demographically, South Africa was more like northeastern Brazil with the slave and "free black" population together outnumbering the whites, although the latter constituted a substantial minority of well over 40 percent of the total population.[42] In the high rate of natural decrease of the slave population it closely resembled both Brazil and the British Caribbean during the eighteenth century.[43] In its hostility to manumission it closely resembled the U.S. South and the British Caribbean, sharing with these societies the lowest manumission rates in the history of large-scale slavery.[44] Finally, in cultural terms, it was closest to the U.S. South, having a relatively large, settled white population with a strong puritanical tradition; an even sex ratio, allowing for stable family life among the whites; and an incapacity to resist the "dreadful sin" of miscegenation.[45]

However, the small freedman class that did emerge lived a far less confined and oppressive existence than its U.S. counterpart. (South Africa's barbaric racial policy is very much a product of the nineteenth and twentieth centuries.) While its system of slavery was harsh, in the opportunities and status it allowed the freed blacks it compared favorably with the most open of the Latin American slave societies.[46] What is more, the status of the freedmen in South Africa not only closely resembled that of Latin America but did so for much the same reasons. The freed blacks were not needed as a buffer the way they were in the British and French Caribbean and in Surinam, so this was not the reason for their relatively better status.

The condition of the freed slaves in South Africa bears an unusual resemblance to that of their counterparts in Lima and Buenos Aires. First, they were all overwhelmingly urban in location or origin.[47] At the same time, competition from white artisans, though it existed, was never as severe and oppressive as in the U.S. South.[48] The demographic profiles also are almost identical. There were more females; the age distribution showed the same high dependency ratio; there was a disproportionate number of persons of mixed racial origins; the vast majority of manumissions were purchased; and there was a strong correlation between the mode of acquisition and the form of manumission[49] (see Table 10.1 in the next chapter).

Finally, the economic, political, and social constraints were about the same in all these areas. While looser than in the U.S. South, they should not be idealized. A small minority of freedmen were able to become modestly prosperous, whereas the great majority lived at or below contemporary standards of poverty. They usually had little or no say in municipal affairs and of course were excluded from important decision-making processes and offices.[50] Finally, they suffered discrimination resulting from both racial prejudice and their former slave status. There were also laws that regulated their behavior somewhat more severely than that of freeborn persons (although these were never as onerous as they were in the United States). Strikingly similar were the sumptuary laws aimed mainly at the freedwomen: in Lima, they were forbidden "silk, pearls, gold slippers ornamented with silver bells, canopied beds, and rugs or cushions to sit on at church";[51] in South Africa, jealous white women decided that freed women, by their dress and manner, had become "unseemly and vexing to the public" and in 1765 they were forbidden to wear "colored silk clothing, hoopskirts, fine laces, adorned bonnets, curled hair or earrings."[52] One can understand the vexation over silks, but forbidding a mulatto to walk in public with her hair in curls a hundred fifty years before the invention of the straightening iron was an early and ominous indication of the white South African talent for fine-tuned racial sadism.

The South African case highlights two important aspects of the release from slavery. One is the fact that there is not necessarily any association between the rate of manumission and the status of the manumitted. The rate in Buenos Aires was two and a half to eight times greater than in Cape Town, yet the status of freedmen was similar and quite unlike their status in the U.S. South, which had a manumission rate more like that of the Cape. The second important implication of this comparison of freedman status at the Cape and elsewhere is that the status of freedmen, and to some extent the manumission rate, was more sensitive to what Hoetink calls "different sets of secondary economic, demographic, and social conditions" than to broad macrosocioeconomic configurations.[53]

(5) Let us now move to the fifth group of societies, in which the master

class was not only racially distinct but constituted a small minority—between 10 and 15 percent of the total population. The overwhelming majority of the population were slaves. There was a strong prohibition on manumitting slaves, masters wishing to do so sometimes requiring legislative permission. Even so, a freedman group did emerge, largely through concubinage. A minority of freedmen purchased their freedom, but this was extremely difficult given the capitalistic nature of these societies, the high replacement value of slaves, and the hostility of planters to the idea. There was no institutionalization of the wala relationship: the large number of slaves and the capitalistic mode of production meant that personal relationships rarely developed between field slaves and members of the master class.

The freedman population was demographically peculiar, especially during the early and middle periods of these slave formations. There were far more women than men and a disproportionate number of children. The male freedmen tended to be older persons, since they were able to purchase their freedom only after a lifetime of saving, or they had been unscrupulously granted their freedom when they had become too old to be worth their keep.

What was most distinctive about this group of societies was that in spite of the hostility toward manumission, the master class viewed the freedman group with some ambivalence. This was partly because of the strong sexual and illegitimate kinship ties between the two groups. But it resulted primarily from the racial insecurity of the minority master class (see Table 9.1) and its fear of slave revolts. The racially mixed "freed coloreds" were seen as a vital buffer between the masters and the mass of black slaves. The freedman class strongly identified with the master class and exploited its buffer status to good effect. Notoriously, freedmen were among the cruelest masters. Because almost all whites were slaveholders involved with the plantation economy, there was not a large group of free white artisans who resented the freedmen as economic competitors. Where such a group existed, as in Barbados and the French Antilles, it was too small to constitute a major source of repression for the freed group, and its interests always took second place to the grudgingly recognized value of the freedman as a racial buffer.

With this leverage the free coloreds in all these societies increasingly improved their civil status until they attained full citizenship and had equal legal status with all other free persons. Yet they continued to suffer the stigma of slave and partial black ancestry. All the French and British Caribbean slave societies, as well as Surinam (but not Curaçao), fell into this group, as did the Mascarene Islands (Mauritius, Reunion, Rodrigues, Seychelles, and their dependencies) during the eighteenth century and the Dutch slave system of the Banda Islands south of Ceram.[54]

(6) The sixth and last group of societies is a group with only one

Table 9.1 Freedmen as percentage of total population and of free population in selected societies.

Society	1764-1768 Total	1764-1768 Free	1773-1776 Total	1773-1776 Free	1784-1790 Total	1784-1790 Free	1800-1808 Total	1800-1808 Free	1812-1821 Total	1812-1821 Free	1827-1840 Total	1827-1840 Free
Puerto Rico	—	—	48.4	54.1	—	—	43.8	47.7	43.6	50.9	—	—
Curaçao	—	—	—	—	—	—	—	—	32.0	62.1	43.4	71.5
Brazil	—	—	—	—	—	—	—	—	—	—	—	—
Minas Gerais	—	—	—	—	35.0	65.0	41.0	62.5	40.3	60.2	—	—
São Paulo	—	—	3.3	19.3	—	—	18.8	25.0	22.7	30.0	23.2	27.7
Martinique	2.3	13.6	—	—	3.7	25.4	7.1	40.0	9.4	50.1	24.9	76.2
Saint Domingue	—	—	4.0	39.6	—	—	—	—	—	—	—	—
Jamaica	1.7	16.4	2.1	19.4	—	—	2.9	25.0	—	—	—	—
Barbados	0.5	2.7	0.6	2.8	1.0	4.9	2.6	12.2	3.3	15.7	6.5	25.5
United States												
Upper South	—	—	—	—	1.8	2.7	2.7	3.9	3.4	4.9	3.7	5.1
Lower South	—	—	—	—	0.6	1.1	0.8	1.4	1.7	3.0	1.6	2.9
Cuba	—	—	20.3	27.3	—	—	—	—	—	—	15.1	25.4

SOURCE: Adapted from David W. Cohen and Jack P. Greene, *Neither Slave nor Free* (Baltimore: Johns Hopkins University Press, 1972), tables 1 and 2, pp. 4, 10.

member: the slave states of the United States. Berlin tells us: "Once free, blacks generally remained at the bottom of the social ladder, despised by whites, burdened with increasingly oppressive racial proscriptions, and subjected to verbal and physical abuse. Free negroes stood outside the direct governance of a master, but in the eyes of many whites their place in society had not been significantly altered. They were slaves without masters."[55] There was literally no place for the freedman in this slave formation.

The South was unusual, too, in the wholly irrational fear of the freedmen who were seen as marginal and "dangerous" persons, an "anomalous caste." Although obviously harmless politically, "in the white mind the free negro was considerably more dangerous than the slave" and whites "uniformly identified them with the most rebellious."[56] Like witches and other marginals among primitives, the freedmen became classic scapegoats, easy prey for every troubled white free person. Bills to expel all free blacks were repeatedly introduced all over the South, although not all states enacted them. Seven states required freedmen to leave the state, and thirteen made their immigration illegal.[57]

How do we account for this remarkable situation? One of the causes was the peculiar economic condition prevailing in the South during the nineteenth century, when the freedman group attained some numerical significance: a booming agrarian slave system with an insatiable demand for slaves but no external source of supply, existing within the context of a wider continental economy in which wage labor was the norm. The economic structure, however, better explains the hostility to manumission and its low rate than the hostility to the small freedman class. We have already seen, in our discussion of the Caribbean cases, that hostility toward manumission did not necessarily imply complete hostility to freedmen. Nor, in this instance, can the racial differences between freedmen and white have been the determining or even the most important factor.

The main reasons for the peculiarly oppressed status of the freed class in the South were the unusual demographic structure of the area; the economic fears of the large free white artisan and working class; the absence of a formalized wala relationship; the puritanical tradition; and the familial and sexual values of the whites, especially as reflected in their attitudes toward women.

The demographic mix of the South was unusual. The slave population, although large, was always a minority (rarely above a third of the total) and was unusual in reproducing itself. There was relatively less political fear of black slaves than, say, in the Caribbean with its large slave populations and its traditions of massive slave revolts. Thus there was little need for a racial buffer, and the freedmen could not exploit that role. At the same time, the large white lower-class population, especially the growing immigrant group during the nineteenth century, saw the freedmen who converged disproportionately in the urban areas as economic competitors. Unlike ancient Greece and many parts of Latin America in the eighteenth and nineteenth centuries, the urban economy was not growing so fast that the demand for skilled labor ran ahead of the supply. Nor was there any cultural disdain for skilled labor. On the contrary, the white immigrants came from societies in which there was a proud tradition of skilled work. They were strongly opposed to any lowering of the status of crafts by their association with slaves or freed blacks. Instead, the most low-paying semiskilled activities were soon identified as "nigger work," while the better-paying skilled crafts were exclusively confined to white workers. In this economic struggle racism became an easy weapon in the hands of the white artisans.

But the hostility of the white working class cannot sufficiently explain the unusual status of the southern freedman for, as Berlin has shown, despite their disproportionate location in the urban areas, the majority of the freedmen actually remained in the rural parts of the South.

The absence of a formal wala relationship is another factor explaining the freedman's oppressed status. While ties of economic dependence continued in the rural areas, such ties were difficult to establish in a system where most slaves were field hands in what were highly capitalistic rural firms. There were several more reasons why masters did not wish formally and openly to continue their relationship with ex-slaves even when the latter had been house slaves or concubines whom they had known well. These reasons must be considered independently of their contribution to the absence of a formal wala relationship.

One is that southern masters genuinely felt that the presence of freedmen set a bad example to the slaves. In most other slaveholding societies, of course, masters welcomed this example as a means of motivating their slave population to work harder. However, the southern masters chose a different incentive scheme, that of rewarding the slave materially within the context of slavery. Once they had selected this kind of reward system, slaveholders felt obliged to remove freedmen or to depress their status so as to avoid making manumission a competing incentive mechanism. (This is in part why many states demanded that the freedmen remove themselves altogether from the state.)

There were other reasons for the demand that the freedmen go elsewhere: the marital traditions of the planter class, their attitudes toward the women of their class, and their fundamentalist religious values. In all other slaveholding societies the sexual exploitation of slave women was either fully sanctioned by social and religious law (as in Islamic lands and other societies that practiced polygamy and formal concubinage) or the moral system, along with social practice, accommodated such exploitation (as in the Catholic slaveholding societies of medieval Europe and Latin America). In the Protestant slaveholding societies of the Caribbean the church had almost no impact, this being a part of the general erosion of moral values among the whites, and the high male-female sex ratio among the whites made concubinage not just a biological necessity but in most areas required practice on the plantations.

The U.S. South shared with other slaveholding societies the exploitation of slave women and the inclination of masters to manumit their concubines and children. The intense shame that the master class felt about this sexual relationship was absolutely unique to the South, however. The guilt, with its disastrous consequence for the freedmen, had three sources. First, there was the puritanical tradition, which condemned fornication with the threat of fire and brimstone. Second, there was a highly developed sense of racial purity frequently codified in laws against miscegenation. And third, there was a strong moral commitment to a patriarchal family life, in which the women of the master class were placed on a pedestal and became symbolic not only of all that was virtuous, but as W. J. Cash has argued, of "the very notion of the South itself." The cult of southern womanhood was of course directly derived from slavery and the sense of racial superiority. Any assault on the dignity and honor of the idolized woman was an assault on the entire system.[58]

But southern males were no less pleasure-loving than the men of any other slaveholding society. Their hedonism, however, conflicted with their religious values, making the southern master alive to a deep sense of sin and wickedness: "the Southerner's frolic humor, his continual violation of his strict precepts in action, might serve constantly to exacerbate the sense of sin in him, to keep his zest for absolution always at white heat, to make him humbly amenable to the public proposals of his preachers, acquiescent in their demands for the incessant extension of their rule."[59] Equally, his hedonistic exploitation of the slave women was an assault on the integrity of the idolized women, all of whom were constantly reminding him of his wickedness when they were not displacing their bitterness in acts of cruelty toward comely female slaves.[60]

The result of all this was that the freed group, with its disproportionate number of mixed-blood members, was a living reproof, a caste of shame, confronting the white males with the fact that they repeatedly violated not only their puritanical precepts but the honor of their women. It was not guilt about slavery that accounts for the exceptional hostility toward freedmen, as Berlin and others claim, or any real fear of them as a political threat, but guilt about their own violation of their own social order. The "zest for absolution always at white heat" made it imperative that the freedmen be scourged from their midst—or, if not scourged, punished, victimized, and defiled like scapegoats.

Nothing like this had previously existed in the long annals of human slavery.

10

Patterns
of
Manumission

IN DISCUSSING the frequency of manumission, we need to recall the distinction between intragenerational and intergenerational mobility. The vast majority of societies tended to manumit their slaves over time, replacing them with fresh recruits, so that there often was an intergenerational tendency toward release from slavery when there was little intragenerational manumission. Intragenerational mobility was clearly far more important to a slave population than intergenerational mobility. Over three or four generations the descendants of most slaves were released—but to most slaves the pragmatism of Lord Keynes would have been far more meaningful, namely, that in the long run, we are all dead. The fact that his great-grandchildren might be free perhaps was of some consolation to the first-generation or second-generation slave, but there are limits to the capacity of human beings to postpone gratification. Most slaves in postprimitive societies would have preferred release within their lifetime, and their extraordinary efforts to secure freedom, not just for their children but for themselves, is an impressive testament to the human drive toward independence. Indeed, the most comprehensive body of evidence on manumission in any premodern society, that on Delphi, makes it abundantly clear that, given a choice, human beings will take freedom for themselves at the expense of their children. Keith Hopkins claims that "parents even left children behind in slavery to win freedom for themselves as adults."[1] Studies on eighteenth-century slavery in the Americas and in South Africa reveal that not only did many parents face this tragic plight but many adult children had to leave their parents in slavery.[2]

There are two kinds of issues involved in the frequency of manumission. One concerns variations in the rate of manumission across societies. The second addresses the varying rates among different groups of individuals within societies, regardless of the overall rate of manumission. We begin with the latter.

The Incidence of Manumission

What factors determine which slaves are released from slavery and which are not? We have already come across most of them in our discussion of the treatment of slaves. The most important variables are sex, status of parent, age, skill, means of acquisition, color, and residence (where relevant). Tables 10.1 and 10.2 present raw data on a select number of societies.

In nearly all slaveholding societies female slaves were manumitted at a higher rate than males, whatever the overall manumission rate, primarily because of their frequent sexual relations with the master or with other free males. Prostitution was also an important source of income for slaves, and in many cases for owners, and a path to manumission; it was usually closed to male slaves, although there were exceptions, perhaps the most notable being the Barbary states from the sixteenth to the eighteenth century, where sodomy was widespread and male prostitution, as well as male concubinage (sometimes involving female owners), was common.[3] Data on the extent of female slave prostitution are hard to come by, but the literary evidence suggests that while servile prostitution frequently occurred, it was more pronounced in certain areas. It was very common in ancient Greece and Rome and must have accounted for a good part of the peculium used by women to buy their freedom at Delphi; it was also an important way to accumulate the redemption fee in sixteenth- and seventeenth-century Valencia.[4] Perhaps the most extraordinary case is that of Cape Town in eighteenth-century South Africa, where the slave lodgings of the puritanical Dutch East India Company became notorious as the best and biggest whorehouse in town.[5]

Another factor favoring the female slave in the manumission process was the mother-child bond, which under slavery was not only stronger than the father-child relation, but may often have been the only parental bond. Hence mothers tended to be bought out of bondage by previously freed children to a much greater degree than were fathers. Women in their maternal role also had far more numerous opportunities to establish close personal bonds with their owners, whom they might have reared. Probably the most important reason why women were manumitted at a greater rate than

Table 10.1 Percentage distribution of those manumitted, by color, gender, age, and form of manumission in selected cities.

	Buenos Aires 1776–1810	Bahia 1684–1745	Bahia 1813–1853	Paraty 1789–1822	Lima 1580–1650	Mexico City 1580–1650
Color						
Negro	51.3	54.4	80.1	50.6	—	—
Mulatto	48.7	45.6	19.9	49.4	—	—
Total	(1,316)	(945)	(657)	(320)	—	—
Gender						
Female	58.8	66.9	67.3	65.5	67.7	61.5
Male	41.2	33.1	32.7	34.5	32.3	38.5
Total	(1,482)	(1,150)	(686)	(325)	(294)	(104)
Age						
0–5	14.6	9.2	—	22.0	36.0	41.5
6–13	7.1	35.6	—	19.8	15.9	12.3
14–45	67.0	52.3	—	43.3	35.5	33.9
46 and over	11.3	2.9	—	14.9	12.6	12.3
Total	(937)	(763)	—	(268)	(214)	(65)
Form of manumission						
Gratis	29.3	—	31.5	26.1	33.8	39.3
Purchased	59.8	—	46.0	31.4	47.8	36.4
Conditional	10.9	—	22.5	42.5	18.4	24.3
Total	(1,356)	—	(561)	(325)	(299)	(107)

SOURCE: Lyman L. Johnson, "Manumission in Colonial Buenos Aires, 1776–1810," *Hispanic American Historical Review* 59 (1979): 262. Copyright © 1979 Duke University Press, Durham, N.C.

men is that in all societies so-called free women were far more dependent than free men. Masters took fewer risks in losing the services of female slaves by freeing them than they took in freeing male slaves. Despite all this, in many cases, especially in ancient Greece and Rome, the Americas, and South Africa, women were obliged to pay full replacement costs for their freedom.[6]

The status of parents has already been discussed at length,[7] and we saw that there was considerable variation in the ways in which mixed (free/slave) parenthood influenced manumission. Apart from the Islamic lands, only a small minority of the children of masters by their slaves in the advanced slave systems received their freedom. This remained true even where, as in many parts of Latin America and South Africa, such children constituted a disproportionate number of those who were actually manumitted.

In most slaveholding societies slaves who managed to acquire some skill, or who were already skilled when enslaved, were better able to accumulate

Table 10.2 Preliminary analysis of 1,237 manumissions recorded and surviving from Delphi.

Approximate dates	Slaves freed (number)	Adults[a] (percent) Male	Female	Children (number) Male	Female	Origins (percent) Not known	Home-born	Known aliens[b]	Slaves conditionally released[c] (percent)	Acts of manumission (number)	Acts of multiple manumission[d] (percent)	Slaves multiply manumitted (percent)
201–153 B.C.	495	39	61	23	17	62	11	27	30	411	14	29
153–100 B.C.	378	37	63	38	32	27	44	29	25	303	14	27
100–53 B.C.	123	36	64	15	19	46	46	8	37	93	19	39
53–1 B.C.	128	41	59	16	23	62	36	2	52	96	21	39
A.D. 1–47	63	25	75	9	16	56	41	3	61	45	24	46
A.D. 48–100	50	23	77	4	3	82	18	0	40	26	35	66
Total percent	—	37	63			50	29	21	32	—	16	33
Total numbers	1,237	371	627	105	110	621	357	259	400	974	159	404

SOURCE: Keith Hopkins, *Conquerors and Slaves* (Cambridge: Cambridge University Press, 1978), p. 140.
a. Twenty-four ex-slaves of unknown sex are excluded.
b. Known aliens came from a wide variety of places, especially the Balkans, Asia Minor, Syria, Palestine, and other regions in Greece.
c. The conditions of release were not known for forty-five slaves (3.6 percent of the total), who are excluded here.
d. These were acts in which more than one slave was released by an owner at one time.

the peculium necessary to purchase their freedom. Nonetheless, skilled slaves were usually the most expensive slaves, hence their redemption fee would have been much higher and the master's willingness to free them, or to do so unconditionally, much lower. The influence of skill must always be considered in relation to the kind of work performed, especially as it reflected the slave's freedom of movement. Lyman L. Johnson found that in Buenos Aires "a crucial variable in determining whether a slave could accumulate sufficient capital to purchase manumission was independence from the direct supervision of the slaveowner, not gross earning capacity."[8] The more skilled male slaves were hired out at negotiated salaries paid directly to the owner, while the female slaves engaged in hawking or other "petty entrepreneurial occupations" had more control over their earnings, returning a fixed sum to their owners. Skilled women, partly for this reason, had a higher manumission rate than their more skilled male counterparts. Probably this variable of control over income played as decisive a role in ancient Greece and Rome and in the Americas and South Africa as it did in Buenos Aires.

While the interactive effect of control of earnings was critical, I do not mean to suggest that skill was never independently important. A great deal depended on just how skilled the slave was and how vital it was for the master to motivate him. Where slaves were very highly skilled and a single unit of their output generated considerable earnings, the slave's negotiating position may have been so strong that the master's control of his income became of minor importance. In such situations the slave could actually demand manumission as a long-term reward for efficient performance. The most dramatic example of this was the *mükâtebe* system in the textile and silk-weaving industry of Bursa, and to a lesser extent in Istanbul from the middle of the fourteenth to the seventeenth century. The world-famous brocades and velvets made in Bursa required not only highly skilled labor but a substantial amount of time and patience. Masters were so eager to motivate their slaves that they entered into a semicontractual obligation in which manumission was guaranteed after the completion of a defined amount of production, that is, "after so many yards of brocade or the finishing of a particularly beautiful piece of velvet."[9] Needless to say, only a small minority even of urban slaves ever found themselves in this kind of a bargaining position.

In nearly all slaveholding societies the age distribution of freed slaves was different from that of the freeborn or slave population. We need to determine whether age accounted in part for the incidence of manumission or whether its distribution was merely a reflection of other factors. A commonly held view is that masters in modern slave systems freed old and superannuated slaves in order to avoid the expense of looking after them in their nonproductive years. Some recent studies, on Latin America and South Africa, largely disprove this view. The practice certainly existed in these societies, but it applied to only a small minority of the slaves manumitted.[10] Although the available data are not as "hard," it seems that the practice was more prevalent in the U.S. South and the Caribbean.[11] The same must have been true of republican Rome, though the pattern changed during the imperial period; and it must have been true of Delphi between 200 B.C. and A.D. 100, where the 32 percent of slaves freed conditionally usually had to await the death of their master or mistress—sometimes both—before they actually became free.[12]

More important than the old-age problem, however, was the fact that a disproportionate number of freed slaves were children in one subset of societies on which we have data. At first glance this might seem an act of generosity on the part of the master, but in reality it was nothing of the sort. I do not have enough data to prove my point, but I strongly suspect that masters tended to free children rather than adults in societies that had extremely high mortality rates among slave children and in which adult slaves could be readily recruited from outside. It is hardly an accident that the tendency was most pronounced in Bahia (see Table 10.1) and the non-Latin Caribbean, as well as in Cuba during the nineteenth century, where infant and child mortality in general was notoriously high. On the other hand, in Delphi during the last two centuries before Christ and in late eighteenth-century Buenos Aires, where adults outnumbered children nearly four to one, the impressionistic data suggest that these were naturally reproductive slave populations during these periods and that children were not easily manumitted. It is significant that the price of girl slaves not only increased relative to boys between 200 B.C. and 1 B.C., but actually went beyond that of boys in absolute terms. From what we know of the demography and price movements of modern slave populations, we can safely assume that this extraordinary increase in the relative replacement price of girl slaves is indicative of increased reproductivity in the slave population.[13]

The means of acquisition also influenced the incidence of manumission in nearly all slaveholding societies. In general, slaves who were inherited were manumitted at a far higher rate than those who were bought. This variable is closely related to the origin of the slave: those slaves who were locally born (Creoles) were more likely to win their freedom than those brought in from outside. These variables, however, were weaker in their effect than skill and control of income. Imported slaves who already possessed some skills or who developed them after being purchased were more likely to acquire the peculium to buy their freedom than locally born slaves, including those of the household, who had no appropriate opportunities. This was true of the Africans who worked in the mining areas of Latin America and had more extensive opportunities to acquire a larger peculium than many of their urban Creole counterparts.

Ethnicity sometimes overcame the disadvantages of alien status, although it was itself a weak factor. Indeed, it is mainly in Islamic lands and in medieval Europe that ethnicity significantly influenced the incidence of manumission. In the Islamic world, Turkish and European slaves were more likely to be manumitted than Ethiopians, and the latter more so than sub-Saharan Africans.[14] In medieval Europe, European slaves (especially Greeks and Slavs) were more likely to be manumitted than Asians.[15] What appears at first look to be an ethnic bias, on closer inspection often turns out to be the operation of some other variable. Arab masters during the caliphate favored Turkish slaves, not primarily because they were Turkish, but because of their unusual riding and military skills. This, in turn, accounts for their much higher rate of manumission than slaves of other ethnic groups.[16] Similarly, the much higher incidence of manumission among Asian slaves in South Africa is best explained by the badly needed skills they brought with them.[17]

At the same time, it must be made clear that a bias in favor of an ethnic group often became self-fulfilling—such slaves would be granted opportunities to acquire skills to confirm the prejudice in their favor. Although masters in the New World were aware of ethnic differences among their African slaves and had formulated well-known stereotypes about them, they rarely acted on the basis of their stereotypes with a consistency that would have markedly benefited some groups of Africans as opposed to others. One possible exception was the stereotype held by both Brazilian and West Indian masters, that slaves from the Senegambia area were more intelligent and made better craftsmen and house slaves. This may have created a bias in favor of manumission for such slaves, but I have seen no firm evidence to support such a view.[18]

We saw in the last chapter that there was a disproportionate number of persons of mixed race among the freed population. This has led to what is known as the somatic theory of manumission, the view that masters favored slaves who appeared to be close to their own somatic norm. Several of the recent studies employing statistical techniques have either called this theory into question or have qualified it. When the more important variables such as skill, origin, and means of acquisition are controlled, the differences in the incidence of manumission between black and mulatto slaves were considerably reduced. Thus Johnson found in his study of Buenos Aires that mulattoes who were purchased were no more likely to be favorably treated than blacks; further, that it was because mulattoes were more likely to be Creole rather than foreign, urban rather than rural, brought up in the household rather than elsewhere, and "more aware of opportunities for manumission," that they had a better chance to acquire skills and to purchase their freedom. Black slaves with these characteristics were almost—though not completely, for color did count for something—as likely to be freed.[19] Richard Elphick and Robert Shell used much the same arguments against the somatic theory.

Cultural familiarity and access to skills were also the critical factors in South Africa.[20] In Brazil the somatic explanation carried far more weight. *Pardos,* or persons of mixed parentage, made up between 10 and 20 percent of the slave population, but 46 percent of the manumitted. Even here, though, the advantage was much greater among children, a fact already mentioned. The higher manumission rate among pardos largely reflected the greater willingness of masters to manumit children. The advantage of the pardos was less the result of their color than of the fact that they had a normal age structure, while the age-selectively imported blacks had an abnormally small number of children.[21]

In Jamaica the somatic theory also receives only qualified support. It was certainly the case that "the chances of manumissions increased as the slaves approached whiteness,"[22] nonetheless Barry Higman found several puzzling correlations once he went beyond this strong zero-order relationship. He found it necessary to postulate two patterns of manumission—one rural, the other urban. The somatic factor held up strongly in the rural areas, but principally because the masters tended to recruit skilled slaves on the plantations mainly from the mixed-blood slaves. In the urban areas the same bias existed, but the range of skills was greater and the bias of whites in determining access to skills not so strong; the result was that the number of blacks manumitted in Kingston far exceeded those of mixed parentage.[23]

These comments about the relationship between color and incidence of manumission hold equally for the relation of freedom to urbanism. In almost all slaveholding societies with significant urban sectors there is a strong association between urban residence and incidence of manumission. What Frederick P. Bowser observes of Latin America holds true for most other areas: "manumission, in an age when few questioned the morality of slavery, was largely an urban phenomenon."[24] In Jamaica[25] the percentage of slaves living in urban areas was the variable showing the strongest correlation with manumission ($r = 0.89$); and in South Africa, as indicated in the last chapter, the Cape Town–based Dutch East India Company manumitted its slaves at twelve times the rate of the mainly rural private owners. Even among rural owners, all the slaves manumitted were either Cape born or from the urban areas of India and the Indonesian archipelago.[26] The same high correlation exists between urban residence of the slave population and the manumission rate in ancient Greece[27] and Rome[28] and, of course, would be expected in the essentially urban-industrial slave systems of Han China[29] and the Islamic lands other than sub-Saharan Africa.[30]

The critical factor at work here was the fact that the urban areas offered more plentiful opportunities for slaves either to acquire skills or to exercise some control, even if marginal, over the disposal of their earnings—or both. Where such opportunities existed in nonurban areas, the difference in the rates between rural and urban areas declined dramatically and in a few cases may even have been reversed. Two examples will illustrate: the Visigothic kingdom during the late sixth and seventh centuries, and the Colombian Chocó during the late seventeenth and eighteenth centuries.

Visigothic Spain was a large-scale slave society in which there was little convergence of rural slavery and the colonate as elsewhere in late Roman and postimperial Europe.[31] There were two kinds of slaves, the *servi rustici,* the mass of agricultural slaves who were considered legally inferior, and the *servi idonei,* their superiors. The latter were skilled and personal slaves, many of whom rose to positions of high responsibility in the palatine service and administration.[32] And yet in what Charles Verlinden calls "a curious reversal of social relation" the rural *inferiores* were manumitted in much larger numbers than the idonei.[33]

There were several reasons for this. One was that the rustici were allowed to work the soil as tenant farmers, and although they were thoroughly exploited, they were able to control their earnings and peculium to a greater degree than the idonei. The latter were under the watchful eye of their masters; while they were encouraged to engage in many lucrative activities, they had few opportunities to accumulate a peculium of the size necessary to cover their replacement costs (which were much greater than those of the rustici). Several plagues during this period created a severe labor shortage in the kingdom. This no doubt lowered the rate of manumission for all slaves, but it did so to a lesser degree for the rustici. The latter ran away in great numbers and could successfully make their escape because the competition for labor was so severe that masters were prepared to risk strict legal penalties and not ask questions of strange persons who turned up at their villa asking for land to farm. To entice the slaves of other owners and to keep their own, masters offered the incentive of manumission and the opportunity slowly to accumulate a peculium to redeem themselves; rural slaves were allowed full control over movable property, including cattle. None of these options were open to the idonei who, though materially much better off, remained fully slaves right up to the period of the reconquest, long after the rustici had virtually all become serfs or small "free" farmers.

In the Colombian Chocó the manumission rate was high, with the most frequent form being by means of a self-purchase similar to the Cuban *coartacion* installment plan: "Slaves could work in the placer beds during their 'free time,' including religious holidays following mass, and keep what they earned."[34] The installment arrangement benefited the masters, since they had a highly motivated work force. The extra work the slaves put in meant increased overall production, since it was the masters who bought the ore produced. There were no urban areas in the region, but the manumission rate of these rural mining slaves was still greater than that of slaves in almost all the urban regions of Latin America. Household slaves, although they "received good treatment as well as affectionate friendship," like their Visigothic counterparts were "carefully watched" and obviously had few opportunities to accumulate the peculium necessary to purchase their freedom.[35]

Rates and Patterns

We turn now to a consideration of the overall, or societal, rates of manumission and the factors accounting for variation in them. An immediate problem is that the available data on the frequency of manumission are mainly of a qualitative nature; in most cases only rough, nonnumerical estimates are possible. Once again, I examine two sets of societies: those in the Murdock world sample and my own list of the most important slaveholding societies. There are no numerical data on any of the societies in the Murdock sample, and the available information permits nonnumerical assessments on only forty-nine of the slave societies (see Table 10.3). These are

Table 10.3 Estimated manumission rate in societies selected from Murdock's world sample. Murdock number and name of society are given for those societies on which there is enough information.

Infrequent	*Not uncommon*	*Frequent*
4. Lozi	12. Ganda	5. Mbundu
7. Bemba	14. Nkundo Mongo	23. Tallensi
15. Banen	16. Tiv	25. Wodaabe Fulani
18. Fon	17. Ibo	26. Hausa
19. Ashanti	28. Azande	30. Otoro
20. Mende	38. Bogo	33. Kaffa
21. Wolof	39. Kenuzi Nubians	36. Somali
22. Bambara	44. Hebrews	40. Teda nomads
29. Fur	81. Tanala	41. Tuareg
70. Lakher	87. Toradja	45. Babylonians
104. Maori		49. Romans
131. Handa		67. Lolo
132. Bella Coola		85. Iban
133. Twana		112. Ifugao
147. Comanche		115. Manchu
159. Goajiro		116. Koreans
177. Tupinamba		134. Yurok
181. Cayua		142. Pawnee
		153. Aztec
		161. Callinago
		167. Cubeo
Number of societies		
18	10	21
Percent of total		
37	20	43

categorized by whether manumission was "infrequent," "not uncommon," or "frequent."

This classification should be viewed with caution, representing, as it does, my subjective assessment of the available literary and anthropological materials, in which figures are rarely cited. The category "infrequent" is obvious: I refer here to societies in which the slaveholders expressed open reluctance or even hostility to manumitting their slaves and in which the obstacles placed in the way of the slaves' release were formidable, say, payment of over twice their market value and the complete loss of their peculium in addition to the requirement of special service. By "not uncommon" I mean a general impression from the available data that manumission was an established practice, but was reserved for exceptional slaves with respect to intragenerational mobility; however, it was achieved by many slaves of the fourth or later generations. Finally, the group ranked "frequent" includes all societies in which the free constituted a significant proportion of all those people ever enslaved, roughly over 25 percent, in which manumission was granted to all slaves who could afford it, in which the redemption price was not above the slave's market value, in which masters or special institutions were supportive of such efforts, and in which the intergenerational turnover from slave to nonslave status took three generations or less. Table 10.3 gives the frequency distribution of this variable in the Murdock world sample.

For the advanced slave systems of the world I have created two subtables. One consists of the small number of modern slave societies on which there are sufficient quantitative data to make numerical estimates of the manumission rate for given periods (see Table 10.4). The manumission rate is calculated simply as the annual percentage of the total enslaved population legally released from slavery. The second subtable lists all the advanced slave systems for which numerical estimates are not possible. For this group I use the same technique as in categorization of the Murdock world sample except that the richer qualititative data permit five rather than three categories (see Table 10.5).

THE SIGNIFICANT VARIABLES

What accounts for the varying rates of manumission across societies? I found no worldwide correlation between the manumission rate and any single variable. All the important variables operated not only interactively but in complex, often contradictory ways in different kinds of societies, and even in the same society at different periods of time. Thus in many societies a high level of miscegenation between free persons (especially masters) and slaves was strongly correlated with a high manumission rate; nearly all Islamic and Latin American societies show this, while in most matrilineal

Table 10.4   The manumission rate in several modern slave societies.

Area	Period	Rate (percent)
South Africa[a]	18th century	0.17
Northeast Brazil[b]	1684–1745	1.0
Buenos Aires[c]	1778	0.4
Buenos Aires[d]	1810	1.3
Colombia Chocó[e]	1782–1808	3.2
Jamaica[f]	1829–1823	0.1
U.S. South[g]	1850	0.04

SOURCES:

a. Richard Elphick and Robert Shell, "Intergroup Relations: Khoikhoi, Settlers, Slave and Free Blacks, 1652–1795," in Richard Elphick and Hermann Giliomee, eds., *The Shaping of South African Society, 1652–1820* (London: Longmans, 1979), p. 136.

b. Stuart B. Schwartz, "The Manumission of Slaves in Colonial Brazil: Bahia, 1684–1745," *Hispanic American Historical Review* 54 (1974): 606n7.

c. Lyman L. Johnson, "Manumission in Colonial Buenos Aires, 1776–1810," *Hispanic American Historical Review* 54 (1974): 277.

d. Ibid.

e. William F. Sharp, *Slavery on the Spanish Frontier: The Colombian Chocó, 1680–1810* (Norman: University of Oklahoma Press, 1976), p. 142.

f. Barry W. Higman, *Slave Population and Economy in Jamaica, 1807–1834* (Cambridge: Cambridge University Press, 1976), pp. 177–256.

g. Robert W. Fogel and Stanley L. Engerman, *Time on the Cross: The Economics of American Negro Slavery* (Boston: Little, Brown, 1974), p. 150.

slaveholding societies, the U.S. South, and the British Caribbean, miscegenation had just the opposite effect.

Other variables had no effects, not even contradictory ones. Of these ineffectual variables, the two most surprising were religion and race. We have already seen that religion had little effect on the treatment of slaves or on the status of freedmen. The same holds true for manumission rates. The effect of religion was evaluated by way of two questions. First, did the fact that masters and slaves shared the same or separate creeds significantly influence the manumission rate? Second, did the major world religions vary significantly in their effects on the rate of manumission? The two questions obviously are closely related and apply only to the advanced postliterate slave systems, since in all preliterate societies, on the one hand slaves were obliged to adopt the religion of their masters, and on the other hand no religion in such societies ever developed a stand on manumission.

Sharing or nonsharing of creeds between masters and slaves was found to have no correlation with the rate of manumission.

Exploration of the second question shows that all the monotheistic religions revealed striking similarities in their teachings, practices, and hypocrisies. All eventually came to define manumission as an act of piety; all went

Table 10.5 Estimated manumission rate in selected large-scale slave societies.

Name of slave society	Period (approximate)	Very low	Low	Moderate	High	Very high
Ashanti	19th century	X				
Dahomey	18th century	X				
Sokoto caliphate	19th century				X	
Nagaoundere (North Cameroon)	19th century			X		
Merina (Madagascar) kingdom	19th century	X				
Zanzibar	Late 19th century				X	
São Tomé	1500–1550		X			
	1550–1650				X	
	1650–1876					
Mascarene Islands	18th–19th centuries	X				
Greece						
Rural and mining areas	Early 5th century B.C.– 2nd century A.D.		X			
Urban areas	Early 5th century B.C.– 2nd century A.D.				X	
Italy						
Rural areas	3rd century B.C.– 2nd century A.D.		X			
	3rd century A.D.– 6th century A.D.			X		
Urban areas	3rd century B.C.– 2nd century A.D.					
	3rd century A.D.– 6th century A.D.			X		
Visigothic Spain	A.D. 415–711			X		
Muslim Spain	A.D. 711–1492				X	
Sicily	200 B.C.–A.D. 1		X			
Iraq						
Rural areas	9th–10th centuries A.D.	X				
Urban areas	9th–10th centuries A.D.					
Late medieval Mediterranean islands, especially Crete, Rhodes, Cyprus	14th–15th centuries			X		
Majorca	15th century				X	
Madeira	15th–17th centuries			X		
Santiago (Cape Verde)	15th–17th centuries		X			
	18th–19th centuries				X	
Toradjas (central Celebes)	19th century		X			
Korea	Koryŏ and early Yi			X		
	Mid-late Yi				X	
Banda Islands	18th–19th centuries		X			

Table 10.5 (continued)

Name of slave society	Period (approximate)	Very low	Low	Moderate	High	Very high
Hispanic Mexico						
Urban areas	16th century				X	
Sugar and mining areas	16th century		X			
Surinam	18th–19th centuries	X				
Curaçao	18th–early 19th centuries				X	
Barbados	1700–1834	X				
Leeward Islands	1700–1834	X				
Martinique	1700–1789	X				
	1789–1830			X		
Guadaloupe	1700–1830	X				
Saint Domingue	1700–1789	X				
	1789–1800			X		

out of their way to reject the view that conversion implied manumission. All insisted, however, that conversion be a precondition of manumission. Except in isolated cases none of these religions seem to have had any influence. Only when economic and political expediency coincided with piety did religion seem to count.

A few examples will suffice. Judaism expressed uneasiness about the enslavement of Hebrews by Hebrews and dictated that all Jewish bondsmen be freed at the end of their sixth year of servitude. Not only were most Jewish slaves likely to have been fellow Jews, but the suspicion, long held, that Jewish masters neglected their religious dictates and kept Jewish slaves in perpetuity was recently given dramatic support by the papyric discovery of F. M. Cross. The papyrus concerns a group of Samarian nobles massacred by Alexander's soldiers and the translation clearly indicates that Jewish slaves received no special treatment and were being held in perpetuity.[36]

Christianity had no effect on the rate of manumission in medieval Europe. Indeed, church-owned slaves were often the last to receive their freedom[37] and in many parts of Europe churchmen strongly opposed manumission, piously stating that "to set them free would be positively reprehensible since in view of their evil nature it would expose them to a greater danger of sin."[38] Baptized slaves of Jewish masters did, in theory, automatically receive their freedom, but Jewish-owned Christian slaves were too few in number to make any difference to the overall rate of manumission. While in some cases this rule was applied, especially in Christian Spain up to the sixteenth century,[39] one is left to wonder how it happened that Jewish masters were able to keep any slaves at all. The answer is that the rule was neglected by Jewish masters with the connivance of the state authorities. There were frequent quarrels between church and state over Jewish ownership of baptized slaves, especially in fifteenth-century Sicily.[40] What Marc Bloch wrote of Europe following the end of the Western Roman Empire holds for all Christendom at all times: "If the frequency of manumissions at this time was considerable, it is because, as well as being a good act about whose nature slave owners were far from indifferent, the freeing of slaves constituted an operation from which economic conditions of the moment had removed all danger, revealing nothing but its advantages."[41] Exactly the same could be said of the large-scale manumission of slaves in thirteenth-century Sweden, where it was at the urging not of the church (which was too compromised by its large-scale holding of slaves on the Continent to take a stand), but of the Crown, which urged the remaining slave owners to reconcile notions of Christian equality before Christ with what was economically harmless.[42]

Elsewhere Christian piety merely camouflaged economic motives. In late medieval Genoa, for example, Verlinden found a persistent pattern of "hypocrisy" among manumitting masters.[43] Almost all students of Latin American slavery are now agreed that the church made no difference in explaining either the individual incidence of manumission or the relatively higher rates of manumission compared to the U.S. South and non-Latin Caribbean.[44]

The ineffectiveness of Christianity with regard to the manumission rate is most dramatically revealed by the case of South Africa during the late seventeenth and early eighteenth centuries. In 1618 the Council of Dort had ruled that all baptized persons should be manumitted and enjoy equal rights with Christians. When Cape Colony was founded later in the century, the Dutch Reformed Church maintained that principle, but it never received the force of law, and a recent study shows that during this and later periods "most baptized slaves were not freed, most manumitted slaves were not baptized."[45] When in 1770 the government in Batavia directed that slaves should be actively proselytized and baptized, real conflict was generated at the Cape between the old religion and the new institution of slavery. "In practice," write Elphick and Shell, "this did not result in higher manumission rates, but it did result in lower baptism rates."[46]

The situation was more complex with Islam. As in Christianity and Judaism, the conversion of the slave was not a reason for manumission. Islam also forbade the enslavement of fellow Muslims born into the religion or converted before being captured. But the history of Islam shows that political and economic factors triumphed over religious sentiment whenever the two were in conflict. On the whole, religion might have counted slightly more in favor of the slave of the Muslim master; more than that it would be reckless to claim. What is certain is that religion was never the decisive factor in the manumission rate of Muslim countries. More important were the kinds of socioeconomic structures in lands converted to Islam. In most such societies slavery was primarily of the urban, commercial character, and manumission rates were always higher. In the Sudan and Sahel, where slaves were important in pastoralism and agriculture, the rate of manumission probably was already high prior to the Islamic conquest, and in any event, as we shall argue shortly, may be adequately explained without the religious factor. Even in the heartland of Islam among the pastoral Arabs, it is probable that the pattern of converting slaves into agricultural dependents—a common practice among pastoralists—long predated Muhammad. Where slavery already existed, Islam reinforced existing tendencies and gave new meaning to the act of manumission. And where a major increase in the role of slavery accompanied an Islamic conquest, the kind of slavery introduced was usually of the sort that thrived on and even required a high rate of manumission: a civilization dependent on slaves for its manpower, its military force, its administrative apparatus, and even its executive elite simply could not have survived had not such slaves been motivated by the prospect of eventual manumission.

The practices of the Barbary states of Morocco, Algiers, Tunis, and Tripoli from the end of the sixteenth century to the early nineteenth century are very revealing.[47] There are numerous horror stories by European escaped slaves telling of the Muslim masters forcing their slaves to convert to Islam.[48] It is also true that most slaves who were pressured to apostatize received their freedom, although it was not automatic. What is more, the manumission rate among Christian captives must be judged high. Several of the regencies depended heavily on the Renegades (as the apostates were called) not only to man their bureaucracies at all levels, but also to run their industries and lead their armies and fleets.[49]

A closer look, however, reveals that it was not religion that was at work, but the demand for skilled manpower. Unskilled Christian slaves were actually discouraged from apostatizing. As Stephen Clissold notes, "Whilst certain categories would be cajoled or persecuted into apostatizing—boys likely to make good soldiers or seamen, skilled artisans and technicians, beautiful women destined for the harem, commanders, priests and other distinguished figures whose conversion would confer prestige—the rank and file would often be forcibly discouraged."[50]

THE INSIGNIFICANCE OF RACE

Before we consider the reasons for variations in the manumission rate, we must dispose of another commonly held view, namely, that racial difference or absence of difference between masters and slaves influenced the manumission rate. This view was recently restated by Keith Hopkins, who argues that "the existence of color difference reinforced hereditary status. The low visibility of status distinctions in the classical world *must have helped manumission*" (emphasis added).[51]

Actually Hopkins is making two points: perceived racial differences reinforced hereditary status; and such differences influenced the rate of manumission. The first is right; the second is wrong. Neither in the Murdock sample of world societies, nor in the group of advanced slave systems, have I found any relationship between master-slave racial differences, however perceived, and the rate at which slaves were freed. Throughout medieval Europe, especially in Scandinavia during the early and mid-Viking period, perceived racial differences between masters and slaves, while significant, were small compared to other areas; yet the manumission rate was low. Or, to take the most dramatic case, in the large-scale slave system of medieval Korea all slaves were of the same race and ethnic group as their masters, yet the manumission rate was only moderate.

On the other hand, we know that the manumission rate was high in the vast majority of the Islamic lands that had slavery. In all of them there were marked perceptions of racial differences between masters and slaves.[52] Variations in the Americas alone sufficiently demonstrate the absence of any correlation between racial differences and the manumission rate. To compare within these cultural groups, the Colombian Chocó had one of the highest rates of manumission in the hemisphere—many times higher than the rate in Buenos Aires, which had the same sort of racial differences. During the late eighteenth century New England masters manumitted their slaves at a much higher rate than their southern counterparts. The manumission rate in Curaçao was many times greater than that of Surinam, although the two racial groups involved were identical: Dutch planters and West African slaves.

It is clear that the racial factor bears no relation to the manumission rate. In both of our samples, however, racial difference between master and slave did significantly influence the status of freedmen. The most obvious explanation is that usually the person or group of persons who made the decision to free the slave—the masters—were not the same as the person or group of persons who determined whether he would be accepted or not—all those of free birth.[53]

In more general terms, the decision to grant or to permit slaves to purchase their freedom was an individual one, largely determined in the advanced slave systems by economic and/or political factors, whatever the cultural rationalizations, whereas the decision to *accept* the freedman was a collective one, strongly influenced by traditional values and prejudices.

Intercultural Patterns

Because of the complex ways in which variables interact in determining the manumission rate, it is best to approach the problem in a manner similar to that employed in our analysis of freedman status. Except at a rather high level of generality, no single variable or single configuration of variables can account for the differentials in these rates across time and place. I have searched instead for several configurations of variables operating in different groups of societies and have discovered six causal patterns or societal conditions under which manumission occurred.

DOMESTIC ASSIMILATION

The typical case here is the small, lineage-based, patrilineal society in which there was little or no division of labor between slaves and nonslaves, and noneconomic motives were at least as important as economic ones in the keeping of slaves. Slaves here constituted a small part of the population and were often prestige symbols or political retainers. Female slaves, the majority, were used primarily as a means of reproduction. They were also released from slavery earlier and in greater proportion than male slaves. The slave population was assimilated by means of intermarriage and adoption into the master's clan, although this could take many generations. Market factors played only a minor role in determining the rate of manumission. There was a stable equilibrium: the supply of slaves was limited, but so was the demand. The replacement price of the average slave, while stable, was usually out of the reach of most slaves. Besides, masters were generally reluctant to manumit first-generation slaves. An exceptional few might by one means or another redeem themselves, but redemption was usually not worth the price for a first-generation slave, since the social environment was such that he had to remain socially attached to, and dependent on, his master. On the other hand, slaves of later generations might feel more secure in detaching themselves, but by then might not want to because of ties of sentiment and kinship developed with the master's family.

MATRILINEAL CIRCUMVENTION

There is one subgroup of kin-based societies that differs from the above pattern, and it is in discussing this group that we come to the second socioeconomic context of manumission, the condition of matrilineal circumvention. Unlike the first group, there was a very low rate of manumission both intragenerationally and intergenerationally. Slavery, in other words, was highly hereditary, and it was only the exceptional individual who escaped under any circumstances, no matter how many generations his ancestors might have been enslaved. Even more than in domestic assimilation slaves were recruited for reproductive and political reasons rather than for economic reasons. These were matrilineal societies in which slavery was a means of circumventing the system of descent that assigned the patria potestas over a man's children to his wife's brother. The children of slave concubines and slave wives were the only ones over whom a natural father had direct control. In this way slave lineages were deliberately created, and control over them was inherited patrilineally, in contrast with the prevailing rule of matrilineal inheritance. For this reason slaves remained slaves forever. The greater the number of generations a slave's ancestors had been in the society, the more difficult it was for him to secure his freedom, because the greater would be the number of agnates who had proprietorial powers in him. In contrast to the first group of societies, not only was there a very low overall rate of manumission, but first-generation slaves usually had a better chance of redeeming themselves than slaves of later generations.

The Ashanti of West Africa, the Yao of East Africa, the Kongo of Zaire, the Imbangala of Angola, the Luvale of what is now Zambia, and the Goajiro of South America all exemplified this pattern. Among the Luvale "slave status was permanent," and because children by slave women "increased the number of people in a village and hence the following of the headman," there was great reluctance to manumit them.[54] As noted in Chapter 8, the Kongo slave, even if released by his owner and returned to his native matrilineal group, became a slave of his own group. Although second-generation slaves (*mavala*) attained a status somewhat more favorable than those of the first generation, there was no further mobility toward "freedom" or full membership in the host society.[55] Slavery was an important institution among the Yao during the nineteenth century. When J. C. Mitchell studied a Yao group in the mid-twentieth century, long after slavery was abolished, he found that "slave descent still markedly affects social relationships."[56]

DOMESTIC EXCLUSIVENESS

Here the critical factor was the combination of a primitive socioeconomic system and the operation of a strong endogamous principle either within the free group or between the free and slave group (the free not necessarily being endogamous among themselves). This category includes societies such as the Vai of West Africa and most of the nonmatrilineal slaveholding communities of aboriginal northwestern America. One of the best examples of this group of slaveholding societies is the Merina of Madagascar before the founding of the Imerina kingdom during the closing years of the eighteenth century. Slavery was important in the prekingdom communities and was to grow to massive proportions during the nineteenth century. The manumission rate was very low, almost nonexistent, although Maurice Bloch exaggerates the uniqueness of this low level of manumission for Africa; we have already seen that low rates were typical of those African societies operating under conditions of matrilineal circumvention. Bloch attributes the low rates to the endogamous nature of Merina kinship. He writes: "If both parents did not come from the same group then the offspring always belonged to the lower group. This meant that marriage was unlikely to occur between free and slave persons and that in any case the children would belong to the lower group, that is, they would be slaves."[57]

This explanation lacks sufficiency. There were many societies in which the free group was highly endogamous or in which the principle of *deterior condicio* operated, which nonetheless exhibited high rates of manumission. In India from the period of Buddha there was a fairly high rate of manumission, in spite of both the internal endogamy of the master class and the endogamy of this class as a whole vis-à-vis slaves and ex-slaves. In imperial China up to the twelfth century, the operation of the principle of deterior condicio did not prevent a high level of manumission. To cite the best-known case, the highly chauvinistic endogamy of the ancient Greeks relative to all non-Greeks, exemplified in the Athenian citizenship law of 451 B.C.,[58] did not prevent unusually high rates of manumission. What is crucial is the combination of either internal or external endogamy among the free and a closed, primitive socioeconomic order. In Athens the existence of a relatively large urban center and a large free, noncitizen population—the metics—meant that there was more than enough social space to absorb the manumitted. No such social space existed in prekingdom Merina and the other closed, small-scale societies in this group. Manumission there was utterly meaningless, since the freedman had nowhere to go and yet could not be assimilated by his master's group.

ECONOMIC FORCES were of little significance in the first three kinds of societies discussed above. In the remaining groups to be considered, market forces and the productive uses of slaves became the most critical variables determining the volume and pattern of manumission. They operated, however, in quite different ways—both independently and in interaction with other variables.

PREDATORY CIRCULATION

In the fourth group of societies the manumission process operated under what may be termed conditions of predatory circulation. Here slaves played a pivotal role in what were economically more complex societies than those of the first three groups. They continued to be used as reproducers, but they were also the major producers of the elite's wealth and, as retainers, directly supported their power. Slaves reproduced the system economically as well as demographically, in that the wealth they generated was used to acquire yet more slaves. As soldiers, manumitted slaves and sometimes even persons still in slavery assisted the elite in its raids for more slaves. There was a high volume of intergenerational mobility, as well as a significant amount of intragenerational movement from slave to nonslave statuses.

The high volume of manumission resulted, first, from the manumission of almost all concubines and their children. Second, since male slaves and their spouses worked largely on their own as agriculturalists and pastoralists, the need to motivate them was strong. Incentive was provided by the high probability of manumission, reinforced by religious assimilation of the slave class and by religious emphasis on manumission as an act of piety. Since slaves usually were given "free" days to provide for themselves, and since their replacement cost was not excessive, many were able to accumulate a peculium and redeem themselves. With the masters' encouragement of this practice, a high turnover of the slave population was typical of this group.

The system of demographic and economic reproduction, at the core of the manumission rate, created a large demand for slaves to replace those manumitted. The demand was met by predatory raids, largely supported by manumitted slaves and by those hoping for manumission, and by a buoyant external market sometimes the result of unstable political frontiers. Almost all the states of early Islam, the medieval Islamic states of the southern Sahara, and most of the Islamic states of the Sahel and Sudan (especially during the nineteenth century) fall into this category. I also include the interesting case of advanced agricultural slavery in Crete during the fourteenth and fifteenth centuries; more doubtful is the example of Sardinia during the late Middle Ages.[59]

COMMERCIAL REPRODUCTION

Although there was a substantial external supply of slaves, the demand continued to escalate, owing to changes in the mode of production and the use of slaves as the prime agents of economic change. The manumission rate varied regionally, depending upon whether the slave was located in the agricultural, mining, or urban commercial sector. Thus, in ancient Athens, especially between the sixth and third centuries B.C., there was a low rate of manumission in the Laurium mines and the agricultural sectors where slaves were used; similarly, in Rome, seldom were slaves of the latifundia manumitted. Masters needed a cheap, stable work force and were reluctant to release their slaves. Even if the masters were willing, the latifundia slaves rarely were able to save enough to redeem themselves. The lack of close contact between masters and slaves also meant that few slaves were granted their freedom. In urban areas, however, the commercial and industrial uses of slaves required a highly motivated slave population. Again, manumission was one method of motivation. Further, the practice of hiring out slaves meant that they had a better chance to accumulate savings. Manumission was profitable for the masters, for it not only ensured a loyal, hard-working, skilled and semiskilled work force but it also enabled the masters to liquidate their capital in older slaves in order to procure more vigorous younger slaves. The use of the paramonē technique in Greece and other devices such as the operae in Rome meant that the economic services of the slave were usually not lost even after he was freed.[60]

The sensitivity of the manumission rate to market forces in this group of societies is illustrated not only by the declining rates of manumission in Greece during the second and first centuries B.C. but by the changes of the rate in late fifteenth-century Spain and nineteenth-century Cuba. During the late fifteenth century the Turkish advance on the Levant led to a decrease in the supply of slaves, and a consequent rise in their purchase price and increase in the redemption fee charged by masters. The number of manumissions declined immediately. In 1441 a slave was required to pay as much as 20 percent above market value for his freedom and in addition he had to perform many onerous operae.[61] The changes in the relative size of the Cuban "free colored" population between the last quarter of the eighteenth century and the abolition of slavery in 1886 also illustrate this sensitivity. From 20.3 percent of the total population in 1774, the proportion of freedmen declined to a low of 15.1 percent between 1827 and 1841, then climbed back to 20 percent in 1877. This coincided with the change in Cuba's economy, from one that was primarily pastoral and full of small family farms to an order that was dominated by large-scale plantations. The increased demand for plantation labor, and the obstructions to the supply of slaves from Africa, had a depressing effect on manumission rates. Not only were restrictions placed on the *coartacion,* the Cuban counterpart to the Athenian paramonē system, but many more slaves were now in the plantation sector and as a result were less capable of building up a peculium of any significance. The increased redemption fee resulting from the increased purchase price of slaves aided in creating an environment that was unfavorable to manumission.[62]

An interesting hypothesis, formulated recently to explain the rate of manumission, is of some relevance to this group of societies, especially their urban and commercial sectors. Ronald Findlay's theory,[63] which he derives from Zimmern,[64] is that the complex nature of the tasks performed by slaves in these economies makes the use of force a very poor instrument to increase production. Instead, the "carrot" of incentive payment is employed: this is the peculium the slave is able to accumulate by working on his own. The master behaves "rationally," in economic terms, in attempting to find the optimal combination of incentive payments and supervisory costs that will maximize the total earnings he can wring from his slave. He assumes that such incentive earnings are acquired by the slave for the purposes of manumitting himself or a loved one. The major economic problem for Findlay is "what determines the proportion of a worker's life spent in slavery." Using purely deductive methods, he develops a model in which "the owner trades off a shorter period of exploitation of his human asset against a higher return per unit of time over the reduced period of exploitation." The model predicts that "the length of time it would take for a slave to purchase his freedom out of savings from his incentive payments" varies inversely with the rate of interest. In layman's terms, where there is a relative scarcity of capital, the master finds it more profitable to permit his slave to buy his freedom earlier in return for more intensive and productive work during his period of slavery; where capital is abundant, there is no such incentive to the master. Findlay claims that Latin American societies fall into the former group, whereas the U.S. South falls into the latter.

There are a number of flaws in this argument and it has almost no support from the comparative data. In the first place, it was not always true that incentive payments were made with the assumption that they were to be used for the purchase of the slave's freedom. As Findlay recognizes from the work of Fogel and Engerman,[65] such incentive payments were made in the U.S. South, but with the implicit understanding that they would *not* be used for the redemption of the slave. Second, there is the simple fact that even in these highly commercial and urban societies a substantial minority, and in many cases, a majority of slaves manumitted did not themselves pay for their freedom. It was either granted freely by the masters, who were sometimes their sexual partners or fathers, or it was bought for them by loved ones already out of slavery.[66] This was true in the ancient Near East, ancient Greece and Rome, late medieval Spain, quite possibly late medieval Italy, all the important Latin American societies, and the Dutch commercial slave colony of Curaçao.

DOMINANT LARGE-SCALE RURAL ECONOMY

In this group of societies large-scale rural slavery was of overwhelming significance for the entire system. Slaves were concentrated on large farms of either the latifundic or plantation type. Significant urban sectors were absent or, where present, accounted for only a small minority of the total slave population. There was a high and continuously growing demand for slaves; supply constantly lagged behind demand, so that the replacement cost was always extremely high. Most of these systems depended heavily on an external supply of slaves, both to replace those who were rapidly used up and to increase the population. The high proportion of foreign-born slaves pushed down the manumission rate. But even where the slave population was self-reproducing, high replacement costs in themselves sufficiently accounted for the low manumission rate. For all but an insignificant minority of slaves the simple economic reality of their high market value combined with a dearth of opportunities, if not to acquire skills, to accumulate or control earnings, dictated that self-purchase was an impossibility. Significantly, a substantial proportion, though always a minority, of the few who did gain their freedom received it gratis. In these systems masters opted for incentive schemes other than manumission and were, in principle, opposed to manumission even where the unusual slave might be able to afford it.

I include in this group medieval Korea; the advanced sugar plantation system of the Madeira Islands during the fifteenth century, as well as the cotton-based slave system of Santiago in the Cape Verde Islands from the fifteenth to the end of the seventeenth centuries; the Mascarene Islands of the Indian Ocean during the eighteenth century; the Banda Islands of the Pacific during the eighteenth century; eighteenth- and early nineteenth-century South Africa; the British and French Caribbean during the eighteenth century; the Dutch colony of Surinam during the eighteenth and early nineteenth centuries; and the U.S. South from the late seventeenth century to the abolition of slavery in 1865.

It should be noted that while most of these societies were plantation systems, a plantation economy was neither necessary nor sufficient for this pattern. Brazil, for instance, had a large plantation system but is not in this group, partly because of the substantial proportion of slaves in nonplantation areas, both urban and mining. South Africa, on the other hand, had an economy that was based more on latifundia than on plantations; yet the pattern of demand and supply of slaves, as well as the overwhelmingly rural location of the slave population, places it in this group.

In all these systems the masters used physical punishment "as an integral part of their system for maintaining social discipline and regulating work activity," as Stephen Crawford writes of the U.S. South.[67] There were occasional incentives other than manumission, however: better material conditions; mobility up the occupational scale; days off to work on provision grounds, the returns from which, though largely controlled by the slaves, were usually barely beyond what was needed for subsistence.[68]

The Overarching Factors

Now that we have examined the major patterns of manumission, we may ask once again whether it is possible to detect any causal factors operating on a higher level of determination. In other words, is there a pattern behind the patterns we have just discussed? I think there is, and it is this: for all but the small lineage-based societies, manumission rates tended to be highest in those societies that were subject to periodic structural shocks. Those shocks might be of an economic or political (military) nature, or of course both.

ECONOMIC DISTURBANCES

When a slave system experienced a major economic slump, for example, masters found themselves with capital tied up in assets—their slaves—which generated earnings that were either less than their maintenance costs or much less than what could be earned from other investments. In such situations the best way for the masters to liquidate was to encourage the slaves to buy their freedom. When, as was usually the case, this could be done without losing the services of most of the ex-slaves, all the better.

Furthermore, the converse of this was not always true. It was frequently the case that a rapidly expanding slave economy meant high replacement costs and low manumission rates, but this depended on the nature of the slave economy.Where initial investments were high, the economic process highly routinized, and the returns to capital realized over a long period, an expanding economy almost certainly resulted in a considerably reduced manumission rate. This was the case during the eighteenth century in all the societies classified above as dominant rural economies. The U.S. South best illustrates the lack of high manumission rates. It is significant that even here the period of highest rates occurred toward the end of the eighteenth century with the declining fortunes of the older, upper South and the massive structural change in the North. In the upper South manumission rates, though never high in absolute terms, were at their peak during the brief postrevolutionary slump; in the North, of course, the far greater returns to investment in the expanding free-wage industrial system culminated in the rapid abolition of slavery at the same time. The sudden rapid growth of the new South, however, and the cotton revolution, coming after the abolition of the slave trade, immediately pushed the manumission rate down to its lowest levels by the end of the second decade of the nineteenth century.

The Brazilian economy also had lower manumission rates in its plantation sectors, as we have already seen. Not only was its rural economy subject to a far greater number of economic slumps, providing more frequent incentives for a flight of capital from slaves, but it was much more diversified than the U.S. South. The lack of integration meant that the massive downturn in the northeastern regions of Brazil at the start of the nineteenth century was not significantly influenced by the expansion of the central and southwestern regions during this period. Unlike the U.S. South, the replacement cost of slaves was not out of the reach of those seeking to purchase their freedom. The interregional slave trade was of minor significance in Brazil, as much because of the continuation of the Atlantic slave trade as because of the lack of national integration in the economy. In addition to all this, the other major element of the Brazilian colonial economy, the mining sector, was chronically subject to wild fluctuations.

Although other scholars have pointed to these factors in explaining the relatively high overall manumission rates in Brazil, it is Carl N. Degler who has most systematically articulated the thesis. "In short," he writes, "in colonial Brazil the master sometimes had good reason to free his slaves—to be rid of their expense in bad times—while the undermanned society and economy had a place and a need for the former slave."[69] There is one important caveat: the boom-or-bust pattern only operated where there was a well-functioning external supply of slaves, or where reenslavement was possible. The masters, being themselves aware of the cyclic nature of the economy, would clearly not rid themselves of slaves during difficult times if none were forthcoming when conditions changed for the better. Brazil and Korea respectively best exemplify the conditions of abundant external supply and of massive reenslavement.

The significance of frequent economic shocks to the rate of manumission is further illustrated by a comparison of Surinam, with its low overall rate, and Curaçao, where the rate was high. Behind the more specific causal patterns we have already discussed, Harry Hoetink found this more general determinant: "By the middle of the eighteenth century, recurrent periods of commercial depression had caused a relatively large number of manumissions in Curaçao; in Surinam, on the other hand, manumissions were few until the last quarter of the eighteenth century, when they increased, partly because of the favorable attitudes of one governor, but also as a result of the economic crisis which began in the 1770's."[70] Similarly in Cuba, the precarious, diversified preplantation economy had an extremely high manumission rate judging from the size of the freed group in 1774 (20 percent of the total population). With the structural shift of the economy to an expanding plantation system, however, the manumission rate apparently declined considerably. There are no precise statistical data to support this thesis, but the available statistics (as well as other kinds of data) strongly suggest such a development.[71]

In the operation of economically induced structural changes, there is an overarching pattern of determination. Economic fluctuations were not the only inducers of structural shock. More random in their occurrence, but in many ways even more impressive in their effects on manumission rates, were politically induced shocks. Of these the most important in their effects were military disturbances, both internal and external.

MILITARY DISTURBANCES

In Chapter 8 we saw that the political mode of manumission was frequently used in times of warfare. Almost all societies that kept slaves used manumission at some time, both as a means of motivating slaves to help in the defense of the master's territory or to invade the territory of others. Civil wars were also important in the history of mass manumissions. In all such conflicts slaves tended to benefit from both sides.

Because military manumissions occurred relatively infrequently, there has been a tendency to underestimate their significance. Yet the large numbers of slaves manumitted on these occasions often contributed substantially to the size of the freed population. This was especially true of the modern

Americas. It is desirable therefore to briefly review the evidence in both the premodern and the modern world.

We have already had occasion to note that in ancient Greece and Rome as well as medieval Europe, while slaves in principle were prevented from participating in military affairs, exceptions were made in times of crisis. On such occasions (especially in Rome) the principle was upheld by first manumitting all slaves who were selected for military service. No estimate is possible of the numbers or proportions of slaves freed in this manner, but we know that in times of major conflict such as the Persian, Peloponnesian, and Punic wars large numbers of slaves gained their freedom. There are many occasions in European history also when large numbers of slaves won their freedom by joining successful invading armies. Perhaps the most dramatic example is the large number of fugitive slaves who became free by associating themselves with the Visigothic invaders of Roman Spain.[72]

In Islamic lands the institution of military slavery was an essential feature in both the rise and spread of Islam, a point I have repeatedly made.[73] In general, the officer corps, where they were recruited as slaves, eventually won their manumission. The same was not normally true of the mass of slave regulars. At the same time, there is no doubt that the hope of eventual manumission was held out to those slaves who distinguished themselves in battle. Hence the near-universal Islamic practice of military slavery was an important factor contributing to the high rate of manumission in these societies.

In the premodern non-Islamic world the most striking case of periodic mass emancipation of slaves for military reasons was that of medieval Korea. Ironically, one of the major reasons for enslavement in Korea was evasion of the military draft.[74] For those enslaved persons who desired freedom enough to risk the hazards of internal and external warfare, military crises offered frequent opportunities for realization of their goal. In the internal struggles for power between various factions of the aristocracy, and between aristocrats and the Crown, slaves desiring manumission benefited when the Crown was strong; for the Crown favored the emancipation of slaves as a means of breaking the economic base of the large-scale, slaveholding aristocrats.[75]

The many invasions by foreign powers throughout the history of Korea also offered opportunities for mass emancipations. During the Mongol invasions of the thirteenth century (1231–1258) slave registrations, which were the official proof of slave status, were burned as a means of encouraging slaves to join in the defense of the country. For many of the slaves so emancipated, however, freedom must have been temporary or else it was not inherited by their children, since we find a massive increase in the number of slaves under the Mongol rulers.[76]

The opportunities for manumission offered by the settlement schemes for the northern border areas of Korea under Sejong (1419–1450) and Sejo (1456–1468) must be classed as military; the schemes were motivated largely by the need to protect these regions from the frequent invasions of the Jurchen tribes. Slaves from the southern provinces were induced to settle there with the incentive of manumission.[77]

It was the Japanese invasions between 1592 and 1598 that offered the greatest opportunities for mass emancipation. Large numbers of slaves simply took advantage of the social chaos to make good their escape; others did not even have to do this, as their masters fled or were economically ruined by the destruction of their estates; still others destroyed the slave registers.[78] While these invasions shook the foundations of mass slavery in Korea, they did not lead to its abolition. As Susan S. Shin has commented, "It would be simplistic to attribute the disappearance of hereditary servitude to a temporary disruption, however devastating. What requires explanation is not the decline of slavery during the war, but also its failure to reemerge later on the previous scale."[79] Still, she does not deny the fact that most fugitives at this time eluded reenslavement: there were 352,000 state-owned slaves in 1484 compared with only 190,000 in 1655. Whatever the factors accounting for the subsequent decline of slavery in Korea, it is in keeping with the country's tradition of mass manumission following invasion that the final abolition of slavery in 1910 was imposed by Japan after its conquest.

It is in the modern Americas that the role of warfare has been most seriously underestimated as a factor contributing to the rise of the freed groups. Military manumission may indeed have been the earliest form of release on a significant scale in the post-Columbian history of the hemisphere. Slaves accompanied the conquistadors in their conquests of the New World.[80] According to Frederick P. Bowser, a number of them "distinguished themselves through military prowess and profited by the free-and-easy atmosphere of the conquest period to gain their freedom."[81] So many apparently received their freedom by this means that by 1530 freed blacks were considered a problem in Lima.

From the very earliest period of Brazilian history slaves seized their opportunities to gain freedom from both combating sides. Carl N. Degler cites the Portuguese willingness to arm slaves as one of the more dramatic contrasts with the United States.[82] Slaves fought on both sides during the quarter of the seventeenth century that the Dutch tried to wrest Brazil from the Portuguese, and they would do so again when the French invaded Rio de Janeiro.[83] Degler sums up the record as follows:

> In fact in the armed conflicts within Brazil itself, in the eighteenth and nineteenth centuries, blacks, both slave and free, were to be found bearing arms. Sometimes the black slaves fought on both sides, as they did in the war of independence in 1823–24. Even bandits and magnates in Minas Gerais during the mining boom used armed slaves to exert their power. When fights in

Minas occurred in the early eighteenth century between the miners and "invaders" from Sao Paulo in the so-called war of Emboabas, Negro slaves fought in considerable numbers against the *paulistas.* In southern Brazil, during the revolt there against the central government, called the war of the Farrapos, 1835–45, slaves also took part, and the imperial armies threatened to punish those slaves who fought with the rebels. Perhaps the most striking example of the role of the armed slave in the wars of Brazil, aside from the Dutch episode of the seventeenth century, was the participation of slaves in the Paraguayan War of 1865–70. When the war was over, some 20,000 slaves were given their freedom for their participation in the struggle.[84]

Elsewhere in Latin America much the same pattern existed. The greater the frequency of internal and external wars, the greater the number of slaves who won their freedom.[85] The Caribbean was always the most vulnerable part of the Spanish empire, so it is no surprise that from very early on, blacks in great numbers were participating in warfare there and winning their freedom, however precarious it turned out to be. One-tenth of the Spanish forces who faced Sir Francis Drake when he attacked Cartagena in 1586 were free blacks; and ten years later there was an entire unit of free blacks under a black captain participating in the Panama campaign against him.[86] Throughout the preabolition history of Cuba there were numerous cases of mass manumissions resulting from warfare. Hundreds of slaves were freed in the 1760s during and after the English invasion; in the late 1790s the Crown liberated a thousand of its slaves in the copper mining region of Santiago del Cobre.[87]

A quantitative assessment of the kind of effect that political manumission could have on the manumission rate is provided by the case of Buenos Aires between 1806 and 1807. On average, ninety-two slaves were manumitted annually by nonmilitary means between 1806 and 1810. During the British invasions of 1806 and 1807, however, an additional eighty-four slaves won their freedom "as a result of their heroism against the British."[88] In other words, an average of 31 percent of the total manumissions in the two years 1806 and 1807 resulted from military action. Lyman Johnson follows the traditional approach in excluding these manumissions in his calculations, on the grounds that "they were special cases unrelated to the normal manumission process."[89] My own view, however, is that there was nothing abnormal about this kind of manumission; it was sporadic, but each occasion was on such a large scale that over the entire course of Latin American slavery the result must have contributed substantially to the total number of persons ever manumitted. What is more, the frequency of these events increased considerably during the wars of independence—so much so that, as Leslie Rout comments, the wars "dealt a body blow to slavery" in most parts of Latin America.[90]

It is easy to underestimate the significance of the use of slaves in warfare and the ensuing military manumissions in the non-Latin areas of the hemisphere. Non-Latin masters in the Caribbean and the United States may have found the necessity to arm slaves even more repugnant than did their Latin counterparts, but like the latter, and like the Romans and Greeks hundreds of years earlier, principle was quickly abandoned during periods of crisis.

In the Caribbean the various northern European imperial powers did not hesitate to use slaves in their numerous wars against each other, starting in the early years of the seventeenth century. The nucleus of the freed black group in Jamaica was formed in part by slaves of the Spanish who refused to leave the island with their masters when the British expelled them, after a five-year struggle, in 1660.[91]

Roger Norman Buckley, author of the only major study of the military role of blacks in the Caribbean, opens his pathbreaking work with this statement:

> With the advent of African plantation slavery during the first half of the sixteenth century, the military potential of slaves was immediately recognized and quickly exploited by the rival nations. All over the Caribbean world blacks were employed as service troops and even as front-line soldiers. Indeed, with white immigration largely discouraged by the plantation system, expanding negro slavery, and a deadly climate, the military use of slave labor rapidly became indispensable to West Indian warfare. To accommodate such a need, dramatic modifications of the slave order were instituted, such as the widespread manumission of slave soldiers.[92]

From very early on, the Europeans recognized the difficulty of keeping all-white regiments in the islands in view of their extremely high mortality rate. Partial Africanization of the British army took place throughout the eighteenth century. During the revolutionary era the conflicts between France and Britain, which were inevitably played out in the Caribbean (where they were later complicated by the Haitian slave revolt), resulted in the large-scale use of slaves in West Indian warfare. Almost all the British islands had corps of slave soldiers by 1795. In the face of strong planter opposition Britain in that same year took the unusual action of raising two black regiments, which were to be permanently stationed in the area and treated as part of the British military system.

Yet there was great confusion about the exact status in law of the black soldiers. They apparently believed themselves to be freedmen, while the planters and the white officers considered them to be slaves. The confusion was compounded by the fact that the officers, while declaring the black soldiers to be legally slaves, in actuality treated them on equal terms with their white counterparts. To make matters worse, most of the recruits were newly arrived Africans. In 1807 the matter was finally settled when Whitehall decided that all blacks in the king's service were free persons. "Thus," Buckley comments, "about 10,000 West India soldiers were enfranchised in what must certainly have been one of the largest number of slaves freed by a single act of manumission in preemancipation society in the Caribbean."[93]

There were parallels in the history of North American slavery. During early colonial times slaves were regularly recruited in the defense of the colonies against Indians and foreign Europeans. Usually their reward was freedom. By the late seventeenth century the colonial legislatures had become increasingly alarmed at the sight of armed slaves, and throughout most of the eighteenth century there were laws prohibiting their employment as soldiers. Even so, in times of emergency the laws, as always, were suspended and blacks were recruited. Unlike the Caribbean, freedmen were used much more frequently than slaves on these occasions. Hence manumission was less the consequence of desperation measures.[94]

The situation began to change dramatically at the start of the American Revolution.[95] It is one of the ironies of American history that the first person to die at the hands of the British in the events that led up to the American War of Independence was a runaway slave, Crispus Attucks, who fell on the night of August 5, 1770. Five years later the irony was compounded into one of the nation's most infamous moments when the Massachusetts Committee of Safety prohibited the recruitment of slaves on the grounds that such action was "inconsistent with the principles that are to be supported, and reflect dishonor on this country."[96] It might well be that the first part of the statement was unwittingly truthful. Needless to say, the legislatures quickly changed their position when the crisis worsened, especially when the British began to promise slaves their freedom if they would fight with the redcoats. All the northern states then actively recruited slaves, with the promise of freedom as the war continued, but only one southern state, Maryland, could bring itself to make and keep this pledge. In all, some five thousand blacks served on the American side during the war and about one thousand fought with the British. Although many obtained the promised freedom, a large number were deceived. Virginia, for example, sold all the state-owned slaves who had served in the navy, and many masters attempted to reenslave the veterans. The British proved themselves more honorable in the whole nefarious episode; not only did they free more slaves than the colonists, who had just won their own freedom, but over fifteen thousand slaves were carried off by the British when they evacuated the area, and many of them were later freed.

During the early decades of the nineteenth century significant numbers of slaves gained their freedom in the wars that flared periodically. Several thousand did so during the British-American wars, by joining ranks with the British.[97] Later, in the American Civil War some two hundred thousand slaves served on the Union side, winning their freedom in the process. Since this war resulted in the abolition of slavery, its events do not fall within the purview of military action as a means of preabolition manumission.[98]

It is clear, then, that although sporadic in its occurrence, warfare was one of the major reasons for the growth of the freed group not only in premodern times but in most of the major slave systems of the Americas. We are justified in concluding that structural shocks due to economic fluctuations, or military conflicts, or a combination of both were the major underlying causes of manumission throughout the posttribal world. At the highest level of generalization, we may say that the greater the frequency of such shocks the higher the rate of manumission. Below this causal level it is not possible to generalize about variations in the manumission rate in all slave systems. These must be explained in terms of the middle-range causal patterns uncovered in the earlier portion of this chapter. The major structural fluctuations not only overrode the more specific causal patterns, in this way facilitating manumission and ensuring the growth of the freed group, but they also stimulated the growth rate in the stable patterns. In the United States during and immediately after the revolutionary period, for example, not only did the structural shock of the revolution itself generate a massive increase in the manumission rate, but constraints on the usual methods of release were removed. In the ensuing "manumission fever" many more slaves than usual were released. What Ira Berlin observes of both North and South holds for most systems in other countries during periods of structural shock:

> The relaxation of the strictures against manumission reflected the main thrust of anti-slavery activity, but Southern abolitionists pressed their cause with equal vigor in the courts. Although freedom suits provided only piecemeal emancipation, establishing a single precedent often led to emancipation of many slaves.[99]

Conclusions

In the last three chapters we have examined the nature, meaning, and forms of manumission on the one hand, and on the other, the factors accounting for its incidence and the frequency of its occurrence. It is time now to relate this discussion to the preceding analysis of the nature of slavery.

The problem of slavery and manumission has been discussed on three levels: the cultural, the ideological, and the social. In cultural terms enslavement, slavery, and manumission were symbolically interpreted as three phases in an extended rite of passage. Enslavement was separation (or symbolic execution), slavery was a liminal state of social death, and manumission was symbolic rebirth. Accompanying this cultural process in the internal relations of slavery is an ideological dialectic. The master gives the slave physical life either directly (if he was the original enslaver) or indirectly (if he purchased or inherited him), in return for which the slave is under obligation to reciprocate with total obedience and service. In the act of repaying his debt, the slave loses social life. This loss, however, is not a part of the repayment to the master; it is rather one of the terms of the transaction—the exchange of physical life for total obedience. With manumission the master makes another gift to the slave, this time the gift of social life, which is ideologically interpreted as a repayment for faithful service.

Completion of the gift-exchange triad in this way forms the basis of a new triad, for the ex-slave now comes under another obligation to the ex-master, which he repays by faithful dependence. His redemption fee, if he pays one, is not and within the terms of the relationship cannot be ideologically interpreted as a repayment, for the money was not his own. In any case, it is not possible to sell freedom in a conveyance transaction; whatever it is that the ex-slave gains, it is never the same as what the master loses. Rather, the redemption fee is interpreted as a token gift, meant as a signal of gratitude to the master for the gift of freedom. As such, it is the initiation of a new dialectic of domination and dependence.

These symbolic and ideological interpretations are ritually and legally expressed in the different social modes of manumission. Seven such modes have been identified as the most universal forms of release.

The status and condition of freedmen have been considered, and it was found that in utilitarian terms, manumission universally extended and indeed deepened the ties of dependency between ex-slave and ex-master. A master class never lost, but invariably gained, by the change in status. In most cultures the ties were formalized in a dependency relationship that I have called wala, the Arabic term, to distinguish it from genuine patron-client relationships between free persons. It was determined, further, that the legal status and the prestige of the freedman in the community at large varied independently of each other. In all societies the freedman suffered some stigma, but the intensity and the duration differed. In some cases the stigma persisted for generations; in others it disappeared by the third generation. The movement from freedman to fully accepted freeman was usually an intergenerational process which took as long as, and often longer than, the movement from enslavement to manumission.

The main factors determining the pace of politicolegal and prestigious assimilation of the freedman were found to be race, the type of socio-economic system, demographic composition of the population (especially the master-slave ratio and the sex ratio of the master class), and the degree of formalization of the ex-master/ex-slave relationship (which itself is partially shaped by cultural factors, mainly laws and religion). With the exception of race, which does adversely influence the status of freedmen where perceived differences between masters and slaves exist, these variables influence freedman status independently, in conflicting ways; in addition, there are complex interactive effects. For this reason there were no meaningful worldwide correlations (again with the exception of the race variable). Instead there were causal configurations with respect to specific subgroups within the universe of slaveholding societies. Six such subgroups were identified and the configurations of the determinants of freedman status for each group were discussed.

The variations in the incidence and rates of manumission, both intrasocietal and intersocietal, were next considered. Sex, age, parental status, somatic similarity, residence (mainly rural versus urban), skill, control of earnings, and mode of acquisition were found to be the major correlates of individual variations in the incidence of manumission, with a high level of interaction among these variables. While each had some direct effect, and in extreme cases could override other variables, in general access to skill and opportunity to control part of earnings were found to be the major determinants of incidence.

Regarding the intersocietal variations in the rates of manumission, none of the variables either by themselves or interactively could explain them; nor could racial or religious factors. Use of the same approach as in the analysis of freedman status uncovered six causal patterns identified as domestic assimilation, matrilineal circumvention, domestic exclusiveness, predatory circulation, commercial reproduction, and the dominant large-scale rural economy.

Delineation of these causal patterns made it possible to distinguish the forest from the trees. Only then was it found that, at a higher level of determination, there was indeed one major worldwide causal factor that applied to all posttribal slave systems. Manumission rates varied positively with the frequency of structural shocks a system experienced, and these shocks were either of an economic or a politicomilitary nature. The structural determinants operated independently of the more stable patterns or else stimulated in them whatever propensities for manumission existed.

An important finding is that the conditions influencing freedman status differ from those influencing the rate of manumission, sometimes in extreme ways. The manumission rate was largely a function of individual opportunity structures and decision making; the status of the freed was largely the result of collective responses. The two sets of determinants were not unrelated, although their interaction was complex. In some cases hostility to freedmen was congruent with masters' unwillingness to free slaves, and this was reflected in low manumission rates. But in other situations hostility to freedmen was used as a bargaining device by masters to enhance postemancipation dependency; in such situations the manumission rates were high. Thus a high rate of manumission no more implied highly favorable freedman status than a low rate of manumission implied unfavorable freedman status. The rate of manumission was low in both the eighteenth-century British Caribbean and the American South, yet the conditions of the freedman differed radically. The rate of manumission was high in both Greece and Rome, but in both countries the fate of freedmen and their descendants differed markedly. There was considerable hostility to freedmen in late medieval Italy, especially in Venice and Florence, but the manumission rate was relatively high, as was the level of postemancipation dependency. Racial attitudes and, more crudely, master-slave racial differences were important variables explaining differences in freedman status, although they played little part in determining the manumission rate.

We see now how untenable are the recent claims of James L. Watson that "the eventual fate of the person who enters society as a slave is not relevant when one is constructing a definition of slavery as an institution" and that "it is less than helpful to conceive of slavery as an institution for the incorporation of outsiders."[100] To the contrary, it is not possible to understand what slavery is all about until we understand it as a process including the act of manumission and its consequence. Enslavement, slavery, and manumission are not merely related events; they are one and the same process in different phases. To separate one from the other in an imposed schema is as gross an error as the attempt of a biologist to classify as distinct entities larva, chrysalis, and imago.

Nor is there the slightest trouble with the claim that the process of slavery both incorporated and natally alienated persons. One answer to this apparent contradiction is that already offered by Kopytoff and Miers: individuals may be incorporated in some respects while excluded in others. Black Americans have been thoroughly included on the level of the manorial household, even from the days of slavery. As Genovese and others have shown, as long as black Americans "knew their place" they were paternalistically, sometimes even lovingly, accepted as "our people" by the master class and their associates. But even while knowing their place, they were ruthlessly excluded from what European sociologists of the twenties, and more recently Daniel Bell, have called "the public household"—all those areas of society where power is competed for and status and honor are claimed, conferred, and accepted.[101]

The issue is still more complex than this. The paradoxical incorporation and alienation of the slave, the implication of the act of manumission in the act of enslavement, the status of the freedman and the status of the slave, all hint strongly at the critical role of contradiction in the unfolding of this complicated drama known as slavery. Such contradiction should not be "resolved" by only a schematic decomposition of the process, by distinguishing, say, between private and public households. We miss a great deal by resorting to such a method—not that it is wrong, but it is incomplete. The contradiction is an inherent part of the internal relations of slavery, as it is of all social processes. So far we have only intimated this. We must now confront the matter squarely.

11

The
Ultimate
Slave

HEGEL HAS WRITTEN that "the distinctive difference of anything is ... the boundary, the limit, of the subject; it is found at that point where the subject matter stops, or it is what the subject matter is not."[1] It is in this sense that the historical existence of elite slaves presents us with a crucial test. Such slaves, to be sure, were found in nearly all areas of the premodern world where slavery became an important institution: slaves and freedmen played significant military, administrative, and executive roles in the Persian empire,[2] in dynastic Korea, and in early modern Russia.[3] But it was the *familia Caesaris* of early imperial Rome, the elite slaves of the Islamic states and empires, and the palatine eunuchs of Byzantium and imperial China that provide the most extreme cases of persons who were at once slaves and figures of high political and administrative importance.

One immediately begins to question whether these individuals were really slaves. What could an important slave *dispensatores* or freedman *procurator* possibly have in common with a rural slave or freedman? What could a favored Mamluk in ninth-century Baghdad either before or after his manumission have in common with a lowly African Zandj toiling in the dead lands of lower Mesopotamia? Or to take the most extreme contrast possible, in what sense is the word "slave" meaningful when applied to both a grand vizier of the Ottoman Empire and an Ethiopian domestic slave in the household of a modest merchant?

We seem here to be at the very limit of the concept of slavery, if not well beyond it, and it might seem far more prudent simply to exclude these exceptional cases. Such a solution would be wholly inadmissible, for it is precisely at the limits that one tests the sharpness of one's constructs. And there is something else: the limiting cases raise issues of analytic value not immediately apparent in the less problematic cases.

The Familia Caesaris

To begin with the Roman case, the *familia Caesaris* was an extremely heterogeneous group with several subdivisions based on legal status, occupation, and region of service. The difference between those who were slaves and those who had been manumitted was the pivotal legal distinction and the basis of a fivefold status division.[4] P. R. C. Weaver's analysis places at one end of the spectrum the *servus vicarius*, the slave of the emperor's slaves; next the *liberti servus*, the slave of one of the emperor's freedmen; after this the *liberti libertus*, the freedman of a freedman of the emperor. Then came the two most important legal subclasses: the *Caesaris servi*, or direct slaves of the emperor; and finally the *Augusti liberti*, the freedmen of the emperor.

While these distinctions were legally important, it should be obvious already that what was really critical was proximity to the emperor, and occupation. A Caesaris servus might have been a slave, but even in purely legal terms his position was far superior to all freedmen of freedmen. Indeed, many Caesaris servi were superior both in rank and power to their freedmen counterparts, the Augusti liberti. Although manumission was relevant, our problem is not solved by claiming that the most important members of this group were eventually manumitted. In any case, the claim is downright wrong.

The second division of the familia was functional. Basically, the distinction was between the domestic staff—those in the personal service of the emperor—and the imperial civil service. Within both there was a wide range of occupations—the palatine staff, for example, being quite distinct from those who administered the emperor's *patrimonium* (crown property) in other parts of Rome, in Italy, and in the provinces. At the same time, the distinction between domestic and civil service cannot be pressed too hard, especially during the early period of the empire when there was considerable overlapping of the emperor's patrimonium and the public property. Nor, further, should one equate power too closely with position on the occupational hierarchy. While the emperor's chamberlain, for instance, because of his access to the person of the emperor, often achieved great influence, he was also a willing target for bribes and a source of valuable information. In the early empire many chamberlains sold daily accounts of the emperor's mood and passed on what became known as "fumus" (smoke), rumors—

many of them invented—that were avidly bought up by anxious senators and other wealthy suitors and lobbyists.

There is no need to go into the details of the imperial organization. It is enough to observe the established fact that "the *Familia Caesaris* was an essential part of the power structure of the empire until the increasing militarization of the third century swept its power away."[5] At various times during this period slaves and freedmen held some of the most powerful positions in the empire, including the three greatest offices: *libertus a rationibus,* the financial secretary and head of the *fiscus,* which controlled all the state property entrusted to the emperor; *libertus a libellis,* the secretary who handled all petitions and grievances addressed to the emperor; and *libertus ab epistulis,* the secretary of state. Under Claudius, when these offices were at their most powerful, all three were held by freedmen—the notorious triumvirate of Narcissus, Pallas, and Callistus. Through these and many other positions they controlled all the revenues collected from the imperial provinces, all those from the emperor's domain, and all taxes except those belonging to the senatorial or military treasuries.[6] Although they were excluded from positions in the army, the fiscus nonetheless "controlled the expenditure for the army and navy, for the conveyance of corn, for the establishment and repair of public works, and for the general administration of Rome, Italy, and the imperial provinces."[7] The *libertus a libellis* controlled all patronage of the arts, and a great deal more; even a Seneca, scornful as he was of their influence, found it politic to flatter the freedman whom Claudius had appointed *a libellis.*

Nor did the influence of these appointees end with their control of the major executive positions or access to the emperor. While it was true that they were largely barred from the top administrative posts in the imperial civil service, they were occasionally appointed to minor governorships; and in their roles as deputies and auxiliaries to the heads of departments they were in positions to influence, and sometimes control, incompetent or corrupt magistrates. As A. M. Duff comments, a great deal depended on the character of these equestrian (upper middle class) heads of departments:

> Each of these departments had its under-secretary with a large staff of clerks and accountants. Each staff was recruited from the slaves and freedmen of the Emperor, and the under-secretaries also were nearly always freedmen, even after general transfer of the headships to the knights. Of course it depended on individual character whether much could be made of these subordinate posts. If the director of a department were both honest and vigilant, his under-secretary would find that he could not make any profit except that brought in by his salary. If the director however were unwary, his subordinate could carry on a vast illicit traffic; whereas, if he were dishonest, his subordinate would sooner or later learn his secret and make him pay a high price for his silence.[8]

What accounts for this extraordinary development? The first and most obvious cause is the utter novelty of the problem that confronted the Roman ruling class as a result of its territorial expansion beyond the Italian peninsula. The need to govern an empire on this scale had never before arisen. Rome itself lacked the volume of skilled manpower—the managerial expertise, in effect—to run such an empire. Although the excesses of imperial slaves and freedmen have been widely publicized, it should not be forgotten that they were the exceptions to the general rule. The normal pattern seems to have been one in which slaves and freedmen executed their tasks with commendable efficiency. The remarkable thing about Rome and its empire during the first three centuries after Christ is not its extravagance, for in this it was hardly unique, but the simple, stark fact that it worked. The originality and dexterity with which it met its administrative challenges is simply incredible, and the imperial freedmen and slaves must take a large part of the credit.

But why slaves and ex-slaves? Even if Rome did not have the skilled manpower, why were not free foreigners recruited, as Athens had used metics in the fifth century B.C. (in the economic sector) when her citizen body lacked similar resources? The answer is, first of all, that these persons were needed not only in great numbers but in a great hurry. Furthermore, the persons whom Rome needed most to perform these skilled administrative jobs were precisely the persons who were most likely to be quite content in their natal communities. It was only by means of enslavement that they could be compelled to move in order to meet Rome's bureaucratic needs.

In the second place, the very novelty of the administrative challenge made the use of slaves mandatory. Slaves, as the ultimate human tools, are the ideal persons to be employed in major structural transformations. It is a truism that people who perform bureaucratic and other middle-class roles tend to be very conservative with respect to the nature and functioning of their jobs. In republican Rome birth, citizenship, status, and seniority were the major criteria for recruitment into public life. If the empire was to run properly, not only were wholly new occupations to be created, but the principle of merit had to be given some recognition. It was natally alienated persons who could most readily be employed in this way: ever ready to move physically, and occupationally, not only upward but laterally, downward, and out; ever ready to retrain for entirely new positions and to accept, without complaint, whatever was offered in remuneration.

The third reason for using slaves now becomes obvious; they were cheap. Slaves were the most flexible, adaptable, and manipulable category of workers imaginable; furthermore, Stanley Engerman has shown that, quite apart from matters of efficiency, it was possible to increase the profit or surplus gained from them by, on the one hand, reducing their maintenance costs, and on the other hand, raising (beyond what is possible with free employees) their total volume of work.[9] The East German classicist Elisabeth Welskopf makes much the same point in her study of slavery in the ancient Orient and Western world. Slavery, she observes, made possible a more effective utilization of the principle of specialization and cooperation, it allowed for an extension of the workday, and it also permitted a greater constancy of work and thus a more efficient use of working time. Total product, and surplus, were increased even if productivity, in the narrow sense, remained constant or even declined.[10] What was true of the proletarian use of slaves held even more for bureaucratic and executive use.

Yet another saving was realized by using slaves, one that was particularly relevant to elite occupations. Slavery considerably reduced the recruitment and replacement costs of labor. Weaver has shown that by the middle of the first century A.D. the familia Caesaris had become a largely self-perpetuating order. It was a tightly knit, highly efficient "closed shop," which recruited largely by birth. Another reason why it would be simplistic to make too much of the legal distinction between slaves and freedmen is the fact that "the emperor was able to recruit into the Familia as *servi* from *all* the children born to Imperial slaves before manumission."[11]

We should be careful not to forget the most obvious advantage of using slaves: the fact that they could be literally whipped into shape. We are likely to neglect this in considering the elite slaves, since it is true that they did not have drivers behind them as they worked. Nonetheless, naked force did apply. The slave or freedman could not only be moved about and used without any regard to his feelings on the matter, but in the event that he was inefficient and corrupt, he could be punished in the most degrading and painful manner possible. Augustus, like other emperors who used slaves, was not unmindful that he had the power to torture unto death the most elevated of his slaves and freedmen, a power that he not infrequently used.

By this mention of the role of naked force we have begun to support our argument that imperial freedmen and slaves were indeed slaves in the terms in which I have defined the concept. This is reinforced when we consider the fifth reason why the familia Caesaris developed. Slaves offered the only solution to the unsolved legal problem of having individuals to act as one's agents. With his vast personal fortune to administer, the emperor, like other members of the Roman ruling class, needed persons who in law had no separate legal identity but were simply living surrogates of their masters. Weaver, agreeing with Boulvert, notes:

> Certain financial posts in the administration were always held by slaves despite or rather because of the important responsibilities involved. Boulvert has well pointed out that this was precisely because the slave's lack of separate legal personality enabled him to handle funds directly on behalf of his

master, whereas free persons not *in potestate,* at least in the time of the jurist Gaius could not act as representatives on behalf of another with the same direct effects.[12]

If the above arguments explain why slaves and freedmen were used on a large scale, they still do not sufficiently account for the fact that these persons came to occupy the high and commanding positions that a few of them did.

The Emperor Augustus had two principal reasons for promoting his slaves and freedmen to the powerful offices they held. One was his desire to exercise total power and control over all important affairs. His slaves, as extensions of his own person, and his freedmen, as loyal servants, were ideally suited to do this. As natally alienated persons with no other anchor in Roman society or as freedmen owing their status solely to the emperor, their interests were completely identified with his own and he could use and abuse them as he wished.

Second, Augustus genuinely did not wish to offend the honor of the upper-class Romans. To have even requested them to perform some of these roles in early imperial Rome would have been an insult. Why so? The Roman upper class, even before the days of the empire, had always regarded secretarial and accounting work as dishonorable. In her study of the freedmen of Cicero, Susan Treggiari observed that "a considerable though subordinate part of the life of a Roman of the upper classes was played by his servants, who ministered to his comfort, supported his *dignitas,* and were essential agents in his political work."[13]

It is worth elaborating at this point on the Roman notion of honor. Not just secretarial work but any form of direct personal service was considered dishonorable by upper-class Romans. This is quite distinct from patron-client relationships, which were compatible with, and in fact highly correlated with, a highly developed system of honor. The Roman ruling class was no exception; the institution of the *clientela* thrived and was a free, mutually beneficial relationship that promoted the honor and *gloria* of both patron and client, especially in political affairs.[14]

Donald Earl gives a good summary. The Roman elite held that *virtus* was the quintessential human quality. What they called *gloria,* or public distinction, was to be won by the "objective expression of *virtus,"* which they called *virtutes,* that is, good deeds and high moral integrity. "Above all, *virtus* formed the ancestral foundation of the Roman state and attached both to the people and the empire of Rome. For men to struggle with each other over *virtus* and to compete for *gloria* was not merely natural but a mark of felicity. *Virtus* demanded recognition and honor; to insist on and to strive for them was praiseworthy."[15] Further, Romans strongly believed that "the highest field in which *virtus* could be exercised, *virtutes* displayed, and *gloria* won was the service of the state."[16] Service to the state, however, specifically excluded personal service to anyone, including the emperor. To obtain political office or to have a distinguished military career were the highest attainable goals. Although the statement is somewhat oversimplified, it is generally true that toward the end of the republican era the rise of the *novi homines,* the new elite that was rapidly to replace the old patrician aristocracy, was ideologically reinforced not only by the replacement of *nobilitas* by *virtus* as the highest Roman ideal but also by the acceptance of the pursuit of wealth as a legitimate exercise of virtus and display of virtutes (although wealth always ranked lower than public service).[17]

With such an ideology, the view of Tacitus is now more understandable, that *"virtus belonged to the free man since it involved an exercise of the will and the display of qualities not open to the slave."*[18] Precisely because the powerful imperial offices during the early empire were so closely associated with the person of the emperor, his upper-class peers could not have been asked to function in these offices without being deeply dishonored. As Duff observes: "Even if knights could become the agents of the Emperor they could not perform the work of his private secretaries. The sorting of petitions to Caesar and the management of his correspondence were naturally for his slaves and freedmen to perform."[19]

Thus the assumption of vast power by the imperial slaves and freedmen was partly an outcome of the Roman elite's own traditions and values. They were trapped by their too keenly developed sense of honor. Obviously, the more powerful and wealthy the slave or freedman, the more he would be held in contempt and denied all claim to honor. The literary sources leave us in no doubt about this. There is nothing in ancient or modern literature more brutally scathing, not to mention more uproariously funny, than Petronius' satire on dinner with Trimalchio, the epitome of the freedman upstart and nouveau riche.[20] We read of Trimalchio's grotesquely furnished house, with a series of frescoes on his wall depicting his life from the slave market to his entry into Rome under the sponsorship of Minerva, followed by a panel of Trimalchio as an apprentice accountant, then as a paymaster, climaxed by "a picture of Mercury grasping Trimalchio by the chin and hoisting him up to the lofty eminence of the official's tribunal."[21] The high point of the entire evening is Trimalchio's staged entry into his dining room:

> We were nibbling at these splendid appetizers when suddenly the trumpets blared a fanfare and Trimalchio was carried in, propped up in piles of miniature pillows in such a comic way that some of us couldn't resist smiling. His head, cropped close in a recognizable slave cut, heavily swathed already in bundles of clothing, was wrapped in a large napkin bounded by an incongruous senatorial purple stripe with little tassels dangling down here and there. On the little finger of his left hand he sported an immense gilt ring; the ring on the last joint of his fourth finger looked to be solid gold of the kind the lesser nobility wear, but was actually, I think, an imitation, pricked out

with small steel bars ... He was picking his teeth with a silver toothpick when he first addressed us."[22]

As Arrowsmith comments, Trimalchio, having the right to wear neither the senatorial purple stripe nor the gold ring, "does the next best thing, wearing an imitation steel ring and transferring the purple stripe from the toga to the napkin."

At least there is a great deal of raucous good humor in this contemptuous depiction of the wealthy freedman—which, one suspects, is too wickedly funny not to have been based on real life. There is, however, nothing the least bit funny about the scathing comments of other Latin authors.[23] What Tacitus wrote of the notorious Felix, the freedman of Claudius who became the tyrannical governor of Judea and the persecutor of Saint Paul, must have been typical of how all Romans of honorable birth and status viewed these favored imperial freedmen. "With all manner of brutality and lust, he exercised the power of a monarch in the spirit of a slave."[24]

Not only were freedmen denied all claims to honor by what should have been their class peers, not only were they "rejected by the aristocracy" and "integrated in an inferior milieu,"[25] but their legal privileges came entirely from their proximity to power, and it is this more than any other form of evidence that confirms my thesis that they were always considered people without honor. As Garnsey tells us:

> The legal privileges of the Imperial freedmen are to be explained purely in terms of their proximity to the seat of power. *They were gained independently of dignitas or a social standing which could be acknowledged by judges and officials.* Similarly these privileges did not gain for the freedman a status which could be justified in terms of the prevailing social values. *Imperial freedmen were not held to be honestiores* [of noble or honorable background].[26]

We have said enough to demonstrate that in at least two crucial respects the familia Caesaris does meet our definition of slavery: its members were elevated to their positions not in spite of but because they were originally or currently natally alienated and bereft of honor. The question of their power is still problematic, and to define it we must begin by specifying the object of power. The object may be third parties or the master himself—in this case, the emperor. It will be recalled that in defining the powerlessness of the slave we emphasized that this is an individualized condition, one that exists essentially in relation to the master. The slave is not necessarily powerless with respect to third parties. Everything, clearly, depends on the power of the master: if the master is all powerful and the slave is his surrogate and personal agent, it is inevitable that, acting under his authority, the slave too will be powerful. Even when the slave is given a free hand and exercises it ruthlessly, he acts on behalf of his master; for ultimately, all that he owns accrues on his death to his master's patrimonium. There is clear evidence that several of the emperors in their relations with their most powerful and notorious freedmen and slaves were actually using the latter's ruthlessness for their own ulterior ends. According to Suetonius, Vespasian, a strong emperor, deliberately appointed his most rapacious freedmen to proconsulships in the provinces with the expectation that they would amass as great a fortune as possible—fortunes he would later appropriate by the simple expedient of execution.[27]

The crucial issue, the real challenge to my thesis, comes when we examine the relationship between the imperial slave or freedman and his master. Here the facts are unequivocal: there can be no doubt that some members of the familia Caesaris exercised considerable influence over their masters. The influence of Pallas, Narcissus, and Callistus over Claudius is perhaps the most nefarious; but there is also that of Helius, Halatus, and Polyclitus over Nero; of Icelus over Galba; of Moschus over Ortho; of Asiaticus over Vitellius; and of Cleander over Commodus. The list is a long one.[28]

We saw in the introduction that power has three aspects: coercion, authority, and influence. It is now evident that what the imperial slaves and freedmen exercised above all was great influence. Despite the serious risk of schematism, it would be foolish to neglect one important implication of power that rests overwhelmingly on influence: it is essentially psychological in nature and rests solely on the character of one person, the master. It has no independent objective bases such as the power of the master himself or of his upper-class peers; and it is not diffuse, not embedded in a network of mutually reinforcing alliances, but is highly specific.

Of necessity, the power of freedmen and slaves was utterly precarious; it existed solely at the whim, feeblemindedness, or design of the master. Nothing makes this clearer than the fate of powerful freedmen on the death of their masters. Often a carnage ensued as the new emperor cleared the deck and settled scores. Narcissus, who had plotted the downfall of Messalina, was removed by Agrippina, the mother of Nero, as soon as Claudius departed; Vespasian crucified Asiaticus, his predecessor's favorite; Otho executed Galba's favorite, Icelus, to public rejoicing; and so on.

If this was power, then we had better recognize it as a very peculiar and perverse form of power indeed and specify its limitations: that its source was wholly influential; that it was completely noninstitutional in origin, practice, and termination; that it had no authority whatsoever; and that it required natal alienation and dishonor.

Having come this far in the direction of schematism, let us now approach the problem from a different perspective. Whatever its limitations and peculiarities, power is power. It must surely have offered little comfort to Sulpicius Camerinus and his family that Helius, left master of Rome by Nero during the latter's tour of Greece, exercised power purely as a surrogate of his master. The fact remains that Helius acted, and as a result the noble Sulpicius soon lost his head.

Further, the relationship between imperial master and slave or freedman was not wholly asymmetric. In some cases the master needed his freedman almost as much as his freedman needed him—and not merely to satisfy his personal whim and passions, since these surely could have been satisfied by a host of eager free persons.[29]

So it seems that, except in a preliminary manner, we cannot view power as a static entity. It is a relationship, an ongoing social process. Not its essence—which can only be a metaphor—but its dialectics must be exposed. Before we attempt to do so, however, let us consider our other cases, first that of the Islamic ghilmān.

The Islamic Ghilmān

From the founding of the Islamic empires and republics in the eighth century until the gradual abolition of slavery in the twentieth century, slave and freedman have played an even more important role than their counterparts in early imperial Rome. Use of the slave *ghilmān* was already well established in the first centuries of Islam. They were used as guards and attendants in the service of all high-ranking Arabs.[30] Unlike Rome, slaves of all ranks also came to play a crucial role in the military and, as soldiers, were a critical element in the establishment and expansion of the Islamic states.[31]

During the caliphate the regiments of ghilmān soon became powers unto themselves. Frequently they ceased being the guards and became the masters of the caliph. They not only removed and seated caliphs but played a commanding role in politics. In Egypt, for example, the Turkish slaves sent by al-Malik al-Sahih soon seized power for themselves and founded the Mamluk kingdom.[32] In the Mamluk institutions of the caliphate and Egypt and in the janissaries of the Ottoman Empire, we find the two most extreme developments of servile power in the Islamic world; it is on these that we shall concentrate.

Both involved the recruitment of aliens, their conversion to Islam, rigorous training in military academies, and eventual passing or graduation into the army and other high-status positions in the executive and administrative branches of their respective polities. The ghilmān, it may be contended, were above all honored and powerful persons. Paul Rycaut, a British ambassador to the court of Sultan Mahomet during the mid-seventeenth century, observed of the "Kul, which is the Grand Signior's Slave," that "it is more honorable than the condition and name of Subject."[33] And Halil Inalcik is typical of many modern historians when he writes: "In Ottoman society, to be a slave of the Sultan was an honour and a privilege."[34] That the ghilmān exercised great power on behalf of their proprietors and rulers, there can be no doubt. Many commentators, in fact, have gone out of their way to stress the differences between the ghilmān and other slaves. It would be absurd to deny that there were indeed great differences. Slaves were no more homogeneous a category of persons than, say, soldiers or merchants or women. But in emphasizing the differences, the commentators often go to contradictory extremes. For instance, Inalcik claims that "there is no resemblance at all between these [ordinary agricultural slaves] and the ghulāms belonging to the military class."[35] If there is "no resemblance at all," clearly the ghilmān were not slaves. Then why do commentators insist on calling them slaves? Clearly something is amiss, and suggesting, as Inalcik does, that the issue is semantic does not help much.

The semantic issue largely arises from the fact that alongside the master-slave relationship there existed throughout the Islamic world a highly developed and structured patron-client relationship, with which honor was closely bound. As Stanford Shaw notes, in his study of the Ottoman Empire: "Many of the dealings between individuals in the Ottoman system involved the practice of *intisap,* a tacit relationship *established by mutual consent* between a powerful individual and a weaker one . . . It was considered to be in extremely bad taste—in fact a violation of one's personal honor—for either party to break the relationship or fail to live up to its obligations when required" (emphasis added.)[36] It was inevitable that the master-slave and patron-client relationships should influence each other, a fact that largely accounts for the semantic confusion. The intisap was sometimes *metaphorically* expressed as a master-slave relationship, and vice versa. A zealous client might declare to his lord, "I am your slave." Indeed, even today in parts of the Middle East a person will formally address another, especially a respected social superior, as "your obedient slave." But it would be as ridiculous an error to confuse such formalities with genuine expressions of slavishness as would, say, an Islamic observer of the British deducing that bureaucrats are literal servants because of such formalities as "your obedient servant" at the end of letters. The point is that a clear distinction was always made throughout the Islamic world between the intisap or, more generally, the patron-client relationship, and the master-slave relationship.

How were they distinguished? First and foremost, by the origin and character of the two relationships. The intisap was established "by mutual consent"; the master-slave relationship was forced, with the slave a conquered person. The threat of naked violence was the ultimate basis of support for the latter; freely recognized mutual benefit was the ultimate basis of support for the former. Second, the slave was always a natally alienated person—one who, by definition, came from an alien society, and preferably one who was originally an infidel. Deracination was the very essence of the ghulām's existence. Nothing more tellingly demonstrates this than the method of recruitment of both the Mamluks and their janissary counterparts. From the early days of the caliphate we find the tendency to recruit elite slaves from groups who were infidels and of a different ethnic and "racial" type. It is important to understand that the rulers were not simply making a virtue of necessity: perhaps so with the mass of soldiers given the acute manpower shortages that were soon to beset the Arab aristocracy and later Islamic rulers,[37] but not in filling the elite positions. There the use of deracinated persons was a deliberate policy, elements of which can be traced back as far as Umayyad times.[38] It was during the early Abbasid period, however, that the policy took its final shape.

The favored group were the ethnic Turks from Transoxania,[39] and there is a general agreement among Muslim and Western scholars that this emphasis began with Mùtasim. Free Iranians (Xurasânians) were also recruited to perform high-status roles and were available and willing to fill all the available elite positions in the caliphate, but conflict soon developed between the two groups, from which the natally alienated Turks emerged triumphant.[40]

Why did the caliphs prefer their Turkish Mamluks to free aliens and even fellow Arabs? The answer goes straight to the heart of the distinction between the patron-client relationship and the master-slave relationship, and it is similar to that which accounts for the rise of the familia Caesaris under Augustus, namely, that the highly developed sense of honor among the Arab aristocracy meant that the caliph could not secure persons to serve him in the highly personal capacities he needed while at the same time executing his wish with the selflessness and total loyalty he demanded. Ibn Khaldun went so far as to argue that it was this trait in the Arab character that accounts for their dependence on other peoples for the development of their civilization. And he implied as much in accounting for the dependence on others in their rise to power, when he wrote that "every Arab regards himself as worthy to rule, and it is rare to find one of them submitting to another."[41] To claim that this was the only reason (which Khaldun did not) would of course be an oversimplification. But assuredly it was a significant contributing factor, one of which the caliphs were fully aware.

An anecdote from the Abbasid period provides a telling illustration. A prominent member of the Abbasid family complained to the Caliph al-Mahdī that the preferential treatment accorded to the Mamluk freedmen was creating resentment among his kinsmen and a morale problem in the Khuräsänī army. To this al-Mahdī replied:

> The mawālī deserve such a treatment, for only they combine in themselves the following qualities. When I sit in public audience, I may call a mawlā and raise him and seat him by my side, so that his knee will rub my knee. As soon, however, as the audience is over, I may order him to groom my riding

animal *and he will be content with this and will not take offence.* But if I demand the same thing from somebody else, he will say: "I am the son of your supporter and intimate associate" or "I am a veteran in your ('Abbāsid) cause (da'wā)" or "I am the son of those who were the first to join your ('Abbāsid) cause." *And I shall not be able to move him from his (obstinate) stand* (emphasis added).[42]

David Ayalon, who cites this passage, also points out that the reason why the caliph did not employ members of his own family in his all-important information service was because *"this kind of occupation would humiliate them* and he therefore employed his mawālī in their stead" (emphasis added).[43]

In addition to the problem of honor, there was the caliph's strong belief that natally alienated persons, having no basis of existence in their new societies except their masters, were likely to be totally loyal to him. Unlike freely contracted clients, the mawālī sometimes preferred suicide or death with their master to life without him. When al-Muhallabī, governor of the province of al-Ahwāz, faced certain defeat, he told his mawālī to escape while they could and leave him to his fate. They replied: "By God! If we do so, we would cause you great injustice. You have manumitted us from slavery and elevated us from a humble position and raised us from poverty to riches. And after all that, how can we abandon you and leave you in such a state?" Instead, they fought by their lord's side until they had all been killed. Ayalon sums up as follows:

> It was thus the combination of their complete dependence on their master, who was the sole arbiter of their fate (for they had nobody else, relative or otherwise to whom they could resort) and their unbounded gratitude to him for raising them from nothingness and anonymity to the peak of power and wealth which made the freedman so faithful and loyal to him. It should be noted in this connection that the ties between slave and patron were not severed with the slave's manumission. Mutual loyalty (walā) constituted the basis of their relations.[44]

The same emphasis on natal alienation and reincorporation into society as the living surrogate of the sultan existed in all other areas of the Islamic world. Thus P. Hardy observes of Muslim India: *"Deracinated,* the Turkish ghulāms of the period of the Ghurid conquest found membership of the conquering elite *the only satisfying role possible* in a compartmentalized society from which they were divided by religion and attitude of caste" (emphasis added).[45]

Nowhere, however, was the emphasis on natal alienation more extraordinary than in the case of the janissaries, who were largely recruited on the basis of the *devshirme,* the levy of children or "tribute of blood" from the subjected Christian peoples.[46] The devshirme has been defined by Basilike

Papoulia as "the forcible removal, in the form of a tribute, of children of the Christian subjects from their ethnic, religious, and cultural environment and their transformation into the Turkish-Islamic environment with the aim of employing them in the service of the Palace, the army, and the state, whereby they were on the one hand, to serve the Sultan as slaves and freedmen and on the other to form the ruling class of the State."[47] What is perhaps most unusual about the devshirme is that, in a very basic way, it contradicted one of the sacred precepts of the *Saria,* the holy law according to which Christian subjects acquired the status of *Dhimni,* thereby giving them freedom of religious worship. Paul Wittek comments that it is one of the unsolved mysteries of Islamic history that the Ottoman sultan who saw himself as the most pious defender on earth of the Islamic faith should so blatantly defy one of the fundamental laws of his creed.[48]

The mystery vanishes, however, once one recognizes that to the Ottoman sultan the ultimate good was the maintenance of a powerful empire in the service of Allah. Breaking the Saria was surely a minor and pardonable offense in light of what it made possible: the creation of a corps of people who, by being natally alienated, socially killed during the process of slavery and redefined and recreated as surrogates of the sultan, were made into the mightiest force in the service of Allah.

In contrast to all this, the free client was anything but natally alienated. He had many satisfying roles in his society; among the most important were his familial relationships, of which he was intensely proud and to which he owed his first loyalty. Indeed, the ghulām relationship was needed precisely because of the intensity of familial loyalties—and by this I mean family relationships of all kinds, those referring to family of orientation (parents and other ancestors) as well as family of procreation (children and other descendants). The distinction is important because in addition to being natally alienated, the ghilmān, like all other slaves, were prevented or strongly discouraged from passing on their status to their children. Like all slaves, they were *genealogical isolates.* C. E. Bosworth cites a contemporary account of the Persian ghilmān that explains their loyalty as a result of the fact that "there are no ties of Affection or Kindred between them."[49]

The most effective way of preventing such kinship ties from later developing was, of course, by means of castration, and it is therefore no accident that some of the most successful ghilmān were eunuchs. There are in fact cases of slaves voluntarily having themselves castrated in order to ensure promotion. (The same, incidentally, was true of the eastern Roman empire.) Another factor is that homosexuality was almost the norm among ghilmān all over the Islamic world.[50] The incapacity to pass their status on to their children remained true (with one or two exceptions, always strongly censured) even in the Mamluk kingdom of Egypt.[51] The ghilmān, unlike clients, were in cultural theory socially dead persons. Having no independent existence outside of their masters, they were both feared and resented: feared because they were so identified with the all-powerful sultan or caliph that to injure them was to injure him; resented because they had no standing as independent human beings, no roots in the families that created the empires.

We have established that the ghilmān were natally alienated persons, and we have seen too that one reason why they were created was that honorable persons could not have been expected to hold the same relationship wiith the caliph as was required of the Mamluk. There is evidence to support my view that honor, in the sense in which I have defined it, was not accorded even the most powerful of the ghilmān, even long after the institution was well established. It is still a matter of some controversy among students of Ottoman history whether the janissaries were manumitted after the *čīkma*, or passing-out from their training schools,[52] as were the Mamluks, but there is one striking element of support for my argument. It is an anecdote concerning the famous Grand Vizier Ibrāhīm Pasha, who as a favorite slave of the Sultan Sulaymān exercised great power in the Ottoman Empire between 1523 and 1536. The celebrated Ibn Fenārī was judging a case one day in the imperial *dīwān* (court) when Ibrāhīm Pasha, who was acquainted with the facts, presented himself as a witness:

> "O Mullā, this case is incontrovertible and I am witness to it; it leaves no room for delay." (Ibn Fenārī) said: "Your testimony is unacceptable under the Sharī'a." The vizier was horrified and said: "Why is my testimony not acceptable?", to which he replied, "Because you are an unmanumitted slave." The vizier rose and went to the Sultan; he was held in great esteem by Sultan Sulaymān Khan. He complained to him and wept, saying: "May God make you immortal, O Sultan. Mullā ibn Fenārī has dishonoured and disgraced me in the imperial *dīwān*, saying thus and so. *The honour of your slaves, the viziers, is as the honour of your exalted person"* (emphasis added).[53]

The sultan, however, claimed there was nothing he could do about the insult, since the mullā was acting properly in law. The only comfort he could offer his vizier was to manumit him, so that he was entitled to present evidence. Insult was added to injury in that it was the same mullā who was called upon to draw up the manumission papers, and he did this as if to emphasize the vizier's lack of honor "in the presence of the leading men in the imperial dīwān saying":

> "Take this, your document of manumission. Now your testimony is acceptable." And this (i.e. his humiliating Ibrāhīm Pasha by giving him his document of manumission in the presence of the dīwān) was an odder piece of daring than the first (i.e. his having raised the matter of Ibrāhīm Pasha's status in the first place).[54]

Repp cites this anecdote as support of V. L. Ménage's thesis that the janissaries were not automatically manumitted. What the anecdote also demonstrates is that in relation to his lord and his class peers, the second most powerful man in the most powerful empire of the time was without honor because he was a slave. And it is clear too that the vizier himself accepted this view, because the honor he felt and claimed was not his own but a surrogate honor, that of *"your* exalted person."

There is still the problem of the ghilmān's formidable power to contend with. In our discussion of the familia Caesaris we noted that the slave or freedman remained powerless with respect to the master. Daniel Pipes argues this position forcefully in support of his claim that the ghilmān were true slaves. He notes that since the vizier was always subject to the pādishāh's arbitrary decision to reduce him to the status of a kitchen assistant, "so long as he personally remained under his master's control nothing else affected his status as a true slave."[55] However, once the balance of power changed and the ruler had no other basis of support but his ghulām, the latter could forcefully manumit himself and then ceased to be a slave. Direct control is the critical factor for Pipes, who shows that he understands the dynamics of the relationship when he adds:

> Behind the trust and loyalty between the ruler and these slaves lies a complex, adversary relationship; the more he trusts them, the more power they acquire, the greater their independent power grows, and the less loyal they become . . . The master's military dependence on his military slaves thus has two contrary implications; he never voluntarily relaxes control over them but they have the means to escape his control against his will. The double-edged sword of politics cuts both ways.[56]

Pipes is clearly on the right track here, but the explanation is hardly complete. It does not take account of the incredible fact that the ghilmān usually continued to recognize themselves as slaves long after they had assumed all but formal control of the empire and, in the case of the Mamluk kingdom of Egypt, had insisted that only slaves could succeed them. Clearly this is not just a semantic issue, but how is it possible for a ruler to be a slave? Is it not a contradiction in terms? It is, but only if we emphasize the personal relationship. What is required to solve the paradox is a twofold shift, one of focus and one of method. We begin to understand how it is possible for a king to be a slave when we shift our focus from personal interaction to the dynamics of power as a thing-in-itself, and when we move from a mechanistic to a dialectic method of analysis. But before doing so, and as a transition to this new approach, let us consider our third and in many ways most extraordinary case.

Political Eunuchism in Byzantium and China

The final case straddles historically the two already discussed. It is the most extreme, and at the same time the most revealing of the three, and involves a category of slaves found not only in the late Roman and Islamic world but in almost all slave systems where the master exercised absolute power vis-à-vis the nonslave members of his society. Political eunuchism presents what at first glance seems a remarkable paradox: the fact that rulers who claim absolute power, often with divine authority, seem to prefer—even to need—slaves who have been castrated. Furthermore, their reliance becomes so total that they often end up being dominated by these deformed persons who otherwise are universally despised. Is the high correlation between the presence of slave eunuchs and sacral absolutism merely accidental? If not, what accounts for this strange association? Why is the power relationship between master and slave so frequently inverted? The powerful court eunuch in Byzantium, imperial China, and many areas of the Islamic world as well as Africa seems to challenge virtually everything I have said about the nature of slavery. Yet this phenomenon, when properly understood, actually strengthens my argument and, further, illuminates many of the subtler aspects of the dialectics of slavery. The absolute ruler, we shall see, requires the ultimate slave; and the ultimate slave is best represented in the anomalous person of the eunuch.

The cornerstone of my argument will be the Byzantine case, and to a lesser extent the Chinese, partly because they are the most extreme and best known, but also because the Byzantine case has been the subject of a searching recent analysis by the historical sociologist Keith Hopkins, an analysis that is a convenient point of departure for my own exploration of the problem.

The widespread use of slaves as guards of the harems in the elite households of polygamous societies is common knowledge. Less well known is the fact that slave eunuchs played a key role in the political, administrative, and sometimes even military life of most of the major bureaucratic empires. Karl A. Wittfogel called them "a formidable weapon of autocracy for supervising and controlling the ranking officialdom."[57] Actually they were much more than that; they were often also an equally potent weapon in the absolute monarch's control and neutralization of the aristocratic classes. Although the castration of human beings was practiced in Assyria from the latter part of the second millennium, political eunuchism developed no earlier than the eighth century B.C. and became a fully established institution among the later Achaemenid Persians.[58] The Japanese historian of imperial China, Taisuke Mitamura, in a volume devoted to the subject, has shown how the eunuchs "formed an indispensable part of the Chinese system of absolute rule." Eunuchs were partly responsible for the fall of the Han dynasty.[59] Seven of the last nine emperors who reigned during the T'ang dynasty owed their throne to the palace eunuchs, and the remaining two were murdered by them. In Ming times, when their power reached its peak, it has been estimated that their numbers exceeded one hundred thousand, of whom seventy thousand were in the capital.[60] Although Muhammad specifically condemned castration,[61] eunuchs nonetheless came to play a major role in the military, political, and administrative life of all the major Islamic states and empires. Quite possibly under Byzantine influence, the court of Muslim leaders very early had organized corps of eunuchs.[62] A black eunuch named Kafur became master of both Egypt and Syria during the tenth century; many white eunuch generals led the Muslim attack on the Byzantines, and in one engagement in 919 both the admirals commanding the opposing Fatimid and Byzantine fleets were eunuchs. The corps of eunuchs was a major force among the Fatimids; one of them once acted as a regent of the empire, and many were involved in the numerous plots and counterplots that plagued the system. Both black and white (especially Georgean) eunuchs dominated the palace of the Persian shah from the early seventeenth century till the fall of the Safawid dynasty in 1737. In Turkey, eunuch influence began to grow in the palace during the reign of Murad (1421–1451).[63] White and black eunuchs competed for influence, especially in the control of the harem, with the blacks triumphing in 1582. Outside the harem, however, several white eunuchs rose to the highest offices in the empire: between 1501 and 1623 at least six grand viziers were eunuchs.[64]

In black Africa, eunuchs played a major role in Ethiopia and all the Islamic emirates and republics. Ethiopia has an unenviable reputation as a major source of eunuchs throughout the world from ancient times. As late as the twentieth century a well-known governor of Sidam province in Ethiopia was a eunuch.[65] In 1800, eunuchs representing the Prince of Muscat took control of both civil and military power in Zanzibar in an attempt to curtail the independence of the local elite.[66] The Fulani-controlled kingdom of Nupe was another major source of eunuchs for North Africa and the Middle East, although as in Ethiopia there was also a keen demand for them at court.[67] All the emirates of northern Nigeria relied on eunuchs for political and military purposes, and Bornu was ruled by one for fifty years.[68] Bagirmi not only employed eunuchs in a wide variety of military and civil roles at the officer level, but was later to become itself an important exporter of eunuchs.[69] During the early part of the nineteenth century the ruler of Bagirmi, Muhammad-el-Fadhl, was completely dominated by his chief eunuch, Muhammad Kurra.[70] In almost all these emirates the privilege of keeping eunuchs was jealously guarded by the rulers.[71]

Nor was the use of eunuchs in important court positions restricted to the Islamic states of Africa. In the pagan kingdom of Igala, for example, the corps of eunuchs was the dominant of the two main palatine groups. It not only attained a "much higher degree of corporate organization" than its free counterpart, but the chief eunuch was in charge of all the king's ritual acts and of his personal welfare and treasure; by virtue of his control over access to the king, he became the most influential executive officer in the realm. Significantly, only the king was permitted to keep eunuchs.[72]

Let us now examine the development of political eunuchism in Byzantium. Even after the demise of the imperial slaves and freedmen, the emperor's chief personal attendant or chamberlain continued to be a powerful person. It was out of this office that the position of grand chamberlain grew in the Western empire and later in Byzantium. What was new about the grand chamberlain in Byzantine times was the fact that he was always a eunuch, that he attained enormous power, and that he controlled a tightly knit palatine corps of slaves, all of whom were castrated. There had, of course, been a scattering of eunuchs during the earlier periods, such as the eunuch Spores whom Nero "married." Castration became a regular feature only under Elagabus and Gordian, and with the reforms of Diocletian the requirement that the grand chamberlain be a eunuch became entrenched.[73]

Formally, the grand chamberlain was one of the *dignitates palatine,* his role being that of the emperor's main attendant and supervisor of the palatine service. What was true of his earlier, noneunuch counterpart in the Western empire held equally for the Byzantine grand chamberlain. Dunlap has observed:

> He was powerful, not because of the importance of his duties, but because his position made it possible for him so to ingratiate himself with the Emperor as to wield very great influence. Consequently, all other officials stood in dread of him. But they *also despised and hated him,* for he was a eunuch, a social outcast, with whom they would normally have held no relations. Furthermore he was, after all, but the Emperor's body-servant, not a minister of the Empire, and officials of high position can hardly have regarded him otherwise than as an interloper in their ranks.[74]

Keith Hopkins goes further, claiming that "in the Eastern Empire especially, the real power lay in the hands not of the emperor nor of his aristocrats, but of his chief eunuch; or alternatively that the corps of eunuchs as a group wielded considerable if not predominant power at court."[75]

Two questions now arise. Why, especially after the well-known record of freedmen favorites in the Western empire did the eastern emperors continue to use and rely so heavily on their chamberlains? And second—the question that more specifically concerns Hopkins, and me—Why eunuchs? Hopkins underplays, without dismissing, the purely psychological explanation, on the grounds that both strong and weak emperors continued to use and allowed themselves to be used by their chief eunuchs.[76] It should be noted, however, that to reject the argument that political eunuchism was due solely to the weak character of the emperor is not to deny that psychological factors were crucial as the base of the eunuchs' power. The fact that a person is of strong character does not mean that he is not open to influence. All human beings need company, and need persons they can implicitly rely on. Further, the vanities of the strong offer as many possibilities for exploitation as the insecurities of the weak. The fact of intimate contact with the emperor must always have been a critical element in explaining the influence of eu-

nuchs. As C. P. Fitzgerald observes in his discussion of the extreme influence of the eunuchs in Han China: "When the heir to the throne, as was
often the case in the 2nd century A.D., was a boy born and bred in the palace, under the care and in the company of eunuchs from his childhood, the
Emperor became the plaything of these servitors, who knew his foibles, coloured all he ever learned of the outer world, and prejudiced him against
those ministers who attempted to oppose their influence."[77]

Another factor explaining the position of the eunuchs is their role as
scapegoats and fronts for unpopular acts by the emperor. In this regard,
Hopkins argues, the grand chamberlain and his corps of eunuchs were like
the court Jews of seventeenth-century Germany. This makes sense, but it
still does not sufficiently answer the question, Why eunuchs? Hopkins next
argues that, given the absolute power of the emperor and the continued resentment and potential threat to his power presented by the aristocratic
class, the eunuchs acted as necessary "lubricants" in the power structure.
Again, true enough; but equally, it is clear that noneunuch freedmen or even
free persons from the lower classes or lower middle classes could have performed this role, as they did in the absolutist courts of early modern
Europe.

After acknowledging these problems, Hopkins moves to his major explanation. The divine nature of the emperor's power, and the extraordinary development of court ritual, meant that the emperor was increasingly isolated
from his subjects. "Absolute power," Hopkins observes, "is correlated with
absolute isolation."[78] The eunuchs became the necessary intermediaries between the isolated semigod and his administrators, providing him with information and secondhand contact. Furthermore, the eunuchs, given the
disdain in which they were held, could not be assimilated into the aristocracy. They could be relied on as totally loyal henchmen who could have no
interest in supporting potential rivals, since they had little to gain from
changing their allegiance and everything to lose. The crux of Hopkins' analysis—his main answer to the question, Why eunuchs?—then was, in addition to the sociological factors that made an intermediary necessary, the unassimilability of the eunuchs. He sums up his argument as follows:

> The tension between absolutist monarch and the other powers of the state;
> the seclusion of a sacred emperor behind a highly formalised court ritual; the
> need of both parties for intermediaries; the exploitation by eunuchs of this
> channel for the appropriation to themselves of some of the power of control-
> ling the distribution of favours; the non-assimilability of eunuchs into the
> aristocracy; the cohesive but non-corporate nature of their corps; and the
> expertise which resulted from the permanence of their positions as compared
> with the amateurish, rivalrous and individualistic strivings of aristocrats; all
> these factors in combination and in interaction can account for the increas-
> ing power with which eunuchs were invested, and the continuity with which
> they, as a body, held it.[79]

This analysis certainly takes us a long way toward an answer to our question. But all these arguments could be used to explain the rise of chief officers in the courts of the absolutist kings of early modern Europe, yet none of these were eunuchs. Surely, the long record of the conspiratorial tendencies of eunuchs in Byzantium itself, plus the record of their earlier counterparts, the freedmen, could not have been lost on the Byzantine emperors. An emperor who rose to the throne as a result of the murderous conspiracy of the chief eunuch of his predecessor might have had many good reasons for wanting to have his own chief eunuch, but a belief that eunuchs were unshakably loyal could hardly have been one of them.

Hopkins' main argument, the unassimilability of the eunuchs, is certainly on the right track, but it is open to several serious reservations. For by emphasizing this feature, Hopkins implies that one of the major problems facing the emperor was the threat to his power presented by the aristocrats and that the eunuchs were the servants least likely to fall prey to a coalition with this competing group. Hopkins may have been unduly influenced by Steven Runciman's classic work on Byzantium in formulating this argument, for it was Runciman's view that the corps of eunuchs was the "great weapon" of the emperors against the pretentions of the nobility.[80] Wittfogel, however, long ago dismissed this view on the grounds that "since eunuchism was already fully institutionalized in Byzantium in the 4th century, it cannot have been instituted as a weapon to combat a feudal tendency, which was certainly no issue in the bureaucratic regime of Eastern Rome and which, even in the West, only became an issue several centuries later." He emphasized bureaucratic efficiency instead to explain the prominence of the eunuchs in both Byzantium and China.[81] More recent work tends to support this view.[82] We have already seen that the familia Caesaris was a highly efficient group. There are many other examples of nonaristocratic but nonservile and certainly noneunuch groups performing efficiently on behalf of an autocratic ruler. So the question remains, What was it about eunuchs that made them so attractive?

Part of the answer I suggest is not so much their unassimilability or their efficiency as their genealogical isolation, in other words their incapacity to reproduce themselves. The comparative data on absolute imperial states show clearly that the rulers of such empires have three kinds of concerns that are critical to the maintenance of their power. One is to prevent the alliance of different centers of power against them, such as the major bureaucratic and the aristocratic groups; the second is to develop an efficient bureaucracy; and the third is the equally urgent need to prevent the growth of an autonomous, self-perpetuating bureaucracy. Here the question is not one of alliance of the bureaucracy with the aristocracy, or the assimilation of the former by the latter, but the emergence of the bureaucracy as a class in itself, and for itself only. S. N. Eisenstadt, in his study of the political systems of empires, makes this point well. He observes that all highly developed bureaucracies have a strong tendency toward "autonomous power and status." This is facilitated by a basic contradiction in the exercise of power in such polities: the rulers' commitment on the one hand to the promotion of flexibility and universalism, all of which serve their purpose of monopolizing (or at any rate controlling) "free-floating resources" and, on the other hand, their continued strong commitment to traditionalism and to restraint of the ambitions of the very groups who have been made necessary by the universalistic thrust.[83] Ideally, rulers under these circumstances employ either service-oriented bureaucracies, or, when these prove ineffective, strongly subjugated bureaucracies.[84] Eisenstadt notes that "alien groups" are generally recruited for subjugated bureaucracies; over time, however, even such groups are likely to form their own self-perpetuating orders. Eunuchs, I suggest, are ideal in this respect because they cannot pass on their status; there is no one to pass it on to. At the same time, as eunuchs they develop a very strong esprit de corps and thereby, as Hopkins makes clear, a strong corporate identity, which is good for both morale and efficiency.

With this sociological explanation of political eunuchism, along with the traditional psychohistorical explanation, we have come closer to explanatory sufficiency, but still not quite exhausted the problem. Hopkins, for one, is too good a historical sociologist not to recognize this failure of sufficiency in his explanation. Indeed, toward the end of his analysis he emphasizes what he calls "the full paradox of the political power of eunuchs": the fact that they were physically weird and considered the lowest of the low among human beings, associated with male prostitution, transvestite dancing, public displays of their person, and downright nastiness and obscenity.[85]

The paradox becomes still greater when we realize that the low esteem in which eunuchs were held and their association with obscenity and dirt was well-nigh universal. In ancient India we learn from the Hindu epic *Mahabharata* that "Mlechchhas [barbarians] are the dirt of humanity; oil-men are the dirt of Mlechchhas; eunuchs are the dirt of oil-men; and they who appoint Ksatriyas as priests in their sacrifices are the dirt of eunuchs."[86] This is pretty strong language; yet it is typical of the views held of eunuchs the world over. It is an established medical fact that eunuchs undergo many physical changes, which do indeed make them appear abnormal.[87] They tend to grow fat, and their skin has an effeminate quality under which thin lines appear as they grow older. In the vivid terms of one observer, they come to look like "mummified old women." Their voices remain girl-like for a long time, then as they grow older come to sound like harsh female shrieking. They waddle rather than walk. They perspire excessively. Modern studies suggest that no cognitive changes result from the operation, but surely the trauma of castration must have had an emotionally destabilizing effect on every person who has experienced it.

This is the core of truth around which every group of people builds a vast body of myth, some of it quite fantastic, about the eunuch. That such stereotypes exist is, of course, as important as the reality they claim to describe. Besides, it is often difficult to distinguish fact from fiction. We cannot be sure that what holds for eunuchs in modern times, with improved hygienic conditions, should be taken as the objective norm whereby we judge earlier descriptions. For instance, eunuchs are incontinent and one Chinese stereotype of them is that they reeked so of urine that one could smell them from 300 meters—"stinky as a eunuch" being a common term of abuse.[88] This is clearly an exaggeration, but perhaps not a great one if we recall that taking a daily shower is very much a twentieth-century practice. Everybody stank, no doubt, in the preindustrial world, not least of all kings and queens; but the added effluvium of urine-soaked clothes must have been quite offensive.

The unique thing about eunuchs, of course, and the source of much of the mythmaking, was that they had been castrated—which, added to their secondary sex changes, did create an anomalous kind of third sex. A castrated man is always considered a freak of sorts. People everywhere react with horror, and in typically human fashion the sense of horror does not induce pity, but rather disgust and fear. The result is some extremely fanciful notions about the capabilities and emotional instabilities of eunuchs. In China they were supposed to be gentle and warmhearted, but at the same time cowardly, oversensitive, and addicted to opium smoking and gambling.

Islamic peoples held an almost identical set of beliefs about eunuchs, some "authorities" holding that they stank not only from incontinence but from excessive perspiration, others claiming that they ceased to sweat from their armpits after castration.[89] They were supposed to be intellectually superior, especially if white, but morally degenerate if black. Their character was like that of women and children, and they loved to play with birds and eat. "They are avaricious, indiscreet, as quick to lose their temper as to show their joy or to weep, inclined to gossip and slander. They despise the common people and accept only the powerful and rich as masters."[90]

To return now to Byzantium, we find that the horror of eunuchs, and the stereotypes, were no different. Hopkins claims Saint Basil's view of eunuchs to be typical of fourth- and fifth-century attitudes:

> "Lizards and toads . . . the dishonest race of detestable eunuchs, neither men nor women, but made with lust for women, jealous, corruptible, quick-tempered, effeminate, slaves of the belly, avaricious, cruel, fastidious, temperamental, niggardly, grasping, insatiable, savage and envious. What else can I say? Born to the knife, how can their judgement be straight when their legs are crooked? They do not pay for their chastity; the knife has done it. Without a hope of fulfillment they are made with desires which spring from a *natural dirtiness*" (emphasis added).[91]

The paradox then is simply this: how could persons who were considered such foul, miserable specimens have been allowed to associate with monarchs who were not just absolute but in many cases considered semidivine, heaven's proxies on earth? How could an emperor who sat daily beside an empty throne held to be occupied by the living spirit of Jesus be served solely by creatures considered to be such obscene perverts? Psychological and sociological explanations seem incapable of ever fully penetrating this cultural mystery.

Like most paradoxes in human cultures, the answer is to be found in the terms of the paradox itself. Indeed, the clue to the answer quietly screams at us in the very last word of the passage from Saint Basil. It is the word "dirtiness." The emphasis on dirt and filth in the description of eunuchs should have been obvious, but it has clearly been overlooked by Hopkins and others who have considered this matter. No one who is at all acquainted with the rich and still-blossoming field of symbolic anthropology would have failed to recognize at once the enormous significance of Saint Basil's remark, as well as those of the numbers of other people cited above. As Mary Douglas has shown, dirt, the most extreme symbol of defilement and pollution, is intimately related to the nature of the sacred and to the representation of the most fundamental conflicts in the social order.

To anticipate, then, I intend to argue that it is the very dirtiness, grotesqueness, and ineradicable defilement of the slave eunuch that explain his ritual necessity for any absolutist monarch who either rules with semidivine powers or who interprets his rule as a holy mission. In her seminal work, *Purity and Danger,* Douglas shows persuasively how human notions of pollution are used in complex ways to deal with the mysteries and anomalies that life presents. "Uncleanliness or dirt is that which must not be included if a pattern is to be maintained. To recognize this is the first step toward insight into pollution."[92]

But it is only the first step, for dirt also figures in a wholly creative way in the affirmation of what is pure and sacred. This is particularly true of the ways of dealing with those marginal and transitional states found in all human societies that are the sources of the greatest supernatural danger. Drawing on Arnold Van Gennep's classic study, Douglas writes: "Danger lies in transitional states, simply because transition is neither one state nor the next, it is indefinable. The person who must pass from one to another is himself in danger and emanates danger to others. The danger is controlled by ritual."[93] People who are in a marginal state are treated as dangerous outcasts and are expected to behave outrageously. To have been at the margin is to have been in contact with a dangerous kind of power. "Dirt, obscenity and lawlessness are as relevant symbolically to *the rites of seclusion* as other ritual expressions of their condition." It is the duty of all to protect themselves from the danger emanating from the marginal person who "has no place in the social system."[94] The polluting person is always someone who has crossed some line that should never have been crossed, or who brings together what should have remained wholly separate.

Two further findings of Douglas are worth noting. One is that the human body is a major source of symbolism for notions of pollution, notions that focus on the entry and exit points of the body. In this way the body is frequently a symbol of the entire social order. The tendency to protect what enters and what leaves the body by means of strong taboos on food and feces increases the strength and the tightness of social boundaries: "The rituals work upon the body politic through the symbolic medium of the physical body."[95] Another finding of Douglas is that the search for purity creates an insoluble problem. For the truth is that life is amorphous and there are no clear-cut categories. Decay is part of the order of things; death is necessary for life. And the profane may equally be necessary if the sacred is to exist. A way must somehow be found of affirming these unpleasant realities. Hence the apparent paradox that "religions often sacralize the very things which have been rejected with abhorrence."[96] Dirt pollutes, it is true; but dirt, like compost, nullifies—and in its undifferentiated state it becomes the basis for the renewal of life. This extreme dualism is what makes dirt such a powerful symbol, for it suggests the link between life and death, between the sacred and the profane.

This is a good point at which to consider the second major branch of symbolic anthropology which bears on our subject, that of structuralism. Beginning with the view that "binary oppositions are the intrinsic processes of human thought," Edmund Leach, following Claude Lévi-Strauss, has argued that the two most fundamental oppositions are those between life and death and between maleness and femaleness.[97] God and the sacred belong to the order of eternal life; man and nature belong to the profane order that dies. The central problem of all religions is "to re-establish some kind of bridge between man and God." And like Douglas, Leach argues that this is usually achieved by the use of mediating symbols. By containing within themselves both polarities, these symbols resolve the crisis: "Mediation is achieved by introducing a third category which is 'abnormal' or 'anomalous' in terms of ordinary 'rational' categories. The myths are full of fabulous monsters, incarnate gods, virgin mothers. The middle ground is abnormal, non-rational, holy. It is typically the focus of all taboo and ritual observance."[98]

It is at this point that the two subschools of symbolic anthropology part company: the one emphasizing the essentially deductive methodological strategies of structural analysis, the other emphasizing the inductive method of comparative anthropology. I see no reason to take sides. One crucial link between the two, it seems to me, lies in Douglas' emphasis on the body as a major primary source of pollution symbolism. In the same way that myths—the primary data base of the structuralists—are a source of binary oppositions, so are the symbols derived from the body. With this brief intellectual foray, let us return to our problem.

Why eunuchs? Because the eunuch's body and status together create a powerful binary symbol and the ideal mediating symbol. Let us consider more closely the Chinese case. Mitamura tells us that as a result of their castration eunuchs "were found to be generally neither masculine nor feminine, adult [n]or juvenile, good [n]or bad."[99] There was a strong, totally nonrational polarity in the image of the eunuch held by the Chinese. On the one hand their body was seen as rotting and death-like. Castrated criminals were called *fu hsing* in Ming China, a term derived either from "the putrid smell of the wound" or from the belief that if the man were castrated "he would be like a rotten tree, unable to bear fruit."[100] Even more suggestive is the literal meaning of the ideographs used to represent eunuchs. The characters mean, literally, "to put him down in the silk-worm room," and Mitamura comments that "the comparison was to the silk worms that lay like dead bodies in dark, tightly closed rooms where the temperature was kept high and the air smelled of death. Thus the eunuchs lived in a kind of subterranean world."[101] The obvious Freudian interpretation is that the dying worms suggest the macabre notion of glowing, decaying phalli. How horrible and at the same time how powerful a symbol of marginality this is!

This is only one side of the body symbolism of the eunuch. The Chinese also held the diametrically opposed view of the eunuch's body as something pure. Thus the most common words for the adult eunuchs were *ching* or *cheng*—both of which mean, remarkably, "pure of body." Those who were castrated from childhood were called *t'ung cheng*, "pure from birth."[102] This was not a simple, arbitrary quirk of language. During the Ming dynasty it was customary to bury eunuchs, like monks, separately from their relatives, since eunuchs were considered "akin to priests." The eunuchs themselves referred to their castration "as the act of entering the priesthood."[103] Here we have a clear identification of the holy, the immortal, and the pure with the profane, the mortal, and the filthy. The Chinese clearly recognized the mediative role of the eunuch and the polluting effect of a marginal existence. This is evidenced most clearly in the eunuchs' role as mediators between the divine emperor and his subjects and explains why the palatine eunuchs were called "cattlemen." Mitamura writes:

> The monarchs were regarded as agents of God, and the original God-man relationship of ruler and ruled applied. *A clear line separated the monarchs and the people.* Neither God nor the monarch was to reveal what he actually was to the people—the secret door between the two worlds was always shut. But the monarch was only a man, so he led his private life behind doors in mysterious ways . . . Since ordinary commoners could not serve in the inner recesses of the palace, who could? None were more suitable than the eunuchs, the "cattlemen."[104]

Because they were the perfect slaves, the eunuchs could perform their role as intermediaries not just as representatives but as surrogates of the emperor: "The relationship between a monarch and a eunuch was very much like that of a man and his shadow. Separation was impossible, but it was always the eunuch who was labeled as evil while the monarch was regarded as blameless."[105] The eunuch in his ambiguity both affirmed and displaced the mortal reality of the emperor and his ruthlessness. He provided a way of acknowledging and overcoming the opposition between life and death, sacred and profane, good and evil. The person of the eunuch served exactly the same symbolic purpose for the elite Chinese that the four myths analyzed by Lévi-Strauss served for the Winnebago Indians of North America—"in order to be overcome the opposition between life and death should first be acknowledged, or else the ambiguous state will persist."[106] As Douglas pointed out, religion makes sacred the very thing it declares to be dirty and polluting. The dirtiness and death-like decay of the eunuch had to be affirmed. "Thus the eunuch system was instituted in the name of divinity, allowing the monarch to enjoy his earthly privileges. It was quite natural then that there should be four eunuch stars placed west of the Emperor's constellation in the heavenly order of things."[107]

The eunuchs resolved another profound contradiction in elite Chinese culture: that between men and women. It should not be forgotten that the earliest and most common role of the eunuch was as keeper of the harem, or as the Turks put it, "chief of the abode of felicity." Chinese culture exhibits a greater than usual ambivalence in male attitudes toward women, itself a reflection of deep-seated conflicts in the relationship. The nagging and jealous wife is an almost obsessive theme in Chinese literature. So too was the theme of the powerful woman and the henpecked husband. Indeed, orthodox Chinese historians of the Ming dynasty refer to an entire period as the rise of the "fearsome wives."[108] This was largely male projection, resulting from their conflict over the role of women as deeply respected and influential mothers and as totally subdued wives; between their conception of women as imprisoned dolls with dwarfed feet, the embodiment of the neo-Confucian ideal of fidelity and obedience, and their ideal of the sexy, intelligent, and aggressive concubine.

These were, of course, idealistic categories. The real world in China, as everywhere else, was amorphously noncategorical. Women never behaved the way they were supposed to. The revered mother was often a very strong personality; the pure wife often betrayed her carnal knowledge by demanding her sexual rights. If these traits of dominance and sexuality were hallmarks of the concubine and the harlot, intense gender confusion and anxiety no doubt resulted. And when the master of the household was a polygynist with a vast number of wives and concubines, what could he do? "The mere thought staggers the imagination," Mitamura comments. Nevertheless, he explains the role of the eunuch purely in terms of the need for a guardian and troubleshooter in the harem.

I argue that this was the *least* important reason for the presence of eunuchs. It was common knowledge in China, as in Rome and the Islamic world, that the castrated condition of the eunuch did not prevent his gratifying the sexual needs of the women whose chastity he was supposed to protect. Premodern man, especially polygynous premodern man, knew very well that the male reproductive organ is not an indispensable requirement for female sexual gratification. From this realization, black eunuchs were preferred to white in the harems of the Islamic courts; for it was explicitly hoped that if castration did not deter sexual relations between the keeper and the master's concubines, the presumed physical unattractiveness of African men might. Needless to say, there is no reason to believe that it did. The eunuch's sexual deformity, then, was certainly not the only reason for his role as keeper. Rather, he was the closest approximation in the human species to an androgynous being. His body, as a binary symbol, both acknowledged and resolved symbolically most of the conflicts surrounding male-female relationships. The eunuch appeared to be both male and female, both weak and strong, both dirty and pure, both a sex object (as homosexual and heterosexual lover) and asexual, and both mother and wife. Nero's marriage to Spores was only the tip of the psychologically submerged iceberg. Significantly, both in China and in Byzantium several of the emperors were in the habit of referring to the eunuchs who reared them as their mothers.

It was no accident that it was during the Ming dynasty that we find both the rise of "the fearsome wives" and the high point of eunuch influence in China. However, there is abundant evidence that male-female conflicts were endemic in China from the earliest historical periods, and there is fragmentary evidence that the use of the eunuch as a symbolic medium to resolve the polarization surrounding sex roles goes far back indeed. In his work on Chou China the sinologist Herrlee Creel tells us that, from the earliest recorded times, "moralists had little good to say of women, but they delighted to tell of kings and princes who met their doom through female intrigue. One of the worst things which could be said of a man was that 'he follows the words of his woman.' "[109] The symbolic association between women and eunuchs emerges vividly in a passage from the early Chinese *Book of Poetry:*

> A wise man builds up the wall (of a city),
> But a wise woman overthrows it.
> Admirable may be the wise woman,
> But she is (no better than) an owl.
> A woman with a long tongue
> Is a stepping-stone to disorder.
> Disorder does not come from Heaven—
> It is produced by women.
> Those from whom come no lessons, no instruction,
> Are women and eunuchs.[110]

Finally, now, the explanation of political eunuchism in Byzantium can be completed. As in China, there was an unbridgeable gulf between the semidivine emperor and his subjects. Hopkins, who emphasized the need for an intermediary, did not explain why these intermediaries had to be grotesque eunuchs, persons considered by their subjects as "lizards and toads," "neither men nor women," and all the other epithets that were applied to them.

Now we begin to understand. No *ordinary* god-fearing individual could be expected to cross the boundary between sacred emperor and mortal subject. By the inversion of natural logic so typical of symbolic reasoning, it was not because eunuchs were grotesque and obscene that they were chosen as intermediaries; rather, it was because they were intermediaries, because they continuously crossed the dangerous boundary, that they were grotesque. The same inversion of logic appears in witchcraft accusations all over the world: unusual characters are selected as the scapegoats, then their anomalies are taken as proof of their contact with forbidden powers.

But if contact with the sacred pollutes—or, more properly, if crossing the boundary between the sacred and the profane is sanctioned by being considered polluting and dangerous—it is also true that this contact invests the intermediary with enormous power. Intimacy with the powerful invests the servant with power, whether eunuch or not, whether slave or not, but this is an additional source of power, one that comes from supernatural contagion.

The matter does not end here. There is yet another great gulf which was perversely crossed in Byzantium: that between the sacred god and the profane man who acted as the incarnation of the divine on earth. The Byzantine emperor did not claim to be god in essence, as did the emperors of the earlier Western empire. That clearly was not possible in what was supposed to be the Christian God's kingdom on earth. And yet to say, as Dunlap does, that "the principle of the 'divine right of kings' was substituted for that of the inherent rights of divinity"[111] is something of an anachronism. The divine claims of the Byzantine emperors went much farther than those of the monarchs of early modern Europe. The Byzantine emperor claimed to be the vice-regent of God on earth. Exactly what this meant was never clear, but it certainly partook more of genuine divinity than anything claimed by the kings of modern Europe. The emperor was Christ incarnate. The "real" and spiritual emperor was Christ, hence the flesh-and-blood emperor "must necessarily be a materialization, a symbol: the materialization in our tangible world of an incorporeal substance, the symbol by which it can express itself here below. So it is that we find a state which had for its monarch neither a god nor a man, but an actor, a figurine."[112]

One of the serious problems of playing this extraordinary role was that blasphemy was a constant risk. More important, the emperor himself crossed the dangerous line that demarcated the sacred and eternal from the mortal and profane. He was to God as his eunuchs were to him. What Mitamura says of this parallelism in imperial China holds equally for Byzantium, that "the inhuman characteristics of the eunuchs fitted well with those of their masters."[113] The Byzantine emperor was an anomalous person who was at once totally powerful for having crossed the boundary and made contact with God, but also utterly polluted for having done so. It is this alone that explains two otherwise quite incomprehensible aspects of the history of the Byzantine emperors: the contempt in which they were held by their subjects, in spite of their awesome semidivinity; and the frequency with which they were assassinated.

All Byzantine emperors had nicknames, most of them insulting. In view of the bed-wetting and smell of the eunuchs, and the identification of the emperor with his chief eunuch, the nickname by which one of the Constantines was known throughout his life becomes doubly significant: he was called "Copronymus," which means "the Pisser."[114] Furthermore, during the Brumalia festivals emperors were a favorite target of satirical attack. In A.D. 600, during one of these holiday processions, "a man wrapped in a black robe and wearing a wreath of garlic was led through the streets on a donkey and hailed as the Emperor Maurice."[115] Of course, in every society, the high and the mighty are the object of satiric displacement. But the vehemence of the popular conception of the emperor in Byzantium went beyond all known limits—and this in a society where the emperor was supposed to sit beside Christ. It is significant, too, that this presumably semidivine figure was often represented in songs as an obscene lecher. The following example refers to the marriage of the Emperor Maurice, when an elderly man, to a young princess:

> A cow he found, dainty and delicate,
> And like young cocks do, he set about her;
> He now makes children without number,
> Like the shavings of a carpenter—
> But no one's allowed to grumble; he's shut their mouths up.
> Holy Father, Holy Father! Terrible and ugly!
> Give him one over the head, to bring him down a peg or two!
> Then I'll offer up his great ox as a sacrifice to You![116]

That this was no ordinary venting of popular resentment is indicated by the second remarkable fact in the history of the emperors. René Guerdan summarizes the dismal record as follows: "Of one hundred and nine sovereigns, sixty five were assassinated, twelve died in convent or prison, three died of hunger, eighteen were castrated or had their eyes put out, their noses or hands cut off, and the rest were poisoned, suffocated, strangled, stabbed, thrown down from the top of a column or ignominiously hunted down."[117] The accounts of how some of these semidivine emperors were killed must rank among the most brutal tales of collective sadism in the annals of human history.[118] Why was this so? Like convicted witches, they were considered dangerous creatures who had to be tortured before being killed. Quite apart from the way in which they were killed, it was not unusual for absolutist monarchs who claimed divine authority, or essence, to perform polluting acts as part of their sacralization. There is the well-known incest of the pharaohs with their sisters. Ritual incest was also an essential part of the sacralization of the Bushong kings of Africa, one of whom claimed that he was the "filth" of his nation.[119]

Paradoxically, the isolation of the emperor may not have resulted so much from his withdrawal from his people because he was so divine, but from the necessity of his subjects to withdraw from him because he was so polluting. What an awesome realization this must have been. How was it possible for the person who held the highest office in the land, the guardian of Christ's kingdom on earth, to defile in this way?

The chief eunuch resolved this and many other contradictions that centered on the emperor. The pollution incurred by the emperor in crossing the line between the sacred and the profane could be explained as resulting from the dirtiness of his chief eunuch, who thus became a symbolic as well as a political scapegoat. As in China, the anomalous bisexuality of the eunuch's body and his social marginality as slave both acknowledged and resolved many of these conflicts. The slave eunuch, the ultimate slave, was the incarnation of the emperor, even as the emperor was the incarnation of Christ. Further, the anomalous body of the eunuch acknowledged and resolved many of the deep-seated polarities in the Byzantine body politic: by being both all-powerful and completely powerless, he incorporated the relationship between the emperor and his subjects; by being both sacred and profane, he incorporated the contradiction between the heavenly kingdom and the flawed earthly kingdom; by being equal to the mightiest and most honored in the land, yet being nothing more than a despised, alien eunuch-slave, he incorporated the chronic class inequity, especially the conflict between rural small farmer and rapacious aristocrat; and by being male and female, he not only lent further force to his mediative role in a general way, but may have incorporated the anomalous independence of the emperor and the empress. In a more direct way, he may also have performed somewhat the same symbolic role of resolving tensions between male and female status that eunuchs in China did, for in spite of the lowly Christian conception of women, Byzantine upper-class women were in reality among the most liberated of any society preceding the twentieth century.[120]

The end result is the greatest irony of the political culture of Byzantium: it was not the fact that the Basileus in his semidivine absolutism became absolutely isolated; rather, it was that the emperor was so isolated that he was probably inaccessible as a meaningful state symbol. The absolute and divine monarch, as formal symbol of the state, had to be made accessible by a surrogate symbol. In Byzantium, as in imperial China, the true symbol was not the ultimate emperor but his chief eunuch, the ultimate slave.

Before closing this subject, we must take account of the experience of the Tudor court of early modern England. In the office of the king's chief chamberlain, the so-called Groom of the Stool, are several parallels that superficially might seem to contradict the argument advanced above. In a truly superb piece of sociohistorical analysis, David Starkey has shown how the personal servants of the Tudor king, especially those who served in his Privy Chamber, came to play a vital political role in the kingdom.[121] By being in constant attendance on the king, the Groom of the Stool came to regulate all access to him and in this way attained great power. Furthermore, the Groom of the Stool (who literally was just that—a groom who assisted the monarch as he eased himself at the stool), by virtue of the unique intimacy with the king involved in his ostensibly menial task, attained prestige in his community, since some of the charismatic power of the king's body was believed to rub off on him.

The apparent challenge to our thesis is the argument that the Groom of the Stool was neither slave nor eunuch, that indeed he had *first* to be a highly honorable person before being appointed to his menial task and in the process his already honorable status was enhanced. Starkey writes: "The Groom of the Stool had (to our eyes) the most menial tasks; his standing though, was the highest ... Clearly then, the royal body service must have been seen as entirely honorable, without a trace of the demeaning or the humiliating."[122]

Far from contradicting our interpretation of political eunuchism, Starkey's analysis serves to confirm it. As Starkey makes clear, the Groom of the Stool solved an important problem in Tudor government: that of acting as representative of the king before his aristocrats and other local leaders, at a time when the principle of delegation of authority was almost nonexistent. He did this by what Starkey calls "representation through intimacy." Prolonged intimate contact with the person of the monarch meant that the groom became a "full royal alter ego." Proud aristocrats who would not accept the king's order from formally appointed officials immediately recognized his personal servant and accepted him as a substitute.

The Tudor monarch was not divine. Rather he or she claimed to rule by divine right, and the difference was absolutely clear to all his subjects who mattered politically. The king's person had considerable charisma—but charisma was not divinity, whatever the more ignorant of the peasantry might have thought. Among those charged with the government of Britain, and certainly among the aristocracy, there was never any ambiguity on the matter. The gulf between the sacred and the profane was never crossed by the king. Neither he nor his groom were open to the sanction of pollution as a result of crossing prohibited boundaries.

Nor was there any unbridgeable gulf between monarch and subject. There is no comparison between the absurdly elaborate court ritual and isolation of the Chinese and Byzantine emperors and the courtly tradition and position of the Tudor monarchs. Whatever their faults may have been, the Tudors were a thoroughly human group of monarchs who sought to rule their people directly, circumventing all who came in their way, especially the nobility. Consider, for example, the case of Elizabeth I: even with due allowance for time and mythmaking, she still comes across today as a lusty character of flesh, blood, and will—virgin or not.

Hence the groom's main role was not that of a mediator between monarch and people, but that of a special kind of delegate, a "symbol-agent" for communicating between monarch and subject where time and affairs of state elsewhere prevented him from attending in person. Body symbolism, of course, played an important role here, as Starkey clearly recognizes. But it was the king's body, not his groom's, that remained both formally and substantively symbolic of the body politic. Attending the king as he evacuated his bowels became a symbolically honorable task because it was the symbolic equivalent of protecting one of the vital vulnerable points of the body politic. Dirt or filth here is, symbolically, wholly creative. It is, in Mary Douglas' fine imagery, like compost. To feed, clothe, and assist the monarch with his toilet is symbolically equivalent to feeding, sheltering, and protecting the state.

The Dynamics of Total Domination

What have we learned from these case studies? In purely schematic terms our criteria for identifying slavery have held up remarkably well. In relation to their masters, all three types of slaves discussed here were indeed powerless and totally dependent on them, however powerful they might have been in relation to other persons. Further, in all cases they were natally alienated persons. Not only were they natally alienated from their ancestors and often from their community of origin, but also from their descendants. Even more than ordinary slaves, these were genealogical isolates. It is remarkable that even in the Mamluk kingdom, where the slave often rose to the throne over the murdered body of his master, the tradition of genealogical isolation, of not passing one's status on to one's children, and of recruiting only from persons alienated from their community and kinsmen, persisted with only a few strongly frowned-upon exceptions.

And while they may have been greatly honored by their doting masters, none of these slaves were in themselves honorable persons. It is, of course, possible to honor any person, or any animal (such as a cow), or any thing (such as a totem). But to be honored does not imply that one is honorable. Indeed, to the degree that elite slaves used their masters' power in relation to others, to that degree were they despised. It was precisely because they were without honor that they had risen to their positions in the first place. And though honored, and no doubt craving honor, none of them were ever able to bestow honor or to confirm it, at least not to anyone who mattered. To the aristocrats who controlled the rules of the honor game, elite slaves were always contemptible and unassimilable isolates and outsiders. True honor is possible only where one is fully accepted and included, where one is considered by one's potential peers as wholly belonging. This the elite slave never achieved—even, astonishingly, when he himself was a monarch.

Finally, if we consider not the content of what the elite slave did, but the structural significance of his role, we find immediately that it is identical with that of the most miserable of field slaves. He was always structurally marginal, whether economically or socially, politically or culturally. His marginality made it possible for him to be used in ways that were not possible with a person who truly belonged. The latifundia slave was brought in to subvert and change the rural economy of Rome; and the imperial slave or freedman was brought in to change and refashion the political structure and administration of society. To concentrate on the content of their role and the trappings of their different positions is to make too much of the arbitrary specificities of experience, neglecting in the process the structural dimension. Imperial and latifundia slave in Rome; Turkish palace slave in ninth-century Iraq and Zandj; Albanian grand vizier and Ethiopian domestic in seventeenth-century Turkey; and grand chamberlain and urban craftsman in Byzantium were alike in being located in the interstices of the social structure, and in the margins of the culture of the societies they served.

However, in the very process of defending the viability of our criteria for identifying slavery, we have already hinted at its limitation, which is its schematism. Such schematism has its place in any comparative science of history and society, and I make no apology for it. It is the essential heavy plow that must first clear the ground, turn the rough soil, and demarcate the boundaries. An analysis becomes defective not by its use, but by its exclusive use, by failure to recognize what it reveals: that the ground underneath differs from the pebbles and rocks above.

Power, we have seen, is no static element that can be used, along with others, to define a stationary social set. It must be treated differently. The master asserts total power over his slave and demands from him total obedience. To what ends does he employ his power? Does he have other sources of power? Through his slaves he can control others, but does he have either the independent structural bases or the psychological will and strength of character to control his slave? And how do his slaves react to his claims? Do they come to see that without them the master is powerless; and seeing this, do they in turn have the audacity and will to seize control of the relationship? Is the emperor, in other words, naked without the clothes his slaves provide, and do they dare to test their strength?

All this depends, of course, on the context within which the relationship is played out and the interaction with third parties. Clearly there is a wide range of possibilities. At one end is what may be called purely *functional domination*. Here slavery is what it appears to be: the slave is used to serve the master's ends. The master has independent bases of power, the support of third parties, and is secure in his domination. Most slavery falls at or near this end of the continuum. But a significant minority of relationships fall at the other extreme of the range, frequently including the relationship between absolutist master and chief personal slave. It is difficult to dominate another person when that other person is either the main basis of one's power or, more frequently, the sole means of communication with the basis of one's power. Isolation is vulnerability; the control of communication is power. Sublation of the relationship immediately becomes a possibility.

12

Slavery
as Human
Parasitism

THROUGHOUT THIS WORK I have spoken of masters and slaves, and I have called slavery a relation of domination. But language is more than simply a mode of expression; it also fashions thought. My analysis has attempted to penetrate the dictates of thought inherent in the language and other symbols used by the subjects I have studied. I have therefore devoted a great deal of attention to the symbolic aspects of slavery. For cultural systems, as anthropologists have long taught us, are at bottom only silent languages.

Interpreting slavery as a relation of domination rather than as a category of legal thought has been an important departure. But now, as a concluding reflection, it is vital to ask whether this conception of the social process we call slavery has disposed of all the hidden conceptual accretions of language. Consider the term "master." According to the Oxford dictionary, the word has twenty-nine shades of meanings grouped under four basic headings: "A man having control or authority," as the captain of a merchant vessel; "a teacher or one qualified to teach," such as a great artist; a "title of rank or compliment," such as a college head; and attributive uses and combinations in the sense of "superior," for example "the mastermind." Who after reading the Oxford dictionary would not want to be a master? And is it any wonder that for generations the dominant school of historical scholarship on slavery in America led by U. B. Phillips, one of the country's distinguished historians, had thoroughly persuaded itself and its audience that the great achievement of American slavery was the civilizing of the black race, its tutorship and elevation from savagery to civilization. The saddest aspect of this bizarre historiography is its sincerity. It was not only insensitivity to the descendants of black slaves that led to such obtuse conclusions, but insensitivity to the cognitive imperatives of language. The ease with which it is possible to shift from the meaning of "master" as "a man having control or authority" to that of "a teacher or one qualified to teach" reflects the ease with which it is possible to shift from our conception of the slave plantation as a brutal system of exploitation and human degradation to a pastoral college for the edification of poor savages eager to learn the superior arts of the civilized "master."

My conception of slavery as a relation of domination avoids many of these pitfalls. Nevertheless, there remain problems with the term "domination," which according to the dictionary means "ascendancy, sway, control," not to mention "angelic powers of the fourth rank." Domination and its companion exploitation—those two most potent weapons in the logocracy of the left—focus upon the dominator or exploiter as the active agent in the relationship and place upon the exploited the further burden of passivity. Interpreting the relation from the perspective of the dominated, as I have done in this work, goes some way toward redressing the balance—but at the expense of struggling with language.

Is there a better way of rephrasing this conception, what I have called the "relation of domination"? The conceptual apparatus of social biologists provides the answer. One of their major classes of social behavior is symbiosis, and within it one of the most significant subclasses is parasitism.[1] Where I speak of a relation of domination, social biologists refer to a relation of parasitism.[2] My feeling on this is not that we learn from social biologists through parallels, but that the way they conceptualize what they study can inform us. Furthermore, we need use the social biologist's approach only as a first step toward an understanding of the more complex dialectics of human parasitism.

Conceiving of slavery as a relation of parasitism has many advantages. Parasitism emphasizes the asymmetry of all such unequal relations: the degree to which the parasite depends on the host is not necessarily a direct measure of the extent to which the host is exploited in supporting the parasite. A parasite may be only partially dependent on its host, but this partial dependence may entail the destruction of the host. Or the host may be totally dependent on the parasite, but the parasitism may only partially influence the host—or may have no effects beyond being a minor nuisance, in which case the relation approaches what biologists call commensalism.

The crucial advantage of this approach is that it offers a useful way of conceptualizing the complexities of dependence. It took the arcane philosophical language of Hegel to uncover what quickly becomes apparent when the conceptual framework of parasitism is used: the dominator, in the process of dominating and making another individual dependent, also makes himself (the dominator) dependent.

At the same time, the paradox of domination can be expressed without taking the argument to its limits. Parasitism suggests a continuum ranging from minor dependence or exploitation to major "Hegelian" dependence on the part of the dominator and grave survival risks for the dominated. The various combinations of parasitic-dependent and parasitized-exploited may be graded on a continuum ranging from a point just prior to true mutualism to one just this side of total parasitism.

We move closer to the uniquely human aspects of parasitism when we begin to consider the personal satisfaction that the parties experience in their interaction. A significant step in this direction has been provided by the sociologist Anatol Rapoport, who in a fascinating theoretical analysis of human parasitism has shown that while the behavior of the parasitized party is what common sense suggests—he recognizes that the situation is harmful for him under any circumstances and that it is always in his best interest to get out of it—the behavior of the parasite is not so easily understood.[3]

Rapoport derives two important conclusions from his model. His principal deduction is that parasitism is a function of the terms of exchange and that it is always the outcome of an unstable situation. Stable transactions occur only where individuals keep more than they give of whatever they produce and exchange. Wherever individuals are obliged to give more than they keep, there are unstable terms of trade inevitably culminating in parasitism, the condition in which one party produces nothing and consumes a part of the other's product. The inherent instability of the slave relation has been one of the major findings of this work. Where Rapoport, using the language of theoretical economics, speaks of imbalance and disequilibrium, I have spoken of tension and conflict and of dialectical structure.

A second implication of Rapoport's model is that it is incorrect to assume, in commonsense terms, that "it pays to be a parasite if you are sufficiently lazy." Parasitism is most rewarding for the parasite when both he and the parasitized party minimize laziness. Indeed, if maximizing leisure or laziness is the parasite's major objective, he is often better off cooperating with the other party in the attainment of the social optimum (the optimal joint utilities of himself and the other person)—in other words, to give up extreme parasitism and move toward mutualism. Effective parasitism is hard work! The southern U.S. slaveholders were basically right in always insisting on this in their defense of the system of slavery, though they did not, of course, express their views in these terms.[4] Where they were completely wrong was in their equally vehement claim that their hardworking parasitism was in the best interest of their parasitized slaves and of all non-slaveholding freemen.[5] The empirical evidence lends further support to Rapoport's deductions in that it is precisely those societies in which slave-holders sought to maximize leisure—for example, the Toradjas of the central Celebes, some of the Fulani slave systems of West Africa, and all of the northwest coast Indians who kept slaves—that we find the relation moving closer to, though never of course reaching, cooperation and mutualism between holder/parasite and slave/host.

On the macrosociological level the parasitism framework is also valuable as a heuristic device. Instead of individual holders and slaves constituting the units in the relationship, the institution of slavery is conceived of as a single process that operates on the total social system. The systemic parasiti-zation of the slaveholder's culture and society naturally reinforces the direct personal parasitism of the slaveholder on his slave. In this sense the slave may be said to suffer both personal and institutional parasitism.

Slavery began as the violent and permanent overpowering of one person by another. Distinctive in its character and dialectics, it originated as a substitute for certain death and was maintained by brutality. Depending on the number of slaves involved and the kind of society in which the slaveholder lived, a variety of means of acquisition and enslavement were utilized by the slaveholder and his associates in recruiting persons to be parasitized. The slave was natally alienated and condemned as a socially dead person, his existence having no legitimacy whatever. The slave's natal alienation and genealogical isolation made him or her the ideal human tool, an *instrumentum vocal*—perfectly flexible, unattached, and deracinated. To all members of the community the slave existed only through the parasite holder, who was called the master. On this intersubjective level the slaveholder fed on the slave to gain the very direct satisfactions of power over another, honor enhancement, and authority. The slave, losing in the process all claim to autonomous power, was degraded and reduced to a state of liminality.

THE SLAVEHOLDER camouflaged his dependence, his parasitism, by various ideological strategies. Paradoxically, he defined the slave as dependent. This is consistent with the distinctively human technique of camouflaging a relation by defining it as the opposite of what it really is. The slave resisted his desocialization and forced service in countless ways, only one of which, rebellion, was not subtle. Against all odds he strove for some measure of regularity and predictability in his social life. Because his kin relations were illegitimate, they were all the more cherished. Because he was considered degraded, he was all the more infused with the yearning for dignity. Because of his formal isolation and liminality, he was acutely sensitive to the realities of community. The fierce love of the slave mother for her child is attested in every slaveholding society; everywhere the slave's zest for life and fellowship confounded the slaveholder class; and in all slaveholding societies the existential dignity of the slave belied the slaveholder's denial of its existence.

The slaveholder retaliated ideologically by stereotyping the slave as a lying, cowardly, lazy buffoon devoid of courage and manliness: the slave became, in his holder's mind, the "Graeculus" of ancient Rome, the "Zandj" of medieval Iraq, the "Quashee" of eighteenth-century Jamaica, the "Sambo" of the U.S. South, and the "Diimaajo" ("he who does not give birth") of the Fulani. The slave retaliated not only existentially, by refusing to be among his fellow slaves the degraded creature he was made out to be, but also directly on the battlefront of the political psychology of his relation with the slaveholder. He fed the parasite's timocratic character with the pretense that he *was* what he was supposed to be. Still, in his very pretense there was a kind of victory. He served while concealing his soul and fooling the parasite. As the Jamaican slaves put it in their favorite proverb, "Play fool, to catch wise."

Jamaican slaves were not alone in seeing through the slaveholder's ideological inversion of reality, yet behaving as if they did not. All slaves, like oppressed peoples everywhere, wore masks in their relations with those who had parasitized them. It is in their statements to one another, whether via folk sayings or—infrequently—in folk literature, that they revealed what they knew and what they were. Occasionally a slave, feeling he had nothing to lose, would remove the mask and make it clear to the slaveholder that he understood perfectly the parasitic nature of their interaction. Never was this more forthrightly stated than in the response of an old eighteenth-century Canadian slave to his unscrupulous master's disingenuous offer to set him free. "Master," the withered slave demurred, "you eated me when I was meat, and now you must pick me when I am bone."[6]

The ideological inversion of reality was the creation of the slaveholder class, so it is not surprising that few of them expressed reservations about its veracity; almost all masters, in fact, genuinely believed that they cared and provided for their slaves and that it was the slaves who, in the words of one southern ex-slave owner, had "been raised to depend on others."[7] Even among southerners, though, reality sometimes broke through ideological self-deception. This was most marked during the crisis engendered by the Civil War, and the ensuing discussions of how to solve "the Negro Problem." As Lawrence J. Friedman has skillfully shown, southerners forced to examine the realities of their dependence on slaves—and its ideological underpinnings—simply turned away from the truth and ended up with hopelessly contradictory positions.[8] The nearest to the truth that the southerner was prepared to accept was that the relationship was one of mutual dependence. It was a Presbyterian minister, John B. Adger, who articulated this proximity to reality when he stated:

They [the Negroes] belong to us. We also belong to them. They are divided among us and mingled up with us, eating from the same storehouses, drinking from the same fountain, dwelling in the same enclosures, forming parts of the same families . . . See them all around you, in these streets, in all these dwellings; a race distinct from us, yet closely united to us; brought in God's mysterious providence from a foreign land, and placed under our care, and made members of our state and society; they are not more truly ours than we are truly theirs.[9]

Adger's position, itself only a half-truth, was stoutly rejected by nearly all slaveholders. They refused to see their slaves as anything but hopeless parasites and dependents who could only survive in a slave relation under the "superior mind" of the master, who would "direct the labor" and ensure his slaves' happiness.[10]

Southern slaveholders were hardly exceptional in their ideological self-deception. The same inversion of reality was to be found among slaveholders everywhere, from the most primitive to the most advanced of slaveholding societies. Ancient Roman slaveholders were generally no different, although enlightened Romans were more given to pragmatism and aristocratic candor than the elite members of other advanced societies. It is not surprising, then, that among this class of slaveholders are the rare cases of open acknowledgment of the reality behind the ideology. To cite Seneca's celebrated observation: "As many slaves, so many enemies." But it was another Roman of the first century A.D., Pliny the Elder, who in one of his few inspired moments made himself unique among the slaveholders of all time by laying bare the parasitic nature of the relation between slaveholders and slaves:

We use other people's feet when we go out, we use other people's eyes to recognize things, we use another person's memory to greet people, we use someone else's help to stay alive—the only things we keep for ourselves are our pleasures.[11]

However firm their belief in their ideological definition of the slave relation, slaveholders simply could not deny the stark fact that their slaves served under duress: a combination of punishments and rewards was essential. While it was true that the whip struck not just the body of the slave but his soul, slaveholders everywhere knew that incentives were better than punishments to promote efficient service. Treating the slave well was one kind of inducement, though it also supported the slaveholder in a variety of ways. The well-looked-after slave redounded to the generosity and honor of his holder, emphasized the slave's apparent "dependence," and gave credence to the paternalism that the parasite craved. For precisely these reasons the slave, even while accepting and allowing himself to be spurred by these incentives, also resented them. Both masters and slaves knew implicitly what the Eskimos have stated explicitly in one of their pithiest sayings: "Gifts make slaves, as whips make dogs."

One invaluable weapon emerged in all slaveholding groups: no matter how much the slave struggled, he remained illegitimate. Indeed, the struggle itself forced upon him a need that no other human beings have felt so acutely: the need for disenslavement, for disalienation, for negation of social death, for recognition of his inherent dignity.

And so it was that freedom came into the world. Before slavery people simply could not have conceived of the thing we call freedom. Men and women in premodern, nonslaveholding societies did not, could not, value the removal of restraint as an ideal. Individuals yearned only for the security of being positively anchored in a network of power and authority. Happiness was membership; being was belonging; leadership was the ultimate demonstration of these two qualities. It is an abuse of language to refer to membership and belonging as a kind of freedom; freedom is not a faculty or a power to do something. Remember the paradox that what the manumitted slave gained was never the same thing as what the master gave. The same conclusion has been arrived at, a priori, by philosophers. As Maurice Cranston lucidly argues:

> It is a tautology that a man cannot do a thing if he cannot do it. But a man does not say he is free to do a thing simply because he possesses the power or faculty to do so. When he says he can do something, he may mean he has a skill ("I can play Canasta"); or he may mean he has an opportunity ("I can send you some eggs"). He says he is free to do it *only when he wants to refer to the absence of the impediments in the way of doing it* (emphasis added).[12]

Slaves were the first persons to find themselves in a situation where it was vital to refer to what they wanted in this way. And slaveholders, quick to recognize this new value, were the first class of parasitic oppressors to exploit it. In the vast majority of slaveholding societies they regularly took advantage of the slave's discovery of freedom. Only under special circumstances in a few kin-based societies, and a minority of the most advanced modern ones, did slaveholders deem it outside their best interests to exploit their slave's yearning for freedom as a preferred form of incentive. In these rare exceptions the masters resorted to either compensatory emphasis on material incentives or brutal employment of the whip or both.

In all but a small minority of slaveholding societies, then, manumission became an intrinsic part of the process of slavery. In analyzing its meaning and dialectical relation to slavery, I have not only explored how the tension inherent in the relationship was resolved, but have moved, of necessity, from its purely intersubjective to its institutional aspects. Slavery, we have seen, was an institutional process moving through three phases: enslavement, institutionalized liminality, and disenslavement.

Regarding enslavement, we have seen that demand and supply factors reinforced each other in all slaveholding societies. Similarly, while we normally think of manumission as being the result of the negation of slavery, it is also true that manumission, by providing one of the major incentives for slaves, reinforced the master-slave relationship. In material terms, no slaveholding class ever lost in the process of disenslavement or manumission: either the material compensation more than made up for the replacement cost of the slaves or, more frequently, the slave was made over into another, even more loyal and efficient retainer—or the master gained in both instances. There was also a direct two-way link between enslavement and manumission. The rate of the latter was frequently dependent on the volume and elasticity of the former; at the same time, on the demand side, the volume of manumission partly determined the number of persons to be enslaved.

Nor did the slaveholder lose ideologically. Indeed, in institutional terms the entire process was represented as an elaborate cycle of gift exchange, in which the slaveholders found it necessary to draw upon the social and cultural resources of their community. Thus as direct, personal parasitism on the slave was secured and legitimized, the slave relation was transformed into an institutional process in parasitic involvement with the socioeconomic and cultural components of the total social system.

An examination of the nature of the parasitism on the systemic level is outside the scope of this work.[13] I can only hint at its range and complexity. Social and cultural systems always paid a price for becoming involved with slavery, but that price could range from the insignificant to the totally destructive. Up to a certain point it was possible for slavery to flourish without marked social or cultural consequences; this was the case, for example, in tenth- and early eleventh-century England and Han China. Beyond that point, however, no social system could survive without major changes.

The particular configuration of socioeconomic and cultural parasitism determined the kind of slave society that emerged. There was no simple, uniform process. This is not to say, however, that there were no patterns beneath these seemingly random configurations, or that we cannot explain why given slaveholding societies developed specific systemic patterns. Understanding what they were and how they came to be is a goal for future research, in which the nature and dynamics of slave societies will be explored on a broader scale than the interpersonal level I have examined here.

It has been my objective in this book to come to a definitive statement of the fundamental processes of slavery, to grasp its internal structure and the institutional patterns that support it. Throughout this work, however, the ghost of another concept has haunted my analysis, and in this final chapter I have tried to exorcise it. That is the problem of freedom. Beyond the sociohistorical findings is the unsettling discovery that an ideal cherished in the West beyond all others emerged as a necessary consequence of the degradation of slavery and the effort to negate it. The first men and women to struggle for freedom, the first to think of themselves as free in the only meaningful sense of the term, were freedmen. And without slavery there would have been no freedmen.

We arrive then at a strange and bewildering enigma: are we to esteem slavery for what it has wrought, or must we challenge our conception of freedom and the value we place upon it?

Appendixes

Notes

Index

Appendix A

Note on Statistical Methods

In order to make statistically informed statements about the nature of slavery for the entire range of conditions in which it occurred, I have employed the sample of 186 world cultures developed by the eminent cross-cultural anthropologist George P. Murdock. Over the course of a long career it became apparent to Murdock that "what is needed in cross-cultural research is not samples of great size, nor rough approximations to representative samples, nor random samples drawn from the total universe of known cultures, but rather 'stratified' samples carefully adapted to the facts of ethnographic variation and distribution."[1]

Although I cannot consider them all here, formidable theoretical and methodological problems are posed in adapting this philosophy to my specific venture. However, it is important to note that there were three major objectives of Murdock's sample: first, to represent in 186 cases the entire range of known cultural variations; second, to do so while eliminating "as far as possible the number of cases where similarities are presumably due to the historical influences of diffusion or common derivation"[2] (Murdock employed the most advanced techniques available in coping with "Galton's problem," as this is usually called); third, to select societies on which reliable ethnographic and historical data exist.

A major advantage of using this sample, apart from the fact that it is the product of more than half a lifetime of research by a major scholar assisted by a large research team, is that other scholars have also used it for their own specific researches and have made their codings available. In addition, Murdock and his team have prepared a code of general ethnographic data for all 186 societies.[3] To these I have added my own codings. The previous nine sets of data prepared by Murdock and other scholars constitute a pool of literally hundreds of variables against which other variables can be cross-tabulated. I hope to do this in another study; my main concern in this work was the sample itself. All research materials and codings employed in this work are, with the exception of one table, entirely my own.

From the list of 186 societies I set about selecting my own sample. Murdock had already indicated the subset of slaveholding societies (column 37 of part 2 of his *Ethnographic Atlas*). The relevant variable was coded by Murdock as follows for "Type of Slavery":

(0) Insufficient information
(1) Absence or near absence
(2) Incipient or nonhereditary
(3) Reported but type not identified
(4) Hereditary and socially significant.

I retrieved all the societies listed in categories (2), (3), and (4).

My first task involved a preliminary search of the most readily available data on the retrieved list of societies that were coded in the Murdock atlas as (2) or (4), plus a few cases that had been coded (3), "Reported but type not identified." Often, because of my specialized interest in slavery, I was able to locate much richer data than Murdock. (The more general sources Murdock used sometimes did not provide sufficient data to enable him to code a society with any specificity.) The result of this initial work was the sample of sixty-six slaveholding societies listed in Appendix B.

My next research task was a more thorough familiarization with the ethnographic and historical sources, after which I drew up a preliminary questionnaire schedule. This questionnaire I pretested with a subsample of the slaveholding societies, found it to be far too ambitious in light of the available sources, and accordingly trimmed the size and revised the categories. Even with this amended schedule, it was not always possible to code all the variables. The final version was a forty-three-item schedule. All but one of my variables were of the nominal (divisible into class or categories) or ordinal (also capable of being ranked or ordered) type. The single exception was a question on the size of the slave population. Significantly, the response rate for this variable was so poor that I had to drop it from the analysis. Travelers and field anthropologists, like the authors of journals and archival documents on which historians draw, rarely counted. In three or four cases the available data on slavery were so meager or of such poor quality that only about half the variables could be coded.

The questions attempted to categorize information in six main areas: demography; origins, means of enslavement, and acquisition of slaves; main uses of slaves and methods of organization; legal and social status of slaves; frequency of manumission and status of freedmen; and frequency and type of warfare in the society. A typical question from the demographic section is, What was the sex ratio of the slave population? The precoded options for response were

(1) More men than women
(2) About even
(3) More women than men.

On socioeconomic issues I asked questions such as the following: How was the status of children determined? The choices here were

(1) Free if mother free
(2) Free if father free
(3) Free if either parent free
(4) Free only if both parents free
(5) Always free.

A final example taken from the questions dealing with the means of enslavement is the following: Rank order the following seven methods of enslavement using code 1 to indicate the most important method of enslavement, code 8 the absence of that method, code 9 the fact that the method was used but could not be ranked.

The next task involved coding the sixty-six slaveholding societies, using the revised questionnaire schedule. Three coders did the first coding of the data, after which I recoded each society to ensure that all of the variables (with one exception) were coded twice. Where my own interpretation differed from that of the first coder, I carefully reviewed the available data and made a final decision. The single variable that was coded only once was that on warfare. I did not decide to include such a code until after my coders had completed their work, so it was coded only once, by me. No statistical use was made of this code in the present work.

The data were coded in 1974 and 1975, and the first set of analyses conducted in 1975 and 1976. Since that time there has been a virtual explosion in studies of slavery all over the world by scholars in many areas, especially in the Americas and Africa. I have responded to this growing mountain of data by periodically recoding and reanalyzing the materials. Fortunately, in most cases the new information has supplemented the old, so that what has been primarily involved has been the insertion and coding of previously missing information. In a few cases new studies have meant a radical reinterpretation of the traditional view of slavery in a given society. The most dramatic case in point is the Lozi. When we first coded this society, the classic work of the late British anthropologist Max Gluckman still dominated our view of the Lozi past. To be sure, there were indications that Gluckman's view of Lozi traditional society was both too static and too idealized, but in the end we accepted Gluckman's view that slavery among the Lozi was a minor and thoroughly benign institution. Work that has become available since 1974 shows that this view could not have been farther from the truth. The Lozi, as indicated in Appendix C, had a large-scale slave system with an unusually harsh system of exploitation when assessed in African terms. Fortunately, I have not encountered any other case where recent reinterpretations have been as extreme as this. Nevertheless, I should be very surprised if, ten years from now, we did not have to change our coding of several cases in the light of new studies. (Incidentally, the capability for recoding without exorbitant expense is another major advantage of using a small sample.)

Two further points should be emphasized. First, the statistical analysis was always regarded as a *supplementary analytical device*. Even those societies that were coded were studied in the traditional manner also. In the process of recoding the sixty-six societies I became fully immersed in the available literature, and my notes were used in the essentially illustrative and humanistic analysis that dominates this work.

Second, the societies listed in Appendixes B and C do not exhaust the number of cases studied. Many specialist studies of slavery do not appear in either list—for example a number of case studies in the collections edited by Miers and Kopytoff, Meillassoux, Watson, and Lovejoy. Nor do the many Hispanic slaveholding societies of South America, which do not qualify as large-scale slave systems; they nonetheless provide interesting comparisons.

Although many research facilities were used in the various stages of research, coding, and analysis, I must draw special attention to two of them, without which this work would have taken even longer than it did. One is the Human Relations

Area Files (HRAF) in New Haven. We made three main uses of this facility. First, the bibliographic resources were invaluable for our preliminary researches. We were able to go straight to the major ethnographies on each of the sixty-six societies studied. In almost all cases the HRAF bibliography was adequate for the necessary background material. However, in only a small number of cases did the bibliography provide us with *all* the information available on the specific problem of slavery. The core HRAF bibliography, then, was followed up with a specialist search for works dealing specifically with slavery.

Our second and third uses of the HRAF resources had to do with the files themselves. In my pretesting of the questionnaire schedule, the files proved to be invaluable. At that point, however, the limits of the HRAF resources had been reached, and I used them for only one further purpose: to consult a number of essential ethnographies written in Asian and less well known European languages that are available in translation only in the HRAF files. In addition, I took advantage of several HRAF manuscript ethnographies that are accessible nowhere else.

For the final coding of the questionnaire schedule, and in my own notes for the humanistic analysis of the data, I went to the original works referred to in the files, not to mention the specialist literature on slavery that our own group generated. In this regard we were fortunate in having another major research facility at our disposal: the library of Harvard's Peabody Museum of Archaeology and Ethnology (which halfway through our studies moved to new quarters and became known as the Tozzer Library). For comparative ethnographic and ethnohistorical research, Tozzer must certainly rank as one of the best libraries of its kind in the world. Just as valuable as its virtually exhaustive collection of ethnographic materials is its index of authors, books, *and* journal papers. Months, possibly years, of research effort were saved by making full use of these extraordinary facilities.

The reader not acquainted with statistical methods may wonder how these data were analyzed. Without attempting a short course in statistics, I do want to make one or two general remarks. In recent years there has been a great deal of talk about quantitative history. I fully support this development, and not simply because discretion urges support for the inevitable: such studies complement rather than threaten the interpretive approach to history and comparative sociology.

Several statistical techniques are available for handling nominal and ordinal variables and, in elementary form, it is these that I have used in analyzing the coded data. Cramer's V is a common measure of association between nominal variables. It ranges from a score of 0 (no relationship) to 1 (perfect association). Gamma (G) and Spearman's rho are both symmetric measures of association for ordinal variables ranging from minus 1 (perfect negative association) through 0 (no relationship) up to plus 1 (perfect positive association). Any standard elementary textbook in statistics will explain the rationale and mathematical bases of these measurements. The chi square and probability statistic (p) are measures derived from inferential statistics; purists hold that they are relevant only if one's units constitute a random sample. It is rare, however, to find a genuinely random sample in the social sciences. We usually assume that our sample approximates the demands of randomness. The probability statistic assesses the degree to which the observed and measured association is due to chance; more properly, the degree to which we may confidently infer that the particular association observed in the sample holds for the parent population. Thus if $p = 0.05$, it means that there are five chances in a hundred that the observed association is just a fluke; if 0.005, the chances are five in a thousand; if 0.5, the chances are one in two. It is up to the researcher and his reader to decide where he or she is going to draw the line. In this work I have accepted as statistically significant only relationships at the 0.05 level or better. Put another way, whenever I report a relationship as significant I mean that, at the very worst, there is only a 5 percent probability that the reported relationship could have been due solely to chance.

In recent years a powerful new technique has been made available to scholars who analyze categorical data, that of the so-called log-linear models. Unfortunately, I did not have access to an economically feasible program at the time I conducted the major part of my analysis; nor had I acquired full competence and confidence in the theoretical underpinnings of the new method. By the time this situation changed, I had completed the final draft of this book. Nevertheless, with the assistance of one of my programmers, Hiroshi Ishida, I reanalyzed my statistical data using the new methodology. Happily, the log-linear modeling technique fully supported the findings arrived at with the use of the more traditional methods.

Appendix B

The Sixty-six Slaveholding Societies in the Murdock World Sample

Ref. no.	I.D. no. in Murdock sample	Name of society	Location	Approximate dates
1	4	Lozi	Western Zambia	Late 1800s
2	5	Mbundu of the Bai-lundo subtribe	West central Angola	Late 1800s
3	6	Suku of the Feshi territory	Southwestern Zaire	1900–1920
4	7	Bemba	Northern Zambia	Late 1800s
5	8	Nyakyusa near Mwaya and Masoko	Southwestern Tanzania	1900–1934
6	10	Luguru around Moro-goro	Southeastern Tanzania	1900–1925
7	12	Ganda of the Kyad-dondo district	Central Uganda	Late 1800s
8	14	Nkundo-Mongo of the Illanga group	Western Zaire	Late 1800s–1930
9	15	Banen of the Ndiki sub-tribe	Central Cameroon	1900–1935
10	16	Tiv of Benue province	Central Nigeria	1900–1920
11	17	Ibo of the Isu-Ama division	Southeastern Nigeria	1900–1935
*12	18	Fon of the city and en-virons of Abomey	Dahomey	1800s
*13	19	Ashanti of Kumasi state	Ghana	1800s
*14	20	Mende near the town of Bo	Sierra Leone	Early 1900s
*15	21	Wolof of Upper and Lower Salum	Gambia	Late 1800s–early 1

Ref. no.	I.D. no. in Murdock sample	Name of society	Location	Approximate dates
*16	22	Bambara between Segou and Bamako	Southeastern Mali	1800–1910
17	23	Tallensi	Northern Ghana	1900–1934
*18	25	Wodaabe Fulani	Southwestern Niger	Late 1800s–early 1900s
*19	26	Hausa of Zaria or Zaz-zau	Northern Nigeria	Late 1800s–early 1900s
*20	27	Massa	Lake Chad region	Late 1800s
21	28	Azande of the Yambio chiefdom	Southwestern Sudan	Early 1900s
*22	29	Fur around Jebel Marra	West central Sudan	Late 1800s–early 1900s
23	30	Otoro of the Nuba hills	East central Sudan	Late 1800s–early 1900s
24	33	Kaffa	Southwest Ethiopia	Early 1900s
25	36	Somali of the Dolba-hanta subtribe	Northern Somalia	Early 1900s
26	38	Bogo, or Belen	Red Sea hinterland	Early 1900s
27	39	Kenuzi Nubians	Egyptian Sudan	Late 1800s–early 1900s
28	40	Teda nomads of Tibesti	Northeast Chad	Early 1900s
*29	41	Tuareg of Ahaggar	Southern Algeria	1850–1950
30	44	Hebrews of the kingdom of Judah	Palestine	620 B.C.
31	45	Babylonians of the city and environs of Babylon	Mesopotamia	1750 B.C.
32	46	Rwala Bedouins	Northern Saudi Arabia	Early 1900s
*33	49	Romans of the city and environs of Rome	Italy	Early 100s
34	64	Burusho of Hunza state	Dardistan and Kashmir	1900–1945
35	65	Kazak of the Great Horde	Turkestan	Late 1800s
*36	67	Lolo of Taliang Shan mountains	Southwest China	1900–1945
37	68	Lepcha of Lingthem and vicinity	Tibet	1900–1937
38	70	Lakher	West central Burma	1900–1930
39	75	Khmer of Angkor	Cambodia	1292
40	81	Tanala of the Menabe subtribe	Madagascar	1900–1925
41	85	Iban of the Ulu Ai group	Borneo	Early 1900s
*42	87	Toradja of the Bare'e subgroup	Central Celebes	Late 1800s–early 1900s
43	104	Maori of the Nga Puhi tribe	New Zealand	Early 1800s

Ref. no.	I.D. no. in Murdock sample	Name of society	Location	Approximate dates
44	112	Ifugao of the Kiangan group	Northern Philippines	Early 1800s
45	115	Manchu of the Aigun district	Northern Manchuria	Early 1900s
46	116	Koreans of Kanghwa Island	Northwestern South Korea	Late 1800s
47	119	Gilyak	Southeastern Siberia	Late 1800s
48	120	Yukaghir of the Upper Kolyma River	Northern Siberia	Late 1800s
49	121	Chukchee of the Rein-deer group	Northeastern Siberia	Late 1800s
50	123	Aleut of the Unalaska branch	Southwestern Alaska	Late 1700s
51	131	Haida of the village of Masset	Northern northwest Canada	Late 1800s
52	132	Bella Coola	Central British Colum-bia	Late 1800s
53	133	Twana	Northern Washington state	Mid 1800s
54	134	Yurok	Northern coastal Cali-fornia	Mid 1800s
55	138	Klamath	Southern Oregon	Mid 1800s
56	142	Pawnee of the Skidi band	Northern south Oregon	Mid 1800s
57	145	Creek of the Upper Creek division	Northern central Geor-gia	1780–1820
58	147	Comanche	Northern central Texas	Late 1800s
59	153	Aztec of the city and environs of Tenoch-titlan	Central Mexico	Early 1500s
60	159	Goajiro	Northern Colombia and Venezuela	Early 1900s
61	161	Callinago of Dominica	Eastern Caribbean	1600–1650
62	167	Cubeo of the Caduiari River	Northwest Amazonia	1900–1940
63	177	Tupinamba in the vicin-ity of Rio de Janeiro	Eastern coastal Brazil	Mid 1500s
64	181	Cayua of southern Mato Grosso	Argentina	Late 1800s
65	183	Abipon	Argentine Chaco	Mid 1700s
66	185	Tehuelche	Patagonia	Late 1800s

* Indicates a large-scale slave society also listed in Appendix C.

Appendix C

The Large-Scale Slave Systems

Large-scale slave systems were those in which the social structure was decisively dependent on the institution of slavery. This dependence was often, but not necessarily, economic. Although a critical mass of slaves was important, the proportion need not have constituted a majority. Indeed, slaves were usually no more than a third of the total population (as in the U.S. South and ancient Greece) and in some cases may have been no more than 15 to 20 percent (as in many of the Islamic states). It should also be borne in mind that a static estimate of a slave population can be very misleading, in that systems with high rates of assimilation to freedman status could, at any given point in time, show what appears to be a low proportion of slaves in sharp contrast with the proportion of the total population ever enslaved.

With these important caveats, the following are crude estimates of the size of various world slave populations. Apart from the modern Americas and South Africa, most of these estimates are educated guesses; others have been calculated from rough noncensus estimates. The source of the figures used is indicated in the last column, by a reference number keyed to the Notes to Appendix C.

Name and location of large-scale slave society	Approximate date span of society[a]	Estimated proportion of slaves (percent)	Reference note on sources
EUROPE			
Greek states, especially Athens, Corinth, Aegina, and Chios	5th century B.C. to early Roman period	30–33	1
Roman Italy	225–200 B.C.	10	2
	100 B.C.–A.D. 300	30–35	
Roman Empire	A.D. 1–150	16–20	3
Sicily	150 B.C. to A.D. 150	>66	4
Visigothic Spain	A.D. 415–711	>25	5
Muslim Spain	A.D. 756–1492	>20	6
Mediterranean Spain	13th century	>20	7
Central Crete	1350–1500	>20	8
Southwestern Cyprus	1300–1500	>20	9
Majorca	14th–15th centuries	>18	10
Iceland	870–950	>20	11
Western England	9th century to 1080	>20	12
ATLANTIC ISLANDS			
Madeira	1450–1620	30–50	13
Canary Islands	1490–1600	>30	14
AFRICA			
Algiers	1500–1770	>25	15
Early states of western Sudan			
Pre-Islamic Ghana	4th century to 1076	?	—
Islamic Ghana	1076–1600	>30	16
Mali	1200–1500	>30	17
Segou	1720–1861	>40	18
Songhay	1464–1720	>40	19
States of central Sudan			
Darfur	1600–1874; 1898–1916	40	20
Wadai	19th century	50	21
Bagirmi	16th–19th centuries	50	22
Borno	1580–1890	40	23
Kanem	1600–1800	30	24
Hausa city-states	1600–1800	30	25

Name and location of large-scale slave society	Approximate date span of society[a]	Estimated proportion of slaves (percent)	Reference note on sources
Fulani Jihad states of western and central Sudan			
Tokolor			
Fouta-Jalon			
Kita			
Masina			
Liptako			
Sokoto caliphate (Hausaland)	1750–1900	30–>66	26
Banchi			
Adamawa			
Jakhanke diaspora communities			
Tuareg of Sahara and Sahel			
Adrar		14	
Ahaggar		16–33	
Air	1800–1965	33	27
Ioullemeden		50	
Gourma		75	
Wolof and Sereer states of Senegambia			
Period of Jolof dominance	1300–1630	>30	28
Post Jolof	1630–1900	33	29
Sherbro of coastal Sierra Leone	19th century	>40	30
Mende chiefdoms of Sierra Leone	Late 19th century	50	31
Vai Paramount chiefdoms	1826–1890	75	32
	1890–1920	50–60	33
Temme chiefdoms	19th and early 20th centuries	>50	34
Ashanti and Gyaman kingdoms	18th and 19th centuries	33	35
Dahomey	Late 18th and 19th centuries	>33	36
Yoruba Empire of Oyo and Yoruba city-states, especially Ife	1600–1836 / 18th and 19th centuries / 1486–1897	33–>50	37
Yoruba state of Benin			

Name and location of large-scale slave society	Approximate date span of society[a]	Estimated proportion of slaves (percent)	Reference note on sources
"House," or city-states and satellites of lower Niger and Delta areas: true Kalabari, Nembe, Bonny, Okrika, non-Ijo groups (especially Abah, southern Ibo, and Efik), and other coastal Ibibio	18th and 19th centuries	>50	38
Duala of the coastal Cameroon	19th century	>50	39
Four petty kingdoms of the Mpongwe (Gabon River)—Glass, Quaben, Denis, and George	1820–1842 1842–1856	50 50–70	40
Decadent Kongo kingdom	1700–1900	>50	41
Decadent Kasanje kingdom of Angola	Late 18th and 19th centuries	>50	42
Cokwe of interior Angola	1850–1900	>50	43
Mataka chiefdom of East Africa	1800–1885	>50	44
Luvale chiefdoms of Zimbabwe	19th century	>50	45
Lozi state	1864–1906	50–75	46
Arab-Swahili slave systems of Eastern Africa	1820–1890		
Zanzibar	1811 1835 1844	75 66 80	47
Zanzibar and Pemba	1880–1890s	90	
Mombasa and Malindic	1840–1885	80–90	48
Imerina (Madagascar)	1780–1895	50	49
European-dominated slave systems of sub-Saharan Africa and Indian Ocean			
Cape Verde Islands, especially Santiago	1500–1878	66	50
São Tomé	1506 1550–1567 1864	66 66 32	51 52 53

Name and location of large-scale slave society	Approximate date span of society[a]	Estimated proportion of slaves (percent)	Reference note on sources
Portuguese settlements of Angola, including coastal towns from Cabinda to Mocamedes and inland agricultural areas, especially in and around Cazengo, Colunbo Alto, and Pungo Andongo	1830–1900	>75	54
Portuguese settlements in Mozambique, especially urban centers and Zambezia	1750–1910	50–>80	55
South Africa	1701	40	56
	1750	53	
	1773	53	
	1798	54	57
	1820	41	
Mascarene Islands			
Reunion	1713	55	58
	1735	88	59
	1779	76	
	1825	72	60
	1848	54	
Mauritius	1735	77	
	1767	80	
	1797	83	61
	1827	73	
	1835	75	
Seychelles	1789	82	62
ASIA AND OCEANIA			
Iraq (lower Mesopotamia, especially in the dead lands)	9th–10th century	>50	63
Atjehneses of Sumatra	17th century	?	64
Hukawng Valley and triangular areas of Burma	Late 19th–early 20th centuries	>30	65
Thailand	1600–1880	25–33	66
Norsus (Lolos) of Yunnan province (southwestern China)	Late 19th century to early 1940s	47	67

Name and location of large-scale slave society	Approximate date span of society[a]	Estimated proportion of slaves (percent)	Reference note on sources
Korea			
Unified Silla period	A.D. 660–918	50?	68
Koryŏ dynasty	918–1392	>33	69
Early Yi dynasty	1400s	30–37	70
Northern section of Seoul	1663	75	71
Kumhwa County	1672	25	72
Coastal Ulsan	1729	50 }	73
	1810	17 }	
Toradja group in central Celebes (To Lage, Onda'e, Palande, and Pada)	1900	>50	74
Banda Islands	1621–1860	>80	75
SPANISH CARIBBEAN			
Española	1560–1570	90–92	76
Spanish Jamaica	1600–1655	37	77
Cuba	1500–1550	>90	78
	1550	37 }	79
	1600–1606	66 }	
	1650–1774	>25	80
	1792	31 }	
	1804	36 }	
	1817	36 }	81
	1827	41 }	
	1841	43 }	
	1861	29 }	
Trajin slave portage system of the Isthmus	1510–1620	90	82
Panama City	1607	66	83
Coastal and mining areas of Venezuela, especially pearl-fishing centers of Cubagua and La Margarita, and Buria mines of the interior	1510–1600	>90	84
Colombian Chocó	1763	30 }	
	1778	39 }	85
	1781	39 }	
	1808	20 }	

Name and location of large-scale slave society	Approximate date span of society[a]	Estimated proportion of slaves (percent)	Reference note on sources
European-dominated urban and rural areas of Mexico, non-Indian population	1570–1650	50	86
Mining areas	1590s	13.5	87
DUTCH SLAVE SYSTEMS OF THE CARIBBEAN AREA			
Surinam	1790	91	
	1805	90	
	1831	86	88
	1850	77	
	1862	29	
Curaçao	1700	30	89
	1789	65	90
	1816	47	
	1833	39	91
	1857	32	
	1862	29	
Saint Eustatius	1786	53	
	1817	67	92
	1829	71	
Saint Martin	1770	84	93
	1816	72	
Bonaire	1806	28	94
	1828	37	95
	1857	31	96
	1862	21	97
BRITISH CARIBBEAN			
Jamaica	1658	24	
	1664	57	
	1673	53	
	1730	91	
	1758	89	98
	1775	89	
	1800	88	
	1834	82	
Barbados	1643–1645	24–26	99

Name and location of large-scale slave society	Approximate date span of society[a]	Estimated proportion of slaves (percent)	Reference note on sources
	1673	61	
	1710	77	
	1731	80	100
	1768	80	
	1810	79	
	1833–1834	81	
Antigua	1678	48	
	1720	84	
	1756	90	101
	1775	94	
	1834	83	
Saint Kitts	1678	43	
	1720	72	
	1756	89	102
	1775	92	
	1834	91	
Nevis	1678	52	
	1720	81	
	1756	89	103
	1775	92	
	1834	81	
Montserrat	1678	27	
	1720	69	
	1756	86	104
	1775	88	
	1834	82	
Barbuda	1790	99.9	105
Anguilla	1790	83–87	106
British Virgin Islands	1756	84	107
Windward and Southern Islands			
Dominica	1763	77	108
	1773	83	
	1788	90	
	1805	83	109
	1832	80	
Saint Vincent	1763	83	
	1787	89	110
	1817	95	
	1834	95	

Name and location of large-scale slave society	Approximate date span of society[a]	Estimated proportion of slaves (percent)	Reference note on sources
Grenada	1777	96	} 111
	1817–1834	90	
Saint Lucia	1772	86	
	1816–1818	92	} 112
	1834	92	
Tobago	1770	93	
	1775	95	} 113
	1820	98	
Trinidad	1797	56	
	1802	69	
	1810	67	} 114
	1825	55	
	1834	50	
Cayman Islands	1802	58	115
British Honduras (Belize)	1745	71	
	1779	86	
	1790	76	
	1816	72	} 116
	1826	46	
	1832	42	
Guyana: Dutch period, 1700–1796; British period, 1796–1834			
Essequibo region	1701	92	} 117
	1767	90	
Berbice region	1762	87	118
British Guiana as a whole	1796–1800	86	119
	1816	93	120
	1832–1834	88	121
Bahamas	1671	40	122
	1783	49	123
	1786	67	124
	1820	68	125
	1831	57	126
Bermuda	1670	25	
	1687	33	
	1699	38	
	1721	42	
	1731	43	} 127
	1774	47	
	1822–1823	49	
	1833	43	

Name and location of large-scale slave society	Approximate date span of society[a]	Estimated proportion of slaves (percent)	Reference note on sources
FRENCH CARIBBEAN			
Martinique	1664	54	
	1696	65	
	1727	77	
	1751	83	128
	1784	86	
	1816	81	
	1831	67	
	1848	60	
Saint Dominigue (Haiti)	1681	35	
	1739	89	
	1754	90	129
	1775	86	
	1784	90	
	1789	89	
Guadeloupe	1700	62	
	1788	84	130
	1834	76–83	
French Guiana	1665	33	
	1700	87	
	1765	70	131
	1815	97	
	1820	94	
	1830	84	
DANISH WEST INDIES			
Saint Thomas	1686	53	
	1691	59	
	1720	88	
	1754	94	
	1848	25	
Saint Croix	1742	92	132
	1745	93	
	1755	87	
	1848	97	
Saint John	1728	85	
	1739	87	
	1787	92	

Name and location of large-scale slave society	Approximate date span of society[a]	Estimated proportion of slaves (*percent*)	Reference note on sources
BRAZIL			
Brazil as a whole	1530–1650	>66	133
	1798	48	
	1817–1818	50.5	
	1850	31	134
	1864	16	
	1872	15	
Major slaveholding areas			
Minas Gerais	1735	98	
	1749	99	135
	1823	33	
	1872	18	
Bahia	1702	>50	136
	1823	35	137
	1872	12	
Pernambuco	1580–1700	>66	
	1823	59	
	1872	21	
Espirito Santo	1823	50	138
	1872	27	
Rio de Janeiro	1823	33	
	1872	37	
U.S. SOUTH			
The South as a whole	1690	c15	
	1700	c22	
	1720	c25	
	1730	c24	
	1740	c30	139
	1750	c38	
	1760	c39	
	1770	c40	
	1780	c39	
	1790	33.5	
	1800	33	
	1810	33.5	
	1820	34	140
	1830	33	
	1840	35	
	1850	35	
	1860	34	

Name and location of large-scale slave society	Approximate date span of society[a]	Estimated proportion of slaves (percent)	Reference note on sources
Virginia	1715	24	
	1756	41	
	1790	42	
	1810	45	
	1830	45	
	1860	40	
South Carolina	1708	57	
	1720	64	
	1740	50	
	1790	43	
	1810	47	
	1830	54	
	1860	57	
North Carolina	1790	26	
	1810	30	
	1830	33	141
	1860	33	
Georgia	1760	33	
	1773	45	
	1790	35	
	1810	41	
	1830	42	
	1860	44	
Mississippi	1810	55	
	1830	48	
	1860	55	
Alabama	1830	38	
	1860	45	
Louisiana	1810	45	
	1830	51	
	1860	47	

a. In the great majority of cases the date span given refers to the entire period of large-scale slavery. In a few cases the dates are confined to those periods for which estimates are possible.

Notes

Introduction: The Constituent Elements of Slavery

1. *Basic Concepts in Sociology*, trans. H. P. Secher (Secaucus, N.J.: Citadel Press, 1972), p. 117. This translation is a much better rendering of the original than that of Parsons and Henderson, which converts Weber's definition into a probabilistic expression of action theory: Max Weber, *The Theory of Social and Economic Organization*, ed. Talcott Parsons and A. M. Henderson (New York: Free Press, 1947), p. 152.

2. See David V. I. Bell, *Power, Influence, and Authority* (New York: Oxford University Press, 1975), p. 26. Bell's work is extremely enlightening, especially his discussion of influence.

3. *The Social Contract*, ed. Charles Frankel (New York: Hafner Publishing Co., 1947), bk. 1, chap. 3, p. 8. Note how Rousseau's formulation of the concept of authority and its relation to power anticipates Weber's almost identical position.

4. *Basic Concepts in Sociology*, pp. 71–83. See also Weber's *Theory of Social and Economic Organization*, pp. 324–400.

5. *The Phenomenology of Mind*, trans. J. B. Baillie (London: Swan Sonnenschein, 1910), pp. 228–240.

6. *Grundrisse*, trans. Martin Nicolaus (London: Penguin and New Left Books, 1973), pp. 325–326.

7. Ibid.

8. *Die Produktionsverhältnisse im alten Orient und in der griechisch-römischen Antike* (Berlin: Deutsche Akademie der Wissenchaften, 1957), pp. 158–177.

9. See the useful distinction between violence and organized force in Sorel, *Reflections on Violence*, trans. T. E. Hulme (New York: Collier Books, 1961), p. 175.

10. "From Sundown to Sunup: The Making of the Black Community," in George P. Rawick, ed., *The American Slave: A Composite Autobiography* (Westport, Conn.: Greenwood Publishing Co., 1972), vol. 1, p. 59. Stephen Crawford arrives at the same conclusion in his quantitative analysis of the slave narratives: "Quantified Memory: A Study of the WPA and Fisk University Slave Narrative Collections" (Ph.D. diss., University of Chicago, 1980), chap. 3.

11. Cited in John S. Bassett, *Slavery in the State of North Carolina* (Baltimore: Johns Hopkins University Press, 1899), pp. 23–24.

12. Cover, *Justice Accused: Antislavery and Judicial Process* (New Haven: Yale University Press, 1975), p. 78.

13. The Romans, it is true, were unique in promoting the idea that it was possible for a slave to exist without a master. The idea of a masterless slave was a legal concept, one that provided a means for getting around a few tricky legal problems—for example, those related to abandoned or unlawfully manumitted slaves and to the fraudulent sale of freemen (often with their own complicity)—but difficult to make sense of sociologically. As the legal historian Alan Watson observed, "The idea of a slave without a master is not an easy concept." In reality, all that being a *servus sine domino* meant was either that a potential relation of slavery existed, although the person in question—for example, the abandoned slave—was not at the time actually in a slave relationship or in a position to claim free status, or that the person was actually in a relation of slavery but was potentially a free person and could legally claim such a status. Legal technicalities aside, in actual practice all Roman slaves had at least one master. The technicalities referred to very temporary situations. Those who were illegally enslaved and could prove it had their illegal masters quickly removed (there was always a presumption in favor of freedom) and therefore ceased to be slaves; those who were corporately owned by the state (such as the *servi poenae*) would not only have been very surprised to learn that they had no masters but, had they been privy to such legal niceties, would have considered the fiction of their masterless status a grim piece of judicial humor. See W. W. Buckland, *The Roman Law of Slavery* (Cambridge: Cambridge University Press, 1908), p. 2; and Watson, *The Law of Persons in the Later Roman Republic* (Oxford: Clarendon Press, 1967), chap. 14.

14. André Bourgeot, "Rapports esclavagistes et conditions d'affranchissement chez les Imuhaġ," in Claude Meillassoux, ed., *L'esclavage en Afrique précoloniale* (Paris: François Maspero, 1975), p. 91.

15. Pierre Bonte, "Esclavage et relations de dépendence chez les Touareg Kel Gress," in Meillassoux, *L'esclavage en Afrique précoloniale*, p. 55.

16. *Histoire de l'esclavage dans l'antiquité* (Paris: Hachette, 1879), p. 408.

17. *Contribution à une théorie sociologique de l'esclavage* (Paris: Mechelinck, 1931), p. 243.

18. *Searching for the Invisible Man: Slaves and Plantation Life in Jamaica* (Cambridge, Mass.: Harvard University Press, 1978), pp. 367–384. Craton, much to his own disappointment, found that "references to external events dating back beyond present lifetimes were, in fact, remarkably absent" and that "the attempt to trace precise lineage . . . led to disappointment in nearly every case. At best the information was inaccurate; at worst there was ignorance or even indifference" (pp. 374–375).

19. Rawick, *The American Slave*, vol. 2, pt. 1, p. 207.

20. Ibid., p. 58.

21. Winthrop D. Jordan, *White over Black: American Attitudes toward the Negro, 1550–1812* (Baltimore: Penguin Books, 1969), pp. 45–48. Jordan observes that the distinction between owning and selling someone's labor as opposed to their person "was neither important nor obvious at the time" (p. 48).

22. Ibid., p. 56.

23. Ibid., p. 94.

24. Ibid., p. 97.

25. Finley, "Slavery," *Encyclopedia of the Social Sciences* (New York: Macmillan Co. and Free Press, 1968), vol. 14, pp. 307–313.

26. Lévy-Bruhl, "Théorie de l'esclavage," in M. I. Finley, ed., *Slavery in Classical Antiquity* (Cambridge: W. Heffer and Sons, 1960), pp. 151–170.

27. *The Present State of the Ottoman Empire, 1668* (London: Arno Press, 1971), p. 25.

28. Plato, *Gorgias,* in Benjamin Jowett, ed. and trans., *The Dialogues of Plato* (New York: Random House, 1937), vol. 2, p. 543.

29. Rawick, *The American Slave,* vol. 18, p. 44.

30. *History of Slavery in Virginia* (Baltimore: Johns Hopkins University Press, 1902), p. 28.

31. Ibid., p. 34. See also Jordan, *White over Black,* pp. 52–91.

32. See E. G. Pulleyblank, "The Origins and Nature of Chattel Slavery in China," *Journal of the Economic and Social History of the Orient* 1 (1958): 204–211.

33. For the classic comparative study of debt-servitude see Bruno Lasker, *Human Bondage in Southeast Asia* (Chapel Hill: University of North Carolina Press, 1950), esp. chap. 3. On the ancient world see M. I. Finley, "La servitude pour dettes," *Revue historique de droit français et étranger* 43 (1965): 159–184 (ser. 4).

34. *Leviathan* (London: J. M. Dent & Sons, 1914), p. 44.

35. Ibid., pp. 44, 47.

36. "Bentham," in J. S. Mill, *Utilitarianism (and Other Essays)*, ed. Mary Warnock (London: Collins, 1962), pp. 100–101.

37. *The Phenomenology of Mind,* pp. 228–240.

38. Genovese, *The Political Economy of Slavery* (London: MacGibbon & Kee, 1966), p. 32. Cf. David Brion Davis, *The Problem of Slavery in an Age of Revolution, 1770–1823* (Ithaca, N.Y.: Cornell University Press, 1975), pp. 561–564.

39. Genovese, *The Political Economy of Slavery,* p. 32. This is a paraphrase of the more radical but untenable section of Hegel's thesis. See my discussion in Chapter 3.

40. Ibid., p. 33. See Genovese's more recent discussion of the psychology of master and slave in his *The World the Slaveholders Made* (New York: Vintage Books, 1971) pt. 1, pp. 5–8, and pt. 2.

41. I deliberately avoid getting involved with the thesis of Stanley Elkins regarding the personality of American slaves as set forth in his *Slavery: A Problem in American Institutional and Intellectual Life* (Chicago: University of Chicago Press, 1962). As already indicated, I am concerned with discussing the problem of honor relative to the political psychology of slavery, not with problems of human personality—on which I can offer neither theoretical expertise nor relevant data. See Ann J. Lane, ed., *The Debate over Slavery: Stanley Elkins and His Critics* (Urbana: University of Illinois Press, 1971).

42. *Amphitryo,* in Plautus, *The Rope and Other Plays,* ed. and trans. E. F. Watling (New York: Penguin Books, 1964), p. 234.

43. *The Ghost,* in Plautus, *The Rope and Other Plays,* pp. 67–68.

44. Rawick, *The American Slave,* vol. 2, pt. 1, p. 11.

45. Ibid., pp. 39–40.

46. Plautus, *The Rope and Other Plays*, pp. 116–117.

47. Rawick, *The American Slave*, vol. 2, pt. 2, p. 113.

48. *Life and Times of Frederick Douglass* (1892; reprint ed., New York: Bonanza Books, 1972), p. 143.

49. Ibid.

1. The Idiom of Power

1. Karl Marx, *Capital* (London: Lawrence & Wishart, 1954), vol. 1, p. 80.

2. *The Prince* (London: Oxford University Press, 1903), p. 69; chaps. 15–18 passim.

3. *Capital*, vol. 1, pp. 80–87.

4. Robert H. Lowie, "Some Aspects of Political Organization among the American Aborigines," *Journal of the Royal Anthropological Institute* 78 (1948): 11–24. Reprinted in Ronald Cohen and John Middleton, eds., *Comparative Political Systems* (Garden City, N.Y.: Natural History Press, 1967), p. 73.

5. "The Social and Psychological Aspects of Chieftainship in a Primitive Tribe: The Nambikuara of Northwestern Mato Grosso," *Transactions of the New York Academy of Sciences* 7 (1944): 16–32. Reprinted in Cohen and Middleton, *Comparative Political Systems*, pp. 45–62. Quote on p. 52.

6. See Jean Buxton, "'Clientship' among the Mandari of the Southern Sudan," *Sudan Notes and Records* 37 (1957): 100–110. Reprinted in Cohen and Middleton, *Comparative Political Systems*, pp. 229–245. See also the papers on the Tuareg by Edmond and Suzanne Bernus, Pierre Bonte, and André Bourgeot, in Claude Meillassoux, ed., *L'esclavage en Afrique précoloniale* (Paris: François Maspero, 1975). On kinship and power among the Imuhaġ groups see pp. 85–90.

7. Marx, *Capital*, vol. 1, pp. 77, 82.

8. "Notes on Comparative Economics," *British Journal of Sociology* 5 (1954): 118–129. Steiner was, of course, building on the work of Marcel Mauss, who himself fully recognized the role of gift exchange as a means of ritualizing power among preindustrial peoples. See Mauss, *The Gift*, trans. Ian Cunnison (New York: W. W. Norton, 1967). I shall return to this problem in Chapter 8.

9. In his *Structural Anthropology* (Garden City, N.Y.: Doubleday, Anchor Books, 1967), Lévi-Strauss discusses the dangers of neglecting such models and, at the same time, of not recognizing their limitations. See pp. 274–275.

10. "Changes in Property Relations," in *Transactions of the Third World Congress of Sociology* 1–2 (1956): 175. See also Friedmann's very useful review of the concept under "Property" in the *Dictionary of the History of Ideas* (New York: Charles Scribner's Sons, 1973), vol. 3, pp. 650–656. See also J. Valkhoff, "Les rapports de la propriété au XXème siècle au point de vue juridico-sociologique," in *Transactions*, p. 188.

11. *The Law of Primitive Man* (New York: Atheneum, 1973), p. 58.

12. See W. N. Hohfeld, *Fundamental Legal Conceptions as Applied to Judicial Reasoning and Other Essays*, ed. W. W. Cook (New Haven; Yale University Press, 1923). One of the best reassertions of Hohfeld's principles is Max Radin, "A Restatement of Hohfeld," *Harvard Law Review* 51 (1938): 1141–64.

13. For a useful review of this school of thought see G. B. J. Hughes, *Jurisprudence* (London: Butterworth & Co., 1955), pp. 161–166, 344–347.

14. Alf Ross, *On Law and Justice* (London: Stevens & Sons, 1958), pp. 158–160.

15. For a more detailed discussion of this issue see O. Kahn-Freund's introduction to Karl Renner, *The Institutions of Private Law and Their Social Functions* (London: Routledge & Kegan Paul, 1949).

16. For a review of ancient and modern definitions up to the 1930s see G. Landtman, *The Origin of the Inequality of the Social Classes* (London: Routledge & Kegan Paul, 1938), pp. 228–229.

17. *History of Slavery and Serfdom* (London: Black, 1895), p. 265.

18. *Slavery as an Industrial System* (The Hague: Martinus Nijhoff, 1910), p. 6 and chap. 1, passim. Nieboer concludes his lengthy discussion with an infelicitous, inaccurate, but often-quoted definition: "Slavery is the fact that one man is the property or possession of another beyond the limits of the family proper" (p. 30). Cf. L. T. Hobhouse, *Morals in Evolution* (London: Chapman & Hall, 1906), pp. 282–283. Edward Westermarck is the major critic of this definition among the early twentieth-century comparativists, but only on the unpersuasive grounds that "the master's right of disposing of his slave is not necessarily exclusive." See his *Origin and Development of the Moral Ideas* (London: Macmillan & Co., 1906–1908), vol. 1, p. 670.

19. *Report to the League of Nations Advisory Committee of Experts on Slavery*, Geneva, April 5, 1938, vol. 6, p. 16.

20. "Slavery as an Institution, Open and Closed Systems," in James L. Watson, ed., *Asian and African Systems of Slavery* (Oxford: Basil Blackwell, 1980), p. 809.

21. Although Finley begins with the observation that "as a commodity, the slave is property," he immediately embarks on a subtle and penetrating specification of what kind of property the slave is, a definition that identifies as the critical elements of the slave condition the "unilateral" power of the master, the "deracination" of the slave, and the master's control of the slave's "person and his personality" (which clearly implies a condition of dishonor, although Finley does not use the term). There remain some differences between his interpretation and mine, but they are largely matters of emphasis and conceptualization. M. I. Finley, *Ancient Slavery and Modern Ideology* (New York: Viking Press, 1980), pp. 73–75.

22. A similar point was made by U. B. Phillips, as Stanley Engerman has kindly reminded me. In *Life and Labor in the Old South* (Boston: Little, Brown, 1963), p. 160, Phillips opens his chapter entitled "The Peculiar Institution" as follows: "For a man to be property may seem barbaric and outrageous. But in this twentieth century thousands of divorced husbands are legally required to pay periodic alimony to their ex-wives, and if one seeks escape from the levy upon his earnings, he may be clapped into prison until he gives adequate pledges of compliance. The woman has a property right which the law maintains. This institution of alimony has developed somewhat unawares; and so, in some degree, did Negro slavery."

23. *Jurisprudence*, p. 442.

24. See, for example, Barry Hindess and Paul Q. Hirst, *Pre-Capitalist Modes of Production* (London: Routledge & Kegan Paul, 1975), pp. 109–177. For a critique of these authors' theoretical views on slavery, see Orlando Patterson, "Slavery and Slave Formations," *New Left Review* 117 (1979): 49–52.

25. Wang Yi-T'ung, "Slaves and Other Comparable Social Groups during the Northern Dynasties (386–618)," *Harvard Journal of Asiatic Studies* 16 (1953): 313–314.

26. Olga Lang claims that there were as many as two million of these female and child "slaves" in China before World War II; she distinguishes them from girls sold as concubines. *Chinese Family and Society* (New Haven: Yale University Press, 1946), pp. 259–260. H. D. Lamson, discussing the Mui Tsai practice during the early part of this century, writes that "economic pressure; the demand for concubines, prostitutes, and household slaves; the practice of buying a future wife for a male child at an early age when they can be secured more cheaply; and the low value set upon females, encourage the persistence of traffic in children." *Social Pathology in China* (Shanghai: Commercial Press, 1934), p. 262. For a more recent discussion see James L. Watson, "Transactions in People: The Chinese Market in Slaves, Servants, and Heirs," in Watson, *Asian and African Systems of Slavery,* pp. 223–250. Watson claims that in many parts of China before 1949, especially in the south, "nearly every peasant household was directly or indirectly affected by the sale of people" (p. 223).

27. It is well established that early Roman fathers could sell their children into slavery. More controversial is my suggestion that it was possible to sell them into nonslave status. I arrive at this conclusion as the only satisfactory explanation of what Alan Watson calls "a strange provision" of the code of XII Tables: "If a pater sold a son *three times* the son was to be *free from* the pater" (emphasis added). To sell someone into slavery was usually a lifetime transaction. It is, of course, possible that a father who sold his son once could buy him back and then sell him a second time. But it is beyond the limits of credulity to imagine that a father would have been either willing or able to sell, repurchase, and resell his son into slavery three times. Even if we allow for the occasional existence of such paternal perversity, the practice could hardly have been so frequent that it was necessary to enact a law against it. The only reasonable explanation of this "strange provision," then, is the existence of the practice, similar to the Chinese custom, of selling children into temporary nonslave statuses. On the sale of children into slavery see Alan Watson, *Rome of the XII Tables* (Princeton, N.J.: Princeton University Press, 1975), p. 44; on the "strange provision" see p. 45.

28. "Sonjo Bride-Price and the Question of African 'Wife Purchase,'" in E. E. Le Clair, Jr., and H. K. Schneider, eds., *Economic Anthropology* (New York: Holt, Rinehart and Winston, 1968), pp. 259–282.

29. It is significant that even in the modern world the fiction is usually dropped when dealing with degraded persons other than slaves, or with dehumanizing situations. Thus men who employ prostitutes speak of hiring or buying not their services but their bodies. We say of a woman who sits naked before a group of gawking men in a peep show that she sells her "body"; we say of the same woman who sits nude before a group of students at an art college that she rents her "services" as a model. A revealing development in the terminology of today's large bureaucracies is the use by personnel officers of the term "bodies" to describe employees in the organization. One increasingly hears statements such as the following: "Our biggest problem is a lack of bodies in the technical department." It is difficult to resist the conclusion that language has caught up with reality.

30. Mintz proposes that Marx was uncomfortable with the relationship be-

tween slavery and capitalism, given his conception of the role of "free" labor in capitalism. See Mintz, "The So-Called World System: Local Initiative and Local Response," *Dialectical Anthropology* 11 (1977): 253–270. For an extremely helpful discussion of the complexities involved in use of the terms "slave," "proletarian," and "free labor," see also Mintz, "Was the Plantation Slave a Proletarian?" *Review* 2 (1978): 81–98.

31. Michael S. Jacobs and Ralph K. Winter, Jr., "Antitrust Principles and Collective Bargaining by Athletes: Of Superstars in Peonage," *Yale Law Journal* 81 (1971): 3.

32. "So You Want to Own a Ball Club," *Forbes,* April 1, 1977, p. 37. Cited in D. Stanley Eitzen and George H. Sage, *The Sociology of American Sports* (Dubuque, Iowa: Wm. C. Brown Co., 1978), p. 188.

33. Jacobs and Winter, "Antitrust Principles," p. 2.

34. Dan Kowel, *The Rich Who Own Sport* (New York: Random House, 1977), pp. 19–20. See also the reference to Vida Blue as "The property of Oakland through 1978," p. 134.

35. See Roger Noll, ed., *Government and the Sports Business* (Washington, D.C.: Brookings Institution, 1974), pp. 3–4 and p. 217, where it is observed that "because professional sports does require that employees maintain their bodies in acceptable physical condition, owners are always going to insist on having some control over players in this area."

36. Watson, *Rome of the XII Tables,* p. 38.

37. *Ashanti Law and Constitution* (Oxford: Clarendon Press, 1929), p. 33.

38. Ibid., p. 34. It should be emphasized that Rattray was discussing colonial Ashanti during the early twentieth century. The situation was far more complex during the nineteenth century, when Ashanti was an imperial state with an advanced premodern economy.

39. I. M. Diakanoff, building on I. J. Gelb, defines the slave of early Mesopotamia as "a person entirely devoid not only of property in means of production, but also of the features of a subject of any personal rights." Diakanoff, "Slaves, Helots, and Serfs in Early Antiquity," *Acta Antiqua Academiae Scientiarum Hungaricae T. XXII* (1974), fasc. 104, p. 55. See also Gelb, "From Slavery to Freedom," in Bayerische Akademie der Wissenschaften, *Gesellschaftsklassen im Alten Zweiströmland und in den angrenzenden Gebieten* 75 (Munich, 1972): 87–88.

40. *Stone Age Economics* (London: Tavistock Publications, 1974), pp. 92–93.

41. Land, of course, was dominant in the Roman economy, as Finley and others have shown. See M. I. Finley, ed., *Studies in Roman Property* (Cambridge: Cambridge University Press, 1976). On the importance of slaves as a source of wealth and the relation of this source to land, see Finley, *The Ancient Economy* (Berkeley: University of California Press, 1973), chap. 3. See also Keith Hopkins, *Conquerors and Slaves* (Cambridge: Cambridge University Press, 1978), pp. 49–64, 99–118.

42. *The Law in Classical Athens* (Ithaca, N.Y.: Cornell University Press, 1978), p. 133.

43. The Oxford classicist J. Walter Jones makes this point well in *The Law and Legal Theory of the Greeks* (Oxford: Clarendon Press, 1956). He notes that there was no "technical precision" among the Greeks in the distinction between possession and ownership and that their conception of property was highly relativistic. "What

was recognized . . . was not an absolute right but one relatively better as between the two parties, leaving open the question whether some third party might not have a title superior to that of either litigant in the particular case" (p. 203). And he observes, further, that "Greek notions of ownership were nearer to those of feudal Europe or modern England than to those of Roman law" (p. 214).

44. Kahn-Freund's introduction to Renner, *The Institutions of Private Law and Their Social Functions,* pp. 24–25.

45. Ibid.

46. W. W. Buckland, *The Roman Law of Slavery* (Cambridge: Cambridge University Press, 1908), p. iv.

47. In addition to the references given in note 41 see Richard Duncan-Jones, *The Economy of the Roman Empire* (Cambridge: Cambridge University Press, 1974), pp. 24–25, 272–273, 323–324. On the importance of slaves in agriculture see K. D. White, *Roman Farming* (London: Thames & Hudson, 1970), pp. 350–362, 368–376.

48. On the development of the English law of property see F. Pollock and F. W. Maitland, *The History of English Law* (Cambridge: Cambridge University Press, 1968), vol. 2, bk. 2, chap. 4. See in particular the discussion of seisin, pp. 29–80. See also A. K. R. Kiralfy, ed., *Potter's Historical Introduction to English Law and Its Institutions* (London: Sweet & Maxwell, 1958), pt. 3, chap. 7.

49. M. I. Finley, "Was Greek Civilization Based on Slave Labour?" in M. I. Finley, ed., *Slavery in Classical Antiquity* (Cambridge: W. Heffer and Sons, 1960), pp. 53–72. More recently, Finley has observed that in both Greece and Rome the *permanent* work force on "establishments larger than the family unit, whether on the land or in the city," was composed of slaves. *Ancient Slavery and Modern Ideology,* p. 81. Although nonslave labor remained important in Italy, as Peter Garnsey has emphasized, the slave latifundia were of major importance in its economy, whereas such units were never important in Greece. Where slaves took part in agriculture, they were largely a supplementary work force, although their significance should not be underestimated. See Garnsey, "Non-slave Labour in the Roman World," paper presented at the International Conference of Economic Historians, Edinburgh, August 13–19, 1978. On slaves in Athenian agriculture see Michael H. Jameson, "Agriculture and Slavery in Classical Athens," *Classical Journal* 72 (1977–1978): 122–141.

50. For a discussion of the problem of status see John Crook, *Law and Life of Rome* (Ithaca, N.Y.: Cornell University Press, 1967), pp. 36–37. Of course, the entire field of law relating to persons was richly developed to meet such problems. For a fuller treatment of the law of persons see Alan Watson, *The Law of Persons in the Later Roman Republic* (Oxford: Clarendon Press, 1967). See also R. W. Leage, *Roman Private Law,* ed. A M. Prichard (London: Macmillan Co., 1961), ed. 3, pt. 2. On the relationship between status and legal privilege see Peter Garnsey, *Social Status and Legal Privilege in the Roman Empire* (Oxford: Oxford University Press, 1970).

51. Real freedom for the Greeks meant membership by birth in the community "citizenship"—not the simple negation of slavery. See M. I. Finley, *The Ancient Greeks* (New York: Viking Press, 1964), pp. 40–43.

52. See Herbert F. Jolowicz, *Historical Introduction to the Study of Roman Law* (Cambridge: Cambridge University Press, 1952), pp. 272–276. See also note 54 below.

53. *Introduction to Early Roman Law* (Oxford: Oxford University Press, 1944), vol. 2. pp. 159–161. See also Jolowicz, *Historical Introduction,* pp. 142–144.

54. There is a continuing controversy about whether early Roman law had a relative conception of property. For a review of the literature see György Diósdi, *Ownership in Ancient and Preclassical Roman Law* (Budapest: Akadémiai Kiadó, 1970), pp. 94 ff.

The traditional and most widely accepted view is that the early conception was relativistic. Strongly contesting this view are scholars such as Alan Watson and Diósdi (although these two differ on other issues). I find the arguments of Watson and Diósdi unpersuasive. This is, admittedly, a subject into which the outsider is best advised to tread warily, but since the matter rests more on clear thinking and sociological sensitivity than on specialized knowledge of the available, quite sparse data, I shall hazard a few comments.

According to Diósdi, the early expression of property was an absolute one; what was lacking was the "notion," in legal form, of the concept. This is a strange position for a Marxist to take. He supports his position with two principal arguments. One that he claims is "irrefutable" is that the relative conception of property is incompatible with the all-embracing totality of the *patria potestas.* His argument, however, rests on a spurious conception of the nature of relative property. This form of property does not exclude the possibility of absolute power; it is distinctive, rather, in including the actuality of countervailing claims and powers in a legal thing. The essential character of the relative conception of property is its realistic assumption that all claims and powers exist with respect to other persons. This allows for the possibility of absolute power, in which case no other person has competing claims and powers in the object. Whether totally exclusive power ever exists in practice is a moot point; it is best to see it as one extreme of a network of claims, privileges, and powers, at the other end of which is total powerlessness, which may also be no more than a theoretical possibility. Patria potestas falls somewhere near the absolutist end of the continuum of relative power. Whatever the actual situation, it is certainly fallacious to argue that the idea of relative property does not contain the possibility of total power.

Diósdi's other argument is that the expression *ego—meum esse aio* in the *legis actio sacramento in rem* could not possibly imply a relativistic conception of property, as common sense clearly indicates, because "it is inconceivable that ancient Roman peasants would have understood this simple and clear declaration in such a sophisticated way." This assertion gives everything away, for as we have already seen, modern anthropological studies have made it abundantly clear that the relative conception of property prevails among contemporary preliterate peoples far less sophisticated than the early Romans. See Diósdi, *Ownership,* chaps. 7–9, esp. pp. 98 and 122.

55. See Raymond Monier, "La date d'apparition du 'dominium' et de la distinction juridique des 'res' en 'corporales' et 'incorporales,' " in *Studi in onore Siro Solazzi* (Naples: E. Jovene, 1948), pp. 357–374.

56. Buckland, *The Roman Law of Slavery,* p. 3.

57. Claude Meillassoux, "Introduction," in Meillassoux, ed., *The Development of Indigenous Trade and Markets in West Africa* (London: Oxford University Press, 1971), pp. 49–86. See also the introduction and case studies in Meillassoux, *L'esclavage en Afrique précoloniale* and Martin Klein and Paul E. Lovejoy, "Slavery in

West Africa," in Henry A. Gemery and Jan S. Hogendorn, eds., *The Uncommon Market: Essays in the Economic History of the Atlantic Slave Trade* (New York: Academic Press, 1979), pp. 184–212. Philip Burnham, "Raiders and Traders in Adamawa: Slavery as a Regional System," in Watson, *Asian and African Systems of Slavery,* pp. 43–72.

58. "African 'Slavery' as an Institution of Marginality," in Suzanne Miers and Igor I. Kopytoff, eds., *Slavery in Africa* (Madison: University of Wisconsin Press, 1977), p. 64 and more generally pp. 65–66.

59. *The Political Economy of Slavery* (London: MacGibbon & Kee, 1966), esp. pp. 15–31.

60. Robert W. Fogel and Stanley L. Engerman, *Time on the Cross: The Economics of American Negro Slavery* (Boston: Little, Brown, 1974), vol. 1, esp. pp. 67–78, 86–106. For the more informed criticisms of this work see Paul A. David et al., *Reckoning with Slavery* (New York: Oxford University Press, 1976). See the rejoinder by Fogel and Engerman, as well as further responses from Gavin Wright, Thomas L. Haskel, D. F. Schaefer and M. D. Schmitz, Paul A. David, and P. Temin in *American Economic Review* 69 (1979): 206–226. See also the final response by Fogel and Engerman, "Explaining the Relative Efficiency of Slave Agriculture in the Antebellum South: Reply," *American Economic Review* 70 (1980): 672–690.

61. Contrary to common misconceptions, the free white in the South was independent, relatively well off, and sometimes politically quite militant in relation to the southern plantocracy on matters not directly relating to blacks. In several southern states secession did not result merely from a strong sense of solidarity on the part of the planter class but from their doubts about the white working class; secession was a drastic way of smothering an impending political crisis. See Michael P. Johnson, *Toward a Patriarchal Republic: The Secession of Georgia* (Baton Rouge: Louisiana State University Press, 1977); also Fletcher M. Green, "Democracy in the Old South," *Journal of Southern History* 12 (1964): 2–23; and Jonathan M. Winer, "Planter Persistence and Social Change: Alabama, 1850–1870," *Journal of Interdisciplinary History* 7 (1976): 235–260.

On the sociological and economic reasons for the yeoman white farmers' refusal to become involved with the cotton economy see Gavin Wright and Howard Kunreuther, "Cotton, Corn, and Risk in the Nineteenth Century," *Journal of Economic History* 25 (1975): 526–551. For a useful selection of older views on the subject see Harold D. Woodman, ed., *Slavery and the Southern Economy* (New York: Harcourt, Brace & World, 1966), pp. 113–161.

A similar case is that of the notorious radicalism of the South African freeburghers, especially the trekboers during and after the period of slavery. See Richard Elphick and Hermann Giliomee, eds., *The Shaping of South African Society, 1652–1820* (London: Longmans, 1979), chaps. 2 and 10; and George M. Frederickson, *White Supremacy: A Comparative Study in American and South African History* (New York: Oxford University Press, 1981), pp. 33–37.

62. "Between Slavery and Freedom," *Comparative Studies in Society and History* 6 (1964): 233–249.

63. See Richard S. Dunn, *Sugar and Slaves: The Rise of the Planter Class in the English West Indies, 1624–1713* (Chapel Hill: University of North Carolina Press, 1972), pp. 67–83, 96, 128–130, 154, 165. In Barbados during the seventeenth century,

"when the white servants found themselves toiling in the same field gangs with black slaves, they became wild and unruly in the extreme" (p. 69). In 1647 there was an attempted white servant rebellion that resulted in the execution of eighteen of the plotters. The buildings of the planters were like fortifications "equipped with bulwarks and bastions from which they could pour scalding water upon the attacking [white] servants and slaves" (p. 69). See also Ramiro Guerra y Sánchez, *Sugar and Society in the Caribbean* (New Haven: Yale University Press, 1964), pp. 1–27; and Richard B. Sheridan, *Sugar and Slavery: An Economic History of the British West Indies, 1623–1775* (Lodge Hill, Barbados: Caribbean Universities Press, 1974), chap. 5 and pp. 128–141.

64. See Max Weber, *The Agrarian Sociology of Ancient Civilizations* (London: New Left Books, 1976), pp. 310–329. The "scale of migration by the Italian poor" was, according to Keith Hopkins (p. 64), "amazing"; between 80 and 8 B.C. about half of all free rural adult males migrated to the towns. See Hopkins, *Conquerors and Slaves*, pp. 64–74. On hired laborers, slavery, and farm management see White, *Roman Farming*, pp. 332–383. On the Roman "myth of the peasant" (the romantic upper-class view of traditional rural life and Roman origins) and for a more complex interpretation of nonslave agricultural labor see Garnsey, "Non-slave Labour in the Roman World."

2. Authority, Alienation, and Social Death

1. *Thucydides on the Nature of Power* (Cambridge, Mass.: Harvard University Press, 1970), pp. 153–154.

2. *The Republic*, 9: 578 in Benjamin Jowett, ed. and trans., *The Dialogues of Plato* (New York: Random House, 1937), vol. 1, pp. 836–837.

3. Siegfried Lauffer, "Die Sklaverei in der griechisch-römischen Welt," in *Rapports* II, Eleventh International Congress of Historical Sciences, Stockholm, August 21–28, 1960 (Uppsala: Almquist and Wiksell, 1960), p. 76.

4. Max Weber, *Basic Concepts in Sociology*, trans. H. P. Secher (Secaucus, N.J.: Citadel Press, 1972), pp. 81–83. For a detailed analysis of Weber's use of this concept see Reinhardt Bendix, *Max Weber: An Intellectual Portrait* (London: Methuen & Co., 1966), pt. 3.

5. G. B. J. Hughes, *Jurisprudence* (London: Butterworth & Co., 1955), pp. 161–166. Hans Kelsen states the issue bluntly: "Law is a coercive order." "The Pure Theory of Law," in M. P. Golding, ed., *The Nature of Law* (New York: Random House, 1966), p. 112.

6. After criticizing Weber, Fortes points to the role "played by ceremony and ritual in the confirmation of status." Drawing on the seminal work of Everett Hughes, he notes that all statuses require a "mandate from society" (Hughes's term) and adds that "ritual mobilizes incontrovertible authority behind the granting of office and status and this guarantees its legitimacy and imposes accountability for its proper exercise." "Ritual and Office in Tribal Society," in Max Gluckman, ed., *Essays on the Ritual of Social Relations* (Manchester: Manchester University Press, 1962), p. 86.

7. *The Rites of Passage*, trans. M. B. Vizdeom and G. L. Caffee (London: Rout-

ledge & Kegan Paul, 1960). For a critical assessment of this work see Max Gluck-man, "Les rites de passage," in Gluckman, *Essays on the Ritual of Social Relations,* pp. 1-52.

8. Victor Turner, *The Forest of Symbols* (Ithaca, N.Y.: Cornell University Press, 1967), pp. 30-32, esp. chap. 4. For a more general and theoretical statement see his "Symbolic Studies," *Annual Review of Anthropology* 4 (1975): 145-161.

9. Claude Meillassoux, *L'esclavage en Afrique précoloniale* (Paris: François Maspero, 1975), esp. pp. 11-26.

10. Ibid., pp. 20-21.

11. See Henri Lévy-Bruhl, "Théorie de l'esclavage," in M. I. Finley, ed., *Slavery in Classical Antiquity* (Cambridge: W. Heffer and Sons, 1960), pp. 151-169.

12. Iris Origo, " 'The Domestic Enemy': The Eastern Slaves in Tuscany in the Fourteenth and Fifteenth Centuries," *Speculum* 30 (1955): 321-366.

13. See Mircea Eliade, *The Sacred and the Profane* (New York: Harvest Books, 1959), pp. 20-65.

14. *Bella Coola Indians* (Toronto: University of Toronto Press, 1948), vol. 1, p. 159.

15. *The Religious System and Culture of Nias, Indonesia* (The Hague: Uitgeverij Excelsior, 1959), p. 45.

16. *Slavery among the Indians of North America* (Moscow: U.S.S.R. Academy of Sciences, 1941), p. 80.

17. On Ashanti, see Robert S. Rattray, *Ashanti Law and Constitution* (Oxford: Clarendon Press, 1929), p. 29. On Ur see Bernard J. Siegel, *Slavery during the Third Dynasty of Ur,* Memoirs of the American Anthropological Association, no. 66 (1947), pp. 1-54. Siegel, after examining the available data, asserts, "We can thus conclude that the earliest notion of 'slave' was incorporated with the idea of 'foreigner,' " pp. 8-9. This linguistic usage persisted even when the vast majority of slaves were recruited from impoverished families. On the sources of slaves see pp. 9-27.

18. On the words used for "slaves" and their sources see William L. Wester-mann, *The Slave Systems of Greek and Roman Antiquity* (Philadelphia: American Philosophical Society, 1955), pp. 5-12. Also M. I. Finley, "Was Greek Civilization Based on Slavery?" in Finley, *Slavery in Classical Antiquity,* p. 146.

19. P. R. C. Weaver, "Vicarius and Vicarianus in the Familia Caesaris," *Journal of Roman Studies* 54 (1964): 118.

20. W. W. Buckland, *The Roman Law of Slavery* (Cambridge: Cambridge University Press, 1908), pp. 291-312.

21. See Peter P. Spranger, *Historische Untersuchungen zu den Sklavenfiguren des Plautus und Terenz* (Wiesbaden: Akademie Mainz, 1961), p. 65.

22. Lev. 25:44.

23. Maimonides, *The Code: Book Twelve, The Book of Acquisition,* ed. Isaac Klein (New Haven: Yale University Press, 1951), p. 809, and on the laws concerning heathen slaves, pp. 264-282.

24. See Maurice Keen, *The Laws of War in the Late Middle Ages* (London: Routledge & Kegan Paul, 1965), p. 137; and David Brion Davis, *The Problem of Slavery in Western Culture* (Ithaca, N.Y.: Cornell University Press, 1966), pp. 48, 100-101.

25. Robert Roberts, *The Social Laws of the Qorân* (London: Williams & Norgate, 1925), p. 54.

26. Ali Abd Elwahed, *Contribution à une théorie sociologique de l'esclavage* (Paris: Mechelinck, 1931), pp. 139, 166–167.

27. "Slavery and Emancipation in Two Societies," in M. G. Smith, ed., *The Plural Society in the British West Indies* (Berkeley: University of California Press, 1965), pp. 116–161.

28. "Conceptions of Slavery in the Nineteenth Century Sokoto Caliphate," paper presented at the Conference on the Ideology of Slavery in Africa, York University, Toronto, April 3–4, 1980.

29. Virginia Gutierrez de Pineda, *Organización social en la Guajira* (Bogota: Instituto Etnologico Nacional, 1950): 172.

30. Carlos Bosch Garcia, *La esclavitud prehispánica entre los Aztecas* (Mexico City: Colegio de Mexico, Centro de Estudios Históricos, 1944), p. 22.

31. *Slavery in Pharaonic Egypt* (Cairo: L'Institut français d'archéologie orientale, 1952), chap. 2.

32. Helmut Wiesdorf, *Bergleute und Hüttenmänner im Altertum bis zum Ausgang der römischen Republik: Ihre wirtschaftliche, soziale, und juristische Lage* (Berlin: Akademie-Verlag, 1952), p. 63.

33. E. G. Pulleyblank, "The Origins and Nature of Chattel Slavery in China," *Journal of the Economic and Social History of the Orient* 1 (1958): 204–211.

34. On Korea during the Koryŏ period, the major study in English is Ellen S. Unruh, "Slavery in Medieval Korea" (Ph.D. diss., Columbia University, 1978). Two useful general histories that deal with slavery during this period are Han Woo-Keun, *History of Korea* (Seoul: Eul-Yoo Publishing Co., 1970); and Takashi Hatada, *A History of Korea* (Santa Barbara, Calif.: ABC-Clio Press, 1969). On the Yi dynasty the major relevant studies in English are Susan S. Shin, "Land Tenure and the Agrarian Economy in Yi Dynasty Korea: 1600–1800" (Ph.D. diss., Harvard University, 1973); John Somerville, "Success and Failure in Eighteenth Century Ulsan: A Study in Social Mobility" (Ph.D. diss., Harvard University, 1974); and Edward W. Wagner, "Social Stratification in Seventeenth-Century Korea: Some Observations from a 1663 Seoul Census Register," in *Occasional Papers on Korea* 1 (1974): 36–54. Other works, including several in Korean (translated for the author) are cited in later references.

On Russian slavery the most important work in English is that of Richard Hellie, *Slavery in Russia, 1450–1725* (forthcoming); see also his "Recent Soviet Historiography on Medieval and Early Modern Russian Slavery," *Russian Review* 35 (1976): 1–32. Of special interest are two other works: George Vernadsky, "Three Notes on the Social History of Kievan Russia," *Slavonic Review* 22 (1944): 81–92; and (although it is based entirely on secondary sources) J. Thorsten Sellin, *Slavery and the Penal System* (New York: Elsevier, 1976).

35. Cited in Herbert Passin, "The Paekchŏng of Korea," *Monumenta Nipponica* 12 (1956–1957): 31.

36. In addition to the works by Shin and Wagner cited above see Susan S. Shin, "The Social Structure of Kùmhwa County in the Late Seventeenth Century," in *Occasional Papers on Korea* 1 (1974): 9–35.

37. Vernadsky, "Three Notes," pp. 81–82.

38. Ibid., pp. 88–92.

39. Sellin, *Slavery and the Penal System*, p. 121.

40. Hellie, *Slavery in Russia*, msp. XI-10.

41. Ibid., msp. XI-9.

42. Ibid., pp. XI-10–XI-11.

43. I draw heavily on several works in making these assertions, particularly Sellin, *Slavery and the Penal System*, and Michael R. Weisser, *Crime and Punishment in Early Modern Europe* (Sussex: Harvester Press, 1979). Sellin's work is itself largely an elaboration of the thesis that "the demands of the labor market shaped the penal system and determined its transformation over the years, more or less unaffected by theories of punishment in vogue." This thesis had been developed in two earlier works, those of Georg Rusche and Otto Kirchheimer, *Punishment and Social Structure* (New York: Columbia University Press, 1939); and Gustav Radbruch, "Der Ursprung des Strafrechts aus dem Stande der Unfreien," reprinted in *Elegantiae juris criminalis* (Basel: Verlag für Recht und Gesellschaft, 1950). See also Sidney W. Mintz, "The Dignity of Honest Toil: A Review Article," *Comparative Studies in Society and History* 21 (1979): 558–566.

44. Cited in Sellin, *Slavery and the Penal System*, p. 47.

45. Not all contemporary penal reformers attempted to disguise the fact that the punishment they were calling for as a replacement for the death penalty was slavery, pure and simple. Thus the Milanese noble and penal reformer Cesare Beccaria in his influential tract, *Of Crime and Punishments*, stated bluntly that the alternative to the death penalty that he was advocating was "slavery for life." See Sellin, *Slavery and the Penal System*, pp. 65–69.

46. "Mafakur: A Limbic Institution of the Margi," in Suzanne Miers and Igor I. Kopytoff, eds., *Slavery in Africa* (Madison: University of Wisconsin Press, 1977), pp. 85–102.

47. Ibid., p. 100.

48. Theda Perdue, *Slavery and the Evolution of Cherokee Society, 1540–1866* (Knoxville; University of Tennessee Press, 1979), pp. 3–18.

49. Burton Raffel, ed. and trans., *Beowulf* (New York: New American Library, 1963). All citations are from this edition.

50. Ibid., lines 1060–62.

51. Ibid., lines 2210–11.

52. Ibid., lines 2279–87.

53. For the classic statement see John Dollard, *Caste and Class in a Southern Town* (New Haven: Yale University Press, 1937).

54. For one of the best statements of this view see Edmund R. Leach, *Aspects of Castes in South India, Ceylon, and North-West Pakistan* (Cambridge: Cambridge University Press, 1960).

55. Typical of this approach is James H. Vaughan who, "following anthropological usage," defines caste as "a hereditary endogamous group who are socially differentiated by prescribed behavior." See his "Caste Systems in the Western Sudan," in Arthur Tuden and Leonard Plotnicov, eds., *Social Stratification in Africa* (New York: Free Press, 1970), pp. 59–92. See also in the same volume Jacques Maquet, "Rwanda Castes," pp. 93–124.

56. On the Margi see Vaughan's two previously cited papers: "Mafakur: A

Limbic Institution of the Margi," and "Caste Systems in the Western Sudan"; on the Somali see Enrico Cerulli, "Il diritto consuetudinario della Somalia settentrionale (Migiurtini)," *Somalia, scritti vari editi ed inediti* 2 (1959): 1–74. On Korea see Passin, "The Paekchŏng of Korea."

57. See Robert S. Starobin, *Industrial Slavery in the Old South* (New York: Oxford University Press, 1970); Claudia Dale Goldin, "The Economics of Urban Slavery, 1820–1860" (Ph.D. diss., University of Chicago, 1972); and Stanley L. Engerman, "A Reconsideration of Southern Economic Growth, 1770–1860," in *Agricultural History* 49 (1975): 343–361. On Jamaica see Barry Higman, *Slave Population and Economy in Jamaica, 1807–1834* (Cambridge: Cambridge University Press, 1976), chaps. 2–4, 10.

58. While the vast majority of outcaste groups were despised, a few were not, among them the *enkyagu* of the Margi.

59. *The Maori,* Memoirs of the Polynesian Society, no. 5 (1924), p. 251.

60. Raymond Firth, *Primitive Economics of the New Zealand Maori* (Wellington, N.Z.: R. E. Owen, Government Printer, 1959), p. 214.

61. Lionel Caplan, "Power and Status in South Asian Slavery," in James L. Watson, ed., *Asian and African Systems of Slavery* (Oxford: Basil Blackwell, 1980), pp. 177–180.

62. "The Tupinamba," in Julian H. Steward, ed., *Handbook of the South American Indians* (Washington, D.C.: Government Printing Office, 1948), vol. 3, p. 120.

63. Ibid.

64. A. M. Wergeland, *Slavery in Germanic Society during the Middle Ages* (Chicago: University of Chicago Press, 1916), p. 16.

65. H. R. P. Finberg, *The Agrarian History of England and Wales* (Cambridge: Cambridge University Press, 1972), p. 507.

66. J. C. Miller, "Imbangala Lineage Slavery," in Miers and Kopytoff, *Slavery in Africa,* pp. 205–233.

67. Carlos Estermann, *The Ethnography of Southwestern Angola* (New York: Africana Publishing Co., 1976), pp. 128–129.

68. Laura Bohannan and Paul Bohannan, *The Tiv of Central Nigeria* (London: Ethnographic Survey of Africa, 1953), pt. 8, pp. 45–46.

69. K. Nwachukwu-Ogedengbe, "Slavery in Nineteenth Century Aboh (Nigeria)," in Miers and Kopytoff, *Slavery in Africa,* p. 141.

70. Arthur Tuden, "Slavery and Social Stratification among the Ila of Central Africa," in Tuden and Plotnicov, *Social Stratification in Africa,* p. 52.

71. Edmund R. Leach, *Political Systems of Highland Burma* (London: Bell, 1954), p. 304.

72. N. Adriani and Albert C. Kruyt, *De Bare'e Sprekende Toradjas van Midden-Celebes* [The Bare'e-speaking Toradja of Central Celebes] (Amsterdam: Nood-Hollandsche Uitgevers Maatschappij, 1951), vol. 2, p. 142.

73. On Jamaica see Orlando Patterson, *The Sociology of Slavery: Jamaica, 1655–1838* (Rutherford, N.J.: Fairleigh Dickinson University Press, 1969), chap. 6. On the U.S. South see Eugene D. Genovese, *Roll, Jordan, Roll* (New York: Pantheon, 1974), esp. bk. 2. See also the detailed discussion of the slaves' cultural life in Charles W. Joyner, "Slave Folklife on the Waccaman Neck: Antebellum Black Cul-

ture in the South Carolina Low Country" (Ph.D. diss., University of Pennsylvania, 1977), chap. 3.

74. *Language and Myth* (New York: Dover Publications, 1953), p. 3.

75. There were, however, many peculiarly servile names, the best-known being perhaps "Rufio." This and other names suggest the national origins of the slaves, but as Gordon, Solin, and others have pointed out, it is dangerous to draw conclusions about the ethnic origins of Roman slaves on the basis of the available distribution of ethnic names. Slaves were often named for the place of purchase, which tells us nothing about their origin—a good case in point being the common slave name "Corinthus." Greek or hellenized names were often taken for cultural reasons. In an exceptional case a captive was allowed to keep his original name, the most famous example being Spartacus. Whatever the new name, the overwhelming tendency was for the slave's master or superior to select it. Principally for this reason slave names "do not often take the form of nicknames derived from physical characteristics." See Mary L. Gordon, "The Nationality of Slaves under the Early Roman Empire," in Finley, *Slavery in Classical Antiquity,* pp. 171–211; Lily Ross Taylor, "Freedman and Freeborn in the Epitaphs of Imperial Rome," *American Journal of Philology* 82 (1961): 113–132; and, more recently, Heikki Solin, *Beiträge zur Kenntnis der griechischen Personennamen in Rom* (Helsinki: Societas Scientiarum Fennica, 1971).

76. Hellie, *Slavery in Russia,* mspp. XI-19–XI-27.

77. On the ancient Near East see Isaac Mendelsohn, *Slavery in the Ancient Near East* (Oxford: Oxford University Press, 1949), p. 31; on China see Pulleyblank, "The Origins and Nature of Chattel Slavery in China," p. 217; on Egypt see Bakir, *Slavery in Pharaonic Egypt,* pp. 103–107, 114.

78. Ralph A. Austen, "Slavery among the Coastal Middlemen: The Duala of the Cameroon," in Miers and Kopytoff, *Slavery in Africa,* p. 312. See also K. Nwachukwu-Ogedengbe, "Slavery in Nineteenth Century Aboh (Nigeria)," in the same volume, p. 140.

79. Edward Sapir and Morris Swadesh, *Native Accounts of Nootka Ethnography* (Bloomington: Indiana University Research Center in Anthropology, Folklore, and Linguistics, 1955), p. 177. When a Nootka slave escaped or was ransomed, a potlatch was given for him and he was assigned a new name. Carl O. Williams, *Thraldom in Ancient Iceland* (Chicago: University of Chicago Press, 1937), pp. 35–36.

80. Genovese, *Roll, Jordan, Roll,* pp. 443–450. See also Newbell N. Puckett, "American Negro Names," *Journal of Negro History* 23 (1938): 35–48. On the significance of name-changing upon emancipation see Ira Berlin, *Slaves without Masters* (New York: Vintage Books, 1976), pp. 51–52. On the struggle to retain African names in colonial South Carolina, the linguistic compromises worked out between masters and slaves (especially in the use of African day-names), and the ultimate disappearance of African names with the Americanization of the slave population see Peter H. Wood, *Black Majority: Negroes in Colonial South Carolina* (New York: Alfred A. Knopf, 1974), pp. 181–186. For an enslaved African's account of his reactions with each new master see Olaudah Equiano, *The Interesting Narrative of the Life of Olauda Equiano, or Gustavus Vasa, The African, Written by Himself* (Norwich, England: Printed and Sold by the Author, 1794), pp. 62, 87.

81. *The Black Family in Slavery and Freedom* (New York: Pantheon, 1976), pp. 230–256.

82. William F. Sharp, *Slavery on the Spanish Frontier: The Colombian Chocó, 1680–1810* (Norman: University of Oklahoma Press, 1976), p. 114.

83. Ibid., pp. 114–115.

84. Colin A. Palmer, *Slaves of the White God; Blacks in Mexico, 1570–1650* (Cambridge Mass.: Harvard University Press, 1976), p. 39.

85. David De Camp, "African Day-Names in Jamaica," *Language* 43 (1967): 139–149. See also Patterson, *The Sociology of Slavery,* pp. 174–181.

86. Michael Craton, *Searching for the Invisible Man: Slaves and Plantation Life in Jamaica* (Cambridge, Mass.: Harvard University Press, 1978), p. 157.

87. Ibid., p. 158.

88. Higman, *Slave Population and Economy in Jamaica,* p. 173.

89. My discussion here of the French Antilles relies heavily on Gabriel Debien, *Les esclaves aux Antilles françaises, XVIIe–XVIIIe siècles* (Basse-Terre, Fort-de-France: Société d'histoire de la Guadeloupe et Société d'histoire de la Martinique, 1974), pp. 71–73.

90. See Bernard Lewis, "The African Diaspora and the Civilization of Islam," in Martin L. Kilson and Robert I. Rotberg, eds., *The African Diaspora* (Cambridge, Mass.: Harvard University Press, 1976), pp. 37–56.

91. During the eighteenth century the South Carolina masters attempted to regulate slave clothing by law, but the attempt was abandoned because of a lack of interest of the masters in its enforcement. For a detailed discussion of the limited symbolic role of costume in the slave culture of South Carolina see Joyner, "Slave Folklife," pp. 206–219. Joyner found no evidence to support Genovese's claim that slaves preferred the color red. Over time the rough cotton "osnaburgs" became identified as "nigger cloth." American slaves, too, soon developed peculiar styles of dressing. See Genovese, *Roll, Jordan, Roll,* pp. 550–561. In Mauritius slaves were not permitted to wear shoes. The colonists declared that doing so "was tantamount to proclaiming their emancipation" (Burton Benedict, "Slavery and Indenture in Mauritius and Seychelles," in Watson, *Asian and African Systems of Slavery,* p. 141).

92. For further discussion see Victor Ehrenberg, *The People of Aristophanes* (New York: Schocken Books, 1962), p. 184.

93. We do not know when this incident, referred to by Seneca, occurred. See Seneca, *On Mercy* (Cambridge, Mass.: Harvard University Press, Loeb Classical Library, 1970), 1.24.1. Plautus also refers to the slaves' different style of dress although, of course, the setting is supposedly Greece. Plautus, *Amphitryo,* 114, in Plautus, *The Rope and other Plays,* ed. and trans. E. F. Watling (New York: Penguin Books, 1964), p. 232.

94. There is still some controversy concerning exactly what the *abbuttum* or Babylonian slave-mark was, though it is certain that it was a mark of degradation. For a discussion of the subject see G. R. Driver and John C. Miles, eds., *The Babylonian Laws* (Oxford: Clarendon Press, 1960), vol. 1, pp. 306–309, 422–423.

95. Sellin, *Slavery and the Penal System,* pp. 49–50.

96. Ibid., p. 120.

97. Cited in Kenneth Stampp, *The Peculiar Institution* (London: Eyre & Spottiswoode, 1964), p. 185.

98. Ibid., p. 205.

99. Craton, *Searching for the Invisible Man,* p. 198.

100. C. R. Boxer, *The Golden Age of Brazil, 1695–1750* (Berkeley: University of California Press, 1969), p. 172.

101. Kenneth Little, "The Mende Farming Household," *Sociological Review* 40 (1948): 38.

102. A. A. Dim Delobsom, *L'empire du Mogho-Naba: Coutumes des Mossi de la Haute-Volta* (Paris: Domat-Montchrestien, 1943), p. 64.

103. On the psychoanalysis of hair and hairdressing see Charles Berg, *The Unconscious Significance of Hair* (London: Allen & Unwin, 1951). For a sympathetic critique of this work and a useful statement of the anthropological symbolism of hair see E. R. Leach, "Magical Hair," in John Middleton, ed., *Myth and Cosmos* (Garden City, N.Y.: Natural History Press, 1967), pp. 77–108. For a general study of hair and hair symbolism see Wendy Cooper, *Hair: Sex, Society, and Symbolism* (London: Aldus Books, 1971). And for a useful review of the anthropological literature on hair "as private asset and public symbol" see Raymond Firth, *Symbols: Public and Private* (Ithaca, N.Y.: Cornell University Press, 1973), pp. 262–298. As important as the content in hair symbolism is the structural principle that hair shaving always implies a transitional status. I shall have more to say about this in a later chapter.

104. Raymond Breton, "Father Raymond Breton's Observation of the Island Carib: A Compilation of Ethnographic Notes Taken from Breton's Carib-French Dictionary Published in 1665," trans. and ed. Marshall McKusick and Pierre Verin (New Haven: HRAF, 1957?), p. 42 (manuscript). See also Raymond Breton and Armand de la Paix, "Relations de l'Ile de la Guadeloupe," in Joseph Rennard, ed., *Les Caraibes, La Guadeloupe, 1635–1656* (Paris: Librairie Generale et Internationale, 1929), pp. 45–74; Irving Rouse, "The Carib," in Steward, *Handbook of the South American Indians*, vol. 4, pp. 552–553.

105. There is a vast literature on this subject. For a good overview see the papers collected in Magnus Mörner, ed., *Race and Class in Latin America* (New York: Columbia University Press, 1970). See also Charles Wagley, "On the Concept of Social Race in the Americas," *Actas del XXXIII Congreso Internacional de Americanistas* 1 (1959): 403–417; and Carl N. Degler, *Neither Black nor White: Slavery and Race Relations in Brazil and the United States* (New York: Macmillan Co., 1971). For an excellent study of the complexities of race, class, and color in a Caribbean slave society see Verena Martinez-Alier, *Marriage, Class, and Colour in Nineteenth-Century Cuba* (Cambridge: Cambridge University Press, 1974). For an interesting but flawed theory of the role of somatic perception in the development of race relations during and after slavery see Harry Hoetink, *The Two Variants of Caribbean Race Relations* (London: Oxford University Press, 1967). See also David Lowenthal, *West Indian Societies* (New York: Oxford University Press, 1972), esp. chap. 7; Florestan Fernandes, "Slaveholding Society in Brazil," in Vera Rubin and Arthur Tuden, eds., *Comparative Perspectives on Slavery in New World Plantation Societies* (New York: New York Academy of Sciences, 1977), pp. 311–342; and Leslie B. Rout, Jr., *The African Experience in Spanish America* (New York: Cambridge University Press, 1976), esp. chaps. 5 and 12.

106. For a discussion of the social psychology of hair and hair color, and the priority status of "good hair" over "good color," see the work of the Jamaican sociologist Fernando Henriques, *Family and Colour in Jamaica* (London: MacGibbon & Kee, 1968), esp. chaps, 1, 2, 13, and 14. As Henriques observes: "A dark person with

good hair and features ranks above a fair person with bad [that is, African-type] hair and features" (p. 55).

107. Woodville K. Marshall, ed., *The Colthurst Journal: Journal of a Special Magistrate in the Islands of Barbados and St. Vincent, July 1835–September 1838* (Millwood N.Y.: K.T.O. Press, 1977), p. 100. Resentment of the beautiful curls of some mulatto women also existed in South Africa.

108. Ibid.

109. See Rex M. Nettleford, *Identity, Race, and Protest in Jamaica* (N.Y.: William Morrow and Co., 1972), esp. chaps. 1, 3, and 5. On Trinidad see Bridget Brereton, *Race Relations in Colonial Trinidad, 1870–1900* (Cambridge: Cambridge University Press, 1979), and for the modern period Selwyn D. Ryan, *Race and Nationalism in Trinidad and Tobago* (Toronto: University of Toronto Press, 1972).

110. See, for example, James B. Christensen, *Double Descent among the Fanti* (New Haven: Human Relations Area Files, 1954), p. 96; and J. S. Harris, "Some Aspects of Slavery in Southeastern Nigeria," *Journal of Negro History* 27 (1942): 96.

111. Meyer Fortes, *The Web of Kinship among the Tallensi* (London: Oxford University Press, 1949), p. 25.

112. Perdue, *Slavery and the Evolution of Cherokee Society*, p. 11.

113. Meyer Fortes, *The Dynamics of Clanship among the Tallensi* (London: Oxford University Press, 1945), p. 52.

114. J. C. Miller, "Imbangala Lineage Slavery," in Miers and Kopytoff, *Slavery in Africa*, p. 213.

115. Rattray, *Ashanti Law and Constitution,* pp. 40–41.

116. André Bourgeot, "Rapports esclavagistes et conditions d'affranchissement chez les Imuhaġ," in Meillassoux, *L'esclavage en Afrique précoloniale,* pp. 85, 90.

117. On the psychology of witchcraft in West Africa see M. J. Field, *Search for Security: An Ethnopsychiatric Study of Rural Ghana* (London: Faber & Faber, 1960). See also the classic paper of S. F. Nadel on the subject, "Witchcraft in Four African Societies: An Essay in Comparison," *American Anthropologist* 54 (1952): 18–29.

118. *Rural Hausa: A Village and a Setting* (Cambridge: Cambridge University Press, 1972), p. 42.

119. *The Cubeo: Indians of the Northwestern Amazon* (Urbana: University of Illinois Press, 1963), Illinois Studies in Anthropology, no. 2, p. 130.

120. *Roll, Jordan, Roll,* p. 514.

121. *Journal of a West Indian Proprietor, Kept during a Residence in the Island of Jamaica* (London: 1834), p. 240.

122. For the classic statement of this view see Max Weber, *The Sociology of Religion,* trans. Ephraim Fischoff (Boston: Beacon Press, 1964), esp. chaps. 1, 3, and 14. See in particular Weber's discussion of the means by which Rome, like China and other Far Eastern states, developed "more inclusive associations, especially of the political variety," while retaining the power and significance of familial religious organizations and ancestral gods (pp. 15–16). See also Robert N. Bellah, *Beyond Belief* (New York: Harper & Row, 1970), chap. 2.

123. *Untersuchungen über die Religion der Sklaven in Griechenland und Rom* (Wiesbaden: Akademie Mainz, 1960), vol. 2, p. 144.

124. Ibid., vol. 3, pp. 173–195.

125. *Custom and Conflict in Africa* (Oxford: Basil Blackwell, 1955), p. 125; also chap. 5.

126. Bömer, *Untersuchungen über die Religion der Sklaven,* vol. 3, p. 44.

127. W. K. C. Guthrie, *The Greeks and Their Gods* (Boston: Beacon Press, 1950), p. 84; also chap. 7.

128. Bömer, *Untersuchungen über die Religion der Sklaven,* vol. 1, pp. 32–86.

129. For a good discussion of the saturnalia see E. O. James, *Seasonal Feasts and Festivals* (London: Thames & Hudson, 1961), pp. 175–177.

130. Bömer, *Untersuchungen über die Religion der Sklaven,* vol. 1, pp. 87–98.

131. R. H. Barrow, *Slavery in the Roman Empire* (London: Methuen & Co., 1928), p. 164.

132. Ibid., p. 168.

133. Bömer, *Untersuchungen über die Religion der Sklaven,* vol. 1, pp. 110–171.

134. *Conquerors and Slaves* (Cambridge: Cambridge University Press, 1978), pp. 212–213. See also Robert E. A. Palmer, *Roman Religion and Roman Empire: Five Essays* (Philadelphia: University of Pennsylvania Press, 1974), pp. 114–120.

135. Hopkins, *Conquerors and Slaves,* chap. 5.

136. *Aspects of Antiquity* (New York: Viking Press, 1969), p. 207.

137. For the classic analysis of the religions of salvation see Weber, *The Sociology of Religion,* chaps. 9–12.

138. Early Christianity, as Weber pointed out, was essentially a religion of urban artisans "both slave and free" (ibid., p. 95). See also Ernst Troeltsch, *The Social Teachings of the Christian Churches,* vol. 1 (London: Macmillan & Co., 1931); A. D. Nock, *Early Gentile Christianity and Its Hellenistic Background* (New York: Harper Torchbooks, 1957); Philip Carrington, *The Early Christian Church,* vol. 1 (Cambridge: Cambridge University Press, 1957). For a good recent treatment of Constantine's conversion and its consequences see J. H. W. G. Liebeschuetz, *Continuity and Change in Roman Religion* (Oxford: Clarendon Press, 1979), pp. 277–308.

139. See Ambrogio Donini, "The Myth of Salvation in Ancient Slave Society," *Science and Society* 15 (1951): 57–60. For a review of slavery in Christian thought see Davis, *The Problem of Slavery,* esp. chaps. 3 and 4.

140. J. G. Davies, "Christianity: The Early Church," in R. C. Zaehner, ed., *The Concise Encyclopedia of Living Faiths* (Boston: Beacon Press, 1959), p. 56.

141. Ibid., pp. 55–58.

142. For one of the best-known statements of the view that Christianity is primarily a religion built on the response to Jesus' crucifixion see John Knox, *The Death of Christ* (London: Collins, 1967). See also Christopher F. Evans, *Resurrection and the New Testament* (Naperville, Ill.: Alec R. Allenson, 1970).

143. Rom. 6:10.

144. Undoubtedly the most probing modern analysis of Paul's ethical dualism is Maurice Goguel's *The Primitive Church,* trans. H. C. Snape (London: Allen & Unwin, 1964), pp. 425–455.

145. Ibid., p. 428.

146. Ibid., p. 449.

147. On the chronic dualism of Saint Augustine see Karl Jaspers' brilliant critique in his *Plato and Augustine* (New York: Harvest Books, 1957), esp. pp. 109–119. Still valuable is J. N. Figgis, *The Political Aspects of St. Augustine's City of God* (London: Longmans, 1921). See my own interpretation in Orlando Patterson, *Ethnic*

Chauvinism: The Reactionary Impulse (New York: Stein & Day, 1977), pp. 231–241.

148. See Weber, *The Sociology of Religion,* esp. chaps. 9 and 10.

149. We need not become involved here with the spent debate on the role of the Catholic church in Latin American slavery. See Davis, *The Problem of Slavery,* pp. 223–261; also Rout, *The African Experience in Spanish America,* chap. 5; Boxer, *The Golden Age of Brazil,* chaps. 5–7; and Palmer, *Slaves of the White God,* chap. 4, esp. the cases cited on pp. 113–114.

150. See William Lou Mathieson, *British Slavery and Its Abolition* (London: Longmans, 1926), pp. 109–114; Elsa V. Goveia, *Slave Society in the British Leeward Islands at the End of the Eighteenth Century* (New Haven: Yale University Press, 1965), pp. 263–310; and Patterson, *The Sociology of Slavery,* pp. 33–51. Although formally Catholic, the situation in the French Caribbean was more like that of the British islands. See Debien, *Les esclaves aux Antilles françaises,* pp. 249–295.

151. *Sugar and Slaves: The Rise of the Planter Class in the English West Indies, 1624–1713* (Chapel Hill: University of North Carolina Press, 1972), p. 249.

152. Albert J. Raboteau, *Slave Religion* (New York: Oxford University Press, 1980), p. 141.

153. Ibid., p. 149.

154. See John B. Boles, *The Great Revival, 1787–1805* (Lexington: University Press of Kentucky, 1972); also his *Religion in Antebellum Kentucky* (Lexington: University Press of Kentucky, 1976). On the ways in which Christian conscience was reconciled to bondage see H. Sheldon Smith, *In His Image, But—* (Durham, N.C.: Duke University Press, 1972).

155. Genovese, *Roll, Jordan, Roll,* p. 186.

156. See Edgar T. Thompson, "God and the Southern Plantation System," in S. S. Hill, ed., *Religion and the Solid South* (Nashville, Tenn.: Abingdon Press, 1972), pp. 51–91; and James L. Peacock, "The Southern Protestant Ethic Disease," in J. K. Morland, ed., *The Not So Solid South* (Athens: University of Georgia Press, 1971).

157. *The Religion of the Slaves* (Helsinki: Finnish Academy of Science and Letters, 1976), p. 139.

158. Genovese, *Roll, Jordan, Roll,* bk. 2, pt. 1.

159. Lawrence W. Levine, *Black Culture and Black Consciousness* (New York: Oxford University Press, 1978), chaps. 1 and 3.

160. See Levine, *Black Culture and Black Consciousness,* p. 33; and Raboteau, *Slave Religion,* p. 250. Alho's careful study of the spirituals and slave narratives does not support the view that the Exodus myth or identification with the children of Israel were the dominant themes in the religious beliefs of slaves. See Alho, *The Religion of the Slaves,* pp. 75–76.

161. Alho, *The Religion of the Slaves,* p. 79.

162. Goguel, *The Primitive Church,* pp. 454–455.

163. *Redemption in Black Theology* (Valley Forge, Pa.: Judson Press, 1979).

3. Honor and Degradation

1. J. W. Duff and A. M. Duff, eds., *Minor Latin Poets* (Cambridge, Mass.: Harvard University Press, 1934), p. 4.

2. Ibid., pp. 68–69, line 413.

3. Ibid., pp. 42–43, line 211.

4. Ibid., line 212.

5. Ibid., pp. 40–41, line 196.

6. *The Gift*, trans. Ian Cunnison (New York: W. W. Norton, 1967), p. 36.

7. *The Antichrist*, in Walter Kaufmann, ed., *The Portable Nietzsche* (New York: Viking Press, 1954), p. 570.

8. "Of Honor and Reputation," in *Essays Civil and Moral* (New York: Collier, 1909); Harvard Classics, vol. 30, p. 136.

9. Carl O. Williams, *Thraldom in Ancient Iceland* (Chicago: University of Chicago Press, 1937), pp. 38–39.

10. The standard work on the subject is still the collection of essays edited by J. D. Peristiany, *Honour and Shame: The Values of Mediterranean Society* (London: Weidenfeld & Nicolson, 1965). More general in their application are the essays of Julian Pitt-Rivers on which I draw. See his "Honor," in the *Encyclopedia of the Social Sciences*, ed. 2 (New York: Macmillan Co., 1968), vol. 6, pp. 503–511. For a recent review of the literature see John Davis, *People of the Mediterranean* (London: Routledge & Kegan Paul, 1977), pp. 89–101.

11. Davis, *People of the Mediterranean*, p. 98.

12. Pitt-Rivers, "Honor," p. 505.

13. *Fundamental Principles of the Metaphysics of Ethics* (London: Longmans, 1959), p. 14.

14. Plato, *The Republic*, VI.11. 548–549. The term "timocracy" is derived from the Greek word for honor (*timé*). It is true that Plato had Sparta in mind when speaking of timocracy and the timocratic character; however, his description not only applies to ancient Athens but to the kind of culture and character we have in mind when speaking of honorific cultures or the honorific syndrome among all other peoples. According to Plato, in addition to the desire to excel, "the timocratic character has the following traits[:] . . . he must be more self-willed than Glaucon and rather uncultivated, though fond of music; one who will listen readily, but is no speaker. Not having a properly educated man's consciousness of superiority to slaves, he will treat them harshly; though he will be civil to free men, and very obedient to those in authority. Ambitious for office, he will base his claims, not on any gifts of speech, but on his exploits in war and the soldierly qualities he has acquired, through his devotion to athletics and hunting. In his youth he will despise money, but the older he grows the more he will care for it, because of the touch of avarice in his nature; and besides his character is not thoroughly sound for lack of the only safeguard that can preserve it throughout life, a thoughtful and cultivated mind." From Francis M. Cornford, ed. and trans., *The Republic of Plato* (Oxford: Clarendon Press, 1941), p. 266.

15. Yves d'Evreux, *Voyage dans le nord de Brésil, fait durant les années 1613 et 1614*, ed. Ferdinand Denis (Paris: A. Franck, 1864), p. 46.

16. Ibid., p. 56.

17. *Thraldom in Ancient Iceland*, p. 163.

18. The extent and structural significance of slavery among the Germanic peoples is a controversial issue requiring further research. For the moment it is safest to say that in most areas slavery was of the domestic variety and that slaves, while used economically, were essentially a supplementary work force. The claim of some

Marxist writers, such as H. Gråtopp, that a slave mode of production existed in Scandinavia during the Middle Ages, is highly questionable. What seems more reasonable is that slavery was of far greater economic significance among the Icelanders, Danes, Norwegians, and Swedes during the Viking Age (800–1300) than has been previously suspected. For the most representative of the Marxist approaches see Gråtopp, "Slavesamfunnet i Norge og birkebeinerevolusjonen," [Slave Society in Norway and the Revolution of Birkebeine] *Røde fane* 6 (1977): 1–2. For a recent synthesis see Thomas Lindkvist, *Landborna i Norden under äldre medeltid* [Tenants in the Nordic Countries during the Early Middle Ages] (Uppsala: University of Uppsala, 1979), pp. 66–72, 129–139. See also Peter Foote and David M. Wilson, *The Viking Achievement* (London: Sidgwick & Jackson, 1970), pp. 65–78. The situation was different among the Anglo-Saxon kingdoms of England; I am convinced that slavery on a large scale existed in the southwestern states of the late Old English period.

19. A. M. Wergeland, *Slavery in Germanic Society during the Middle Ages* (Chicago: University of Chicago Press, 1916), p. 36.

20. Williams, *Thraldom in Ancient Iceland,* p. 13.

21. Ibid., p. 16.

22. Ibid., p. 93.

23. Dafydd Jenkins, ed., *Cyfraith Hywel* [Law of Hywel] (Llandysul, Wales: Gwasg Gomer, 1976), p. 15. For a general treatment of the subject see Sir John E. Lloyd, *A History of Wales* (London: Longmans, 1911), vol. 1, chap. 9.

24. H. R. P. Finberg, *The Agrarian History of England and Wales* (Cambridge: Cambridge University Press, 1972), p. 430.

25. For two excellent recent reviews of the literature on African slavery see Paul E. Lovejoy, "Indigenous African Slavery," in Michael Craton, ed., *Roots and Branches: Current Directions in Slave Studies, Historical Reflections* 6 (1979): 19–61; and Frederick Cooper, "The Problem of Slavery in African Studies," *Journal of African History* 21 (1979): 103–125.

26. See Ronald Cohen, *The Kanuri of Bornu* (New York: Holt, Rinehart and Winston, 1966); Allan Hoben, "Social Stratification in Traditional Amhara Society," in Arthur Tuden and Leonard Plotnicov, eds., *Social Stratification in Africa* (New York: Free Press, 1970), pp. 197–198; and M. G. Smith, "The Hausa System of Social Status," *Africa* 29 (1959): 239–252.

27. Tuden and Plotnicov, "Introduction" in Tuden and Plotnicov, *Social Stratification in Africa,* pp. 1–29.

28. This is fully documented in all the papers collected in Ronald Cohen and John Middleton, eds., *Comparative Political Systems* (Garden City, N.Y.: Natural History Press, 1967). See also Helen S. Codere, "Kwakiutl Society: Rank without Class," *American Anthropologist* 59 (1957): 473–486.

29. See Victor C. Uchendu, *The Igbo of Southeastern Nigeria* (New York: Holt, Rinehart and Winston, 1965), esp. chaps. 1, 9, and 10.

30. See Claude Meillassoux, ed., *L'esclavage en Afrique précoloniale* (Paris: François Maspero, 1975), p. 64; and Suzanne Miers and Igor I. Kopytoff, eds., *Slavery in Africa* (Madison: University of Wisconsin Press, 1977), pp. 40–48.

31. John J. Grace, "Slavery and Emancipation among the Mende in Sierra Leone, 1896–1928," in Miers and Kopytoff, *Slavery in Africa,* p. 419.

32. Ibid., p. 420.

33. *Freedom in Fulani Social Life: An Introspective Ethnography* (Chicago: University of Chicago Press, 1977), p. 117.

34. Ibid., pp. 127-128.

35. *Ethno-conchology: A Study of Primitive Money* (Washington, D.C.: U.S. National Museum Report, 1887, 1889), p. 331.

36. Catharine McClellan, "The Interrelations of Social Structure with Northern Tlingit Ceremonialism," *Southwestern Journal of Anthropology* 10 (1954): 94.

37. Philip Drucker gives a brief description in *Indians of the Northwest Coast* (Garden City, N.Y.: Natural History Press, 1963), pp. 131-143. For the classic account see Franz Boas, *The Social Organization and the Secret Societies of the Kwakiutl Indians* (Washington, D.C.: U.S. National Museum Report, 1895), pp. 311-338. The standard modern account is Helen S. Codere, *Fighting with Property: A Study of Kwakiutl Potlatching and Warfare, 1792-1930* (New York: J. J. Augustin, 1950). And for a dissenting view emphasizing the problem of cultural contact and change see Stuart Piddocke, "The Potlatch System of the Southern Kwakiutl: A New Perspective," in *Southwestern Journal of Anthropology* 21 (1965): 244-264.

38. N. Adriani and Albert C. Kruyt, *De Bare'e Sprekende Toradjas van Midden-Celebes* [The Bare'e-speaking Toradja of Central Celebes] (Amsterdam: Nood-Hollandsche Uitgevers Maatschappij, 1951), vol. 2, p. 96.

39. Ibid., p. 145.

40. Ibid., p. 146.

41. Ibid., p. 143.

42. See in particular Hsien Chin Hu, "The Chinese Concepts of Face," *American Anthropologist* 46 (1944): 45-64. The Chinese have two concepts of face: *mien-tzŭ*, which refers to status, power, and wealth; and *lien*, which refers to moral worth, honor, and integrity. To deny the latter is the greatest of insults.

43. E. G. Pulleyblank, "The Origins and Nature of Chattel Slavery in China," *Journal of the Economic and Social History of the Orient* 1 (1958): 204.

44. Ellen S. Unruh, "The Landowning Slave: A Korean Phenomenon," *Korean Journal* 16 (1976): 30.

45. Dang Trinh Ky, *Le nantissement des personnes dans l'ancien driot annamite* (Paris: Domat-Montchrestien, 1933), p. 45.

46. Ibid.

47. Dev Raj Chanana, *Slavery in Ancient India* (New Delhi: People's Publishing House, 1960), p. 54.

48. Ibid., p. 176.

49. Ibid., p. 69.

50. M. I. Finley, *The World of Odysseus* (London: Penguin Books, 1962), pp. 32-33, 125-128, 131-142.

51. M. I. Finley, "Was Greek Civilization Based on Slave Labour?" in M. I. Finley, ed., *Slavery in Classical Antiquity* (Cambridge: W. Heffer and Sons, 1960), pp. 53-72; Rodolfo Mondolfo, "The Greek Attitude to Manual Labor," *Past and Present* (1952), no. 2, pp. 1-5.

52. *The Hellenic World: A Sociological Analysis* (New York: Harper Torchbooks, 1969), pp. 42, 49-51. While Gouldner's work was received with hostility by many classicists, few would argue with the view that honor was a central preoccupa-

tion of ancient Greek culture. See, for example, H. D. F. Kitto, *The Greeks* (London: Penguin Books, 1951), pp. 245–248. On Greek competitiveness see E. R. Dodds, who describes ancient Greek culture as a "shame" culture in his book, *The Greeks and the Irrational* (Berkeley: University of California Press, 1951). Of special interest too is A. W. Adkins, *Merit and Responsibility: A Study in Greek Values* (Oxford: Oxford University Press, 1960).

53. "Greek Theories of Slavery from Homer to Aristotle," in Finley, *Slavery in Classical Antiquity,* p. 114.

54. *Ancient Slavery and the Ideal of Man* (Cambridge, Mass.: Harvard University Press, 1975), p. 8.

55. Ibid., p. 19.

56. "The Murder of Slaves in Attic Law," *Classical Philology* 32 (1937): 214–215.

57. Ibid.

58. Douglas M. MacDowell, *The Law in Classical Athens* (Ithaca, N.Y.: Cornell University Press, 1978), pp. 79–83. On the law of homicide see pp. 109–122; on hubris, pp. 129–132; and on the testimony of slaves, pp. 245–247. It is difficult to come to grips with the ancient Greek concept of hubris. However, insofar as it applies to slaves, we may note the case of a man called Ktesikles, who during a festival hit another man with his riding whip. A charge of impious action during a festival was brought against him. Ktesikles defended himself on the grounds that he was drunk at the time. However, the jury found against him, concluding that he had acted "from hybris, not from wine—*treating free men as slaves,*" and he was condemned to death. Cited in MacDowell, *Athenian Homicide Law* (Manchester: University of Manchester Press, 1963), p. 195, emphasis added. The jury's judgment is revealing in that it defines hubris as "treating free men as slaves"; hence if we are to believe that slaves could suffer hubris, we must conclude that a man could be condemned to death for treating a slave like a slave, which is an absurdity.

59. M. I. Finley, *Ancient Slavery and Modern Ideology* (New York: Viking Press, 1980), pp. 93–122.

60. Victor Ehrenberg, *The People of Aristophanes* (New York: Schocken Books, 1962), p. 165.

61. Ibid., p. 187.

62. Ehrenberg, *The People of Aristophanes,* p. 186.

63. Finley, *Ancient Slavery and Modern Ideology,* p. 107.

64. Finley's assessment of the available data on the role of slaves as governesses and nursemaids is important in itself. While I share his view that Vogt's use of these data to demonstrate humanity in master-slave relationships is misguided, Vogt's own review at least shows the importance of slaves in these roles. See Finley, *Ancient Slavery and Modern Ideology;* and Vogt, *Ancient Slavery and the Ideal of Man,* pp. 103–121.

65. I cite, with some trepidation, Philip E. Slater's analysis of the family in classical Greece, *The Glory of Hera: Greek Mythology and the Greek Family* (Boston: Beacon Press, 1968), esp. chap. 1. See also Kitto, *The Greeks,* pp. 219–236.

66. *Social Status and Legal Privilege in the Roman Empire* (Oxford: Oxford University Press, 1970).

67. Ibid., p. 234.

68. Ibid.

69. Ibid., p. 224.

70. Horace, *Epistle*, II, 156–157.

71. *Civilization and the Caesars* (Ithaca, N.Y.: Cornell University Press), p. 14.

72. Peter Garnsey, *Social Status and Legal Privilege in the Roman Empire* (Oxford: Oxford University Press, 1970), p. 1.

73. F. W. Walbank, "Polybius and Rome's Eastern Policy," *Journal of Roman Studies* 53 (1963): 1–4.

74. For a thorough analysis of changing Greek attitudes see Bettie Forte, *Rome and the Romans as Greeks Saw Them,* American Academy of Rome, Papers and Monographs 24 (1972), esp. pp. 9–12, 86–87, 219–225.

75. C. M. Bowra, "Melinno's Hymn to Rome," *Journal of Roman Studies* 47 (1957): 27–28.

76. H. Hill, "Dionysius of Halicarnassus and the Origins of Rome," *Journal of Roman Studies* 51 (1961): 89.

77. Ibid.

78. Nicholas Petrochitos, *Roman Attitudes to the Greeks* (Athens: University of Athens, 1974).

79. Ibid., pp. 40–41.

80. Ibid.

81. Ibid., p. 53.

82. I have discussed Roman universalism at some length in my *Ethnic Chauvinism: The Reactionary Impulse* (New York: Stein & Day, 1977), chap. 2.

83. On slaves as tutors in Roman comedy see Peter P. Spranger, *Historische Untersuchungen zu den Sklavenfiguren des Plautus und Terenz* (Wiesbaden: Akademie Mainz, 1960), pp. 90–91. On the significance of the servus callidus see C. Stace, "The Slaves of Plautus," *Greece and Rome* 15 (1968): 66. On the dangers of relying too heavily on this kind of data see Finley, *Ancient Slavery and Modern Ideology*, pp. 105–108.

84. Cited in R. H. Barrow, *Slavery in the Roman Empire* (London: Methuen & Co., 1928), p. 42.

85. Keith Hopkins, *Conquerors and Slaves* (Cambridge: Cambridge University Press, 1978), p. 112.

86. Cited in Finley, *Ancient Slavery and Modern Ideology*, p. 104.

87. See Abou A. M. Zied, "Honour and Shame among the Bedouins of Egypt," in Peristiany, *Honour and Shame*, pp. 245–259.

88. *Arabian Highlands* (Ithaca, N.Y.: Cornell University Press, 1952), p. 373.

89. *The Arab of the Desert: A Glimpse of Badawin Life in Kuwait and Saudi Arabia* (London: Allen & Unwin, 1951), p. 502.

90. "Slavery in Arabia" (Philadelphia: Institute for Israel and the Middle East of the Dropsie College for Hebrew and Cognate Learning, 1952), p. 11 (manuscript).

91. *Plantation Slavery on the East Coast of Africa* (New Haven: Yale University Press, 1977), p. 76.

92. Ibid., pp. 77–78.

93. Ibid., pp. 153–156, 182–200, 215–242.

94. See Bernard Lewis, *Race and Color in Islam* (New York: Harper Torchbooks, 1971). For a more sophisticated treatment of the problem of Islam and slav-

ery than that offered in his earlier work, see Frederick Cooper, "Islam and Cultural Hegemony: The Ideology of Slaveowners on the East African Coast," paper presented at the Conference on the Ideology of Slavery in Africa, York University, Toronto, April 3–4, 1980.

95. "Slaves, Fugitives, and Freedmen on the Kenya Coast, 1873–1907" (Ph.D. diss., Syracuse University, 1976), p. 110.

96. Ibid., p. 116.

97. Ibid., pp. 137–282; Cooper, *Plantation Slavery,* pp. 200–210.

98. *The World the Slaveholders Made* (New York: Vintage Books, 1971), p. 131.

99. *The Waning of the Old South Civilization, 1860-1880's* (Athens: University of Georgia Press, 1968), pp. 50–51.

100. James Boswell, *The Life of Samuel Johnson,* C. G. Osgood, ed. (New York: Charles Scribner's Sons, 1945), p. 353.

101. *Romanticism and Nationalism in the Old South* (New Haven: Yale University Press, 1949), pp. 213–216.

102. *The Militant South* (Boston: Beacon Press, 1964), pp. 34–35.

103. Ibid., p. 36.

104. Ibid., pp. 66–71.

105. Cited in ibid., pp. 66–67.

106. "The Southern Gentleman as He Saw Himself," in Willard Thorpe, ed., *A Southern Reader* (New York: Alfred A. Knopf, 1955), p. 250. See also the other selections in sec. 8 of this work.

107. Osterweis, *Romanticism and Nationalism,* p. 213.

108. Stanley Elkins, *Slavery: A Problem in American Institutional and Intellectual Life* (Chicago: University of Chicago Press, 1959), p. 82.

109. Orlando Patterson, *The Sociology of Slavery; Jamaica, 1655-1838* (Rutherford, N.J.: Fairleigh Dickinson University Press, 1969), chap. 6.

110. See Claude Meillassoux's discussion of these systems in the introduction to his *The Development of Indigenous Trade and Markets in West Africa* (London: Oxford University Press, 1971).

111. For the standard account see Joseph Vogt, "The Structure of Ancient Slave Wars," in his *Ancient Slavery and the Ideal of Man,* pp. 39–92.

112. On the revolt of the Zandj see A. Popovic, "Ali B. Muhammad et la révolte des esclaves à Basra" (Ph.D. diss., University of Paris, 1965).

113. On the early slave revolts of Jamaica see Orlando Patterson, "Slavery and Slave Revolts: A Sociohistorical Analysis of the First Maroon War, 1665–1740," *Social and Economic Studies* 19 (1970): 289–325. For another interpretation of the same revolts see Mavis C. Campbell, "Marronage in Jamaica, Its Origins in the Seventeenth Century," in Vera Rubin and Arthur Tuden, eds., *Comparative Perspectives on Slavery in New World Plantation Societies* (New York: New York Academy of Sciences, 1977), pp. 389–419. For a romantic interpretation of these revolts see Carey Robinson, *The Fighting Maroons* (Kingston, Jamaica: William Collins and Sangster, 1969). On Haiti see C. L. R. James, *The Black Jacobins* (New York: Vintage Books, 1963); Hubert Cole, *Christophe: King of Haiti* (London: Eyre & Spottiswoode, 1966); and Leslie F. Manigat, "The Relationship between Marronage and Slave Revolts and Revolution in St. Dominigue-Haiti" in Rubin and Tuden, *Comparative Perspectives on Slavery,* pp. 420–438. There is a large and growing literature on slave re-

volts and marronage in the New World. See in particular Richard Price, ed., *Maroon Societies*, ed. 2 (Baltimore: Johns Hopkins University Press, 1979). (The afterword and bibliography are particularly useful.) See also Eugene D. Genovese, "Rebelliousness and Docility in the Negro Slave," in his *Red and Black: Marxian Explorations in Southern and Afro-American History* (New York: Vintage Books, 1971), pp. 73–101; and his *From Rebellion to Revolution* (New York: Random House, 1981). See also Gerald W. Mullin, *Flight and Rebellion* (London: Oxford University Press, 1972).

114. See the very useful collection of papers on the Elkins thesis in Ann J. Lane, ed., *The Debate over Slavery: Stanley Elkins and His Critics* (Urbana: University of Illinois Press, 1971).

115. G. W. F. Hegel, *The Phenomenology of Mind* (London: Allen & Unwin, 1910, 1961), pp. 228–240. For references to the views of Eugene D. Genovese and David Brion Davis on this work see the Introduction, note 38. G. A. Kelly observes that "as a form of consciousness, lordship and bondage was continuously indispensable to Hegel's dialectical deduction of the formation of subjective mind and had occupied him from his earliest attempts to construct a system." Kelly, "Notes on Hegel's Lordship and Bondage," *Review of Metaphysics* 19 (1966): 781. See also Jean Hyppolite, *Genesis and Structure of Hegel's Phenomenology of Spirit*, trans. Samuel Cherniak and John Heckman (Evanston, Ill.: Northwestern University Press, 1974).

116. Hegel, *The Phenomenology of Mind*, p. 234.

117. *Introduction to the Reading of Hegel* (New York: Basic Books, 1969), p. 19. See also Aimé Patri, "Dialectique du maître et de l'esclave," *Le contrat social* 5 (1961).

118. Hegel, *The Phenomenology of Mind*, p. 237.

119. See in particular Karl Marx, *Economic and Philosophic Manuscripts of 1844* (Moscow: Foreign Languages Publishing House, 1961), pp. 142–170; and Herbert Marcuse, *Reason and Revolution* (New York: Humanities Press, 1954), p. 113.

120. Hegel, *The Phenomenology of Mind*, pp. 238–240.

121. It is interesting to read what a slave has to say on this matter. Solomon Northup not only cites numerous cases of masters basking in the degradation of their slaves, but gives a chilling instance of how the degradation and brutalization of the slave influenced the children of the master class. Northup's master's eldest son, a boy between ten and twelve years of age, took special delight in tormenting the dignified old slave Uncle Abram: "It is pitiable, sometimes, to see him chastising, for instance, the venerable Uncle Abram. He will call the old man to account, and if in his childish judgment it is necessary, sentence him to a certain number of lashes, which he proceeds to inflict with much gravity and deliberation. Mounted on his pony, he often rides into the field with his whip, playing the overseer, greatly to his father's delight." Solomon Northup, *Twelve Years a Slave* (Baton Rouge: Louisiana State University Press, 1968), p. 201.

122. For general accounts of the larger Caribbean systems see Gabriel Debien, *Les esclaves aux Antilles françaises, XVIIᵉ-XVIIIᵉ siècles* (Basse-Terre, Fort-de-France: Société d'histoire de la Guadaloupe et Société d'histoire de la Martinique, 1974); Patterson, *The Sociology of Slavery;* B. W. Higman, *Slave Population and Economy in Jamaica, 1807-1834* (Cambridge: Cambridge University Press, 1976); Jerome S. Handler and Frederick W. Lange, *Plantation Slavery in Barbados* (Cambridge, Mass.: Harvard University Press, 1978); Woodville K. Marshall, ed., *The*

Colthurst Journal: Journal of a Special Magistrate in the Islands of Barbados and St. Vincent, July 1835–September 1838 (Millwood, N.Y.: K.T.O. Press, 1977); Michael Craton, *Sinews of Empire* (Garden City, N.Y.: Doubleday, Anchor Books, 1974); and Richard S. Dunn, *Sugar and Slaves: The Rise of the Planter Class in the English West Indies, 1624–1713* (Chapel Hill: University of North Carolina Press, 1972).

There is as yet no study of the large-scale slave system of the Banda Islands. Indeed, even specialists are often not aware of the existence of slavery there. Yet the Banda slave systems were among the most advanced and destructive ever developed. The only relevant works I know are J. A. Van der Chijs, *De vestiging van het Nederlandsche gezag over de Banda-eilanden, 1599–1621* [The Imposition of Dutch Rule over the Banda Islands] (Batavia: Albrecht & Co., 1886); V. I. van de Wall, "Bijdrage tot de Geschiedenis der Perkeniers, 1621–1671," [Contribution to the History of the Perkeniers, 1621–1671] *Tijdschrift voor Indisch Taal-, Land-, en Volkenkunde* 74 (1934); Bruno Lasker, *Human Bondage in Southeast Asia* (Chapel Hill: University of North Carolina Press, 1950), pp. 33–34, 75–76; J. C. Van Leur, *Indonesian Trade and Society* (The Hague: W. van Hoeve, 1955), pp. 122–123, 141–144, 183, 208–209; and H. W. Ponder, *In Javanese Waters* (London: Seeley, Service & Co., 1944?), pp. 100–118.

123. This solution, however, was not available to the isolated master class of the Banda Islands. Even as the masters brutalized their slaves and regarded them as totally degraded objects, the slaves in turn held their dependent masters in utter contempt. Both groups struggled in an escalating social squalor of mutual degradation, resulting in what Lasker aptly calls "a weird exhibit in the museum of human folly" (p. 34).

124. Long before the present wave of slave studies emphasized this fact, it was recognized by G. G. Johnson in her neglected classic, *Ante-Bellum North Carolina: A Social History* (Chapel Hill: University of North Carolina Press, 1937), for example, p. 522. For more recent works see John Blasingame, *The Slave Community* (New York: Oxford University Press, 1972), pp. 184–216; E. D. Genovese, *Roll, Jordan, Roll* (New York: Pantheon, 1974), pp. 658–660; and Lawrence W. Levine, *Black Culture and Black Consciousness* (New York: Oxford University Press, 1978), pp. 121–135.

125. *The Confessions of St. Augustine,* trans. F. J. Sheed (Kansas City: Sheed, Andrews and McMeel, 1970), p. 56.

4. Enslavement of "Free" Persons

1. On the Tupinamba see Alfred Métraux, "The Tupinamba," in Julian H. Steward, ed., *Handbook of the South American Indians* (Washington, D.C.: Government Printing Office, 1948), vol. 3, pp. 118–126; on the Aztecs see Carlos Bosch Garcia, *La esclavitud prehispánica entre los Aztecas* (Mexico City: Colegio de Mexico, Centro de Estudios Históricos, 1944), chaps. 3 and 10.

2. Theda Perdue, *Slavery and the Evolution of Cherokee Society, 1540–1866* (Knoxville: University of Tennessee Press, 1979), chaps. 1 and 2; and U. P. Averkieva, *Slavery among the Indians of North America* (Moscow: U.S.S.R. Academy of Sciences, 1941), chap. 7.

3. Many ancient peoples other than the Carthaginians sacrificed their prisoners of war—for example, the Etruscans, early Greeks, insular Celts, Asiatic Gauls, Scythians, and Thracians. See Mars M. Westington, *Atrocities in Roman Warfare to 133 B.C.* (Chicago: University of Chicago Libraries, 1938), pp. 12–13, 118–119; and, more recently, Pierre Ducrey, *Le traitement des prisonniers de guerre dans la Grèce antique* (Paris: Editions E. De Boccard, 1968), pp. 204–206.

4. On Greek massacre see Ducrey, *Le traitement des prisonniers de guerre,* pp. 56–73, 117–130. See also W. Kendrick Pritchett, *Ancient Greek Military Practices* (Berkeley: University of California Press, 1971), pp. 71, 72, and 73. On Rome see Westington, *Atrocities in Roman Warfare,* passim. On human sacrifice in Rome after 225 B.C. see Robert E. A. Palmer, *Roman Religion and Roman Empire: Five Essays* (Philadelphia: University of Pennsylvania Press, 1974), pp. 154–171. I return to this subject in Chapter 8.

5. On the Nkundu see Gustave E. Hulstaert, *Le mariage de Nkundo,* Memoires de l'institut royal colonial belge, no. 8 (1938), pp. 334, 335–336. On the Luvale see C. M. N. White, "Clan, Chieftainship, and Slavery in Luvale Political Organization," *Africa* 27 (1957): 66.

6. Bernard J. Siegel, *Slavery during the Third Dynasty of Ur,* Memoirs of the American Anthropological Association, no. 66 (1947), p. 44.

7. Carl O. Williams, *Thraldom in Ancient Iceland* (Chicago: University of Chicago Press, 1937), p. 25.

8. Gerald W. Hartwig, "Changing Forms of Servitude among the Kerebe of Tanzania," in Suzanne Miers and Igor I. Kopytoff, eds., *Slavery in Africa* (Madison: University of Wisconsin Press, 1977), p. 270.

9. James H. Vaughan, "Mafakur: A Limbic Institution of the Margi," in Miers and Kopytoff, *Slavery in Africa,* p. 91.

10. A. G. B. Fisher and H. J. Fisher, *Slavery and Muslim Society in Africa* (London: C. Hurst & Co., 1970), pp. 34, 67.

11. See Maurice Keen, *The Laws of War in the Late Middle Ages* (London: Routledge & Kegan Paul, 1965), pp. 137, 156.

12. "Christian Captives at 'Hard Labor' in Algiers, Sixteenth to Eighteenth Centuries," *International Journal of African Historical Studies* 13 (1980): 618. See also Stephen Clissold, *The Barbary Slave* (London: Paul Elek, 1977), pp. 5, 14–15, 102–129, 137–148.

13. Siegel, for example, asserts the traditional view that a major source of slavery during the Third Dynasty of Ur was captives of war. *Slavery during the Third Dynasty of Ur,* p. 11.

14. Chou ku-Cheng, "On Chinese Slave Society," in Office of Historical Studies, *Selected Essays on Problems Concerning Periodization of the Slave System and Feudal System in Chinese History* (Peking: Joint Publishing Co., 1956), pp. 61–67. (In Chinese.)

15. See, for example, Kuo Mo-jo, "A Discussion on the Society of the Chou Dynasty," in Office of Historical Studies, *Selected Essays,* pp. 85–100. See also Kuo Pao-chun, "Description of Historical Facts on Various Slaves as Sacrifices in the Yin and Chou Dynasties," ibid., pp. 58–60; as well as Kuo Mo-jo's response, "Tu liao Chi Yin-Chou hsuan-jen Shih-shih" [My Comments on 'Description of Historical Facts of Various Slaves as Sacrifices in the Yin and Chou Dynasties']; ibid., pp. 54–58. (In Chinese.)

16. Tung Shu-yeh, "On the Issues of Periodization of Ancient Chinese History," in Office of Historical Studies, *Selected Essays,* pp. 131–161. (In Chinese.)

17. Chien Po-tsan, "On the Problems Concerning the Official and Private Slaves and Maids of the Western and Eastern Han Dynasties," in Office of Historical Studies, *Selected Essays,* pp. 388–418. (In Chinese.)

18. C. M. Wilbur, *Slavery in China during the Former Han Dynasty, 206 B.C.–A.D 25* (Chicago: Field Museum of Natural History, 1943).

19. Ibid., p. 96.

20. C. M. Wilbur, "Industrial Slavery in China during the Former Han Dynasty (206 B.C.–A.D. 25)," *Journal of Economic History* 30 (1943): 59.

21. E. G. Pulleyblank, "The Origins and Nature of Chattel Slavery in China," *Journal of Economic and Social History of the Orient* 1 (1958): 201, 205.

22. Wang Yi-T'ung, "Slaves and Other Comparable Social Groups during the Northern Dynasties (386–618)," *Harvard Journal of Asiatic Studies* 16 (1953): 302.

23. Ibid., pp. 302, 306–307.

24. *Slavery in the Ancient Near East* (Oxford: Oxford University Press, 1949), pp. 1–3.

25. V. V. Struve, "The Problem of the Genesis, Development, and Disintegration of the Slave Societies in the Ancient Orient," in I. M. Diakanoff, ed., *Ancient Mesopotamia* (Moscow: Nauka, 1969), esp. pp. 20, 23–24, 29.

26. I. M. Diakanoff, "The Commune in the Ancient East as Treated in the Works of Soviet Researchers," in Stephen P. Dunn and Ethel Dunn, eds., *Introduction to Soviet Ethnography* (London: Social Science Research Station, 1974), p. 519. Although Diakanoff asserts that the use of POWs in agriculture was dangerous and impractical in early Mesopotamia, he nonetheless calls this early period the "slave-owning system of production."

27. I. I. Semenov, "The Problem of the Socioeconomic Order of the Ancient Near East," in Dunn and Dunn, *Introduction to Soviet Ethnography,* p. 592. See also pp. 576–577.

28. "Prisoners of War in Early Mesopotamia," *Journal of Near Eastern Studies* 32 (1973): 72. See also pp. 90–93.

29. See, for example, his remarks on culture shock (ibid., p. 91).

30. M. Dandamayev, "Foreign Slaves on Estates of the Achaemenid Kings and Their Nobles," Proceedings of the 25th Congress of Orientalists, Moscow, 1960 (Moscow: n.p., 1963), p. 151.

31. Ducrey, *Le traitement des prisonniers de guerre.*

32. Ibid., pp. 54–55 and passim.

33. Ibid., chap. 3. Westington also made this distinction in his discussion of ancient Rome. See his *Atrocities in Roman Warfare,* chap. 7.

34. For an excellent treatment of this subject see Richard Elphick, *Kraal and Castle* (New Haven: Yale University Press, 1977), esp. pp. 180–181.

35. Pritchett, *Ancient Greek Military Practices,* p. 69.

36. Ibid., pp. 68, 70.

37. Westington, *Atrocities in Roman Warfare,* chap. 7.

38. *The Greeks* (London: Hutchinson, 1967), p. 139.

39. Ibid.

40. M. I. Finley, *Ancient Slavery and Modern Ideology* (New York: Viking Press, 1980), p. 72.

41. Ibid.

42. Sherburne F. Cook and Woodrow Borah, *Essays in Population History: Mexico and the Caribbean,* 2 vols. (Berkeley: University of California Press, 1971, 1974); Philip D. Curtin, "The Slave Trade and the Atlantic Basin: Intercontinental Perspectives," in Nathan Huggins, Martin Kilson, and Daniel Fox, eds., *Key Issues in the Afro-American Experience* (New York: Harcourt Brace Jovanovich, 1971); M. J. MacLeod, *Spanish Central America: A Socioeconomic History, 1520-1720* (Berkeley: University of California Press, 1973); C. O. Sauer, *The Early Spanish Main* (Cambridge: Cambridge University Press, 1966). Still helpful after fifty years is Ruth Kerns Barber, *Indian Labor in the Spanish Colonies* (Albuquerque: University of New Mexico Press, 1932), esp. chap. 7. Though highly journalistic in tone, there is much that is useful in L. R. Bailey, *Indian Slave Trade in the Southwest* (New York: Tower Publications, 1966). The most valuable and moving source, of course, is the classic work of Bartolemé de las Casas, *History of the Indies,* trans. and ed. Andrée Collard (New York: Harper & Row, 1971).

43. Kenneth R. Andrews, *The Spanish Caribbean: Trade and Plunder, 1530-1630* (New Haven: Yale University Press, 1978), pp. 6–13.

44. Ibid., p. 9.

45. Ibid., p. 19.

46. The origins of the Toradja slaves are buried in myth and obscurity. The Toradjas themselves claim that the slaves were originally descended from credit bondsmen, but N. Adriani and Albert C. Kruyt, the standard ethnographers, dismiss that explanation as improbable. However, their own speculation that the slaves were originally a conquered race is equally implausible. See Adriani and Kruyt, *De Bare'e Sprekende Toradjas van Midden-Celebes* [The Bare'e-speaking Toradja of Central Celebes] (Amsterdam: Nood-Hollandsche Uitgevers Maatschappij, 1950), vol. 1, pp. 137–140.

47. Raymond Firth, *Primitive Economics of the New Zealand Maori* (Wellington, N.Z.: R. E. Owen, Government Printer, 1959), p. 109.

48. See virtually all the case studies in Miers and Kopytoff, *Slavery in Africa;* and in Claude Meillassoux, ed., *L'esclavage en Afrique précoloniale* (Paris: François Maspero, 1975). On Dahomey see M. J. Herskovits, *Dahomey: An Ancient West African Kingdom* (New York: J. J. Augustin, 1938), vol. 1, p. 99. On Ashanti see Ivor Wilks, *Asante in the Nineteenth Century* (London: Cambridge University Press, 1975), pp. 83–85, 176–177, 679–680.

49. Averkieva, *Slavery among the Indians of North America,* pp. 82–92.

50. M. I. Finley, "The Black Sea and Danubian Regions and the Slave Trade in Antiquity," *Klio* 40 (1962): 56. See also William L. Westermann, *The Slave Systems of Greek and Roman Antiquity* (Philadelphia: American Philosophical Society, 1955), pp. 1–12. Greece of the Homeric period falls into my first group of societies. See M. I. Finley, *The World of Odysseus* (London: Penguin Books, 1962), pp. 61–62.

51. Keith Hopkins, *Conquerors and Slaves* (Cambridge: Cambridge University Press, 1978), pp. 102–106. I am not concerned here with the still controversial issue of the role of warfare in the emergence of large-scale slavery in ancient Rome, on which see Finley, *Ancient Slavery and Modern Ideology,* pp. 82–92.

52. Max Weber's assertion that "the final offensive wars of the second century . . . were in fact little more than slave raids" may have been putting the matter a little

too strongly. *The Agrarian Sociology of Ancient Civilizations* (London: New Left Books, 1976), p. 399. Warfare continued to provide slaves throughout the period of the empire, but, as William V. Harris has recently pointed out, "The relative importance of this source declined severely after the change of external policy which took place in the last years of Augustus' life." "Towards a Study of the Roman Slave Trade," in J. H. D'Arms and E. C. Kopff, eds., "The Seaborne Commerce of Ancient Rome: Studies in Archeology and History," in Memoirs of the American Academy in Rome, vol. 36 (1980), p. 122. See also Finley, *Ancient Slavery and Modern Ideology*, p. 128.

53. See Pierre Ducrey, *Le traitement des prisonniers de guerre*, chaps. 2B, 2C, and 3B.

54. The means of enslavement of the Africans brought to the New World still needs to be thoroughly explored. Of the Senegambian region Philip D. Curtin has written that "at least 80 per cent . . . were captives." *Economic Change in Precolonial Africa* (Madison: University of Wisconsin Press, 1975), p. 154. It would be wrong to assume that the same held for the other areas of West Africa throughout the period of the trade. A safer claim is that under the pressure of European demand the majority of the slaves shipped from Africa until the early decades of the eighteenth century were war captives. On the effect of demand for slaves by Europeans, see Karl Polanyi, *Dahomey and the Slave Trade* (Seattle: University of Washington Press, 1966). On Ashanti see the classic work of N. Walton Claridge, *A History of the Gold Coast and Ashanti* (ed. 1, 1915; reprint ed. London: Frank Cass & Co., 1964), esp. vol. 1, pt. 3. On Benin see Philip A. Igabafe, "Slavery and Emancipation in Benin, 1897–1945," *Journal of African History* 16 (1975): 409–429. See also James D. Graham, "The Slave Trade, Depopulation, and Human Sacrifice in Benin History," *Cahiers d'études africaines* 6 (1965): 317–334, for a dissenting, if rather forced, view. On the Yoruba see the standard work of J. F. Ade Ajayi and R. S. Smith, *Yoruba Warfare* (Ibadan: Cambridge University Press, 1964), esp. pt. 1. On Mauritius and the other Mascarene Islands see J. M. Filliot, *La traité des esclaves vers les Mascareignes au XVIII siècle* (Paris: Orstom, 1974).

55. Colin A. Palmer writes: "It is generally acknowledged that the mortality rate of the slaves in Spanish America during the sixteenth and seventeenth centuries was quite high. As a result, the colonies depended on the slave trade to replenish their supply of slaves, rather than upon internal reproduction." *Slaves of the White God: Blacks in Mexico, 1570–1650* (Cambridge, Mass.: Harvard University Press, 1976), p. 27. See also Andrews, *The Spanish Caribbean*, pp. 31–37.

56. Robert W. Fogel and Stanley L. Engerman, *Time on the Cross: The Economics of American Negro Slavery* (Boston: Little, Brown, 1974), pp. 13–29.

57. Ibid., p. 23.

58. Curtin, *Economic Change in Precolonial Africa*, p. 154.

59. See Mungo Park, *Travels in the Interior Districts of Africa* (London: W. Bulmer, 1799) esp. chap. 12.

60. See note 54 above.

61. Charles Verlinden, *L'esclavage dans l'Europe médiévale* (Bruges: De Tempel, 1955), vol. 1, pp. 62–65, 251–258, 403–418, 548–561, 615–629.

62. Ibid., vol. 1, bk. 2, chaps. 1 and 3.

63. Ibid., vol. 2, passim.

64. On early Islam see Paul G. Forand, "The Development of Military Slavery under the Abbasid Caliphs of the Ninth Century A.D. (Third Century A.H.) with Special Reference to the Reigns of Mu'Tasim and Mu'Tadid" (Ph.D. diss., Princeton University, 1961), chap. 2. On Muslim Spain see Verlinden, *L'esclavage dans l'Europe médiévale*, vol. 1. chap. 3. On Muslim Africa see Fisher and Fisher, *Slavery and Muslim Society in Africa*, pp. 14–36; also the articles in Meillassoux, *L'esclavage en Afrique précoloniale.*

65. The relation of manumission to the Islamic emphasis on external sources of supply and hence prisoners of war will be discussed in Chapter 8.

66. Henry A. Ormerod, *Piracy in the Ancient World* (Liverpool: University Press of Liverpool, 1924), p. 67.

67. "From Freedom to Slavery," in Bayerische Akademie der Wissenschaften, *Gesellschaftsklassen im Alten Zweiströmland und in den angrenzenden Gebieten* 18 (Munich, 1972), p. 84.

68. Ormerod, *Piracy in the Ancient World*, chap. 1. My thinking on piracy in the Mediterranean is based mainly on this work. On piracy there during modern times see Clissold, *The Barbary Slaves*, esp. chap. 4.

69. Ormerod, *Piracy in the Ancient World*, chap. 6.

70. Ibid., chap. 7. Finley cautions us not to overemphasize piracy as a source of slaves in the ancient world. See his "The Black Sea and Danubian Regions and the Slave Trade in Antiquity," pp. 57–58. Harris also de-emphasizes kidnapping. See his "Towards a Study of the Roman Slave Trade," p. 124. Several scholars, however, give greater weight to kidnapping. Westermann regarded it as the major means of enslavement in the Hellenistic world. See his *The Slave Systems of Greek and Roman Antiquity*, pp. 28–29. Peter P. Spranger finds that kidnapping looms large as a source of slaves in the plays of Plautus, where a common motif for a happy ending in the comedies was the successful parental search for a kidnapped child. See his *Historische Untersuchungen zu den Sklavenfiguren des Plautus und Terenz* (Wiesbaden: Akademie Mainz, 1961), pp. 70–72. On the Roman republic see also Westermann, *The Slave Systems of Greek and Roman Antiquity*, pp. 63–69, and for slavery under the empire pp. 85, 126. John Crook has observed that the Augustan peace, far from stamping out *suppressio* (the Roman term for kidnapping) may well have encouraged it. See his *Law and Life of Rome* (Ithaca, N.Y.: Cornell University Press, 1967), p. 59. According to Marc Bloch, kidnapping by soldiers and professional bandits was a major source of slaves in the fourth century. See *Slavery and Serfdom in the Middle Ages: Selected Essays*, trans. William R. Beer (Berkeley: University of California Press, 1975), p. 2.

71. On Viking raids and kidnapping see Erik I. Bromberg, "Wales and the Medieval Slave Trade," *Speculum* 17 (1942): 263–269; P. H. Sawyer, *The Age of the Vikings* (London: Edward Arnold, 1962), chap. 6; Gwyn Jones, *A History of the Vikings* (London: Oxford University Press, 1968), sec. 3; Peter Foote and David M. Wilson, *The Viking Achievement* (London: Sidgwick & Jackson, 1970), chap. 6, esp. pp. 229–230. On thirteenth- and fourteenth-century Spain see Verlinden, *L'esclavage dans l'Europe médiévale*, vol. 1, pp. 258–268. Since all members of an enemy population were considered fair game for enslavement, the distinction between POWs and kidnapped was especially thin during the Middle Ages and even during early modern times. See, for example, Vicente Graullera Sanz, *La esclavitud en Va-*

lencia en los siglos XVI y XVII (Valencia: Instituto Valenciano de Estudios Históricos, 1978), pp. 41–45.

72. Verlinden, *L'esclavage dans l'Europe médiévale,* vol. 2, bk. 1, chap. 3A; bk. 2, chaps. 1–2.

73. Sidney M. Greenfield, "Madeira and the Beginnings of New World Sugar Cane Cultivation and Plantation Slavery: A Study in Institution Building," in Vera Rubin and Arthur Tuden, eds., *Comparative Perspectives on Slavery in New World Plantation Societies* (New York: New York Academy of Sciences, 1977), pp. 536–552; idem, "Plantations, Sugar Cane, and Slavery," in Michael Craton, ed., *Roots and Branches: Current Directions in Slave Studies, Historical Reflections* 6 (1979): 85–119.

74. Friedman, "Christian Captives," pp. 616–632; Norman R. Bennett, "Christian and Negro Slavery in Eighteenth-Century North Africa," *Journal of African History* 1 (1960): 65–82; and Clissold, *The Barbary Slaves,* esp. chaps. 1–4.

75. To repopulate their countryside, the Thais organized slave raids against the Khas and other weaker peoples. Slaves were also bought from professional Chinese raiders. See Andrew Turton, "Thai Institutions of Slavery," in James L. Watson, ed., *Asian and African Systems of Slavery* (Oxford: Basil Blackwell, 1980), pp. 254–258. Bruno Lasker lists "raids both by pirates and by professional traders" as one of the four main forms of enslavement in Southeast Asia; see his *Human Bondage in Southeast Asia* (Chapel Hill: University of North Carolina Press, 1950), pp. 16–21.

76. Wilbur, *Slavery in China,* pp. 93, 217–218.

77. Hayakawa Jirō, "The Position and Significance of the Slave System after the Taika Restoration," in Rekishi Kagaku Kyōgikai, ed., *Kodai Kokka To Doreisei* [Ancient State and Slave Systems] (Tokyo: Azekura Shobō, 1972), pp. 92–108. (In Japanese.)

78. See Frederick Cooper, *Plantation Slavery on the East Coast of Africa* (New Haven: Yale University Press, 1977), esp. pp. 114–136. Cooper argues that Arab masters did not themselves engage in direct trading until the late nineteenth century. Before this time agents for the Arab and Swahili owners raided and kidnapped slaves in the interior, disrupting traditional social orders in a way that further increased the supply of slaves. For a more detailed analysis see Rodger F. Morton, "Slaves, Fugitives, and Freedmen on the Kenya Coast, 1873–1907" (Ph.D. diss., Syracuse University, 1976), chap. 1.

The Arabs were established along the east coast of Africa by the tenth century, and a contemporary account indicates that Arab traders from Oman were leading raids into Africa and kidnapping adults and children. For a history of the trade in slaves on the coast from ancient times see R. W. Beachey, *The Slave Trade of Eastern Africa* (New York: Harper & Row, 1976), esp. chaps. 1 and 8. Joseph E. Harris states explicitly that most slaves were taken not in genuine wars, but in raids—some organized, some indiscriminate—conducted for this purpose. See his *The African Presence in Asia* (Evanston, Ill.: Northwestern University Press, 1971), pp. 10–15. All the evidence from the interior of Africa suggests that most slaves were originally kidnapped or taken in small raids. This was true, for example, of the Luvale of Northern Rhodesia, on which see White, "Clan, Chieftainship, and Slavery in Luvale Political Organization," pp. 58–75.

79. On the Portuguese slave trade in its African colonies during the second half

of the nineteenth century see James Duffy, *A Question of Slavery* (Oxford: Clarendon Press, 1967). The American journalist Henry W. Nevinson gives a vivid contemporary account of the kidnapping of Africans by Portuguese traders in *A Modern Slavery* (New York: Schocken Books, 1968). See also William G. Clarence-Smith, *Slaves, Peasants, and Capitalists in Southern Angola, 1840-1926* (Cambridge: Cambridge University Press, 1979), pp. 64, 66, 68. On the South African slave trade see Anna J. Böeseken, *Slaves and Free Blacks at the Cape, 1658-1700* (Cape Town: Tafelberg Publishers, 1977), pp. 1-2, 61-76; and James C. Armstrong, "The Slaves, 1652-1795," in Richard Elphick and Hermann Giliomee, eds., *The Shaping of South African Society, 1652-1820* (London: Longmans, 1979), pp. 76-84.

80. On Visigothic Spain see Verlinden, *L'esclavage dans l'Europe médiévale*, vol. 1, pp. 78-79; on Spain between the thirteenth and fifteenth centuries see ibid., pp. 277-278, 426; and on sixteenth- and seventeenth-century Valencia see Sanz, *La esclavitud en Valencia*, pp. 106-113.

81. Wilbur, *Slavery in China*, p. 39; Wang Yi-T'ung, "Slaves and Other Comparable Social Groups," pp. 311-312, 317.

82. Wang Yi-T'ung, "Slaves and Other Comparable Social Groups," p. 307.

83. Mary Smith, *Baba of Karo* (London: Faber & Faber, 1954), p. 262. The statement is attributed to Mai-Sudan.

84. One of the most blatant such cases is that of the Damel of Kayor, who attempted to reduce his subjects to slavery. See Claude Meillassoux, introduction to his edition of *The Development of Indigenous Trade and Markets in West Africa* (London: Oxford University Press, 1971), pp. 56-57.

85. Young women, especially in Perak, were raided in districts where the village chief was weak—for example, Kampar, Sungkei, and Pulan Tiga during the nineteenth century. These raids usually took place on the occasion of a birth or marriage of a member of the raja's family. Ostensibly they were to become attendants and wards at court, but many unmarried girls ended up as slave prostitutes. The husbands of those who were married became slaves of the raja. See W. E. Maxwell, "The Law Relating to Slavery among the Malays," *Journal of the Straits Branch of the Royal Asiatic Society* (1890): 252-253; and R. O. Winstedt, *The Malays: A Cultural History* (New York: Philosophical Library, 1950), p. 54.

86. Lasker, *Human Bondage in Southeast Asia*, p. 34. See also H. W. Ponder, *In Javanese Waters* (London: Seeley, Service & Co., 1944?), pp. 105-117.

87. Philip D. Curtin, *The Atlantic Slave Trade: A Census* (Madison: University of Wisconsin Press, 1969), table 77, p. 268.

88. Curtin, *Economic Change in Precolonial Africa*, pp. 156-168.

89. Henry A. Gemery and Jan S. Hogendorn, "Elasticity of Slave Labor Supply and the Development of Slave Economies in the British Caribbean: The Seventeenth Century Experience," in Rubin and Tuden, *Comparative Perspectives on Slavery*, pp. 72-83.

90. By the early seventeenth century "panyarning" or kidnapping was well established on the west coast of Africa. The European traders of course denied this, claiming that most Africans were taken "legally," meaning as prisoners of war or bought captives. See Daniel P. Mannix and Malcolm Cowley, *Black Cargoes* (London: Longmans, 1963), pp. 42-45. For an account by a participant see Daryll Forde, ed., *Efik Traders of Old Calabar* (London: Oxford University Press, 1956), pp. 27-65.

For accounts by some of the victims see Philip D. Curtin, ed., *Africa Remembered* (Madison: University of Wisconsin Press, 1967). According to Mahdi Adamu, kidnapping was second to true POWs as the source of slaves taken in the central Sudan; but apart from the fact that his evidence is weak, the area to which he refers contributed only a small fraction of the slaves for the Atlantic slave trades. See Adamu, "The Delivery of Slaves from the Central Sudan to the Bight of Benin in the Eighteenth and Nineteenth Centuries," in Henry A. Gemery and Jan S. Hogendorn, eds., *The Uncommon Market: Essays in the Economic History of the Atlantic Slave Trade* (New York: Academic Press, 1979), esp. pp. 166–172.

91. In addition to the references given in note 79 above see Joseph C. Miller, "Some Aspects of the Commercial Organization of Slaving at Luanda, Angola: 1760–1830," in Gemery and Hogendorn, *The Uncommon Market,* pp. 77–106. See also Herbert S. Klein, *The Middle Passage: Comparative Studies in the Atlantic Slave Trade* (Princeton, N. J.: Princeton University Press, 1978), pp. 37–42.

92. J. D. Fage, *A History of West Africa* (Cambridge: Cambridge University Press, 1969), p. 94.

93. In addition to works cited previously, see the four papers in part one of Stanley L. Engerman and Eugene D. Genovese, eds., *Race and Slavery in the Western Hemisphere; Quantitative Studies* (Princeton, N.J.: Princeton University Press, 1975); Curtin, *The Atlantic Slave Trade;* Walter Rodney, *A History of the Upper Guinea Coast, 1545–1800* (Oxford: Clarendon Press, 1970); Michael Mason, "Population Density and 'Slave Raiding': The Case of the Middle Belt of Nigeria," *Journal of African History* 10 (1969): 551–564; and the chapters by Gemery and Hogendorn as well as Lovejoy and Hogendorn in Gemery and Hogendorn, *The Uncommon Market.*

94. See J. F. Ade Ajayı and Michael Crowder, eds., *A History of West Africa* (London: Longmans, 1971), chaps. 10–12; Claridge, *A History of the Gold Coast and Ashanti,* vol. 1, pt. 3; and Polanyi, *Dahomey and the Slave Trade.*

95. Forde, *Efik Traders of Old Calabar,* pp. 27–65. See also G. I. Jones, *The Trading States of the Oil Rivers: A Study of Political Development in Eastern Nigeria* (London: Oxford University Press, 1963), pp. 33–35, 89–95.

96. K. Madhu Panikkar, *The Serpent and the Crescent* (Bombay: Asia Publishing House, 1963), chap. 10.

97. Much has been written on the Yoruba presence in Cuba during the nineteenth century. The numbers of these "lucumi" slaves, as they were called, rose from 8 percent of the slaves on the sugar and coffee plantations during the period 1800–1820 to 34.5 percent (the single largest group of Africans) during 1850–1870. See Manuel Moreno Fraginals, "Africa in Cuba: A Quantitative Analysis of the African Population in the Island of Cuba," in Rubin and Tuden, *Comparative Perspectives on Slavery,* pp. 189–191. See also Fernando Ortiz, *La lampa afro-cubano: Los negros esclavos* (Havana: Ruis, 1916), pp. 30–48; and W. R. Bascom, "The Yoruba in Cuba," *Nigeria* 39 (1950):15–24.

98. Klein, *The Middle Passage,* chaps. 2–4.

99. Hartwig, "Changing Forms of Servitude among the Kerebe of Tanzania," p. 270.

100. See Victor C. Uchendu, "Slaves and Slavery in Igboland, Nigeria," in Miers and Kopytoff, *Slavery in Africa,* p. 125.

101. Finley, *The World of Odysseus,* p. 61.

102. In the great majority of the most primitive societies, female captives were rapidly absorbed as wives, although there was variation even at this level in their treatment. Nieboer's claim that female captives ceased to be slaves as soon as they were married cannot be supported. The Tupinamba, for example, made wives of the captives they spared, but this did not negate the fact that they were slaves and could eventually be killed and eaten. See Métraux, "The Tupinamba," p. 112. Among the Cubeo, wives who were originally taken as captives (though highly valued in view of the crucial role of women in their economy) were nonetheless considered slaves. See Irving Goldman, "Tribes of the Uaupes-Caqueta Region," in Steward, *Handbook of the South American Indians,* vol. 3, p. 786; see also Goldman, *The Cubeo: Indians of the Northwestern Amazon* (Urbana: University of Illinois Press, 1963), Illinois Studies in Anthropology, no. 2, esp. pp. 53–58. The Trumai Indians of Brazil went to war mainly to capture women and thereby bolster their population, on which see R. F. Murphy and Buell Quair, *The Trumai Indians of Brazil* (New York: J. J. Augustin, 1955), p. 15. The classic instance of the systematic capture of women for marriage is the pre-Columbian Caribs of the Caribbean. Although the children of these women were all free, the women themselves were regarded as slaves and were distinguished from freeborn women by the fact that only the latter wore anklets. See Irving Rouse, "The Caribs," in Steward, *Handbook of the South American Indians,* vol. 4, pp. 553–556. For a vivid description of a slave raid among the Hausa with its emphasis on female captives see Smith, *Baba of Karo,* pp. 68–82.

103. Pierre Ducrey, *Le traitement des prisonniers de guerre,* p. 112.

104. *Atrocities in Roman Warfare,* p. 125.

105. William V. Harris claims that the Roman slave population was lopsidedly male, although many factors other than warfare would account for this. See his "Towards a Study of the Roman Slave Trade," pp. 119–120.

106. See Speros Vryonis, Jr., "Byzantine and Turkish Societies and Their Sources of Manpower," in V. J. Parry and M. E. Yapp, eds., *War, Technology, and Society in the Middle East* (London: Oxford University Press, 1975), pp. 125–152; C. E. Bosworth, "Recruitment, Muster, and Review in Medieval Islamic Armies," ibid., pp. 59–77; and David Ayalon, "The European-Asiatic Steppe: A Major Reservoir of Power for the Islamic World," Proceedings of the 25th Congress of Orientalists, Moscow, 1960 (Moscow: n.p., 1963), pp. 47–52.

107. In most Islamic societies slaves were used as concubines or household help. See Reuben Levy, *The Sociology of Islam* (Cambridge: Cambridge University Press, 1931–1933), pp. 105–127; and R. Brunschvig, "Abd," *Encyclopedia of Islam,* ed. 2 (Leiden: E. J. Brill, 1961), vol. 1. For a typical case see Gabriel Baer, "Slavery in Nineteenth Century Egypt," *Journal of African History* 8 (1967): 417–441. Although domestic labor and concubinage were the main uses of female slaves, they were rarely the only ones, a point emphasized by Baer. One area of the modern Islamic world where male slaves may have existed in proportionately greater numbers (though never more than women) was eighteenth-century North Africa, especially Algiers, where most slaves were Christians taken captive by pirates. For a very good discussion of these captives and their fate see Friedman, "Christian Captives," pp. 616–632. See also Bennett, "Christian and Negro Slavery in Eighteenth Century North Africa," pp. 65–82.

108. 'Abd al-Muhsin Bakīr, *Slavery in Pharaonic Egypt* (Cairo: L'institut français d'archéologie orientale, 1952), p. 65; and Gelb, "Prisoners of War in Early Mesopotamia," p. 72. This shift in favor of male captives does not mean, however, that male slaves ever came to outnumber females. One conclusion that may be drawn from Gelb's own data is that even after male POWs were taken in greater numbers than female, only women were certain to be enslaved; men met a variety of fates.

109. J. A. Lencman, *Die Sklaverei im mykenischen and homerischen Griechenland* (Wiesbaden: Franz Steiner Verlag, 1966), pp. 256-259.

110. K. Nwachukwu-Ogedengbe, "Slavery in Nineteenth Century Aboh (Nigeria)," in Miers and Kopytoff, *Slavery in Africa*, pp. 137-139.

111. Svend E. Holsoe, "Slavery and Economic Response among the Vai," in Miers and Kopytoff, *Slavery in Africa*, pp. 287-300.

112. Ralph A. Austen, "Slavery among Coastal Middlemen: The Duala of the Cameroon," in Miers and Kopytoff, *Slavery in Africa*, pp. 305-329.

113. See the narratives in Curtin, *Africa Remembered.* It is significant that the one period of the African slave trade in which women and children outnumbered adult males was between 1816 and 1818, among Africans transported to Cuba. Herbert S. Klein, who reports this unusual development, finds it difficult to explain. The comparative data suggest that the real reason for the change was that these Africans were prisoners of genuine warfare rather than victims of organized kidnappers. See Klein, *The Middle Passage*, pp. 222-224.

114. *The Economy of the Roman Empire: Quantitative Studies* (Cambridge: Cambridge University Press, 1974), pp. 5-6. A review of newly discovered and traditional evidence suggests that the state's interest in the grain trade "extended only to fulfilling the needs of the dole and of government personnel." Lionel Casson, "The Role of the State in Rome's Grain Trade," in D'Arms and Kopff, "The Seaborne Commerce of Ancient Rome," pp. 21-29.

115. Cited in Ormerod, *Piracy in the Ancient World*, p. 207.

116. Forand, "The Development of Military Slavery," chap. 2.

117. Ibid., p. 18.

118. V. L. Ménage, "Devshirme," *Encyclopedia of Islam*, ed. 2 (Leiden: E. J. Brill, 1961) vol. 2, pp. 210-213; Speros Vryonis, Jr., "Isidore Glabas and the Turkish Devshirme," *Speculum* 31 (1956): 433-443; and for the most exhaustive study, Basilike D. Papoulia, *Ursprung und Wesen der 'Knabenlese' im osmanischen Reich* (Munich: R. Oldenbourg, 1963).

119. Fisher and Fisher, *Slavery and Muslim Society in Africa*, pp. 149-153.

120. Wilks, *Asante in the Nineteenth Century*, pp. 63-70. On the Oyo see I. A. Akinjogbin, "The Expansion of Oyo and the Rise of Dahomey, 1600-1800," in Ajayi and Crowder, *History of West Africa*, chap. 10.

121. Fisher and Fisher, *Slavery and Muslim Society in Africa*, p. 151.

122. Ibid., p. 150.

123. Polanyi, *Dahomey and the Slave Trade*, p. 24; Akinjogbin, "The Expansion of Oyo."

124. William E. Henthorn, *Korea: The Mongol Invasions* (Leiden: E. J. Brill, 1963), pp. 212-213.

125. Garcia, *La esclavitud prehispánica entre los Aztecas*, pp. 35-38.

126. Cited in William Y. Adams, *Nubia: Corridor to Africa* (Princeton, N.J.: Princeton University Press, 1977), pp. 231–232, 451.

127. Fisher and Fisher, *Slavery and Muslim Society in Africa*, p. 153.

128. Robert S. Rattray, *Ashanti Law and Constitution* (Oxford: Clarendon Press, 1929), pp. 47–55.

129. On debt as a source of slavery among the less advanced peoples such as the Batak, the tribes of the Podang Highlands, and the interior tribes of Nias, as well as other tribes such as the Dyaks, the Buginese, the Makassarese, and those of the Lesser Sunda Islands, see G. A. Wilken, *Handleiding voor de vergelijkende volkenkunde van Nederlandsch-Indië* [Manual for the Comparative Ethnology of the Netherlands East Indies], ed. C. M. Pleyte (Leiden: E. J. Brill, 1893), pp. 421–430.

130. Debt-bondage was of course forbidden in Islamic law, but that law was neglected by the Arab rulers of the area, who simply continued the practice of the former Hindu rulers. See W. E. Maxwell, "The Law Relating to Slavery," pp. 249–256; and Winstedt, *The Malays*, pp. 54–55.

131. Mendelsohn, *Slavery in the Ancient Near East*, pp. 14–19, 23–24; and Siegel, *Slavery in the Third Dynasty of Ur*, pp. 11–12. So important was debt as a source of slavery in early Mesopotamia that I. I. Semenov coined the term "debt-slave mode of production relationship" to define these systems. He was certainly aware of the difficulties involved, but added that "we must reconcile ourselves to this." Unfortunately, he made no attempt to distinguish between debt-bondsmen and genuine slaves. See Semenov, "The Problem of the Socioeconomic Order of the Ancient Near East," esp. pp. 588–589, 598–604.

132. Although apparently against strict religious law, debt was the main source of fellow Hebrew slaves for Hebrew masters in both biblical and talmudic times (more so for males than for females). See "Slavery," in *The Jewish Encyclopedia*, pp. 403–404; "Slavery," in *Encyclopedia Judaica*, pp. 1656–58. A few writers deny the importance of debt as a source of Hebrew slavery, most conspicuously J. Kahana Kagan in *The Three Great Systems of Jurisprudence* (London: Stevens & Sons, 1955), pp. 54–56. This is, however, a rather polemical work, concerned largely with an unstructured comparison of laws without reference to their social setting.

133. In Korea the influence of debt was largely indirect. Most persons became slaves to avoid the ruinous tax and corvée labor demanded by the government. See Takashi Hatada, *A History of Korea* (Santa Barbara, Calif.: ABC-Clio Press, 1969), pp. 58–67. The decline of most commoners to slavery in Kùmhwa County in the late seventeenth century was due "probably [to] impoverishment." See Susan S. Shin, "The Social Structure of Kùmhwa County in the Late Seventeenth Century," in *Occasional Papers on Korea* 1 (1974): 9–35.

134. Because of the high interest rate and the fact that the debt-slave's service often could not repay even the interest, most debt-slavery became perpetual—hence genuine slavery. See Lasker, *Human Bondage in Southeast Asia*, pp. 150–154; and Turton, "Thai Institutions of Slavery," pp. 262–272.

135. Roberta A. Dunbar, "Slavery and the Evolution of Nineteenth Century Damagaram," in Miers and Kopytoff, *Slavery in Africa*, p. 162.

136. M. I. Finley, "La servitude pour dettes," *Revue historique de droit français et étranger* 43, ser. 4, pp. 159–184.

137. Douglas M. MacDowell, *The Law in Classical Athens* (Ithaca, N.Y.: Cornell University Press, 1978), pp. 79–80; and Westermann, *The Slave Systems of*

Greek and Roman Antiquity, pp. 4–5, 30, 44. On Hellenistic Egypt see Westermann, pp. 50–51; also Iza Biezunska-Malowist, *L'esclavage dans l'Egypte gréco-romaine, première partie: Période ptolémaïque* (Warsaw: Polska Akademia Nauk, 1974), vol. 1, pp. 29–49. As Biezunska-Malowist demonstrates, the issue of debt-slavery in Hellenistic Egypt remains extremely controversial.

138. W. W. Buckland, *The Roman Law of Slavery* (Cambridge: Cambridge University Press, 1908), p. 402.

139. Crook, *Law and Life of Rome*, pp. 170–178.

140. Dang Trinh Ky, *Le nantissement des personnes dans l'ancien droit annamite* (Paris: Domat-Montchrestien, 1933), pp. 18–20; and Wilbur, *Slavery in China*, pp. 85–90.

141. Wilbur, *Slavery in China*; and Pulleyblank, "The Origins and Nature of Chattel Slavery in China," pp. 206–208.

142. On classical Greece see Robert Schlaifer, "Greek Theories of Slavery from Homer to Aristotle," in M. I. Finley, ed., *Slavery in Classical Antiquity* (Cambridge: W. Heffer and Sons, 1960), p. 107; also MacDowell, *The Law in Classical Athens*, p. 256. On Ptolemaic Egypt see Biezunska-Malowist, *L'esclavage dans l'Egypte gréco-romaine*, vol. 1, pp. 29–49. In contrast to Rome, penal slaves were not used in the mines in Ptolemaic Egypt; see Biezunska-Malowist, p. 81.

143. Buckland, *The Roman Law of Slavery*, p. 403.

144. Ibid., pp. 403–412; Crook, *Law and Life of Rome*, pp. 272–273; and Harris, "Towards a Study of the Roman Slave Trade," p. 124.

145. Tran-Van Trai, *La famille patriarcale annamite* (Paris: P. Lapagesse, 1942), pp. 17–18.

146. Enslavement as a punishment for crime was more common in earlier times. Among the laws believed established by Ki-ja in the twelfth century B.C. was one that made enslavement the punishment for those who committed theft or adultery. See Cornelius Osgood, *The Koreans and Their Culture* (New York: Ronald Press, 1951), p. 216. During the period of the Three Kingdoms (57 B.C. to A.D. 660) the families of persons guilty of treason were enslaved. Other crimes so punished included robbery and the killing of valuable domestic animals. The number of crimes for which enslavement was the penalty decreased over the centuries; by early Yi, persons were enslaved only for armed robbery and treason.

147. Jirō, "The Position and Significance of the Slave System," pp. 92–108.

148. Pulleyblank, "The Origins and Nature of Chattel Slavery in China," pp. 204–206.

149. Ibid., pp. 209–211. Wilbur, *Slavery in China*, pp. 72–85. See also Ma Cheng-feng, *Chinese Economic History* (Shanghai: Commercial Publishing Co., 1937), vol. 2, pp. 229–232. (In Chinese.)

150. J. Thorsten Sellin, *Slavery and the Penal System* (New York: Elselvier, 1976), chaps. 3–9.

151. "Der Ursprung des Strafrechts aus dem Stande der Unfreien," cited in Sellin, *Slavery and the Penal System*, p. viii.

152. Ibid., chaps. 4–7.

153. Ibid., chap. 9.

154. J. S. Harris, "Some Aspects of Slavery in Southeastern Nigeria," *Journal of Negro History* 27 (1942): 40–41.

155. MacDowell, *The Law in Classical Athens*, p. 256.

156. Carol P. MacCormack, "Wono: Institutionalized Dependency in Sherbro Descent Groups," in Miers and Kopytoff, *Slavery in Africa*, p. 195.

157. Mannix and Cowley, *Black Cargoes*, pp. 40–41.

158. Sellin, *Slavery and the Penal System*, pp. 43–44, 65–69.

159. Bernd Baldus, "Responses to Dependence in a Servile Group," in Miers and Kopytoff, *Slavery in Africa*, pp. 439–440.

160. H. D. Lamson, *Social Pathology in China* (Shanghai: Commercial Publishing Co., 1934), pp. 562–566. For a recent study of the differences in the treatment of boys and girls and the institution of child slavery in modern pre-Communist China see James L. Watson, "Transactions in People: The Chinese Market in Slaves, Servants, and Heirs," in his *Asian and African Systems of Slavery*, pp. 223–250.

161. Mendelsohn, *Slavery in the Ancient Near East*, pp. 5–6.

162. Harris, "Towards a Study of the Roman Slave Trade," pp. 123–124. See also Westermann, *The Slave Systems of Greek and Roman Antiquity*, p. 86, and, on the Greek city-states, p. 6. See Biezunska-Malowist, *L'esclavage dans l'Egypte gréco-romaine*, vol. 1, pp. 49–50, on Hellenistic Egypt, and on Roman Egypt, vol. 2 (1977), pp. 21–26; also R. H. Barrow, *Slavery in the Roman Empire* (London: Methuen & Co., 1928), pp. 8–9.

163. On infanticide in general see Maria W. Piers, *Infanticide* (New York: W. W. Norton, 1978). On primitive female infanticide see W. T. Divale and Marvin Harris, "Population, Warfare, and the Male Supremacist Complex," *American Anthropologist* 78 (1976): 521–538. See the ensuing controversy in the comments by L. A. Hirschfeld, James Howe, and Bruce Levin, and by Chet Lancaster and Jane Lancaster, *American Anthropologist* 80 (1978): 110–117; and H. H. Norton, ibid., 665–667. On India see K. B. Pakrasi, *Female Infanticide in India* (Calcutta: Editions Indian, 1970).

164. G. R. Driver and John C. Miles, eds., *The Babylonian Laws* (Oxford: Clarendon Press, 1960), vol. 1, pp. 390–391.

165. Crook, *Law and Life of Rome*, p. 58.

166. See his "Slavery and the Law in Muscovy," paper presented at the Third International Conference on Muscovite History, Oxford, September 1–4, 1975. For more details see idem, "Slavery in Russia," pp. 46–53 (manuscript).

167. Wyatt MacGaffey, "Economic and Social Dimensions of Kongo Slavery (Zaire)," in Miers and Kopytoff, *Slavery in Africa*, pp. 246–247.

168. E. A. Thompson, "Slavery in Early Germany," in Finley, *Slavery in Classical Antiquity*, p. 197.

169. Hatada, *A History of Korea*, pp. 56–57. For the early Yi period see Susan S. Shin, "Changes in Labor Supply in Yi Dynasty Korea: From Hereditary to Contractual Obligation" (August 1976), p. 5 (manuscript).

170. Leopold von Schrenck, *Die Völker des Amur-Landes: Reisen und Forschungen im Amur-Lande in den Jahren 1854–1856* (St. Petersburg: Kaiserliche Akademie der Wissenschaften, 1881–1895), vol. 3, p. 646.

171. Harris, "Towards a Study of the Roman Slave Trade," p. 124.

172. On Slavic slaves and their reputation see Verlinden, *L'esclavage dans l'Europe médiévale*, vol. 1, p. 213. Volume 2 (1977) of this work discusses at great length slaves of Slavic origin in Italy, the Italian colonies, and Byzantium. On the sale of fellow Slavs by Slavs see pp. 132–133. The word "slave" is derived from

"Slav" and came into general use throughout Europe from about the eighth century as a result of the large number of Slavic slaves. For a detailed discussion see Verlinden, vol. 2, pp. 999–1010. See also Iris Origo, " 'The Domestic Enemy': The Eastern Slaves in Tuscany in the Fourteenth and Fifteenth Centuries," *Speculum* 30 (1955): 326, 332.

173. Bosworth, "Recruitment, Muster, and Review in Medieval Islamic Armies," pp. 64–65. One late Ottoman source has it that the Christian population of Bosnia not only avidly accepted Islam "but requested that their children should nevertheless be eligible for the devshirme." See Ménage, "Devshirme," p. 211.

174. On the Ibos, who are typical preliterates, see Harris, "Some Aspects of Slavery in South Eastern Nigeria," p. 48. On Rome see Crook, *Law and Life of Rome*, p. 62. (Exceptions were made, especially in cases of marriage to elite slaves, on which see Chapter 11.) On ancient India see Dev Raj Chanana, *Slavery in Ancient India* (New Delhi: People's Publishing House, 1960), pp. 36, 94. On China see Wang Yi-T'ung, "Slaves and Other Comparable Social Groups," p. 321. On medieval Europe see Verlinden, *L'esclavage dans l'Europe médiévale*, vol. 1, pp. 74, 419; vol. 2, p. 51.

5. Enslavement by Birth

1. On the Mexican slave population the work of G. Aguirre Beltrán is still the most valuable. See *La población negra de Mexico, 1519-1810*, ed. 2 (Mexico City: Fondo de Cultura Económica, 1972). See also Luz Maria Martínez Montiel, "Integration Patterns and the Assimilation Process of Negro Slaves in Mexico," in Vera Rubin and Arthur Tuden, eds., *Comparative Perspectives on Slavery in New World Plantation Societies* (New York: New York Academy of Sciences, 1977), pp. 446–454. On Peru see Frederick P. Bowser, *The African Slave in Colonial Peru, 1524-1650* (Stanford, Calif.: Stanford University Press, 1973); also his "The Free Person of Color in Mexico City and Lima: Manumission and Opportunity, 1580–1650," in Stanley L. Engerman and Eugene D. Genovese, eds., *Race and Slavery in the Western Hemisphere: Quantitative Studies* (Princeton, N.J.: Princeton University Press, 1975), pp. 331–368. On Latin America generally see Rolando Mellafe, *Negro Slavery in Latin America* (Berkeley: University of California Press, 1975), chap. 6.

I claim no originality for the distinction between biological and social reproduction. See, for example, Igor I. Kopytoff and Suzanne Miers, "Introduction," in Suzanne Miers and Igor I. Kopytoff, eds., *Slavery in Africa* (Madison: University of Wisconsin Press, 1977), pp. 59–61.

2. For a discussion of the issues raised here, both in general terms and in the specific context of Cuba, see Jack E. Eblen, "On the Natural Increase of Slave Populations: The Example of the Cuban Population, 1775-1900," in Engerman and Genovese, *Race and Slavery*, pp. 211–247.

3. Orlando Patterson, *The Sociology of Slavery: Jamaica, 1655-1838* (Rutherford, N.J.: Fairleigh Dickinson University Press, 1969), chap. 4; George W. Roberts, *The Population of Jamaica* (Cambridge: Cambridge University Press, 1957), pp. 30–42; Herbert S. Klein and Stanley L. Engerman, "Fertility Differentials between Slaves in the United States and the British West Indies: A Note on Lactation Prac-

tices and Their Possible Implications," in *William and Mary Quarterly,* ser. 3, 35 (1978): 357–374; and Robert W. Fogel and Stanley L. Engerman, "Recent Findings in the Study of Slave Demography and Family Structure," *Sociology and Social Research* 63 (1979): 566–589. Detailed statistical support for my thesis that Jamaican slave women were in gynecological revolt against the system is given in Richard S. Dunn, "Two Thousand Slaves: Black Life at Mesopotamia, Jamaica, and at Mount Airy, Virginia, 1760–1860," paper presented at a symposium on New World Slavery: Comparative Perspectives, Rutgers University, May 1–2, 1980.

4. Evidence on the biological reproductivity of the Roman slave population is fragmentary and does not permit anything approaching a reasonable estimate. The secondary literature on the subject is, as a result, highly contentious. See the frequently cited passages in W. D. Hooper and H. B. Ash, trans. and eds., *Cato and Varro: On Agriculture* (Cambridge, Mass.: Loeb Classical Library, Harvard University Press, 1935), pp. 9, 13–14, 227–228, 409. The strongest claim for natural reproduction of the slave population from the period of the republic is made by K. D. White, *Roman Farming* (London: Thames & Hudson, 1970), p. 370. Against which see Keith Hopkins, *Conquerors and Slaves* (Cambridge: Cambridge University Press, 1978), pp. 102, 106n16. See also M. I. Finley, *Ancient Slavery and Modern Ideology* (New York: Viking Press, 1980), p. 130; and William L. Westermann, *The Slave Systems of Greek and Roman Antiquity* (Philadelphia: American Philosophical Society, 1955), pp. 72, 76–77, 85–86. For the classic view of the unreproductive slave of the late republican era see Max Weber, *The Agrarian Sociology of Ancient Civilizations* (London: New Left Books, 1976), pp. 398–399.

5. Stanley J. Stein, *Vassouras: A Brazilian Coffee County, 1850–1900* (Cambridge, Mass.: Harvard University Press, 1957), pp. 70, 155–156; and C. R. Boxer, *The Golden Age of Brazil, 1695–1750* (Berkeley: University of California Press, 1969), pp. 8–9, 174–175.

6. William V. Harris, "Towards a Study of the Roman Slave Trade," in J. H. D'Arms and E. C. Kopff, eds., "The Seaborne Commerce of Ancient Rome: Studies in Archeology and History," in Memoirs of the American Academy in Rome, vol. 36 (1980), pp. 118–124.

7. Patterson, *The Sociology of Slavery,* pp. 145–146. See also Barry W. Higman, *Slave Population and Economy in Jamaica, 1807–1834* (Cambridge: Cambridge University Press, 1976), pp. 75–76.

8. W. W. Buckland, *The Roman Law of Slavery* (Cambridge: Cambridge University Press, 1908), p. 397; and R. H. Barrow, *Slavery in the Roman Empire* (London: Methuen & Co., 1928), p. 14.

9. Robert S. Rattray, *Ashanti Law and Constitution* (Oxford: Clarendon Press, 1929), pp. 39–40. The same was true of other Akan groups: on the Fanti see J. M. Sarbah, *Fanti Customary Laws* (London: William Clowes & Sons, 1904), p. 56.

10. John J. Grace, "Slavery and Emancipation among the Mende in Sierra Leone, 1896–1928," in Miers and Kopytoff, *Slavery in Africa,* p. 421; idem, *Domestic Slavery in West Africa* (New York: Harper & Row, 1975), p. 39.

11. Joseph C. Miller, "Imbangala Lineage Slavery," in Miers and Kopytoff, *Slavery in Africa,* pp. 219–220.

12. Wyatt MacGaffey, "Economic and Social Dimensions of Kongo Slavery (Zaire)," in Miers and Kopytoff, *Slavery in Africa,* p. 246.

13. Kalervo Oberg, "Crime and Punishment in Tlingit Society," *American Anthropologist* 36 (1934): 149.

14. Ronald Olson, *Social Structure and Social Life of the Tlingit in Alaska* (Berkeley: University of California Press, 1967), p. 55.

15. T. F. McIllwraith, *The Bella Coola Indians* (Toronto: University of Toronto Press, 1948), vol. 1, p. 161.

16. Virginia Gutierrez de Pineda, *Organización social en la Guajira* (Bogotá: Instituto Etnologico Nacional, 1950), pp. 144-145.

17. Enrico Cerulli, "Testi di diritto consuetudinario dei Somali Marrēhân," *Somalia, scritti vari editi ed inediti* 2 (1959): 83.

18. Enrico Cerulli, "Il diritto consuetudinario della Somalia Settentrionale (Migiurtini)," *Somalia, scritti vari editi ed inediti* 2 (1959): 22.

19. Ibid., p. 21.

20. James H. Vaughan, "Mafakur: A Limbic Institution of the Margi," in Miers and Kopytoff, *Slavery in Africa*, p. 89.

21. Ibid., p. 97.

22. J. S. Harris, "Some Aspects of Slavery in Southeastern Nigeria," *Journal of Negro History* 27 (1942): 48n15.

23. M. I. Finley, *The World of Odysseus* (London: Penguin Books, 1962), p. 67.

24. *The Law and Legal Theory of the Greeks* (Oxford: Clarendon Press, 1956), p. 282.

25. Jeffrey R. Brackett, *The Negro in Maryland* (Baltimore: N. Murray, Publication Agent, Johns Hopkins University, 1889), pp. 32-33. An act of 1664 stated that children of free women and slaves should be slaves "as their fathers were." In 1681, however, such children were again allowed to be free although the owner of the slave and the clergyman who performed the parents' marriage were fined. In 1715 whites were forbidden to marry slaves.

Brackett, like other commentators, was puzzled by the Somali rule and commented: "There must have then been no free blacks in the colony—or we are left to reason that children followed the condition of the father instead of the mother, entirely contrary to custom, as we find it later" (p. 33). We know, however, that there were free blacks in Maryland at that time. It is possible that the children of female slaves by free men continued to be slaves and that the law's main concern was with the children of free or indentured white women by black slaves. Were this the case, the rule of status inheritance in Maryland between 1664 and 1681 would have been Chinese. The Roman rule held, however, only when it served the slaveholders' interests. Thus in 1794 a male slave petitioned for freedom in the county court, on the grounds that his great-grandmother, Hannah Allen, was "a white, Scotch woman." The county court granted the petitioner his freedom on the basis of the Roman rule. His owner, however, appealed; in 1798 the general court reversed the county court and returned the petitioner to slavery. No reason was given for the decision. See Helen T. Catterall and James J. Hayden, eds., *Judicial Cases concerning American Slavery and the Negro* (New York: Octagon Books, 1968), vol. 4, p. 55. Compare the response of the Bermuda court to a similar petition discussed in note 68 below.

26. A. Leon Higginbotham, Jr., *In the Matter of Color, Race, and the American Legal Process: The Colonial Period* (New York: Oxford University Press, 1980), pp. 44, 128.

27. In both cases the children were freed only after reaching their majority, and they had to be baptized Christians. The baptismal requirement was neglected in South Africa, and in both areas the Somali rule had become a dead issue by the 1690s. On the French Antilles see Leo Elisabeth, "The French Antilles," D. W. Cohen and Jack P. Greene, eds., *Neither Slave nor Free* (Baltimore: Johns Hopkins University Press, 1972), pp. 139-140. On South Africa see Anna J. Böeseken, *Slaves and Free Blacks at the Cape, 1658-1700* (Cape Town: Tafelberg Publishers, 1977), pp. 44-60, 80-97.

28. Stephen Baier and Paul E. Lovejoy, "The Tuareg of the Central Sudan," in Miers and Kopytoff, *Slavery in Africa,* p. 400.

29. "Esclavage et relations de dépendence chez les Touareg Kel Gress," in Claude Meillassoux, ed., *L'esclavage en Afrique précoloniale* (Paris: François Maspero, 1975), p. 53.

30. On which see André Bourgeot, "Rapports esclavagistes et conditions d'affranchissement chez les Imuhaġ," in Meillassoux, *L'esclavage en Afrique précoloniale,* p. 90.

31. G. P. Murdock, *Africa: Its Peoples and Their Culture History* (New York: McGraw-Hill, 1959), pp. 408-409.

32. Buckland, *The Roman Law of Slavery,* p. 398.

33. Ibid.

34. Ibid., pp. 398, 412-413.

35. Ibid., pp. 400-401.

36. Dev Raj Chanana, *Slavery in Ancient India* (New Delhi: People's Publishing House, 1960), p. 98.

37. "Plato and Greek Slavery," *Mind,* April 1939, p. 186.

38. Ibid., p. 196.

39. A. M. Wergeland, *Slavery in Germanic Society during the Middle Ages* (Chicago: University of Chicago Press, 1916), pp. 19-34.

40. Ibid., p. 155.

41. Carl O. Williams, *Thraldom in Ancient Iceland* (Chicago: University of Chicago Press, 1937), p. 130.

42. Ibid., p. 108.

43. A. R. Williams, ed., *Llyfr Iorwerth* [The Book of Iorwerth] (Cardiff: University of Wales Press, 1960), p. 68, par. 102. (In Welsh.)

44. Ibid., p. 122, par. 101, line 18.

45. Gearóid MacNiocaill, *Ireland before the Vikings* (Dublin: Gill and Mac-Millan, 1972), p. 9.

46. Hayakawa Jirō, "The Position and Significance of the Slave System after the Taika Restoration," in Rekishi Kagaku Kyōgikai, ed., *Kodai Kokka To Doreisei* [Ancient State and Slave Systems] (Tokyo: Azekura Shobō, 1972), pp. 92-108. (In Japanese.)

47. Niida Noboru, *Chūgoku hōseishi Kenkyū* [A Study of Chinese Legal History] (Tokyo: Tokyo University Press, 1962). (In Japanese.) I draw heavily on this work in the following pages.

48. See also Wang Yi-T'ung, "Slaves and Other Comparable Social Groups during the Northern Dynasties (386-618)," *Harvard Journal of Asiatic Studies* 16 (1953): 327-329.

49. Ibid., p. 330.

50. Ibid.

51. See Byung-Sak Ku, *Hanguk Sahoe Pŏpchesa Tüksu Yŏngu* [A Study on the History of Law in Korea] (Seoul: Tongo Ch'ulp'ansa, 1968), pp. 100–103. (In Korean.)

52. N. Adriani and Albert C. Kruyt, *De Bare'e Sprekende Toradjas van Midden-Celebes* [The Bare'e-speaking Toradja of Central Celebes] (Amsterdam: Nood-Hollandsche Uitgevers Maatschappij, 1950), vol. 1, pp. 139–141; Maurice Bloch, "Modes of Production and Slavery in Madagascar: Two Case Studies," in James L. Watson, ed., *Asian and African Systems of Slavery* (Oxford: Basil Blackwell, 1980), p. 108.

53. Charles Verlinden, *L'esclavage dans l'Europe médiévale* (Bruges: De Tempel, 1955), vol. 1, p. 73.

54. Iris Origo, " 'The Domestic Enemy': The Eastern Slaves in Tuscany in the Fourteenth and Fifteenth Centuries," *Speculum* 30 (1955): 344.

55. Higginbotham, *In the Matter of Color*, p. 159.

56. G. R. Driver and John C. Miles, eds., *The Babylonian Laws* (Oxford: Clarendon Press, 1960), vol. 1, pp. 226–227, 253–256, 332–333, 350–356; and Isaac Mendelsohn, *Slavery in the Ancient Near East* (Oxford: Oxford University Press, 1949), p. 104.

57. Mendelsohn, *Slavery in the Ancient Near East*, p. 104.

58. For citations in the Qoran on this subject see A. J. Wensinck, *A Handbook of Early Mohammedan Tradition* (Leiden: E. J. Brill, 1927), pp. 141–143. See also Robert Roberts, *The Social Laws of the Qorân* (London: Williams & Norgate, 1925), pp. 10–11, 59–60. On the capacity of Tuareg women to take slave spouses see Edmond Bernus and Suzanne Bernus, "L'évolution de la condition servile chez les Touaregs sahéliens," in Meillassoux, *L'esclavage en Afrique précoloniale*, p. 34.

59. Joan Dyste Lind, "The Ending of Slavery in Sweden: Social Structure and Decision Making," *Scandinavian Studies* 50 (1978): 68.

60. Verlinden, *L'esclavage dans l'Europe médiévale*, vol. 1, p. 274.

61. Mellafe, *Negro Slavery in Latin America*, pp. 111–123; Colin A. Palmer, *Slaves of the White God: Blacks in Mexico, 1570–1650* (Cambridge, Mass.: Harvard University Press, 1976), p. 62; and Bowser, "The Free Person of Color," pp. 331–363.

62. On Jamaica see Edward Brathwaite, *The Development of Creole Society in Jamaica* (Oxford: Clarendon Press, 1971), pp. 169–175. On the eastern Caribbean see Elsa V. Goveia, *Slave Society in the British Leeward Islands at the End of the Eighteenth Century* (New Haven: Yale University Press, 1965), pp. 215–232.

63. Carol P. MacCormack, "Wono: Institutionalized Dependency in Sherbro Descent Groups," in Miers and Kopytoff, *Slavery in Africa*, p. 185.

64. Ibid., p. 198.

65. Arthur Tuden, "Slavery and Stratification among the Ila of Central Africa," in Arthur Tuden and Leonard Plotnicov, eds., *Social Stratification in Africa* (New York: Free Press, 1970), pp. 47–58.

66. Martin A. Klein, "Servitude among the Wolof and Sereer of Senegambia," in Miers and Kopytoff, *Slavery in Africa*, pp. 344–345.

67. Cyril O. Packwood, *Chained on the Rock: Slavery in Bermuda* (New York: Eliseo Torres and Sons, 1975), pp. 56–57.

68. Marc Bloch, *Slavery and Serfdom in the Middle Ages: Selected Essays*, trans.

William R. Beer (Berkeley: University of California Press, 1975), pp. 38–40. Serfs were normally required to marry serfs belonging to their lord. In exceptional cases marriage with the serf of another master was permitted, but usually only after the payment of a fee. Such unions were referred to as "formariage." As in Bermuda, complications developed where the serfs in formariage had an uneven number of children. The practice continued in France down to 1789. It is not clear when Bermuda changed to the Roman rule, although this must have happened some time during the eighteenth century. In 1791 a black successfully petitioned the governor for her freedom on the grounds that she was descended from a white woman in spite of the fact that she was "herself remarkably black" (Packwood, *Chained on the Rock,* pp. 174–175).

69. Brooke Low, *The Natives of Borneo,* ed. H. Ling Roth (London: Anthropological Institute of Great Britain and Ireland, 1892–1893), p. 33.

6. The Acquisition of Slaves

1. Claude Meillassoux, "Introduction," in Claude Meillassoux, ed., *The Development of Indigenous Trade and Markets in West Africa* (London: Oxford University Press, 1971), p. 53. See also Meillassoux, "Le commerce précolonial et la développement de l'esclavage à Gūbu du Sahel (Mali)," ibid., pp. 182–195; Emmanuel Terray, "Commerce précolonial et organization social chez les Dida de Côte d'Ivoire," ibid., pp. 145–152; and Philip D. Curtin, "Pre-colonial Trading Networks and Traders: The Diakhanké," ibid., pp. 228–239.

2. Meillassoux, "Introduction," pp. 60–61.

3. Ibid., pp. 61–62.

4. Stuart Piggot, *Ancient Europe: From the Beginnings of Agriculture to Classical Antiquity* (Chicago: Aldine, 1965), p. 172.

5. Cyril Fox, *A Find of the Early Iron Age from Llyn Cerrig Bach, Anglessey: Interim Report* (Cardiff: National Museum of Wales, 1945).

6. U. P. Averkieva, *Slavery among the Indians of North America* (Moscow: U.S.S.R. Academy of Sciences, 1941), pp. 79–81. Frances Knapp and R. L. Childe tell us that the Flatheads of British Columbia formed a large proportion of bought slaves among the Tlingits of southeastern Alaska. *The Thlinkets of Southeastern Alaska* (Chicago: Stone and Kimball, 1896), p. 43.

7. For the best recent work on the largely neglected Indian Ocean slave trade see R. W. Beachey, *The Slave Trade of Eastern Africa* (New York: Harper & Row, 1976). Useful too is his volume entitled *A Collection of Documents on the Slave Trade of Eastern Africa* (New York: Barnes & Noble Books, n.d.). Also of value is Joseph E. Harris, *The African Presence in Asia: Consequences of the East African Slave Trade* (Evanston, Ill.: Northwestern University Press, 1971). In addition, I have drawn on the following: Frederick Cooper, *Plantation Slavery on the East Coast of Africa* (New Haven: Yale University Press, 1977), esp. chaps. 1 and 4; Rodger Morton, "Slaves, Fugitives and Freedmen on the Kenya Coast, 1873–1907" (Ph.D. diss., Syracuse University, 1976), and Moses D. E. Nwulia, *Britain and Slavery in East Africa* (Washington, D.C.: Three Continents Press, 1975).

8. Beachey, *The Slave Trade of Eastern Africa,* p. 2.

9. Ibid., pp. 2–4. For other periods see also Frank M. Snowden, Jr., *Blacks in Antiquity* (Cambridge, Mass.: Harvard University Press, Belknap Press, 1970), pp. 19, 127, 184–185.

10. Beachey, *The Slave Trade of Eastern Africa,* pp. 260–262. It need hardly be emphasized that these are very rough estimates based on data of widely varying reliability.

11. M. I. Finley, "The Black Sea and Danubian Regions and the Slave Trade in Antiquity," *Klio* 40 (1962): 51–59.

12. William V. Harris, "Towards a Study of the Roman Slave Trade," in J. D. D'Arms and E. C. Kopff, eds., "The Seaborne Commerce of Ancient Rome: Studies in Archeology and History," in Memoirs of the American Academy in Rome, vol. 36 (1980), pp. 117–140.

13. The major authority on slave trading in medieval and early modern Europe is Charles Verlinden, *L'esclavage dans l'Europe médiévale* (Bruges: De Tempel, 1955, 1975), vols. 1 and 2.

14. Ibid., vol. 1, pp. 320–370.

15. Ibid., vol. 2. See also J. H. Galloway, "The Mediterranean Sugar Industry," *Geographical Review* 67 (1977): 177–194, esp. pp. 188–190.

16. Erik I. Bromberg, "Wales and the Medieval Slave Trade," *Speculum* 17 (1942): 263–269; B. G. Charles, *Old Norse Relations with Wales* (Cardiff: University of Wales Press, 1934); Gwyn Jones, *A History of the Vikings* (London: Oxford University Press, 1968), pt. 3; P. H. Sawyer, *The Age of the Vikings* (London: Edward Arnold, 1962), esp. chaps. 6–9; Peter Foote and David M. Wilson, *The Viking Achievement* (London: Sidgwick & Jackson, 1970), esp. chaps. 2, 6, 7; Eric Oxenstierna, *The Norsemen* (Greenwich, Conn.: Graphic Society Publishers, 1965), esp. pp. 92–94; Johannes Brondsted, *The Vikings* (London: Penguin Books, 1960), pp. 24–69. On Scandinavian slavery see note 24.

17. Cited in Foote and Wilson, *The Viking Achievement,* p. 67.

18. Oxenstierna, *The Norsemen,* p. 160.

19. Jones, *A History of the Vikings,* p. 148.

20. For detailed discussions of the archeological and other evidence in Birka, Hedeby, Kaupang, and other towns see Sawyer, *The Age of the Vikings,* chap. 8; and Foote and Wilson, *The Viking Achievement,* chap. 6.

21. Sawyer, *The Age of the Vikings,* p. 186. See also the remarks in Eric Oxenstierna, *The World of the Norsemen* (London: Weidenfeld & Nicolson, 1967), pp. 136–137.

22. Oxenstierna, *The Norsemen,* p. 294.

23. For the best treatments in English see Sawyer, *The Age of the Vikings,* chap. 7; and Jones, *A History of the Vikings,* pt. 3.

24. On slavery in Scandinavia see Carl O. Williams, *Thraldom in Ancient Iceland* (Chicago: University of Chicago Press, 1937); Joan Dyste Lind, "The Ending of Slavery in Sweden: Social Structure and Decision Making," *Scandinavian Studies* 50 (1978): 57–71; and Foote and Wilson, *The Viking Achievement,* chap. 2. A good recent account in Swedish is Thomas Lindkvist, *Landborna i Norden under äldre medeltid* [Tenants in the Nordic Countries during the Early Middle Ages] (Uppsala: University of Uppsala, 1979), chap. 5. Compare Perry Anderson, *Passages from Antiquity to Feudalism* (London: Verso, 1978), pp. 173–181. For a useful review of the

literature see Thomas Lindkvist, "Swedish Medieval Society: Previous Research and Recent Developments," *Scandinavian Journal of History* 4 (1979): 253-268.

25. Sawyer, *The Age of the Vikings*, pp. 97-98. For a somewhat more critical view of the numismatic and archeological evidence see Foote and Wilson, *The Viking Achievement*, chap. 6. Another useful assessment is Jones, *A History of the Vikings*, pp. 3-10.

26. There is a vast literature on the Viking ships. Acknowledged as the best account in English is Sawyer, *The Age of the Vikings*, chap. 4. For a more recent review see Foote and Wilson, *The Viking Achievement*, chap. 7. See also Jones, *A History of the Vikings*, pp. 182-195 (for bibliography, p. 183n2). Useful for its excellent graphics is Oxenstierna, *The Norsemen*.

27. J. C. Russell, *Late Ancient and Medieval Populations* (Philadelphia: American Philosophical Society, 1958), pp. 71-131.

28. F. M. Maitland, *Domesday Book and Beyond* (Cambridge: Cambridge University Press, 1897; reprint ed., 1960); and Georges Duby, *Rural Economy and Country Life in the Medieval West* (Columbia: University of South Carolina Press, 1968), pp. 37-39.

29. Jones, *A History of the Vikings*, chap. 5, esp. p. 279; and Lindkvist, *Landborna i Norden*, pp. 129-139. On this decline of the European population in the early tenth century and for a good general summary of medieval demographic estimates see B. H. Slicher Van Bath, *The Agrarian History of Western Europe* (London: Edward Arnold, 1963), pp. 77-78.

30. This estimate of 1 percent is based on the experience of the U.S. South during most of the eighteenth century. The annual forced immigration of slaves to meet the needs of the masters beyond the natural reproduction of the slave population was approximately 1 percent of the total slave population until about 1790. Between 1790 and 1807, when the slave population grew at an unusually high rate in anticipation of abolition of the trade, the annual forced immigration rose to approximately 1.9 percent of the total slave population. For these estimates I am grateful to Robert W. Fogel, who provided them in a personal communication.

31. *Economic Change in Precolonial Africa* (Madison: University of Wisconsin Press, 1975), p. 66.

32. A. G. B. Fisher and H. J. Fisher, *Slavery and Muslim Society in Africa* (London: C. Hurst & Co., 1970), p. 60.

33. Curtin, *Economic Change in Precolonial Africa*, p. 156.

34. "The Trans-Saharan Slave Trade: A Tentative Census," in Henry A. Gemery and Jan S. Hogendorn, eds., *The Uncommon Market: Essays in the Economic History of the Atlantic Slave Trade* (New York: Academic Press, 1979), pp. 23-76.

35. Cited in Jonathan Derrick, *Africa's Slaves Today* (New York: Schocken Books, 1975), p. 24 and chap. 2 generally.

36. Robin Maugham, *The Slaves of Timbuktu* (London: Sphere Books, 1967), p. 12. This work provides several vivid eyewitness accounts of Timbuktu and other slave-trading centers during December 1958. See also Derrick, *Africa's Slaves Today*, chap. 6.

37. Curtin, *Economic Change in Precolonial Africa*, pp. 153-156.

38. There are several good general histories of the Atlantic slave trade: Daniel P. Mannix and Malcolm Cowley, *Black Cargoes* (London: Longmans, 1963); Basil

Davidson, *Black Mother* (London: Victor Gollancz, 1961); and James Pope-Hennessy, *Sins of the Fathers* (New York: Capricorn Books, 1969). Eric Williams' classic study of the economic roots of the trade is still essential reading: *Capitalism and Slavery* (New York: Capricorn Books, 1966). Also still useful are C. M. Macinnes, *England and Slavery* (London: Arrowsmith, 1934); and W. E. Ward, *The Royal Navy and the Slavers* (New York: Schocken Books, 1970). For two excellent short surveys see Christopher Fyfe, "The Dynamics of African Dispersal: The Transatlantic Slave Trade," in Martin L. Kilson and Robert I. Rotberg, eds., *The African Diaspora* (Cambridge, Mass.: Harvard University Press, 1976), pp. 57–74; and Philip D. Curtin, "The Atlantic Slave Trade, 1600–1800," in J. F. Ade Ajayi and Michael Crowder, eds., *A History of West Africa* (London: Longmans, 1971), pp. 302–330. See also the special issue of *Revue française d'histoire d'outre mer,* nos. 226–227 (1975).

Until recently the major gaps in the literature on the history of the trade have been with regard to Dutch and Scandinavian participation, but these are now being rapidly filled. See, on the Dutch trade, James Postma, "The Dutch Participation in the African Slave Trade: Slaving on the Guinea Coast, 1675–1795" (Ph.D. diss., University of Michigan, 1970). For a summary see Postma's, "The Origin of African Slaves: The Dutch Activities on the Guinea Coast, 1674–1795," in Stanley L. Engerman and Eugene D. Genovese, eds., *Race and Slavery in the Western Hemisphere: Quantitative Studies* (Princeton, N.J.: Princeton University Press, 1975), pp. 33–41. See also P. C. Emmer, "The History of the Dutch Slave Trade: A Bibliographical Survey," *Journal of Economic History* 32 (1972): 728–747; and E. Vanden Boogart and P. C. Emmer, "The Dutch Participation in the Atlantic Slave Trade," in Gemery and Hogendorn, *The Uncommon Market,* pp. 353–375. On the Scandinavian slave trade see S. E. Green-Pedersen, "The Scope and Structure of the Danish Negro Slave Trade," *Scandinavian Economic History Review* 19 (1971): 149–197. For more specialized studies see note 39.

39. *The Atlantic Slave Trade: A Census* (Madison: University of Wisconsin Press, 1969) and his "Measuring the Atlantic Slave Trade," in Engerman and Genovese, *Race and Slavery,* pp. 107–128. For important recent advances see, in the same volume, Roger Anstey, "The Volume and Profitability of the British Slave Trade, 1761–1807," pp. 3–31; E. Philip Le Veen, "A Quantitative Analysis of the Impact of British Suppression Policies on the Volume of the Nineteenth Century Atlantic Slave Trade," pp. 51–81; K. G. Davies, "The Living and the Dead: White Mortality in West Africa, 1684–1732," pp. 83–98; and the very insightful "Comment" of George Shipperson, pp. 99–106.

For the most ambitious cliometric studies since Curtin's *Census* see Herbert S. Klein, *The Middle Passage: Comparative Studies in the Atlantic Slave Trade* (Princeton, N.J.: Princeton University Press, 1978); Gemery and Hogendorn, *The Uncommon Market;* D. Eltis, "The Export of Slaves from Africa, 1820–1843," *Journal of Economic History* 37 (1977): 409–433; Richard N. Bean, *The British Trans-Atlantic Slave Trade, 1650–1775* (New York: Arno Press, 1975); Jean Mettas and Serge Daget, eds., *Repertoire des expéditions négrières françaises au XVIII siècle* (Paris: Société français d'histoire d'outre-mer, 1978); and Robert Louis Stein, *The French Slave Trade in the Eighteenth Century: An Old Regime Business* (Madison: University of Wisconsin Press, 1979). For a review of more recent work by Stein, Klein, and others, see Orlando Patterson, "Recent Studies in Caribbean Slavery and the Slave Trade," *Latin American Research Review* 17 (1982).

40. See Chapter 5, note 3. See also Robert W. Fogel, Stanley L. Engerman, Stephen C. Crawford, J. F. Olson, and Richard H. Steckel, "Why the U.S. Slave Population Grew So Rapidly: Fertility, Mortality, and Household Structure," 1975 (mimeographed).

41. Klein, *The Middle Passage*, pp. 65–67, 194–199, 240–241; and Stein, *The French Slave Trade*, pp. 96–101, 194–195, 205–206.

42. Bean, *The British Trans-Atlantic Slave Trade*, chap. 4, esp. fig. 4–1 and appendixes A and B.

43. Ibid., p. 122.

44. Ibid., p. 73. For an economic model using fishery as an analogy see R. P. Thomas and Richard N. Bean, "The Fishers of Men: The Profits of the Slave Trade," *Journal of Economic History* 34 (1974): 885–894. For another econometric approach which, however, stops short of claiming that the trade was good for Africa demographically, see Henry A. Gemery and Jan S. Hogendorn, "The Atlantic Slave Trade: A Tentative Model," *Journal of African History* 15 (1974): 223–246. A much stronger critique of Bean is implicit in the paper by these two authors cited in note 46. Curtin, in *The Atlantic Slave Trade*, asserted that for Africa "the net demographic effect of the three Atlantic migrations was population growth, not decline" (p. 271), but he has backed away from this position in later works.

45. Philip D. Curtin, "The African Diaspora," in Michael Craton, ed., *Roots and Branches: Current Directions in Slave Studies, Historical Reflections* 6 (1979): 15.

46. Henry A. Gemery and Jan S. Hogendorn, "The Economic Costs of West African Participation in the Atlantic Slave Trade," in Gemery and Hogendorn, *The Uncommon Market*, pp. 143–161. See also, in the same volume, Joseph C. Miller, "Some Aspects of the Commercial Organization of Slaving at Luanda, Angola: 1760–1830," pp. 77–106; Mahdi Adamu, "The Delivery of Slaves from the Central Sudan to the Bight of Benin in the Eighteenth and Nineteenth Centuries," pp. 163–180 and James Postma, "Mortality in the Dutch Slave Trade, 1675–1795," pp. 239–260. For a balanced study of the effects of the slave trade in one area of West Africa, and a good review of previous work on the subject, see Michael Mason, "Population Density and 'Slave Raiding': The Case of the Middle Belt of Nigeria," *Journal of African History* 10 (1969): 551–564. In more general terms see Walter Rodney, "African Slavery and Other Forms of Social Oppression on the Upper Guinea Coast in the Context of the Atlantic Slave-Trade," *Journal of African History* 7 (1966): 431–443; idem, *How Europe Underdeveloped Africa* (London and Dar-es-Salaam: Bogle-L'Ouverture Publications and Tanzania Publishing House, 1972); idem, *A History of the Upper Guinea Coast, 1545–1800* (Oxford: Clarendon Press, 1970); idem, "Slavery and Underdevelopment," in Craton, *Roots and Branches*, pp. 275–286. See my commentary on this article, ibid., pp. 287–292. See also J. D. Fage, "Slavery and the Slave Trade in the Context of West African History," *Journal of African History* 10 (1964): 393–404. For a review of these problems emphasizing both the academic and the ideological issues involved see Curtin, "The African Diaspora," pp. 1–17, esp. pp. 11–16.

47. See Harris, "Towards a Study of the Roman Slave Trade," pp. 125–126.

48. Robert W. Fogel and Stanley L. Engerman, *Time on the Cross: The Economics of American Negro Slavery* (Boston: Little, Brown, 1974), vol. 1, pp. 44–58.

These figures have been strongly contested; see Paul A. David et al., *Reckoning with Slavery* (New York: Oxford University Press, 1976).

49. For the strongest advocate of the slave-breeding thesis see Richard Sutch, "The Breeding of Slaves for Sale and the Westward Expansion of Slavery, 1850–1860," in Engerman and Genovese, *Race and Slavery*, pp. 173–210. For a critique of the breeding thesis see Fogel and Engerman, *Time on the Cross*, vol. 1, pp. 78–86; and for a sharper, more detailed critique aimed specifically at Sutch see Robert W. Fogel, Stanley L. Engerman, Richard H. Steckel, and Stephen C. Crawford, *The Demography of American Negro Slavery*, chap. 3 (manuscript).

50. *The Destruction of Brazilian Slavery, 1850–1888* (Berkeley: University of California Press, 1972), p. 47.

51. Ibid., p. 65.

52. Klein, *The Middle Passage*, chap. 5.

53. See Bancroft, *Slave Trading in the Old South* (New York: Frederick Ungar, 1959).

54. See D. Eltis, "The Traffic in Slaves between the British West Indian Colonies, 1807–1833," *Economic History Review*, ser. 2, 25 (1972), no. 1.

55. Barry W. Higman, *Slave Population and Economy in Jamaica, 1807–1834* (Cambridge: Cambridge University Press, 1976), pp. 45–68.

56. For a good recent study see Jack Goody and S. J. Tambiah, *Bridewealth and Dowry* (Cambridge: Cambridge University Press, 1973), pp. 2–47.

57. See, for example, M. J. Herskovits, *Dahomey: An Ancient West African Kingdom* (New York: J. J. Augustin, 1938), vol. 1, chaps. 16 and 17.

58. Victor C. Uchendu, "Slaves and Slavery in Igboland, Nigeria," in Suzanne Miers and Igor I. Kopytoff, eds., *Slavery in Africa* (Madison: University of Wisconsin Press, 1977), p. 125.

59. Ralph A. Austen, "Slavery among Coastal Middlemen: The Duala of the Cameroon," in Miers and Kopytoff, *Slavery in Africa*, p. 311.

60. Kenneth Little, *The Mende of Sierra Leone* (London: Routledge & Kegan Paul, 1951), p. 37.

61. Stephen Baier and Paul E. Lovejoy, "The Tuareg of the Central Sudan," in Miers and Kopytoff, *Slavery in Africa*, p. 400.

62. Martin A. Klein, "Servitude among the Wolof and Sereer of Senegambia," in Miers and Kopytoff, *Slavery in Africa*, p. 345.

63. Gustave E. Hulstaert, *Le mariage de Nkundo*, Memoirs de l'Institut Royal Colonial Belge, no. 8 (1938), pp. 147–148.

64. On the ancient Near East see Isaac Mendelsohn, *Slavery in the Ancient Near East* (Oxford: Oxford University Press, 1949), p. 4; on ancient India, Der Raj Chanana, *Slavery in Ancient India* (New Delhi: People's Publishing House, 1960), pp. 21, 35, 37; and on pharaonic Egypt, Abd al-Muhsin Bakīr, *Slavery in Pharaonic Egypt* (Cairo: L'institut français d'archéologie orientale, 1952), pp. 13, 70. On the legal complexities in Roman law of the *servi dotales* (slaves who were part of a woman's dowry) see W. W. Buckland, *The Roman Law of Slavery* (Cambridge: Cambridge University Press, 1908), pp. 262–265. On medieval Europe see Iris Origo, " 'The Domestic Enemy': The Eastern Slaves in Tuscany in the Fourteenth and Fifteenth Centuries," *Speculum* 30 (1955): 324. In the Caribbean the relatively few white women tended to outlive their spouses, with the result that widows were often extremely wealthy and much sought after by aspiring, "interested" white men of lesser

means. To "marry and bury" became a common term, although women benefited more than men. See the entry of February 12, 1802, in *Lady Nugent's Journal of Her Residence in Jamaica from 1801-1805,* ed. Philip Wright (Kingston: Institute of Jamaica, 1966), pp. 58-59. On Brazil see Gilberto Freyre, *The Masters and the Slaves* (New York: Alfred A. Knopf, 1964), p. 320. On the U.S. South see the account of the master class in U. B. Phillips, *Life and Labor in the Old South* (Boston: Little, Brown, 1963), chaps. 12-14. See also Clement Eaton, *The Growth of Southern Civilization, 1790-1860* (New York: Harper Torchbooks, 1963), p. 187.

65. John Crook, *Law and Life of Rome* (Ithaca, N.Y.: Cornell University Press, 1967), p. 61.

66. Williams, *Thraldom in Ancient Iceland,* p. 33.

67. Karl Polanyi, Conrad M. Arensberg, and Harry W. Pearson, eds., *Trade and Market in the Early Empires* (Chicago: Gateway, Henry Regnery Co., 1971), p. 350. See also pp. 264-266.

68. Mendelsohn, *Slavery in the Ancient Near East,* p. 41.

69. Bruno Lasker, *Human Bondage in Southeast Asia* (Chapel Hill: University of North Carolina Press, 1950), p. 53.

70. Little, *The Mende of Sierra Leone,* p. 37.

71. Fisher and Fisher, *Slavery and Muslim Society in Africa,* pp. 158-159.

72. Ibid., pp. 156-158.

73. The most recent and thorough treatment of this subject is Marilyn Gerriets, "Money and Clientship in Ancient Irish Law" (Ph.D diss., University of Toronto, 1978), chap. 3, esp. pp. 67-72; on the equivalent values see p. 95.

74. Ibid., pp. 67-72.

75. Nerys Wyn Patterson, personal communication.

76. Williams, *Thraldom in Ancient Iceland,* pp. 34-35.

77. Oxenstierna, *The Norsemen,* p. 93.

78. Lasker, *Human Bondage in Southeast Asia,* p. 45.

79. Fisher and Fisher, *Slavery and Muslim Society in Africa,* pp. 164-165. For a more detailed statement of the horse value of slaves and other equivalences in the Saharan slave market see Austen, "The Trans-Saharan Slave Trade," pp. 69-71.

80. Lasker, *Human Bondage in Southeast Asia,* p. 45.

81. The standard works on the links between Mediterranean slavery and slave trading with New World slavery and the Atlantic slave trade are Charles Verlinden, "Les origines coloniales de la civilisation atlantique: Antécédents et types de structure," *Journal of World History* 1 (1953): 378-398; and his *The Beginnings of Modern Colonization* (Ithaca, N.Y.: Cornell University Press, 1970).

82. For the classic labor of love in this scholarly tradition see Fernand Braudel, *La Méditerranée et le monde méditerranéen à l'époque de Philippe II,* 2 vols. (Paris: Librairie Armand Colin, 1966).

7. The Condition of Slavery

1. Susan Treggiari, "The Freedmen of Cicero," *Greece and Rome* 16 (1969): 202.

· 2. Ibid., p. 196. For a broader treatment of the reasons for manumission in Rome see Treggiari, *Roman Freedmen during the Late Republic* (Oxford: Clarendon

Press, 1969), pp. 1–20. On the ancient world more generally see M. I. Finley, *Ancient Slavery and Modern Ideology* (New York: Viking Press, 1980), chap. 3.

3. See in particular Paul E. Lovejoy and Stephen Baier, "The Desert-Side Economy of the Central Sudan," *International Journal of African Historical Studies* 8 (1975): 555–581; Martin A. Klein and Paul E. Lovejoy, "Slavery in West Africa," in Henry A. Gemery and Jan S. Hogendorn, eds., *The Uncommon Market: Essays in the Economic History of the Atlantic Slave Trade* (New York: Academic Press, 1979), pp. 181–212; and M. G. Smith, *The Economy of Hausa Communities of Zaria* (London: Her Majesty's Stationery Office, 1955). For an interpretation that departs somewhat from Smith's see Jan S. Hogendorn, "The Economics of Slave Use on Two 'Plantations' in the Zaria Emirate of the Sokoto Caliphate," *International Journal of African Historical Studies* 10 (1977): 369–383.

4. John J. Grace, "Slavery and Emancipation among the Mende in Sierra Leone, 1896–1928," in Suzanne Miers and Igor I. Kopytoff, eds., *Slavery in Africa* (Madison: University of Wisconsin Press, 1977), p. 422; idem, *Domestic Slavery in West Africa* (New York: Harper & Row, 1975), pp. 14, 41. Among the more advanced pre-European states, however, such slaves were sometimes sold under special circumstances, especially as a form of punishment. See Hogendorn, "The Economics of Slave Use," pp. 379–380.

5. William W. Westermann, *The Slave Systems of Greek and Roman Antiquity* (Philadelphia: American Philosophical Society, 1955), pp. 86–87. For a discussion of the attitude of the state toward locally born slaves, and the reasons for its laws respecting this group during Ptolemaic times, see Iza Biezunska-Malowist, *L'esclavage dans l'Egypte gréco-romaine, première partie: Période ptolémaïque* (Warsaw: Polska Akademia Nauk, 1974), chap 3.

6. On Tuareg color values and racial attitudes toward their slaves see Johannes Nicolaisen, *Ecology and Culture of the Pastoral Tuareg* (Copenhagen: National Museum of Copenhagen, 1963), p. 16. The Ahaggar word *Ibenharen* refers to the racial origin of their Negro slaves and is often used as a term of abuse.

7. Bernard Lewis, *Race and Color in Islam* (New York: Harper Torchbooks, 1971); idem, "The African Diaspora and the Civilization of Islam," in Martin L. Kilson and Robert I. Rotberg, eds., *The African Diaspora* (Cambridge, Mass.: Harvard University Press, 1976), pp. 37–56.

8. This contempt led to the custom of many of the rajas raiding their own villages, as discussed in Chapter 4. See John M. Gullick, *Indigenous Political Systems of Western Malaya* (London: Athlone Press, 1958), pp. 102–104; and L. R. Wheeler, *The Modern Malay* (London: Allen & Unwin, 1928), p. 99.

9. Until the middle of the eighth century southern barbarians and the border and tribal peoples were "looked on as not quite human." See E. G. Pulleyblank, "The Origins and Nature of Chattel Slavery in China," *Journal of Economic and Social History of the Orient* 1 (1958): 209. During the period of the Northern dynasties the Liao people of the northern part of present-day Szechuan were a major source of slaves. See Wang Yi-T'ung, "Slaves and Other Comparable Social Groups during the Northern Dynasties (386–618)," *Harvard Journal of Asiatic Studies* 16 (1953): 306–308. Eunuchs, who came to play a vital role in Chinese imperial politics, were largely recruited from alien races; see Taisuke Mitamura, *Chinese Eunuchs: The Structure of Intimate Politics* (Rutland, Vt.: Charles E. Tuttle Co., 1970). Having made these observations, I should emphasize that the typical Chinese slave was Chi-

nese, given the penal origin of most slaves. There is no evidence that any ethnic or racial group became identified with slavery. What C. P. Fitzgerald wrote of Chinese culture as a whole applies equally to those who are descendants of slaves: "The apparent identity of type, and the real identity of culture over an area so vast and so definitely divided in climate and configuration, is the outstanding achievement of Chinese civilization." *China: A Short Cultural History* (London: Cresset Press, 1965), p. 10.

10. Although Mongoloid in most respects, the Lolos have certain distinctive somatic traits that readily distinguish them from their Han Chinese slaves. These include "dark skin, hooked nose, and big ear lobes." For a discussion of relations between black Lolo masters and their white Lolo and Han slaves see Yueh-hwa Lin, *Liang-shan I-chia* [The Lolo of Liang-shan] (Shanghai: Commercial Press, 1947), chap. 7.

11. Carl O. Williams, *Thraldom in Ancient Iceland* (Chicago: University of Chicago Press, 1937), p. 74. See also Peter Foote and David M. Wilson, *The Viking Achievement* (London: Sidgwick & Jackson, 1970), pp. 65, 75–76.

12. Williams, *Thraldom in Ancient Iceland,* pp. 74–75. This story, of course, suggests more an ideology of innate slavishness and innate nobility than of association between these "virtues" and a given racial type. More likely, both views were held. Ideally they would be in harmony, as in the case of the noble blond king or swarthy slave; where they were not, the innately endowed qualities held sway. As Foote and Wilson observe, "Scandinavians decidedly favoured the postulate that heredity accounts for most things" (*The Viking Achievement,* p. 77).

13. See K. J. Dover, *Greek Homosexuality* (New York: Vintage Books, 1980), pp. 68–73, 78–81; and A. N. Sherwin White, *Racial Prejudice in Imperial Rome* (Cambridge: Cambridge University Press, 1967). On the racial aspect of Greco-Roman attitudes to slaves of whatever race see the recent remarks of Finley, *Ancient Slavery and Modern Ideology,* p. 118.

14. Snowden states that "the Greeks and Romans developed no doctrines of white superiority," and that "the intense color prejudice of the modern world was lacking." *Blacks in Antiquity* (Cambridge, Mass.: Harvard University Press, Belknap Press, 1970), pp. 182–183. However, Snowden seems to be unaware of some of the subtler aspects of the sociology of racial and ethnic relations. One of these is that the absence of an articulated doctrine of racial superiority does not necessarily imply behavioral tolerance in the relations between peoples of somatically different groups. It is sometimes the case that a forcefully articulated denial of racial prejudice and a formal ideology of racial tolerance go hand in hand with behavioral prejudice. (Brazil is a well-known example.) More subtle, but no less pervasive and vicious in their social consequences, are the color values of middle-class, brown and light-skinned West Indians. In their formal ideology these individuals not only condemn racial and color prejudice but present themselves to the world as models of racial and color harmony. In actual practice, this group until recently was highly sensitive to the most minute color gradations and practiced color prejudice on a massive scale. See Orlando Patterson, "Toward a Future That Has No Past: The Fate of Blacks in the Americas," in *Public Interest* 27 (1972): 25–62; Fernando Henriques, *Family and Colour in Jamaica* (London: MacGibbon & Kee, 1968); and Rex M. Nettleford, *Identity, Race, and Protest in Jamaica* (New York: William Morrow and Co., 1972),

pp. 19–37. On color values in Cuban slave society see Verena Martinez-Alier, *Marriage, Class, and Colour in Nineteenth-Century Cuba* (London: Cambridge University Press, 1974), esp. chap. 5.

15. There is nothing amusing or tolerant about Juvenal's remarks, as Snowden suggests in *Blacks in Antiquity*, p. 194. Juvenal was implying more than the fact that there would be more mulattoes were it not for abortion when he wrote in his thoroughly nasty sixth satire on women (*Satirae* VI. 598–601): "For if she chose to distend and torture her womb with leaping boys, you would perhaps be the father of an Ethiopian and before long, a swarthy heir would fill the chief place in your will, a fellow you would not like to meet in the morning." Juvenal clearly equates blacks with the grotesque and the criminal, for in the previous satire he speaks scornfully of wine being served by "the bony hand of a black Moor, one whom you would not like to meet in the middle of the night, while you are driving through the tombs on the steep Latin way" (ibid., V. 54–55).

16. One's response to artistic objects is, of course, subjective. Certainly a few of the artistic representations of Negroes by Greco-Roman artists are not only beautiful in themselves but suggest an appreciation of negroid beauty by artists (for example, the popular janiform vases with their conjoined heads of a black woman and a white woman); but most of them are hideous and implicitly racist in their perspective (for example, the detail of a black woman dancing between a maenad and a satyr on a fourth-century B.C. askos). See Jean Vercoutter, Jean Leclant, Frank M. Snowden, Jr., and Jehan Desanges, *The Image of the Black in Western Art* (New York: William Morrow and Co., 1976), vol. 1, plates 193 and 220. Snowden's comments on the dancing black woman (p. 176) are simply incomprehensible.

17. David Ayalon, "The Muslim City and the Mamluk Military Aristocracy," in Ayalon, ed., *Studies on the Mamlūks of Egypt* (London: Variorum Reprints, 1977), pp. vii, 314. C. E. Bosworth suggests that in many parts of the Islamic world "white-skinned Europeans were prized even more highly than Turks." "Recruitment, Muster, and Review in Medieval Islamic Armies," V. J. Parry and M. E. Yapp, eds., *War, Technology, and Society in the Middle East* (London: Oxford University Press, 1975), p. 66. On Muslim Spain see Pierre Guichard, *Structures sociales "orientales" et "occidentales" dans l'Espagne musalmane* (Paris: Mouton, 1977), pp. 77–80, 122–124. See also V. L. Ménage, "Devshirme," *Encyclopedia of Islam*, ed. 2 (Leiden: E. J. Brill, 1965), vol. 2, pp. 210–213.

18. The homosexual use of slaves remained an important aspect of Islamic slavery right down to modern times. It was particularly common among elite masters and high-status slaves. See Paul Rycaut, *The Present State of the Ottoman Empire, 1668* (London: Arno Press, 1971), pp. 33–35. The practice was almost the norm among the mamluks, on which see David Ayalon, *L'esclavage du mamelouk* (Jerusalem: Oriental Notes and Studies, 1951), p. 14. In the Jebala area of Morocco, where homosexuality was common, so-called boy-markets were to be found as late as the early part of this century, when Carleton S. Coon studied the area. While the market el Had Ikanen of Ktama was notorious, similar boy-markets existed in other parts of the Jebala, especially among the Benzi Zerwali tribesmen. See Coon's *Tribes of the Rif* (Cambridge, Mass.: Peabody Museum of American Archeology and Ethnology, 1931), pp. 110–111.

19. Gabriel Baer, in his study of slavery in nineteenth-century Egypt, classified

slaves according to their color and sex. At the top of the hierarchy of female slaves were Greek and Circassian girls; "second best" were the Abyssinians; and at the bottom were blacks, some of whom were eunuchs. "Slavery in Nineteenth Century Egypt," *Journal of African History* 3 (1967): 417–441. For a more detailed analysis of the relative prices of slaves of different races in the Muslim market see Ralph A. Austen, "The Trans-Saharan Slave Trade: A Tentative Census," in Gemery and Hogendorn, *The Uncommon Market,* pp. 69–71.

20. Africans, however, were used in a wide variety of roles in India including those of soldier, statesman, and confidant. In the thirteenth-century sultanate of Delhi, Queen Raziya became so intimate with her Habshi slave Jalal-ud-din Yagut that the queen's father and other offended aristocrats killed him. The most famous African in India's history was Malik Ambar, an Ethiopian who was trained and promoted by Genghis Khan and later led the Indian counterassault against the Mogul armies. At his death he was regent-general of the Deccanis kingdom. See Joseph E. Harris, *The African Presence in Asia: Consequences of the East African Slave Trade* (Evanston, Ill.: Northwestern University Press, 1971), esp. chap. 7. In Ottoman Turkey the chief eunuch, or "Head of the Blessed Chamber," was usually a Negro. See C. Orhonly, "Khāsī," *Encyclopedia of Islam,* ed. 2 (Leiden: E. J. Brill, 1978), vol. 4, pp. 1087–93. References to black slaves in China go back to the fourth century A.D. These "K'unlun" slaves, as they were called, were "very popular," especially in T'ang times. See C. M. Wilbur, *Slavery in China during the Former Han Dynasty, 206 B.C. to A.D 25.* (Chicago: Field Museum of Natural History, 1943), p. 93.

21. One of the spiciest scandals in Jonsonian England was the affair of the Duchess of Queensberry with her black protégé and former slave, Soubise. Soubise later became the most sensational Don Juan in the bedrooms of upper-class British ladies. For his naughty excesses the duchess eventually packed him off to India, where he founded a riding school. Black servants were de rigeur among the royal and noble families of eighteenth-century England and, according to James Walvin, "became so common among the aristocracy that the Duke of Dorset, whose family had employed them for the past 200 years, abandoned the practice in favor of Chinese servants." See Walvin, *Black and White: The Negro and English Society, 1555-1945* (London: Allen Lane, Penguin Press, 1973), pp. 53–56. See also the portrait by Mignard of the Duchess of Portsmouth with her black page, reproduced in Walvin, *Black and White,* facing p. 83.

22. "Théorie de l'esclavage," in M. I. Finley, ed., *Slavery in Classical Antiquity* (Cambridge: W. Heffer and Sons, 1960), pp. 151–169.

23. Lin, *Liang-shan I-chia,* pp. 81–82. This reluctance to enslave fellow ethnics is true of other primitive Asian tribes (for example, the Gilyak), but the opposite is the case among the advanced Asian civilizations. On the Gilyaks' "abhorrence" of endoservitude see Leopold von Schrenck, *Die Völker des Amur-Landes: Reisen und Forschungen im Amur-Lande in den Jahren 1854-1856* (St. Petersburg: Kaiserliche Akademie der Wissenschaften, 1881–1895), vol. 3, p. 646.

24. Svend E. Holsoe, "Slavery and Economic Response among the Vai," in Miers and Kopytoff, *Slavery in Africa,* p. 290.

25. There were, however, client relationships between different groups of Tuareg. Furthermore, it is not entirely true that fellow Tuaregs were never enslaved. L. Cabot Briggs mentions the case of Moussa ag Amastan, who was leader of the

Ahaggar from 1905 to 1921 and had as one of his numerous concubines a Tuareg slave girl whom he had acquired during a raid into the Niger Bend country. Briggs further observes that "although the case was exceptional, it was by no means unique." "The Tuareg," in Briggs, *The Living Races of the Sahara Desert* (Cambridge, Mass.: Peabody Museum of American Archeology and Ethnology, 1958), p. 98.

26. This we would expect from the fact that crime is an important source of slaves in such societies, for example the Ibos. Even where slaves are procured primarily through warfare, slavery remains intraethnic, since most such wars are "internal" or within the tribe or language group. Typical of the small-scale intraethnic slavery arising from interclan warfare are the precontact Cherokees. See the recent study of slavery among this group by Theda Perdue, *Slavery and the Evolution of Cherokee Society, 1540-1866* (Knoxville: University of Tennessee Press, 1979), pp. 6-18. After white contact, however, the Cherokees rapidly adopted the practice of plantation slavery, using black slaves.

27. Kalervo Oberg, *The Social Economy of the Tlingit Indians* (Seattle: University of Washington Press, 1973), p. 84.

28. Alison Burford, *Craftsmen in Greek and Roman Society* (Ithaca, N.Y.: Cornell University Press, 1972).

29. Ibid. See also M. I. Finley, *The Ancient Economy* (Berkeley: University of California Press, 1973), esp. chaps. 1, 2, 5, 6; and William L. Westermann, "Industrial Slavery in Roman Italy," *Journal of Economic History* 2 (1942): 149-163.

30. "The Contributions of Slaves to and Their Influence upon the Culture of Early Islam" (Ph.D. diss., Princeton University, 1942), p. i.

31. Lynn White, Jr., *Medieval Technology and Social Change* (Oxford: Clarendon Press, 1962), p. 116.

32. See, for example, Arthur Tuden and Leonard Plotnicov, eds., *Social Stratification in Africa* (New York: Free Press, 1970), pp. 15-18, 59-92.

33. Orlando Patterson, *The Sociology of Slavery: Jamaica, 1655-1838* (Rutherford, N.J.: Fairleigh Dickinson University Press, 1969), pp. 15-51. On the Caribbean slave societies generally see L. J. Ragatz, "Absentee Landlordism in the British Caribbean, 1750-1833," *Agricultural History* 5 (1931): 7-26. For a more equivocal view see Douglas Hall, "Absentee Proprietorship in the British West Indies to about 1850," *Jamaican Historical Review* 4 (1964): 15-35. Supporting Hall's view that absenteeism varied in its impact is Richard B. Sheridan, in his *Sugar and Slavery: An Economic History of the British West Indies, 1623-1775* (Lodge Hill, Barbados: Caribbean Universities Press, 1974), pp. 385-387. The reservations of Hall and Sheridan relate more to the personal qualities of absentees and locals than to the structural effects of absenteeism. I remain firmly convinced that absenteeism was an unmitigated disaster for slaves insofar as their material treatment was concerned. By way of contrast see Eugene D. Genovese's discussion of the relative absence of the problem in the U.S. slave South, with the exception of the local absenteeism of the Mississippi Valley. *Roll, Jordan, Roll* (New York: Pantheon, 1974), pp. 10-13. See also Genovese's *The World the Slaveholders Made* (New York: Vintage Books, 1971), pp. 28-31, 42-44, 77-79. On the French Caribbean see Gabriel Debien, *Les esclaves aux Antilles françaises, XVIIe-XVIIIe Siècles* (Basse-Terre, Fort-de-France: Société d'histoire de la Guadaloupe et Société d'histoire de la Martinique, 1974),

p. 493; and his *Plantations et esclaves à Saint-Dominque,* University of Dakar Publications of the History Section, no. 3 (1963), pp. 9–15, 49–55. On Cuba see Franklin W. Knight, *Slave Society in Cuba during the Nineteenth Century* (Madison: University of Wisconsin Press, 1970), p. 69.

On the whole, absenteeism was more of the internal form in South America; that is, owners lived in the more desirable urban centers away from their plantations. Where this happened the results were often, though not always, deleterious for the slaves. A detailed discussion of the effects of local absenteeism in the Chocó area of Colombia is given in William F. Sharp, *Slavery on the Spanish Frontier: The Colombian Chocó, 1680–1810* (Norman: University of Oklahoma Press, 1976), pp. 24, 123, 131–132. On Brazil see C. R. Boxer, *Salvador de Sa and the Struggle for Brazil and Angola* (London: Athlone Press, 1952), pp. 14–15.

Absenteeism is only one of several factors accounting for the brutal treatment of slaves, so I am not suggesting that there is a perfect correlation between the two variables. A great deal depends on the interaction of other (usually economic) variables. Thus the presence of planters in the Vassouras region of Brazil in no way worked in favor of the slaves, on which see Stanley J. Stein, *Vassouras: A Brazilian Coffee County, 1850–1900* (Cambridge, Mass.: Harvard University Press, 1957), esp. chaps. 5–7.

34. On the Somali see Ioan M. Lewis, *Peoples of the Horn of Africa* (London: International African Institute, 1955), pp. 126–128. Until quite recently there were many slave villages owned by various pastoral Arab tribes in Saudi Arabia, Yemen, and the Hadramaut. These villages specialized in agriculture, especially date growing. See Sylvia Bailes, "Slavery in Arabia" (Philadelphia: Institute for Israel and the Middle East of the Dropsie College for Hebrew and Cognate Learning, 1952), p. 5 (manuscript); and Carleton S. Coon, *Caravan: The Story of the Middle East* (New York: Holt, 1951), p. 161. Regarding this practice among the Manchu, Owen Lattimore in his classic study suggests that such absenteeism was an outgrowth of military colonization during the period of conquest and expansion. Chinese slaves were placed on large farms, which the Manchus lacked the skill to manage. The disadvantage for the Manchus, according to Lattimore, was that "it encouraged the wealthy, especially those who had become successful in official careers, to become absentee landlords." Eventually the lands were usurped by descendants of the slaves. Lattimore, *Manchuria: Cradle of Conflict* (New York: Macmillan, 1935), p. 180.

35. E. A. Thompson, "Slavery in Early Germany," in Finley, *Slavery in Classical Antiquity,* pp. 18, 26–28.

36. Lovejoy and Baier, "The Desert-Side Economy of the Central Sudan," pp. 551–581.

37. Robert S. Rattray, *Ashanti Law and Constitution* (Oxford: Clarendon Press, 1929), p. 229.

38. Carol P. MacCormack, "Wono: Institutionalized Dependency in Sherbro Descent Groups," in Miers and Kopytoff, *Slavery in Africa,* pp. 189–190.

39. Kenneth Little, *The Mende of Sierra Leone* (London: Routledge & Kegan Paul, 1951), p. 83.

40. Polly Hill, "From Slavery to Freedom: The Case of Farm Slavery in Nigerian Hausaland," *Comparative Studies in Society and History* 18 (1976): 395–426; and Hogendorn, "The Economics of Slave Use," pp. 369–383.

41. I. M. Diakanoff, "The Commune in the Ancient East as Treated in the Works of Soviet Researchers," in Stephen P. Dunn and Ethel Dunn, eds., *Introduction to Soviet Ethnography* (London: Social Science Research Station, 1974), pp. 521–522. See also M. Dandamayev, "Foreign Slaves on the Estates of the Achaemenid Kings and Their Nobles," Proceedings of the 25th Congress of Orientalists, Moscow, 1960 (Moscow: n.p., 1963), pp. 147–154. Many scholars strongly dispute the claim that these tenant farmers in the ancient Near East can be called slaves. See, in particular, I. J. Gelb, "From Freedom to Slavery," in Bayerische Akademie der Wissenschaften, *Gesellschaftsklassen im Alten Zweiströmland und in den angrenzenden Gebieten*, 18 (Munich, 1972).

42. For examples see, on the Kerebe, Gerald W. Hartwig, "Changing Forms of Servitude among the Kerebe of Tanzania," in Miers and Kopytoff, *Slavery in Africa*, pp. 266–267. On the Mende, see Little, *The Mende of Sierra Leone*, p. 39. On ancient India, Dev Raj Chanana, *Slavery in Ancient India* (New Delhi: People's Publishing House, 1960), p. 32. On the ancient Near East, Bernard Siegel, *Slavery during the Third Dynasty of Ur*, Memoirs of the American Anthropological Association, no. 66 (1947), p. 40; Isaac Mendelsohn, *Slavery in the Ancient Near East* (Oxford: Oxford University Press, 1949), p. 67; *Jewish Encyclopedia* (New York: Funk & Wagnalls, 1905), vol. 11, p. 406. On ancient Greece, Douglas M. MacDowell, *The Law in Classical Athens* (Ithaca, N.Y.: Cornell University Press, 1978), p. 80, also pp. 133–137. On Rome, John Crook, *Law and Life of Rome* (Ithaca, N.Y.: Cornell University Press, 1967), pp. 188–189; and W. W. Buckland, *The Roman Law of Slavery* (Cambridge: Cambridge University Press, 1908), chaps. 8–10. On Visigothic Spain see P. D. King, *Law and Society in the Visigothic Kingdom* (Cambridge: Cambridge University Press, 1972), p. 170; and Charles Verlinden, *L'esclavage dans l'Europe médiévale* (Bruges: De Tempel, 1955), vol. 1, p. 88. On Islamic law in general see R. Brunschvig, "Abd," *Encyclopedia of Islam*, ed. 2 (Leiden: E. J. Brill, 1960), vol. 1, pp. 28–29. On the United States see John C. Hurd, *The Law of Freedom and Bondage in the United States* (Boston: Little, Brown, 1858); W. E. Moore, "Slave Law and Social Structure," *Journal of Negro History* 26 (1941): 171–202; Kenneth Stampp, *The Peculiar Institution* (London: Eyre & Spottiswoode, 1964), chap. 5; on the Caribbean, E. V. Goveia, *Slave Society in the British Leeward Islands at the End of the Eighteenth Century* (New Haven: Yale University Press, 1965), chap. 3.

43. Ellen S. Unruh, "The Landowning Slave: A Korean Phenomenon," *Korean Journal* 16 (1976): 31.

44. Unruh's strictures deserve the greatest attention. Normally I would have no problem accepting her thesis that the Korean case is exceptional. It is not my aim to set forth generalizations that admit no exceptions, for such phenomena are not to be found even in the physical universe. Having said this, however, I must nonetheless point out certain aspects of the Koryŏ period that lend a rather different interpretation to what Unruh calls "the landowning slave, a Korean phenomenon."

Following the Mongol invasions and occupation in the thirteenth century, and the marauding of both Japanese and dissident internal agents, there was a great expansion of private agricultural estates and increasing ambiguity in the countryside between slave status and free status. What suffered most were the precise definitions of base and honorable status. Moreover, there were radical changes in the land-tenure system at this time: private ownership of land and expropriation of both crown lands and peasant holdings by the growing nobility were rampant. Many peasant landholders became slaves and attached themselves to lords to avoid murderous taxes, ruinous military service, and the devastation of bandits. This, then, was a period of transition which saw a large segment of the peasant class descending into slavery. It is understandable that for a while they would continue to hold formal claims to their land; but in actuality these claims meant nothing, and it was only a matter of time before even the formal claims were lost to the rapacious absentee lords. Seen in these terms, it is doubtful that Korea is after all an exception. In addition to Unruh see William E. Henthorn, *Korea: The Mongol Invasions* (Leiden: E. J. Brill, 1963); and Han Woo-Keun, *History of Korea* (Seoul: Eul-Yoo Publishing Co., 1970), p. 181. On the early Yi period see Byung-Sak Ku, *Hanguk Sahoe Pŏpchesa Tŭksu Yŏngu* [A Study on the History of Law in Korea] (Seoul: Tongo Chu'lp'ansa, 1968), chap. 4. (In Korean.)

45. "Slavery and the Law in Muscovy," paper presented at the Third International Conference on Muscovite History, Oxford, September 1–4, 1975. See also Hellie's more recent *Slavery in Russia, 1450-1725* (forthcoming).

46. Ruth Pike, "Sevillian Society in the Sixteenth Century: Slaves and Freedmen," *Hispanic American Historical Review* 47 (1967): 353–356. A similar fear of black competition in the U.S. South resulted in monopolization of the most highly skilled jobs by working-class whites. See Ira Berlin, *Slaves without Masters* (New York: Vintage Books, 1976), pp. 60, 229–233, 240–241, 349–351.

47. On Visigothic Spain, for example, see Verlinden, *L'esclavage dans l'Europe médiévale*, vol. 1, pp. 88–89. The issue presented many complex conceptual and sociological problems, which I take up in the next chapter.

48. Crook, *Law and Life of Rome*, p. 189. The issue of what principles, if any, determined the disposal of the peculium upon manumission in ancient Rome is still controversial.

49. Robert Schlaifer, "Greek Theories of Slavery from Homer to Aristotle," in Finley, *Slavery in Classical Antiquity*, p. 111, presents the benign view of the laws. I personally have read the translation of the laws by Augustus Merriam and they do impress me as benign: see his "Law Code of the Kretan Gortyna," *American Journal of Archeology* 1(1885): 324–350; 2(1886): 24–45. However, I have been warned by an eminent specialist that even the translation of these laws remains ambiguous, to say nothing of their sociological interpretation. The claim that Gortyna was a specially humane case of advanced slavery must therefore be viewed, for the time being, with caution, perhaps even with skepticism.

50. *Ashanti Law and Constitution*, pp. 40–41. Note, however, that the Ashanti case is not without its problems. Ivor Wilks presents an interpretation of Ashanti slavery that is much less "domestic" and far more "commercial" than Rattray's. See Wilks, *Asante in the Nineteenth Century* (Cambridge: Cambridge University Press, 1975).

51. *Ashanti* (Oxford: Clarendon Press, 1923), p. 230.

52. Ibid., pp. 43–44.

53. Ibid.

54. Varro, *The Agriculture*, I, 17.5, in W. D. Hooper and H. B. Ash, trans. and eds., *Cato and Varro: On Agriculture* (Cambridge, Mass.: Loeb Classical Library, Harvard University Press, 1935), p. 227.

55. David Brion Davis, *The Problem of Slavery in Western Culture* (Ithaca, N.Y.: Cornell University Press, 1966), pp. 104–105.

56. See the theoretical discussions and illustrative case studies in R. F. Winch and L. W. Goodman, eds., *Selected Studies in Marriage and the Family* (New York: Holt, Rinehart and Winston, 1968). Among the traditional Dahomeans sixteen different kinds of marriage were recognized. See M. J. Herskovits, *Dahomey: An Ancient West African Kingdom* (New York: J. J. Augustin, 1938), vol. 1.

57. "Slavery and Emancipation among the Mende," in Miers and Kopytoff, *Slavery in Africa,* p. 421. This disruption of the union of slaves may have been unusual even for the Mende and was true of *some* masters only during the unsettled period that Grace studied.

58. Brunschvig, "Abd," p. 27.

59. Ibid., p. 29.

60. Enrico Cerulli, "Il diritto consuetudinario della Somalia settentrionale (Migiurtini)," in *Somalia, scritti vari editi ed inediti* 2 (1959): 21.

61. Rattray, *Ashanti Law and Constitution,* p. 38.

62. Once again a distinction must be made between the traditional domestic slavery described by Rattray and the more complex situation during the nineteenth century described by Wilks. The Ashanti laws at that time may well have been the same for house-born slaves, but different for trade slaves and those working in the mines.

63. G. R. Driver and John C. Miles, eds., *The Babylonian Laws* (Oxford: Clarendon Press. 1960), vol. 1, p. 47.

64. Mendelsohn, *Slavery in the Ancient Near East,* pp. 40–41.

65. Siegel, *Slavery during the Third Dynasty of Ur,* p. 40.

66. For a detailed discussion of this problem during the T'ang dynasty see Niida Noburu, *Chūgoku hōseishi Kenkyū* [A Study of Chinese Legal History] (Tokyo: Tokyo University Press, 1962), pp. 100–113. (In Japanese.)

67. Westermann, *Slave Systems of Greek and Roman Antiquity,* p. 23.

68. R. H. Barrow, *Slavery in the Roman Empire* (London: Methuen & Co., 1928), p. 158.

69. H. R. P. Finberg, *The Agrarian History of England and Wales* (Cambridge: Cambridge University Press, 1972), p. 435.

70. Marc Bloch, *Slavery and Serfdom in the Middle Ages: Selected Essays,* trans. William R. Beer (Berkeley: University of California Press, 1975), p. 14.

71. This is discussed at great length by Verlinden for both France and the Iberian peninsula. See in particular his *L'esclavage dans l'Europe médiévale,* vol. 1, pp. 30–42. On the church's role in medieval Italy, as well as the unions of slaves, see ibid., vol. 2 (1977), pp. 80–96, 192–207, 526.

72. See Stephen C. Crawford, "Quantified Memory: A Study of the WPA and Fisk University Slave Narrative Collection" (Ph.D. diss., University of Chicago, 1980), chaps. 5 and 6.

73. The hacienda region of Córdoba in Veracruz, Mexico, was typical of the nonplantation areas of Latin America, on which see Cathy Duke, "The Family in Eighteenth-Century Plantation Society in Mexico," in Vera Rubin and Arthur Tudens, eds., *Comparative Perspectives on Slavery in New World Plantation Societies* (New York: New York Academy of Sciences, 1977), vol. 292, pp. 226–258. On the Jesuit haciendas of colonial Peru, "families were rarely divided" although the system was harsh and highly regimented; see Nicholas P. Cushner, "Slave Mortality and Reproduction on Jesuit Haciendas in Colonial Peru," *Hispanic American Historical*

Review 55 (1975): 177–199 (quote on p. 189). The Jesuits kept slave families intact for economic rather than humanitarian reasons and were often more inhuman masters than their lay counterparts. There is evidence that Jesuit hacienda owners in Córdoba, Argentina, engaged in deliberate slave breeding in the middle of the eighteenth century; see Rolando Mellafe, *Negro Slavery in Latin America* (Berkeley: University of California Press, 1975), pp. 140–141. On the instability of slave unions in the advanced plantation areas of Latin America, see Stanley J. Stein, *Vassouras,* pp. 155–157; and Manuel Moreno Fraginals, *The Sugarmill: The Socioeconomic Complex of Sugar in Cuba* (New York: Monthly Review Press, 1976), pp. 142–143.

74. Bailes, "Slavery in Arabia," p. 7.

75. Virginia Gutierrez de Pineda, *Organizatión social en la Guajira* (Bogotá: Instituto Etnologico Nacional, 1950), p. 142.

76. Ivan Veniaminov, *Zapiski ob ostrovakh Unalashkinskago otdĩela* [Notes on the Islands of the Unalaska District] (St. Petersburg: Izdano Izhdiveniem Rossiĭsko-Amerikanskoĭ Kompanii, 1840), vol. 2, p. 85.

77. Ronald Olson, *Social Structure and Social Life of the Tlingit in Alaska* (Berkeley: University of California Press, 1967), p. 53.

78. Aurel Krause, *The Tlingit Indians,* trans. Erna Gunther (Seattle: University of Washington Press, 1956), p. 159.

79. Ibid., p. 280.

80. *The Social Organization and the Secret Societies of the Kwakiutl Indians* (Washington, D.C.: U.S. National Museum Report, 1895–1897), p. 664.

81. U. P. Averkieva, *Slavery among the Indians of North America* (Moscow; U.S.S.R. Academy of Science, 1941), p. 101. See also Oberg, *The Social Economy of the Tlingit Indians,* pp. 116–128.

82. Herrlee G. Creel, *The Birth of China* (New York: Frederick Ungar, 1937), pp. 204–216. See also Kuo Mo-jo, "Nu-li-chih shih-tai" [The Period of Slave Systems]; and idem, "Tu liao Chi Yin-Chou hsuan-jen Shih-shih" [My Comments on "Descriptions of Historical Facts on Various Slaves as Sacrifices in the Yin and Chou Dynasties"], both in Office of Historical Studies, *Selected Essays on Problems concerning Periodization of Slave Systems and Feudal Systems in China* (Peking: Joint Publishing Co., 1956), pp. 1–58. (In Chinese.)

83. Hayakawa Jiró, "The Position and Significance of the Slave System after the Taika Restoration," in Rekishi Kagaku Kyōgikai, ed., *Kodaii Kokka To Doreisei* [Ancient State and Slave Systems] (Tokyo: Azekura Shobō, 1972), pp. 92–108. (In Japanese.)

84. On human sacrifice in early and later Ur and in early dynastic Egypt see Jack Finegan, *Archeological History of the Ancient Middle East* (Boulder, Colo.: Westview Press, 1979), pp. 32, 53, 189. All over Asia and southern European Russia there is evidence of widespread human sacrifice between the seventh century B.C. and the ninth century A.D. See Ivan Lopatin, *The Cult of the Dead among the Natives of the Amur Basin* (The Hague: Mouton, 1960), pp. 103–104.

85. The Eurasiatic Scythians were typical. See Anatoli M. Khazanov, "O kharaktere rablov ladeniia u skifor" [On the Character of Slavery among the Scythians], in *Vestnik drevnie istorii* 119 (1972): 159–170.

86. Johannes Brondsted, *The Vikings* (London: Penguin Books, 1960), pp. 301–305. On the sacrifice of slaves to the gods see pp. 284–285.

87. Carlos Bosch Garcia, *La esclavitud prehispánica entre los Aztecas* (Mexico City: Colegio de Mexico, Centro de Estudios Históricos, 1944), pp. 40–49.

88. Herskovits, *Dahomey*, pp. 50–56.

89. James H. Vaughan, "Mafakur: A Limbic Institution of the Margi," in Miers and Kopytoff, *Slavery in Africa*, p. 98.

90. Rattray, *Ashanti Law and Constitution*, p. 38. Ivor Wilks has argued strongly (and understandably) that during the nineteenth century a great deal of what was called human sacrifice by Europeans was really capital punishment. While this is no doubt true, it does not alter the fact that there was indeed human sacrifice during this and previous periods, though on a scale much smaller than that claimed by the missionaries and other contemporary commentators. See Wilks, *Asante in the Nineteenth Century*, pp. 592–599.

91. Bruno Lasker, *Human Bondage in Southeast Asia* (Chapel Hill: University of North Carolina Press, 1950), p. 287; and Andrew Turton, "Thai Institutions of Slavery," in James L. Watson, ed., *Asian and African Systems of Slavery* (Oxford: Basil Blackwell, 1980), p. 270.

92. S. W. Baron, *The Social and Religious History of the Jews* (New York: Columbia University Press, 1937), vol. 1, p. 59.

93. Bloch, *Slavery and Serfdom in the Middle Ages*, pp. 14, 35; Churchill Babington, *The Influence of Christianity in Promoting the Abolition of Slavery in Europe* (Cambridge: Cambridge University Press, 1846), p. 57; and Verlinden, *L'esclavage dans l'Europe médiévale*, vol. 1, p. 296.

94. Iris Origo, " 'The Domestic Enemy': The Eastern Slaves in Tuscany in the Fourteenth and Fifteenth Centuries," *Speculum* 30 (1955): 340.

95. Glenn R. Morrow, "The Murder of Slaves in Attic Law," *Classical Philology* 32 (1937): 224–225. See also Douglas MacDowell, *Athenian Homicide Law* (Manchester: Manchester University Press, 1963), p. 21.

96. Buckland, *The Roman Law of Slavery*, pp. 36–38.

97. Verlinden, *L'esclavage dans l'Europe médiévale*, vol. 1, pp. 466–467.

98. Cited in Morrow, "The Murder of Slaves in Attic Law," p. 313.

99. J. R. Dickson, *The Arab of the Desert: A Glimpse of Badawin Life in Kuwait and Saudi Arabia* (London: Allen & Unwin, 1951), p. 504.

100. Williams, *Thraldom in Ancient Iceland*, p. 111.

101. Schlaifer, "Greek Theories of Slavery," p. 108.

102. See, for example, the case of the Sherbro of Sierra Leone, among whom it is held that any human blood spilled in violence defiles the land. MacCormack, "Wono," pp. 188–189.

103. Morrow, "The Murder of Slaves in Attic Law," p. 214.

104. See MacDowell, *Athenian Homicide Law*, pp. 20–21, for a thorough review of the complexities involved.

105. Morrow, "The Murder of Slaves in Attic Law," p. 223.

106. E. Grace, "Status Distinctions in the Draconian Law," *EIRENE* (1973): 18.

107. Ibid., p. 23.

108. Ibid., pp. 23–24.

109. On the meaning and prevalence of torture in Greco-Roman slavery see Finley, *Ancient Slavery and Modern Ideology*, pp. 94–95.

110. Buckland, *The Roman Law of Slavery*, pp. 31–36.

111. Ibid., p. 32, table 8.3.

112. Barrow, *Slavery in the Roman Empire,* p. 46.

113. J. S. Boston, *The Igala Kingdom* (Ibadan: Oxford University Press, 1968), pp. 162–175.

114. Lewis, *Peoples of the Horn of Africa,* p. 126.

115. W. E. Maxwell, "The Law Relating to Slavery among the Malays," *Journal of the Straits Branch of the Royal Asiatic Society,* no. 22 (1890): 259, 273.

116. Verlinden, *L'esclavage dans l'Europe médiévale,* vol. 1, pp. 81–82.

117. Ibid., pp. 460–461.

118. For example, on the Somali see Cerulli, "Il diritto consuetudinario," p. 22.

119. Williams, *Thraldom in Ancient Iceland,* pp. 103–104.

120. Verlinden, *L'esclavage dans l'Europe médiévale,* vol. 1, p. 90.

121. Rattray, *Ashanti Law and Constitution,* p. 44.

122. James B. Christensen, *Double Descent among the Fanti* (New Haven: Human Relations Area Files, 1954), p. 39.

123. For a detailed discussion of the many legal problems created by such transactions in Roman society see Buckland, *The Roman Law of Slavery,* chaps. 6–9.

124. Crook, *Law and Life of Rome,* p. 189.

125. Buckland, *The Roman Law of Slavery,* pp. 159, 163.

126. Orlando Patterson, "Slavery and Slave Revolts: A Sociohistorical Analysis of the First Maroon War, 1665–1740," *Social and Economic Studies* 19 (1970): 289–325.

127. On Iceland see Williams, *Thraldom in Ancient Iceland,* pp. 109–110; on Norway see Foote and Wilson, *The Viking Achievement,* p. 70.

128. Maxwell, "The Law Relating to Slavery," p. 297; see also R. O. Winstedt, *The Malays: A Cultural History* (New York: Philosophical Library, 1950), p. 101.

129. On the Ashanti see Rattray, *Ashanti Law and Constitution,* p. 42. On the Nyinba see Nancy E. Levine, "Opposition and Independence: Demographic and Economic Perspectives on Nyinba Slavery," in Watson, *Asian and African Systems of Slavery,* pp. 205–206.

130. A. Cameron, "Inscriptions Relating to Sacral Manumission and Confession," *Harvard Theological Review* 22 (1939): 165.

131. Westermann, *The Slave Systems of Greek and Roman Antiquity,* p. 155.

132. Cited in Babington, *The Influence of Christianity,* pp. 57–58.

133. Origo, " 'The Domestic Enemy,' " pp. 350–351.

134. Maxwell, "The Law Relating to Slavery," p. 291.

135. MacCormack, "Wono," p. 189.

136. A. M. Wergeland, *Slavery in Germanic Society during the Middle Ages* (Chicago: University of Chicago Press, 1916), p. 61.

137. Origo, " 'The Domestic Enemy,' " pp. 349–350.

138. Robert S. Rattray, *Ashanti Proverbs* (Oxford: Clarendon Press, 1929), pp. 41–42.

139. On ancient Rome see Barrow, *Slavery in the Roman Empire,* pp. 59–60. On the Colombian Chocó see Sharp, *Slavery on the Spanish Frontier,* pp. 138–139.

140. On the Tuareg practice see André Bourgeot, "Rapports esclavagistes et conditions d'affranchissement chez les Imuhaġ," in Claude Meillassoux, *L'esclavage en Afrique précoloniale* (Paris: François Maspero, 1975), pp. 85–86.

141. Martin A. Klein, "Servitude among the Wolof and Sereer of Senegambia," in Miers and Kopytoff, *Slavery in Africa*, p. 347.

142. Bailes, "Slavery in Arabia," p. 8.

143. Bourgeot, "Rapports esclavagistes," p. 86.

144. N. Adriani and Albert C. Kruyt, *De Bare'e Sprekende Toradjas van Midden-Celebes* [The Bare'e-speaking Toradja of Central Celebes] (Amsterdam: Nood-Hollandsche Uitgevers Maatschappij, 1950), vol. 1, pp. 233–234.

145. Arthur Tuden, "Slavery and Social Stratification among the Ila of Central Africa," in Tuden and Plotnicov, *Social Stratification in Africa*, p. 57.

146. Crawford, "Quantified Memory," p. 77 and chap. 3 generally.

147. Ibid., chaps. 5 and 6.

148. Ibid., pp. 82–85.

149. Ibid., pp. 62, 146, 179, 187.

150. Ibid., p. 227.

151. Cited in Chanana, *Slavery in Ancient India*, p. 57.

152. Ibid., p. 56.

153. Ibid.

154. *A Diary from Dixie* (Boston: Houghton Mifflin Co., 1949).

155. "We Wear the Mask," in Jay David, ed., *Black Defiance* (New York: William Morrow and Co., 1972), p. 63.

8. Manumission: Its Meaning and Modes

1. I use the term *manumission* to connote the legal release of an individual from slavery either by the master or by a superior authority, such as the state. Manumission constituted the means of release for almost all ex-slaves. While some running away and rebellion occurred, in the vast majority of slaveholding societies insignificant numbers of slaves were released by these means.

In no way do I mean to slight the importance of rebellion and other forms of resistance by slaves. I have discussed these issues elsewhere and shall return to them in a later work. See Orlando Patterson, "Slavery and Slave Revolts: A Sociohistorical Analysis of the First Maroon War, 1665–1740," *Social and Economic Studies* 19 (1970): 289–325.

2. See the detailed discussion in W. W. Buckland, *The Roman Law of Slavery* (Cambridge: Cambridge University Press, 1908), pp. 714–723.

3. Ibid., p. 714.

4. Ibid., p. 715.

5. For a review of the main issues see Raymond Firth, *Symbols: Public and Private* (Ithaca, N.Y.: Cornell University Press, 1973), pp. 368–381.

6. Marcel Mauss, *The Gift*, trans. Ian Cullison (New York: W. W. Norton, 1967), pp. 3–5.

7. Marshall Sahlins, *Stone Age Economics* (London: Tavistock Publications, 1974), p. 220.

8. Mauss, *The Gift*, p. 63.

9. Sahlins, *Stone Age Economics*, pp. 149–183.

10. Firth, *Symbols*, pp. 381–382.

11. See the more detailed statement in his and Henry Hubert's, *Sacrifice: Its Nature and Function,* trans. W. D. Hall (Chicago; University of Chicago Press, 1964). For recent developments in the anthropological study of sacrifice see M. F. C. Bourdillon, ed., *Sacrifice* (New York: Academic Press, 1980).

12. Mauss, *The Gift,* p. 13.

13. Ibid., p. 14.

14. Wyatt MacGaffey, "Economic and Social Dimensions of Kongo Slavery (Zaire)," in Suzanne Miers and Igor I. Kopytoff, eds., *Slavery in Africa* (Madison: University of Wisconsin Press, 1977), p. 244.

15. Among many North American Indian tribes the captive who escaped and returned to his tribe was treated with utter contempt and regarded as socially dead. This was particularly true of militaristic tribes, such as the Iroquois and the Haida. See W. C. Macleod, "Debtor and Chattel Slavery in Aboriginal North America," *American Anthropologist* 27 (1925): 378.

16. Gerald W. Hartwig, "Changing Forms of Servitude among the Kerebe of Tanzania," in Miers and Kopytoff, *Slavery in Africa,* p. 271.

17. Liebeschuetz, *Continuity and Change in Roman Religion* (Oxford: Clarendon Press, 1979), pp. 70–72. For a more detailed discussion of the traditional Lares cult see Robert E. A. Palmer, *Roman Religion and Roman Empire: Five Essays* (Philadelphia: University of Pennsylvania Press, 1974), pp. 114–120. On the prominent role of freedmen in the Lares cult see Franz Bömer, *Untersuchungen über die Religion der Sklaven in Griechenland und Rom* (Wiesbaden: Akademie Mainz, 1957), vol. 1, pp. 32–36. See also Keith Hopkins, *Conquerors and Slaves* (Cambridge: Cambridge University Press, 1978), pp. 211–215.

18. Peter Foote and David M. Wilson, *The Viking Achievement* (London: Sidgwick & Jackson, 1970), p. 73.

19. Dev Raj Chanana, *Slavery in Ancient India* (New Delhi: People's Publishing House, 1960), pp. 80, 116–117.

20. *Slavery in Germanic Society during the Middle Ages* (Chicago: University of Chicago Press, 1916), p. 150. See also Carl O. Williams, *Thraldom in Ancient Iceland* (Chicago: University of Chicago Press, 1937), pp. 129–130.

21. "The Manumission of Slaves in Colonial Brazil: Bahia, 1684–1745," *Hispanic American Historical Review* 54 (1974): 619.

22. Ira Berlin, *Slaves without Masters* (New York: Vintage Books, 1976), p. 149.

23. Wergeland, *Slavery in Germanic Society,* pp. 115–116.

24. Ibid., pp. 133–134.

25. Ibid., p. 157.

26. G. R. Driver and John C. Miles, eds., *The Babylonian Laws* (Oxford: Clarendon Press, 1960), vol. 1, p. 226.

27. Examples of selective testamentary manumission among seventeeth-century Mexican masters are given in Colin A. Palmer, *Slaves of the White God: Blacks in Mexico, 1570–1650* (Cambridge, Mass.: Harvard University Press, 1976), p. 174.

28. Williams, *Thraldom in Ancient Iceland,* pp. 13–14.

29. A. Playfair, *The Garos* (London: David Nutt, 1909); and W. W. Hunter, "Garo Hills," in his *Imperial Gazetteer of India* (London: Trubner, 1885), vol. 5, p. 30.

30. N. Adriani and Albert C. Kruyt, *De Bare'e Sprekende Toradjas van Mid-*

den-Celebes [The Bare'e-speaking Toradjas of Central Celebes] (Amsterdam: Nood-Hollandsche Uitgevers Maatschappij, 1950), vol. 3, pp. 201, 261, 505, 523. Compare the practice of the Goldi, in which a wife lies with her husband's corpse or on his grave as a substitute for previous human sacrifice. Ivan Lopatin, *The Cult of the Dead among the Natives of the Amur Basin* (The Hague: Mouton and Co., 1960), p. 103.

31. Aurel Krause, *The Tlingit Indians,* trans. Erna Gunther (Seattle: University of Washington Press, 1956), pp. 112, 153, 161; and Kalervo Oberg, *The Social Economy of the Tlingit Indians* (Seattle: University of Washington Press, 1973), p. 34.

32. U. P. Averkieva, *Slavery among the Indians of North America* (Moscow: U.S.S.R. Academy of Sciences, 1941), p. 112.

33. Philip Drucker, *The Northern and Central Nootkan Tribes* (Washington, D.C.: Government Printing Office, 1951), p. 47.

34. Carlos Bosch Garcia, *La esclavitud prehispánica entre los Aztecas* (Mexico City: Colegio de Mexico, Centro de Estudios Históricos, 1944), pp. 71–72.

35. Martin A. Klein, "Servitude among the Wolof and Sereer of Senegambia," in Miers and Kopytoff, *Slavery in Africa,* p. 348.

36. David Daube, "Two Early Patterns of Manumission," *Journal of Roman Studies* 36 (1946): 59, 73. See also Buckland, *The Roman Law of Slavery,* p. 443.

37. Buckland, *The Roman Law of Slavery,* p. 443.

38. Palmer, *Roman Religion and Roman Empire,* pp. 157–158.

39. R. H. Barrow, *Slavery in the Roman Empire* (London: Methuen & Co., 1928), p. 175.

40. "The Economics of Human Sacrifice," *African Economic Review* 11 (1975): 8.

41. Richard Hellie, *Slavery in Russia, 1450–1725* (forthcoming), chap. 5, pp. 27–30. It is significant that for some favored slaves enslavement ended legally with the death of the master.

42. Robert N. Bellah, *Beyond Belief* (New York: Harper & Row, 1970), pp. 20–39. For the classic sociological treatment of this problem see Max Weber, *The Sociology of Religion,* trans. Ephraim Fischoff (Boston: Beacon Press, 1964), esp. chaps. 9–12, 15–16.

43. Churchill Babington, *The Influence of Christianity in Promoting the Abolition of Slavery in Europe* (Cambridge: Cambridge University Press, 1846), pp. 47–48.

44. Ibid., pp. 76–77. For a good discussion of this development and possible ulterior motives for the new view of manumission see Marc Bloch, "How and Why Ancient Slavery Came to an End," in his *Slavery and Serfdom in the Middle Ages: Selected Essays,* trans. William R. Beer (Berkeley: University of California Press, 1975), pp. 14–15.

45. Joan Dyste Lind, "The Ending of Slavery in Sweden: Social Structure and Decision Making," *Scandinavian Studies* 50 (1978): 65–66. On Norway and other parts of Scandinavia see Foote and Wilson, *The Viking Achievement,* pp. 71–72. On the pagan practice of burying slaves alive with their dead master or sacrificing them on the occasion of his death see Gwyn Jones, *A History of the Vikings* (London: Oxford University Press, 1968), p. 149; and for the most convenient translation of Ibn Fadlan's celebrated account of a mortuary sacrifice of a slave girl see ibid., pp. 425–430. Eric Oxenstierna has suggested that this ceremony may have been the wedding of a slave girl to her master, which the Arab traveler confused with a sacri-

fice! If there is any truth to this hypothesis, it certainly lends strong support to my thesis that manumission and sacrifice were closely related. See his *The Norsemen* (Greenwich, Conn.: Graphic Society Publishers, 1965), pp. 108–109.

46. 1 Cor. 7:11.

47. A. J. Wensinck, *A Handbook of Early Mohammadan Tradition* (Leiden: E. J. Brill, 1927), p. 142.

48. Robert Roberts, *The Social Laws of the Qorân* (London: Williams & Norgate, 1925), p. 59.

49. R. Brunschvig, "Abd," *Encyclopedia of Islam* (Leiden: E. J. Brill, 1961), vol. 1, p. 15.

50. This holds only for the Migiurtini group. The Marrehan follow the usual Islamic practice of freeing the child of a slave concubine. See Enrico Cerulli, "Testi di diritto consuetudinario dei Somali Marrēhân," *Somalia, scritti editi ed inediti* 2 (1959): 83.

51. Muslim Spain and the nineteenth-century Adamawa of the northern Cameroons are typical. See Pierre Guichard, *Structures sociales "orientales" et "occidentales" dans l'Espagne musulmane* (Paris: Mouton, 1977), pp. 77–80, 122–124; and Philip Burnham, "Raiders and Traders in Adamawa: Slavery as a Regional System," in James L. Watson, ed., *Asian and African Systems of Slavery* (Oxford: Basil Blackwell, 1980), p. 48.

52. Barbara Isaacman and Allen Isaacman, "Slavery and Social Stratification among the Sena of Mozambique," in Miers and Kopytoff, *Slavery in Africa*, p. 111.

53. Leopold von Schrenck, *Die Völker des Amur-Landes* (St. Petersburg: Kaiserliche Akademie der Wissenschaften, 1881–1895).

54. Driver and Miles, *The Babylonian Laws*, vol. 1, pp. 305–306; and Isaac Mendelsohn, *Slavery in the Ancient Near East* (Oxford: Oxford University Press, 1949), pp. 50–52.

55. *Conquerors and Slaves*, pp. 166–171.

56. William L. Westermann, "Two Studies in Athenian Manumission," *Journal of Near Eastern Studies* 5 (1946): 101. See also K. J. Dover, *Greek Homosexuality* (New York: Vintage Books, 1980), pp. 153–179.

57. Buckland, *The Roman Law of Slavery*, p. 609.

58. On Jamaica see Edward Brathwaite, *The Development of Creole Society in Jamaica* (Oxford: Clarendon Press, 1971), pp. 167–175. On the eastern Caribbean see Elsa V. Goveia, *Slave Society in the British Leeward Islands at the End of the Eighteenth Century* (New Haven: Yale University Press, 1965), pp. 215–221. On the French Caribbean see Leo Elisabeth, "The French Antilles," in D. W. Cohen and Jack P. Greene, eds., *Neither Slave nor Free* (Baltimore: Johns Hopkins University Press, 1972), pp. 134–171; and Gabriel Debien, *Les esclaves aux Antilles françaises, XVIIe–XVIIIe siècles* (Basse-Terre, Fort-de-France: Société d'histoire de la Guadeloupe et Société d'histoire de la Martinique, 1974), pp. 369–391. On South Africa see Anna J. Böeseken, *Slaves and Free Blacks at the Cape, 1658–1700* (Cape Town: Tafelberg Publishers, 1977), pp. 77–79. For evidence that strongly questions the traditional view that most concubines and their progeny were freed in Latin America see Schwartz, "The Manumission of Slaves in Colonial Brazil," pp. 621–622. It has recently been shown for Buenos Aires that economic factors largely explain the higher incidence of female manumissions; see Lyman L. Johnson, "Manumission in Colo-

nial Buenos Aires, 1776–1810," *Hispanic American Historical Review* 59 (1979): 263, 276–277.

59. Roberts, *The Social Laws of the Qorân*, p. 50.

60. Edmund R. Leach, *Political Systems of Highland Burma* (London: Bell, 1954), p. 305.

61. Lev Iâkovlevich Schternberg, *Giliâki, orochi, gol'dy, negidal'tsy, aïny: stat'i i materialy* [The Gilyak, Orochi, Goldi, Negidal, Ainu: Articles and Materials] (Khabarovsk: Dal'giz, 1933).

62. K. Nwachukwu-Ogedengbe, "Slavery in Nineteenth Century Aboh (Nigeria)," in Miers and Kopytoff, *Slavery in Africa*, p. 151.

63. Foote and Wilson, *The Viking Achievement*, p. 72.

64. Mendelsohn, *Slavery in the Ancient Near East*, p. 81. On legal aspects of the process see Driver and Miles, *The Babylonian Laws*, vol. 1, pp. 227–228.

65. Wergeland, *Slavery in Germanic Society*, p. 114.

66. Wang Yi-T'ung, "Slaves and Other Comparable Social Groups during the Northern Dynasties (386–618)," *Harvard Journal of Asiatic Studies* 16 (1953): 360–362.

67. On the medieval Germans see Wergeland, *Slavery in Germanic Society*, p. 133–134; on the Somali see Enrico Cerulli, "Il diritto consuetudinario della Somalia settentrionale (Migiurtini)," *Somalia, scritti vari editi ed inediti* 2 (1959): 23.

68. "Two Early Patterns of Manumission," p. 63: see also pp. 72–73.

69. Buckland, *The Roman Law of Slavery*, pp. 449–451.

70. Westermann, "Two Studies in Athenian Manumission," p. 96.

71. Buckland, *The Roman Law of Slavery*, pp. 441–442, 451–452; Susan Treggiari suggests that this was the oldest form of Roman manumission, but I disagree (for reasons already given). See Treggiari, *Roman Freedmen during the Late Republic* (Oxford: Clarendon Press, 1969), p. 24.

72. Mauss, *The Gift*, p. 66.

73. On Greece see Westermann, "Two Studies in Athenian Manumission." Most authors rank manumissio vindicta second in frequency to manumissio testamento in ancient Rome, but Treggiari reverses this order. See her *Roman Freedmen during the Late Republic*, p. 31.

74. Bömer, *Untersuchungen über die Religion der Sklaven*, vol. 2, p. 120.

75. Ibid., pp. 13–14.

76. William W. Westermann, *The Slave Systems of Greek and Roman Antiquity* (Philadelphia: American Philosophical Society, 1955), p. 35.

77. F. Sokolowski, "The Real Meaning of Sacral Manumission," *Harvard Theological Review* 47 (1954): p. 173.

78. *Untersuchungen über die Religion der Sklaven*, vol. 2, p. 15.

79. Mendelsohn, *Slavery in the Ancient Near East*, p. 104.

80. On Visigothic Spain see Charles Verlinden, *L'esclavage dans l'Europe médiévale* (Bruges: De Tempel, 1955), vol. 1, p. 83. More generally on Europe see Bloch, *Slavery and Serfdom in the Middle Ages*, pp. 12–14.

81. The pagoda slaves of Burma were outcastes and considered extremely unclean. Their descendants, unlike those of other kinds of slaves, suffered great stigma. James G. Scott, *The Burman: His Life and Notions* (London: Macmillan, 1912), pp. 428–429.

82. W. R. G. Horton, "The Osu System of Slavery in a Northern Ibo Village-Group," *Africa* 26 (1956): 311–335; and Victor C. Uchendu, "Slaves and Slavery in Igboland, Nigeria," in Miers and Kopytoff, *Slavery in Africa,* p. 130.

83. The view of Mary Douglas on the symbolism of purity and pollution is extremely suggestive in explaining the peculiar aversion to cult slaves. See the discussion in chapter 11.

84. Bömer, *Untersuchungen über die Religion der Sklaven,* vol. 2, p. 120.

85. Ibid., vol. 1, p. 22.

86. Hopkins, *Conquerors and Slaves,* p. 144.

87. Ibid., pp. 146, 158, 163.

88. Buckland, *The Roman Law of Slavery,* pp. 444–447.

89. Ibid., pp. 554–555.

90. Verlinden, *L'esclavage dans l'Europe médiévale,* p. 300.

91. Brunschvig, "Abd," p. 30.

9. The Status of Freed Persons

1. For discussions of the wala relationship see Reuben Levy, *The Sociology of Islam* (Cambridge: Cambridge University Press, 1931–1933), pp. 114–116; Brunschvig, "Abd," *Encyclopedia of Islam* (Leiden: E. J. Brill, 1961), vol. 1, pp. 30–31; David Ayalon, *L'esclavage du mamelouk* (Jerusalem: Oriental Notes and Studies, 1951), esp. p. 34; idem, "Preliminary Remarks on the Mamelūk Military Institution in Islam," in V. J. Parry and M. E. Yapp, eds., *War, Technology, and Society in the Middle East* (London: Oxford University Press, 1975), pp. 44–57. The term *Mawla* is frequently used in Arabic to describe both ex-master and freedman. It also has several other meanings not all related and sometimes not made clear by the context. This is a complex and confusing subject best left to expert Arabists. For an excellent discussion of the semantic problems posed by the term and of the sociological status of the freedman in Islamic history see Daniel Pipes, "Mawlas: Freed Slaves and Converts in Early Islam," *Slavery and Abolition* 1 (1980): 132–177. For more details see Chapter 11.

2. See Thomas Wiedemann, *Greek and Roman Slavery* (Baltimore: Johns Hopkins University Press, 1981), pp. 41–49 for a discussion and translation of typical Greek cases.

3. William L. Westermann, "Two Studies in Athenian Manumission," *Journal of Near Eastern Studies* 5 (1946): 92–104; and Keith Hopkins, *Conquerors and Slaves* (Cambridge: Cambridge University Press, 1978), chap. 3. For a succinct comparison of Greece and Rome see M. I. Finley, *Ancient Slavery and Modern Ideology* (New York: Viking Press, 1980), pp. 97–98.

4. This discussion of the patron-freedman relationship is based mainly on Susan Treggiari, *Roman Freedmen during the Late Republic* (Oxford: Clarendon Press, 1969), pp. 68–81. On the legal complexities of this relationship see W. W. Buckland, *The Roman Law of Slavery* (Cambridge: Cambridge University Press, 1908), esp, chaps. 11–14. Freedmen during the imperial period are discussed in chapter 11, where more references are given. For a useful collection of translated Latin sources see Wiedemann, *Greek and Roman Slavery,* pp. 50–60.

5. Treggiari, *Roman Freedmen during the Late Republic*, p. 75.

6. Ibid., p. 81.

7. These are thoroughly documented in Verlinden, *L'esclavage dans l'Europe médiévale* (Bruges: De Tempel, 1955, 1977), vols. 1 and 2. See also Marc Bloch, *Slavery and Serfdom in the Middle Ages: Selected Essays,* trans. William R. Beer (Berkeley: University of California Press, 1975), pp. 14–19.

8. Thomas Lindkvist, *Landborna i Norden under äldre medeltid* [Tenants in the Nordic Countries during the Early Middle Ages] (Uppsala: University of Uppsala, 1979), esp. pp. 133–136. See also Joan Dyste Lind, "The Ending of Slavery in Sweden: Social Structure and Decision Making" *Scandinavian Studies* 50 (1978): esp. 65–67; and Peter Foote and David M. Wilson, *The Viking Achievement* (London: Sidgwick & Jackson, 1970), pp. 71–74.

9. Foote and Wilson, *The Viking Achievement*, p. 74.

10. Harry Hoetink, "Surinam and Curacao," in D. W. Cohen and Jack P. Greene, eds., *Neither Slave nor Free* (Baltimore: Johns Hopkins University Press, 1972), p. 68.

11. Frederick P. Bowser, "Colonial Spanish America," in Cohen and Greene, *Neither Slave nor Free,* pp. 23–24.

12. Ibid.

13. A. J. R. Russell-Wood, "Colonial Brazil," in Cohen and Greene, *Neither Slave nor Free,* pp. 91–92.

14. Lyman L. Johnson, "Manumission in Colonial Buenos Aires, 1776–1810," *Hispanic American Historical Review* 59 (1979): table 1, pp. 262, 273.

15. "The Manumission of Slaves in Colonial Brazil: Bahia, 1684–1745," *Hispanic American Historical Review* 54 (1974): 632–633.

16. Anna J. Böeseken, *Slaves and Free Blacks at the Cape, 1658–1700* (Cape Town: Tafelberg Publishers, 1977), pp. 82–84.

17. Richard Elphick and Robert Shell, "Intergroup Relations: Khoikhoi, Settlers, Slaves, and Free Blacks, 1652–1795," in Richard Elphick and Hermann Giliomee, eds., *The Shaping of South African Society, 1652–1820* (London: Longmans, 1979). pp. 141–142.

18. Ibid.

19. *Slaves without Masters* (New York: Vintage Books, 1976), p. 53.

20. Henry W. Farnam, *Chapters in the History of Social Legislation in the United States to 1860* (Washington, D.C.: Carnegie Institution of Washington, 1938), p. 206.

21. Berlin, *Slaves without Masters,* pp. 149–151.

22. Ibid., p. 224.

23. This is particularly well illustrated by variations in the significance of manumission among different groups of Tuaregs. See, for example, André Bourgeot, "Rapports esclavagistes et conditions d'affranchissement chez les Imuhaġ," in Claude Meillassoux, ed., *L'esclavage en l'Afrique précoloniale* (Paris: François Maspero, 1975), pp. 92–93.

24. Barbara Isaacman and Allen Isaacman, "Slavery and Social Stratification among the Sena of Mozambique," in Suzanne Miers and Igor I. Kopytoff, eds., *Slavery in Africa* (Wisconsin: University of Wisconsin Press, 1977), pp. 111.

25. "Slavery among Coastal Middlemen: The Duala of the Cameroon," in Miers and Kopytoff, *Slavery in Africa,* pp. 312–313.

26. Igor I. Kopytoff and Suzanne Miers, "African 'Slavery' as an Institution of Marginality," in Miers and Kopytoff, *Slavery in Africa,* pp. 18–29.

27. Ibid., p. 20. In the light of this unambiguous statement, the criticism recently leveled at Kopytoff and Miers by Martin A. Klein and Paul E. Lovejoy—that emphasis on " 'assimilationist' tendencies misrepresents the condition of many slaves in the past"—is manifestly unfair. A careful reading of the case studies in Miers and Kopytoff's excellent volume, including the fine pieces by Klein and Lovejoy themselves, reveals that the criticism is not deserved by any of the contributors either. For the criticism in question see Klein and Lovejoy, "Slavery in West Africa," in Henry A. Gemery and Jan S. Hogendorn, *The Uncommon Market: Essays in the Economic History of the Atlantic Slave Trade* (New York: Academic Press, 1979), pp. 181–182.

28. *Les Bambara du Ségou et du Kaarta* (Paris: La Rose, 1924).

29. Hilliard d'Auberteuil, *Considerations sur l'état présent de la colonie française de St. Dominigue* (Paris: n.p., 1976–1977), vol. 2, p. 73. Cited in Gwendolyn Mildo Hall, "Saint Domingue," in Cohen and Greene, *Neither Slave nor Free,* p. 184.

30. *Roman Freedmen during the Late Republic,* pp. 36–68.

31. Ibid., pp. 61, 65. See also Finley, *Ancient Slavery and Modern Ideology,* pp. 97–98.

32. Wang Yi-T'ung, "Slaves and Other Comparable Groups during the Northern Dynasties (386–618)," *Harvard Journal of Asiatic Studies* 16 (1953): 329.

33. Jacob J. Rabinowitz, "Manumission of Slaves in Roman Law and Oriental Law," *Journal of Near Eastern Studies* 19 (1960): 42–45.

34. Ernst Levy, "Captivus Redemptus," *Classical Philology* 38 (1943): 176.

35. *Slavery during the Third Dynasty of Ur,* Memoirs of the American Anthropological Association, no. 66, 1947, p. 4.

36. *Slavery in Ancient India* (New Delhi: People's Publishing House, 1960), p. 113.

37. M. I. Finley, "The Servile Statuses of Ancient Greece," *Revue internationale des droits de l'antiquité* 7 (1960): 165–189; idem, "Between Slavery and Freedom," *Comparative Studies in Society and History* 6 (1964): 233–249; Rodolfo Mondolfo, "The Greek Attitude to Manual Labor," *Past and Present* no. 2 (1952): 1–5; Alison Burford, *Craftsmen in Greek and Roman Society* (Ithaca, N.Y.: Cornell University Press, 1972); W. L. Westermann, "Slavery and the Elements of Freedom in Ancient Greece," *Quarterly Bulletin of the Polish Institute of Arts and Sciences* 2 (1943): 1–14; idem, "The Freedmen and the Slaves of God," *Proceedings of the American Philosophical Society* 92 (1948): 55–64; and Hopkins, *Conquerors and Slaves,* pp. 133–171.

38. On Latin America see Bowser, "Colonial Spanish America," p. 50; and C. R. Boxer, *The Golden Age of Brazil, 1695–1750* (Berkeley: University of California Press, 1969), pp. 1–2. On South African attitudes see Isobel E. Edwards, *Towards Emancipation: A Study of South African Slavery* (Cardiff: Gomerian Press, 1942), pp. 15, 18. Reinforcing attitudes of disdain for manual or skilled labor was the high level of mobility and egalitarianism among whites in eighteenth-century South Africa, on which see Hermann Giliomee and Richard Elphick, "The Structure of European

Domination at the Cape, 1652–1820," in Elphick and Giliomee, *The Shaping of South African Society,* pp. 376–378.

39. On Lima see Frederick P. Bowser, "The Free Person of Color in Mexico City and Lima: Manumission and Opportunity, 1580–1650," in Stanley Engerman and Eugene D. Genovese, eds., *Race and Slavery in the Western Hemisphere: Quantitative Studies* (Princeton, N.J.: Princeton University Press, 1975), p. 356. On Buenos Aires see Johnson, "Manumission in Colonial Buenos Aires," p. 286 n16. Note, however, that the ownership of skilled slaves by whites of slender means was equally important as an explanation of the ability of skilled slaves to become master craftsmen. On the role of the eastern slaves in the development of early Cape architecture in South Africa see Elphick and Shell, "Intergroup Relations," p. 453.

40. "Slave and Citizen: The South African Case," *Race* 10 (1973): 25–46. See also George M. Frederickson, *White Supremacy: A Comparative Study in American and South African History* (New York: Oxford University Press, 1981), chap. 2.

41. See in particular Giliomee and Elphick, "The Structure of European Domination at the Cape"; and Greenstein, "Slave and Citizen." Compare Frederick P. Bowser, *The African Slave in Colonial Peru, 1524–1650* (Stanford, Calif.: Stanford University Press, 1973); and Colin A. Palmer, *Slaves of the White God: Blacks in Mexico, 1570–1650* (Cambridge, Mass.: Harvard University Press, 1976), chaps. 2–3.

42. James C. Armstrong, "The Slaves, 1652–1795," in Elphick and Giliomee, *The Shaping of South African Society,* esp. pp. 90–98. Cf. Caio Prado, Jr., *The Colonial Background of Modern Brazil* (Berkeley: University of California Press, 1967); and Florestan Fernandes, "Slaveholding Society in Brazil," in Vera Rubin and Arthur Tuden, eds., *Comparative Perspectives on Slavery in New World Plantation Societies* (New York: New York Academy of Sciences, 1977), pp. 311–342.

43. Armstrong, "The Slaves," p. 88; cf. George W. Roberts, *The Population of Jamaica* (Cambridge: Cambridge University Press, 1957), pp. 29–42.

44. Elphick and Shell, "Intergroup Relations," pp. 135–145; and Böeseken, *Slaves and Free Blacks at the Cape,* pp. 77–97.

45. See, in particular, Sheila Patterson, "Some Speculations on the Status and Role of the Free People of Colour in the Western Cape," in Meyer Fortes, ed., *Studies in African Social Anthropology* (New York: Academic Press, 1975), pp. 160–205; and the classic interpretation by I. D. MacCrone, *Race Attitudes in South Africa: Historical, Experimental, and Psychological Studies* (Johannesburg: Witwatersrand University Press, 1965). But contrast Giliomee and Elphick, "The Structure of European Domination at the Cape," pp. 363–365, and the discussion on the U.S. South that follows.

46. For details see Elphick and Shell, "Intergroup Relations," pp. 145–155; and Böeseken, *Slaves and Free Blacks at the Cape,* pp. 77–78.

47. Bowser, "The Free Person of Color," p. 334.

48. Elphick and Shell, "Intergroup Relations," pp. 152–155.

49. Johnson, "Manumission in Colonial Buenos Aires," pp. 265–266, 271–272; and Elphick and Shell, "Intergroup Relations," p. 139.

50. It is only fair to note that in South Africa almost all free persons were excluded from participating in the administration of the Dutch East India Company.

51. Bowser, "The Free Person of Color," p. 354.

52. Elphick and Shell, "Intergroup Relations," p. 146.

53. I find it difficult to follow Hoetink's discussion in its entirety, but I agree with this part of the argument. See his "Surinam and Curacao," pp. 79–82.

54. Elsa V. Goveia, *Slave Society in the British Leeward Islands at the End of the Eighteenth Century* (New Haven: Yale University Press, 1965), pp. 215–229. On Surinam see Hoetink, "Surinam and Curacao," pp. 80–81; on Barbados see Jerome S. Handler and Arnold A. Sio, "Barbados," p. 233; on the French Antilles see Elisabeth, "The French Antilles," p. 166; on Jamaica see Douglas Hall, "Jamaica," pp. 203–204, all in Cohen and Greene, *Neither Slave nor Free*. On the Mascarene Islands see Burton Benedict, "Slavery and Indenture in Mauritius and Seychelles," in James L. Watson, ed., *Asian and African Systems of Slavery* (Oxford: Basil Blackwell, 1980), pp. 135–138. On the Banda Islands see Bruno Lasker, *Human Bondage in Southeast Asia* (Chapel Hill: University of North Carolina Press, 1950), pp. 34, 75. And for a useful if rather too colorful account see H. W. Ponder, *In Javanese Waters* (London: Seeley, Service & Co., 1944?), pp. 100–137.

55. *Slaves without Masters,* p. xiii.

56. Ibid., p. 188.

57. Eugene D. Genovese, "The Slave States of North America," in Cohen and Greene, *Neither Slave nor Free,* p. 259; and Robert W. Fogel and Stanley L. Engerman, *Time on the Cross: The Economics of American Negro Slavery* (Boston: Little, Brown, 1974), vol. 1, p. 37.

58. W. J. Cash, *The Mind of the South* (New York: Vintage Books, 1960), p. 118.

59. Ibid., p. 59.

60. For two of the most detailed examinations of slavery and sexuality see Winthrop D. Jordan, *White over Black: American Attitudes toward the Negro, 1550–1812* (Baltimore: Penguin Books, 1969), pp. 136–178; and Earl E. Thorpe, *Eros and Freedom in Southern Life and Thought* (Durham, N.C.: Seeman Printery, 1967). On the explosiveness of the issue, especially during the Civil War, see Forrest G. Wood's discussion of the miscegenation controversy of 1864 in his *Black Scare: The Racist Response to Emancipation and Reconstruction* (Berkeley: University of California Press, 1968), pp. 53–79.

10. Patterns of Manumission

1. *Conquerors and Slaves* (Cambridge: Cambridge University Press, 1978), p. 166.

2. See for example Lyman L. Johnson, "Manumission in Colonial Buenos Aires, 1776–1810," *Hispanic American Historical Review* 59 (1979): 262, table 1; and Richard Elphick and Robert Shell, "Intergroup Relations: Khoikhoi, Settlers, Slaves, and Free Blacks, 1652–1795," in Richard Elphick and Hermann Giliomee, eds., *The Shaping of South African Society, 1652–1820* (London: Longmans, 1979), pp. 137–138.

3. See Stephen Clissold, *The Barbary Slaves* (London: Paul Elek, 1977), pp. 42–44. Muslim women who had sexual relations with their slaves faced the death penalty, yet the practice was not uncommon. Marriage to freed apostates was permitted (see pp. 44–46).

4. On ancient Greece see the speech by a supporter of Demosthenes attacking Stephanos for disgracing his citizenship by marrying Neaira, a freedwoman and former slave prostitute, in Thomas Wiedemann, *Greek and Roman Slavery* (Baltimore: Johns Hopkins University Press, 1981), pp. 45–46. See also W. L. Westermann, *The Slave Systems of Greek and Roman Antiquity* (Philadelphia: American Philosophical Society, 1955), pp. 13–14. On Rome see Joel Schmidt, *Vie et mort des esclaves dans la Rome antique* (Paris: Editions Albin Michel, 1973), pp. 57–58. On Valencia see Vicente Graullera Sanz, *La esclavitud en Valencia en los siglos XVI y XVII* (Valencia: Instituto valenciano de estudios historicos, 1978), pp. 147, 159.

5. Elphick and Shell, "Intergroup Relations," p. 127.

6. Hopkins, *Conquerors and Slaves,* p. 139; and Johnson, "Manumission in Colonial Buenos Aires," pp. 275–276. In Brazil Stuart B. Schwartz claims that "men and women paid for freedom in exact proportion to their numbers." See his "The Manumission of Slaves in Colonial Brazil: Bahia, 1684–1745," *Hispanic American Historical Review* 54 (1974): 624–625. On South Africa see Elphick and Shell, "Intergroup Relations," pp. 137, 144; figs. 4.1, 4.4.

7. See Chapter 5.

8. "Manumission in Colonial Buenos Aires," p. 276.

9. Alan Fisher, "Chattel Slavery in the Ottoman Empire," *Slavery and Abolition* 1 (1980): 37–38. See also Halil Inalcik, "Ghulām: Ottoman Period," *Encyclopedia of Islam,* ed. 2, p. 1090.

10. Schwartz, "The Manumission of Slaves in Colonial Brazil," pp. 618–619; Johnson, "Manumission in Colonial Buenos Aires," pp. 269–270; and Elphick and Shell, "Intergroup Relations," pp. 136–138.

11. Ira Berlin, *Slaves without Masters* (New York: Vintage Books, 1976), pp 152–153. In Westmoreland parish, Jamaica, this seems to have been true of black slaves (as opposed to those of mixed blood) whose average age at manumission was forty-two years. For a Jamaican of the early nineteenth century this was very old. See Barry W. Higman, *Slave Population and Economy in Jamaica, 1807–1834* (Cambridge: Cambridge University Press, 1976), p. 178.

12. On republican Rome see Susan Treggiari, *Roman Freedmen during the Late Republic* (Oxford: Clarendon Press, 1969), p. 35. On imperial Rome and Delphi see Hopkins, *Conquerors and Slaves,* pp. 127, 149–152.

13. In the period 201 B.C.–153 B.C. the average price of a boy slave was 235 drachmas, whereas that of a girl was 160 drachmas; by the period 53 B.C. to 1 B.C. a boy sold for 330 drachmas, while a girl's price was 333. See Hopkins, *Conquerors and Slaves,* p. 159, table 111.3.

14. "Ghulām," *Encyclopedia of Islam,* vol. 3, pp. 1079–91.

15. Charles Verlinden, *L'esclavage dans l'Europe médiévale* (Bruges: De Tempel, 1955), vol. 1, pp. 460–461.

16. David Ayalon, "The European-Asiatic Steppe: A Major Reservoir of Power for the Islamic World," Proceedings of the 25th Congress of Orientalists, Moscow, 1960 (Moscow: n.p., 1963), pp. 47–52.

17. Elphick and Shell, "Intergroup Relations," p. 144.

18. In his highly romantic treatment of the subject Gilberto Freyre claims that in Brazil slaves from Muslim Africa were "culturally superior" to "the great majority of the white colonists" and that the women were eagerly sought as friends, concu-

bines, and housekeepers. *The Masters and the Slaves* (New York: Alfred A. Knopf, 1964), pp. 264–271.

19. Johnson, "Manumission in Colonial Buenos Aires," pp. 265–266, 271–272.

20. Elphick and Shell, "Intergroup Relations," p. 139.

21. Schwartz, "The Manumission of Slaves in Colonial Brazil," pp. 612, 618.

22. Higman, *Slave Population and Economy in Jamaica*, p. 176.

23. Ibid., pp. 177–178.

24. "The Free Person of Color in Mexico City and Lima: Manumission and Opportunity, 1580–1650," in Stanley L. Engerman and Eugene D. Genovese, eds., *Race and Slavery in the Western Hemisphere: Quantitative Studies* (Princeton, N.J.: Princeton University Press, 1975), p. 334.

25. Higman, *Slave Population and Economy in Jamaica*, p. 77.

26. Elphick and Shell, "Intergroup Relations," pp. 143–144.

27. See Michael H. Jameson, "Agriculture and Slavery in Classical Athens," *Classical Journal* 72 (1977–1978): 134–135.

28. Treggiari, *Roman Freedmen during the Late Republic*, p. 36.

29. C. M. Wilbur, *Slavery in China during the Former Han Dynasty, 206 B.C.–A.D. 25* (Chicago: Field Museum of Natural History, 1943), pp. 240–252.

30. "Ghulām," pp. 1079–91.

31. I draw here on Verlinden, *L'esclavage dans l'Europe médiévale*, vol. 1, pp. 61–101; and P. D. King, *Law and Society in the Visigothic Kingdom* (Cambridge: Cambridge University Press, 1972), pp. 159–183.

32. King, *Law and Society,* p. 163.

33. *L'esclavage dans l'Europe médiévale*, vol. 1, p. 84.

34. Based on William F. Sharp, *Slavery on the Spanish Frontier: The Colombian Chocó, 1680–1810* (Norman: University of Oklahoma Press, 1976), pp. 142–146.

35. On the domestic slaves see ibid., pp. 137–138. Slaves in the other mining areas of Latin America did not fare as well as those in the Colombian Chocó. In both the gold-mining area of Minas Gerais and the diamond district of Brazil, mortality rates were horrendously high. Even there, however, slaves were allowed to mine in their spare time; they seized opportunities for stealing the ore, with the result that some of them were able to be manumitted. See C. R. Boxer, *The Golden Age of Brazil, 1690–1750* (Berkeley: University of California Press, 1969), pp. 177, 217–218.

36. Personal communication from Professor F. M. Cross of the Harvard Semitic Museum, who kindly discussed and translated the critical passages from the papyrus.

37. Verlinden, *L'esclavage dans l'Europe médiévale*, vol. 1, p. 84. On the church's role in the late empire see pp. 31–42.

38. Iris Origo, " 'The Domestic Enemy': The Eastern Slaves in Tuscany in the Fourteenth and Fifteenth Centuries," *Speculum* 30 (1955): 327–328.

39. On thirteenth-century Spain see Verlinden, *L'esclavage dans l'Europe médiévale*, vol. 1, p. 303. On sixteenth- and seventeenth-century Valencia see Sanz, *La esclavitud en Valencia*, p. 132.

40. On which see Verlinden, *L'esclavage dans l'Europe médiévale*, vol. 2 (1977), pp. 254–255.

41. "How and Why Ancient Slavery Came to an End," in Marc Bloch, ed., *Slavery and Serfdom in the Middle Ages: Selected Essays*, trans. William R. Beer (Berkeley: University of California Press, 1975), p. 15.

42. See Joan Dyste Lind, "The Ending of Slavery in Sweden: Social Structure and Decision Making," *Scandinavian Studies* 50 (1978): 66–69.

43. Verlinden, *L'esclavage dans l'Europe médiévale,* vol. 2, pp. 540–549.

44. In Brazil there was "no coherent body of Church doctrine or ecclesiastical statute that regulated slavery," and the issue of manumission was largely neglected by the church. See Schwartz, "The Manumission of Slaves in Colonial Brazil," pp. 610–611. Johnson states the matter even more bluntly: "The colonial societies of Latin America tolerated manumission, but the process was not encouraged actively by either Church or State." "Manumission in Colonial Buenos Aires," p. 261.

45. Elphick and Shell, "Intergroup Relations," p. 122.

46. Ibid.

47. I draw on Clissold, *The Barbary Slaves,* esp. pp. 86–101; Ellen G. Friedman, "Christian Captives at 'Hard Labor' in Algiers, Sixteenth to Eighteenth Centuries," *International Journal of African Historical Studies* 13 (1980): 616–632; and Norman R. Bennett, "Christian and Negro Slavery in Eighteenth-Century North Africa," *Journal of African History* 1 (1960): 65–82.

48. Friedman, in "Christian Captives," suggests that these tales were grossly exaggerated; so does Bennett in "Christian and Negro Slavery." But Clissold's account in *The Barbary Slaves* suggests that even by the standards of the age conditions were quite brutal for the mass of slaves.

49. There were variations. Morocco relied least on the Renegades; Tunis was totally dependent on them during the eighteenth century. See Clissold, *The Barbary Slaves,* p. 100.

50. Ibid., pp. 91–92.

51. Hopkins, *Conquerors and Slaves,* p. 148. See also Westermann, *Slave Systems of Greek and Roman Antiquity,* pp. 11, 23.

52. Bernard Lewis, *Race and Color in Islam* (New York: Harper Torchbooks, 1971), passim.

53. Although freedmen were ideologically assimilated into their former masters' lineages in West Africa and, compared to other areas, relatively well treated, it is significant that large numbers of them flocked to the quarters of the invading Europeans when they made their grab for Africa at the end of the nineteenth century, on which see Martin A. Klein and Paul R. Lovejoy, "Slavery in West Africa," in Henry A. Gemery and Jan S. Hogendorn, eds., *The Uncommon Market: Essays in the Economic History of the Atlantic Slave Trade* (New York: Academic Press, 1979).

54. C. M. N. White, "Clan, Chieftainship, and Slavery in Luvale Political Organization," *Africa* 27 (1957): 71–72.

55. Wyatt MacGaffey, "Economic and Social Dimensions of Kongo Slavery (Zaire)," in Suzanne Miers and Igor I. Kopytoff, eds., *Slavery in Africa* (Madison: University of Wisconsin Press, 1977), p. 244.

56. J. C. Mitchell, *The Yao Village* (Manchester: Manchester University Press, 1956), p. 72; and Edward Alpers, "Trade, State, and Society among the Yao in the Nineteenth Century," *Journal of African History* 10 (1969): 410–414.

57. Maurice Bloch, "Modes of Production and Slavery in Madagascar: Two Case Studies," in James L. Watson, ed., *Asian and African Systems of Slavery* (Oxford: Basil Blackwell, 1980), p. 108.

58. Plutarch, *Pericles,* 37.3.

59. On this group of societies see Claude Meillassoux, ed., *L'esclavage en*

Afrique précoloniale (Paris: François Maspero, 1975); and idem, *The Development of Indigenous Trade and Markets in West Africa* (London: Oxford University Press, 1971), esp. his introduction, and chaps. 5 and 7. See also Jean Bazin, "War and Servitude in Segou," *Economy and Society* 3 (1974): 107–143; Klein and Lovejoy, "Slavery in West Africa," pp. 181–212; Paul E. Lovejoy, "Indigenous African Slavery," in Michael Craton, ed., *Roots and Branches, Current Directions in Slave Studies: Historical Reflections* 6 (1979): esp. pp. 39–43; Polly Hill, "From Slavery to Freedom: The Case of Farm Slavery in Nigerian Hausaland," *Comparative Studies in Society and History* 18 (1976): 395–426; and M. G. Smith, "Slavery and Emancipation in Two Societies," in M. G. Smith, ed., *The Plural Society in the British West Indies* (Berkeley: University of California Press, 1965), pp. 116–161.

On slavery, warfare, and manumission in early Islam see Paul G. Forand, "The Development of Military Slavery under the Abbasid Caliphs of the Ninth Century A.D. (Third Century A.H.) with Special Reference to the Reigns of Mu'Tasim and Mu'Tadid" (Ph.D. diss., Princeton University, 1961), esp. chaps. 3 and 5; Samuel S. Haas, "The Contributions of Slaves to and Their Influence upon the Culture of Early Islam" (Ph.D. diss., Princeton University, 1942), esp. chap. 2; David Ayalon, *L'esclavage du mamelouk* (Jerusalem: Oriental Notes and Studies, 1951); P. M. Holt, "The Position and Power of the Mamluk Sultan," *Bulletin of the School of Oriental and African Studies* 38 (1975): pt. 2; and "Djaysh," *Encyclopedia of Islam*, ed. 2, vol. 2, pp. 504–511.

On fourteenth- and fifteenth-century Crete see Verlinden, *L'esclavage dans l'Europe médiévale*, vol. 2, pp. 826–832, 876–878; on Sardinia see ibid., pp. 343–346, 353–358.

60. See the references cited in Chapter 9, note 37. In addition, on the low level of manumission at Laurium see Siegfried Lauffer, *Die Bergwerkssklaven von Laureion* (Wiesbaden: Akademie Mainz, 1956).

61. Verlinden, *L'esclavage dans l'Europe médiévale*, vol. 1, pp. 524–526.

62. Franklin W. Knight, "Cuba," in D. W. Cohen and Jack P. Greene, eds., *Neither Slave nor Free* (Baltimore: Johns Hopkins University Press, 1972), pp. 278–308.

63. "Slavery, Incentives, and Manumission: A Theoretical Model," *Journal of Political Economy* 83 (1975): 923–933.

64. A. Zimmern, "Was Greek Civilization Based on Slave Labor?" *Sociological Review* 2 (1909): 1–19, 159–176.

65. Robert W. Fogel and Stanley L. Engerman, *Time on the Cross: The Economics of American Negro Slavery* (Boston: Little, Brown, 1974), esp. pp. 148–155, 240–246. The authors observe that manumission existed as a kind of "long-run reward" but that the slave's chance of receiving it was "quite low." In 1850 the manumission rate was 0.45 per 1,000 slaves (see p. 150). For further details see Stephen C. Crawford, "Quantified Memory: A Study of the WPA and Fisk University Slave Narrative Collection" (Ph.D. diss., University of Chicago, 1980), chaps. 2 and 3.

66. The argument suffers from the limitations of all monocausal explanations: a number of other variables both independently and interactively may undermine the relationship between the price of capital and the period of time it takes the slave to buy his freedom. A still more basic criticism may be made, however. The length of time a slave takes to redeem himself is a very poor index of the overall volume of manumission in any of the societies with which we are concerned. In most of them

the bought slave is at such a tremendous disadvantage that he rarely is able to buy his freedom. He may, in addition, be reluctant to purchase his freedom before he is socially competent. Legal and cultural variation in the amount of time considered proper before a slave may be manumitted plays havoc with economic calculation like Findlay's.

One could try to improve the usefulness of the model by confining it to locally born male slaves working in skilled or semiskilled occupations in the urban sectors, all other things remaining equal. But even with this restriction the model fails. The price of freedom varies directly and positively with the purchase price of slaves. In the class of societies to which I have confined the model, masters had little or no control over the supply of slaves. Furthermore, many social and cultural factors influenced the manumission rate—religion, the sex ratio, the kind of political system, to name a few.

Perhaps the biggest problem with Findlay's model is his "assumption that slaves [were] not able to borrow for the purchase of their freedom." He cites the case of an Athenian prostitute (mentioned by Westermann) who borrowed money from her clients, then adds, incredibly, that "her case, however, must be exceptional." In truth, in all these societies, whether Greek or Roman or Spanish American, there were well-developed institutions that enabled slaves to borrow funds to purchase their freedom.

67. "Quantified Memory," p. 88.

68. On the Caribbean see Sidney W. Mintz, *Caribbean Transformations* (Chicago: Aldine Publishing Co., 1974), chap. 7.

69. *Neither Black nor White: Slavery and Race Relations in Brazil and the United States* (New York: Macmillan Co., 1971), p. 45.

70. "Surinam and Curacao," in Cohen and Greene, *Neither Slave nor Free,* pp. 79–80.

71. See Knight, "Cuba," esp. pp. 284–285. Cf. Herbert S. Klein, *Slavery in the Americas: A Comparative Study of Virginia and Cuba* (Chicago: University of Chicago Press, 1967), esp. pp. 63–65, 194–201. Klein does not suggest any marked decrease in the manumission rate but does support the view that there was growing opposition to the high rate.

72. Verlinden, *L'esclavage dans l'Europe médiévale,* vol. 1, p. 61.

73. For references see Chapter 11.

74. See Chapter 4.

75. See Han Woo-Keun, *History of Korea* (Seoul: Eul-Yoo Publishing Co., 1970), p. 129; and William E. Henthorn, *A History of Korea* (New York: Free Press, 1971), p. 89.

76. William E. Henthorn, *Korea: The Mongol Invasions* (Leiden: E. J. Brill, 1963), pp. 113, 175, 213–214.

77. See Byung-Sak Ku, *Hanguk Sahoe Pŏpchasa Tŭksu Yŏngu* [A Study on the History of Law in Korea] (Seoul: Tongo Ch'ulp'ansa, 1968). (In Korean.)

78. The standard work is Hiraki Mokoto, *Nobi Chongyanggo: yimjinran-chung ranhurŭl chungsimŭro* [A Study of Manumission of Slaves during and after the Japanese Invasion of 1592: 1592–1670] (Seoul: National University, 1967). (In Korean.)

79. "Changes in Labor Supply in Yi Dynasty Korea: From Hereditary to Contractual Obligation," August 1976, pp. 17–18 (manuscript).

80. See Leslie B. Rout, Jr., *The African Experience in Spanish America* (New

York: Cambridge University Press, 1976), pp. 75-77. There were also black freedmen, on which see Peter Gerhard, "A Black Conquistador in Mexico," *Hispanic American Historical Review* 58 (1978): 451-459.

81. "Colonial Spanish America," in Cohen and Greene, *Neither Slave nor Free,* p. 20. For more on Peru see Louis Millones, "Gente negra en el Peru: Esclavos y conquistadores," *América indígena* 31 (1971); also for more details see Bowser, *The African Slave in Colonial Peru, 1524-1650* (Stanford, Calif.: Stanford University Press, 1973). On Chile, and for one of the most dramatic cases of freedom gained through distinction in the conquest, see Rolando Mellafe, *La introducción de la esclavitud negra en Chile: Tráfico y rutas* (Santiago: University of Chile, 1959), pp. 49-50.

82. Degler, *Neither Black nor White,* p. 76.

83. In the Dutch-Portuguese war for Brazil most of the Luso-Brazilian forces consisted of "mulattoes, Negroes, Amerindians, and half-breeds of various kinds," and C. R. Boxer adds that "the natural chagrin of the Dutch at the loss of north-east Brazil was greatly increased by their realization that they had been defeated by what was in great part a coloured army." See Boxer, *Four Centuries of Portuguese Expansion, 1415-1825* (Johannesburg; Witwatersrand University Press, 1963), pp. 51-52.

84. *Neither Black nor White,* pp. 76-77.

85. For a review of the role of blacks and mulattoes in southern South America see Rout, *The African Experience in Spanish America,* pp. 167-172.

86. Kenneth R. Andrews, *The Spanish Caribbean: Trade and Plunder, 1530-1630* (New Haven: Yale University Press, 1978), p. 36.

87. Klein, *Slavery in the Americas,* pp. 200-201.

88. Johnson, "Manumission in Colonial Buenos Aires," pp. 278-279.

89. Ibid., p. 278n***.

90. *The African Experience in Spanish America,* p. 181.

91. See S. A. G. Taylor, *The Western Design: An Account of Cromwell's Expedition to the Caribbean* (Kingston: Institute of Jamaica and the Jamaica Historical Society, 1965), pp. 98-102. Most of these blacks would form the nucleus of the Maroons, who were to remain an independent force in Jamaica throughout the period of slavery and long afterward. See Orlando Patterson, "Slavery and Slave Revolts: A Sociohistorical Analysis of the First Maroon War, 1665-1740," *Social and Economic Studies* 19 (1970): 289-325.

92. *Slaves in Red Coats: The British West India Regiments, 1795-1815* (New Haven: Yale University Press, 1979), p. vii. Most of what follows on the Caribbean is based on Buckley's work.

93. Ibid., p. 79.

94. For a good study of the military role of blacks in the seventeenth-century United States see Benjamin Quarles, "The Colonial Militia and Negro Manpower," *Mississippi Valley Historical Review* 45 (1959): 643-652. See also Lorenzo J. Greene, *The Negro in Colonial New England* (New York: Atheneum, 1968), pp. 126-127. Blacks were used in the army and obtained their freedom by this means for a much longer period in Louisiana than in New England, on which see Roland McConnell, *Negro Troops in Antebellum Louisiana* (Baton Rouge: Louisiana State University Press, 1968); see also Berlin, *Slaves without Masters,* pp. 112-130.

95. The standard work is Benjamin Quarles, *The Negro in the American Revolu-*

tion (Chapel Hill: University of North Carolina Press, 1960). See also Berlin, *Slaves without Masters,* pp. 15–50; and Jack D. Foner, *Blacks and the Military in American History* (New York: Praeger Publishers, 1974), pp. 3–19.

96. Cited in Foner, *Blacks and the Military,* p. 6.

97. Ibid., pp. 20–31. See also Frank A. Cassell, "Slaves of the Chesapeake Bay Area and the War of 1812," *Journal of Negro History* 57 (1972): 144–155. Cassell claims that between three thousand and five thousand slaves fled from Virginia and Maryland in 1813 and 1814 and that the slaves always "saw the British as being benevolent" (p. 152).

98. See instead Benjamin Quarles, *The Negro in the Civil War* (Boston: Little, Brown, 1953); and, more recently, James M. McPherson, *The Negro's Civil War* (New York: Vintage Books, 1965).

99. Berlin, *Slaves without Masters,* p. 33.

100. "Slavery as an Institution: Open and Closed Systems," in Watson, *Asian and African Systems of Slavery,* p. 9.

101. Daniel Bell, "The Public Household: On 'Fiscal Sociology' and the Liberal Society," *Public Interest* 37 (1974): 29–68. I use the term more in the older sense of "an arena for the conflict of political forces in the society," in which common needs are defined, justified, and met.

11. The Ultimate Slave

1. G. W. F. Hegel, *The Phenomenology of Mind* (London: Allen & Unwin, 1949), p. 69.

2. James D. Dunlap, *The Office of the Grand Chamberlain in the Later Roman and Byzantine Empires* (New York: Macmillan Co., 1924), pp. 166–167.

3. On Korea see William E. Henthorn, *A History of Korea* (New York: Free Press, 1971), p. 112. On Russia see Richard Hellie, "Muscovite Slavery in Comparative Perspective," *Russian History* 6 (1979): 133–209. For a more detailed discussion, especially of the role of slaves in the army, see Hellie's forthcoming work, *Slavery in Russia, 1450-1725,* chap. 13.

4. The two major sources on which I draw for this part of the discussion are P. R. C. Weaver, *Familia Caesaris: A Social Study of the Emperor's Freedmen and Slaves* (Cambridge: Cambridge University Press, 1972); Gérard Boulvert, *Domestique et fonctionnaire sous le haut empire romain: La condition de l'affranchi et de l'esclave du prince,* Les belles lettres, annales littéraires de l'université de Besançon, vol. 151 (1974). Although somewhat dated, A. M. Duff, *Freedmen in the Early Roman Empire* (Oxford: Clarendon Press, 1928) is still useful.

5. Weaver, *Familia Caesaris,* p. 17. See also Boulvert, *Domestique et fonctionnaire,* pp. 1–8, 200–209.

6. See Boulvert, *Domestique et fonctionnaire,* pt. 1, chap. 2.

7. Duff, *Freedmen in the Early Roman Empire,* p. 153. On exclusion of the fiscus from military service see Boulvert, *Domestique et fonctionnaire,* pp. 230–231.

8. Duff, *Freedmen in the Early Roman Empire,* p. 159.

9. "Some Considerations Relating to Property Rights in Man," *Journal of Economic History* 33 (1973): 43–65. In a personal communication Engerman wondered

just how far it was possible or desirable to cut down on the maintenance costs of administrative slaves. The question is an important one, but I have not been able to find any data on which to base a response.

10. E. C. Welskopf, *Die Produktionsverhältnisse im alten Orient und in der griechisch-römischen Antike* (Berlin: Deutsche Akademie der Wissenschaften, 1957), pp. 121-156.

11. Weaver, *Familia Caesaris,* p. 178.

12. Ibid., p. 205. For a detailed discussion see Boulvert, *Domestique et fonctionnaire,* pp. 84-109, 180-197.

13. "The Freedmen of Cicero," *Greece and Rome* 16 (1969): 95. See also her *Roman Freedmen during the Late Republic* (Oxford: Clarendon Press, 1969), pp. 142-153.

14. For a discussion see Donald Earl, *The Moral and Political Tradition of Rome* (London: Thames & Hudson, 1967), esp. pp. 15-17.

15. Ibid., pp. 81-82.

16. Ibid.

17. Ibid., pp. 12-13, 44-58.

18. Ibid., p. 81 (emphasis added). Tacitus, *Germania,* 20.2, cited by Earl.

19. Duff, *Freedmen in the Early Roman Empire,* p. 151.

20. Petronius, *The Satyricon,* trans. W. Arrowsmith (Ann Arbor: University of Michigan Press, 1959), pp. 25-79.

21. Ibid., p. 27 (Petronius, *Sat.* 29).

22. Ibid., p. 30 (Petronius, *Sat.* 32).

23. See for example D. Iunii Iuvenalis, *Satirae,* trans. J. D. Lewis (London: Trubner & Co., 1882).

24. Tacitus, *Hist.* 5.9. Cited in Duff, *Freedmen in the Early Roman Empire,* p. 173. On the attitude of other authors see Boulvert, *Domestique et fonctionnaire,* pp. 231-232.

25. For a detailed discussion of what he calls the "sociological inferiority of freedmen" see Boulvert, *Domestique et fonctionnaire,* pp. 231-256.

26. Peter Garnsey, *Social Status and Legal Privilege in the Roman Empire* (Oxford: Oxford University Press, 1970), p. 122 (emphasis added).

27. Duff, *Freedmen in the Early Roman Empire,* p. 180.

28. Ibid., pp. 173-186, summarizes.

29. In this regard the case of Claudius is perhaps the most instructive. See Vincent M. Scramuzza, *The Emperor Claudius* (Cambridge, Mass.: Harvard University Press, 1940), esp. pp. 35-50, 85-89.

30. The term *ghulām* (singular; plural *ghilmān*) means literally a young man or boy, and by extension a servant—usually, but not necessarily, a slave or freedman with strong ties of personal loyalty to his master. See "Ghulām," *Encyclopedia of Islam,* ed. 2 (Leiden; E. J. Brill, 1965), vol. 2, pp. 1079-91.

31. Concerning military slavery in the Islamic world I have drawn primarily on Daniel Pipes, "From Mawla to Mamlūk: The Origins of Islamic Military Slavery" (Ph.D. diss., Harvard University, 1978). This is a first-rate piece of scholarship marred only by the author's insistence that elite military slavery was unique to Islamic civilization, what he calls the "Islamicate." Pipes concedes that slaves were recruited from outside and trained for the military in other parts of the world, and he

is also aware of the role of administrative slaves elsewhere. What he insists on is the uniqueness of the combination of qualities that specified a professional regiment of soldiers occupying high status and power in a society. Pipes is not necessarily wrong, but makes too much of the distinctiveness. This leads him into an empty kind of schematism that is unfortunate in the way it prompts the author to make wholly insupportable assertions. Typical of such statements is this one: "Government slaves cannot build up a power base of their own and almost never threaten their masters; military slaves, however, can develop such a base from their own corps and with it they stand up to the ruler" (p. 25). The familia Caesaris and, as we shall see later, the corps of eunuchs in Byzantium did exactly this for several centuries.

I have also drawn heavily on Paul G. Forand, "The Development of Military Slavery under the Abbasid Caliphs of the Ninth Century A.D. (Third Century A.H.) with Special Reference to the Reigns of Mu'Tasim and Mu'Tadid" (Ph.D. diss., Princeton University, 1961), which is a sound work though less sociologically sophisticated than that of Pipes. The most prolific and, on the Mamluks, the most authoritative author is David Ayalon: I have drawn principally on the following of his works: *Studies on the Mamlūks of Egypt* (London: Variorum Reprints, 1977); *L'esclavage du mamelouk* (Jerusalem: Oriental Notes and Studies, 1951); *Gunpowder and Firearms in the Mamlūk Kingdom* (London: Vallentine, Mitchell, 1956); "The European-Asiatic Steppe: A Major Reservoir of Power for the Islamic World," Proceedings of the 25th Congress of Orientalists, Moscow, 1960 (Moscow: n.p., 1963), pp. 47–52. Also valuable is P. M. Holt's "The Position and Power of the Mamluk Sultan," *Bulletin of the School of Oriental and African Studies* 38, pt. 2 (1975): 237–249. The best short review of the military in the Islamic world must surely be the series of articles under "Djaysh" in the *Encyclopedia of Islam*, ed. 2, vol. 2, pp. 504–509. Of special value also are the papers in V. J. Parry and M. E. Yapp, eds., *War, Technology, and Society in the Middle East* (London: Oxford University Press, 1975). On the janissaries the standard work is now Basilike D. Papoulia, *Ursprung und Wesen der 'Knabenlese' im osmanischen Reich* (Munich: R. Oldenbourg, 1963). Important in its own right is V. L. Ménage, "Some Notes on the Devshirme," *Bulletin of the School of Oriental and African Studies* 29 (1966): 64–78.

32. According to Pipes, persons of slave origin directed Islamic governments in over fifty cases, including two female ex-slave rulers. "From Mawla to Mamlūk," pp. 38, 253.

33. Paul Rycaut, *The Present State of the Ottoman Empire, 1668* (London: Arno Press, 1971), p. 8.

34. *The Ottoman Empire* (New York: Praeger Publishers, 1973), p. 87. It is significant that most specialists on the janissaries, including Papoulia, concur that they were genuine slaves (although there is disagreement on whether and when they ceased to be slaves). Pipes confronts the issue directly and concludes that they remained genuine slaves as long as they were under the control of their masters. He notes that the reluctance of historians of Islam to call the ghilmān slaves springs from their mistaken assumption that slavery implies low status. See his "From Mawla to Mamlūk," pp. 25–39.

35. *Encyclopedia of Islam*, ed. 2, vol. 2, p. 1090.

36. *History of the Ottoman Empire and Modern Turkey* (Cambridge: Cambridge University Press, 1976), p. 166.

37. Manpower shortages and reliance on the conquered peoples of the periphery and semiperiphery of the central Islamic lands to meet these manpower needs is a continuous theme in the history of the major Islamic states. See Samuel S. Haas, "The Contributions of Slaves to and Their Influence upon the Culture of Early Islam" (Ph.D. diss., Princeton University, 1942), chap. 2, which deals with warfare. See also Ayalon, "The European-Asiatic Steppe"; idem, *Studies on the Mamlūks of Egypt*, chaps. 2–5; Speros Vryonis, Jr., "Byzantine and Turkish Societies and Their Sources of Manpower," in Parry and Yapp, *War, Technology, and Society in the Middle East*, pp. 125–152.

38. Forand, "The Development of Military Slavery," pp. 5–15.

39. For a geographic delineation see ibid., pp. 21–22.

40. Ibid., pp. 27–29.

41. Ibn Khaldun, *An Arab Philosophy of History,* trans. Charles Issawi (London: John Murray, 1950), p. 57.

42. Cited in David Ayalon, "Preliminary Remarks on the Mamlūk Military Institution in Islam," in Parry and Yapp, *War, Technology, and Society in the Middle East*, p. 49. Emphasis added.

43. Ibid.

44. Ibid., p. 50.

45. "Ghulām, iii: India," *Encyclopedia of Islam*, ed. 2, vol. 2, p. 1085.

46. Paul Wittek, "Devshirme and Shari'a," in Stanford Shaw, ed., "Selected Readings on Ottoman History" (Cambridge, Mass.: Harvard University Library, 1965), vol. 2, pp. 645–653 (manuscript).

47. Papoulia, *Ursprung und Wesen*, p. 1; see also p. 116. The translation of this particular passage is by Ménage, "Some Notes on the Devshirme," p. 64. See also idem, "Devshirme," *Encyclopedia of Islam*, ed. 2, vol. 2, pp. 210–213.

48. Wittek, "Devshirme and Shari'a," p. 645.

49. C. E. Bosworth, "Ghulām, ii: Persia," *Encyclopedia of Islam*, ed. 2, vol. 2, p. 1083. Daniel Pipes notes: "Being outsiders also increases their susceptibility to being molded; the owner can isolate foreigners by eliminating any ties outside his household and by forcing them to depend entirely on the small world of the master and his fellow slaves." *From Mawla to Mamlūk*, p. 21.

50. On eunuchism see Ayalon, "Preliminary Remarks," pp. 50–51. See also "Khasi," *Encyclopedia of Islam*, ed. 2 (Leiden: E. J. Brill, 1978), vol. 4, pp. 1087–93.

51. Ayalon calls the Mamluk aristocracy of Egypt "a one generation nobility only, all its members having been born in the steppe and being Muslims of the first generation." *Studies on the Mamlūks of Egypt*, p. 313.

52. On what R. C. Repp calls "the vexed problem of the status in law" of the janissaries, see Papoulia, *Ursprung und Wesen*, pp. 4–10, where she argues that the passing-out ceremony did involve a form of manumission; in contrast see Ménage, "Some Notes on the Devshirme." See also, in support of Ménage, R. C. Repp, "A Further Note on the Devshirme," *Bulletin of the School of Oriental and African Studies* 31 (1968): 137–139.

53. Repp, "A Further Note on the Devshirme," pp. 138–139.

54. Ibid.

55. Pipes, *From Mawla to Mamlūk*, p. 31.

56. Ibid., pp. 35–36.

57. *Oriental Despotism* (New Haven: Yale University Press, 1957), p. 356.

58. See Richard Millant, *Les eunuques: A travers les ages* (Paris: Vigot Frères, 1908), esp. chaps. 4 and 5; and Dunlap, *Office of the Grand Chamberlain,* pp. 166–167.

59. *Chinese Eunuchs: The Structure of Intimate Politics* (Rutland Vt.: Charles E. Tuttle Co., 1970), pp. 152, 160; and for more on their role on the fall of the Han dynasty see C. P. Fitzgerald, *China: A Short Cultural History* (London: Cresset Press, 1965), pp. 250–255.

60. Mitamura, *Chinese Eunuchs,* p. 11; and Fitzgerald, *China,* pp. 305, 468–474.

61. The prohibition, however, was hardly a strong one, since Muhammad himself accepted a eunuch as a slave. Cengiz Orhonlu, "Khasi," *Encyclopedia of Islam,* ed. 2, vol. 4, p. 1089.

62. Ayalon, "Preliminary Remarks," pp. 50–51.

63. Orhonlu, "Khasi."

64. Ibid., pp. 1091–93. Eunuchs were used in Islamic lands until modern times. See Otto Meinardus, "The Upper Egyptian Practice of the Making of Eunuchs in the Eighteenth and Nineteenth Century," *Zeitschrift für Ethnologie* 94 (1969): 47–58.

65. Ethiopian eunuchs are mentioned in many ancient texts, including the Bible. On the celebrated Ethiopian eunuch baptized by Philip see Frank M. Snowden, Jr., *Blacks in Antiquity* (Cambridge, Mass.: Harvard University Press, Belknap Press, 1970), pp. 204, 206–207. On the eunuch governor of Sidam, and a good general account of the use of and trade in eunuchs in northeast Africa and the Middle East, see R. W. Beachey, *The Slave Trade of Eastern Africa* (New York: Harper & Row, 1976), pp. 169–174.

66. A. G. B. Fisher and H. J. Fisher, *Slavery and Muslim Society in Africa* (London: C. Hurst & Co., 1970), p. 143.

67. S. F. Nadel, *A Black Byzantium* (London: Oxford University Press, 1942), p. 107.

68. Fisher and Fisher, *Slavery and Muslim Society in Africa,* p. 147.

69. Ibid., pp. 145–147.

70. Beachey, *The Slave Trade of Eastern Africa,* p. 170.

71. Fisher and Fisher, *Slavery and Muslim Society in Africa,* p. 148.

72. J. S. Boston, *The Igala Kingdom* (Ibadan: Oxford University Press, 1968), pp. 163–175, 197–236. Political eunuchism was also well developed among the Yoruba, although this was partly due to direct Muslim influence, on which see Natalia B. Kochakova, "Yoruba City-States (at the Turn of the Nineteenth Century)," in H. J. M. Claessen and Peter Skalnik, eds., *The Early State* (New York: Mouton, 1978), p. 506.

73. For the development of the grand chamberlain's position I have drawn mainly on Dunlap, *Office of the Grand Chamberlain,* chaps. 1–3.

74. Ibid., p. 180.

75. *Conquerors and Slaves* (Cambridge: Cambridge University Press, 1978), p. 172.

76. Ibid., pp. 180–181.

77. *China,* p. 251.

78. *Conquerors and Slaves,* p. 187.

79. Ibid., p. 191.

80. *Byzantine Civilization* (London: E. Arnold, 1933), p. 187.

81. Wittfogel, *Oriental Despotism*, p. 357.

82. See Evelyne Patlagean, *Pauvreté economique et pauvreté sociale à Byzance, 4e-7e siècles* (Paris: Mouton, 1977), p. 285.

83. S. N. Eisenstadt, *The Political Systems of Empires* (New York: Free Press, 1963), pp. 133–149.

84. Ibid., pp. 285–286.

85. Hopkins, *Conquerors and Slaves*, pp. 193–196.

86. Cited in Louis L. Gray, "Eunuchs," *Encyclopedia of Religion and Ethics* (New York: Charles Scribner's Sons, [1908–1927]), vol. 5, p. 582.

87. For a review of the modern medical literature, see Hopkins, *Conquerors and Slaves*, pp. 193–194.

88. Mitamura, *Chinese Eunuchs*, pp. 36–38.

89. Orhonlu, "Khāsi," pp. 1089–90.

90. Ibid.

91. Hopkins, *Conquerors and Slaves*, p. 195.

92. Mary Douglas, *Purity and Danger* (London: Routledge & Kegan Paul, 1966), p. 40.

93. Ibid., p. 96.

94. Ibid.

95. Ibid., chap. 7. Quotation on p. 128.

96. Ibid., quotation on p. 159; chap. 10 passim.

97. Edmund R. Leach, "Genesis as Myth," in John Middleton, ed., *Myth and Cosmos* (Garden City, N.Y.: Natural History Press, 1967), pp. 1–13.

98. Ibid., p. 4.

99. Mitamura, *Chinese Eunuchs*, p. 42.

100. Ibid., p. 57.

101. Ibid., p. 47.

102. Ibid., p. 37.

103. Ibid., p. 127.

104. Ibid., p. 48.

105. Ibid., p. 50.

106. Claude Lévi-Strauss, "Four Winnebago Myths: A Structural Sketch," in Middleton, *Myth and Cosmos*, p. 24.

107. Mitamura, *Chinese Eunuchs*, pp. 48–49.

108. Ibid., pp. 88–95.

109. Herrlee G. Creel, *The Birth of China* (New York: Frederick Ungar, 1937), p. 287.

110. Ibid., pp. 287–288.

111. Dunlap, *Office of the Grand Chamberlain*, p. 178.

112. René Guerdan, *Byzantium: Its Triumphs and Tragedy* (New York: Capricorn Books, 1962), p. 18.

113. Mitamura, *Chinese Eunuchs*, p. 52.

114. Guerdan, *Byzantium*, p. 28.

115. H. W. Haussing, *A History of Byzantine Civilization* (New York: Praeger Publishers, 1971), p. 126.

116. Ibid.

117. Guerdan, *Byzantium,* p. 135.
118. See, for example, ibid., p. 39.
119. Cited in Douglas, *Purity and Danger,* pp. 159–160.
120. Guerdan, *Byzantium,* pp. 34–38.
121. "Representation through Intimacy: A Study of the Symbolism of Monarchy and Court Office in Early-Modern England," in Ioan M. Lewis, ed., *Symbols and Sentiments* (New York: Academic Press, 1977), pp. 187–224.
122. Ibid., p. 212.

12. Slavery as Human Parasitism

1. The social biologist Edward O. Wilson writes: *"Symbiosis* is defined in the sense usually employed by American biologists, to include all categories of close and protracted interactions between individuals of different species, rather than in the narrower European sense of an exclusively beneficial interaction. Accordingly, three principal kinds of symbiosis can be recognized: parasitism, in which one partner benefits as the other suffers; commensalism, in which one partner benefits and the other is not affected either way; and mutualism, in which both species benefit." *The Insect Societies* (Cambridge, Mass.: Harvard University Press, 1971), p. 389.
2. Ibid., pp. 349–377.
3. Anatol Rapoport, *Fights, Games, and Debates* (Ann Arbor: University of Michigan Press, 1960), pp. 62–71. The following is a summary of the analysis in, as far as possible, plain English.

The model is a simple Ricardo type with the usual stylized assumptions: only two producers, X and Y, seeking to maximize their utilities both through their own production and through exchange of products with each other. There are two important assumptions: (1) The terms of exchange are fixed (by custom, law, contract, agreement of any sort). Each producer must exchange a part of his product, q, and keep the remaining fraction, p (so that $p = 1 - q$). (2) The terms of exchange are equal. The first producer exchanges q portion of his product x, and the second producer exchanges q portion of his product y. Given the usual assumptions about utility (declining marginal utility of increased consumption and constant marginal disutility, β, of increased work) Rapoport's model derives the production levels (x,y) under different "terms of trade" (p,q). Parasitism is the outcome where either $x = 0$ and $y > 0$, or $y = 0$ and $x > 0$, such that one producer receives a portion of the other's product while producing nothing himself.

Rapoport shows that equilibrium exists only at the "balance point" defined by the intersection of the following two equations:

$$px + qy = p/\beta - 1, \qquad qx + py = p/\beta - 1.$$

However, p must be greater than β (the parameter of "laziness") or else the system is not feasible—that is, no one will produce anything.

Rapoport's central observation is that the balance point may be either stable or unstable. In the stable case, X's optimal production line is steeper than Y's. This is the situation of commensalism, or stable economic exchange. Neither individual can exploit the other; any change in production will return to balance.

In the unstable case, Y's optimal production line is steeper. One producer will find it advantageous to produce nothing and simply consume a portion of the other's product—parasitism. Rapoport argues that stability occurs only if p is greater than q (if you keep more than you give), whereas instability, culminating in parasitism, always results when q is greater than p. Parasitism, in other words, is a function of the terms of exchange.

For the case of slavery perhaps the most problematic of Rapoport's assumptions is not that exchange is fixed, but rather that exchange is equal. My colleague John Padgett, however, has shown that Rapoport's analysis still holds, even with relaxation of this constraint (by allowing $px = py$). The conditions for stability in this case become $px + py > 1$, and the conditions for parasitism become $px + py < 1$. As before, the system is feasible only if $px > \beta x$ and $py > \beta y$.

This qualification should be borne in mind when considering the three most important conclusions that Rapoport draws form his analysis:

"1. In the stable case, both parties are better off at the social optimum than they are at the (stable) point of balance.

2. In the unstable case, the host is always better off at the social optimum.

3. The parasite would be better off at the social optimum if β were greater than a certain critical value, but he is better off as a parasite if β is smaller than this critical value."

Although Rapoport's key *analytic* finding concerns the terms of trade and its relation to the conditions of stability versus instability, his most important substantive finding, and the one that is most relevant here, is the third conclusion listed above. Parasitism pays only when β, the parameter of laziness, is minimized, never when it is maximized.

It is important to emphasize that the social optimum is not necessarily the same thing as the attainment of the joint maximum product measured in standard economic terms. The problem of reconciling the two has long been a major concern of liberal economic commentators, and the issue has always been closely linked with debate over the relative merits of forced and "free" labor. A recent paper by Stanley Engerman is highly relevant: see "Coerced and Free Labor: Property Rights and the Development of the Labor Force," paper presented at the Conference on the Evolution of the Right to Property, June 16–20, 1980. Engerman observes, for example, that "the exercise of freedom of choice by individuals need not lead to the maximization of conventionally measured economic outputs. Individuals with freedom of choice as to work input and occupations may not produce as much as those compelled workers to whom such choices are precluded. If it is the aim of "society" to increase the output of conventionally measured goods, it does not follow that this would be achieved with free, rather than compelled, labor" (mimeographed, p. 5). This cogent observation is of relevance not only to students of slavery but to social scientists who are studying the development process in the Third World.

Returning to Rapoport's model, while it has carried us beyond biological parasitism in taking into consideration the uniquely human variable of utility, its limitations should also be noted. It is clearly of most value for the analysis of slavery where the slaveholder's main concern is with the extraction of a material surplus from the slave. While this was the case in most of the advanced slave systems of the world, we have seen that it was not true even of a number of these systems—and certainly not true of most small-scale slaveholding societies. The model is inappropriate in those societies where the slaveholder seeks mainly to extract from the slave such intangibles as loyalty, sexual gratification, honor, and even love. A purely economic model of parasitism not only neglects the important ideological and symbolic aspects of the parasitic relation but, more seriously, it can be highly misleading when uncritically applied to the extraction of noneconomic gains.

Take, for example, the classic case of the slave concubine. The slaveholder invariably demands and usually gets both sexual gratification and love. In return he generally gives protection, material support, and sometimes prestige. In Rapoport's model, assuming the right balance of utilities, the relationship becomes symbiotic and stable. A more extreme case would be one in which the slave concubine is obliged to support herself, say by hiring out as a weaver or a prostitute. At the same time, she is hopelessly in love with the master and enthralled by his prestige. The master gives nothing in return; he offers no love; he takes sexual gratification and a portion of her earnings as well. Nonetheless the slave is so enraptured that what she gives is not a loss. It is, in fact, a positive utility which may be so great that it more than compensates for the disutility of enslavement. Both holder and slave gain from the relationship which, in Rapoport's terms, as well as those of social biology, becomes one of mutualism. Our moral sensibilities are strongly offended by such a conclusion and we remain inclined to view such a master as a parasite.

Human beings are social animals, and to the extent that they are, the social biologist's conception of parasitism is appropriate. They are also economic men and women, and to this extent the utility model of Rapoport is appropriate. But they are, above all, moral persons. In this last respect neither of the above perspectives is appropriate. As moral creatures we rightly pass judgment on others' actions independent of their own conception of their utilities. The master remains a moral parasite, however well he treats his slave; the slave remains a parasitized victim, however much he or she enjoys thralldom.

4. The relevance of this discussion to the recent debate on the economics of slavery should be obvious. See Paul A. David et al., *Reckoning with Slavery* (New York: Oxford University Press, 1976); Robert W. Fogel and Stanley L. Engerman, *Time on the Cross: The Economics of American Negro Slavery* (Boston: Little, Brown, 1974), chaps. 5 and 6; idem, "Explaining the Relative Efficiency of Slave Agriculture in the Antebellum South: A Reply," *American Economic Review* 67 (1977): 275–296; Thomas L. Haskel, "Explaining the Relative Efficiency of Slave Labor in the Antebellum South: A Reply to Fogel and Engerman," *American Economic Review* 69 (1979): 206–207; D. F. Schaefer and M. D. Schmitz, "The Relative Efficiency of Slave Agriculture: A Comment," *American Economic Review* 69 (1979): 208–212; Paul A. David and Peter Temin, "Explaining the Relative Efficiency of Slave Agriculture in the Antebellum South: Comment," *American Economic Review* 69 (1979): 213–218; Gavin Wright, "The Efficiency of Slavery: Another Interpretation," *American Economic Review* 69 (1979): 219–226; Robert W. Fogel and Stanley L. Engerman, "Explaining the Relative Efficiency of Slave Agriculture in the Antebellum South: Reply," *American Economic Review* 70 (1980): 672–690.

Fogel and Engerman have persuasively demonstrated that the slaves were forced to work much harder than they would have done had they been free. They have also explained why their extraordinary level of effort has for so long been misinterpreted by both liberal and conservative commentators, as well as proslavery and antislavery debaters: the fact that "the fundamental form of exploitation of slave labor was through speed-up (increased intensity per hour) rather than through an increase in the number of clock-time hours per year" (see Fogel and Engerman, "Explaining the Relative Efficiency of Slave Agriculture: A Reply"). Fogel and Engerman have also demonstrated how, and why, the parasitism of the slaveholder class involved hard work on their part. Idle planters, they have shown, constituted a "distinct minority" of the planter class. Confusion on this issue has been due to the fact that during the last decades of slavery one of the major problems facing the parasitic class was how to provide efficient management especially on the large plantations. "Far from being cavalier fops," they write, "the leading planters were, on the whole, a highly self-conscious class of entrepreneurs who generally approached their governmental responsibilities with deliberation and gravity— a manner which accorded with their self-image" (see Fogel and Engerman, *Time on the Cross,* vol. 1, pp. 200–202).

A good part, though certainly not all, of the heat surrounding the debate over *Time on the Cross* was largely semantic. We are not only ambivalent about the term "master," as I indicated earlier, but in capitalist America the term "efficient" has positive moral overtones, even among liberal and left-wing economists. Hence any reference to "efficient masters" was bound to be explosive. It is interesting to contemplate what would have been the response had Fogel and Engerman said the same thing but referred not to "efficient masters" but to "zealous parasites."

5. The issue of the extent to which the parasitism of the slaveholder class adversely influenced free nonslaveholding southerners and the overall economic development of the South is still controversial. See Stanley L. Engerman, "A Reconsideration of Southern Economic Growth, 1770–1860," *Agricultural History* 49 (1975): 343–361. See also the other papers in this issue of the journal, especially those of Eugene D. Genovese and Harold D. Woodman. An earlier special number of this journal on "The Structure of the Cotton Economy of the Antebellum South" is also valuable: see *Agricultural History* 44 (1970). Of particular importance in this issue is the highly suggestive paper by William N. Parker, "Slavery and Southern Economic Development: An Hypothesis and Some Evidence," pp. 115–125. See also the related paper by Stanley L. Engerman, "The Antebellum South: What Probably Was and What Should Have Been," pp. 127–142. A convenient though now slightly dated summary of these issues may be found in Harold D. Woodman, ed., *Slavery and the Southern Economy* (New York: Harcourt, Brace & World, 1966). On past debate over the effects of slavery on the nonslaveholder see pp. 113–161, and on the relationship between slavery and the economic development of the South, see pp. 179–233.

The work of Claudia Dale Goldin on the economics of urban slavery is also highly relevant to both the problem of southern economic development and the degree to which the slave system influenced the free nonslaveholding southern population. See her "Economics of Urban Slavery: 1820–1860" (Ph. D. diss., University of Chicago, 1972). On the first issue Goldin concludes that "slavery and Southern cities were not incompatible during the period 1820–1860" and that in general "the growth in the demand for urban slave services appears to have been strong" (p. 111). The southern slave system, she concludes, "was extremely flexible, and it is in the cities that this flexibility is most apparent" (p. 116). On the second issue, the effect of the system on nonslaveholders, Goldin is less positive, but in general she is of the opinion that the slave system had an adverse effect on the interests of free nonfarm, working-class whites. Slave labor kept wages low and slaves were used as "scabs" to break up strikes: "The slave owners were numerous and powerful, and they passed laws protecting slave labor from the encroachments of free white labor" (p. 31). Ironically, the planter class was so successful in controlling the wage of sections of the white urban working class that by the 1850s it had become cheaper to employ them than to continue using slaves, especially when the rising prices of slaves and of slave hire rates were taken into account. The resulting movement of slaves from the cities to the rural areas did not mean the decline of urban slavery. Rather, "it was far more a function of the availability of low cost substitute labor" (pp. 112–113).

The relationship between slavery, the exploitation of the free nonslaveholder, and economic development has not been explored with anything approaching the same depth in other areas of the Americas or Africa. For discussions of the issues with respect to the English-speaking Caribbean see George L. Beckford, *Persistent Poverty* (New York: Oxford University Press, 1972); Clive Thomas, *Dependence and Transformation: The Economics of the Transition to Socialism* (New York: Monthly Review Press, 1974); Walter Rodney, "Slavery and Underdevelopment," in Michael Craton, ed., *Roots and Branches: Current Directions in Slave Studies, Historical Reflections* 6 (1979): 279–286; and my "Commentary" on this paper in ibid., pp. 287–292.

For an examination of these relationships in the case of Puerto Rico, see Sidney W. Mintz, *Caribbean Transformation* (Chicago: Aldine, 1974), chaps. 3 and 4. And for an even stronger statement of the effects of the expanding slave system of nineteenth-century Puerto Rico on "free" labor and Puerto Rican development in general, see Francisco Scarano, "Slavery and Free Labor in the Puerto Rican Sugar Economy, 1815–1873," in Vera Rubin and Arthur Tuden, eds., *Comparative Perspectives on Slavery in New World Plantation Societies* (New York: New York Academy of Sciences, 1977), pp. 553–563.

On Cuba see Manuel Moreno Fraginals, *The Sugarmill* (New York: Monthly Review Press, 1976), pp. 17–30, 131–153. On Brazil see Florestan Fernandes, "Slaveholding Society in Brazil," in Rubin and Tuden, *Comparative Perspectives on Slavery*, pp. 311–342; Stanley J. Stein, *Vassouras: A Brazilian Coffee County, 1850–1900* (Cambridge, Mass.: Harvard University Press, 1957), esp. chap. 5; Robert Conrad, *The Destruction of Brazilian Slavery, 1850–1888* (Berkeley: University of California Press, 1972), esp. chap. 3; Celso Furtado, "The Slavery Economy of Tropical Agriculture in Sixteenth- and Seventeenth-Century Brazil," in Eugene D. Genovese, ed., *The Slave Economics* (New York: John Wiley & Sons, 1973), pp. 9–22.

6. Cited in Robin W. Winks, *The Blacks in Canada: A History* (Montreal: McGill University Press, 1971), p. 53.

7. Joseph E. Brown in the Jackson (Mississippi) *Daily Clarion*, June 20, 1867. Cited in Lawrence J. Friedman, *The White Savage: Racial Fantasies in the Postbellum South* (Englewood Cliffs, N.J.: Prentice-Hall, 1970), p. 24.

8. *The White Savage*, pp. 21–36.

9. Cited in ibid., p. 25.

10. Ibid., p. 31.

11. Pliny the Elder, *Natural History,* 28, 14. Cited in Thomas Wiedemann, *Greek and Roman Slavery* (Baltimore: Johns Hopkins University Press, 1981), p. 73.

12. *Freedom* (New York: Basic Books, 1953), p. 19.

13. This problem is usually expressed in terms of the dependence of society on slavery. I treat the issue instead as one of systemic invasion by a parasitic slave institution. The conceptual difference is important, but the basic idea is the same. See Orlando Patterson, "Slavery and Slave Formations," *New Left Review* 117 (1979): esp. pp. 47–67. See also Carl N. Degler, "Note: Starr on Slavery," *Journal of Economic History* 19 (1959): 271–277; and M. I. Finley, "Was Greek Civilization Based on Slave Labour?" in M. I. Finley, ed., *Slavery in Classical Antiquity* (Cambridge: W. Heffer and Sons, 1960), pp. 53–72.

Related to this issue are Marxian attempts to define a "slave mode of production," on which see Perry Anderson, *Passages from Antiquity to Feudalism* (London: Verso, 1978), chap. 1; Barry Hindess and Paul Q. Hirst, *Pre-Capitalist Modes of Production* (London: Routledge & Kegan Paul, 1975), pp. 109–177; R. A. Padgug, "Problems in the Theory of Slavery and Slave Society," *Science and Society* 40 (1976): 3–27; and Martin A. Klein and Paul E. Lovejoy, "Slavery in West Africa," in Henry A. Gemery and Jan S. Hogendorn, eds., *The Uncommon Market: Essays in the Economic History of the Atlantic Slave Trade* (New York: Academic Press, 1979), esp. pp. 207–212. I consider all attempts to formulate a slave mode of production theoretically misguided, for reasons partially adumbrated in my "Slavery and Slave Formations," esp. pp. 47–55. See also Claude Meillassoux, *L'esclavage en Afrique précoloniale* (Paris: François Maspero, 1975), Introduction, esp. pp. 18–25.

Appendix A: Note on Statistical Methods

1. G. P. Murdock and D. R. White, "Standard Cross-Cultural Sample," *Ethnology* 8 (1969): 329.

2. Ibid.

3. G. P. Murdock, "Ethnographic Atlas: A Summary," *Ethnology* 6 (1967): 109–236.

Appendix C: The Large-Scale Slave Systems

1. M. I. Finley, "Was Greek Civilization Based on Slave Labour?" in M. I. Finley, ed., *Slavery in Classical Antiquity* (Cambridge: W. Heffer and Sons, 1960), pp. 58–59; and Antony Andrews, *The Greeks* (London: Hutchinson, 1967), p. 135.

2. Keith Hopkins, *Conquerors and Slaves* (Cambridge: Cambridge University Press, 1978), p. 68; and M. I. Finley, *Ancient Slavery and Modern Ideology* (New York: Viking Press, 1980), p. 80.

3. William V. Harris, "Towards a Study of the Roman Slave Trade," in J. H. D'Arms and E. C. Kopff, eds., "The Seaborne Commerce of Ancient Rome: Studies in Archeology and History," in Memoirs of the American Academy of Rome, vol. 36 (1980), p. 118.

4. Francis M. Crawford, *Southern Italy and Sicily and the Rulers of the South*

(London: Macmillan & Co., 1905), p. 293. See also M. I. Finley, *Ancient Sicily* (New York: Viking Press, 1968), pp. 137–147, 162.

5. Inferred from Charles Verlinden, *L'esclavage dans l'Europe médiévale* (Bruges: De Tempel, 1955), vol. 1, pp. 62, 82, 85; and from P. D. King, *Law and Society in the Visigothic Kingdom* (Cambridge: Cambridge University Press, 1972), esp. pp. 160–162. King notes that the smallest churches had ten slaves and considered themselves "pauperrima" (poverty-stricken). Larger churches "numbered their slaves in hundreds or thousands" (p. 160n3).

6. Inferred from Verlinden, *L'esclavage dans l'Europe médiévale,* pp. 181–188.

7. Inferred from ibid., pp. 278–289.

8. Inferred from ibid., vol. 2 (1977), pp. 876–884; and from J. H. Galloway, "The Mediterranean Sugar Industry," *Geographical Review* 67 (1977): figs. 1 and 2; p. 190.

9. Inferred from Verlinden, *L'esclavage dans l'Europe médiévale,* vol. 2, pp. 884–892; and from Galloway, "The Mediterranean Sugar Industry," figs. 1 and 2; p. 190.

10. Calculated in Verlinden, *L'esclavage dans l'Europe médiévale,* vol. 2, p. 351. I have rounded off Verlinden's figure of 17.94 percent. He emphasizes the fact that this is a very conservative minimum estimate. In all probability, slaves constituted well over a quarter of the total Majorcan population, especially in the rural areas.

11. Slaves would have been most in demand during the period of colonization and settlement, roughly 870–930, during which period it was estimated that some twenty thousand persons went to Iceland. See Peter Foote and David M. Wilson, *The Viking Achievement* (London: Sidgwick & Jackson, 1970), pp. 52–53. The period of settlement was scarcely more than one and a half human generations when late ninth- and tenth-century demographic conditions are considered. The mean population would hardly have been greater than ten thousand, and Carl O. Williams has estimated that the slave population at any one time during the period of settlement was about two thousand. See his *Thraldom in Ancient Iceland* (Chicago: University of Chicago Press, 1937), p. 36. Hence the slave population was at least 20 percent of the total and certainly much greater during the first half of the colonization.

12. According to the Domesday statistics, on which see F. W. Maitland, *Domesday Book and Beyond* (Cambridge: Cambridge University Press, 1897; reprint ed., 1960), 9 percent of the entire British population were slaves in 1086. However, in the western counties the proportion rose to over 20 percent: Gloucestershire's slave population was 24 percent, and Cornwall's 21. At this time slavery was already long on the decline, hence during the Anglo-Saxon and late old English period, when these regions were either autonomous states or nearly so, slaves must have accounted for well over a third of the total population in many of them (especially in Gloucestershire, where Bristol thrived as one of the major slave marts of the western European world).

13. Inferred from Sidney M. Greenfield, "Madeira and the Beginnings of New World Sugar Cane Cultivation and Plantation Slavery: A Study in Institution Building," in Vera Rubin and Arthur Tuden, eds., *Comparative Perspectives on Slavery in New World Plantation Societies* (New York: New York Academy of Sciences, 1977), pp. 536–552; and from T. Bentley Duncan, *The Atlantic Islands: Madeira, the*

Azores, and Cabo Verde in Seventeenth Century Commerce and Navigation (Chicago: University of Chicago Press, 1972).

14. Inferred from Juan de Abreau de Galindo, *The History of the Discovery of the Canary Islands* (London: Dodsley and Durham, 1764).

15. While all the Barbary states came to rely on slaving and slavery during this period, Algiers alone developed a large-scale dependence on the institution. In 1580 between twenty-five thousand and thirty-five thousand persons in a total population of one hundred thousand were slaves. While this ratio rose and fell during the two and a half centuries of Barbary slavery, it was apparently the average for the entire period. See Stephen Clissold, *The Barbary Slaves* (London: Paul Elek, 1977), p. 53. For an excellent analysis of the vital economic and sociopolitical role of slavery see Ellen G. Friedman, "Christian Captives at 'Hard Labor' in Algiers, Sixteenth to Eighteenth Centuries," *International Journal of African Historical Studies* 13 (1980): 616–632. Although not classified as large-scale slavery, Morocco's heavy dependence on military and administrative slaves makes it a marginal case, on which see Allan R. Meyers, "The Abid 'L-Buhari: Slave Soldiers and Statecraft in Morocco, 1672–1790" (Ph.D. diss., Cornell University, 1974).

16. Inferred from Nehemia Levtzion, "The Early States of the Western Sudan to 1500," in J. F. Ade Ajayi and Michael Crowder, eds., *A History of West Africa* (London: Longmans, 1971), vol. 1, pp. 114–151, esp. pp. 139–140; and from Paul E. Lovejoy, "Indigenous African Slavery," in Michael Craton, ed., *Roots and Branches, Current Directions in Slave Studies: Historical Reflections* 6 (1979): 28–29.

17. Inferred from Levtzion, "The Early States of the Western Sudan"; from Lovejoy, "Indigenous African Slavery"; and from A. G. B. Fisher and H. J. Fisher, *Slavery and Muslim Society in Africa* (London: C. Hurst & Co., 1970), pp. 101–102, 137, 139.

18. Inferred from Jean Bazin, "War and Servitude in Segou," *Economy and Society* 3 (1974): 107–143.

19. Inferred from J. O. Hunwick, "Religion and State in the Songhay Empire, 1464–1591," in Ioan M. Lewis, ed., *Islam in Africa* (London: Oxford University Press, 1966), pp. 296–315; from J. P. Olivier de Sardan, "Captifs ruraux et esclaves impérieux du Songhay," in Meillassoux, *L'esclavage en Afrique précoloniale* (Paris: François Maspero, 1975), pp. 99–134; and from Lovejoy, "Indigenous African Slavery," pp. 28–29.

20. Inferred from R. S. O'Fahey, "Slavery and the Slave Trade in Dār Fūr," *Journal of African History* 14 (1973): 29–43; and from Fisher and Fisher, *Slavery and Muslim Society in Africa,* passim.

21. Inferred from Fisher and Fisher, *Slavery and Muslim Society in Africa,* pp. 34–35 and passim; and stated in Lovejoy, "Indigenous African Slavery," p. 41.

22. Ibid.

23. Inferred from E. A. Ayandele, "Observations on Some Social and Economic Aspects of Slavery in Pre-Colonial Nigeria," *Nigerian Journal of Economic and Social Studies* 9 (1967): 329–338; from Ronald Cohen, "Slavery among the Kanuri," in *Slavery in Africa,* special suppl. *Trans-action* (January/February 1967): 48–50; from R. A. Adeleye, "Hausaland and Borno, 1600–1800," in Ajayi and Crowder, *History of West Africa,* vol. 1, pp. 568–579; from Lovejoy, "Indigenous African Slavery," pp. 29–30; and from Fisher and Fisher, *Slavery and Muslim Society in Africa,* p. 59 and passim.

24. Inferred from Fisher and Fisher, *Slavery and Muslim Society in Africa*, passim.

25. Inferred from Adeleye, "Hausaland and Borno," esp. pp. 595–596.

26. For some light on the complicated ethnohistory of the Fulani and their explosive imperialist drive in the mid-eighteenth century until the European invasion at the end of the nineteenth century see G. P. Murdock, *Africa: Its Peoples and Their Culture History* (New York: McGraw-Hill, 1950), pp. 413–421; Levtzion, "The Early States of the Western Sudan," pp. 128–131; Joseph P. Smaldone, *Warfare in the Sokoto Caliphate* (Cambridge: Cambridge University Press, 1977), esp. chaps. 1, 2, 8, 9; Ayandele, "Observations in Pre-Colonial Northern Nigeria"; Fisher and Fisher, *Slavery and Muslim Society in Africa*, pp. 9–13 and passim; Martin A. Klein and Paul E. Lovejoy, "Slavery in West Africa," in Henry A. Gemery and Jan S. Hogendorn, eds., *The Uncommon Market: Essays in the Economic History of the Atlantic Slave Trade* (New York: Academic Press, 1979), pp. 181–212; and Lovejoy, "Indigenous African Slavery," esp. pp. 37–43.

On Masina see M. Johnson, "The Economic Foundations of an Islamic Theocracy: The Case of Masina," *Journal of African History* 17 (1976): 481–495. No figures are cited, but the implication is clear that slaves were well over a third of the population; see in particular pp. 486, 488–491.

The Jakhanke are a diaspora Islamic clerical subgroup of Fulanis living in semiautonomous communities all over Senegambia. The main town, Touba, in Fouta Jaalo, had a slave population of 60 percent in the late nineteenth century. See Lamin O. Sanneh, *The Jakhanke* (London: International African Institute, 1979), esp. pp. 219–240; and Philip D. Curtin, *Economic Change in Precolonial Africa* (Madison: University of Wisconsin Press, 1975), pp. 79–80. Curtin cites estimates for the entire Senegambia region that range from 20 percent to over 75 percent (p. 36).

For more specific estimates see, on the Sokoto caliphate, Allan R. Meyers, "Slavery in the Hausa-Fulani Emirates," in D. F. McCall and Norman R. Bennett, eds., *Aspects of West African Islam*, Boston University Papers on Africa, no. 5, Boston (1971), pp. 176–177; an estimate of one-third to one-half of the population is given. On the emirate of Zaria, M. G. Smith claims that 50 percent of the population were slaves in the late nineteenth century: see his "Slavery and Emancipation in Two Societies," in M. G. Smith, ed., *The Plural Society in the British West Indies* (Berkeley: University of California Press, 1965), pp. 116–161. On Fouta-Djalon see M. S. Baldé, "L'esclavage et la guerre sainte au Fouta-Jalon," in Meillassoux, *L'esclavage en Afrique précoloniale*, pp. 183–220. Baldé cautiously claims that it is impossible to say today whether the slave population was more than 50 percent of the total, but he did find that in 1954–1955 a quarter of all persons in the area were descendants of slaves. This is usually indicative of a former slave population of over 50 percent, as Meillassoux' own analysis of similar data for Gumbu indicates, on which see Claude Meillassoux, "Etat et conditions des esclaves à Gumbu (Mali) au XIX siècle," in Meillassoux, *L'esclavage en Afrique précoloniale*, p. 225. For Adamawa, the most recent study claims that the ratio ranged from 50 percent to 66 percent, on which see Philip Burnham, "Raiders and Traders in Adamawa: Slavery as a Regional System," in James L. Watson, ed., *Asian and African Systems of Slavery* (Oxford: Basil Blackwell, 1980), p. 48.

27. All these figures are from Claude Bataillon et al., *Nomades et nomadisme au Sahara* (Paris: UNESCO, 1965), p. 31, and are cited in Jonathan Derrick, *Africa's*

Slaves Today (New York: Schocken Books, 1975), p. 37. However, Johannes Nicolaisen, a leading authority on the Tuareg, gives a much lower figure for the Air region (see Derrick, p. 37n15). It should be emphasized, however, that this disagreement refers to the situation in the 1960s! There is no argument regarding the near-total dependence on slaves and ex-slaves among nineteenth- and early twentieth-century Tuaregs, among whom we can safely assume slave ratios ranging from 33 to over 75 percent. See the chapters by Edmond and Suzanne Bernus, Pierre Bonte, and André Bourgeot in Meillassoux, *L'esclavage en Afrique précoloniale*, pp. 27–97. See also Johannes Nicolaisen, "Slavery among the Tuareg of the Sahara," *KUML* (1957): 107–113; Stephen Baier and Paul E. Lovejoy, "The Tuareg of the Central Sudan," in Suzanne Miers and Igor I. Kopytoff, eds., *Slavery in Africa* (Madison: University of Wisconsin Press, 1977), pp. 391–411.

28. For the early period we have no estimates, but the states from medieval times were predatory systems centered on slave raiding and trading. See Curtin, *Economic Change in Precolonial Africa;* and Martin A. Klein, "Servitude among the Wolof and Sereer of Senegambia," in Miers and Kopytoff, *Slavery in Africa,* esp. pp. 337–343.

29. Klein, "Servitude among the Wolof and Sereer of Senegambia," pp. 338–339.

30. Carol P. MacCormack, "Wono: Institutionalized Dependency in Sherbro Descent Groups," in Miers and Kopytoff, *Slavery in Africa,* p. 192.

31. John J. Grace, "Slavery and Emancipation among the Mende in Sierra Leone, 1896–1928," in Miers and Kopytoff, *Slavery in Africa,* p. 418. Other estimates place the percentage of Mende slaves somewhat lower. For a discussion of available statistics on the various tribes of Sierra Leone see John J. Grace, *Domestic Slavery in West Africa* (New York: Harper & Row, 1975), pp. 169–172; and Kenneth C. Wylie, "Innovation and Change in Mende Chieftaincy, 1880–1896," *Journal of African History* 10 (1969): 295–308.

32. Svend E. Holsoe, "Slavery and Economic Response among the Vai," in Miers and Kopytoff, *Slavery in Africa,* p. 294.

33. Grace, *Domestic Slavery in West Africa,* p. 172.

34. Inferred from Grace, who states that the Mende population at this time was about 50 percent slaves; he also clearly indicates that the Temme proportion was higher. See his *Domestic Slavery in West Africa,* pp. 169–172; and his "Slavery and Emancipation among the Mende," p. 418. See also Kenneth C. Wylie, "The Slave Trade in Nineteenth Century Temneland and the British Sphere of Influence," *African Studies Review* 16 (1973): 203–217.

35. Ivor Wilks states that the slave plantation region around Kumasi in the early nineteenth century constituted a third of the entire population of Kumasi and its rural environs. In the mining regions of Ashanti during the nineteenth century the proportion would have been greater, since there was a taboo on gold mining by free persons; in other regions it would have been lower. In the Gyaman client kingdom the proportion would have been generally higher than the 33-percent average. See Wilks, *Asante in the Nineteenth Century* (Cambridge: Cambridge University Press, 1975), esp. pp. 93–94, 177–179, 435–436. On the Gyaman see Emmanuel Terray, "La captivité dans le royaume abron du Gyaman," in Meillassoux, *L'esclavage en Afrique précoloniale*, pp. 389–453.

According to A. Norman Klein, there are two different interpretations of the nature and socioeconomic scale of slavery among the Ashanti. See his "The Two Asantes: Competing Interpretations of 'Slavery' in Akan-Asante Culture and Society," in Paul E. Lovejoy, ed., *The Ideology of Slavery in Africa* (Beverly Hills, Calif.: Sage Publications, 1981), pp. 149–167. Klein claims that the British anthropologists Robert S. Rattray and Meyer Fortes have interpreted the institution as a highly integrated, socially important, but economically insignificant process, whereas Wilks sees it as a dynamic, economically significant process during the nineteenth century, the major basis for class formation in Ashanti society.

I think the contrast is exaggerated. Rattray and Fortes were writing about Ashanti slavery during the second quarter of the twentieth century and later, when the institution had already been officially "abolished" by the British and was rapidly waning. Wilks writes of slavery at the height of its development during the nineteenth century. Furthermore, the anthropologists were concerned with the cultural aspects of the institution rather than with its economic and structural significance. These cultural patterns were in all likelihood similar to those that existed during the nineteenth century. It is a sociological truism that the economic aspects and significance of an institution change much faster than its cultural aspects. The two sets of interpretations, then, far from being competing, are actually complementary.

36. In the early twentieth century, when large-scale slavery was already on the decline, 31 percent of the population in the Porto Novo region were slaves. See C. N. Newburg, "An Early Enquiry into Slavery and Captivity in Dahomey," *Zaire* 14 (1960): 57. According to M. J. Heskovits, slaves constituted "the basic labor supply of Dahomey"; see Herskovits, *Dahomey: An Ancient West African Kingdom* (New York: J. J. Augustin, 1938), vol. 1, p. 99. Implicit in Karl Polanyi's analysis is a large-scale economy that could not have had less than a third of its population in slavery; see his *Dahomey and the Slave Trade* (Seattle: University of Washington Press, 1966), esp. pp. 33–59. See also Robin Law, "Royal Monopoly and Private Enterprise in the Atlantic Trade: The Case of Dahomey," *Journal of African History* 18 (1977): 555–577; Catherine Coquery-Vidrovitch, "De la traité des esclaves à l'exportation de l'huile de palme et des palmistes au Dahomey: XIXe siècle," in Claude Meillassoux, ed., *The Development of Indigenous Trade and Markets in West Africa* (London: Oxford University Press, 1971), pp. 107–123.

37. On the Yorubas generally see E. A. Oroge, "The Institution of Slavery in Yorubaland with Particular Reference to the Nineteenth Century" (Ph.D. diss., University of Birmingham, 1971). On the Oyo see Robin Law, *The Oyo Empire* (Oxford: Clarendon Press, 1977), esp. pp. 205–207. Although Philip Igbafe cites no figures, a majority slave population is implicit in the British strategy of a general declaration of emancipation to induce the Benin population back to the city after the invasion; see Igbafe, "Slavery and Emancipation in Benin, 1897–1945," *Journal of African History* 16 (1975): 409–429. See also James D. Graham, "The Slave Trade, Depopulation, and Human Sacrifice in Benin History," *Cahiers d'études africaines* 6 (1965): 317–334; and Babatunde Agiri, "Slavery in Yoruba Society in the Nineteenth Century," in Paul E. Lovejoy, ed., *The Ideology of Slavery in Africa* (Beverly Hills, Calif.: Sage Publications, 1981), pp. 123–148. According to one official report, the slave population was "more than the indigenous people" of Ibadan in 1877 (ibid., p. 136).

38. G. I. Jones, speaking of all these states, asserts that the unskilled laborers

who were "mainly agriculturalists" were slaves during the eighteenth and early nineteenth centuries. See his *Trading States of the Oil Rivers: A Study of Political Development in Eastern Nigeria* (London: Oxford University Press, 1963), pp. 12–13. It is stated explicitly for the Aboh (Abna) that the slave population was over 50 percent, on which see K. Nwachukwu-Ogedengbe, "Slavery in Nineteenth Century Aboh (Nigeria)," in Miers and Kopytoff, *Slavery in Africa*, p. 141. On old Calabar and other states of the Oil Rivers, Jones in his discussion of the Egbo secret society states that slaves constituted "the largest section of the community"; see his "Political Organization of Old Calabar," in Daryll Forde, ed., *Efik Traders of Old Calabar* (London: Oxford University Press, 1956), p. 145; also pp. 134–135, 145–148. See also E. A. Alagoa, "Long-Distance Trade and States in the Niger Delta," *Journal of African History* 11 (1970): 319–329; and idem, "Nineteenth Century Revolutions in the Eastern Delta States and Calabar," *Journal of the Historical Society of Nigeria* 5 (1971): 565–574.

39. Ralph A. Austen, "Slavery among Coastal Middlemen: The Duala of the Cameroon," in Miers and Kopytoff, *Slavery in Africa*, p. 321.

40. K. David Patterson, "The Vanishing Mpongwe: European Contact and Demographic Change in the Gabon River," *Journal of African History* 16 (1975): 224–225; also pp. 226–227.

41. Jan Vansina, *Kingdoms of the Savanna* (Madison: University of Wisconsin Press, 1968), pp. 189–197. Vansina states that between 1720 and 1780 "most of the inhabitants in the Mbanza or in the village seem to have been domestic slaves who were carefully distinguished from 'slaves for export' " (p. 192).

42. Inferred from Joseph C. Miller, "Imbangala Lineage Slavery," in Miers and Kopytoff, *Slavery in Africa*, pp. 205–233; and clearly implied in Vansina, *Kingdoms of the Savanna*, esp. pp. 199–203.

43. Inferred from Joseph C. Miller, "Cokwe Trade and Conquest," in Richard Gray and David Birmingham, eds., *Pre-Colonial African Trade: Essays on Trade in Central and East Africa before 1900* (London: Oxford University Press, 1970), pp. 175–201.

44. Implied in Edward A. Alpers, "Trade, State, and Society among the Yao in the Nineteenth Century," *Journal of African History* 10 (1969): 405–420. This estimate depends on whether one defines the children of slave wives as slaves. They clearly were, as they were in nearly all matrilineal societies. The estimate is also confined to towns and villages under the direct control of the Matakas.

45. C. M. N. White, "Clan, Chieftainship, and Slavery in Luvale Political Organization," *Africa* 27 (1957): 59–75. The same caveat applies here as in the case of the Yao in note 44; that is, I refer only to villages under the direct control of the chiefs. The estimate of over 50 percent is inferred from White's statement that he knew of one village that included twenty-two slaves. From Alpers and Vansina and from ethnographers of the region it is known that the average village had about forty persons, with fifty being considered the maximum for a village among the Yao. See Alpers, "Trade, State, and Society among the Yao," p. 409.

46. Eugene Hermitte, in "An Economic History of Barotseland, 1800–1940" (Ph.D. diss., Northwestern University, 1973) gives an estimate of between 25 and 50 percent, but this is based mainly on oral tradition (p. 214). The more reliable historical evidence indicates a slave population ratio of between 50 and 75 percent. In one

year, 1906, some 30,000 slaves were freed in a total population estimated at 85,000— and this at a time when slavery was already on the decline. For a more recent account of this large-scale slave system see William G. Clarence-Smith, "Slaves, Commoners, and Landlords in Bulozi, c.1875–1906," *Journal of African History* 20 (1979): 219–234, esp. p. 228.

47. Frederick Cooper, *Plantation Slavery on the East Coast of Africa* (New Haven: Yale University Press, 1977), table 2.2, p. 56; p. 70.

48. Ibid., p. 88. For statistical data on slaves in 1897 after the formal abolition of slavery on the Kenya Coast, see Rodger F. Morton, "Slaves, Fugitives, and Freedmen on the Kenya Coast, 1873–1907" (Ph.D. diss., Syracuse University, 1976), pp. 398–406.

49. Maurice Bloch, "Modes of Production and Slavery in Madagascar: Two Case Studies," in Watson, *Asian and African Systems of Slavery*, p. 10.

50. This estimate refers mainly to the nineteenth century and is derived as follows. In 1916, thirty-six years after the abolition of slavery, of a total population of 149,793 persons whites made up 4 percent, blacks 36 percent, and mulattoes 60 percent. Assuming roughly the same proportion during the last decades of slavery, and assuming further that nearly all the blacks and about half the mulattoes were slaves, I arrive at an estimate of approximately 66 percent slaves during this period. The proportion of slaves would have been higher in earlier periods. For the 1916 data see G. R. Prothero, ed., *The Formation of the Portuguese Colonial Empire* (London: His Majesty's Stationery Office, 1920), pp. 5–6. On the historical demography of the islands from 1580 to 1960 see Duncan, *The Atlantic Islands*, p. 255. Although Duncan gives no breakdown of these figures by race and slave/free status, his statements in the text clearly imply a huge slave population. See in particular pp. 19–22 and 234–238. A massive majority of slaves is also implied in Greenfield, "Plantations, Sugar Cane, and Slavery" in Craton, *Roots and Branches*, pp. 111–114.

51. The most thorough analysis of the racial composition of the São Tomé population is to be found in Luis Ivens Ferraz, "The Creole of São Tomé," *African Studies* 37 (1978): 3–68. In 1506 there were one thousand citizens and two thousand slaves. This does not include eight hundred Jewish children, the remainder of some two thousand who had been removed from their parents under the Inquisition and sent to São Tomé to help settle the island with whites. Their mortality rate was so high that their influence on the white population of the island was negligible.

52. According to Ferraz, São Tomé reached its peak of prosperity between 1550 and 1567 (ibid.). The slave population would therefore have increased beyond the 66 percent of the earlier period. At the same time, the manumission rate began to increase substantially during this and later periods, so it is unlikely that the slave population went beyond 75 percent (ibid., pp. 17–18). Between 1567 and 1644 the São Tomé economy went into steep decline. In 1586 there was a sweeping revolt of the slave population, resulting in the exodus of a substantial number of Portuguese. The decline of the economy and the growing rate of manumission resulted in both a steady decline in the proportion of the population that were slaves and the rise of a free population that was overwhelmingly black or mulatto.

53. In spite of its long period of economic decline and stagnation, São Tomé remained a large-scale slave system; slavery was not abolished until 1876. According to Almada Negreiros, in 1864 there were 7,710 freeborn persons, 1,073 libertos, and

4,075 slaves; see *Historia Ethnographica da Ilha de S. Thomé* (Lisbon: José Bastos, 1895), p. 44.

54. No precise figures are available, but it is well attested that these were areas in which the small white minorities were served by a mass of African slaves. The Portuguese "abolition" of slavery in its African colonies in 1869 was meaningless. As Henry W. Nevinson, the best of the contemporary chroniclers, points out, the difference between slave and contracted laborer was "no more than legal cant"; see *A Modern Slavery* (New York: Schocken Books, 1968; 1st ed., 1906), p. 37. In his vivid description of a slave plantation in the interior of Luanda, Nevinson estimates a total of two hundred slaves supervised by a handful of white and near-white overseers, a ratio of at least nine slaves to each overseer. Since there were more free persons in the towns, I have estimated an average of over 75 percent for the slave population. I exclude here the large native African population that lived outside the economic settlements of the Portuguese. For a major modern treatment see James Duffy, *A Question of Slavery* (Oxford: Clarendon Press, 1967), esp. chaps. 2, 4, 7. In an analysis of the Cazengo area David Birmingham finds that in 1895 the subcolony had 131 villages occupied by 7,115 bonded, nonslave Africans and 3,798 slaves working on twenty-eight coffee plantations "owned or managed by ninety-six expatriates." See "The Coffee Barons of Cazengo," *Journal of African History* 19 (1978): 529. In his study of the entire southern Angola region William G. Clarence-Smith states that "slavery was the dominant form of labor relations in the colonial nucleus of southern Angola from 1840 to 1878" and remained "predominant" between 1879 and 1911. See *Slaves, Peasants, and Capitalists in Southern Angola, 1840–1926* (Cambridge: Cambridge University Press, 1979), p. 32. He gives the following estimates of the slave population of the colonial nucleus: 600 slaves in 1854; 2,500 in 1864; 3,000 to 4,000 in the late 1870s; and about 10,000 in 1913 (ibid., pp. 33–34).

55. In the early 1800s the Portuguese colony of Mozambique had "a population of a few hundred Europeans and half-castes, the same number of free Africans, and about 5,000 slaves." R. W. Beachey, *The Slave Trade of Eastern Africa* (New York: Harper & Row, 1976), p. 12. A report to the British Foreign Office in 1875 stated that the capital had a total population of eight hundred Portuguese and mixed persons and five thousand Negroes. It was further stated that more than half the Negroes were either slaves or libertos, with little real difference existing between the two categories. See Duffy, *A Question of Slavery*, p. 68. On the notorious *prazeros*, the estate owners of Zambézia, see pp. 40–41, 54, 130–138. For a more detailed study of this bizarre and ultimately unsuccessful attempt at large-scale plantation slavery, see Allen Isaacman, *Mozambique: The Africanization of a European Institution, the Zambesi Prazos, 1750–1902* (Madison: University of Wisconsin Press, 1972).

56. James C. Armstrong, "The Slaves, 1652–1795," in Richard Elphick and Hermann Giliomee, eds., *The Shaping of South African Society* (London: Longmans, 1979), table 3.6, p. 96.

57. Hermann Giliomee and Richard Elphick, "The Structure of European Domination at the Cape, 1652–1820," in Elphick and Giliomee, *The Shaping of South African Society*, table 10.1, p. 360. Note that this table excludes Khoikhoi and Bastaards. In 1711 there were 1,693 European freeburghers, 63 free blacks, and 1,771 slaves in Cape Colony; in 1820 there were 42,975 freeburghers, 1,932 free blacks, and 31,779 slaves. There were also 26,975 Khoikhoi and Bastaards.

58. André Scherer, *Histoire de la Réunion* (Paris: Presses Universitaires de France, 1964), p. 15.

59. Ibid., pp. 17, 26.

60. Ibid., pp. 62–63. There were 580 whites and 4,494 slaves in 1735; in 1779 the count was 6,464 whites, 465 freedmen, and 22,611 slaves. In 1848, when slavery was abolished, there was a total population of 110,000 of whom fewer than 60,000 were slaves.

61. P. J. Barnwell and A. Toussaint, *A Short History of Mauritius* (London: Longmans, 1949), table 1, appendix 3. In 1735 there were 648 slaves and 190 whites; by 1767 this had increased to 15,027 slaves, 587 freedmen, and 3,163 whites; when slavery was abolished in 1835, there were 76,774 slaves in a total population of 101,469 persons.

62. British Information Services, *Mauritius and Seychelles* (London: Government Printing Office, 1964), p. 3. In 1789, at the height of this micro slave system, there were 69 persons of French ancestry, 3 soldiers, 32 free colored persons, and 487 slaves. Slavery also existed on a substantial scale in the small dependencies of Mauritius, but it is not possible to make any estimates. See, however, Robert Scott, *Limuria: The Lesser Dependencies of Mauritius* (London: Oxford University Press, 1961), esp. pp. 107–135.

63. Iraq during the ninth and tenth centuries was a large-scale slave system in spite of the fact that slaves constituted a majority only in the canal region of lower Iraq and the marsh areas of Al Batiha. However, slaves dominated the army and the administration of the caliphate. Without military and administrative slavery the Abbasid caliphate would simply not have been possible during this period. We know that the majority of the population must have been slaves in the areas of lower Mesopotamia specified above, since a harsh gang system was the norm there, with bands of slaves ranging in size from five hundred to five thousand. There was also a high level of local absenteeism among owners and a mass migration of the nonslave population to the urban areas.

I base these remarks on the most thorough study to date of the Zandj and their revolt of 868–883. See A. Popovic, "Ali B. Muhammad et la révolte des esclaves à Basra (Ph.D. diss., University of Paris, 1965). The greatest concentration of slaves was quite probably at Al Mukhtara in the canal region; this city became the capital of the Zandj rebel state (ibid., p. 66).

While the large-scale slave economy of lower Iraq was based on the use of African slaves, the country's military and administrative structure used mainly Turkish slaves. See Paul G. Forand, "The Development of Military Slavery under the Abbasid Caliphs of the Ninth Century A.D. (Third Century A.H.) with Special Reference to the Reigns of Mu'Tasim and Mu'Tadid" (Ph.D. diss., Princeton University, 1961).

Almost all the major Islamic states relied to some extent on military and administrative slaves, but except for Muslim Spain the dependence was most complete in ninth-century Iraq. Furthermore, none of the other states experienced the same convergence of large-scale sectoral reliance on agricultural slave labor and of military-administrative slavery in the capital. See Daniel Pipes, "From Mawla to Mamlūk: The Origins of Islamic Military Slavery" (Ph.D. diss., Harvard University, 1978). See also the articles under "Djaysh" and "Ghulām" in the *Encyclopedia of*

Islam, ed. 2, vol. 2, esp. pp. 504–511; and the articles in V. J. Parry and M. E. Yapp, eds., *War, Technology, and Society in the Middle East* (London: Oxford University Press, 1975).

64. In the late seventeenth century the Atjehnese relied entirely on imported slaves, mainly Indians from the Coromandel coast, to cultivate their rice. Slaves also did all the deep-sea fishing and gold mining. Clearly, they constituted a substantial proportion of the working population, but no estimates are possible. For a summary of the available data and bibliography see Bruno Lasker, *Human Bondage in Southeast Asia* (Chapel Hill: University of North Carolina Press, 1950), pp. 27–28.

65. Ibid., p. 46. Based on a 1925 report included in *Documents of the Sixth Assembly, League of Nations* (Geneva, 1925), vol. 6.

66. This frequently cited estimate was given by J. B. Pallegoix, *Description du royaume Thai ou Siam, 1854* (Paris: La Mission de Siam, 1854). For an evaluation of this and other estimates see Andrew Turton, "Thai Institutions of Slavery," in Watson, *Asian and African Systems of Slavery,* pp. 274–277. See also Lasker, *Human Bondage in Southeast Asia,* pp. 56–59 and appendix A.

67. Alan Winnington, *The Slaves of the Cool Mountain* (London: Lawrence & Wishart, 1959), p. 32. This estimate refers to the 1940s, when Winnington visited the Norsus and made the first careful on-the-spot study of the group. Although there was a significant level of slavery among the Norsus long before the end of the nineteenth century, the scale and frequency of slave raids increased during and after the Chinese revolution of 1911. As late as 1948, thousands of Han Chinese were still being taken into slavery by the "Nor" or "black-boned" noble class of Norsus. The total population of the Norsus in the 1940s was 56,294, of whom 3,000 were nobles, 26,458 were slaves, and 26,836 were serfs or common nonslave bondsmen.

68. According to Takashi Hatada, "One can safely conclude that all of Silla's agricultural population were slaves." *A History of Korea* (Santa Barbara, Calif.: ABC-Clio Press, 1969), p. 30. Hatada infers this from the literary materials, and his statement seems highly questionable.

69. No hard data are available for the Koryŏ period. Nevertheless, all the literary evidence suggests that the slave population was much greater during the Koryŏ than in subsequent periods when more reliable data existed. At the earliest date of the later periods, the slave population has been estimated at 33 percent of the total (see note 70). An estimate of between 30 and 33 percent was suggested by Ellen Salem in a conversation with me. Her subsequent work, the only major study of Koryŏ slavery in English, generally supports this estimate. "Slavery in Medieval Korea" (Ph.D. diss., Columbia University, 1978).

70. Sudo Yoshiyuki, "Korai makki Yori Chōsen Shoki ni itaru dohi no kenkyū" [A Study of Slavery from the End of the Koryŏ Period to the Early Yi Dynasty], *Rekishigaku kenkyū* 9 (1939): 14. (In Japanese.) During the fifteenth century large-scale slave ownership was apparently concentrated in the southern and central provinces of Korea, on which see Susan S. Shin, "Changes in Labor Supply in Yi Dynasty Korea: From Hereditary to Contractual Obligations" (August 1976), p. 8 (manuscript). The proportion of the population enslaved was again on the increase during the fifteenth century, especially state-owned slaves (ibid., pp. 9–17).

71. Edward W. Wagner, "Social Stratification in Seventeenth-Century Korea; Some Observations from a 1663 Seoul Census Register," in *Occasional Papers on*

Korea 1 (1974): 54. Wagner writes: "The slave population of this small section of Korea already was over 50 percent of the households and over 75 percent of the total in-resident recorded population of about 2,400. Every indication points to the conclusion that this high percentage was climbing still higher in 1663." This high percentage was not typical of Korea as a whole. Closer to the norm was Kùmhwa county, on which see note 72.

72. Susan S. Shin, "The Social Structure of Kùmhwa County in the Late Seventeenth Century," in *Occasional Papers on Korea* 1 (1974): 25.

73. Shin, "Changes in Labor Supply in Yi Dynasty Korea," pp. 20–21. The massive decline in the slave population during the eighteenth century in three coastal districts of Ulsan is typical of changes in the country as a whole. By the latter half of the century, large-scale slavery in Korea had come to an end (although the institution was not to be formally abolished until the Japanese occupation during the first decade of the twentieth century).

74. N. Adriani and Albert C. Kruyt, *De Bare'e Sprekende Toradjas van Midden-Celebes* [The Bare'e-speaking Toradja of Central Celebes] (Amsterdam: Nood-Hollandsche Uitgevers Maatschappij, 1950), vol. 1, p. 138. Not all tribes with slave standings had such high percentages, but the evidence certainly indicates that in all these tribes slaves constituted well over a third of the group.

75. In the early seventeenth century, just prior to the Dutch conquest, the Banda Islands had a total population of 15,000, of whom a third were slaves and other very poor persons. See J. C. Van Leur, *Indonesian Trade and Society* (The Hague: W. van Hoeve, 1955), p. 210. For the best short account in English of the indigenous social structure see pp. 141–144. By 1621 the entire population had been either butchered by the Dutch or forced to flee the islands, in what is without doubt one of the most brutal episodes in European imperial history. The land was then parceled out to what H. W. Ponder calls "a few score families" of Dutchmen and re-peopled by slaves brought in from outside. Each "Perkenier," as the plantation owners were called, lived with his family and "hundreds of slaves" in what amounted to fortified camps. Clearly, the free population of owners was outnumbered at least ten to one in this vicious system, which had only one counterpart: the Caribbean slave systems of about the same era. Slavery was abolished in Indonesia in 1860. The fact that the abolition created a severe labor crisis indicates that the freedman group was only a negligible proportion of the slave population. Ponder, *In Javanese Waters* (London: Seeley, Service & Co., 1944?), pp. 100–118. For the standard work on the Dutch conquest and on the pre-European Bandas, see Jacobus A. Van der Chijs, *De vestiging van het Nederlandsche gezag over de Banda-eilanden (1599–1621)* [The Imposition of Dutch Rule over the Banda Islands] (Batavia: Albrecht & Co., 1886).

76. Kenneth R. Andrews, *The Spanish Caribbean: Trade and Plunder, 1536–1630* (New Haven: Yale University Press, 1978), pp. 14–15. Slaves outnumbered free persons in Española from as early as 1520. By 1525 the Spanish population began to decline precipitously, as settlers moved to the more lucrative areas on the mainland. There were between 1,000 and 2,000 free persons in 1570 and, ten years earlier, between 12,000 and 20,000 slaves. By the early decades of the seventeenth century Española ceased to be a large-scale slave system and became an economic backwater of the Spanish imperial system. The white and free mulatto popu-

lations began to grow in relation to the slaves, and by the 1630s a peasant-type economy—partly pastoral, partly tobacco oriented—emerged. In 1606 the total population had declined to 10,805, of which 89 percent were slaves. After this the slave proportion declined rapidly. In 1750, slaves constituted 14 percent of an estimated total population of 125,000; in 1789, they made up 20 percent of a total of 152,000; and in 1821, about the same percentage in a much reduced population. See Franklyn J. Franco, *Los negros y los mulatos y la nación Dominicana* (Santo Domingo: Editora Nacional, 1969), pp. 48–49, 67, 72; and Pedro A. Perez Cabral, *La communidad mulata* (Caracas: Grafica Americana, 1967), pp. 106–107.

77. There were very few slaves in Jamaica during the sixteenth century, unlike Española. However, as the large-scale slave system of Española rapidly declined, the proportion of slaves in Jamaica increased during the last half-century or so of Spanish rule in the island. The free population always remained in the majority, and the economy was of the agro-pastoral type found in other areas of the Caribbean. Yet the dependence on slaves reached levels that justify Jamaica's classification as a large-scale slave system. In 1611 the total population was 1,510, of whom 558 were slaves; see Andrews, *The Spanish Caribbean*, p. 223. By 1655, the year of British capture, the total population had increased to 2,500. For an account of Jamaica under the Spaniards see Francisco Morales Padrón, *Jamaica Española* (Seville: La Escuela de Estudios Hispano-Americano de Sevilla, 1952); and for a critical appraisal of this work see J. P. Jacobs, "The Spanish Period of Jamaican History," *Jamaican Historical Review* 111 (1957): 79–93.

78. Cuba was a large-scale slave society from its very beginnings until abolition in 1887. However, the kind of slave system changed drastically from one period to another. From discovery to about 1530, the large Indian population was subjected to a murderous form of enslavement in the mines and on the fields. With the decline of the Indian population, there was a shift to black slavery. The agro-pastoral slave system that evolved and lasted until the last quarter of the eighteenth century was undeniably different from the plantation system of the British islands, but it was nonetheless large-scale slavery. Like all such systems, it was both brutal and degrading for those exploited. From the last quarter of the eighteenth century until 1880, Cuba was a large-scale plantation slave system.

79. In 1550 there were 322 free whites, 1,000 free Indians, and 800 black and Indian slaves in Cuba (Andrews, *The Spanish Caribbean*, p. 16). By 1606 there were "some 20,000" black slaves in Cuba, on which see Herbert S. Klein, *Slavery in the Americas: A Comparative Study of Virginia and Cuba* (Chicago: University of Chicago Press, 1967), p. 142. In Havana the slaves outnumbered the free by a ratio of three to one in 1600, according to Andrews, *The Spanish Caribbean*, p. 20. Since 65 percent of the total Cuban population lived in or around Havana at the time, the estimate may hold for the island as a whole. See Philip S. Foner, *A History of Cuba* (New York: International Publishers, 1962), p. 34.

80. When the first census of Cuba was taken in 1774, of the total population of 171,620 persons, 44,333 were slaves (25.8 percent); 96,440 were white free persons; and 30,847 were colored free persons. We know, however, that this is at or near the lowest point in the proportion of the population enslaved after the decline in the nineteenth century. Thus we may estimate the average proportion during this period at between 25 and 33 percent of the total. See Klein, *Slavery in the Americas*, table 2, p. 202.

81. Ibid.

82. This was one of the most savage and deadly slave systems of all time. Between 1500 and 1540 the great majority of the slaves were Indians; after this they were mainly blacks. In the entire provinces of Panama and Veragua there were only four hundred households of Spaniards outside the capital. See Andrews, *The Spanish Caribbean,* pp. 18–22. For more on Indian slavery in Panama and Central America generally during this period see Murdo J. MacLeod, *Spanish Central America: A Socioeconomic History, 1520–1720* (Berkeley: University of California Press, 1973), pp. 46–63.

83. Andrews, *The Spanish Caribbean,* p. 35. In a total population of 5,591 persons there were 3,721 slaves and 1,870 free persons.

84. Ibid., pp. 26–27, 33–34.

85. William F. Sharp, *Slavery on the Spanish Frontier: The Colombian Chocó, 1680–1810* (Norman: University of Oklahoma Press, 1976), table 7, p. 199. The total population of the Chocó in 1763 was 13,963 persons; in 1808 it had increased to 25,000. For Colombia as a whole the proportion of enslaved persons was much smaller than for the Chocó. In 1779 there were only 53,788 slaves (6.7 percent) in a total population of 800,000, excluding Indians. See Jaime Jaramillo Uribe, "Esclavos y señores en la sociedad Colombiana del siglo XVIII," *Anuario colombiano de historia social y de la cultura,* 1 (1963):7.

86. If the Indian population is included, slaves at their highest level constituted only 2 percent of the total Mexican population. However, it is best to see Mexico during this period as having two parallel economies—one centered on the urban, plantation, and mining areas; the other tributary, and of a hacienda type. Black slave labor dominated the first, Indian serf labor the second. The first sector was a large-scale slave system in every sense of the term. See Colin A. Palmer, *Slaves of the White God: Blacks in Mexico, 1570–1650* (Cambridge, Mass.: Harvard University Press, 1976), esp. chaps. 2 and 3. See also Sherburne F. Cook and Woodrow Borah, *Essays in Population History: Mexico and the Caribbean* (Berkeley: University of California Press, 1974), vol. 2, pp. 180–269. And for the major work on the black population of Mexico see G. Aguirre Beltrán, *La población negra de Mexico, 1519–1810,* ed. 2 (Mexico City: Fondo de Cultura Económica, 1972). There were approximately 20,000 slaves in 1553; 20,570 in 1570, including 2,000 runaways; and 80,000 in 1645.

87. Palmer, *Slaves of the White God,* table 14, p. 80. There were 7,547 persons working in the mines, of whom 1,022 were slaves, 4,610 "free Indians," 1,619 repartimiento Indians, and 296 owners.

88. *Encyclopaedie van nederlandsch West-Indie* (Leiden: E. J. Brill, 1914–1917), p. 665. The total population in 1790 was 58,000; it reached a peak of 64,602 in 1805, then declined to 52,963 in 1862.

89. There were over two thousand slaves in Curaçao at this time. The total white population in the early eighteenth century was upward of four thousand, of whom over half were Sephardic Jews. See Johan Hartog, *Curacao: From Colonial Dependence to Autonomy* (Aruba: De Wit, 1968), pp. 129–134.

90. In 1789 there were 3,964 Europeans, 2,776 freedmen, and 12,804 slaves in Curaçao (Hartog, *Curacao,* p. 134).

91. Ibid., p. 179. The total population of Curaçao in 1816 was 12,840 persons; by 1862 it had increased to 19,129.

92. *Encyclopaedie van nederlandsch West-Indie,* p. 627. The total population of Saint Eustatius in 1786 was 7,600 persons; it fell to 2,591 in 1817, and again to 2,273 persons in 1829.

93. Ibid., p. 631. The total population of Saint Martin in 1770 was 4,159 persons; in 1816 it had fallen to 3,559 persons.

94. Johan Hartog, *Geschiedenis van de Nederlandse Antillen: Bonaire: Van Indianen Tot Treristen* [History of the Netherlands Antilles: Bonaire] (Aruba: De Wit, 1957), p. 108. Bonaire, in spite of its small size, was very much a large-scale slave system measured in terms of its dependence on slave labor for essential tasks. In the total population of 1,309 persons there were 364 slaves.

95. Ibid., p. 159. There were 1,476 persons in the island at this time, of whom 90 were whites, 839 freed persons, and 547 slaves.

96. Ibid., p. 161.

97. Ibid. The total population at the abolition of slavery was 3,103 persons.

98. Material on Jamaica in Appendix C and in Table N1 at the end of the Notes section is based on the following: Orlando Patterson, *The Sociology of Slavery: Jamaica, 1655–1838* (Rutherford, N.J.: Fairleigh Dickinson University Press, 1969), table 1, p. 95; George W. Roberts, *The Population of Jamaica* (Cambridge: Cambridge University Press, 1957), pp. 33, 36, 39, esp. tables 4, 5, 6; Douglas Hall, "Jamaica," in D. W. Cohen and Jack P. Greene, eds., *Neither Slave nor Free* (Baltimore: Johns Hopkins University Press, 1972), table 6-1, p. 194; Sheila Dunker, "The Free Coloured and the Fight for Civil Rights in Jamaica, 1800–1830" (master's thesis, University of London, 1960), p. 9. The figures of 20,000 for the white population and 46,200 for the free nonwhite population in 1834 are my own rough approximations. Before 1758 there was a small free nonwhite population, but its numbers were negligible.

99. Jerome S. Handler and Frederick W. Lange, *Plantation Slavery in Barbados* (Cambridge, Mass.: Harvard University Press, 1978), p. 15. The white population at this time was estimated at between 18,300 and 18,600 persons, and the black population between 5,680 and 6,400.

100. Estimates for the years 1673–1731 are taken from Richard B. Sheridan, *The Development of Plantations to 1750* (Lodge Hill, Barbados: Caribbean University Press, 1970), table 3, p. 29; otherwise Appendix C and Table N2 are based on Jerome S. Handler and Arnold A. Sio, "Barbados," in Cohen and Greene, *Neither Slave nor Free,* table 7-1, pp. 218–219.

101. The sources for Appendix C and Table N3 are Richard B. Sheridan, *Sugar and Slavery: An Economic History of the British West Indies 1623–1775* (Lodge Hill, Barbados: Caribbean University Press, 1974), table 8.1, p. 150; Douglas Hall, *Five of the Leewards, 1834–1870* (Lodge Hill, Barbados: Caribbean University Press, 1971), table 1, p. 8; Elsa V. Goveia, *Slave Society in the British Leeward Islands at the End of the Eighteenth Century* (New Haven: Yale University Press, 1965), chap. 4 passim.

102. Sources for the material on the Leeward Islands in Appendix C and Table N4 are as in note 101.

103. See note 102.

104. See note 102.

105. See note 102.

106. See note 102.

107. Sheridan, *Sugar and Slavery,* p. 150 fn. The nine British Virgin Islands at

this time were Tortola, Spanish Town, Jost Van Dyke, Peter's Island, Camains, Scrub Island, Guanna, Beef Island, and Thatch Island. The 1756 total population comprised 1,184 whites and 6,121 slaves. The majority were in Tortola, which had 465 whites and 3,864 slaves, and in Spanish Town, which had 396 whites and 1,204 slaves.

108. Ibid.; Higman, "The Slave Population of the British Caribbean." There is little reliable information.

109. The source for Appendix C and Table N5 is John Davy, *The West Indies before and since Emancipation* (London: W. & F. G. Cash, 1854), p. 499.

110. The sources for Appendix C and Table N6 are Sheridan, *Sugar and Slavery*, p. 458; and George W. Roberts, "Movements in Slave Population of the Caribbean during the Period of Slave Registration," in Rubin and Tuden, *Comparative Perspectives on Slavery*, p. 149, table 1. Inasmuch as I could find no estimate of the white population during the nineteenth century before the census of 1844, I took the average annual decline of the white population between 1787 and 1844 and on this basis calculated the probable size in 1817 and 1834. These estimates exclude the Carib population.

111. Sheridan, *Sugar and Slavery*, p. 458. For the nineteenth century, Grenada followed the pattern of the other Windward Islands except that its white population declined more precipitously and its free colored population was above the norm for the British Caribbean—approximately 10 percent of the total population. On the nineteenth-century slave population see Roberts, "Movements in Slave Population."

112. Appendix C and Table N7 are based on Davy, *The West Indies before and since Emancipation*, p. 277; and Roberts, "Movements in Slave Population," p. 149.

113. Sheridan, *Sugar and Slavery*, p. 457. In 1770 the total population was 3,402 persons; it climbed to 9,034 by 1775 and reached a peak of 15,313 in 1820, after which it began to decline slowly. See also Barry W. Higman, "The Slave Populations of the British Caribbean: Some Nineteenth Century Variations," in Samuel Proctor, ed., *Eighteenth Century Florida and the Caribbean* (Gainesville: University Presses of Florida, 1976), pp. 67–70.

114. The sources for Appendix C and Table N8 are James Millette, *The Genesis of Crown Colony Government, Trinidad, 1783-1810* (Trinidad: Moko Enterprises, 1970), table 9: Carlton R. Ottley, *Slavery Days in Trinidad* (Trinidad: Published by the Author, 1974), appendix 2, p. 152; and Donald Wood, *Trinidad in Transition* (London: Oxford University Press, 1968), p. 32.

115. *Cayman Island: Colonial Annual Report* (London: His Majesty's Stationery Office, 1946), p. 8. In 1802 there were 933 persons in Cayman, of whom 545 were slaves.

116. O. Nigel Boland, "Slavery in Belize," *Journal of Belizean Affairs* 6 (1978): 7, table 1. The slave population rose from 120 in 1745 to its highest level of 3,000 in 1779. It declined to 2,742 in 1816 and again to 1,783 in 1832.

117. R. T. Smith, *British Guiana* (London: Oxford University Press, 1962), p. 21. In 1701 there were 800 slaves and 67 Europeans in the area. The slave population grew to 3,986 in 1767. There is no good estimate of the European population, but it is certain that the proportion of Europeans did not increase.

118. Ibid., p. 19. There was a total population of 4,423.

119. Henry G. Dalton, *The History of British Guiana* (London: Longmans,

1855), vol. 1, pp. 254, 256. At the end of the eighteenth century there were 50,000 to 60,000 slaves in the colony and between 8,000 and 10,000 free persons.

120. Ibid., p. 239. In 1816 there were 77,163 slaves in Demerara and Essequibo, and 24,549 slaves in Berbice. The total free population of the colony was approximately 8,000 persons.

121. Ibid., p. 412. On the eve of abolition there were 82,824 slaves and approximately 11,000 free persons in the colony.

122. Michael Craton, *A History of the Bahamas* (London: Collins, 1962), p. 189. There were 443 slaves in 1671, "comprising 40 percent of the total population."

123. Ibid., p. 166. Craton gives a total 1783 population of 4,058, of whom 2,336 were Negroes. In 1789, however, approximately 500 blacks were free (p. 187). So the slave population must have been about 2,000 in 1783.

124. Ibid. The total population in 1786 was 8,957, of whom 2,948 were whites and approximately 400 were free blacks. This estimate of the free black population is also based on the figure of 500 for 1789.

125. Ibid., appendix D, table A, p. 306, gives a total population of 16,000 in 1820. The average slave population between 1819 and 1822 was 10,908, on which see Higman, "The Slave Populations of the British Caribbean," p. 67.

126. Craton gives a slave population of 9,268 for 1831. The total black population was 12,259, of whom 2,991 were free. He implies a total population of 16,345 (see pp. 187 and 306), hence a slave proportion of approximately 57 percent.

127. Appendix C and Table N9 are based on Cyril O. Packwood, *Chained on the Rock: Slavery in Bermuda* (New York: Eliseo Torres and Sons, 1975), pp. 7, 33–34, 73–82.

128. Appendix C and Table N10 are based on Leo Elisabeth, "The French Antilles," in Cohen and Greene, *Neither Slave nor Free*, pp. 148–151.

129. Appendix C and Table N11 are based on Sheridan, *The Development of Plantations*, table 6, p. 49; Elisabeth, "The French Antilles," pp. 146–151; and Philip D. Curtin, *The Atlantic Slave Trade: A Census* (Madison: University of Wisconsin Press, 1969), table 19, p. 78.

130. The source of Appendix C and Table N12 is Alexandre Moreau de Jonnès, *Recherches statistiques sur l'esclavage coloniale* (Paris: Bourgogne et Martinet, 1842), p. 19.

131. Appendix C and Table N13 are based on Pierre Dupon-Gonin, *La Guyane française* (Geneva: Librairie Droz, 1970), pp. 48–53; and Arthur Dangoise, *Notes, essais et études sur la Guyane française* (Paris: Librairie Générale et Internationale, 1923), p. 41.

132. The sources for Appendix C and Table 14 are Waldemar Westergaard, *The Danish West Indies under Company Rule, 1671–1754* (New York: Macmillan Co., 1917), pp. 318–319; and S. E. Green-Pedersen, "The Scope and Structure of the Danish Negro Slave Trade," *Scandinavian Economic History Review* 19 (1971): 149–177.

133. There are no reliable statistics on Brazil before the end of the eighteenth century. All the available nonquantitative data, plus the few scraps of statistical information, strongly suggest that during the sixteenth century and the first half of the seventeenth century Brazil was a large-scale slave-based plantation system, the New World prototype of the Caribbean slave systems. At the end of the sixteenth century

Brazil was the world's largest producer of sugar, with a slave population estimated at between 13,000 and 15,000. See Frederick Mauro, *Le Portugal et l'Atlantique au XVIIe siècle* (Paris: Ecole Pratique des Hautes Etudes, 1960), p. 179; Caio Prado, Jr., *The Colonial Background of Modern Brazil* (Berkeley: University of California Press, 1967); and Gilberto Freyre, *The Masters and the Slaves* (New York: Alfred A. Knopf, 1964), esp. chap. 1.

134. Appendix C and Table N15 are based on Robert Conrad, *The Destruction of Brazilian Slavery, 1850-1888* (Berkeley: University of California Press, 1972), table 1, p. 283; and Stanley J. Stein, *Vassouras: A Brazilian Coffee County, 1850-1900* (Cambridge, Mass.: Harvard University Press, 1957), pp. 294-296.

135. Appendix C and Table N16 were calculated from C. R. Boxer, *The Golden Age of Brazil, 1695-1750* (Berkeley: University of California Press, 1969), appendix 4, pp. 341-346; and Stein, *Vassouras*, p. 296.

136. Boxer, *The Golden Age of Brazil*, p. 2.

137. Stein, *Vassouras*, p. 296.

138. The estimates for the sixteenth and seventeenth centuries are based on sources given in note 133. Calculations for 1823 and 1872 are from Stein, *Vassouras*, p. 296.

139. Robert W. Fogel and Stanley L. Engerman, *Time on the Cross: The Economics of American Negro Slavery* (Boston: Little, Brown, 1974), vol. 1, pp. 20-29, esp. figs. 4 and 7. There are few hard data on the United States before the census of 1790. The black population of Virginia in 1700, almost all slaves, was approximately 16,000, and the total slave population of all the colonies was only about 27,000. The slave population in 1740 had grown to about 200,000 persons, and by 1780 it had passed the half-million mark. For more detailed figures on the colonial period see Stella H. Sutherland, *Population Distribution in Colonial America* (New York: Columbia University Press, 1936), pp. 169-170.

140. The sources for Appendix C and Table N17 on the U.S. South are the following: Harold D. Woodman, ed., *Slavery and the Southern Economy* (New York: Harcourt, Brace & World, 1966), p. 13, table 1; and U.S. Department of Commerce, Bureau of the Census, *Historical Statistics of the United States, Colonial Times to 1970, Bicentennial Edition (Washington, D.C.*: Government Printing Office, 1975), pt. 1, ser. A 172-194, p. 22.

141. Appendix C and Table N18 were derived from Woodman, *Slavery and the Southern Economy*, p. 13, table 2: and Bureau of the Census, *Historical Statistics of the United States, Colonial Times to 1970*, p. 22.

In 1715 Virginia had a white population of 72,000 and a slave population of 23,000; in 1756 these went up to 173,316 and 120,156 respectively. The white population of Georgia in 1760 was 6,000 and of blacks, 3,000; the respective figures for 1773 were 18,000 and 15,000. Mississippi in 1798 had a white population of 5,000 and a slave population of 3,500. Sources for these figures are John Hope Franklin, *From Slavery to Freedom* (New York: Alfred A. Knopf, 1963), pp. 72, 75, 83; and for Mississippi: Charles S. Sydnor, *Slavery in Mississippi* (Baton Rouge: Louisiana State University Press, 1966), p. vii. South Carolina had a total population of 9,580 in 1708, of whom 4,080 were whites, 4,100 were black slaves, and 1,400 were Indian slaves. In 1720 the free population was 6,525 and slaves numbered 11,828; in 1740 the white population had increased to an estimated 20,000 persons, and slaves were also about 20,000. For data on South Carolina see Peter H. Wood, *Black Majority: Negroes in Colonial South Carolina* (New York: Alfred A. Knopf, 1974), p. 144, table 1, and p. 152, table 4. For estimates on the distribution of the slaves in the South by county and state during the revolutionary period see Sutherland, *Population Distribution in Colonial America,* pp. 174–178, 202, 209, 216–217, 240, 260.

Tables for Notes to Appendix C

Table N1   The Jamaican population, 1658–1834.

Year	Whites	Slaves	Free nonwhites	Total
1658	4,500	1,400	—	5.900
1664	6,000	8,000	—	14,000
1673	8,564	9,504	—	18,068
1730	7,658	74,525	—	82,183
1758	17,900	176,900	3,500	198,300
1775	18,700	192,800	4,500	216,000
1800	30,000	300,000	10,000	340,000
1834	20,000	310,000	46,200	376,200

Table N2   The Barbadian population, 1673–1834.

Year	Whites	Slaves	Free nonwhites	Total
1673	21,309	33,184	—	54,493
1683	17,187	46,602	—	63,789
1710	12,525	41,970	—	54,495
1731	16,113	65,000	—	81,113
1748	15,192	47,025	107	62,324
1768	16,139	66,379	448	82,966
1786	16,167	62,115	833	79,115
1810	15,517	69,110	2,526	87,153
1825	14,630	78,096	4,524	97,250
1833–1834	12,797	80,861	6,584	100,242

Table N3 The population of Antigua, 1678–1834.

Year	Whites	Slaves	Free nonwhites	Total
1678	2,308	2,172	—	4,480
1708	2,909	12,943	—	15,852
1720	3,652	19,186	—	22,838
1745	3,538	27,892	—	31,430
1756	3,435	31,428	—	34,863
1775	2,590	37,808	—	40,398
1817	2,100	31,500	2,200	35,800
1834	2,000	29,100	4,000	35,100

Table N4 The population of the Leeward Islands other than Antigua.

Year	Saint Kitts	Nevis	Montserrat	Barbuda	Anguilla
1678					
Whites	1,897	3,521	2,682	—	—
Slaves	1,436	3,860	492	—	—
1708					
Whites	1,670	1,104	—	—	—
Slaves	3,258	3,676	—	—	—
1720					
Whites	2,800	1,343	1,688	—	—
Slaves	7,321	5,689	3,772	—	—
1745					
Whites	2,377	857	1,117	—	—
Slaves	19,174	6,511	5,945	—	—
1756					
Whites	2,783	1,118	1,430	—	—
Slaves	21,891	8,380	8,853	—	—
1775					
Whites	1,900	1,000	1,314	—	—
Slaves	23,462	11,000	9,834	—	—
1790					
Whites	1,912	—	—	2	300–400
Slaves	20,455	—	—	290	2,000
1812					
Whites	1,600	500	400	—	—
Slaves	19,800	9,200	6,500	600	—
Free colored	1,900	600	400	—	—
1834					
Whites	—	400	300	—	—
Slaves	19,700	8,800	5,000	500	—
Free colored	—	1,700	800	—	—

Table N5 The population of Dominica, 1788–1832.

Year	Whites	Free coloreds	Slaves	Total
1788	1,236	445	14,967	16,648
1805	1,594	2,822	22,083	26,499
1832	791	4,077	19,255	24,123

Table N6 The population of Saint Vincent, 1763–1834.

Year	Whites	Slaves	Total
1763	695	3,430	4,125
1787	1,450	11,853	13,303
1817	1,360	25,218	26,578
1834	1,309	22,997	24,305

Table N7 The population of Saint Lucia, 1772–1834.

Year	Whites	Slaves	Total
1772	2,198	13,278	15,476
1816–1818	1,478	16,285	17,763
1834	1,206	13,348	14,554

Table N8 The population of Trinidad, 1777–1834.

Year	Whites	Free coloreds	Slaves	Indians	Total
1777	340	870	200	—	1,410
1797	2,151	4,474	10,009	1,082	17,716
1802	2,261	5,275	19,709	1,232	28,477
1810	2,495	6,264	20,821	1,683	31,263
1825	3,214	15,003	23,230	727	42,174
1834	3,632	18,724	22,359	—	44,715

Table N9   The population of Bermuda, 1622–1833.

Year	Whites	Slaves	Free blacks	Total
1622	—	—	—	1,200
1629	2,500	300–400	—	2,800–2,900
1670	6,000	2,000	—	8,000
1687	5,333–6,000	2,667–3,000	—	8,000–9,000
1691	4,331	1,971	—	6,302
1699	3,665	2,247	—	5,862
1701	2,000	2,000	—	4,000
1702	—	—	—	6,000
1721	4,850	3,514	—	8,364
1731	4,353	3,248	—	7,601
1774	5,632	5,023	—	10,655
1799	—	4,846	—	—
1822–1823	4,648	5,242	722	10,612
1832	4,181	3,608	1,068	8,857
1833	4,297	4,277	1,286	9,860

Table N10   The population of Martinique, 1664–1848.

Year	Whites	Slaves	Free blacks	Total
1664	2,681	2,704	16	5,401
1696	6,435	13,126	505	20,066
1700	6,597	14,225	507	21,329
1715	8,735	26,865	1,029	36,629
1727	10,959	40,403	1,304	52,666
1731	11,957	46,062	1,204	59,233
1734	12,705	53,080	810	66,595
1738	14,969	47,778	1,295	74,042
1751	12,068	65,909	1,413	79,386
1764	11,634	68,395	1,864	81,875
1776	11,619	71,268	2,892	85,779
1784	10,150	79,198	3,472	92,220
1789	10,636	83,414	5,235	96,158
1802	9,826	75,584	6,578	91,988
1816	9,298	80,800	9,364	99,462
1826	9,937	81,142	10,786	101,865
1831	9,362	86,499	14,055	109,916
1835	9,000	78,076	29,955	116,031
1848	9,490	67,447	36,420	113,357

Table N11 The population of Saint Domingue, 1681–1789.

Year	Whites	Slaves	Free blacks	Total
1681	4,336	2,312	—	6,648
1690	—	—	—	10,250
1703	—	—	500	—
1715	—	—	1,500	—
1739	11,540	117,411	3,588	132,539
1754	14,253	172,188	4,911	191,352
1775	32,650	249,098	7,055	288,803
1784	20,229	298,079	13,257	331,565
1788	27,717	405,528	21,848	455,093
1789	30,831	434,429	24,848	490,108

Table N12 The population of Guadeloupe, 1700–1834.

Year	Whites	Slaves	Free blacks	Total
1700	3,825	6,725	325	10,875
1788	13,466	85,461	3,044	101,971
1834	10,000–15,000	96,684	10,000–15,000	116,684–126,684

Table N13 The population of French Guiana, 1665–1830 (excluding the small Indian population in the colonized area).

Year	Whites	Slaves	Free blacks	Total
1665	848	420	—	1,265
1700	—	—	—	2,000
1765	2,400	5,700	—	8,100
1815	100	15,000	300	15,400
1820	1,004	13,153	1,733	15,890
1830	—	19,100	—	22,666

Table N14   The population of the Danish West Indies, 1686–1848.

Year	Whites	Slaves	Free blacks	Total
Saint Thomas				
1686	300	333	—	633
1691	389	555	—	944
1720	565	4,187	—	4,752
1754	228	3,481	—	c4,000
1775	—	3,979	500	—
1792	—	4,279	—	—
1803	—	5,968	—	—
1835	—	—	—	14,022
1848	—	3,500	—	14,000
Saint Croix				
1742	174	1,906	—	2,080
1745	224	2,905	—	3,129
1755	1,323	8,897	—	10,220
1792	—	22,420	—	—
1803	—	27,161	—	—
1835	—	—	—	26,681
1848	—	26,000	—	—
Saint John				
1728	123	677	—	800
1739	208	1,414	—	1,622
1775	—	2,355	—	—
1787	167	2,200	16	2,383
1803	—	2,598	—	—
1848	—	2,500	—	—

Table N15   The population of Brazil, 1798–1872.

Year	Whites	Free coloreds	Indians	Total free	Slaves	Total
1798	1,010,000	406,000	250,000	1,666,000	1,582,000	3,248,000
1817–1818	1,043,000	585,500	259,400	1,887,900	1,930,000	3,817,900
1850	—	—	—	5,520,000	2,500,000	8,020,000
1864	—	—	200,000	8,530,000	1,715,000	10,245,000
1872	—	—	—	8,419,672	1,510,806	9,930,478

Table N16   The population of Minas Gerais, 1735–1872.

Year	Free	Slave	Total
1735	1,420	96,541	97,961
1740	680	94,632	95,313
1745	903	95,366	96,269
1749	755	88,196	88,951
1823	425,000	215,000	640,000
1872	1,669,276	370,459	2,039,735

Table N17   The population of the U.S. South, 1790–1860.

Year	Total population (approximate)	Total black population	Total slave population	Percent blacks enslaved	Percent total enslaved
1790	1,961,000	689,784	657,327	95	33.5
1800	2,622,000	918,336	857,097	93	33
1810	3,461,000	1,268,637	1,160,977	91.5	33.5
1820	4,419,000	1,642,672	1,508,692	92	34
1830	5,708,000	2,161,885	1,908,384	88	33
1840	6,951,000	2,641,977	2,427,986	92	35
1850	8,983,000	3,352,198	3,116,629	93	35
1860	11,138,000	4,097,111	3,838,765	94	34

Table N18   The population of some major slaveholding states.

State	1790 Total population	1790 Percent slaves	1810 Total population	1810 Percent slaves	1830 Total population	1830 Percent slaves	1860 Total population	1860 Percent slaves
Virginia	692,000	42	878,000	45	1,044,000	45	1,220,000	40
South Carolina	249,000	43	415,000	47	581,000	54	704,000	57
North Carolina	394,000	26	556,000	30	738,000	33	993,000	33
Georgia	83,000	35	252,000	41	517,000	42	1,057,000	44
Mississippi	—	—	31,000	55	137,000	48	791,000	55
Alabama	—	—	—	—	310,000	38	964,000	45
Louisiana	—	—	77,000	45	216,000	51	708,000	47

Index

Aba mbatoea (slave manners), 85
Abandonment, enslavement through, 105, 129–130
Abbasid caliphate: slave armies, 123, 467n63; absentee slave owners, 181; Mamluk freedmen in, 310
'Abd al-Muhsin Bakīr, 42
Abd Elwahed, Ali, 5, 41
Aboh (Nigeria): rituals of enslavement, 53, 55; enslavement methods, 122; concubinal manumission, 230; manumission by adoption, 233; slave population, 465n38
Abolition of slavery, 73; in Europe, 44; in Cuba, 283; in U.S., 293; in Portuguese colonies, 466n54; in Indonesia, 469n75
Abolition of slave trade, 165, 286
Absenteeism: and social recognition, 100; and treatment of slaves, 180–181, 423nn33,34
Achaemenid empire (Persia), 110, 315
Acquisition, mode: and master-slave relationship, 174; and manumission rate, 267. See also Enslavement; Slave Trade
Adamawa (Fulani slave center), 123
Adams, Victoria, 12
Adger, John B., 339
Adonke (slave), 40
Adoption: in kin-based societies, 63–65, 233; between redeemed man and God, 70; and child exposure, 129, 130; manumission by, 232–234, 338; rites, 234; slave assimilation by, 279
Adriani, N., 85, 203, 396n46

Adultery, 128, 188
Africa: marital transactions, 24; marks of servitude, 60; slave trade, 149, 152; slaves as money, 168; slaves of the court, 174; treatment of slaves, 199; sacrifice of slaves, 224; eunuchs, 316. See also East Africa; North Africa; Sub-Saharan Africa; West Africa
Africans: stereotypes, 7; preference for, 114, 422n20, 441n18; in slave trade, 118, 119–120, 122, 159–164, 397n54, 403n113; racism toward, 177; manumission, 267, 278
Age: and loss of honor, 83, 88; and manumission, 264, 266–267, 441n11
Agricultural slavery, 282. See also Rural slaves
Ahaggar (Tuareg group), 422n25
Ainu (Japan), 230; self-enslavement, 131
Air (Niger), 157
Akan-speaking groups, 135–136, 197
Aleut (Alaska), 191
Alexander the Great, 116
Alexandria, 150
Algeria, 157. See also Barbary states; Tuaregs
Algiers: enslavement by ransom, 107; piracy, 117, 402n107; manumission rate, 277; slave population, 460n15
Alho, Ollie, 74, 75, 385n160
Allridge, T. S., 83
al-Mahdī (caliph), 310–311
al-Malik al-Sahih, 308
al-Muhallabī (governor), 311

American Revolution, 292, 293
Americas: capitalistic slave systems, 33; marks of servitude, 61, 62; enslavement of Indians, 112; enslavement of war captives, 114; enslavement of Africans, 118, 122; slave trade, 118-119, 120, 159-164; status inheritance patterns, 138, 144; internal slave trade, 165-166; absentee slave owners, 181; slave unions, 189; concubinal manumission, 231; wala relationship, 246; freedman status, 249-250; ethnicity and manumission, 268; manumission rate, 278, 289. *See also* Caribbean; Northwest coast Indians; U.S. South
Amhara (Ethiopia), 82
Amphitryo (Plautus), 12
Amur group, *see* Gilyaks
Andrews, Anthony, 112
Andrews, Kenneth A., 113
Anglesey, Wales, 149
Anglo-Saxons: notions of property, 30; social and moral role of slaves, 47-48; rituals of enslavement, 52; nature of honor, 82; slave trade, 152; economic role of slaves, 386n18
Angola, 160, 466n54. *See also* Imbangala; Kwanyama; Ndembu
Animal sacrifice, 22, 223
Anstey, Roger, 162
Antilles, 244. *See also* French Antilles
Antonius Pius (emperor of Rome), 192
Apollo (Greek god), 67-68
Arabs: racism, 41, 93, 176, 178, 268; and honor, 92, 93; economics and slavery, 93; enslavement of fellow Arabs, 93; piracy, 116, 117, 399n78; slave tribute to, 124; debt-slavery, 125, 404n130; slave trade, 150; absenteeism of slave owners, 180, 181; killing of slaves, 190, 196; postmortem manumission, 227; incidence of manumission, 268; manumission rate, 277; ghilmān and, 308; dependence on slaves, 310. *See also* Islamic societies
Arakan (Burma), 118
Arawaks (Jamaica), 113
Ardra (West Africa), 123
Argentina, 427n73. *See also* Buenos Aires
Armenians, 152
Arrowsmith, W., 306
Art, 178, 421n16

Artisan class, 254-255
Ashanti (Ghana): personalistic idiom of power, 27-28, 371n38; slaves as foreigners, 40; marks of servitude, 58, 59, 61; fictive kinship system, 63-64; nature of honor, 82; enslavement methods, 119, 123; debt-slavery, 124; status inheritance pattern, 135-137, 139-140, 188; tenant slaves, 181; slave peculium, 185; slave marriage, 187; bride-price, 188; killing of slaves, 191; crimes of slaves, 197; self-defense, 200; granting of sanctuary, 201; change of master, 202; manumission, 232; freedman status, 250, 251; manumission rate, 271, 274, 280; house-born slaves, 427n62; slave population, 462n35
Asia: child exposure, 129; slave trade, 150; technologies from, 180; slaves from, 268. *See also* Middle East; Near East
Assyria, 315
Athens, 386n14; enslavement methods, 111, 113, 115-116; debt-slavery, 125; status inheritance pattern, 140; mining, 181; marriage, 189; killing of slaves, 192; slave as witness, 194; homicide laws, 194-195; treatment of slaves, 198; granting of sanctuary, 201; concubinal manumission, 231; collusive manumission, 236, 237, 242; freedman status, 254; manumission rate, 281, 282. *See also* Greeks
Athletes, professional, 24-26, 371n35
Atjehnese (Southeast Asia), 468n64
Atlantic slave trade, 159-164, 165, 286; volume, 150; organization, 162-163
Atli (character in Icelandic saga), 79
Atonement, 70
Atsi nahsa'i (slaves), 47
Attractiveness, physical, 177
Attucks, Crispus, 292
Augustine, Saint, 72, 101
Augustus (emperor of Rome), 69, 215, 303, 304, 310
Austen, Ralph A., 159, 248
Authoritarianism, 85, 96
Authority: sources, 2, 36-37; as symbolic control, 8-9, 36-38; acquisition, 36; in quasi-filial kin systems, 65; religion and, 73, 74, 75, 76
Averkieva, U. P., 40
Ayalon, David, 311, 448n31

Azores (Portugal), 117
Aztec Indians (Mexico): sources of slavery, 42; treatment of prisoners, 106–107; slave tribute to, 123; killing of slaves, 191; postmortem manumission, 222, 227; manumission rate, 271

Babylonia: prisoners of war, 109–110; child exposure, 130; status inheritance pattern, 145; slaves as dowry, 167; slave unions, 188; manumission, 218, 230, 234, 238; manumission rate, 271; marks of servitude, 381n94. See also Mesopotamia
Bacon, Francis, 78–79
Baghdad, 299, 316
Bagirmi (Chad): slaves as tribute, 124; slaves as money, 169; eunuchs, 316
Bagnes (penal slavery), 44, 45
Bahia (Brazil), 245, 267
Bailes, Sylvia, 93
Balkan peoples, 152
Ballagh, James Curtis, 9
Baltic Sea, 154
Bambara (Mali), 249, 271
Banausic skills, 255
Bancroft, Frederick, 166
Banda Islands (Indonesia): honor and recognition, 99, 100; kidnapping, 118; slave plantations, 181; concubinal manumission, 231; freedman status, 257; manumission rate, 274, 285; mutual degradation, 393n123; slave population, 469n75; treatment of slaves, 392n122, 393n123
Baqt (truce), 124
Barbados (British Caribbean): marks of servitude, 61–62; freedman status, 257; manumission rate, 275; racial differences, 374n63; slave population, 472n99, 477
Barbary states (North Africa): pirates, 117; prostitution, 263; manumission rate, 277; slave population, 460n15. See also Algiers; Morocco; Tunis
Barber, Millie, 12
Barrow, R. H.: on enslavement by birth, 134; on Roman marriage, 189; on Roman manumission, 223, 224
Basil, Saint, 321, 322
Batak (Indonesia), 124, 404n129
Batavia, 276

Batomba (Nigeria), 129
Beachey, R. W., 150
Bean, Richard Nelson, 164
Beccaria, Cesare, 378n45
Bedouins (Sinai), 194
Beja (Arab custom), 203
Bell, Daniel, 296
Bella Coola Indians (northwest coast of America): social death, 39; status inheritance pattern, 136; manumission rate, 271
Bellah, Robert N., 224–225
Bemba (Zambia): marks of servitude, 58; manumission rate, 271
Benghazi (North Africa), 157
Benin (Nigeria), 129, 463n37
Beowulf, 47–48
Berlin, Ira: on master/ex-slave relationship, 246, 259, 260; on manumission in U.S., 293
Bermuda, 147, 411n68, 480
Best, Elsdon, 51
Bhujissa (freeman), 216
Birka (Finland), 154
Birma (attendant to king), 137
Birth, enslavement by, 105, 106, 114, 115, 132–147, 170. See also Status inheritance patterns
Birth defects, 129
Birth rates, 162
Black Americans, 112, 259, 296; military role, 291–292, 446n94
Black Sea area, 116; slave trade, 150–152, 153
Bloch, Marc, 189, 276, 398n70
Bloch, Maurice, 280
Boas, Franz, 191
Böeseken, A. J., 245
Bömer, Franz: on religious lives of slaves, 66; on Apollo as defender of slaves, 67, 68; on sacral manumission, 67, 237, 238; on Roman cults, 69
Bond servants, 26
Bonte, Pierre, 139
Book of Poetry (Chinese), 326
Borgou (Nigeria), 129
Borneo, see Iban
Bornu (Nigeria): nature of honor, 82; enslavement for tribute, 123; status inheritance pattern, 137; slave trade, 157; eunuchs, 316. See also Margi
Bosnia, 407n173

Bosongo (bride-payment), 167
Bosworth, C. E., 312
Boulvert, 303
Bourgeot, André, 203, 204
Bowser, Frederick P., 269
Boy-markets, 421n18
Brahmins, 51
Branding, 59
Brazil: enslavement methods, 120; slave
    populations, 133, 285, 474n133, 482;
    status inheritance pattern, 146; slave
    trade, 163, 286; internal slave trade,
    165–166; slave unions, 189, 190; treat-
    ment of slaves, 198; manumission, 217,
    245, 268, 269, 443n44; wala relation-
    ship, 244; freedman status, 244; reen-
    slavement, 245; manumission rate, 273,
    286, 289–290; preference for African
    slaves, 441n18; military slavery, 446n83.
    See also Minas Gerais; Tupinamba
Breton, Raymond, 60
Bride-price, 24; and status inheritance,
    137, 138, 139; slaves as, 166–167; in
    lineage-based societies, 187, 188
Bridewealth marriage, 166–167
Briggs, L. Cabot, 422n25
Bristol (England), 154, 459n12
British Caribbean: slave naming rituals,
    58; religion and slavery, 72–73; status
    inheritance pattern, 146; slave unions,
    190; concubinal manumission, 231;
    wala relationship, 245; freedman status,
    255, 257; manumission rates, 255, 273,
    285, 291, 295; slave population,
    472n107, 473n111. *See also* Barbados;
    Jamaica
British Columbia, 412n6. *See also* Bella
    Coola Indians
Brumalia festivals, 328
Bryndhild (Icelandic princess), 220
Buckland, W. W.: on slavery and Roman
    law, 29; on debtors in Rome, 125; on
    birth as cause of slavery, 134, 139; on
    manumission, 210–211, 223, 236, 239
Buckley, Roger Norman, 291–292
Buddhism, and honor, 86
Buddhist period (India): nature of honor,
    86; status inheritance pattern, 140;
    treatment of slaves, 207; freedman sta-
    tus, 253; manumission rate, 281
Buenos Aires, 245; freedman status, 255,
    256; manumission rates, 256, 273, 278,
    290, 434n58; incidence of manumission,
    266, 267, 268; skilled slaves, 439n39

Bulgarians, 152
Burial of slaves, with masters, 220
Burma, 118; marks of servitude, 60; en-
    slavement by kidnapping, 117; slaves as
    money, 168, 169; manumission, 238; pa-
    goda slaves, 435n81. *See also* Kachin
Bursa (Turkey), 266
Bushong kings (Africa), 329
Butler, Isaiah, 6
Byzantium, 174; eunuchs, 299, 314–331;
    emperors, 327–328, 330, 331; upper-
    class women, 329; craftsmen, 332

Caesar, Julius, 115, 305
Calabar province (Nigeria), 119
Callicles (character in *Gorgias*), 8
Callinago Caribs (Lesser Antilles), 60,
    271, 402n102
Callisters, 301, 307
Camerinus, Sulpicius, 307, 308
Cameroon, *see* Duala
Camus, Albert, 204
Canada, 338
Canary Islands (Spain), 117, 152
Cannibalism, 52, 81, 107
Cape Colony (South Africa), 276
Cape Town (South Africa): under Dutch,
    255, 263, 269; manumission rate, 256,
    269; prostitution, 263
Cape Verde Islands (Portugal), 117, 285
Capital, 2, 23
Capital crimes, 45
Capitalism, 21, 33, 370n30
Capital punishment, 126, 128, 429n90
Captivus (slave), 40
Cardiff (Wales), 154
Caribbean: migration of free labor from,
    34; rituals of enslavement, 54; marks of
    servitude, 59, 60, 61; religion and slav-
    ery, 72–73; slave stereotypes, 96; sense
    of honor, 97, 99, 100; absenteeism of
    planters, 100; enslavement practices,
    113, 114, 402n102; slave trade, 160–162;
    internal slave trade, 166; treatment of
    slaves, 198; incidence of manumission,
    219, 267, 268, 290, 291; freedman sta-
    tus, 249, 259; slave revolts, 259; slaves
    in warfare, 291; mortality rates, 417n64;
    racial prejudice, 420n14. *See also* Brit-
    ish Caribbean; Dutch Caribbean;
    French Caribbean; Spanish Caribbean;
    names of specific islands

Cartas (letters of manumission), 217
Carthaginians, 107
Cash, W. J., 261
Cassirer, Ernst, 55
Caste: and concept of slavery, 48–51; defined, 378n55
Catholic Church: dualism, 72, 74, 75–76; conversion techniques, 72–73
Caucasians, 178
Celebes, *see* Toradja
Celts (England): status inheritance pattern, 141; slave trade, 149, 152, 154, 156
Central Africa, *see* Africa
Chanana, Dev Raj, 253
Cherokee Indians (southeastern North America): liminal incorporation of slavery, 46–47; group identity, 47; fictive kin system, 63; treatment of prisoners, 107; intraethnic slavery, 423n26
Chesnut, Mary Boykin, 208
Chien (ignoble status), 86, 127
Chien Po-tsan, 108
Childrearing patterns, 85, 88
Children: of prisoners, 9; sale of, 23–24, 129–130; of slaves, 63–64, 65, 409n25, 464n44; as tribute, 123; manumission, 145–146, 267, 269, 434n50; of concubines, 187, 229, 279–280, 434n50; of masters, 392n121
China: children of prisoners, 9; sale of nonslave persons, 23–24, 125, 130, 370n26; extrusive conception of slavery, 42; and penal system, 43, 44, 127; rituals of enslavement, 55; marks of servitude, 58, 59, 60; prisoners of war, 107–108, 110; kidnapping, 117; exposure and sale of infants, 129; self-enslavement, 130; status inheritance pattern, 141–144, 145, 409n25; slaves of court, 174; racial preference in slaves, 176, 178, 419n9, 422n20; slave unions, 188–189; killing of slaves, 191; self-defense, 200; concubinal manumission, 229; political manumission, 235; freedman status, 241, 252; manumission rate, 281; eunuchs, 299, 314–331; free women, 325, 326; social system, 341. *See also* Han dynasties; Lolos; Ming dynasty; Northern dynasties; Oriental societies
Chinese law: enslavement of families of condemned persons, 127; concubinage, and inheritance patterns, 142–143

Chocó (Colombia): change of master, 202; incidence of manumission, 270; manumission rate, 270, 273, 278; mortality rate, 442n35; slave population, 471n85
Chou dynasty (China), 326
Chou ku-Cheng, 108
Christ, Jesus, 70; symbolic meaning of crucifixion, 71, 74, 75, 227; and obedience, 76
Christianity: conflict of good and evil, 47; conversions to, 70, 72, 384n138; salvation, 70–71, 72; dualism, 72, 74, 75–76; fundamentalist, 73–74; marital and family conditions, 189; granting of sanctuary, 201; testamentary manumission, 222, 225, 227; and frequency of manumission, 226, 275–276
Christians: connotation of, 7; enslavement of fellow Christians, 41; enslavement of Muslims, 117; status inheritance patterns, 145; sale of, 189; manumission, 275, 277
Christian Spain: piracy, 116; status inheritance pattern, 141; slave trade, 152; freedman status, 243
Chrysostom, Saint John, 225
Chungnyŏl (king of Korea), 42
Cicero: on honorable prestige, 89, 90; treatment of his slaves, 174, 304
Cimbrian wars, 123
Citizenship: to manumitted slaves, 30–31, 243, 252, 253; freedom as, 372n51
Civil War, 25, 292–293, 338
Clan, 47
Claudius (emperor of Rome), 301, 306, 307
Clifton, Peter, 6
Clissold, Stephen, 277
Clothing: as mark of servitude, 58; regulation, 381n91
Coartacion (installment plan), 270, 283
Cohabitation, and slave status, 140
Coins, English and Frankish, 156
Collusive litigation, manumission by, 236–237
Colombia, 56. *See also* Chocó
Colthurst, John, 62
Columbus, Christopher, 113
Comedy: Greek, 87; Roman, 91
Commensalism, 335, 453nn1,3
Commodus (emperor of Rome), 307
Concubinal manumission, 228–232, 239, 251, 261

Concubines: sale of, 23–24, 129; sexual exploitation, 50; fictive daughters, 64; in kin-based societies, 64; and status inheritance, 142, 145, 146; children of, 187, 229, 251, 279–280, 402n102, 434n50; treatment, 190; male, 263; enslavement, 402n107; parasitic relationship, 455

Conditions of slavery: master-slave relationship, 172–173, 205; slave and community, 172; master and community, 172–173; in work force, 173–174, 206; mode of acquisition and, 174, 175–176; and residence of slave, 174–175; characteristics of slave and, 176–179; skills of slaves and, 179–180; and size of slave population, 180–181, 198–199; and mode of subsistence, 181, 186; peculium and, 182–186, 192, 193; and marriage, 186–190; killing of slaves, 190–193; crimes against slaves, 193–196, 206; crimes against one another, 196–197; legal restraints, 198–199; self-defense, 200–202; granting of sanctuary, 201–202; change of masters, 202–205; in familia Caesaris, 303

Conrad, Robert, 165
Consecration, in sacral manumission, 237
Constantine (emperor of Rome), 189
Contractual manumission, 238–239
Cooper, Frederick, 93
Corinth, 237
Cosmological dualism, 224, 225
Council of Dort, 276
Council of Epaone, 192
Cover, Robert M., 4
Crafts, 255
Cranston, Maurice, 340
Craton, Michael, 6, 57
Crawford, Stephen C., 206
Creel, Herrlee, 326
Cretans, 116
Crete: means of enslavement, 114; status inheritance pattern, 138; slave trade, 152; slave peculium, 185; manumission, 282. *See also* Gortyna
Crimea, 152
Crimes: against slaves, 193–196, 206; slave against slave, 196–197; of slaves, 389n58
Criminals, 9, 86
Critias, 112

Cronia ritual, in Greece, 67
Crook, John, 398n70
Cross, F. M., 275
Crucifixion of Christ: symbolic interpretations, 71, 74, 75; Paul's interpretation, 227
Cuba: branding of slaves, 59; enslavement methods, 120, 403n113; mortality and fertility rates, 133; status inheritance pattern, 146; treatment of slaves, 198; incidence of manumission, 267, 270; manumission rate, 283, 287, 290, 445n71; abolition of slavery, 283; plantation slavery, 401n97; slave population, 470nn78,80
Cubeo Indians (Amazon): fictive kinship system, 64–65; manumission rate, 271; wives as captives, 402n102
Cults: Lares, 68, 69, 215–216; Jupiter Libertas, 69; imperial, 69, 70
Cultural differences, and master-slave relationship, 178
Culture, 37; slavery and, 84–85
Cumal (female slave), 168, 169
Curaçao (West Indies): freedman status, 254; manumission rate, 275, 278, 284, 287
Curtin, Philip D.: on Islam and trade in West Africa, 119, 157; on volume of slave trade, 157, 158, 160; on economics of slave trade, 164
Cyprus, 114, 152
Cyril of Alexandria, Saint, 225

Dahomey (West Africa): kidnapping, 119; bride-payment, 166; royal slave plantations, 181; killing of slaves, 191; manumission rate, 274; marriage, 427n56
Dalles slave mart, 149
Damagaram (Nigeria), 125
Dandamayev, 110
Danes: raids on, 154; economics of slavery, 169, 386n18
Dasa (word for slave), 86
Daube, David, 222–223, 235–236
Davis, John, 70, 80
Death, prospect of, 5; slavery as substitute for, 26, 44, 45, 337, 378n45; of master, 224, 226, 433n41. *See also* Mortality rates
Death penalty, *see* Capital punishment

Debt-servitude, 404n129; difference from slavery, 9, 86, 124–126, 404n131; heredity factor, 9–10, 404n134; and sale of labor, 9, 25; honorable status, 86; in religious law, 404nn130,132
Degler, Carl N., 286, 289–290
Degradation: in kin-based societies, 64, 81, 83; punishment and, 93–94
Delobsom, A. A. Dim, 60
Delos (North America), 149
Delphic manumission records: sacral manumissions, 68, 237, 238; concubinal manumission, 230–231; freedom at expense of children, 262–263; analysis, 265; freedom at death of master, 267
Dependence relationship, see Human parasitism; Master-slave relationship
Dependency on slaves: for childrearing, 88; for independence of master, 97–98; for power, 310; camouflage of, 337, 338–339; by a society, 458n13, 460n15, 470n77
Deracination, 7–8, 309–310, 311
Desai, Moraji R., 698
Destitution, and social death, 41, 42
Deterior condicio (low-status inheritance), 142, 143, 144, 281
Devshirme (tribute of children), 123, 311–312
Diakonoff, I. M., 109, 181, 371n39
Dickson, Harold H. P., 93
Dignitas (honor), 89, 91
Dignity, 100–101
Diimaajo (Fulani slave term), 338
Diocletian (emperor of Rome), 317
Diósdi, Gyorgy, 373n54
Dishonor, see Honor
Dnieper River, 154
Dokladnoe (registered slaves), 183–184
Domestic slavery, 82–83. See also Household slaves
Domination: and power, 1, 2, 332–333; dependency relationship in, 2, 336; and honor, 331–332; and human parasitism, 334–335
Dominium, doctrine of, 30–32, 311
Donini, Ambrosio, 70
Douglas, Mary, 322, 323, 325, 331, 426n83
Douglass, Frederick, 13
Doulos (slavery), 40
Dowry payment, 166–167

Drake, Sir Francis, 290
Driver, G. R., 218, 230
Duala (Cameroon): rituals of enslavement, 55; methods of enslavement, 122; bridewealth, 166; freedman status, 248
Dublin, 154
Ducrey, Pierre, 110, 121
Duff, A. M., 301, 305
Duke, Antera, 119
Dunbar, Paul Lawrence, 208
Duncan-Jones, Richard, 122–123
Dunlap, James D., 317, 327
Dunn, Richard S., 72
Dutch, 289; treatment of slaves, 99, 469n75; enslavement methods, 111, 117, 118, 469n75; slave trade, 160; freedman status, 254, 257, 469n75; manumission rate, 278, 284, 285
Dutch Caribbean: concubinal manumission, 231; wala relationship, 244
Dutch East India Company, 246, 255, 263, 269, 439n50
Dutch Reformed Church, 276
Duties, in jurisprudence, 20–21, 22
Dyongoro (freedman status), 249

Earl, Donald, 304
East Africa: degradation and punishment of slaves, 93–94; piracy, 117, 399n78; enslavement for tribute, 123; slave trade, 150, 159; slaves as money, 168; slave plantations, 181; change of master, 202. See also Zanzibar
East Indies, 99
Eaton, Clement, 94
Economic conditions: role of slaves, 81–82, 83, 87, 93, 386n18; burden of slaves, 99; of freedmen, 253–255, 259; and manumission rate, 259, 279, 281–287, 295, 434n58; demand for slaves, 270, 450n37; and familia Caesaris, 302–303; and urban slavery, 456n5
Egypt: internal source of slavery, 42; rituals of enslavement, 55; marks of servitude, 59, 60; sexual bias in enslavement, 121; slave tribute, 123; penal slavery, 126; slave trade, 150, 157; slaves as dowry, 167; sale of house slaves, 175; treatment of slaves, 178, 421n19; concubinal manumission, 230; freedman status, 253; eunuchs, 316; prisoners of war, 403. See also Mamluk kingdom

Egypt, Ophelia Settle, 8
Ehrenberg, Victor, 88
Eisenstadt, S. N., 319-320
Eliade, Mireca, 39
Elite slaves: and definition of slavery, 14, 299, 306, 309, 315, 331, 333; factors in recruitment, 310, 311-312; honor and, 310, 311, 313, 331-332. *See also* Eunuchs; Familia Caesaris; Ghilmān; Janissaries; Mamluks
Elizabeth I (queen of England), 331
Elkins, Stanley, 96
Elphick, Richard, 273; and somatic theory of manumission, 268; on religion and manumission, 276
Elyokeko (initiating ritual), 53
Emancipation, *see* Abolition of slavery; Freedom; Manumission
Emperor, Byzantine: worship of, 69, 70; power, 317-319; divine right, 327-328, 329; assassination, 328-329
Endogamy, 280-281
Engerman, Stanley L., 162, 163, 273; on interregional movement of slaves in South, 165; on economics of slavery in Rome, 302, 454
England: law of property, 30; enslavement of Europeans, 44; nature of honor, 82; slave trade, 156, 160; slave population, 157, 459n12; racial preference in slaves, 178; killing of slaves, 190; manumission ritual, 217; and American Revolution, 292, 447n97; Groom of the Stool, 330; Tudor monarchs, 330-331; social system, 341. *See also* Anglo-Saxons; British Caribbean
Enslavement: rituals, 8-9, 38, 51-62, 128; transitional phases, 38, 293; marks, 51-62; divine, 71-72; of fellow ethnics, 93, 107, 118, 276, 404n132, 422nn23,25; by capture in warfare, 105, 106-115, 119-120, 170, 396n52, 397n54, 398n71, 400n90, 403n113; by kidnapping, 105, 115-122, 398nn70,71, 399n78, 400nn85, 90; for tribute or tax payment, 105, 122-124, 125; through debt, 105, 124-126; through abandonment, 105, 129-130; through sale of children, 105; self-enslavement, 105, 130-131; by birth, 105, 106, 114, 115, 132-147, 170; of mass populations, 110-112; and demand for slaves, 116; sexual bias,

120-122, 129, 403n108; as punishment, 126-129, 288; through bride and dowry payment, 166-167; slaves as money, 167-171; means versus acquisition of slaves, 169-171; means and master-slave relationship, 175-176; link to manumission, 340-341; and death of master, 433n41. *See also* Acquisition; Slave trade
Equiano, 122
Eskimos, 340
Española, 469n76, 470n77
Ethiopians: marks of servitude, 58; nature of honor, 82; treatment, 177; incidence of manumission, 268; eunuchs, 316, 332, 451n65; preference for, 422n20
Ethnic factors: and master-slave relationship, 178, 199; enslavement of fellow ethnics, 179; in crimes against slaves, 195-196; in manumission rates, 267-268; in recruitment of elite slaves, 310
Ethnographic Atlas, 48-49
Eunuchs, 451nn61,64,65; treatment, 174; castration, 312, 315, 317, 321, 324; role, 315, 316, 324, 325-326, 419n9; genealogical isolation, 319-320, 331; low esteem, 320-321; stereotypes, 320-322; symbolism of pollution, 322-323, 325, 327, 331, 436n83; body symbolism, 324; relationship with monarch, 325; sexual relations, 326. *See also* Political eunuchism
Europe: forms of slavery, 44; branding of slaves, 59; timocratic culture, 95; and Indians in the Americas, 112; enslavement by kidnapping, 116; slave trade, 114, 149, 152-157; internal kidnapping, 117; penal slavery, 127; rituals of enslavement, 128; demand for slaves, 178, 397n54; technologies of skilled slaves, 180; slave marriage, 189; killing of slaves, 192; manumission, 230; freedman status, 250; incidence of manumission, 268; manumission rate, 275, 278, 288. *See also* Medieval period; Middle Ages
Evreux, Father, 81
Excommunication, 192
Exodus myth, and religion of slaves, 385n160
Exposure of children, 129-130

Ex-slaves: Jamaican, 2, 6; American, 6, 8, 12, 392n121; rulers, 449n32

Fage, J. D., 119
Familia Caesaris, 248, 319; divisions, 300–301: power structure, 301, 305, 307, 314; economics, 302–303; recruitment of slaves, 303, 310; legal aspects, 303–304, 306
Fanti (Akan group), 197
Fatimids (Egypt), 316
Felix (governor of Judea), 306
Fezzan (Libya), 157
Fictive kinship systems, 62–65; power relations, 19, 33; naming ceremonies, 55; adoptive and quasi-filial, 63, 65. *See also* Kin-based societies
Finberg, H. R. P., 82
Findlay, Robert, 283–284
Finland, Gulf of, 154
Finley, Moses: on outsider status of slaves, 7; on slaves as property, 21, 34, 369n21; on fear and love in worship, 70; on significance of slavery in Greece, 87, 88, 93; on acceptance of Messenians by Greeks, 112; on kidnapping, 120, 398n70
Firth, Raymond, 37, 51, 212, 213
Fishing communities, 84, 186
Fitzgerald, C. P., 318
Flatheads (British Columbia), 412n6
Flood, Curt, 25
Florence (Italy), 296
Fogel, Robert W., 162, 163, 273; on interregional movement of slaves, 165, 414n30
Foote, Peter, 200
Force, and power, 18, 303
Fortes, Meyer, 37, 63, 375n6
France, 45, 289; penal slavery, 44, 128; branding of galley slaves, 59; enslavement of war captives, 114; slave trade, 152, 160; racial preference in slaves, 178; slave unions, 190, 411n68; freedman status, 243. *See also* French Caribbean
Franklin, John Hope, 95
Franks, 217–218
Freedman status: dangers, 94, 261; pardoned criminals, 126; and ex-master relationship, 240–247, 252, 260; and sex of slave, 240, 251, 260–261; in lineage-based societies, 241, 251; in Islamic societies, 241–242, 252; and occupation, 242, 254–255; freedman's estate, 242; citizenship, 243, 252, 253; legal guardianship, 246; political-legal aspects, 247, 256, 294; prestige ranking, 247, 294; stigmatization, 247, 251, 252, 253, 257, 294; dependency ties, 247, 249, 250, 253, 294; mobility, 248–249; integration, 249, 251, 252, 294, 443n53; and race, 249–250, 251, 254, 256, 257, 259, 278, 294; mode of manumission and, 250, 256; and type of slaveholding society, 250–261; social aspects, 250; economic aspects, 253–255, 259; level of skills and, 254–255; percentage in total population, 258, 259; origins, 341–342; ambiguity, 425n44
Freedom: domain, 14, 341–342; Western and non-Western concept, 27; spiritual, 71: honor and, 94: slave awareness of, 98, 340; purchase of, *see* Peculium; replacement cost, 264, 444n66; as "citizenship," 372n51
French Antilles, 57–58, 138, 230, 231, 257
French Caribbean: slave naming rituals, 57–58; status inheritance pattern, 138; manumission, 219; concubinal manumission, 230, 231; freedman status, 249, 255, 257; manumission rate, 285
French West Indies, 219, 249
Freyre, Gilberto, 441n18
Frials (Norse word for free), 216
Friedman, Ellen, 107
Friedman, Lawrence J., 338
Friedmann, W. B., 20
Frihals (free-neck), 216
Frostathing laws, 216
Fullrettisord (insult), 82
Fundamentalism, 73–75, 76, 260

Gaetisson, Thorkel, 177
Gaius, 139, 193, 304
Galba (emperor of Rome), 307
Galley slaves, 44, 45, 59
Gambia, *see* Wolof
Gandu (Hausa slaves), 64
Garnsey, Peter, 89, 306
Garos (India), 221
Gauls, 223
Geirmund (character in Icelandic saga), 79

Gelb, I. J., 109, 115, 403n108
Gelon (of Syracuse), 111
Gemery, Henry, 119, 162, 164
Genoa, 276
Genocide, 112
Genovese, Eugene, 162; on master-slave relationship, 11, 65; on slavery in U.S. South, 33, 73, 74, 94, 296
Georgia, 73, 94, 475n141, 483
Germanic peoples: rituals of enslavement, 52; marks of servitude, 60; nature of honor, 81; economic role of slaves, 81–82, 386n18; status inheritance patterns, 140, 141; tenant settlements, 181; crimes against slaves, 194; manumission ritual, 217, 218; manumission by adoption, 234; political manumission, 235
Germany, 130
Gerriets, Marilyn, 168
Gewaltverhältnis (power relationship), 36
Ghana. *see* Ashanti; Tallensi
Ghilmān, 448n30, 449n34; honor, 308, 309, 313; power, 308–309, 314; recruitment, 308; deracination, 311; loyalty, 312; eunuchs, 312–313; homosexuality, 312
Ghost, The (Plautus), 12
Gia-Long code (Vietnam), 86
Gibson, Grace, 12
Gift exchange theory: complexities, 212; cycle, 213; earnest and token, 213; balance, 213–214; in manumission, 211–218, 236–237, 243, 294; in human parasitism, 341; in ritualization of power, 368n8. *See also* Human sacrifice
Gilyaks (Siberia): marks of servitude, 58; nonexploitation of female slaves, 229–230; manumission by adoption, 233; enslavement practices, 422n23
Gluckman, Max, 67, 347
Goajiros (Venezuela): internal process of slavery, 38–39, 41–42; penal slavery, 126; status inheritance pattern, 137; killing of slaves, 191; manumission rate, 271, 280
Goguel, Maurice, 71
Goldi (northern Asia), 432n30
Goldin, Claudia Dale, 456n5
Goldman, Irving, 64
Gondola, Nigeria, 137
Gorgias (Plato), 8

Gortyna (Crete): debt-slavery, 125; sanction of peculium, 185, 426n49; granting of sanctuary, 201
Gotland (Baltic Sea), 154
Gouldner, Alvin, 87, 388n52
Governesses, 88
Grace, E., 194
Grace, J. J., 83, 187
Graeca fides (uncreditworthiness), 90
Graeculus (worthlessness), 91, 96, 338
Gray, Robert F., 24
Greek law: property, 29; slave's legal standing, 87; hubris, 389n58
Greeks: master-slave relationship, 4–5; ownership and property, 29, 371n43; socioeconomic dependence on slavery, 30, 372n49; enslavement of fellow Greeks, 30, 179; citizenship, 30; nonslaveholders, 36; slave markets, 40; marks of servitude, 58; slavery and religion, 66–67, 68; honor and value systems, 86–87, 89, 388n52; courts and public opinion, 87; treatment of slaves, 87–88, 174, 175, 177; status of women, 88; honor and punishment, 90; Roman conception of, 90–91; prisoners of war, 107, 110; enslavement of populations, 111; enslavement of war captives, 113, 114; enslavement by kidnapping, 115; killing of slaves, 121; debt-slavery, 125; penal slavery, 126, 128; exposure of children, 129; slave trade, 152; craftsmen, 179, 180, 254–255; slave peculium, 184, 263; crimes against slaves, 194, 195; granting of sanctuary, 201; manumission ritual, 218; testamentary manumission, 227, 237; concubinal manumission, 230–231; manumission by adoption, 234; political manumission, 235; collusive manumission, 236, 237; sacral manumission, 237, 238; freedman status, 241–242, 254, 372n51, 389n58; prostitution, 263; incidence of manumission, 268; manumission rate, 269, 274, 281, 282–283, 284, 288, 296; military slaves, 288; racial prejudice, 420n14. *See also* Athens; Hellenistic Greece; Homeric Greece; Sparta
Greenstein, Lewis J., 255
Gregory the Great, Saint, 225
Gregory of Tours, 201
Groom of the Stool, 330

Grundrisse (Marx), 2
Guadaloupe (Mexico), 275, 481
Guerdan, René, 328
Guinea (West Africa): enslavement
    methods, 119, 120, 123; slave trade, 160
Gumbu (Mali), 461n26
Guthrie, W. K. C., 68
Gutman, Herbert G., 56
Guzz (Turkish tribe), 123

Haas, Samuel S., 180
Hacienda-type farms, 255, 427n73
Hadrian (emperor of Rome), 140
Hagar (biblical character), 230
Haida (northwest coast of America): sta-
    tus inheritance pattern, 136; escaped
    captives, 432n15
Hair: mystical associations, 60; type, 61,
    383n107; and status, 382n106
Haitian slave revolt, 291
Hammurabi, laws of, 188, 230
Han (China), 420n10, 468n67
Hanafis (Muslim legal school): paternity,
    228; manumission, 239
Han dynasties (China): prisoners of war,
    108–109; penal slavery, 127; status in-
    heritance pattern, 141; racism, 176;
    freedmen, 250; eunuchs, 315, 318; social
    system, 341
Hardy, P., 311
Harris, Townsend, 482
Harris, William V., 130, 396n52, 402n105
Hausa (Nigeria): nonslaveholders, 36; fic-
    tive kinship system, 64; nature of
    honor, 82; tenant farming, 181; manu-
    mission rate, 271
Head, the: in enslavement rituals, 52–53,
    54, 216; shorn, 60–61, 128, 215; in man-
    umission rituals, 215, 216, 218
Hebrew Law: intrusive conception of
    slavery, 40–41; killing of slaves, 192;
    debt-bondage, 404n132
Hebrews (Palestine): intrusiveness of slav-
    ery, 40–41; enslavement practices, 41,
    125, 275, 404n132; killing of slaves, 192;
    manumission rate, 271, 275
Hedeby (Scandinavia), 154
Hedonism, 261
Hegel, Georg: on contradictions to total
    power, 2; on political-psychological as-
    pects of slavery, 11; on dialectics of
    slavery, 97–101, 392n115; on limits,
    299; on dependence of dominator, 336

Helius (emperor of Rome), 307, 308
Hellenistic Egypt: marks of servitude, 59;
    penal slavery, 126
Hellenistic Greece: debt-slavery, 125;
    granting of sanctuary, 201
Hellie, Richard, 1, 43, 44, 130, 183
Helotry, 112
Henriques, Fernando, 382n106
Hereditary servitude, 9–10
Hereditary slavery, 84, 279; race and,
    277–278; warfare and, 289. *See also*
    Status inheritance patterns
Heritage, and natal alienation, 5–6
Heshima (respect), 93
Hesiodic Greece, 125
Higginbotham, A. Leon, 138
Higginson, T. W., 75
Higman, Barry, 269, 273
Hill, Polly, 64
Hispaniola, 113
Hjor (Norwegian king), 177
Hobbes, Thomas, 10, 80
Hoebel, E. Adamson, 20
Hoetink, Harry, 244, 256, 287
Hogendorn, Jan, 119, 162, 164
Hohfeld, W. N., 20, 22
Homeric Greece: enslavement practices,
    120; status inheritance pattern, 138
Homosexuality, 231, 312, 421n18
Honor, 367n41, 388n52; and power,
    10–11, 13, 78, 79, 84, 87; sense of, 10,
    82, 92; loss and dishonor, 10–12, 78, 83,
    85, 96, 97; and submission, 77, 78, 95;
    facets, 79; reputation and, 79, 80, 81,
    83, 93; acting honorably versus being
    honorable, 80, 331–332; among tribal
    peoples, 81–85; of aged slaves, 83, 88;
    among advanced premodern peoples,
    86–94; of criminals, 86; and privilege,
    89; and punishment, 89–90, 128; and
    freedom, 94; in U.S. South, 94–97; and
    chivalry, 95, 97; of master, 96; and rec-
    ognition, 99–100; caliphs and, 308–311
Honor payment, 82
Hopkins, Keith, 265; on Augustan Lares
    cult, 69; on slavery and wealth in
    Rome, 92; on Delphic manumissions,
    230–231, 238, 262–263; on race and
    manumission, 277–278; on eunuchs in
    Byzantine power structure, 315, 317,
    318, 319, 320, 322, 327; on migrations
    of Italian poor, 375n64

Horace, 89, 252
Household slaves, 427n62; selling, 175; manumission, 232, 270–271
Hóvamól (Icelander), 82
Hsuiung-nu (China), 108
Hubris (Greek concept), 389n58
Hughes, G. B. J., 22
Human parasitism, 81, 334–342, 453n1; and domain of freedom, 14, 340–341; as relation of domination, 173, 334–339; variables, 206; personal satisfaction in, 336; mutualism, 336–337, 338; institutional aspects, 337, 341; gift exchange theory, 341; on systemic level, 341; Rapoport's theory, 336, 453n3
Human sacrifice, 428n84; alternative to enslavement, 107; in postmortem manumission, 220–228, 433n45; principle of gift exchange, 221, 224, 227; substitution of animals, 221, 223; at death of master, 224, 226; as capital punishment, 429n90. *See also* Potlatch ceremony
Hundley, Daniel R., 95–96
Hunter-gatherer societies, 18
"Hymn to Rome" (Melinno), 90

Iban (Borneo): status inheritance pattern, 147; manumission rate, 271
Iberian Peninsula: enslavement of war captives, 114; slave trade, 160.
Ibn Fenārī, 313
Ibn Khaldun, 310
Ibn Zurdâdhbih, 123
Ibos (Nigeria): marks of servitude, 58; nature of honor, 83; enslavement practices, 120, 126, 128, 423n26; status inheritance pattern, 137; slaves as bride-payment, 166; concubinal manumission, 230; manumission of Osu, 238; manumission rate, 271
Ibrāhīm Pasha, 313
Iceland: rituals of enslavement, 55; nature of honor, 79, 81; ransom and warfare, 107; status inheritance pattern, 141; slave trade, 152, 157; bride-payment, 167; slaves as money, 168, 169; racial ideal, 177; crimes against slaves, 194; crimes of slaves, 196–197, 200; self-defense, 200; postmortem manumission, 220; economic role of slaves, 386n18; slave population, 459n11
Idonei (skilled slaves), 270

Igala kingdom (West Africa), 195, 316
Igbo-speaking groups (Niger), 233
Ila (Central Africa): rituals of enslavement, 53; marks of servitude, 60; status inheritance pattern, 147; change of master, 203–204; freedman status, 251
Iliad (Homer), 121, 230
Illyrians, 116
Imbangala (Angola): rituals of enslavement, 53; fictive kinship system, 63; status inheritance pattern, 136; concubinal manumission, 232; manumission rate, 280
Imerina (Madagascar), 280
Immigration/emigration rates, 132, 414n30
Imperial China, 24, 43
Imuhag (Tuareg group): fictive kinship system, 64; change of master, 203
Inalcik, Halil, 308–309
Incentive, *see* Reward
Incentive payment, 283–284
Incest, 329
Indentured servants, 9, 25, 183
India: caste in, 49; marks of servitude, 60; nature of honor, 80, 86; status inheritance pattern, 140; Mauryan period, 140; slaves as dowry, 167; racial preference in slaves, 178, 311; treatment of slaves, 207; manumission ritual, 216; postmortem manumission, 221; concubinal manumission, 230; freedman status, 253; manumission rate, 281; eunuchs, 320, 422n20
Indian Ocean area: slave trade, 150, 151; plantations, 181
Indians, *see* Northwest coast Indians
Indonesia, 469n75. *See also* Banda Islands; Nias
Ingram, J. K., 21
Initiation ceremonies, 53–54, 191
Innate slavishness, 68, 420n12
Institutional process, 13; enslavement of "free" persons, 105–131; enslavement by birth, 132–147; acquisition of slaves, 148–171
Interbreeding, 134, 135, 137
Intermarriage, 137–138; slave and free, 64, 409n25; and status inheritance pattern, 137–138, 142, 409n25; slave assimilation by, 279

Interregional movement, of slaves, 165, 166
Intisap (tacit relationship), 309
Iranians, 310
Iraq: treatment of slaves, 174; tenant slaves, 181; slave unions, 187; killing of slaves, 190; freedman status, 248; manumission rate, 274; palace slaves, 332; slave population, 467n63. *See also* Mesopotamia
Ireland: Viking raids, 116; status inheritance pattern, 141; slave trade, 152, 154, 156; slaves as money, 168–169
Iroquois (North America), 432n15
Islam: rationalization of slavery, 72; social inferiority of slaves, 93; equality of slaves under God, 93; sense of honor, 97; enslavement of Christians, 117, 196; enslavement of fellow Muslims, 118, 276; and slave trade, 150, 154, 157; testamentary manumission, 222; postmortem manumission, 227; and manumission rate, 276–277
Islamic law: intrusive conception of social death, 41; enslavement of coreligionists, 41, 118; enslavement for debt, 125, 404n130; penal slavery, 128; concubinage, 145; status inheritance, 145; marriage, 187, 188; change of master, 204–205
Islamic societies, economic dependence, 11; marks of servitude, 58; honor, 92–94; ransom and slaves, 107; enslavement of war captives, 114–115; internal kidnapping, 117–118; sexual bias in enslavement, 121; tribute in slaves, 123; debt-slavery, 124–125; penal slavery, 128; social reproduction, 133; status inheritance patterns, 138–139, 145; and slave trade, 150, 157; household slaves, 174; racism, 176, 178; skilled slaves, 180; slave unions, 187, 188; crimes against slaves, 195–196; crimes of slaves, 196; treatment of slaves, 199; change of master, 202–203, 204; testamentary manumission, 222, 239; postmortem manumission, 227; concubinal manumission, 228, 229, 230, 231, 239; manumission by adoption, 232; political manumission, 235; contractual manumission, 239; freedman status, 241, 250, 252; ethnicity and manumission, 268;

manumission rate, 272, 276–277, 278, 282, 288; military slaves, 288, 448n31, 467n63; elite slaves, 299, 308–314, 315, 316, 321, 326, 449n32, 451n64; concubinage, 402n107; homosexual slaves, 421n18; sexual relations with slaves, 440n3; manpower needs, 450n37. *See also* Arabs
Israelites, 75
Istanbul, 266
Italian colonies: enslavement of war captives, 114; slave trade, 152; slave plantations, 181
Italy: penal slavery, 128; killing of slaves, 192; freedman status, 243; manumission rate, 274, 296. *See also* Italian colonies; Roman Empire; Romans
Izard, Michel, 38
Izgoi (aliens), 43

Jahore (Malay), 200
Jakhanke (Fulani subgroup), 461n26
Jamaica: postemancipation, 2–3, 5–6; slave naming rituals, 57; kin terms, 65; religion and slavery, 72; enslavement practices, 113, 120; reproductive and mortality rates, 133, 407n3, 477; slave population, 133, 134, 470n77; status inheritance pattern, 146; internal slave trade, 165–166; absentee slave owners, 180; slave unions, 187; concubinal manumission, 231; incidence of manumission, 269; manumission rate, 273, 291; parasitism, 338; age at manumission, 441n11; military slaves, 446n91. *See also* Caribbean; Worthy Park Plantation
Janissaries, 449n34; natal alienation, 8, 311–312; recruitment, 123, 308, 310, 311–312; race, 248; manumission, 313, 450n52; honor, 314
Japan: enslavement by kidnapping, 117; penal slavery, 127; self-enslavement, 130, 131; status inheritance pattern, 141; killing of slaves, 191; invasion of Korea, 289. *See also* Oriental societies
Jefferson, Thomas, 95
Jelgobi (Upper Volta), 83
Jesuits, 427n73
Jews, 40, 145, 196; in slave trade, 152; manumission rates, 275–276
Jihad (warfare), 115

Johnson, Lyman L., 264, 273; on manumission in Buenos Aires, 266, 268, 290
Johnson, Samuel, 94
Jones, J. Walter, 138
Jordan, Winthrop D., 6–7
Judaism: law and judgment ethic, 71; secular and sacred slaves, 72; manumission, 275
Judgment, ethic of, 71, 74, 75
Jurisprudence: Anglo-American, 20, 21; rights and duties, 20–21, 22; and law, 23, 36
Justification in Paul's theology, 70
Justinian (emperor of Rome), 231, 239
Jutland (Denmark), 244
Juvenal, 91, 178, 421n15

Kachin (Burma): rituals of enslavement, 54, 55; manumission by adoption, 233
Kafur (Muslim leader), 316
Kahn-Freund, Otto, 29
Kallikratidas, 111
Kano (Nigeria), 157
Kant, Immanuel, 80
Karebe (Africa), 230
Kasenje (Angola), 53
Kassi tribe (northwest coast of America), 84
K'atorshniki (slaves), 59
Kel Ahaggar (Tuareg group), 139
Kel Gress (Tuareg group), 4, 139
Kentucky, 59
Kenya (East Africa): racism and slavery, 93; runaways and recapture, 94; enslavement by kidnapping, 117
Kerebe (Tanzania): ransom of slaves, 107; enslavement practices, 120; release ceremony, 215
Keynes, Lord, 262
Khoikhoi (South Africa), 111
Kidnapping, enslavement by, 115–122
Killing of slaves: legal sanctions, 190–193; correlates, 193; by third parties, 193–194; by slaves, 196. *See also* Human sacrifice
Kin-based societies: dependence in, 19; naming ceremonies, 55; fictive kinship, 62–65; adoption, 63–64; sexual exploitation, 64–65, 232; religious institutions, 66–76; enslavement methods, 113; treatment of slaves, 174; sex ratio of slaves, 199; manumission ritual, 215; concubinal manumission, 228, 232; adoption, 233. *See also* Matrilineal societies; Patrilineal societies
Kitāb (payment method), 239
Klein, Herbert S., 162, 165, 403n113
Kojève, Alexandre, 98, 99
Kongmin Wang (Korean ruler), 143
Kongo (Zaire), self-enslavement, 130; slave lineages, 136; manumission ceremony, 215; manumission rate, 280
Kopytoff, Igor, 33, 248, 296, 438n27
Koran, 41, 203, 235, 239
Korea: context of slavery, 39, 42; occupational castes, 49, 50, 86; prisoners of war, 108; enslavement by kidnapping, 117; enslavement for tribute, 123; under Mongols, 123, 288, 425n44; debt-slavery, 125, 404n133; penal slavery, 126–127, 405n146; self-enslavement, 130; status inheritance pattern, 143; slave estates, 181; slave peculium, 183, 184; ownership of land, 183, 184; self-defense, 200; political manumission, 235; freedman status, 252, 253, 425n44; manumission rate, 271, 274, 278, 285, 287, 288–289; reenslavement, 287, 289; decline of slavery, 289; under Sejong and Sejo, 289; elite slaves, 299; slave population, 468nn69,70, 469n73. *See also* Oriental societies
Koryŏ period (Korea): context of slavery, 39, 42; moral connotations of slavery, 42; status inheritance pattern, 143; slave estates, 181; slave peculium, 183, 184; freedman status, 425n44; slave population, 468nn69,70
Kruyt, Albert C., 85, 203, 396n46
Kuka market (Chad), 169
Kul (elite slave), 308
Kumasi (Ghana), 462n35
Kungahälla (Sweden), 156
K'unlun slaves (China), 422n20
Kuo Mo-jo, 108
Kush (North Africa), 123
Kuwait, 93
Kwakiutl Indians (northwest coast of America): social death, 39–40; killing of slaves, 191
Kwanyama (Angola), 53
Kwararafa kingdom (Nigeria), 123
Ky, Dang Trinh, 86

Laberius (Roman writer), 77
Labor, free: in slave societies, 33-34; sale of, 366n21
Lactation practices, 133, 162
Lamson, H. D., 370n26
Land: in peculium, 182, 183; in lineage-based societies, 241; and wealth, 371n41
Lang, Olga, 370n26
Langobards (Germanic group), 217
Lares cult, 68, 69, 215-216
Large-scale slave systems, 353-364. See also Slave populations
Lasker, Bruno, 399n75
La Tene culture (Celtic group), 149
Latifundia slaves: free farmers and, 34, 372n49; degradation of, 64; cults, 68-69; demand for, 116; manumission, 282, 284
Latin America: naming rituals, 56-57; branding of runaways, 59; sense of honor, 97; change of master, 202; concubinal manumission, 231; conditional manumission, 245; freedman status, 254, 255; incidence of manumission, 266, 267, 269; manumission rates, 272, 284; nonplantation areas, 427n73; mining areas, 442n35. See also names of individual countries
Lauffer, Siegfried, 36
Laurium mines (Athens), 181, 187, 198, 282
Law: slave versus indentured servant, 9; conceptions of property, 21, 28-32; slave as person, 22-23; confusion with jurisprudence, 23; dominium, 30-32; and tradition, 36; criminal as slave, 43; courts and public opinion, 87; marriage, 186-190; murder of slaves, 190-193; crimes against slaves, 193-196; crimes of slaves, 196-197; treatment of slaves, 198-199; slave as active agent, 199-205; and manumission, 210-211, 222-223, 228; freedman and, 244; wala relationship, 244, 252. See also Chinese law; Hebrew law; Islamic law; Roman law
Leach, Edmund, 323
Leadership, 18
Leeward Islands, 275, 478
Lencman, J. A., 121
Lesbos (Greece), 111
Lesser Antilles, 60
Leviathan (Hobbes), 10

Lévi-Bruhl, Henri, 7, 38, 178
Levine, Lawrence W., 74
Lévi-Strauss, Claude, 18, 19, 323, 325
Levitas (unworthiness), 90-91
Levy, Ernst, 253
Lewis, Monk, 65
Liang ("good" status), 86
Liao (Szechuan), 419n9
Liberation beer, 218
Libya, 157
Liebeschuetz, J. H. W., 216
Lima (Peru), 245, 256, 289
Liminal incorporation, 45-51, 293
Lind, Joan Dyste, 145
Lindkvist, Thomas, 243
Lineage-based societies, see Kin-based societies; Matrilineal societies; Patrilineal societies
Little, Kenneth, 181
Ljufvina (Russian princess), 177
Lolos (China): marks of servitude, 58; racism, 176, 420n10; treatment of slaves, 178; freedman status, 250; manumission rate, 271
Lombards (Italy): status inheritance pattern, 141, 144; granting of sanctuary, 202
Louisiana, 446n94, 483
Lovejoy, Paul, 41, 438n27
Low, Brooke, 147
Lowie, Robert, 18
Lozi (Zambia): marks of servitude, 58; manumission rate, 271; slave population, 347
Luanda (Angola), 466n54
Lundstedt, Anders V., 20
Luvale (Zambia): ransom and warfare, 107; manumission rate, 280

Maccube (slaves), 83, 84
MacDowell, Douglas M., 29
Machiavelli, Niccolo, 18
McIlwraith, Thomas F., 39
Madagascar, 136, 144. See also Merina
Madeira Islands, 285; source of slaves, 116-117; manumission rate, 274, 285
Mafakur (slavery), 45, 46
Magrizi (Arab geographer), 124
Mahabharata (Hindu epic), 320
Mahomet, Sultan, 308
Maimonides, 41

Majorca: manumission rate, 274; slave population, 459n10
Mälar, Lake, 154
Malay: injury to slaves, 196; self-defense in, 200; granting of sanctuary, 201; slave raids, 400n85
Malaysia: internal kidnapping, 117, 118; debt-slavery, 124; racism, 176; crimes against slaves, 195–196
Male concubinage and prostitution, 263
Mali, 249, 271
Malik Ambar, 422
Mālikis (Muslim legal school), 188
Malindi (Kenya), 94
Malinowski, Bronislaw, 211–212
Mamluk kingdom (Egypt), 308, 310, 450n51
Mamluks: status inheritance pattern, 145, 312, 314, 331, 450n51; freedmen, 248, 310–311; favored status, 299; recruitment methods, 310; mawālī, 310–311; honor, 313; homosexual use, 421n18
Mana (power), 51
Manchu (Manchuria): absenteeism, 180, 424n34; manumission rate, 271
Manning, Patrick, 162
Manumissio censu, 219, 235, 236
Manumission: sacral, 67–68, 237–238; of penal slaves, 127; and social consequences, 132, 133; meaning, 209–214, 340–341, 431n1; conceptual problem, 211; gift-exchange theory, 211–214, 215, 217, 218, 243, 294; origins, 214, 340; release ceremonies, 214–219, 237, 450n52; modes of release, 219–239, 294; post-mortem, 219–228, 433n45; testamentary, 222–223, 225–226, 227, 237, 239, 435n73; concubinal, 228–232, 239, 251, 261, 282; by marriage, 228, 252; by adoption, 232–234, 238; political, 234–236, 287; by collusive litigation, 236–237; skills of slave and, 242, 254–255; conditional and unconditional, 245–246; selective, 246; somatic theory, 268–269; incentives, 285, 444n65; military, 287, 289–293; mass, 288, 289, 290, 292; of janissaries, 313; by death of master, 433n41
Manumission rates: and demand for slaves, 132, 281–282; of children, 145–146, 267, 269; and size of slave population, 255; and freedman status in society, 256, 257, 277–278, 294, 295–296; and economic conditions, 259, 279, 281–287, 295, 434n58, 465n52; variables, 262–263, 264, 272–277, 278–279, 295: gender and, 263–264, 279; parenthood and, 263, 264; race and, 264, 268, 272, 273, 277–278; age and, 264, 266–267, 441n11; form of manumission and, 264; level of skills and, 264–266, 270; means of acquisition and, 267; ethnicity and, 267–268; rural versus urban, 269–271, 274, 282–284; societal, 271–278, 294–295; from Murdock's world sample, 271–272; level of miscegenation and, 272–273; in modern slave societies, 273; religion and, 273–277, 282; in large-scale societies, 274–275; domestic assimilation and, 279; in lineage- and kin-based societies, 279–280; domestic exclusiveness, 280–281; incentive payment and, 283–284; in plantation systems, 284–285, 286; military affairs and, 287–293, 295
Manumissio vindicta, 236, 238, 239, 435n73
Maori (New Zealand): pollution norms, 51; enslavement of war captives, 113, manumission rate, 271
Margi (Nigeria): liminal incorporation, 45–46; occupational castes, 49; ransom and warfare, 107; status inheritance pattern, 137; killing of slaves, 191
Marginality, *see* Liminal incorporation
Marks of servitude, 51–62, 128, 215, 381n94
Maroons (Jamaica), 446n91
Marriage, 427n56; and caste stratification, 49; to slaves, 131, 409n25, 411n68; bride and dowry payments, 166–167, 187, 188; and treatment of slaves, 189–190; religious sanction, 189; manumission by, 228, 229, 252; endogamous, 280–281; formariage, 411n68. *See also* Bride-price; Intermarriage
Martinique, 275, 480
Marx, Karl: on power and domination, 2–3; on forms of social life, 17, 20; on concealment of power in capitalism, 18, 19; on wage labor versus wage slave, 25, 370n30; on freedom through work and labor, 98, 99; on equal exchange, 213

Maryland: status inheritance pattern, 138, 409n25; manumission pattern, 292; runaways, 447n97

Mascarene Islands (Indian Ocean): enslavement of war captives, 114; slave plantations, 181; concubinal manumission, 231; freedman status, 257; manumission rate, 274, 285

Massacre, 106, 107, 120

Master: change of, 201, 202–205; death of, 224, 226; defined, 334–335

Master-slave relationship: and domination, 2, 336; maintenance, 3–4, 205; intimacy, 12; personal relations, 12, 13; and power, 18–19; symbolic control, 37; private and public determinants, 172; intrinsic factors, 173–181; human variables, 206; after manumission, 240–247; in freedman status, 247, 249, 250, 253, 294; with elite slaves, 307, 308; versus patron-client relationship, 309–310. See also Conditions of slavery; Human parasitism

Materialism, and slavery, 11, 19

Matrilineal circumvention, 279–280

Matrilineal societies: adoption, 63–64; status inheritance patterns, 136, 138, 139, 185, 464n44; marriage, 187; manumission, 229, 272–273, 279–280; freedmen, 241, 251

Mauritania (West Africa), 159

Mauritius (Mascarene Islands): enslavement of war captives, 114; freedman status, 257; slave clothing, 381n91; slave population, 467n62

Maurya period (India), 140

Mauss, Marcel, 211; on honor, 78; on ideology of prestation, 212–214; on manumission rituals, 218, 236–237

Mawālī (freedmen), 310, 311, 436n1

Mayan (slave), 233

Mbanza Manteke (Kongo): status inheritance pattern, 136; release ceremony, 215; domestic slaves, 464n41

Mecca, 150

Medieval period: social death, 39; pagans as enemies, 41; rituals of enslavement, 52; branding of slaves, 59; kidnapping, 116; slave trade, 152–157; killing of slaves, 192; manumission, 230; freedman status, 243, 250; incidence of manumission, 268; manumission rates, 275, 278, 282, 284, 285, 288, 296

Medina (Saudi Arabia), 150

Mediterranean area: enslavement practices, 114, 115, 116, 117; child exposure, 129; slave trade, 150–152, 154, 157–158, 160, 170–171; slave plantations, 181; freedman status, 243

Meillassoux, Claude, 33, 38, 148–149

Melior condicio (inheritance of higher status), 144

Ménage, V. L., 313

Mende (Sierra Leone): marks of servitude, 59; nature of honor, 83; old slaves, 88; status inheritance pattern, 136; bridewealth, 167, slaves as money, 168; household slaves, 175, 419n4; tenant slaves, 181; slave unions, 187; concubinal manumission, 230; freedman status, 248; manumission rate, 271; slave population, 462nn31,34

Mendelsohn, Isaac, 109, 234

Mepone (change of master), 203

Merina (Madagascar): status inheritance pattern, 136, 144, 280; manumission rate, 274, 280–281

Mesopotamia, 299; slaves as foreigners, 40, 42; sources of slaves, 44, 403n108; marks of servitude, 62; sense of honor, 97; prisoners of war, 107, 109–110, 395n26; piracy, 115; sexual bias in enslavement, 121; debt-slavery, 125, 404n131; sale of slaves, 175; slave unions, 187; concubinal manumission, 230; manumission by adoption, 234; temple slavery, 238; freedman status, 253; defining slavery in, 371n39. See also Babylonia; Iraq; Third Dynasty of Ur

Metics, 281, 302

Métraux, Alfred, 52

Mexico: naming rituals, 56–57; social reproduction, 133; status inheritance pattern, 146; manumission, 245, 275; hacienda farms, 255; economics of slavery, 471n86. See also Aztec Indians

Middle Ages: abolishment of slavery, 44; penal slavery, 44, 127–128; rise of Protestantism, 72; enslavement methods, 114; church, 189, 201; concubinal manumission, 231; wala relationship, 243; freedmen and descendants, 249; manumission rates, 282; sources of slaves, 398n71; marriage of serfs, 411n68. See also Medieval period

Middle East: slave trade, 150; change of master, 202; manumission modes, 228

Miers, Suzanne, 33, 248, 296, 438n27

Migiurtini Somali (Somalia), 137, 434n50

Miles, J. C., 230

Military capacity, 33

Military manumission, 287, 289–293

Military slavery: origins, 39–40, 467n63; manumission and, 288–293; racial aspects, 446nn83,94; recruitment of elites, 448n31

Mill, John Stuart, 10

Miller, J. C., 136

Minas Gerais (Brazil), 483; branding of slaves, 59; internal slave trade, 165; manumission rate, 289–290; mortality rate, 442n35

Ming dynasty (China): eunuchs, 315, 324, 325; role of free women, 325, 326

Mining areas: manumission rate, 270, 289–290; mortality rate, 442n35

Mintz, Sidney W., 25, 370n30

Miscegenation, 61, 146, 255, 261; and manumission rate, 261, 272–273

Mitamura, Taisuke, 315, 324, 325

Mitchell, J. C., 280

Mithras cult, 69

Moluccas (Spice Islands), 99, 231

Mombasa (Kenya), 94

Money, slaves as, 167–171

Mongols, 123, 288, 425n44

Monteil, Charles V., 249

Moors, 145, 152

Moral connotations of slavery, 42, 47–48, 455n3

Moral responsibility of slave, 22

Moramachi period (Japan), 117

Morocco (North Africa): piracy, 117; slave trade, 157; manumission rate, 277, 443n49; boy-markets, 421n18; slave populations, 460n15

Morrow, G. R., 87, 140, 192, 194

Mortality rates: and enslavement practices, 132, 133, 397n55; in slave trade, 159, 162, 163; in slave populations, 417n64, 465n51; in mining areas, 442n35

Morton, Roger F., 93

Mossi (West Africa), 60

Mother-surrogates, 50

Moyd, Olin P., 75

Mozambique, 160, 228, 466n55

Mubika (slave), 136

Muhammad (prophet), 227, 232, 316, 451n61

Muhammad-el-Fadhl (ruler of Bagirmi), 316

Muhammad Kurra, 316

Mui-tsai institution, 129, 370n26

Mukataba (slave), 239

Mükâtebe system, 266

Mulattoes, 61, 62, 268

Murad (Turkish leader), 316

Murder, *see* Killing of slaves

Murdock, George P., 139, 345

Murdock world sample, 199, 271, 272, 350–352

Muscovy, 43–44

Muslim East Africa, *see* East Africa

Muslim Spain: enslavement of war captives, 114; slave trade, 152, 154; tenant slaves, 181; manumission rate, 274

Muslim traders, 154, 159, 168. *See also* Arabs; Islamic societies

Mutilations, 59

Mutualism, 336–337, 453n1, 455n3

Nagaoundere (Cameroon), 274

Namath, Joe, 24

Names: servile, 55, 380n75; in kin-based societies, 55; surnames, 56–58; following manumission, 56; African, 56, 380n80; of saints, 57–58; features denoted, 58; of slave wives, 189

Naming ceremonies, 53, 54–55

Narcissus, 301, 307

Natal alienation: and heritage of ancestors, 5–6; use of term, 7–8; perpetual nature, 9; flexibility, 32; symbolization, 38; of native populations, 111; janissaries and, 311–312

Natality, restoration of, 235

Ndembu (Angola), 37

Ndizogu (Nigeria), 138

Nduwanga (Mende slave group), 83

Near East: rituals of enslavement, 55; marks of servitude, 58–59; prisoners of war, 107, 110; piracy, 115; penal slavery, 126; exposure and sale of infants, 129; status inheritance patterns, 144–146; slave trade, 150; slaves as dowry, 167; slaves as money, 168; tenant slavery, 181, 425n41; slave peculium, 184; killing of slaves, 191; concu-

Near East (*continued*)
   binal manumission, 231; freedman sta-
   tus, 241, 253; manumission rate, 284
Negroes: prejudice against, 176, 179, 250,
   421n16; free, 259. *See also* Black
   Americans
Nepal: slavery and caste, 51; granting of
   sanctuary, 201
Nero (emperor of Rome), 307, 308, 317,
   326
Netherlands, 44. *See also* Dutch
New England, 278, 446n94
New World, *see* Americas
New York, 138
New Zealand, *see* Maori
Nias (Indonesia), 39
Nicomedes of Bithynia, 123
Nieboer, H. J.: on defining slavery, 21,
   369n18; and treatment of slaves, 181,
   402n102
Nietzsche, Friedrich Wilhelm, 78
Nigeria: nature of honor, 82, 97; internal
   kidnapping, 117-118; treatment of
   slaves, 175; political eunuchs, 316. *See
   also* Aboh; Hausa; Ibos; Margi; Tiv
Nikaya, Majjhima, 207
Nkundu (Zaire): ransom and prisoners,
   107; slaves through bridewealth, 167;
   concubinal manumission, 230; manumission rate, 271
Noburu, Niida, 141
Nonslave persons: sale of, 23-26; work
   ethic in large-scale slave systems, 33-
   34
Nootka (northwest coast of America): rituals of enslavement, 55, 380n79; postmortem manumission, 222
Nordic peoples: slave trade, 154; freedman status, 243-244
Norsemen, 140, 156
Norsus (Lolos), 468n67
North Africa: enslavement of war captives, 107, 114; Barbary pirates, 117;
   slave trade, 157; Christian captives,
   402n107
North America, southeastern, 107
Northern dynasties (China): prisoners of
   war, 109; freedman status, 252
Northup, Solomon, 392n121
Northwest coast Indians: marks of servitude, 60; hereditary slavery, 84; treatment of prisoners, 107; enslavement of

war captives, 113; status inheritance
   patterns, 136; slave trade, 149, 156; killing of slaves, 191; potlatch ceremony,
   214, 222; sacrifice and manumission,
   221-222; manumission by adoption,
   234; parasitism, 337; escapees/return-
   ees, 432n15. *See also* Kwakiutl Indians;
   Nootka
Norway: nature of honor, 82; slave trade,
   152, 154; acquisition of slaves, 157; self-
   defense in, 200; manumission ritual,
   216; wala relationship, 244; freedman
   status, 249; economic role of slaves,
   386n18
Nubians, 123-124
Nursemaids, 50, 88
Nwachukwu-Ogedengbe, K., 233
Nyinba (Nepal), 201

Obedience, ethic of, 74, 76
Obsequium (claims on freedmen), 242
Odysseus, 87, 121
Odyssey (Homer), 121, 230
Oikogeneis (house-born slave), 175
Okigwi (Nigeria), 138
Olivecrona, Karl, 20
Operae (claims on freedmen), 242, 244,
   283
Oriental societies: inheritable slave status,
   9; sense of honor, 86; prisoners of war,
   107; penal slavery, 126-127; exposure
   of infants, 129; slave estates, 181; treat-
   ment of slaves, 199. *See also* China;
   Japan; Korea
Origo, Iris, 201
Ormerod, Henry, 115, 116
Ornaments, as marks of servitude, 58
Osterweis, Rollin G., 94-95
Osu (Ibo cult slaves), 238
Otho (emperor of Rome), 307
Ottoman Empire: piracy, 117; enslave-
   ment for tribute, 123; recruitment of
   slaves, 248, 312; elite slaves, 299; janis-
   saries, 308-309, 313, 449n34
Ottoman Turks, 178
Outcastes, 48-50, 435n81
Outsider status, 7
Ownership: concepts, 20; and property,
   21-22, 28, 371n43; absolute, 28, 29-30,
   31-32
Oxenstierna, Eric, 169
Oyo (Nigeria), 123

Paekchŏng (Korean outcastes), 50
Paganism, 41, 47, 226, 227–228
Palaestra (character in *The Rope*), 12
Palatine slavery, 14
Palestine, 175. *See also* Hebrews
Pallas, 301, 307
Panama: treatment of slaves, 113; slave population, 471n82
Papoulia, Basilike, 311–312, 449n34
Paramonē (down payment), 238, 239, 282
Parasitism, *see* Human parasitism
Pardos (of mixed parentage), 269
Parenthood, and manumission, 263–264
Pascal, Blaise, 78
Pastoral societies: master-slave relationship, 174–175, 180; manumission rate, 277
Paternalism, 93–94, 339
Patrilineal societies: status inheritance patterns, 137, 138, 139; peculium, 186; freedmen, 241, 251; manumission rate, 279
Paul (apostle), 70, 71, 306; on redeemed man and God, 70, 76; on Christ's crucifixion, 71, 74, 75; on manumission, 227
Pawning of persons, 124, 125
Peculium: defined, 182–184; disposal of, 184–185, 210; recognition of, 185–186, 192; and crimes of slaves, 197; and level of skills, 254, 266, 267; prostitution and, 263; and manumission rates, 270, 283
Peloponnesian wars, 114, 115, 288
Penal slavery: as source of slaves, 44, 126–129, 405n146, 419n9; manumission and, 127; demand for labor and, 378n43
Penal systems, 43
Peons, 25, 26
Perak (Malaysia): slave raids, 118, 400n85; debt-slavery, 125
Perdue, Theda, 46–47
Persian Gulf, 150
Persians: enslavement patterns, 110; elite slaves, 299, 315, 316
Persian wars, 115, 288
Personal characteristics, 85, 87; and master-slave relationship, 176, 177. *See also* Ethnic factors; Race
Personal relations, levels, 12, 13
Peru: slave populations, 133; freedman status, 245, 255, 256, 289; Jesuit haciendas, 427n73

Peter the Great, 43
Petrochitos, Nicholas, 90
Petronius, 305–306
Phaniscus (character in *The Ghost*), 12
Pharaonic Egypt: internal source of slavery, 42; rituals of enslavement, 55; marks of servitude, 60; slaves as dowry, 167; concubinal manumission, 230; freedman status, 253; prisoners of war, 403. *See also* Egypt
Philby, Harry St. John Briger, 92–93
Phillips, U. B., 335, 369n22
Pipes, Daniel, 314, 448n31, 449n32
Piracy, *see* Kidnapping
Pitt-Rivers, Julian, 79, 80
Plantation slavery, 46; initiating rituals, 54; economic success, 93, 456n4; stereotypes of slaves, 96; enslavement methods, 116, 117; treatment of slaves, 173–174, 181, 190; manumission rate, 284–285
Plato, 8; on recognition of power, 35; on honor and pride, 81, 90; on inheritance status, 140; on timocratic character, 386n14
Plautus, 12, 40, 381n93, 398n70
Pliny the Elder, 339
Polanyi, Karl, 168
Polis (slaves), 66, 238
Political eunuchism: power relationships, 315; in Byzantium, 315, 317–319, 321–330, 331; in China, 315–316, 318, 327; in Persia, 315, 316; in Turkey, 316; in Africa, 316; sociological aspect, 319–320; in Tudor court, 330–331; among the Yoruba, 451n72
Political manumission, 234–236, 287
Pollution theory, with cult slaves, 322–323, 325, 327, 331, 436n83
Popo (West Africa), 123
Population decline, and slave trade, 157. *See also* Slave populations
Portuguese: kidnapping by, 117, 119; slave trade, 150, 160, 163; manumission rate, 289; "abolition" of slavery, 466n54
Postmortem manumission, 219–228, 433n45
Poteidaians (Greece), 111
Potestas (authority), 188, 189
Potlatch ceremony, 191; honor aspect, 84, 220; prestation in, 214; manumission aspect, 222; assigning new name, 380n79

Poverty: and debt-servitude, 124–126; and sale of children, 129, 130; and self-enslavement, 130–131

Power: relationships, 1, 2, 26, 307, 308, 332; honor and, 10–11, 13, 78, 79, 84, 87; and property concept, 17–21; ritualization, 19, 368n8; personalistic idiom, 18–19, 27–28, 32, 33; materialistic idiom, 19, 28–32; origins, 26; need for recognition, 35; arrogance of, 36; symbols, 37; and total domination, 332–333

Powerlessness, 2, 4, 5, 306

Prestation, 212–213, 214, 215

Prestige ranking, 247

Price of slaves, 163–164, 166, 168, 283, 441n13

Prisoners, *see* Criminals

Prisoners of war: criminal status, 42, 43; and slave status, 43; as source of slaves, 44, 106, 107–115, 119–120, 170, 400n90, 403n113; alternatives to enslavement, 106–107; treatment, 106, 108–109; ransom and exchange, 107; as source of income, 107–108; impressment, 109; in kin-based societies, 113; in large-scale systems, 113–114; sexual bias, 121–122; in agriculture, 395n26. *See also* Warfare

Private slaves, 43

Property: concept of, 17–21, 369n22, 371n43, 373n54; Roman conception, 21, 28–32; Anglo-American conception, 21, 22, 369n22; and slavery, 21–27, 28, 369n21; legal aspects, 28–32; absolute, 29, 32; feudal notions, 30

Prostitutes, 129, 400n85

Prostitution, 177, 263, 370n29

Protestantism, 72, 73, 74

Pubic hair, shorn, 60, 62

Public slaves, branding, 59

Puerto Rico, 187

Pulaaku (stereotype ideal), 84

Pulleyblank, E. G., 86, 108, 127

Punic wars, 288

Punishment: threat of, 3; forms, 59; and preservation of honor, 89–90, 128; and degradation, 93–94; enslavement as, 126–129; as social control, 206, 285; incentives versus, 339–340; sale of slave as, 419n4. *See also* Capital punishment

Purity and Danger (Douglas), 322

Qoran, *see* Koran

Quashee (slave term), 91, 338

Queensberry, Duchess of, 422n21

Rabinowitz, Jacob, 253

Raboteau, Albert, 73, 74

Race: and slave status, 58, 61, 254, 420n14; and range of color, 61; and master-slave relationship, 176–179; and manumission rates, 264, 268, 272, 273, 294; and recruitment of elite slaves, 310; and status, 382n106, 421n19, 441n18. *See also* Miscegenation

Racism, 41, 177–178, 420n14

Radbruch, Gustav, 128

Ransom, 107, 125, 130, 178, 380n79

Rape, 82, 193, 206. *See also* Sexual exploitation

Rapoport, Anatol, 336, 453n3

Rattray, Robert S., 27–28, 136, 185

Rawick, George P., 3

Raziya, Queen (of India), 422n20

Rebel, The (Camus), 204

Rechtsverhältnis (rights relationship), 36

Reconciliation, 70

Redemption, 70, 75; rituals, 214–219

Red Sea area, 116, 150

Reenslavement: to a god, 72; and retaliation, 94; from freedman status, 241, 245; economic conditions and, 287; warfare and, 289, 292

Religion and symbolism: and intrusive conception of slavery, 43–44, 45; in slavery and manumission, 66–68; cults, 68–69; emperor worship, 69, 70; salvation and redemption, 70, 72, 75; Christ's crucifixion, 71, 74, 75, 227; Catholic dualism, 72, 74, 75–76; conversion techniques, 72–73, 276–277; fundamentalism, 73–75, 76, 260; in enslavement practices, 93, 107; and slave marriage, 189; and killing of slaves, 192; and testamentary manumission, 222, 224, 226; and freedman status, 260; and manumission rate, 273–277, 282; in eunuchism, 323, 325; Exodus myth, 385n160

Renegades, 277, 443n49

Renner, Karl, 29

Repp, R. C., 313

Reproduction: rates, 3; as wealth, 33; biological and social, 132–135, 170, 408n4

Residence of slave, and master-slave relationship, 174–175
Reunion (Mascarene Islands), 257
Reward: reinforcement, 3; freedom as, 260, 270, 340, 444n65; treatment as, 339
Rhodes (Greece), 152
Rice, symbolism of, 216
Richard II (character from Shakespeare), 78
Riesman, Paul, 83–84
Rights, in jurisprudence, 20–21, 22
Rigspula, 177
Rigveda, 86
Rio de Janeiro, 165
Rites of passage, 53, 216
Ritual(s): of enslavement, 8–9, 38, 51–62; as symbolic control, 37, 375n6; religious, 66–76; of initiation, 53–54, 191; of gift exchange, 212–213, 236–237; manumission, 214–219, 237; of adoption, 234
Rodrigues (Mascarene Islands), 257
Roman Empire, 70, 76, 122, 144, 152, 224, 225
Roman law: property, 28–30, 32, 373n54; role of slavery, 29; doctrine of dominium, 30–32, 311; intrusive conception of slave, 40; asylum for slaves, 69; principle of privilege, 89, 195; exposure of children, 130; status inheritance, 139; marriage, 189; Twelve Tables, 195, 222; postliminium, 215–216
Romans: social alienation of slaves, 7; conception of ownership and property, 21, 22, 28–30, 31–32, 371n41; sale of children, 24; nonslave persons, 24, 26, 36; socioeconomic order, 28–30, 372n49; and manumission, 30–31, 58, 127, 210, 211, 215, 219, 229, 231; free laborers, 34; etymology of "slave," 40; rituals of enslavement, 54, 55, 58, 380n75; Greek slaves, 55, 89, 90, 91, 92, 174; manumission rate, 58, 271, 274, 282, 283, 284, 288, 296; and religion, 66–67, 68–70, 74, 76; nature of honor, 77, 88–89, 92, 304, 306; value of punishment, 89–90; attitude toward Greeks, 90, 91; enslavement of war captives, 107, 113, 396n52; enslavement of populations, 111–112; enslavement by kidnapping, 116, 121; killing of slaves, 121, 192; economy, 122–123, 403n114; debt-

slavery, 125; penal slavery, 126, 127, 128; political manumission, 127, 219, 235–236, 249, 253; child exposure, 130; slave populations, 133–134, 402n105, 408n4; status inheritance pattern, 139–141, 142, 143, 144, 146, 409n25, 411n68; slave trade, 152; internal trade, 164–165; slaves as dowry, 167; Greek tutors, 174; slaves living apart, 175; racial differences, 177–178; skilled slaves, 180; slave peculium, 184, 263; slave unions, 187, 189; crimes against slaves, 195; crimes of slaves, 196, 197, 241; granting of sanctuary, 201; change of master, 202; freedman status, 216, 241, 242, 243, 248, 249, 252, 253, 305, 306, 307–308; testamentary manumission, 222–223, 224, 227, 238–239, 435n73; concubinal manumission, 231; manumission by adoption, 234; collusive manumission, 236, 435n71; reenslavement, 241; wala relationship, 242, 243, 252, 253; incidence of manumission, 267, 269; military slaves, 288; familia Caesaris, 299, 300–308, 319; upper class, 304; imperial slaves, 332; latifundia slaves, *see* Latifundia slaves; parasitic nature of slaveholding, 339; masterless slave, 366n13; sale of children, 370n27; racial prejudice, 420n14
Roman Spain, 288
Rope, The (Plautus), 12
Ross, Alf, 20, 21
Rousseau, Jean Jacques, 2
Rout, Leslie, 290
Royal families, 141
Royal slaves, 195
Ruffin, Thomas, 3–4
Runaways, 59, 94, 270, 432n15, 447n97
Runciman, Steven, 319
Rural slaves, 242; manumission rate, 269–270, 282, 284–285
Russell, J. C., 156–157
Russia: context of slavery, 39, 42, 44; means of enslavement, 42–43, 45; rituals of enslavement, 55; marks of servitude, 59, 60; penal slavery, 128; self-enslavement, 130; slave trade, 152; slave peculium, 183; elite slaves, 299; human sacrifice, 428n84
Russian Orthodox Church, 43–44
Rustici (agricultural slaves), 270

Ryan, T. C., 224
Rycaut, Paul, 308

Sab group (Somali outcastes), 49, 50, 137, 195
Sacral manumission, 237–238
Sacrifice, see Human sacrifice
Safawid dynasty (Persia), 316
Sahara: master-slave relationship, 36; enslavement of war captives, 114; slave trade routes, 157–160; manumission, 282
Sahel, 252, 277, 282
Sahlins, Marshall, 19, 28, 212, 213
Saint Domingue (Hispaniola), 249–250, 275, 481
Sale of children, 129, 370nn26,27
Sale of nonslave persons, 23–26
Sale of slaves, 23, 175, 419n4. See also Price of slaves; Slave trade
Salvation: religions of, 70; as reenslavement to a god, 72; and manumission, 225
Samas (sun-god), 218
Sambo ideology, 91, 96, 207, 338
Sanctuary, 201–202
Sangir (Indonesia), 118
Santiago (Cape Verde), 274, 285
Santiago del Cobre (Cuba), 290
São Paulo: demand for slaves, 165; manumission rate, 290
São Tomé (West Africa): manumission rate, 274, 465n52; slave population, 465nn51,52,53
Saracens (Spain), 145, 152
Sardinia, 152, 282
Sarhed (honor payment), 82
Saria (holy law), 312
Saudi Arabia: honor in, 92–93; slave trade, 159; change of master, 202–203, 204. See also Arabs
Sawyer, P. H., 154, 156
Scandinavians: law and authority relationships, 36; slave trade, 152–153, 154–156, 160; slave population, 157; slave stereotypes, 176–177; manumission ritual, 217; manumission by adoption, 233; freedman status, 243–244, 245; manumission rate, 278; economic role of slaves, 386n18
Schlaifer, Robert, 87
Schrenck, Leopold von, 229–230

Schternberg, Lev, 233
Self-blame, 12
Self-defense, 200–202
Self-enslavement, 130–131
Sellin, J. Thorsten, 127, 378n43
Semenov, I. I., 109, 404n131
Sena (Mozambique): concubinal manumission, 228; sexual exploitation, 230; freedman status, 247
Seneca, 92, 339
Senegambia (West Africa): enslavement by warfare, 119; status inheritance pattern, 147; slave trade, 160; manumission, 268; slave population, 461n26. See also Wolof
Separation, fear of, 6
Sereer (Gambia): change of master, 202; postmortem manumission, 222
Serfs, 25, 26, 128, 411n68
Servitude: term, 7; hereditary, 9–10; voluntary, 27–28. See also Debt-servitude
Servus vicarius (slave of a slave), 184
Sex ratios: in slave populations, 199; and freedman's acceptance, 250; and manumission, 255
Sexual behavior: of wives of slaves, 6; and caste, 49; adultery, 128, 188; in master-slave relationship, 173; legal sanctions, 187–190; extramarital, 228; of eunuchs, 326; of Muslim women, 440n3
Sexual bias: in enslavement practices, 120–122, 129, 403n108, 441n18; in treatment of slaves, 179; in manumission, 228–232, 239; and freedman status, 240, 251
Sexual exploitation: of concubines, 50, 229, 230; in kin-based societies, 64–65, 232; rape, 82, 193, 206; in developed slave systems, 85, 88; and marriage, 189; legal restraints, 200; and manumission, 229, 230, 232; sanction of, 260–261
Sexual values, and freedman status, 259, 260, 261
Seychelles (Indian Ocean), 257
Shakespeare, William, 78
Sharp, William F., 273
Shaw, Stanford, 309
Shell, Robert, 268, 273, 276
Sherbro (Sierre Leone): punishment of slaves, 128, 429n102; status inheritance pattern, 146–147; tenant slaves, 181; granting of sanctuary, 202

Shild (Danish hero), 47
Shin, Susan, 42, 289
Shorn head, 60–61, 128, 215
Siberia: penal slavery, 128; self-enslave-
   ment, 131. *See also* Gilyaks
Sicilians (Italy): enslavement of, 111; en-
   slavement by, 114; slave trade, 152; ten-
   ant slaves, 181; manumission rate, 274,
   276
Sidam province (Ethiopia), 316
Siegel, Bernard J., 188, 253
Sierre Leone, *see* Sherbro
Sirqu (Babylonia), 145
Sjaelland (Denmark), 244
Skills, level of: and master-slave relation-
   ship, 179–180; and freedman status,
   254–255; and manumission, 264–266,
   267, 269, 270, 439n39
Skin color, *see* Race
Slave: origin of term, 40, 156, 250,
   406n172; stereotypes, 338; origin of
   concept, 376n17
Slave breeding, 427n73
Slave markets, 40, 459n12
Slave populations: mass enslavement,
   110–112; biological reproduction, 132,
   408n4, 414n30; social reproduction, 132;
   birth/death rates, 132, 133; decline,
   133; and demand for slaves, 157; size,
   and treatment of slaves, 180, 198–199,
   206; sex ratios, 199; type, and manumission, 255; and freedman status,
   259–260; of large-scale slave systems,
   353–364
Slave raids, 281, 282, 399nn75,78, 400n85
Slave revolts, 259–260, 291, 465n52
Slavery: constituent elements, 1–14; defining, 13, 21, 369n18, 371n39; internal relations, 17–101, 296; ownership concept,
   21–27; idioms of power and, 27–32;
   contradictions, 32–34, 296; terms for,
   40; and culture, 84–85; and timocracy,
   94–95; dialectics, 97–101; institutional
   process, 104–171; versus debt-servitude,
   124; condition of, 172–208; as relation
   of domination, 334–335; as relation of
   parasitism, 335–336
Slave status: need for new persons, 3; outsider, 7; inheritability, 9; with adoption,
   233; permanent, 280, 404n134; in warfare, 291–292; ambiguity, 425n44. *See
   also* Status inheritance patterns

Slave trade, 113; internal means, 118–119,
   164–166; external means, 148–164;
   intra-African, 149, 156, 160, 399n78,
   403n113; medieval European, 149,
   152–157; volume, 150, 152, 156–157,
   159, 160; Indian Ocean, 150–151; Black
   Sea, 150–152, 153; Mediterranean,
   150–152, 154, 157–158, 160, 170–171;
   routes, 152–154, 157–158, 159; Saharan,
   157–159, 160; Atlantic, 159–164, 165,
   286; mortality rates, 159, 162, 163;
   demography, 160, 162; price of slaves,
   163–164, 441n11; interregional, 165,
   166, 286; abolition, 165, 286
Slavs: Viking raids on, 116; self-enslavement, 131; trading, 155, 156; origin
   of term, 250, 406n172; manumission,
   268
Smith, M. G., 41
Snowden, Frank M., Jr., 177
Social alienation, 7
Social death: conceptions, 38; intrusive
   and extrusive modes, 39–45; as liminal
   state, 46; irrevocability, 215
Social relations, of slaves, 6
Sodomy, 263
Sokolowski, F., 237
Sokoto (Nigeria): enslavement for tribute,
   123; treatment of slaves, 199; manumis-
   sion rate, 274
Solon, 125
Somali (Somalia): occupational castes, 49;
   marks of servitude, 60; honor among,
   84; status inheritance pattern, 137–138,
   141, 409n25, 410n27; absentee slave
   owners, 180; slave unions, 188; crimes
   against slaves, 195; manumission patterns, 228, 235, 249; freedman status,
   249; manumission rate, 271
Somaliland (East Africa), 150
Somatic theory of manumission, 268–269
Sorel, Georges, 3
Sosia (character in *Amphitryo*), 12
South Africa: enslavement methods, 111,
   117, 119; status inheritance patterns,
   138; slave trade, 160; tenant slaves, 181;
   manumission, 231, 232; freedman status, 245, 246, 254, 255, 256, 439n50;
   architecture, 255; racism, 256, 383n107;
   incidence of manumission, 263, 266,
   268, 269; manumission rate, 273, 276,
   285

South America: marks of servitude, 60;
absenteeism, 423n33. *See also* names of
individual countries

South Carolina: treatment of slaves, 6;
master-slave relationship, 12; slave
naming rituals, 56, 57, 58, 380n80;
branding of slaves, 59; status inheritance pattern, 144; freedman status,
246; regulation of clothing, 381n91;
slave population, 475n141, 483. *See also*
U.S. South

Southeast Asia: caste in, 49; enslavement
by kidnapping, 117, 399n75

Spain: enslavement of Europeans, 44; enslavement of war captives, 114; piracy,
116; penal slavery, 128; status inheritance patterns, 141, 144, 145–146; slave
trade, 152, 154, 160; tenant slaves, 181;
slave peculium, 184, 192–193; killing of
slaves, 192; crimes against slaves, 196;
crimes of slaves, 197; change of master,
202; contractual manumission, 239;
freedman status, 243; manumission
rate, 270, 274, 283, 284, 288

Spanish Caribbean: decline of slave population, 113; enslavement methods, 114,
120; manumission, 290

Sparta: enslavement of Athenians, 111;
helotry, 112; timocracy, 386n14. *See
also* Greeks

Spores, 317, 326

Sports, professional, 24–26, 371n35

Spranger, Peter P., 398n70

Starkey, David, 330, 331

Starr, Chester G., 89

Statistical methods, 345–349

Status, *see* Freedman status; Slave status

Status inheritance patterns, 113, 170; and
social reproduction patterns, 134–135,
170; Ashanti pattern, 135–137; of nonslaves, 136; Somali pattern, 137–138,
141, 409n25, 410n27; Tuareg pattern,
136, 138–139, 145; Roman pattern,
139–141, 143, 146, 409n25, 411n68;
Chinese pattern, 141–144, 145, 409n25;
Near East pattern, 144–146; Sherbro
pattern, 146–147; with adoption, 233;
race and, 277–278; ghilmān and, 312.
See also Hereditary slavery

Stearns, Robert E., 84

Steiner, Franz, 19

Stigma, of slavery, 247, 251, 252, 253, 257,
294

Structuralism, 323

Struve, V. V., 109

Submission, 77, 78, 95

Sub-Saharan Africa: nature of honor, 82;
enslavement of war captives, 114; incidence of manumission, 268. *See also*
South Africa

Subsistence mode: and treatment of
slaves, 181; and peculium, 186

Sudan: marks of servitude, 58; internal
kidnapping, 117, 400n90; slave trade,
149, 169; treatment of slaves, 175;
freedman status, 252; manumission
rate, 277, 282

Suetonius, 307

Sugar plantations, 116, 117

Sulaymān Khan (sultan), 313

Sumer, 109. *See also* Mesopotamia

Surinam (South America): freedman status, 255, 257; manumission rate, 275,
278, 285, 287

Suzuki, Peter, 39

Swansea (Wales), 154

Sweden: status inheritance pattern, 140,
145; slave trade, 154, 156; testamentary
manumission, 226; concubinal manumission, 230; manumission rate, 276;
economic role of slaves, 386n18

Symbiosis, 335, 453n1

Symbolic control, authority as, 36–38

Syria, 316

Syrus, Pubilius, 77–78

Taboos, 129

Tacitus, 305, 306

Tallensi (Ghana): fictive kinship system,
63; manumission rate, 271

Tandojai (guardian of the dead), 221

T'ang dynasty (China), 315

Tanzania, *see* Kerebe

Tapu (Maori laws), 51

Tattoos, 58–59

Tax payment, enslavement for, 122–
125

Temple slavery, 49, 237–238

Tenant farming, 181, 199, 425n41

Terence, 40

Testamentary manumission, 237, 239,
435n73; origins, 222–223; salvation and,
225–226, 227

Thailand: enslavement by kidnapping, 117, 399n75; debt-slavery, 125; king's slaves, 174; killing of slaves, 191–192
Theodore (archbishop of Canterbury), 192
Third Dynasty of Ur: slaves as foreigners, 40; sources of slaves, 44; ransom and warfare, 107; slave unions, 188; freedman status, 253. *See also* Mesopotamia
Thirteenth Amendment, 25
Thralldom, 81, 82, 177
Thucydides, 35
Timocracy, 94–97, 100; derivation, 386n14
Tiv (Nigeria): rituals of enslavement, 53; manumission rate, 271
Tlingit (northwest coast of America): marks of servitude, 58; potlatch ceremony, 84, 191, 222; status inheritance pattern, 136; skills, and treatment, 179; sacrifice of slaves, 191, 222; manumission, 222; source of slaves, 412n6
To Anda'e tribe (Toradja group), 85
To Lage tribe (Toradja group), 85, 144
To Pebato (Toradja group), 85
Toradja (Celebes): rituals of enslavement, 54; nature of honor, 84–85; sources of slaves, 113; status inheritance pattern, 144; treatment of slaves, 176; change of master, 203; manumission, 221, 271; sacrifice of slaves, 221; manumission rate, 274; parasitism, 337; origins, 396n46
Towara (Bedouin tribe), 194
Trachalio (character in *The Rope*), 12
Tradition, and law, 36–37
Transoxiania (West Asia), 310
Treatment of slaves, *see* Conditions of slavery
Treggiari, Susan, 174, 242, 243, 252, 304
Tribute, enslavement as, 122–124
Trimalchio, 305–306
Tripoli (North Africa), 277
Trumai Indians (Brazil), 402n102
Tsimshian (northwest coast of America), 136
Ts'ui Tao-ku, 252
Tuaregs (Algeria): master-slave relationship, 4, 46; status inheritance pattern, 136, 138–139, 145; bridewealth, 167; racism, 176, 178–179; tenant slaves, 181; change of master, 203; manumission, 271, 437n23; enslavement of fellow

ethnics, 422n23; slave population, 461n27
Tuden, Arthur, 147
Tudor Court, 330–331
Tung Shu-yeh, 108
Tunis, 277, 443n49
Tunisia, 157
Tupinamba (Brazil): rituals of enslavement, 52; nature of honor, 81; treatment of prisoners, 106–107, 402n102; manumission rate, 271
Turks: enslavement for tax payment, 123; self-enslavement, 131; slave trade, 152; racial differences, 178; incidence of manumission, 268, 283; eunuchs and slaves, 316, 332. *See also* Mamluks
Turner, Victor, 37
Tuscany (Italy): social death, 39; status inheritance pattern, 144; granting of sanctuary, 202
Tutors, Greek, 91, 174
Twelve Tables, Laws of, 195, 222
Twins, 129

Ugaritic manumission, 218
Uí Neill (Irish royal family), 141
Ukodei (adopted slave), 233
Uktena (mythical beast), 47
Unruh, Ellen, 183
Ur, *see* Third Dynasty of Ur
Urban slaves, 254; manumission rate, 269–270, 282; economics, 456n5
U.S. South: incidence of manumission, 3, 267; sexual unions and marriage, 6, 190; black and white servitude, 6–7; economics of slavery, 11, 33, 65, 190; servile personality, 12, 367n41; free laborers, 34, 374n61; nonslaveholders, 36; caste concept, 48; surnames of slaves, 56; kin terms, 65; religion and slavery, 73–75, 260; free persons and slaves, 88, 94; honor and slavery, 94–97, 367n41; European influence, 95; Sambo ideology, 96, 207, 338; slave trade, 160; internal slave trade, 165–166; treatment of slaves, 206–208; manumission rate, 217, 255, 273, 284, 285, 286, 292–293, 295; manumission as control, 217, 232, 285, 444n65; wala relationship, 245, 246, 260; selective manumission, 246–247; freedman status, 255, 256, 259, 260, 261; hostility to manumission,

U.S. South (*continued*)
255, 259; artisans, 255, 256; miscegenation, 255, 261; demographic mix, 259; exploitation of slave women, 260, 261; abolition of slavery, 285, 286; military manumission, 292–293; "achievements" of slavery, 335; parasitism, 336–337; slave populations, 414n30, 475nn139, 141, 483. *See also* names of individual states

Vai (West Africa): sexual bias in enslavement, 122; internal warfare, 178; manumission pattern, 280
Valencia (Spain), 263
Valgard, 154
Van Gennep, Arnold, 37, 322
Varro, 186, 187
Vaughn, James H., 45–46, 137, 378n55
Vebjorn (character in Icelandic saga), 79
Vediovis, cult of, 223
Venezuela, *see* Goajiros
Venice, 296
Verbal abuse, 193
Verlinden, Charles, 192, 270, 276
Vespasian (emperor of Rome), 307
Vietnam: slavery versus debt-servitude, 86, 125, 126; killing of slaves, 191–192; self-defense, 200; concubinal manumission, 230; freedman status, 252
Vikings (Europe): enslavement by kidnapping, 116; slave trade, 152–153, 154–155; ships, 156; killing of slaves, 191; economic role of slaves, 386n18
Violence: and domination, 2, 3; and master-slave relationship, 3–4; in self-hatred, 12
Virginia: indentured servants versus slaves, 9; status inheritance pattern, 138; manumission, 292; runaways, 447n97; slave population, 475nn139, 141, 483. *See also* U.S. South
Virtus (moral integrity), 304–305
Visigothic Spain: status inheritance pattern, 141, 144, 145–146; slave trade, 152; slave estates, 181; privileged slaves, 196; crimes of slaves, 197; freedman status, 243; incidence of manumission, 270; manumission rate, 274, 288
Vitellius (emperor of Rome), 307
Vogt, Joseph, 87

Volga River, 154
Voluntary servitude, 27–28

Wadai (Chad), 124
Wagner, Edward W., 42
Wala relationship, 241–247, 251, 294; and freedman status, 243, 244, 250, 253, 257, 311; intersocietal variations, 244; legal enforcement, 244, 252; absence, 260
Wali (Aswan), 124
Wallon, Henri, 4–5
Wang Yi-T'ung, 143
Warfare: as source of slaves, 106–115, 119–120, 170, 396n52, 397n54; logistics, 106; for wife recruiting, 107, 402n102; atrocities, 120, 212; manumission and, 287, 289–293; slaves in, 290–291. *See also* Prisoners of war
Water, symbolism, 216, 218
Watson, Alan, 366n13, 373n54
Watson, James L., 21, 296, 370n26
Wealth, 2, 28, 33, 371n41
Weaver, P. R. C., 40, 300, 303–304
Weber, Max, 1, 2, 36–37, 375n6, 384n138
Welsh, nature of honor, 82
Welskopf, Elisabeth, 3, 303
Wergeland, Agnes, 217, 218
West Africa: slaves as wealth, 33; slave trade, 114, 119, 128, 148–149, 156, 157, 160, 164, 400n90; selection of slaves, 122; penal slavery, 128; slave peculium, 185; freedman status, 443n53
Westermann, William, 189, 398n70
Westermarck, Edward, 369n18
West Indies, *see* Caribbean
Westington, Mars M., 121
Westrup, C. W., 31
Whipping, 3–4, 12, 56, 94, 128
Wife recruiting, 107, 402n102
Wilbur, C. M., 108, 127
Wilks, Ivor, 429n90
Williams, Carl O., 81
Wilson, David, 200
Winnebago Indians (North America), 325
Witchcraft, 64, 327
Wittek, Paul, 312
Wittfogel, Karl L., 315, 319
Wodaabe Fulani (Niger), 271
Wolof (Gambia): status inheritance pattern, 147; bridewealth, 167; change of master, 202; sacrifice of slaves, 222, 228; manumission rate, 271

Women: in U.S. South, 261; in Byzantium, 325, 326, 329; in China, 325, 326
Wood, Peter, 56
Woodhead, A. Geoffrey, 35
Worthy Park plantation (Jamaica), 6, 57, 59
Wrigley, Philip K., 25–26

Xurasânians (free Iranians), 310

Yangban (aristocrats), 86
Yao (East Africa): stigma of slavery, 251; slave status, 280, 464n45
Yi dynasty (Korea): context of slavery, 39, 42; self-enslavement, 130; status inheritance pattern, 143; slave estates, 181; slave population, 469n73

Yoruba (Nigeria): marks of servitude, 59; enslavement, 120; slaves as money, 168; in Cuba, 401n97; political eunuchism, 451n72
Yuan period (China), 142

Zaire, *see* Kongo; Nkundu
Zambia, *see* Bemba; Lozi; Luvale
Zandj (Iraq): freedman status, 248, 250, 299; marginality, 332; stereotype, 299, 338; revolt, 467n63
Zanzibar: inferior slave status, 93, 94; enslavement by kidnapping, 117; slave trade, 150; manumission rate, 274; elite slaves, 316
Zaria (Nigeria), 461n26
Zimmern, A., 283